Educational Psychology

Educational Psychology
Learning, Instruction, Assessment

Christine B. McCormick
University of New Mexico

Michael Pressley
University at Albany, State University of New York

LONGMAN

An imprint of Addison Wesley Longman, Inc.

New York • Reading, Massachusetts • Menlo Park, California • Harlow, England
Don Mills, Ontario • Sydney • Mexico City • Madrid • Amsterdam

Executive Editor: Priscilla McGeehon
Developmental Editor: Lauren Silverman
Project Editor: Susan Goldfarb
Text and Cover Designer: Rubina Yeh
Art Studio: Erikson/Dillon Art Services
Photo Researchers: Diane Kraut, Leslie Coopersmith
Electronic Production Manager: Alexandra Odulak
Desktop Administrator: Joanne Del Ben
Manufacturing Manager: Hilda Koparanian
Electronic Page Makeup: Americomp
Printer and Binder: RR Donnelley & Sons Company
Cover Printer: Phoenix Color Corp.
Cover: Detail from *Le Dernier Cri* (*The Last Cry*), 1907, by René Magritte. Private Collection.
    © ARS/Art Resource, NY.

Library of Congress Cataloging-in-Publication Data
McCormick, Christine.
    Educational psychology : learning, instruction, assessment /
  Christine B. McCormick, Michael Pressley.
        p.   cm.
    Includes bibliographical references (p.) and indexes.
    ISBN 0-673-46915-8
    1. Educational psychology.   2. Learning, Psychology of.
  3. Knowledge, Theory of.   4. Educational tests and measurements.
  I. Pressley, Michael.   II. Title.
  LB1051.M394   1996   96-5366
  370.15—dc20   CIP

ISBN 0-673-46915-8

2345678910—DOW—999897

Contents

Chapter 3   Representation of Knowledge   53

Chapter 4

Strategies and Metacognitive Regulation of Strategies   79

Chapter 5

The Role of Knowledge in Thinking   107

Part II   **The Construction of Knowledge**

Chapter 6   **Biological Factors Affecting Learning and Development   131**

Special Features

Building Your Expertise
Diversity
Focus on Research
What Do I Do on Monday Morning?

Chapter 7   **Psychological Theories of Learning and Development   153**

Special Features

Building Your Expertise
Diversity
Focus on Research
What Do I Do on Monday Morning?

Chapter 8   **Social Interactional Theories of Learning and Development   181**

Part III   The Classroom Context

Chapter 9   Social Influences in the Classroom   209

Chapter 10 **Schooling Practices   235**

Chapter 11   **Reading and Writing Instruction   265**

Chapter 12   **Mathematics and Science Instruction   293**

Part IV   **Characteristics of Students**

Chapter 13   **Traditional Perspectives on Intelligence
                      and Academic Competence   323**

Chapter 14   **Alternative Assessments of Academic Competence   349**

As active researchers in the field of educational psychology, we have often been disappointed that the texts available for our undergraduate educational psychology courses did not correspond very well to our understanding of current thinking about the processes of learning and teaching. It seemed to us that the typical approach taken in educational psychology texts had not changed much in twenty years and had certainly not kept pace with contemporary perspectives in theory and research. *Educational Psychology: Learning, Instruction, Assessment* fulfills our vision of a text written for undergraduates that reflects advances in the understanding of effective teaching and learning—what we believe to be essentially a "new look" in educational psychology.

This book is organized around the theme of promoting good information processing: helping students construct and use strategic knowledge, develop their metacognitive abilities, acquire knowledge of the world and its cultures, and stay motivated. A good information processing framework is informed by traditional and contemporary theory, by research in educational psychology, by current thinking in curriculum and instruction, and by both conventional and reform-oriented thinking about assessment and individual differences. We believe that the approach taken in this book can be used as a framework for understanding new developments in the field of educational psychology well into the next century.

This text is part of a series of books on educational psychology. The first book, *Advanced Educational Psychology for Educators, Researchers, and Policymakers,* is aimed at advanced graduate students, practicing educational researchers, and policy makers who have a need for state-of-the-science information about educational psychology. The second book, *Cognition, Teaching, and Assessment,* is an abridgement of the first book that focuses more on current theories of education, whereas the advanced book discusses more extensively where the field is moving. This book, the third in the series, introduces students to educational psychology by showcasing the best new research and theories and making the case for their relevance for future educators. One of our reasons for developing the trio of books was our awareness that many graduate students are asked to teach introductory courses in educational psychology. If they have read either the advanced or the intermediate text as part of their graduate study, they will be ready to teach with *Educational Psychology: Learning, Instruction, and Assessment.*

Text Organization

The first part of this book describes the *foundations of good thinking,* with chapters on motivation, representation of knowledge, strategies and metacognitive regulation of strategies, and the role of knowledge in thinking. Students are introduced to a variety of strategy-oriented interventions, from basic strategies to enhance memory to the most up-to-date strategic approaches for developing reading and problem-solving skills. With Chapter 5's detailed coverage of the role of knowledge in teaching, learning, and problem solving, students are also exposed to the full range of ways that knowledge is represented in the mind.

The second part of the book introduces different *theoretical perspectives on the construction of knowledge.* It begins with a chapter on the biological foundations of learning and thinking, an issue of increasing prominence in educational psychology. Following this is a chapter describing traditional learning and developmental theories relevant to educational settings, all of which provide valuable insights into the classroom. Yet another chapter focuses on theories of social interaction as it affects mental development.

The third part of the book examines the *classroom context*. One chapter discusses social influences in the classroom. Another details effective classroom practices and management. Since many classroom practices are specific to content domains, two chapters outline instructional techniques for the content areas of reading, writing, math, and science. Many of the educational interventions designed improve increase reading and writing skills apply to other content domains as well. Similarly, the reasoning and problem-solving skills developed through math and science interventions are germane to other instructional content.

The last part of the book identifies important *student characteristics*. Three of the chapters address student assessment, focusing on traditional assessment techniques (Chapter 13), alternative assessment techniques (Chapter 14), and teacher-designed assessment techniques (Chapter 15). While the implications of student diversity are considered in every chapter, the last chapter deals specifically with the diverse characteristics of learners in the classroom.

Throughout the book, explicit connections are made to our general theme: the challenge of developing good information processing in students. We discuss the significant roles quality of teaching and other environmental variables play in cognitive development and academic achievement.

Text Features

Each chapter begins with a *chapter outline* providing an overview of the topics discussed and concludes with a *chapter summary* in which the major points made in the chapter are briefly reviewed. Key terms are defined in the text, and also in a *glossary* at the back of the book. There are also a number of special features in each chapter.

- *Classroom Predicament*. Students are presented with a classroom dilemma at the beginning of each chapter. These "classroom predicaments" allow students to use critical thinking and reading skills to resolve each situation appropriately by using the concepts and tools provided within that chapter.
- *Return to the Classroom Predicament*. At the end of each chapter, students are presented with ideas to consider as appropriate responses to the predicament that appeared at the start of the chapter. These suggestions act as something of an open-ended "answer key" in which potential applications of the tools gained in the chapter are considered. Students may find ideas that mirror their own thoughts or perhaps offer an alternative resolution.
- *Focus on Research*. These features provide in-depth coverage of research studies, along with questions for students that inspire them to approach the research critically. The ultimate goal is to encourage students to become informed consumers of research findings.
- *Building Your Expertise*. These sections build bridges between newly introduced theoretical concepts, ensuring that concepts taught in one chap-

ter do not get left behind in studying the next. Students learn to approach the text as a holistic resource with intertwining topics and applications rather than as a series of autonomous lessons to be memorized.

- *"What Do I Do on Monday Morning?"* These practical applications of the material addressed in the text are provided to help students make connections between theory and practice and develop the knowledge base necessary to generalize to new situations.
- *Diversity.* These sections discuss the influence of culture and development on the particular educational issues presented in the chapter, complementing the general discussion of student diversity found in Chapter 16.

While we were writing this book, we tested portions of the text on students in our courses at the University of South Carolina, the University of New Mexico, the University of Maryland, and the University at Albany, State University of New York. Our students seemed to grasp the intimate relationships among theory, research, and educational practice. They learned that, as future educators, they would not benefit from a step-by-step, "Here's the recipe" approach to topics in educational psychology. It is not worthwhile for any teacher or text simply to list what educators need to know, no matter how skillfully. Instead, learners must derive their understanding of principles from a base of solid research. They must develop their knowledge, expand their repertoire of strategies, hone their metacognitive abilities, and motivate themselves—in short, they must become good information processors. Our students reported being particularly impressed by the following features of the text:

- The focus on strategies and strategy instruction.
- The emphasis on social interactional theories of learning and development.
- The application of current theories of cognition and instruction to school subjects.
- The proactive emphasis on engaging students in discussions of classroom management.
- The extensive coverage of student assessment—one of the topics they felt they needed the most.
- The integration of issues of development and diversity throughout the text.
- The presentation of Piaget's theory of cognitive development, the behavioral perspective on learning, and social learning theory in a single chapter.

Ancillaries

- The Instructor's Manual, written by Ruth Wharton-McDonald of the University at Albany, State University of New York, provides chapter outlines, learning objectives, concept maps, key terms, teaching and lecture suggestions, and case studies for each chapter.
- The Electronic Portfolio, faculty version, by Harry Noden of the Hudson, Ohio, school system, provides a range of computer network options.

- The Test Bank, written by Barbara L. Snyder of the University of Western Ontario, provides 50 multiple-choice, 20 short-answer, and 5 essay questions per chapter. The Test Bank is also available on TestMaster for DOS or Macintosh-based systems.
- The Student Study Guide, written by Pamela El-Dinery of Georgetown University, includes exercises keyed to learning objectives for each chapter in the text. Learning strategies help students remember important concepts, and practice tests help students prepare for exams.
- The Electronic Portfolio, student version, by Harry Noden, encourages extensive student interaction with the text, offering experimental applications of theories in the classroom and self-review of progress through written responses recorded in an interactive computerized portfolio. It is available for either DOS or Macintosh-based systems.
- *Educational Psychology Video* provides examples of classroom interactions, including "First Day of Class," "Small Group Instruction," "Classroom Behavior Management," "Working with a Discouraged Learner," and "Parent/Teacher Conference."

Acknowledgments

We have many people to thank. Joel Levin encouraged us in the early years of both of our careers. He instilled in us the commitment to move the field forward by learning its past and thinking hard about its future, a commitment reflected in the pages of this text. The following reviewers gave us many wonderful suggestions for the reformulation of the manuscript:

Dave Bass, Valley City State University

George Batsche, University of Florida

Brenna Beedle, Eastern Washington University

Steve Benton, Kansas State University

Karen K. Block, University of Pittsburgh

Kathleen M. Cauley, Virginia Commonwealth University

Theodore Coladarci, University of Maine

James Dickenson, University of Southern Florida

Gail S. Ditkoff, California University of Pennsylvania

Donna Evans, University of North Florida

William R. Fisk, Clemson University

Marlynn M. Griffin, Georgia Southern University

Alison King, California State University, San Marcos

Robert Leahy, Stetson University

Raymond B. Miller, University of Oklahoma

Walter Skinner, Georgia State University

Nancy Smith, Millersville University

Joan S. Timm, University of Wisconsin–Oshkosh

Michael Young, University of Connecticut

Chris Jennison, Lauren Silverman, and their colleagues Shadla Grooms and Nicole Mauter made it a pleasure to work with HarperCollins (now Longman), as did everyone in the New York office who contributed to the three-book project.

Michael Pressley would like to thank his wife, Donna, who was a good sport about all those nights of word processing, and his son, Tim, for being a constant reminder of how important it is to educate the next generation of educators. Christine McCormick has always been inspired to improve education through the examples set by her parents, Jerome C. McCormick and Florence M. McCormick, whose working lives were dedicated to the education of others. She would also like to thank her husband, David Scherer, for his support and patience during this seemingly never-ending project. David, the honeymoon now can begin.

Christine B. McCormick
Michael Pressley

Educational Psychology

Chapter Outline

Chapter 1

An Introduction to Good Thinking and Good Teaching

"I have always known exactly what I was going to do when I grew up—be a teacher. Whenever my younger brother and I played school, I made sure I was always the teacher. I'm really excited about this course. I expect to learn, step-by-step, what I should do when I am in the classroom."

—Roland, sophomore

"I'm taking this course as an elective. I'm pretty sure I don't want to become a teacher, but I am planning to go to graduate school and I expect to become a parent eventually, so I thought it made sense to find out how people of all ages learn. Maybe I'll pick up a few pointers on how to be a better student."

—Ramona, senior

"I'm not sure what I want to do with the rest of my life. I wasn't happy as an accountant so I decided to come back to school. I could possibly want to be a teacher, but I'm exploring other options. Taking this course gives me a chance to find out more about teaching and learning, and I could possibly wind up taking the other courses I need for teacher certification."

—William, post-baccalaureate

"I'm a business major interested in personnel work, and my advisor suggested I take this course since many businesses are heavily involved in employee training and this course would look good on my record."

Tomeka, senior

There are many possible reasons for taking a course in educational psychology. Some students, like Roland, are certain that they want to become teachers. Others, like William, are just checking out teaching as a possible career or, like Ramona, are taking the course because they are interested in understanding how people learn. Still others, like Tomeka, have only a hazy idea of why they are taking the course and are doing so only as a means to an end. Can any educational psychology textbook meet the needs of such a diverse group of students? All of these students, Roland, Ramona, William, and Tomeka, could benefit from understandings gained from the development of the overall theme of this educational psychology textbook—the development of good thinking skills through effective educational intervention.

It is easy to find pessimistic reports about education. Newspapers and magazines publish articles documenting that test scores are down, that increasing proportions of high school students are functionally illiterate, and that even college students are not able to solve simple problems. These reports are especially disturbing because these students need to be able to survive in an increasingly technological world, a world requiring ever higher levels of literacy and mathematical skills. Yet even in the face of such reports it is possible to be optimistic about education, because a great deal is now known about how to create better thinkers.

Much of what is known is based on research that empowers future educators by providing information about educational methods that work. These are not mere tricks of the trade, however. Educational professionals will be most empowered if they are convinced, through research evidence, that particular methods work and if they understand, through theoretical frameworks, why these particular methods work. Educators need to be familiar with educational theories that explain why the relationships observed in research occur. Thus, the major goal of this textbook is to facilitate future educators' construction of knowledge of educational theory and research in a way that will ultimately allow them to use this knowledge in educational contexts.

This goal may disappoint students like Roland, since they will not be handed step-by-step procedures or recipes guaranteed to work in the classroom. This expectation is impossible to meet, since there is no such thing as one best way to teach and learn. Variables among learners—for example, their degree of content knowledge, their level of development, their intellectual ability, and their cultural background—greatly influence the effectiveness of educational interventions. All of these issues are considered in this educational psychology textbook. It is our hope that careful readers of this text will develop an understanding of these variables that will help them solve problems and make decisions in the classroom.

What's Ahead?

This book is organized around the theme of developing good thinking in students. An overview of the book's organization appears in Table 1.1. The first part of the book describes the *foundations of good thinking*. These four chapters elaborate the model of good thinking presented later in this chapter (see Figure 1.1). We begin with a discussion of students' motivation, since enhancing motivation is arguably the first step in developing good thinkers. The chapter on motivation is followed by chapters detailing other aspects of good thinking—the representation of knowl-

Table 1.1

Plan of the Book

1. Introduction to Good Thinking and Good Teaching

Part One Foundations of Thinking	Part Two The Construction of Knowledge	Part Three The Classroom Context	Part Four Characteristics of Students
2. Motivation 3. Representation of Knowledge 4. Strategies and Metacognitive Regulation of Strategies 5. The Role of Knowledge in Thinking	6. Biological Factors Affecting Learning and Development 7. Psychological Theories of Learning and Development 8. Social Interactional Theories of Learning and Development	9. Social Influences in the Classroom 10. Schooling Practices 11. Reading and Writing Instruction 12. Mathematics and Science Instruction	13. Traditional Perspectives on Intelligence and Academic Competence 14. Alternative Assessments of Academic Competence 15. Teacher-Designed Assessments: Traditional and Alternative 16. Diversity of Learners

edge, strategies and metacognitive regulation of strategies, and the role of knowledge in thinking.

The second part of the book introduces different *theoretical perspectives on the construction of knowledge.* It begins with a chapter on biological foundations of learning and thinking, an issue of increasing prominence in educational psychology. Then there is a chapter describing a variety of learning and developmental theories relevant to educational settings, all of which provide valuable insights into the classroom. Still another chapter focuses on theories of social interaction as it affects mental development.

Figure 1.1
Four key components of good thinking: motivation, knowledge strategies, and metacognition.

The third part of the book examines the *classroom context*. One chapter discusses social interactions in the classroom. Another details effective classroom practices and management. Since many classroom practices are content-specific, one chapter outlines instructional techniques for the areas of reading and writing, and another for math and science. There is, of course, a great deal of overlap between these content domains. For example, many of the educational interventions designed to increase reading and writing skills apply to other content domains as well. Similarly, the reasoning and problem-solving skills developed through math and science interventions are germane to other instructional content.

The last part of the book identifies important *characteristics of students*. Three of the chapters address student assessment—one on traditional assessment techniques, one on alternative assessment techniques, and one on teacher-designed assessment techniques. Finally, although the implications of student diversity are considered in every chapter, the book concludes with a chapter further exploring the diverse characteristics of students in classrooms.

You will find a number of special features in each chapter. Beginning with Chapter 2, each chapter begins with a section titled "Classroom Predicament." After reading the chapter, your knowledge will help you to understand this predicament better and will enable you to propose a plan of action for responding to it. The "Focus on Research" feature presents an in-depth description of a research study, which is designed to improve your critical thinking about research investigations. The ultimate goal is to make you a more informed consumer of research findings. In the "Building Your Expertise" feature, connections between theoretical concepts are reviewed and highlighted in order to help you construct new understandings. Often, the implications of theoretical issues introduced in one chapter for the topics presented in a subsequent chapter are discussed in this feature. The "What Do I Do on Monday Morning?" feature presents examples of applications of the material discussed in the text. These examples will help you make connections between theory and practice so that you will begin to develop the knowledge base required to generate additional applications. Finally, the influence of culture and development upon a particular educational issue is highlighted within the context of a general discussion of that issue in the "Diversity" feature. This feature especially complements the discussion of diversity among students in Chapter 16. In addition, the overall organization of each chapter is previewed by a *chapter outline* at the beginning and reinforced by a *chapter summary* at the end.

In the remainder of this chapter, the overall theme of this textbook—the development of good thinking skills through effective instructional intervention—is introduced. The development of good thinking as described throughout this text is an important goal for future educators, for themselves as well as for their future students. In this chapter, the characteristics of good thinking are first described, followed by an introduction to instructional interventions that facilitate the development of good thinking. Then, since what we know about good thinking and effective instruction is derived from research based on educational theory, a summary of educational research methods concludes the chapter. A professional educator possessing at least a rudimentary understanding of research methods can better understand the conclusions drawn from research studies.

What Is Good Thinking Like?

Do you ever read detective books? Perhaps, when you were younger, you read detective stories written for children such as the *Hardy Boys* or *Nancy Drew* series. The detective characters in these books (Frank and Joe Hardy; and Nancy Drew and her friends, George and Bess) exhibited characteristics of good thinking (Dixon, 1972; Pressley, Borkowski, & Schneider, 1989; Pressley, Snyder, & Cariglia-Bull, 1987).

First of all, these young detectives had a rich repertoire of **strategies** for solving crimes. Strategies are plans of action that may result in the solution to a problem. Sometimes the detectives in these books would try to put themselves in the place of the criminal as they analyzed a crime. They had specific tactics for lifting fingerprints from difficult places and for making certain that all of the physical evidence at the scene of a crime was collected. They used strategies such as rehearsal and imagery to remember important information about a crime. One favorite strategy was their approach to remembering a physical description of a person, always beginning at the top of the head and working down to the shoes. These detectives also knew that their memories were fallible, so they used photography to record crime scenes, made drawings when a camera was not available, and took extensive notes.

Strategies are critical for other tasks as well. For example, in writing this chapter, we first planned, which involved thinking about the topic of good thinking in order to retrieve what we knew already. Then we reviewed articles written on the topic that we found by going to the library to find more sources. After this planning phase, we organized our thoughts and created an outline. We juggled the ideas in the outline until the arguments were coherent. Construction of sentences and paragraphs followed. Once we completed a first draft, it was on to revision . . . and more revision . . . and more revision. Some additional searching for information and rewriting of sentences occurred as part of the revision process. In short, we

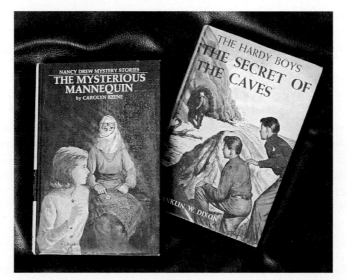

The young detectives in the *Nancy Drew* and *Hardy Boys* books displayed good thinking skills in their adventures.

coordinated a number of specific strategic processes (e.g., planning, writing, and revising) in an overall strategic plan. Good thinkers routinely engage in strategic planning and often coordinate the use of a number of strategies in order to accomplish complex tasks. Examples of strategies useful in the classroom are found in several other chapters of this book.

The Hardy Boys and Nancy Drew also possessed another characteristic of good thinking—**metacognition,** which is knowledge about and awareness of their own thinking (Flavell, 1985). In particular, they knew when and where to use the strategies they had acquired (metacognitive knowledge about strategies). Thus, when first arriving at a crime scene, they knew it was appropriate to use particular strategies to preserve it, such as cordoning it off. Metacognitive knowledge is critical to the regulation of strategies since knowledge of when and where particular strategies are appropriate guides their future application (J. T O'Sullivan & Pressley, 1984). Often, understanding when and where strategies are useful occurs as a result of the learner's **monitoring** when performance is better with a strategy than without it (Ghatala, 1986; Pressley, Levin, & Ghatala, 1984). Chapter 4 provides a more complete discussion of strategies and metacognition about strategies.

Although students will consciously and sometimes quite slowly execute strategies when they are first acquiring them, good thinkers eventually **automatize** the strategies they know. This means that they can quickly recognize when it is appropriate to use particular strategies and can execute them with ease. Thus, a student who is learning a plan-write-revise strategy might at first constantly refer to cue cards indicating how to plan and make revisions. After several years of practice, however, the cue cards are ignored as the student carries out the various steps of the strategy with little apparent effort.

Good thinkers use strategies in conjunction with nonstrategic **knowledge.** Because a criminal investigator knows that glass is a particularly good source of fingerprints, the Hardy Boys and Nancy Drew made certain that glass at a crime scene was undisturbed until it could be examined systematically. The young detectives used the strategies they possessed in particular ways because of their knowledge of the law, of criminals' behaviors, and of physical evidence. The good thinker is much more than a storehouse of information, however. The good thinker can flexibly use many forms of knowledge, including knowledge that is idiosyncratic to their subculture or their particular occupation, religion, and interests. Knowledge is diverse, extensive, complex, and connected to experiences. Different explanations for how knowledge is represented in memory are delineated in Chapter 3. How knowledge influences thinking is addressed in Chapter 5.

No one could read about the Hardy Boys and Nancy Drew without being struck by their **motivation,** another important component of good thinking. They were motivated to acquire more sleuthing strategies and knowledge needed by a detective. They were also motivated to figure out how to adapt what they already knew to new challenges. They were always looking for crimes to solve and were determined to go about their investigations in a systematic way. In Chapter 2, different perspectives on students' motivation are examined.

Other Characteristics of Good Thinking

Good thinking requires a *normally functioning brain* (see Figure 1.2). For instance, a tremendous amount of knowledge must be stored in long-term memory structures.

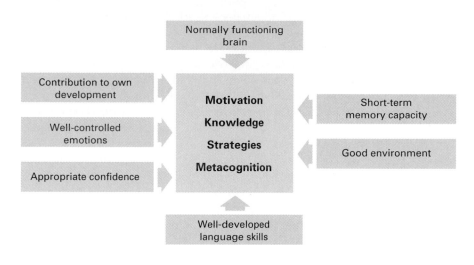

Figure 1.2
Additional components of good thinking.

Loss of long-term memory because of disease or injury results in loss of knowledge and a reduction in the competencies dependent on long-term knowledge. Thinking also depends on **short-term memory,** which is sometimes called consciousness or working memory (Baddeley, 1986). When someone holds a telephone number in memory while searching for a scratch pad, thinking goes on in short-term memory. Short-term memory is active as an author juggles bits and pieces of ideas he or she is trying to combine into sentences and paragraphs. Close your eyes and try to keep in "view" the room you are sitting in; your image is in consciousness, or your short-term memory.

Short-term memory is exactly what the name implies—short term. If a person does not continue to rehearse a phone number, the number will fade from consciousness. If an author is distracted while writing, he or she will lose some of the ideas being juggled. Moreover, short-term memory is limited in terms of the amount of information that can be attended to consciously at any one moment. Only so many numbers can be rehearsed at once. Only so many bits of information can be considered before new pieces of information literally seem to push out some of the information already in short-term memory. Thus, short-term memory is limited in duration and capacity. You have probably noticed how sometimes other things compete for your limited short-term memory capacity when you are trying to pay attention in class. It may be a commotion in the hallway, the person whispering next to you, or even your own plans for the weekend. In fact, you probably shift your attention back and forth between the distractions and the task at hand since you find it difficult to hold so many things in memory at the same time.

An important difference between people is the capacity of their short-term memory (Baddeley, 1986). Short-term memory depends on an intact brain, and when brain structures responsible for short-term memory are damaged, good thinking is difficult at best. The more demanding the task, the more likely it is that the individual with impaired short-term memory will falter (R. A. McCarthy & Warrington, 1990). There are differences in short-term memory capacity even among people with healthy brains. Some people can hold more things in memory and operate on more bits of information simultaneously than can others. As children grow older, they develop an increasing ability to hold information in mind (Case, 1985; Dempster, 1985). This increase in short-term memory capacity accounts for some of the apparent improvements in thinking that come with development. In general, good thinkers have sufficient short-term memory capacity to carry out relatively complex tasks.

Since a healthy brain learns a great deal as a function of experience, it needs a *good environment.* For example, although the acquisition of language is virtually guaranteed by human biology as long as there is some exposure to language (Anastasiow, 1990; Gleitman, 1986), its development is still sensitive to environmental stimulation. Thus, when children are raised in complete isolation, language does not develop normally (Puckering & Rutter, 1987). Even milder forms of deprivation have negative effects on language development. For instance, language acquisition is affected negatively by being reared in a socially disadvantaged home, as a twin, or in a large family. These are situations in which environmental pressures may reduce the amount of time that parents can play and verbally interact with their children (Puckering & Rutter, 1987).

Flexible, *well-developed language skills* support sophisticated thinking. There is a strong association between delayed language and learning disabilities, especially difficulties with reading (Howlin & Rutter, 1987). Some models of thinking emphasize the development of inner speech or self-talk as an important determinant of skill in thinking (Rogoff, 1990; Vygotsky, 1962; Wertsch, 1991).

Good thinkers are *appropriately confident.* They welcome challenges that are well matched to the skills and knowledge they possess. They have high self-efficacy (Bandura, 1986). This means they believe they can accomplish tasks in their environment. They also recognize when they are equal to tasks and when academic tasks might be beyond them or require assistance.

Good thinkers, like the young detectives, have *well-controlled emotions.* For instance, anxiety did not overwhelm the thinking of the Hardy Boys or Nancy Drew, even when they were confronted with great danger. They did not get so excited or agitated at a crime scene that their thinking was clouded.

Good thinkers *contribute to their own education and development* (Bandura, 1986; Scarr & McCartney, 1983). They acquire many strategies and a great deal of knowledge because they place themselves in situations in which they can learn such information. How did the 15-year-old down the block come to know so much more about the inner workings of her computer than her parents? She spends hours at the computer, invests most of her allowance on computer magazines, reads the magazines from cover to cover, figures out how to apply the ideas in the magazine articles to her own computing, and hangs out with other kids at school who are also interested in computing. She is knowledgeable about other topics as well, because she reads the newspaper daily, listens to both popular stations and classical music while working on her computer, and engages in rich conversations with her family. Her friends are no slouches either. Her conversations with them span a whole host of topics, from discussions about whether *Julius Caesar,* now being read in English class, is really history to reflections concerning effective ways to reduce drug and alcohol abuse among classmates. Good thinkers elect to do things that are enriching, and they seek out company that is intellectually engaging. Good thinkers find one another, often with the explicit goal of engaging in activities that will further increase their competence.

In summary, no one characteristic makes a person a good thinker; good thinking is the product of a number of factors in interaction with one another. For instance, by using efficient comprehension and learning strategies, more knowledge is acquired, which in turn can increase confidence and reduce the need to use strategies in the future. With greater knowledge, confidence increases so that knowledge can be used more easily. For example, a young law student who has systematically organized his cases on contract law and has applied a variety of specific learning strategies to acquire the fundamentals of contract law eventually will automatically recognize features of a typical contract that make it nonbinding. He will be able to correct the contract with little effort and without consciously invoking strategies. Likewise, knowledge of traditional contract law will help the student when he is a young attorney. He will be able to recognize features of an atypical contract, ones not encountered previously. Recognizing the inadequacy of his knowledge base, the young attorney might engage in some strategies for coming to terms with these new provisions. One such strategy might include seeking help from a more experienced attorney who has a deeper and broader base of knowledge about contracts.

Characteristics of Not-So-Good Thinking

The same characteristics used to describe good thinking can also be applied to poor thinking. Students who have academic difficulties in school are a diverse group. Some do not have normally functioning brains, although specific disorders are often difficult to pinpoint. Brain abnormalities show up in a variety of ways, including language deficiencies and limited short-term memory capacity (Gaddes, 1985). Weak students use fewer strategies than normal students, and because they have poor metacognition, they know less about when and where it is appropriate to use the strategies they do know (Forrest-Pressley & Waller, 1984; Schneider & Pressley, 1989). Anxiety about academics is common in poor learners (Kasik, Sabatino, & Spoentgen, 1987; B. F. Perlmutter, 1987). Poor learners often hold beliefs that undermine their motivation to try. For instance, they may think their learning problems are due to unchanging ability (Pearl, 1982). Because poor learners acquire less from each lesson than classmates, many aspects of their knowledge base are deficient. Some poor learners have more difficulty than other children in applying what they know to academic work. In short, there are many children who lack one or more elements of good thinking, and impaired interaction between these elements only compounds their difficulties. For example, failing to use strategies decreases how much is learned, which in turn decreases knowledge.

Poor thinking can even be found among college students (Pressley, El-Dinary, & Brown, 1992). For example, they often study and restudy inefficiently. They frequently believe they are ready for tests when they are not. They can completely miss the main point of a reading yet believe they understand the text completely. When searching for material, they often do so ineffectively and fail to find what they are seeking. Often they possess prior knowledge that they could relate to new content, but they do not use it (Pressley, Wood, Woloshyn, Martin, King, & Menke, 1992).

The Development of Good Thinking Through Instruction

The good news is that students can develop good thinking through instruction. School involves learning many different types of information, and no single instructional approach is appropriate for all types of content. Following are brief descriptions of a variety of approaches teachers can use to develop good thinking in their students. These methods focus on helping students develop their knowledge base by constructing their own understandings. Learners construct knowledge as they attempt to make sense of their experiences. They actively seek meaning—forming, elaborating, and testing their understandings through interactions with teachers and peers. More complete discussions of these approaches appear in other chapters of the book.

Direct Explanation and Teacher Modeling: First Steps in Students' Construction of Knowledge

When teachers provide explicit and detailed information about academic processes or concepts and provide explicit modeling of academic processes, they are engaging in **direct explanation and teacher modeling** (Roehler & Duffy, 1984). Consider the teacher who directly explains to students how to write a short essay using a plan-write-revise strategy. The teacher explains and models alternative ways of planning. These include searching one's own knowledge for information to include in the essay, brainstorming with others, and seeking information from library resources. The teacher might also demonstrate ways of organizing the many ideas that are generated, perhaps teaching how to outline an essay before writing it. During the writing phase, the teacher explains how to turn the rough outline into phrases and sentences. Once a good first draft is achieved via planning and writing, then it is time for revision. The teacher explains that revision may require more planning and the search for additional information to put into the essay, followed by development of new phrases and sentences that mesh with what is already in the draft. The teacher conveys much of this information with examples of good writing, which are accompanied by demonstrations of how these examples were constructed using planning, writing, and revising. Students also receive guided practice in each of the steps of the strategy (plan, write, and revise) as well as in the use of the strategy as a whole.

The teacher's explanations and demonstrations are only the beginning of learning. For example, students do not really understand how to write until they write. By writing with the teacher's assistance, students begin to construct an understanding of the writing process (Pressley, Harris, & Marks, 1992). At first, they need a lot of support, but as their understanding of planning, writing, and revising increases through experience, the teacher's presence fades. The teacher's explanations and modeling provide a great start for the students' construction of knowledge.

In addition to explaining and modeling the steps of the strategy, the teacher also provides direct explanation, which imparts substantial information about when and where to apply the strategy as well as how to coordinate using the steps of the strategy. Providing such metacognitive information makes it more likely that students will apply the writing strategy to new situations in which it can be effective (J. T. O'Sullivan & Pressley, 1984). In particular, through direct explanation the teacher focuses on how students' writing is improved through use of the strategy.

The idea is to get students to realize that their successes and failures depend on whether they are making use of the knowledge they possess (Clifford, 1984). Of course, as students write, they construct additional understandings of when the writing strategy is helpful. Again, the teacher's input is just a beginning of the students' construction of knowledge.

In summary, through direct explanation, the teacher combines explanation, modeling, and the provision of metacognitive information, such as when and where to apply the strategy and the usefulness of it. The most critical features of direct explanation are (1) straightforward presentations of well-structured descriptions and demonstrations of what is being taught, followed by (2) opportunities for students to use what they learn, which permits them to construct personalized understandings about the new knowledge.

Other Approaches to Instruction

Each of the three alternative instructional methods that follow can be coordinated with direct explanation. Good teachers interconnect the various types of teaching.

Discovery Learning and Guided Discovery. Discovery learning de-emphasizes instruction (Bruner, 1961; Gagné, 1965; Wittrock, 1966). Teachers facilitate discovery learning by presenting tasks to students that offer rich opportunities for discovery of knowledge and strategies. The teacher's input is often limited to answering student-generated questions about the task (Suchman, 1960). Supporters of discovery learning believe that it promotes motivation by cultivating natural curiosity and that it produces more complete understanding of discovered strategies and knowledge than can be provided through explanation by the teacher. Thus, discovery learning increases the likelihood that students will develop the metacognitive knowledge of when and where to apply the strategies they are learning and the motivation to use them.

Even though there are impressive demonstrations of children's invention of strategies (G. Groen & Resnick, 1977; Svenson & Hedonborg, 1979; Woods, Resnick, & Groen, 1975), there are also difficulties with discovery learning. For example, not all students discover the many strategies they need to know in order to negotiate the academic demands of school. For many students, discovery is inefficient at best, requiring much more time than it would take to learn the same strategies with direct explanation. In addition, learners often discover incorrect strategies. For example, van Lehn (1990) documented more than 100 subtraction strategies discovered by learners that are in fact incorrect. These included "borrowing" from columns when it was not necessary, not writing zeroes in the answers (e.g., generating *2 9* instead of *209*), and only subtracting from some of the columns.

Since pure discovery sometimes produces less learning, less efficient learning, and less "correct" learning, some educators found a way to modify the approach. The result was **guided discovery** teaching, which is more explicit than pure discovery teaching. With guided discovery, the teacher typically poses questions that are intended to lead students to understand ways that a problem can be solved. The questions lead the students to "discover" strategies. Not surprisingly, guided discovery does produce more certain and more efficient learning of strategies and ideas than pure discovery (Gagné & Brown, 1961; Kersh, 1958).

An example of guided discovery is A. Collins and Stevens's (1982) **inquiry teaching.** This approach presents students with a series of questions. Some of the questions focus on features of the concept that make it unique. For example, differences between plants and animals are highlighted by the question, "Is there a difference in the way plants and animals obtain food?" Other questions focus on dimensions that do not discriminate the concepts, such as "Do plants and animals both need to metabolize food?" Teachers can include trick questions to highlight misconceptions students might have, such as, "How long does it take a plant to move food out of the soil into its leaves?" After a series of such questions, the teacher asks the class to state rules that define the concepts under discussion. For the example of the plants and animals, the rule would be that plants manufacture their own food, whereas animals do not. The teacher may provide additional questions as necessary to clarify and refine the rules. This approach can stimulate scientific thinking by encouraging students to realize that by posing questions and constructing answers to them, it is possible to understand important concepts and processes. By thinking about new concepts in different ways and coming to terms with misconceptions, students can gain a deeper understanding of what they are learning. As with other discovery approaches, however, inquiry teaching is not totally efficient. More material can be covered by reading or listening to a lecture than can be covered in the same amount of time devoted to inquiry teaching. Moreover, the method requires a teacher who can really think "on the run," who can pose telling questions and come up with pertinent examples (A. Collins & Stevens, 1982).

Guided Participation. In contrast to discovery approaches, which largely permit students to make their own choices about how they will go about tasks, **guided participation** involves the teacher's extensive and explicit direction of students' processing. Teachers cue students step-by-step about how they should accomplish various tasks, such as solving a problem or writing a letter. The assumption of guided participation is that students will eventually use the steps on their own if they are cued to use them enough times.

For example, Hansen and Pearson (1983) taught a set of reading strategies to fourth-grade students. One process they wanted students to learn was to compare what is in the text with their own lives. The students were cued to do this before each new text was read. The students were also questioned about the text they were reading. These questions required relating personal knowledge to the content of the text and making predictions based on personal knowledge about what might happen next in the text. After ten weeks of instruction, the students' comprehension improved, suggesting that they had started to use independently the processes cued during guided participation.

Scaffolding. In **scaffolding,** the teacher helps students on an as-needed basis. This instructional method is based on theories that adult-child interactions develop mature thought in children (Feurstein, 1980; Vygotsky, 1962, 1978; see also Chapter 8). Adults model good thinking and provide subtle hints and prompts to children when they cannot manage on their own. Sometimes adults direct children's attention to important dimensions of the problems they are attempting to solve. Sometimes adults suggest strategies to children. The idea is that eventually children adopt as their own the thinking processes and patterns that adults have modeled and assisted children in using.

The children eventually internalize the processes that previously were scaf-

Using guided participation, the teacher carefully directs every millimeter of the beginner's swing (or at least tries to!).

folded (S. S. Wood, Bruner, & Ross, 1976) for them by adults. The metaphor of scaffolding is appropriate because scaffolding is an external structure that supports another structure under construction. As the new structure is completed and capable of standing on its own, the scaffolding is removed. This is also what happens in scaffolded adult-child academic interactions. The scaffolding adult provides only enough support for the child to accomplish an academic task—not too much or too little. The adult monitors carefully when the child makes progress toward an academic goal. If a child catches on quickly, the adult's responsive instruction will be less detailed than if the child experiences difficulties applying the strategy and internalizing it.

One way to understand scaffolded instruction is to compare it with direct explanation. Direct explanations flow primarily from the teacher to the students, whereas scaffolded instruction is a result of continuous and mutually responsive

Just as a scaffold is removed when a building no longer needs the support, in scaffolded instruction, adult support is slowly withdrawn as the child begins to learn to accomplish the academic task on his or her own.

interactions between students and teachers. Direct explanations of entire processes are often presented early in instruction, whereas in scaffolded instruction explanations about how to accomplish an academic goal are introduced more gradually as the child and adult attempt to do the academic task in collaboration. More is left for the child to infer during scaffolding than direct explanation, as the teacher using scaffolding attempts to lead the child to important understandings about the task at hand and how that task might be accomplished.

Instruction That Encourages Good Thinking

Skilled teachers typically combine the various teaching methods just described to encourage the learning of strategies, knowledge, and metacognition that comprises good thinking. (See Table 1.2 for a summary of different teaching methods.) For example, when teachers using direct explanation support their students' use of new knowledge through prompts and hints, they are scaffolding their students' learning. In this way, direct explanation can include scaffolding. There are also occasions when a direct explainer sets up classroom situations that promote discovery, with the effective teacher gently nudging students who are not making progress in the discovery process.

Consider the Hardy Boys and Nancy Drew again. The Hardy Boys received instruction in detective work from their father, Fenton Hardy, a famous detective. Nancy Drew received instruction from her father, Carson Drew, a famous criminal lawyer. There can be little doubt that a good deal of direct explanation as well as substantial scaffolding occurred in these interactions between fathers and children. The young detectives were also extremely well read, and they tried hard to discover how what they had learned from books could improve their detective work. In short, the education of these detectives was accomplished through diverse methods. Fenton Hardy and Carson Drew provided very good instruction, but the Hardy Boys and Nancy Drew also did much to create their own instruction, consistently placing themselves in settings in which they could acquire and practice new detective skills.

Table 1.2

Key Characteristics of Teaching Methods

Direct Explanation and Teacher Modeling
- Teacher presents well-structured descriptions and demonstrations.
- Teacher provides opportunities for students to use knowledge after explanations and modeling.

Discovery Learning
- Students are given the opportunity to discover knowledge and strategies.
- Teacher's input is often limited to answering student-generated questions.

Guided Discovery
- Teacher poses questions to lead students to discovery.

Guided Participation
- Teacher uses extensive, explicit cues to direct learning.

Scaffolding
- Teacher provides only the support the student needs.

Methods of Educational Research

One of the goals of this text is to facilitate students' construction of knowledge of educational theories and effective educational practice. Because there is no single theory that completely explains the learning process, multiple theoretical perspectives are presented throughout the text. We demonstrate the soundness of the theories and the effectiveness of educational interventions through presentation of research evidence. Since some key studies are presented in detail, the informed reader needs to be armed with at least a rudimentary understanding of basic research methods.

Educational researchers use diverse research methods. One reason for this is that not all problems can be addressed with a single method. A second reason for variety in methods is the personal preferences and beliefs of investigators. What follows are descriptions of the main types of methods used by educational researchers.

Quantitative Methods

In quantitative investigations, observations are quantified, or turned into numbers, that are then statistically analyzed. There are two main classes of quantitative studies. In **manipulative investigations,** usually called experiments, researchers control variation by randomly assigning people to one educational treatment or another. **Random assignment** means that before the experiment begins, each student has an equal chance of being assigned to any treatment. One way to ensure random assignment of all the students in a class to one of two experimental conditions is to pick the names of all the students one at a time out of a hat. In **nonmanipulative investigations,** researchers systematically analyze naturally occurring differences between people or settings.

Manipulative Investigations. Often educational researchers compare a new or preferred educational intervention with conventional instruction or some other alternative (Campbell & Stanley, 1966). For example, an investigator may compare typical mathematics instruction with mathematics instruction enriched by metacognitive information. A researcher interested in memory strategies may compare the recall performance of students taught to rehearse to learn vocabulary words with those who learned vocabulary words using their own methods. In investigations of reading strategies, the typical comparison is between reading performances by students taught a strategy and those not instructed to use the strategy.

The design for a simple study in which an experimental group is contrasted with a control group contains two cells (i.e., conditions) as shown in Figure 1.3. For each cell in an experiment, two statistics are particularly important. The first is the **mean** for the cell, which is the arithmetic average of all scores. The second is the

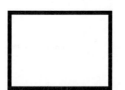

Experimental condition

Control condition

Figure 1.3
Two cells, experimental and control.

standard deviation, which is an index of how much each individual score in the cell differs from the mean for the cell on average. Thus, the standard deviation gives an index of the variation between scores in a cell (see Chapter 13 for a more complete discussion). If every person in the cell had the same score, each would have a score equal to the mean and the standard deviation would be zero.

How do researchers determine whether or not the differences between means are due to chance? They use the means and standard deviations in statistical tests that produce estimates of the likelihood that the experimental and control means differ by chance. These tests determine whether there is a statistically significant difference—one that is unlikely to occur by chance—between the means. If there is a statistically significant difference between the experimental and the control performances, researchers can draw the conclusion that there is a good chance the experimental treatment *caused* the difference in performance. In general, unless there is a 95 percent chance that the difference is not random, social scientists are reluctant to conclude that the difference is real. Often, researchers require even a more stringent standard, such as 99 percent certainty.

Since statistical significance does not tell researchers how large the mean difference between experimental and control conditions is, researchers compute effect size. Why compute effect size if the difference is statistically significant? The reason is that if there are a very large number of participants in a study, it is possible for even small effects to be statistically significant. Effect size, however, is not affected by the number of participants in a study, so it is important to calculate the effect size in order to determine whether the effect is important in a practical sense. One way researchers determine **effect size** is by comparing the size of the difference between the experimental and control means with the size of the standard deviation for the control condition. For example, if the experimental students average 65 percent on a posttest with a standard deviation of 15, and the controls averaged 50 percent with a standard deviation of 20, the effect size would be 0.75 (i.e., 65 − 50 / 20). If the effect size exceeds 0.9, the difference between the means is usually considered to be large; if the effect size is between 0.4 and 0.9, the difference is often described as moderate in size; if effect size is less than 0.4, the difference is considered small (Cohen, 1988).

Educational research studies are often much more complex than the two-cell studies presented so far in which an experimental condition is contrasted with a control condition. For example, if there are three possible instructional innovations, researchers sometimes compare the three innovations directly with each other and each of the three innovations with a control condition receiving typical instruction. This kind of study design would contain four cells (see Figure 1.4).

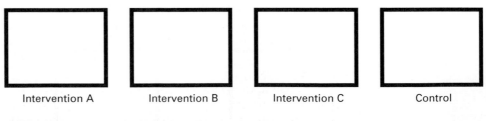

Intervention A   Intervention B   Intervention C   Control

Figure 1.4
Four-cell study: three interventions and one control.

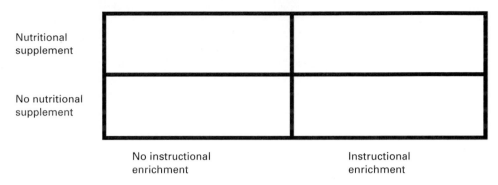

Figure 1.5
Design of a 2-by-2 study.

Sometimes researchers are interested in studying several different variables, each of which can be manipulated. For example, if researchers believe that both nutritional supplements and instructional enrichment promote the learning and thinking of young children, they conduct a factorial study. This study can be set up as a 2- (levels of nutrition) by-2 (levels of instruction) factorial design (see Figure 1.5). In one cell, children receive only the nutritional supplement; in a second, children receive the nutritional and instructional enrichment; in a third, participants are given only the instructional enrichment; and in the fourth (control) condition, children receive neither the nutritional nor the instructional enrichment. This design permits evaluation of whether nutrition, instruction, or nutrition and instruction combined produce differences in children's performances.

Nonmanipulative Investigations. In nonmanipulative studies, random assignment to the variables of interest is not possible. For example, if a researcher is interested in the effects of social class, race, or gender on educational achievement, obviously it is impossible to randomly assign students to these socioeconomic or biologically determined categories. There are two fundamental types of nonmanipulative studies.

Relating Differences Between People to Differences in Performance. The discovery of ways in which people differ increases understanding about human functioning in general. In the late-nineteenth and early-twentieth centuries, psychologists devised tests to classify people as more and less intelligent (see also Chapter 13). In this generation, new methods of brain imaging are revealing differences in brain activity between people, permitting classifications based on neurophysiological structures and functions (see also Chapter 6). Sometimes researchers conduct studies to classify people based on differences in information processing. For instance, people differ in their use of memorization strategies, reading comprehension processes, and problem-solving tactics. People can be classified as rehearsers, elaborative rehearsers, and imagery users. There are active and passive readers. Some problem solvers are planful and others impulsive.

These differences in people can predict important outcomes. Intelligence testing has been important because it predicts success in school. Differences in how students process information consistently predict performance. For example, rehearsers do not remember lists as well as people who integrate list items into memorable mental images. Active readers comprehend better than passive processors. Planfulness in problem solving is a predictor of success at problem solving.

Researchers also use individual differences in information processing to test theories. For example, suppose a researcher hypothesizes that construction of mental images during reading improves understanding of the relationships in the text. If that is true, people who naturally construct mental images while they read should comprehend what they read better. In fact, they do (Sadoski, 1983, 1985). There is a **correlation,** or relationship, between the natural use of mental imagery and text comprehension.

A **correlation coefficient** is used to summarize relationships between two variables. A correlation coefficient can range from −1.00 to +1.00. The greater the absolute value of the correlation coefficient, the greater the relationship between the two variables. For example, a correlation coefficient of 0 implies no relationship between the two variables, whereas either a −1.00 or a +1.00 implies a perfect relationship between the two variables. When the correlation is positive, it means that high values on one variable are associated with high values on the other variable. For instance, more time spent studying for a test is associated with higher test scores. When the correlation is negative, it means that high values on one variable are associated with low values on the other. For instance, increases in test anxiety are associated with lower test performance. See Table 1.3 for more examples.

Correlations provide initial evidence for causal theory. For example, if there had been no correlation between the natural use of mental imagery and text comprehension, the theory that imagery produces comprehension would be in question. The presence of a correlation, however, does not prove a causal theory, for there can be correlation without causation. *Correlation does not imply causation.* For example, perhaps people who naturally use mental imagery are more intelligent or are, in general, deeper thinkers. If so, their greater comprehension could be due to greater intelligence or deeper thinking rather than to their use of mental imagery. In short, studies examining potential correlations between individual differences in performance can be used to separate unlikely from plausible causal hypotheses (Underwood, 1975). Causality is then determined through manipulative studies.

Two characteristics that are evaluated frequently by researchers are gender and age. Age differences are sometimes examined at one point in time among different people at different age levels, such as studying 5-year-olds, 10-year-olds, and 15-year-

Table 1.3

Positive or Negative Correlations?

Examine the following examples to decide whether they illustrate positive or negative correlation:

1. More strategies used, more demonstrations of good thinking
2. More practice with a strategy, less time needed to use it
3. Less knowledge possessed, fewer demonstrations of good thinking
4. More short-term memory capacity, more demonstrations of good thinking
5. More brain abnormalities, fewer demonstrations of good thinking

Answers: 1. Positive; 2. negative; 3. positive; 4. positive; 5. negative.

olds all in 1994. This is done in a **cross-sectional study.** Less frequently, *changes* with age are examined, whereby researchers follow the same people for some time. This is done in a **longitudinal study.** For example, researchers may identify 5-year-olds in 1994 who will be assessed as 10-year-olds in 1999 and 15-year-olds in 2004. Longitudinal developmental studies are less common due to the tremendous cost in time and the greater difficulty in keeping track of participants.

Relating Differences in Settings to Differences in Performance. Differences in schooling environments can affect students' mental processing. For example, some classrooms encourage competition, while others encourage cooperative learning. Some promote substantial questioning, while others less questioning. Some include real conversations about subject matter, whereas others focus on the teacher's drilling and evaluating of students' responses (Mehan, 1979).

Sometimes researchers want to evaluate interventions that are basically differences in educational settings, but they cannot randomly assign people to conditions. For example, it is impossible to assign students randomly to public and private schools. It is even difficult sometimes to assign students to classrooms emphasizing some particular form of instruction compared with another form, for example, competitive versus cooperative classroom environments. What researchers typically do in these cases is to make comparisons between these different settings or interventions. Often, the researcher tries to ensure that the students in the settings being compared are as equal as possible except for the difference in the settings. For example, they might study public and private schools serving the same neighborhoods, or they might check the intelligence scores at the beginning of the year of students enrolled in competitive and cooperative classroom environments. The more equivalent the participants are at the beginning of the study except for the difference in the settings, the more willing researchers are to interpret differences as due to the setting.

One important approach to evaluating the effects of setting is the **cross-cultural study.** Sometimes cultures vary systematically on critical educational variables, such as whether children are formally schooled or whether students are encouraged to challenge their teachers. Cross-cultural researchers sometimes link such cultural differences to differences in students' performance.

Evaluating the Quality of Quantitative Investigations. What are the criteria for determining whether the evidence presented in a quantitative study is convincing or not? One is whether the study has **internal validity,** which means there are no other plausible competing interpretations of the results. A study with internal validity does not have confounding variables (Campbell & Stanley, 1966). **Confounding variables** are variables unrelated to the treatment that may be influencing the outcome. For example, if students in intervention classrooms are receiving free lunches and students in control classrooms are not, it is impossible to be certain that any difference in classroom performance is due to the intervention itself. The free lunch is a confounding variable. In another example, if students taught to use an imagery strategy are led to believe they are being taught this strategy because they are smart, it is impossible to know whether any improved performance is due to the imagery instructions. The difference could simply reflect enhanced self-esteem due to the comments made to them about their intelligence.

In this case, self-esteem is the confounding variable. Sometimes general motivational factors are confounding variables. Perhaps the improvement due to an educational intervention is simply a reaction to novel teaching, that is, due to increases in students' arousal, motivation, or interest (M. L. Smith & Glass, 1987). Perhaps the improvement is due to changes in teachers' expectations, which, in turn, affect students' motivation (R. Rosenthal & Jacobson, 1968). The improvement could even be due to students' awareness that their performance is being used to evaluate the effectiveness of the new instruction (Campbell & Stanley, 1966).

A second important criterion is **external validity.** Externally valid studies resemble the real-life issue the researcher is trying to investigate (Bracht & Glass, 1968). For instance, a study of reading by college students is externally valid to the extent that real college students are reading real texts in a setting that is like the ones in which college students typically read. If the study's participants were not representative of college students (e.g., if the students were enrolled in a remedial English class), if the readings were contrived (e.g., if the passages were from the Graduate Record Exam rather than from textbooks), or if the place where reading occurred was unnatural (e.g., if it took place at a computer screen), the study would lack external validity.

A third important criterion is **reliability,** which is the likelihood of obtaining the same results consistently. Reliability is high when the same results are found on different occasions and low when results differ from occasion to occasion.

Fourth, quantitative researchers value **objectivity,** which is the use of measures that are publicly observable and clearly measurable. The number of times teachers assist students is objective data; if researchers ask the teachers why they intervene, the data are more subjective and open to interpretation.

Fifth, quantitative researchers value **triangulation** (Mathison, 1988), which is a network of multiple indications of a phenomenon. Thus, if observations of overt behavior, teachers' verbalizations, and students' performance all suggest differences in helpfulness between teachers, the researcher is more confident that there are differences in helpfulness among teachers than if only one of the three measures was available.

Educational researchers often choose to observe students' behaviors in a classroom setting.

Qualitative Methods

What are the key differences between quantitative and qualitative approaches to research (Guba, 1990; Hitchcock & Hughes, 1989; K. R. Howe, 1988)? Quantitative approaches are based on the classical scientific method, whereas qualitative approaches depend more on interpretations and weighing the perceptions of participants in a setting. Whereas quantitative researchers do everything possible to obtain *objectivity*, qualitative researchers are more comfortable with *subjectivity*. Quantitative researchers are primarily interested in *testing theories*, and qualitative researchers are primarily interested in *constructing theories*. Qualitative researchers are attempting to develop what is called a **grounded theory**, that is, a theory constructed from interpretations of data (B. Glaser & A. Strauss, 1967).

Development of a Grounded Theory. A. Strauss and Corbin (1990) summarized how to construct grounded theories. The process begins with the *collection of data*. Qualitative researchers use a number of approaches to data collection. For instance, the researcher may observe behaviors in a setting of interest. In the case of a researcher interested in constructing a theory of first-grade reading groups, this may mean many visits to first grades to observe reading groups. Alternatively, the researcher may interview many first-grade teachers about what goes on in their reading groups. In some cases, the observations may be made by the participants themselves, perhaps in the form of diaries or daily journals. Of course, there is also the possibility of combining methods of data collection. Many qualitative studies combine observational and interview data.

In the next step the researcher goes through the data systematically *looking for meaningful clusters and patterns*, that is, behaviors that seem to go together logically. For example, if the teacher pairs off students to read to each other, encourages students to ask one another about difficult words, and suggests that several students read and discuss a library book, these observations suggest a meaningful cluster. The researcher then names the cluster. In this case, perhaps "cooperative reading" would be a reasonable name for this cluster of behaviors.

Analysis of extensive observations and interviews is likely to result in a number of categories. The next step in constructing a grounded theory is to *identify supports for the categories* by reviewing data. The qualitative researcher is always open to (and actually looking for) data inconsistent with an emerging category. Qualitative researchers often begin their data analyses early in the data collection, so that as tentative categories emerge, there is an occasion to look for support or nonsupport of categories with every new opportunity for data collection. The researchers take the emerging categories back to those being observed and interviewed and ask them to evaluate the credibility of the emerging categories. This is called **member checking** (Lincoln & Guba, 1985). Often the subjects of the investigation can provide important refinements and extensions of the categories. As a result of member checking, the researcher may change categories or the names given to them.

Eventually, a stable set of categories emerges based on data collected to date. The next task is to *organize these categories in relation to one another*. For example, the category of "teacher modeling" seems to subsume some of the other categories of behaviors such as teachers' "thinking aloud about how to decode a word," "acting out reading processes," and "acting out deciding to read for fun." Thus, "teacher

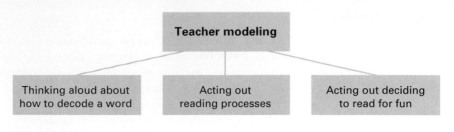

Figure 1.6
Organization of identified categories.

modeling" is higher on an organizational chart than the three categories it subsumes (see Figure 1.6).

Once the researcher has identified categories and placed them in a hierarchical arrangement, it is time to *collect new data.* For the example of the first-grade reading group, it would be time to observe more groups, adjusting the categories and their arrangements in light of new observations, interviews, and so on. Data are collected until no new categories emerge from new observations, no new properties of categories are identified, and no additional adjustments are made to the hierarchical arrangement of the categories.

Once enough data are collected and ordered, the researcher begins *hypothesizing causal relationships between the categories of information.* For instance, some reflection on the interviews with teachers may indicate that teacher modeling is caused by contemporary teacher education practices. That is, teachers may have indicated that they ran reading groups according to what they had learned in college. Alternatively, reflection on the interviews may suggest that teacher modeling is due to tradition. That is, teachers may have claimed that they ran reading groups according to what they had experienced as children. It is also possible that the interviews may indicate that teacher modeling is due to in-service resources. That is, the teachers may have reported that there were many on teacher modeling. Teacher modeling is not only caused by but also in turn causes reactions. For example, perhaps students begin to model reading processes to one another. The qualitative researcher evaluates all the various causal possibilities, actions, and reactions against all of the available data as completely as possible. Those that are supported by the data are retained; those that are not are deleted. This continues until **theoretical saturation,** the point at which all the data are explained adequately.

Eventually, the qualitative researcher must *report the data in a way that can be easily understood.* To tell the story, the researcher must identify a key category or categories, which must be in sufficient detail to reflect the richness of the data analysis. In addition, the researcher should submit the emerging story to member checking, until there is eventually a tale that seems reasonable to researchers and participants.

Evaluating the Quality of Qualitative Investigations. Just as it is possible to evaluate the quality of quantitative studies, it is also possible to evaluate the quality of qualitative studies. Although the evaluations are based on similar dimensions, the language is different (Guba & Lincoln, 1982; Lincoln & Guba, 1985). Thus, rather than worry about internal validity, qualitative researchers are concerned with **credibility.** The stronger the case that the grounded theory captures the reality of the situation studied, the greater the credibility of the study. Rather than be concerned with external validity, the qualitative researcher values **transferability,** which is a measure of how representative the setting is. Evaluating transferability means deciding whether the analysis would apply somewhere else. If transferability is found lacking, the researcher may have to collect data in another setting. **Dependability** is the qualitative researcher's term for reliability. The qualitative researcher must convince others that most people would come to the same conclusions based on the data. **Confirmability** is the term used instead of objectivity. Confirmability is generally high when something like triangulation occurs in the study, that is, when multiple indicators buttress conclusions.

Interaction Between Qualitative and Quantitative Approaches

Qualitative and quantitative approaches may not be as different as they seem. Researchers have come to realize that much of quantitative research involves qualitative decisions (K. R. Howe, 1988; Huberman, 1987). Every quantitative study involves deciding which variables to include and how to measure them, both of which are matters of interpretation. Researchers also make decisions about which statistical tests and criteria to apply, which again involve substantial subjectivity. The way the questions are framed in the introduction of the study, the hypotheses that are tested, and the way the story is told in the discussion section of a quantitative article are also the result of interpretations by the researcher.

Sometimes it is even possible to quantify qualitative data. For example, there is nothing wrong with reporting the proportions of participants who provide a particular rationale and supplementing observations and informal interviews with more formal and more quantifiable measurements.

Summarizing Across Investigations

Every important topic in education results in many studies being conducted. How do researchers make sense of so much data (see Table 1.4)? One method is to be decidedly qualitative. Read everything and try to sort the work and results into categories, figuring out how the categories are related to one another. Then write a review article summarizing what has been found.

There are also quantitative options for summarizing across studies. All quantitative options also require some qualitative sifting, such as figuring out what questions were asked in the literature and which studies asked which questions. The difference in the quantitative approach, however, is that the reviewer attempts to provide a numerical summary of one type or another. One procedure, known as the box-score method, entails counting up the number of studies of an issue reporting a significant effect and the number reporting no effect. This approach ignores much of the quantitative information reported in studies. For example, what if a difference just misses statistical significance? Well, it is a vote against the hypothesis, when in fact, it was almost a vote in favor. What if investigators in the various studies differ in the levels of statistical significance they are willing to interpret as significant or use analyses procedures that differ in sensitivity? For the most part, such distinctions are lost on the box scorer who simply counts up the declared winners (those that are statistically significant) and the losers (those that are not statistically significant).

The most important alternative to the box-score method is **meta-analysis**

Table 1.4

Evaluating Research Studies

As you read a description of a research study, ask yourself what research approach was used. Was it quantitative, qualitative, or both? Depending on your answer, select questions from the following:

- Was the study manipulative or nonmanipulative?
- Was random assignment used?
- Were any statistical tests significant?
- How large was the effect size?
- Are there any confounding variables?
- Were the measures and procedures reliable, valid, and objective?
- Is there evidence of triangulation?
- Can the results be generalized to real-life situations?
- If different age groups were used, is the study longitudinal or cross-sectional?
- Do the data fit the story told?
- Is there evidence of member checking?
- Are the results credible, transferable, dependable, and confirmable?

(Glass, McGaw, & Smith, 1981). With this approach, the effect size is calculated for each test of an issue. Then, the average effect size is calculated based on all of the comparisons reported in the literature. The logic of meta-analysis is that the mean effect size is a more reliable indicator of the actual effect size than the effect size generated in any particular investigation.

Chapter Summary

- Good thinking involves coordination of strategies and knowledge. Good thinkers possess the metacognition to regulate their strategy use effectively and are highly motivated to use their intellectual resources to tackle important academic challenges. Other characteristics of good thinkers include a normal brain, language skills, appropriate confidence, well-controlled emotions, effective use of short-term memory capacity, and the tendency to contribute to their own intellectual development. Good thinking depends on the interaction of any number of these factors.

- Good teaching can promote the development of good thinking in students. Good teachers teach important strategies, make certain students acquire metacognitive understandings about when and where to use strategies, convey a great deal of important knowledge about the world in general, and stimulate academic motivation. Good teaching can be achieved through a variety of teaching methods, including direct explanation and teacher modeling, discovery teaching, guided participation, and scaffolding. Good teaching is the beginning of students' construction of knowledge, stimulating them to use what they know and supporting them as they do. As students use new knowledge, their understanding of it continues to grow.

- Quantitative research focuses on testing theories using objective techniques. There are two major classifications of quantitative studies, manipulative and non-manipulative. The best quantitative studies are simultaneously high on internal and external validity, report outcomes proven to be reliable, and use a variety of objective measures so that triangulation is possible.
- Qualitative research uses subjective interpretation to construct a grounded theory. The best qualitative studies are credible and produce outcomes that are credible, transferable, dependable, and confirmable.

Chapter Outline

Chapter 2

Motivation

Classroom Predicament

The teacher announces to the class that whoever scores the highest on this difficult math assignment will win a prize. One student, Glenda, takes the assignment home, works on it a little, but doesn't really get much done. The teacher is surprised by Glenda's poor performance on the assignment, especially since her test scores and past performance would have predicted that she would be one of a group of top performers on the assignment. The teacher is disappointed in Glenda but decides not to let her know for fear of making her feel bad.

How can you explain Glenda's performance? What is likely to happen on the next difficult assignment? Is she likely to respond the same way to an English assignment? Is Glenda more likely to be a third grader or a tenth grader? Speculate on how this story would be different if it were about a student named Glenn. Reflecting on the information presented in this chapter will help you formulate responses to these questions.

Good thinking, as described in Chapter 1, requires complex interactions among motivation, knowledge, strategies, and metacognition. This chapter focuses on students' motivation. The next three chapters focus on knowledge, strategies and metacognition, and the role of knowledge in thinking, respectively.

Students are not always motivated to learn more or to use what they know already. Some do just enough to get by instead of using every opportunity to learn all they can. Others stop making any attempt to succeed academically altogether. If we wish to create good thinkers, we need to understand academic motivation better and to consider new ways of structuring schooling to enhance rather than destroy academic motivation.

Teachers must be aware that academic motivation is influenced by students' beliefs and perceptions as well as by classroom practices. For example, students' expectations for success and failure and how students explain their performances to themselves influence future performance. Moreover, classroom practices, such as offering rewards and setting goals, also have a considerable impact on students' motivation. For example, classroom environments that stress being the best in the class may have unanticipated effects. How schools and schooling practices can both undermine and promote achievement are themes that recur throughout this chapter.

How Motivation and Achievement Can Be Undermined

Why are some students not motivated to succeed in school? The answer is a complex mix of students' beliefs and perceptions, teachers' behaviors, and classroom practices.

Students' Expectations

Students hold expectations for their school performances that influence their academic motivation. Most children entering elementary school have high expectations for success. When asked how they will do on a task, most early-elementary school children assume that they will do very well (Clifford, 1975, 1978; Flavell, Friedrichs, & Hoyt, 1970; Stipek & Hoffman, 1980). For example, Pressley and Ghatala (1989) asked first and second graders to predict how many answers they would get right on a 30-item, multiple-choice vocabulary test. Nearly all of the children predicted that they would have all or almost all of the correct answers.

The optimism of young children is robust. Even after they fail to do as well as they expected, most children in the very early-elementary school years continue to believe they will do well (Clifford, 1975, 1978; Stipek & Hoffman, 1980). For example, even though none of the children in Pressley and Ghatala's (1989) study made anywhere near perfect scores, more than half of them believed they could make perfect scores if given another chance.

Older elementary school children are usually not so optimistic about their school performance, especially after they perform poorly on academic tasks. In general, students' expectations about themselves as academic achievers and students' interest in school and what they can learn there decline during the elementary years (Harter, 1981; Wigfield, Eccles, MacIver, Reuman, & Midgley, 1991). Later in this chapter we review techniques teachers can use to combat these declining expectations.

Young children's expectations of their school performance are very high. Later in elementary school, these expectations decrease.

Students' Attributions for Success or Failure

Student motivation is influenced not only by performance expectations but also by the explanations students give for their own performances. When you do well on a test, how do you explain your successful performance to yourself? When you perform poorly, how do you explain it to yourself? When people succeed or fail, they explain their success or failure to themselves in various ways. These explanations are called **attributions**. Students frequently explain outcomes by referring to effort, ability, task factors, or luck, and each of these attributions has different motivational consequences (Weiner, 1979). If students make effort attributions, then they believe success is due to their hard work and failure to their lack of effort. If they make ability attributions, they believe success is due to their high ability and failure to their low ability. If they make attributions to task factors, they believe success occurred because the task was easy and failure resulted from unreasonable demands of the task. Finally, if they make attributions to luck, they believe success reflects their good luck and failure their bad luck. Specific examples of these attributions are found in Table 2.1.

Table 2.1

Examples of Attributions for Success and Failure on a Math Test

- *Effort:* "I studied hard for the test"; "I didn't study hard enough or in the right way."
- *Ability:* "I'm smart in math"; "I'm dumb in math."
- *Task:* "Math is an easy subject"; "Math is the hardest subject."
- *Luck:* "I guessed right on some of the problems"; "I missed class the one day we talked about fractions."

The effort attribution is most likely to promote behaviors leading to future success. If you believe that successes and failures are due to effort, then you believe your fate is personally controllable. You can decide to try hard and be successful or to be idle and experience failure. The other explanatory possibilities—ability, task difficulty, and luck—are all out of your control. They are due to your genetic endowment, the teacher's task selection, or the whimsical nature of supernatural forces. Those who believe they can control their destinies are likely to be more motivated to exert effort to pursue goals than those who believe their achievements are out of their control (Bandura, 1982; deCharms, 1968).

Years of failure in school have led some students to conclude that achievement is not controllable. For example, learning disabled children are much more likely than their normally achieving classmates to believe that their achievements reflect low ability (Jacobsen, Lowery, & DuCette, 1986; Pearl, 1982). For many children, failure following great effort leads to discouragement and decreasing expectancies for future success (Covington & Omelich, 1979a, 1979b). Seeing other students experience success as a result of their efforts probably intensifies feelings of personal incapacity (Covington, 1987). This pattern may lead to the development of **learned helplessness**. Students who are learned helpless believe that there is nothing they do that will lead to success (Dweck, 1987). Doing nothing makes these students feel better, since if they fail without trying, they can attribute their failure to not trying instead of having to conclude that they are stupid (Covington & Omelich, 1981, 1984). Is it any surprise that learning disabled students often are passive in school? Trying gets them nowhere; not trying permits an explanation of failure that is not as damaging to the ego as failure following effort.

Ironically, some teachers' well-intentioned responses to students' failure may perpetuate learned helplessness. For example, a teacher may try to reassure a student who has performed poorly on a test by saying something like, "I know you tried hard." What the teacher is actually communicating to the student by this expression of sympathy is something like, "I know this is the best you can do." The student then thinks, "Even the teacher thinks I can't do this; I must be dumb." Even a teacher's response to success can send students the message that the teacher believes them to be incompetent. For instance, a teacher may exclaim, "Good for you, I didn't think you'd get that hard one right!" This sends a message about low ability (Stipek, 1993). Later in the chapter we review some methods for retraining students' attributions.

> ▶ **Diversity**

Gender Differences in Expectations and Attributions

Boys' expectations about their academic performances are often higher than girls' expectations (Crandall, 1969; Harter, 1981; Stipek & Hoffman, 1980; Wigfield, Eccles, MacIver, Reuman, & Midgley, 1991). These sex-based differences in expectations about academic achievement negatively influence girls' willingness to pursue some challenging academic arenas compared with boys' willingness to do so. Mathematics is an important example. During the early-elementary school years, girls surpass boys in mathematics achievement. However, reversal of this pattern begins in junior high and continues for the remainder of schooling. High school girls also take fewer mathematics courses than high school boys because they are less confident in their mathematics abilities and are less likely than males to value careers involving mathematics (Eccles, 1985). How can we explain these patterns? C. S. Dweck (1986) gives the following explanations.

First, high-achieving boys and girls react differently to failure on a task. Girls with high ability are more likely to be devastated by the failure than boys with high ability. This affects the girls' subsequent performances so that later the boys with high ability outperform the girls with high ability on the same task.

Second, girls are more likely to prefer the tasks they are good at than boys. In contrast, boys prefer challenging tasks. Moreover, girls are more likely than boys to attribute any difficulties they have to unchanging abilities rather than to low effort, high task difficulty, or bad luck.

Dweck (1986) reasoned that since mathematics courses given in the post—elementary school years (for example, algebra, geometry, and calculus) are full of new terms, symbols, and concepts, they look very different from elementary school arithmetic and are likely to present initial difficulties. For this reason, girls who are more disrupted by frustration and more likely to avoid the unfamiliar may decide not to pursue mathematics.

Eccles (1989) and her colleagues offer a third explanation. Parents and teachers have lower expectations and valuations of female performance in mathematics than male. Parents have gender-stereotypic expectations about math achievement and valuation (Eccles & Jacob, 1986), and these are communicated to daughters. How teachers undermine female confidence in mathematical abilities is harder to determine. However, there are some consistencies across classrooms in which female confidence is lower than male confidence (Eccles, 1989; Eccles, MacIver, & Lange, 1986).

Girls fare better in classrooms where there is (1) low competition, (2) private and personal contact with the teacher, and (3) little public drill and practice. It is also important for teachers to send the message that math is important for males and females alike, regardless of race or socioeconomic status (Kahle, 1984). Teachers who encourage achievement in mathematics among females do not give into attention-demanding tactics from males (who are more likely to engage in such tactics). Instead, these teachers make certain that all students participate in class discussion and interact productively with one another and with the teacher. Girl-friendly classrooms are supportive of minorities and lower-achieving boys as well (Kahle, 1984; Malcolm, 1984). Fortunately, there is increasing awareness in both students and teachers of the generally small and decreasing difference in male and female mathematical abilities (Hyde, Fennema, & Lamon, 1990).

Does sex-segregated education influence motivation? Some have argued that single-sex educational settings may produce greater academic achievement than coeducation (Coleman, 1961). In particular, some believe that gender biases that negatively affect females are reduced when females are schooled in sex-segregated settings (Bailey, 1993; Willis & Kenway, 1986). Although the evidence is mixed (Marsh, 1989a, 1989b), there is probably a small positive effect of sex segregation on academic achievement, at least at the secondary school level (Lee & Bryk, 1986, 1989).

The Impact of Rewards on Intrinsic Motivation

A teenager coaches young children in soccer to earn extra money. A second grader reads a book to earn a star. Reinforcements, such as the money and the star in these examples, can increase the likelihood of behaviors that precede them. However, rewards also have the potential for undermining performance. Teachers must pay attention to how they use rewards, especially for activities students would do without a reward because they are naturally reinforcing to them (Lepper & Hodell, 1989). For instance, college students who were paid money to work on a puzzle were less willing to work on it later when no reward was offered than students who worked on the puzzle previously without a reward (Deci, 1971). Also, preschoolers who were given a reward for drawing pictures were less interested in drawing pictures later than nonrewarded children (Lepper, Greene, & Nisbett, 1973).

When and why do rewards undermine performance? They do so when initial interest in the rewarded activity is high, or, in other words, when **intrinsic motivation** is high *and* when the reward to perform the behavior is so salient that it seems to be a bribe (Lepper & Hodell, 1989). The detrimental effects of reward primarily appear when they are offered to people simply for doing a task—not for doing a task well (Cameron & Pierce, 1994).

There are clear occasions, however, when teachers can use rewards to motivate performance. Students often are not intrinsically motivated to perform tasks that are good for them. When initial interest in an academic task is low, rewards can increase the likelihood of interest in and performance of the task (Bandura & Schunk, 1981; Lepper & Hodell, 1989). For example, beginning readers are more likely to struggle through an entire book if the reward is to place gold stars next to their names in the teacher's record book. The eventual goal, of course, is for these young readers to become intrinsically motivated to read.

Ego Involvement in Classrooms

It is important for teachers to evaluate the classroom environment in terms of the reward structures they have set up. The reward structures in most classrooms focus on how students do compared with others in the class. Such competitive classrooms foster **ego involvement**, meaning that students feel successful if they outperform others (Ames, 1984; Ames & Ames, 1981). Students in competitive classrooms often believe that success implies high ability and failure implies low ability (Nicholls, 1989). Since most students cannot be the "best" in the class, feelings of failure, self-criticism, and negative self-esteem often occur (Ames, 1984). Also, since trying and failing leads to feelings of low ability, students are less likely to attempt a new classroom task when success is uncertain.

Nicholls (1989) points to several common classroom practices that stimulate ego involvement. These practices may lead some students to conclude that they are not as capable as their peers.

1. Grading on the curve. Only a few students can be on the top of any curve, so most students experience failure in comparison to others in this grading system.
2. Emphasis on percentile rankings on standardized achievement tests. By definition, not every student can score above the national average; the scores of many students will be below average.

Turning play into work: Will this boy's intrinsic motivation to play baseball decrease if he matures into a major-league player earning a high salary?

3. Making grades salient and public. Handing out test papers in order of the grades (highest to lowest) causes many students to experience the public humiliation of failure.

What results can be expected from determining and publicly proclaiming who is smart and who is not? Nicholls believes that many students will go to great lengths to avoid having to try something academic, rather than risk failure, public humiliation, and additional confirmation of low ability compared with other students.

How else can teachers structure reward systems in classrooms? Instead of rewarding students for being better than one another, teachers can reward students for being better than they were previously. Teachers who reward personal improvement on a given task are fostering **task involvement** (Nicholls, 1989). Research on classrooms that foster ego involvement and those that promote task involvement indicates that students in task-oriented classrooms believe that success in school depends on interest, effort, and attempting to learn (Nicholls & Thorkildsen, 1987). In contrast, students in ego-involved classrooms believe that success depends on being smarter than other kids and trying to beat out other students. Moreover, students in task-oriented classrooms express more satisfaction with school and learning in school than students in ego-oriented classrooms. They are also more likely to ask for help that enables them to develop competencies (Butler & Neuman, 1995). This contrasts with the maladaptive behaviors of students associated with ego involvement: working hard only on graded assignments, being upset by low grades, comparing grades with classmates, choosing easier tasks, and copying other students' work (Stipek, 1993).

Students' Perceptions of Intelligence

Students' perceptions of the nature of intelligence also influence motivation. According to Dweck and Leggett (1988), a critical determinant of motivation is whether or not a person believes that intelligence is fixed biologically and not affected by environmental variables. People who believe that intelligence is fixed possess what is called an **entity theory** of intelligence. People who believe that intelligence is modifiable by experience subscribe to an **incremental theory** of intelligence.

Students' views of intelligence influence their persistence on academic tasks (Henderson & Dweck, 1990; Meece, Blumenfeld, & Hoyle, 1988; R. Wood & Bandura, 1989). As long as students are successful, there is little difference in the behaviors of entity and incremental theorists. It is when failure occurs that the differences in their outlooks become apparent. Students who are entity theorists are discouraged when they receive negative feedback since they interpret failure as an indication of low intelligence. Sometimes, they do not continue working on the task in order to avoid additional evidence of low ability. In contrast, students who are incremental theorists direct their energies toward increasing their abilities. They believe that daily efforts lead to small gains. These students persist when faced with obstacles because they see obstacles as a natural part of the learning process.

Students' theories of achievement can be heavily influenced by the behaviors of teachers and by reward structures used in the classroom. Ames and Archer (1988) asked students in the eighth through eleventh grades questions designed to determine whether one of their classes was structured according to incremental or entity theory. The researchers referred to incremental theorists as being **mastery-oriented**, because they focus on mastering material presented in class. They referred to entity theorists as being **performance-oriented**, because they focus on performing well. Students who described their classrooms as mastery-oriented classrooms endorsed the following statements:

> "The teacher makes sure I understand the work."

> "The teacher pays attention to whether I am improving."

> "Students are given a chance to correct mistakes."

> "The teacher wants us to try new things."

> "Making mistakes is part of learning."

> "I work hard to learn."

In contrast, students who described their classrooms as performance-oriented endorsed the following statements:

> "Students want to know how others score on assignments."

> "I really don't like to make mistakes."

"Only a few students can get top marks."

"I work hard to get a high grade."

"Students feel bad when they do not do as well as others." (Ames & Archer, 1988, p. 262)

In addition, students who perceive themselves to be in mastery-oriented classrooms reported using more strategies and more effective strategies, were more open to challenging tasks, were more positive about the class, and were more likely to believe that improvements follow effort. Those perceiving themselves to be in performance-oriented classrooms were more likely to have a negative view of their own ability and to believe that classroom difficulties reflect low ability.

Ames (1990) believes students are better off in mastery-oriented classrooms where the following messages are prominent: (1) Trying hard fosters achievement and intelligence. (2) Failure is a natural part of learning. (3) Being best is not what school is about; getting better is.

■ Building Your Expertise

Are You a Motivated Learner?

Are you generally motivated to learn? Can you apply the theoretical principles you have just read about to a case history you know well—your own? Which factors identified in this chapter influence your motivational level? Reflect on your answers to the following questions:

- *Expectations.* When I enroll in a course, do I expect to be able to do well and learn the material? Alternatively, do I expect that the course will be too difficult for me and that I will have to struggle just to get by?
- *Attributions.* Do I believe I have personal control over my academic successes and failures? Alternatively, do I believe my successes or failures are due to other things beyond my control, such as course difficulty, quality of teaching, and teachers' preferences?
- *Rewards and Intrinsic Motivation.* Do I work hard on academic tasks only to receive a good grade, or do I work so I will feel good about what I have accomplished? Do I study only because I reward myself with treats, or do I feel a sense of accomplishment when I feel I've mastered the material?
- *Ego Versus Task Involvement.* Do I always focus on how well I do in comparison to the rest of the class, or do I focus on how much I have learned?
- *Entity Versus Incremental Intelligence.* Do I believe there is only so much I can learn, or do I believe the more I learn, the more I am capable of learning?
- *Performance-oriented Versus Mastery-oriented.* Is my major goal to do well, or do I just want to make sure I eventually learn the material?

Your answers to these questions may vary depending on the course you are taking, your interest in the course's topic, whether or not the course is in your major, or even the semester or year. How well do your answers to these questions correspond to your actual academic achievement?

How to Create Motivated Students

Motivational researchers have made many suggestions for increasing students' motivation. Some of these include techniques for changing students' perceptions and beliefs. Others focus on changing classroom tasks and practices. If the next generation of teachers designed their classroom environments to be in accord with these recommendations, future generations of students would be much more motivated than the current one.

Facilitating Goal Setting

Sometimes students need help to focus their efforts toward the achievement of a goal. Achieving a goal requires the conscious direction of activities toward some desired end point. Teachers can help students learn how to set appropriate goals. The process of goal setting includes establishing a goal and modifying it if needed (Schunk, 1990). Goal setting guides the formulation of plans of action and the evaluation of progress toward a desired end state. The characteristics of goals can range widely. They can be *specific,* such as "I will learn to speak Spanish so I can travel more easily in Mexico," or more *general,* such as "I will become a better person." Goals also vary in terms of how long they take to accomplish. *Proximal goals,* such as "I will be able to spell these 20 vocabulary words by the end of this evening," can be accomplished in a relatively short period of time. *Distal goals,* such as "In four years, I will finish college and get a good job," can only be accomplished in the relatively distant future.

Do certain kinds of goals lead to better performance? Specific goals and proximal goals tend to be more motivating and lead to more success than general goals and proximal goals because progress is easier to gauge (Schunk, 1990; Stipek, 1993). Nevertheless, general goals can often be made more specific, and distal goals can be broken down into specific subgoals. For example, completing a project for a science fair can be divided into subgoals, such as developing the concept, asking the teacher for advice, getting the materials, beginning the initial experimentation, developing a display, explaining the project to the class, revising the display, and finally submitting the completed project.

● "What Do I Do on Monday Morning?"

Guidelines for Helping Students Set Classroom Goals

- Solicit students' goals whenever possible (Schunk, 1990). It is best if students can set their own goals. It helps them commit to the goal, attach personal value, and see the utility of the task.

- Elicit the involvement of students with teacher-selected goals. If it is not possible for students to set their own goals, then try to give students choices in goals or at least a choice of which goal to achieve first. Be sure to explain how a teacher-selected goal is relevant, and try to get students to describe relevancy by tying the task to something meaningful.
- Convince students of the goal's feasibility (Wentzel, 1989). Students must feel that they can reach the goal. Teachers can make the feasibility of a goal clearer to students by giving information that others have attained the goal, making sure the students have the resources to reach the goal, and letting the students know that others believe the students can succeed.
- Ensure feedback on students' progress toward the goal. It is best to teach students to monitor their own progress through self-observation and self-reflection. Elicit their appraisal through comments such as, "What do you think happened?" instead of "You stopped too soon" or "How did you do?" instead of "Good job, you got them all."

Increasing Students' Self-Efficacy

Students who believe they are capable of reaching a desired goal or of attaining a certain level of performance have a high level of perceived **self-efficacy** (Bandura, 1977a, 1986; Schunk, 1990, 1991; see also the discussion of social learning in Chapter 7). High self-efficacy in any given domain is important because it motivates future attempts at tasks in the same domain. For example, one motivation for a first-year university student to enroll in introductory calculus is previous success in mathematics. If the calculus course goes well, then self-efficacy in mathematics increases even more, which in turn motivates future selection of more mathematics courses. What if the calculus course goes badly? Self-efficacy in mathematics is likely to decline, reducing the likelihood of seeking mathematics credit in the future. Self-efficacy is determined in part by present attempts at learning and performance; it then affects future attempts at learning and performance.

What are the other determinants of self-efficacy besides previous success in the domain? First, there are *social models*. When people who are similar to you can do something, you are more likely to believe you can do it and should attempt to do it (Schunk, 1991). Second, the *opinions of others* provide encouragement and convince you of your competence. How many times did your gym teachers encourage you to try the balance beam because they were sure you could do it? Third, you consistently receive *specific feedback for your efforts*. Although modeling and the opinions of others have an impact on self-efficacy, specific feedback for efforts has a greater impact (Schunk, 1990, 1991).

Self-efficacy is domain-specific. There are students who have high self-efficacy in math and low self-efficacy in writing. There are those with high self-efficacy in most academic areas and low self-efficacy in athletics. Even within a single sport, there are students who have high self-efficacy in playing first base and low self-efficacy in pitching. All of us possess detailed knowledge about what we can do and what is beyond us.

Self-efficacy plays an important role in goal selection and persistence in efforts to attain goals. For example, Bandura and Cervone (1983, 1986) studied college students as they worked an exercise-type machine. The amount of effort students were willing to expend to improve in the task in the future was related to their perceptions of successful improvement based on feedback they had received. Perceptions of effectiveness in a present task increase task efforts in the future (Schunk, 1989, 1990, 1991).

The self-efficacy perspective suggests that it is important to provide students with tasks that are challenging. If students attempt an easy goal, they make progress rapidly, but they do not acquire information about their abilities to tackle more ambitious tasks. If students attempt too difficult a task, there is little success in meeting the goal. This results in diminished self-efficacy and motivation to continue with the task. Only tasks that are challenging for the learner, but not so difficult that progress is impossible, are capable of providing information to students that increases self-efficacy.

Does every attempt to accomplish a goal have great consequences for self-efficacy? This is not the case if a person already has a very strong sense of self-efficacy built up over many years (Bandura, 1986; Schunk, 1991). Suppose a college student has had a great deal of success in writing term papers and has high self-efficacy for this task. In his senior year, the student receives a *C* on his first paper for a new professor. Is there a major effect on the student's self-efficacy about writing? Probably not, or if there is, it is likely a very specific shift, such as, "I have to figure out what this professor wants in a paper." When attempting a new goal, however, the feedback on one occasion can have a dramatic impact on self-efficacy and long-term motivation. If this same student receives a *C* on the first poem he ever wrote, he may feel that he is not a very good poet and may not be motivated to write another poem.

Retraining Attributions for Success and Failure

As discussed earlier in this chapter, many students who experience difficulties with schoolwork attribute their failures to uncontrollable ability factors and, consequently, are not motivated to exert academic effort. Can the attributional tendencies of these students be retrained to controllable factors such as effort?

Students must be persuaded that their academic successes and failures are due to their own efforts. Since low-achieving students probably do not know how best to focus their efforts, it is not enough just to encourage these students to try hard; they must also be taught effective ways to learn. Thus, one technique used with low-achieving children is to train them first to use effective strategies to accomplish intellectual tasks. Then, the next step is to persuade students that their successes and failures on the academic tasks are due to their efforts in using the strategies (M. Carr & Borkowski, 1989; Clifford, 1984). For example, a student who has successfully used a new strategy would be told, "See how your performance improved when you used this strategy? See how *what* you do as you study determines how *well* you will do?" Many educators are already using attributional retraining with their learning-disabled students. For example, in the University of Kansas strategies instructional model, as students are taught comprehension, writing, and memory strategies, there is consistent emphasis on the role of controllable factors, such as strategy use, as a determinant of performance (Deshler & Schumaker, 1988).

Focus on Research

Retraining the Attributions of Low-Achieving Students

Let's examine in detail one study by John Borkowski and his colleagues who attempted to retrain attributional tendencies as part of larger educational programs aimed at students who had experienced academic difficulties. M. Carr & Borkowski (1989) randomly assigned underachieving elementary school students to one of three experimental conditions: (1) In the *strategies and attributional training condition*, students were taught comprehension strategies. They were instructed to read paragraphs and to determine through a self-test whether they understood the content. The students were also taught summarization, topic sentence, and questioning strategies as a means of understanding the text. The attributional part of the training consisted of emphasizing to students that they could understand the text by applying the comprehension strategies. In other words, they were persuaded that their comprehension of text resulted from how they approached the task rather than from their comprehension abilities. (2) Students in the *strategies-only condition* were taught strategies, without the benefit of attributional training. (3) Students in the *control condition* were provided with neither strategies nor attributional training. Think back to Chapter 1. Would this study be considered manipulative or nonmanipulative? (Consider random assignment.) How many experimental cells are there? (The answer is obvious in this example. There are three, of course.)

When tested three weeks later, the students in the strategies and attributional training condition were more likely to use the strategies than students in the other conditions. These students also recalled more text material. In addition, they maintained use of the strategies in the classroom much more than the students in the other conditions of the study. Why was a strategy-only condition included? (The reason was to increase internal validity by ruling out the alternative explanation that strategy training alone was responsible for the results.)

Nurturing Possible Selves

Ask yourself the following question: What am I going to be in 10 years? This question taps into your conception of the "possible self" you might become, which is another way to conceptualize your perceptions and expectations (Cantor, Markus, Niedenthal, & Nurius, 1986; Markus & Nurius, 1986). Students reading this book who are enrolled in teacher preparation programs may anticipate that they will be teachers, administrators, or curriculum developers. Students in music programs may envision themselves as concert soloists, conductors, or teachers. Possible selves should not be frivolous fantasies but rather realistic goals. Possible selves are the results of envisioning, and they can provide the motivation to continue reading this book and complete this educational psychology course, to enroll in more courses next term, and to look for advancement opportunities once school is completed. Possible selves provide direction and energy for behaviors that reduce the distance between the current true self and the possible self that one aspires to become (Markus & Nurius, 1986).

Unfortunately, many students do not have desirable possible selves. For example, consider a 10-year-old boy who expects to become a drug dealer because that is all he sees older boys doing in his neighborhood or a little girl who suspects she will never have a job because she knows no one who has one.

It is important to have a realistic possible self. Many students believe they have

The odds of becoming a professional athlete are extremely small. Nevertheless, many youths direct all their efforts toward this unlikely possible self.

a high probability of becoming professional athletes. In fact, the odds of attaining such a possible self are thousands to one (H. Edwards, 1973). This unrealistic possible self motivates effort directed toward athletic accomplishment, effort that could have been expended in pursuit of a self that is a more realistic possibility.

Attainable dreams can be powerful motivators. For example, Gooden (1989) reported the case of a dishwasher whose dream was to become a chef, a dream that motivated him to make it through cooking school. Gooden also described cases of young black males whose lofty goals, such as becoming a famous scientist or physician, kept them on track academically so that they did eventually become professionals, although they did not attain their specific dreams.

Given the potential of possible selves for motivating interest in and commitment to academic attainment, Day, Borkowski, Dietmeyer, Howsepian, and Saenz (1994) designed an intervention to encourage possible selves that is more likely to keep Hispanic students in grades 3 through 7 on track. Most of the students come from neighborhoods with few, if any, professionals. Thus, there is little opportunity to see Hispanic models in high-status occupations, models that could inspire these students to believe they could become professionals. Even so, these students highly value success in school and have ambitious possible selves: 92 percent expect to graduate from high school, 75 percent expect to graduate from college, and 17 percent expect to graduate from graduate or professional school. On the other hand, they also fear that these dreams may not come true. Half of the students fear that they will end up in jobs that require less than a high school education.

Day and her colleagues (1994) developed a training package designed to help the students maintain their dreams through the many, potentially frustrating steps of the educational process. This training package was aimed at increasing awareness of the many types of jobs these students might attain in their lives and to make it clear that completion of high school is essential for many vocations. In addition, the training package focused on how to cope with negative feedback and failure, including unjustified reactions of others. Consistent with the principles of attribution theory described earlier in this chapter, the training was designed to increase the students' understanding that their successes were under their control and that their academic efforts would pay off.

The results of this intervention are promising. In comparison to control students who did not receive the intervention, those participating in the possible-selves training had greater expectations of success in the future. They were more likely to believe they might attain especially high-status occupations, such as judge or physician, and showed modest improvements in grades (Estrada, 1990).

Fostering Cooperative Learning

Classroom environments are often characterized by social interactions that can have dramatic effects on students' motivation. David Johnson and Roger Johnson (1985) described three types of social structures found in classrooms.

First, a *cooperative* social situation exists when the goals of the separate individuals are linked together so that an individual can obtain his or her goal only if the other participants can achieve theirs. Students working together to put on a play is an example of a cooperative situation. The play is a success only if all students do their part. Second, a *competitive* social situation exists when the goals of the separate individuals are in opposition so that an individual can obtain his or her goal only if the other participants cannot obtain theirs. A spelling bee is an example of a competitive situation. Only one student can win; the others must lose. Finally, an *individualistic* social situation exists when there is no relationship among the goal attainments of the participants. Whether an individual accomplishes his or her goal has no influence on whether other individuals achieve their goals (D. W. Johnson & Johnson, 1985, p. 251). A student working to master the multiplication tables is an example of an individualistic situation. Success at this task has no bearing on the other students in the class.

David Johnson and Roger Johnson argued that most schools are much too competitive and individualistic in orientation with too little emphasis on cooperation. They estimate that **cooperative learning** occurs less than 20 percent of the time in American education (D. W. Johnson & Johnson, 1985). According to the Johnsons, there are four essential characteristics of learning (D. W. Johnson & Johnson, 1985):

Although this young girl is clearly happy to have won the spelling contest, the expressions of some of the other students emphasize the possible negative effects on students' motivation of a competitive classroom climate.

1. Learning should be *interdependent*. Tasks should be divided so different students can take on different parts of tasks. Moreover, task completion must require everyone's help. There must not be tasks where one person can do it all while the rest freeload. Rewards need to be structured so everyone has an incentive to pitch in and help.

2. There should be *face-to-face interactions among students within small learning groups*. The likelihood that all students will participate is greater with small groups than with large groups.

3. *Individual accountability* is essential. Students can assist one another effectively only if there is sufficient awareness among students about who knows how to perform a given task and who needs help.

4. Students need to be taught *interpersonal and small-group skills*. Students who do not naturally interact well in groups need to learn the social skills that permit more productive interactions.

Many studies indicate that cooperative learning produces better learning and more motivated learners than competitive or individualistic learning does (D. Johnson, Maruyama, Johnson, Nelson, & Skon, 1981). Fantuzzo, King, and Heller (1992) found that gains do not follow from rewards alone or from simply working together. It is incentives and working together in the context of cooperative structures that promote the learning of all students in a group. Another supporter of cooperative learning, Robert Slavin, emphasizes that cooperative learning is most likely to be effective if there are *both* group rewards and individual accountability (R. E. Slavin, 1985a). Cooperative learning works because of the mix of components rather than because of one of the components of the intervention. Specific instructional methods for cooperative learning are discussed in Chapter 10.

Stimulating Cognitive Conflict

One paradox of cooperative learning is that if it is done well, the participating students will be in some conflict with one another. For instance, one student may push for one perspective on a problem while another pushes for another perspective. Such cognitive conflict is healthy, motivating, and important to stimulate in students. Students think about the issues more deeply when they are challenged. This leads them to think about things in new ways. When there is conflict between current knowledge and new knowledge, the discrepancy motivates efforts to understand the new perspective (see the discussion of Piaget in Chapter 7). It is likely that knowledge will change as the new perspective is understood.

Lawrence Kohlberg (1969, 1984) translated ideas about cognitive conflict into educational methods. Interested in developing sophisticated moral reasoning in students, Kohlberg presented groups of students with moral dilemmas. Moral dilemmas are problems with alternative perspectives that elicit spirited discussion and conflict. Kohlberg hypothesized that cognitive growth occurs because hearing different ideas results in the learners' reflection on their assumptions, the viewpoints of others, and the differences between their own views and those of others. The students who dealt with these moral dilemmas were engaged in the learning process.

One of the most famous dilemmas that Kohlberg presented was about a character named Heinz whose dying wife could potentially be saved by a new drug.

Cognitive conflict emerging from students' discussions stimulates thinking.

The dilemma is that the druggist who discovered the drug wants a great deal of money for it. Heinz doesn't have the money and considers stealing the drug. The questions posed to students are "Should Heinz steal the drug? Why or why not?" The ensuing discussion exposes students to a variety of perspectives. Students learn that controversial issues are many sided and complex. In Chapter 9, we discuss Kohlberg's stage theory of moral development, which was generated through research with moral dilemmas. For now, it is sufficient to ask whether cognitive conflict generated by moral dilemmas, such as the story of Heinz, increases the sophistication of moral judgment. Enright, Lapsley, and Levy (1983) concluded that, beginning with students in middle school, cognitive conflict works despite the variety of techniques, teacher variations, and treatment lengths.

The use of cognitive conflict to motivate academic engagement is not restricted to moral issues. Indeed, stimulating cognitive conflict is at the heart of some science education interventions. These methods are based on the fact that students have many inaccurate scientific beliefs. For example, the following are common misconceptions about blood and circulation (Arnaudin & Mintzes, 1985; Barrass, 1984):

> All organisms have blood.
>
> Blood is made up only of red cells.
>
> Under the microscope, blood looks like a bunch of red cells clustered closely together.
>
> The heart cleans, filters, makes, and stores blood.
>
> There are air tubes from the lungs to the heart.

Blood is not responsible for transporting nutrients throughout the body.

The heart is one pump, pumping blood from itself to the body.

The heart only pumps oxygenated blood.

Teachers should draw out inaccurate beliefs early during instruction (Nussbaum & Novick, 1982; see also Chapter 12). As teachers present more accurate conceptions, they stimulate conceptual conflicts between the inaccurate prior knowledge and the new information through discussions as well as through demonstrations. Teachers make additional input to elaborate the new scientific understandings and beliefs. Lively and engaging debate continues throughout the process of learning scientific concepts.

Such debate is possible in mathematics as well. Contemporary mathematics educators believe in fostering discussion that simultaneously activates incorrect knowledge and more realistic understandings. They encourage students to discuss and debate problems, generating alternative ways of solving problems (Charles & Silver, 1989).

Praising Students

Teachers often have opportunities to praise students, and they should do so. How they do so, however, determines whether the praise is motivating for students. Brophy (1981) summarized research on praise and offered a set of prescriptions about how teachers should praise for the best effects.

Effective praise is delivered following desirable behaviors by students. That is, the praise should be *contingent* on the behavior. In delivering the praise, the teacher should make clear what it was about the student's behavior that was praiseworthy. In other words, the praise should be *specific*. The teacher should focus attention on the student's behaviors leading to the praise.

Effective praise is *sincere,* reflecting the teacher's attention to the student's accomplishments. The praise implies that the student can be similarly successful in the future if appropriate effort is exerted. The praise also contains a message that the student expended the effort to receive the praise because he or she enjoyed the task or wanted to develop the competencies that were praised.

Unfortunately, effective praise as described by Brophy rarely occurs in classrooms. Instead, praise not connected to noteworthy behavior by students occurs frequently in most classrooms. Much of the praise teachers give does not make clear what the student did well. It may be bland, repetitive, and not informative (e.g., "Good job"; "Nice work"; "Good . . . Good . . . Good"). There is even praise for behavior that really is not praiseworthy. For example, many teachers praise for participation alone (for example, "I'm so glad you are taking part"), rather than for participation consistent with the processes being taught (for example, "You have really thought hard about this").

Encouraging Volition

People differ in the extent to which they can stick with a task and not be easily distracted (Kuhl, 1985). This individual difference is an important determinant of performance on many tasks. In the classroom, this is called **volition** (Corno, 1989).

How can students learn to increase their volitional capabilities? They need to learn to control their attention to the task at hand, especially to ignore distractions in the environment. Schools are filled with distractions, from the antics of the class clown to the sounds of commotion in the hallway.

One way to encourage students to develop volition is to teach them to generate verbal self-instructions to attend to a task. Self-instruction is essentially talking to oneself (see the discussion of cognitive behavior modification in Chapter 7). Many successful interventions involve simply teaching children to tell themselves to ignore distractions (Meichenbaum, 1977; Pressley, 1979). Often, difficulty with a task is accompanied by emotional responses. Students need to learn to suppress these responses, since anxiety and distress can disrupt information processing. They can learn to instruct themselves to remain calm and task-focused (Corno, 1989). For example, they can tell themselves, "I can't worry about this; I can't get irrational." Students also need to learn how to motivate themselves if they begin to become discouraged. They can learn to self-verbalize encouragements (Corno, 1989), such as, "I know this material, and I'll succeed next time," or to think of new strategies for reviewing the material on a next round, such as, "This time I'm going to reread closely and take notes." Self-instruction can have a powerful effect on students' performance in the classroom, particularly for those who are hyperactive and impulsive (Manning, 1988, 1990; Zentall, 1989).

● "What Do I Do on Monday Morning?"

Suggestions on How to Motivate Students

Brophy (1986, 1987) suggested that many teachers do not understand all that they can do and need to do to maximize motivation in their classrooms. Teachers, however, can learn tactics for increasing students' motivation. Brophy proposed the following "greatest hits" list of motivational interventions:

- Teachers should model interest in learning. Teachers should let students know they like learning and find academic activities satisfying.
- Teachers should communicate to students reasons for being enthusiastic about school. When presenting new content, for example, the message should be that the students will find the material interesting; a message that the material is boring should never be sent. Presentations should be staged so that words, tone, and manner make clear that the material at hand is important and worth learning.
- Teachers should create low-anxiety classrooms. What goes on in school should be presented as learning experiences, not tests. It is better for classrooms to be task-oriented than ego-oriented.
- Teachers should induce curiosity and suspense. For example, students should be encouraged to make predictions about what might be in an upcoming text or lesson. Cognitive conflict should be induced. To stimulate students to come up with ways to resolve the contradictions, apparent contradictions in materials or current knowledge should be pointed out.
- Teachers should make abstract material more personal, concrete, and familiar. Relating such material to prior knowledge is a good way to help

students understand it. Moreover, concrete material is easier to understand and remember than abstract material. In addition, people often understand specific cases much better than the abstract principles the cases illustrate (see also Chapters 3 and 4).

- Teachers should provide students with informative feedback, such as contingent praise. As much as possible, students should be given tasks that provide them with automatic feedback on how well they are progressing. For example, not being able to complete a writing assignment on a story provides feedback to the students that their understanding of the story may be incomplete.
- Teachers should design tasks so that there is opportunity for activity. Projects, discussions, role-playing, and simulations all induce student activity.

Making Academic Tasks More Interesting

People pay more attention to content they find interesting (Hidi, 1990; Renninger, 1990; Schiefele, 1991). This prompts educators to transform academic materials so they will grab students' attention. There is a terrible paradox here, however. Sometimes these embellishments result in students' learning something other than what the materials were intended to teach. The areas of instruction studied most completely by interest theorists are learning from text and learning from computers.

Learning from Text. What makes a text interesting? Texts should include characters with whom readers can readily identify, such as characters similar in sex, age, race, religion, and occupation to readers. Texts should also be based on life themes important to the readers and depict intense action and feeling (R. C. Anderson, Shirey, Wilson, & Fielding, 1987).

The textbooks used in school are often dull. One way these texts can be improved is to include interesting anecdotes and examples. Unfortunately, this practice contributes to a lack of coherence in textbooks and can have unintended consequences. For instance, adding intriguing details to a text has a great danger (Garner, Gillingham, & White, 1989; Garner, Alexander, Gillingham, Kulikowich, & Brown, 1991): readers may pay so much attention to what Garner and her colleagues (1991) called the "seductive details" that they neglect the main ideas. The seductive detail is italicized in the following text:

> Some insects live alone, and some live in large families. Wasps that live alone are called solitary wasps. A Mud Dauber Wasp is a solitary wasp. Click beetles live alone. *When a click beetle is on its back, it flips itself into the air and lands right side up while it makes a clicking noise.* [Italics added.] Ants live in large families. There are many kinds of ants. Some ants live in trees. Black ants live in the ground. (Garner, Gillingham, & White, 1989, p. 46)

Garner and her colleagues found that recall of the main ideas was approximately half as likely when the text contained a seductive detail as when readers processed texts with the seductive details deleted.

Learning from Educational Software. Many classrooms now contain microcomputers, and there are growing lists of educational software. Some programs are dressed-up drill-and-practice routines, essentially electronic flash cards. Others incorporate all the bells and whistles of the most elaborate arcade games.

Mark Lepper and his colleagues (Lepper & Malone, 1987; Malone & Lepper, 1987) analyzed the motivational properties of computer software. They had little difficulty demonstrating the motivational appeal of gamelike versions of computer programs compared to drill-and-practice programs that cover the same content. Children are willing to spend much more time with games than with drills. Unfortunately, gamelike programs do not always produce greater academic achievement.

Lepper and Malone described the characteristics of these programs that make them intrinsically appealing and motivating to students. They are appropriately *challenging*—not too easy but not so difficult that they cannot be played competently with some effort. They also *provoke curiosity*. For example, how do the lights and sounds change what appears on the screen? They *provide a sense of control* to players, that is, a feeling that their actions determine what happens in the miniature world of the computer program. The games also involve *fantasy*. In addition, some of the games *offer opportunities to cooperate* with others, which can be motivating. Other games increase motivation by *providing opportunities to compete*. Some games *provide explicit opportunity for recognition*. For example, the program may include a "Hall of Fame" for players who have played exceptionally well.

Unfortunately, the current generation of computer programs is designed to be intrinsically motivating with little thought given to how to facilitate learning of the content. It is all too easy to have a lot of fun with many of the programs without learning much.

In fact, during a school visit we learned from a fifth-grade student a way to trick a math program in order to remain at the microcomputer. The trick was simply to make certain *not* to perform at mastery, since to do that meant that the program would produce a fireworks display in celebration of the student's success. This display would end the student's day at the computer.

Lepper and Malone believe that computer games and software can be programmed to be instructionally effective. They can be programmed to enhance

Many computer programs are motivating but instructionally ineffective.

attention to content, to provide appropriate feedback about learning and performance, to increase the meaningful processing of the program content, and to produce multiple representations of content.

Chapter Summary

- Traditional classrooms are often not motivating environments for students. High expectations turn into low expectations as schooling continues.
- Students' attributions for success and failure influence their motivation. Effort attributions are most likely to lead to improved future performance. Many unsuccessful students, such as the learning disabled, make attributions that they have no control over their performance and consequently become learned helpless.
- Girls are much more likely to react to initial difficulties by avoiding the task situation than boys are. Thus, mathematically competent females who could succeed at advanced math get discouraged and stop taking math.
- Classroom environments can have powerful effects on the cognitive processes affecting motivation. The ego (or competitive or performance) orientation of many classrooms undermines intrinsic motivation to learn and naturally high expectations of success. On the other hand, the classroom with a task (or cooperative or mastery) orientation produces increased student expectancies for success if appropriate effort is exerted. Such classrooms also signal that intelligence is incremental rather than an entity that is fixed.
- When teachers consistently require students to work on tasks that are just beyond their competence, there is a high potential for students to develop the understanding that effort pays off, that is, to develop high self-efficacy with respect to academic tasks. Resolution of cognitive conflict following cognitive effort is likely to increase self-efficacy and long-term academic effort. Teachers can also encourage students to believe that they can do well in school and in life and hence affect the possible selves the students imagine.
- Classrooms filled with praise and other rewards can motivate students in the long term if the reinforcement is informative and clearly flags what the students did that was praiseworthy. Positive reinforcement can decrease long-term motivation, however, if the students infer they are working *only* for rewards.
- Students who are especially prone to distractions can learn to self-instruct to stay on task or to increase volition. Giving themselves instructions such as, "OK, I'm moving along. I'm getting some of this done" or "Don't get anxious, just try another way to work the problem" can have powerful effects on students' performance.
- Educators must engineer tasks so that attention is not diverted to the high-interest part of the presentation at the expense of the intended content.

Return to the Classroom Predicament

Has this chapter helped you understand Glenda's performance better? Glenda really didn't try to complete the math assignment, most likely because her expectations for success were low. Perhaps her mother saw her working on the assignment and said, "Oh, it's a hard math assignment. Don't worry if you don't finish." Even though Glenda had high ability, she had low self-efficacy, at least in the math domain. Since self-efficacy is domain-specific, it would be difficult to predict performance in another academic subject such as English. It is also important to note that the teacher has set up a competitive learning environment, which encourages ego-involvement and performance goals rather than learning goals. This environment fosters the development of learned helplessness in Glenda. If she doesn't try hard, there is no need for her to attribute her performance to ability, which may damage her ego. The teacher's lack of response has the unintended effect of indicating to Glenda that the teacher must really not have expected her to do well, so Glenda will be even more likely not to work hard on the next math assignment. Since gender differences in math expectations increase in high school, Glenda is more likely to be in high school. If someone named Glenn were given this assignment, he would likely be more comfortable with the competitive environment, would pay less attention to the teacher's feedback, and would be more likely to have higher self-efficacy in math.

Chapter Outline

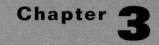

Chapter 3

Representation of Knowledge

Classroom Predicament

Jason has just moved into a new school district in a different state from where he had lived previously. Even though he has never been to this school before, he knows what a student is expected to do. He knows how to talk to his teachers. He knows he will sit in one of the desks in the classroom, but not the big desk at the front of the room. He knows he will need paper and pencils. He knows he should listen to the teacher and not talk to his neighbor while the teacher is talking. He always earned *A*s and *B*s on his report card, so he feels pretty good about what he knows until his social studies class when the students and teacher begin to have a lively discussion. What are they talking about? Are all these students so much smarter and so much better informed than he is? He was pretty smart in his old school; what is going on? He can't even follow the discussion because so few of the topics are familiar to him. They don't ring a bell at all. They are discussing historical events and people about which he has never even heard. Finally, he realizes the discussion is about places and events from this state's history. He really has to catch up.

Why does Jason know how to behave in this new school? Why doesn't he understand the discussion? Can we explain the differences in his knowledge in terms of the kinds of knowledge structures in long-term memory? Reflecting on the information presented in this chapter will help you formulate responses to these questions.

O ne of the components of good thinking described in Chapter 1 is the use of extensive knowledge stored in long-term memory. You may have heard the saying "Ignorance is bliss." For the good thinker, however, "Knowledge is power." Your long-term memory includes memory of the 26 letters of the alphabet. It also includes an understanding of what a mother is, what is meant by *democracy*, what the key characteristics of mammals are, and why the moon revolves around the earth. Even more complex understandings are represented in your long-term memory. For instance, when you stop at a fast-food hamburger restaurant, you know how to behave appropriately, what will be on the menu, and how to go about ordering your food. You also know how to accomplish complex tasks such as driving a car and keying information into a computer from a keyboard.

How do we represent such different kinds of knowledge in our long-term memory? This chapter describes different models of the representation and organization of knowledge in long-term memory. As of yet, we really do not know which of these models is the "best" explanation. Some models explain some types of knowledge better than others. For example, in early childhood you acquired the concept of *mother.* You can also access a visual depiction of your mother from a knowledge representation called an image. Your understanding of what the key characteristics of mammals are can be represented in a network (conceptual or propositional) of related ideas. At the most basic level, connections between ideas may be best described in knowledge representations called neural networks. Your knowledge of how to behave in a fast-food restaurant is best characterized by a knowledge representation called a schema. Your knowledge of how to do such things as drive a car is best represented in productions. These different types of knowledge interrelate, with complex connections between them that are often not very well understood. In this chapter, all of these different ways to represent knowledge are examined.

Concepts

A **concept** is a mental representation of a category of related items (Klausmeier, 1990). Concepts help us organize our experiences by allowing us to group similar things together into categories. Without this ability, it would be difficult to make sense of the many, many different things we experience in our environment. For example, your concept of *dog* helps you lump together the Labrador retriever in the neighborhood, Lassie from television and movies, and greyhounds at the race track (Bower & Clapper, 1989). When you see an animal coming toward you on the street, you can use your concept of *dog* to decide whether or not the approaching animal is a dog, rather than a rat or a lion.

Formation of Concepts

How people classify items into conceptual categories is not completely understood. One perspective, the **feature comparison theory,** is that concepts are defined according to the necessary and sufficient features, the **defining features,** required for an item to qualify as a representative of the concept (Stillings et al., 1987). For example, the defining features of a *grandmother* are being female and having a child who has had a child. According to the feature comparison theory, learning a concept is largely a matter of learning its defining features. For example, a *triangle* is a closed figure in a plane with three straight sides and three interior angles. Having learned these defining features of a triangle, a student can identify examples of triangles such as a slice of pie or a side of a pyramid.

The feature comparison theory explains the formation of clear-cut concepts, ones about which most people find it easy to agree on whether or not an item is an example of the concept. Most of us would recognize a triangle. Most of us recognize a football game when we see it. However, other concepts are not as clear-cut and are referred to as "fuzzy" (Neisser, 1967; Oden, 1987). For instance, it is not clear when a person stops being a juvenile and becomes an adult or when a small business becomes a large business. There is substantial fuzziness to these and other concepts carried around in our heads.

We cannot reduce fuzzy concepts to a set of particular features that uniquely define instances of the concept. For instance, it is difficult to determine what the defining features of adulthood are. Moreover, the harder we look at many clear-cut concepts, the fuzzier they get. For example, most of us would classify a woman who adopted one child, who in turn had a child, as a grandmother. We also apply many noncritical features to our conceptual decisions. For instance, we are more likely to classify women over the age of 40 with gray hair as grandmothers than women under the age of 40 with youthful hair color (Stillings et al., 1987).

In contrast to the feature comparison theory, the **prototype theory** suggests that people classify concepts on the basis of resemblance, not defining features (Rosch, 1975, 1978; Rosch & Mervis, 1975). Thus, *typical* grandmothers are older than 40 and have gray hair. *Atypical* grandmothers (e.g., 35-year-olds who had a child at 17, who in turn had a child at 18) are less readily classified as grandmothers. Because of its typicality, we easily and quickly classify a robin as a bird, but we less certainly classify a penguin as a bird. We are able to make these classifications because we construct a **prototype,** or a very typical member of the category. The more an animal resembles this prototype bird, for example, the more certainly and quickly we would classify it as such. We would respond faster to the question "Is a robin a bird?" than to the same question posed about a less typical example of bird such as a chicken (Rips, Shoben, & Smith, 1973; Rosch, 1973; Rosch & Mervis, 1975). People recall more typical category members before the atypical ones, and children learn the typical category members first (E. E. Smith & Medin, 1981.)

How are such prototypes formed? They are mental averages of the many instances the concept has been previously encountered in the world. Both adults and children construct such mental averages (Lasky, 1974; Posner & Keele, 1968, 1970; Reed, 1972). For example, in Lasky's (1974) study, 8-year-olds and adults observed patterns of geometric forms and later selected patterns they had seen before on a recognition task. One of the patterns, called a prototypical pattern, shared features with previously viewed patterns but was not identical to any one of them. Both adults and children rated a prototypical pattern as having been seen previously, even though it had not been presented. This prototype received even higher ratings than patterns that were actually presented. Thus, the adults and children had formed a prototypical concept and were using it to guide decision making on the recognition test.

Relationships Between Concepts

Our conceptual understandings are related to each other in **semantic networks** in which concepts are stored in nodes with links between the nodes specifying the relationship between the concepts. There are large networks of associations to each of these nodes, with many of the associations being very personal. For example,

The ostrich, which is wingless, flightless, and large, is an atypical example of the concept *bird*. A robin, on the other hand, is a closer match to the bird prototype and would be recognized as an example of the concept *bird* more quickly than an ostrich.

perhaps polar bears are connected to memories of the Arctic exhibit at a zoo you once visited. Polar bears may also bring to mind Klondike ice cream bars, which have a polar bear on the wrapper. Your knowledge of polar bears also is connected to your knowledge of penguins, sea lions, and walruses, with knowledge of all of these animals tied to your knowledge of the Arctic.

Concepts are hierarchically organized. For example, the concept of all living things can be subdivided into animals and plants. Animals can be further subdivided into reptiles, mammals, birds, insects, and so on, each with associated features (e.g., hair, vertebrate, and warm-bloodedness for mammals). Mammals can be divided by genus (e.g., bears, elephants, giraffes, moles, etc.), each with associated features. Each genus is further divided into species (e.g., bears can be polar, black, brown, grizzly, etc.). Each species has its associated features.

Consider the animal concept hierarchy in Figure 3.1. Questions requiring consideration of information at different places in the hierarchy are answered more slowly than questions requiring information coded in nearby nodes (A. M. Collins & Quillian, 1969). For example, the question "Do robins have skin?" takes longer to answer than "Do robins have red breasts?" since the feature of red breasts is stored directly with *robins* and the feature of skin is stored with *animals,* which is farther away in the animal hierarchy.

The associations between nodes are particularly important since activation of any particular part of the network results in **spreading activation** to parts of the hierarchy that are "closer" and more highly associated with the activated concept (A. M. Collins & Loftus, 1975). Activating some content can make it easier to understand related material. Thus, if the word *stone* is read by a person followed by the word *rock, rock* is recognized more quickly than if *stone* had not been activated since the activation of *stone* can spread to *rock,* a highly associated concept (D. Meyer, Schvaneveldt, & Ruddy, 1975; Neely, 1976, 1977). The sentence "The lawyer is in the bank" is understood more quickly if the sentence is preceded by a sentence containing words associated with *lawyer* and *bank,* such as *judge* or *money* (J. R. Anderson, 1984; McKoon & Ratcliff, 1979).

What are the educational implications of semantic networks? Teachers often

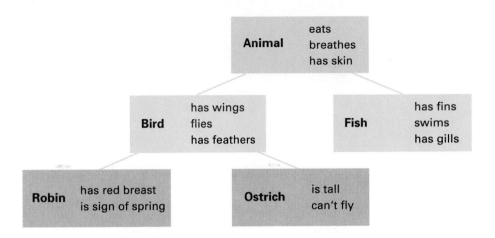

Figure 3.1
Sample hierarchical semantic network, showing animal hierarchy.

encourage students to activate background knowledge about material that is to be presented. They may remind students of what they learned yesterday or ask students to think about everyday experiences that are related to the topic at hand. This encourages spreading activation through a hierarchical network that encodes many associations between concepts. For example, a teacher may introduce a lesson on the Spanish Civil War by asking students to consider what they know about the Civil War in the United States. The students could be asked to think about the kinds of tensions and disagreements that can lead to civil war. This activation should make it easier to understand new content and its relationship to the activated knowledge.

Sometimes students even reap the benefits of spreading activation while taking a test. For example, consider the student who draws a blank when reading a test question, skips the question, and continues with the rest of the test. Later on, another question on the test activates knowledge the student has. The resultant spreading activation brings to mind the answer to the question the student had skipped. There are great advantages to having a well-organized semantic network!

▶ **Diversity**

The Influences of Development and Culture upon the Formation of Hierarchical Concepts

Do children have hierarchical conceptual networks that resemble those of adults? In general, even preschool children possess knowledge about hierarchical relationships between some of the concepts they know. Infants can abstract categories from presentation of a number of examples of category members (Anglin, 1977; Bomba & Siqueland, 1983; M. S. Strauss, 1979), and 2- to 3-year-olds can sort familiar objects into appropriate categories (Carey, 1985; Gelman & Baillargeon, 1983; Horton, 1982; Markman & Callanan, 1983; Sugarman, 1983).

Western-style schooling increases children's use of hierarchical knowledge in tasks requiring categorization.

The knowledge of hierarchical relationships possessed by preschoolers, however, is not always used by them. Children often prefer to use *thematic relationships* rather than categories to group objects even though they can be categorized (Bruner, Olver, & Greenfield, 1966; Kagan, Moss, & Sigel, 1963). Thus, when given a group of objects that can be sorted into categories (e.g., tiger, elephant, monkey, giraffe, banana, orange, grapes, and apple), preschoolers often sort according to themes (e.g., monkeys eat bananas, elephants and giraffes live in the same house at the zoo, a tiger could eat an apple, mommy puts oranges and grapes in her fruit salad). Unlike adults, children also underextend—for example, using *duck* to refer only to one's pet duck—and overextend—for example, using *duck* to refer to any bird larger than a robin—their use of concepts (L. Bloom, 1973; E. V. Clark, 1973).

Research in other cultures indicates the influence of experience on the use of categories. Specifically, attendance in Western-style schools increases the use of hierarchical, categorical knowledge. D. Sharp, Cole, and Lave (1979) found that rural Mexicans without formal schooling classified objects on the basis of functional properties. For example, when given a triad of chicken, horse, and egg, they grouped chicken and egg together as related objects. In contrast, rural Mexicans with some formal schooling used categories comparable to Western-educated adults. They grouped chicken and horse together as examples of the conceptual category of *animal.*

● "What Do I Do on Monday Morning?"

Concept Learning in School

Important concepts in a culture are often transmitted through schooling. For example, in English class students learn the concepts of *noun* and *verb,* and in mathematics class they learn the concepts of *square* and *prime number.* What are some ways to teach concepts?

A teacher may elect to teach a concept directly by first presenting the name and definition of the concept. This definition will include the defining features of the concept. For example, the defining features for *square* are a four-sided figure with four equal sides and four right angles. Then the teacher presents examples and nonexamples of the concept. Students develop concepts by seeing examples of what a concept is and what it isn't. The examples the teacher uses can be either actual ones or ones depicted in pictures. For the concept *square,* examples might be a large square white gift box and a children's small, square wooden block. Nonexamples for *square* might be a rectangular shoe box and a round orange. Then, the teacher points out both the defining features and the irrelevant characteristics of the concept. For example, color and size are irrelevant for squares. Finally, the students are asked to find their own examples of the concept and receive feedback on the correctness of their choices.

Tennyson and Park (1980, p. 59) suggest three rules for presenting examples and nonexamples of a concept: (1) arrange the examples from easy to difficult, clear-cut to hard to classify, since more typical examples are easier to learn; (2) select examples that differ in terms of irrelevant features, in order to explore the full range of irrelevant characteristics; and (3) point out the similarities and differences between the examples and nonexamples, in order to clarify which are defining features and which are irrelevant characteristics.

The teacher may also elect a discovery approach (see Chapter 1), in which the teacher presents examples and nonexamples and asks students to discover the definition of the concept and to determine the defining features and irrelevant characteristics. The students can work on this independently or in groups, with the teacher answering student-generated questions. In a guided discovery approach, the teacher supports the students' discovery of the defining features and irrelevant characteristics of the concept through teacher-generated questions.

Many concepts learned in school, such as the concepts of *democracy* and *irony,* are abstract or fuzzy and are difficult to learn through concrete examples. In this case, students learn the definition and apply it in a number of different situations. For example, once the concept of *democracy* is defined, students categorize descriptions of governments as democratic or not. It is often possible to teach abstract concepts by making them more concrete through the use of analogies or illustrations in diagrams or graphs. For example, the concept of *sonar* can be explained as analogous to the system bats use to detect movement, and the relationship between supply and demand in the economy can best be conveyed through graphs.

Propositions

We often develop understandings and build our knowledge base when we read about ideas presented in written materials such as books, magazines, and newspapers. Researchers trying to explain how students represent the knowledge they derive when they read textual materials suggest that **propositions** are the building blocks of knowledge. Similar to the basic premise of semantic networks, this perspective of knowledge representation also emphasizes connections between ideas. Propositions are descriptions that specify relationships between things and properties of things (H. H. Clark & Clark, 1977; Kintsch, 1974). They are the smallest complete unit of thought that can be judged true or false. Each proposition contains a subject (or object) and a verb and/or preposition that specifies a relationship. Thus, the proposition "The book is inside the desk" specifies a relationship between a book and a desk. Although the representation of propositions on paper is as sentences, their representation in our heads is in terms of the abstract meaning of the sentence, not necessarily the sentence itself.

Complex ideas comprised of several idea units in interaction can be expressed in multiple propositional units (Kintsch, 1982). Consider the sentence "Donna quietly worked on the difficult assignment." There are three units of meaning in this sentence: *Work is being done quietly, Donna worked on the assignment,* and *The assignment is difficult.* Each of these three propositions is a *microproposition,* since it was directly derived from the text.

A reader processes a text into its micropropositions (Kintsch, 1983; van Dijk & Kintsch, 1983) and combines them to capture the full meaning of the text. Of course, no one remembers everything about a text. No one remembers a text word for word unless they have struggled to learn it in that manner. What people remember is the gist, the main idea of the text, which is encoded into *macropropositions.* Macropropositions are derived from the micropropositions and not directly from the text. Thus, a macroproposition for the passage containing the sentence about Donna's working might be *Donna does her schoolwork* or even *Donna works hard.*

Suppose that you are beginning a paragraph-long text. The first sentence is broken down into micropropositions. From these you generate a macropropositional representation that captures the main meaning of the sentence. You hold this macroproposition in short-term memory (the memory store of limited duration and capacity described in Chapter 1) as you process the next sentence. You then attempt to link the macroproposition from the first sentence to the micropropositions of the second sentence. Ultimately, a new set of macropropositions emerges from this analysis. Sometimes you need to generate **bridging inferences** that reconcile the meaning of the previous macroproposition with the new micropropositions. These inferences produce coherence between the previous text and the new text and are derived largely from your world knowledge. For instance, if you are reading about a student's working on an English assignment in a text that never mentions a pencil or pen, you may still infer a pencil or pen when you read the sentence "The student started to write."

Later, if you had to recall the paragraph, you would recall the most important ideas first (Kintsch & Keenan, 1973). Your recall would reflect bridging inferences made during reading as well as some inferences made during recall, inferences again based on what you already know. After a while, you would recall only the most important information in the text.

Once a macrostructure is formed, later exposure to some part of the macrostructure activates other parts of it (Kintsch, 1988; van Dijk & Kintsch, 1983). There is spreading activation, much like that described earlier in the discussion of how semantic networks link concepts. Spreading activation between propositions occurs because propositions are linked via **propositional networks.** Any two propositions that share common elements are directly linked in such networks (Hayes-Roth & Thorndyke, 1979). For example, the propositions representing "George Washington visited the colonial army at Valley Forge," "George Washington was the first president of the United States," and "George Washington's wife's name was Martha" are all linked through *George Washington.*

Neural Networks

Both concept and propositional models of knowledge representation describe connections between units of information in similar ways. For concepts, the connections are in a semantic network; for propositions, the connections are in a propositional network. The **connectionist model** suggests that the basic building block of understanding is not concepts or propositions but rather the connections between units of information. These connections are represented in networks linking neuronlike units called **neural networks.** Neural networks have three basic characteristics (Bechtel & Abrahamsen, 1991; Martindale, 1991). First, units of information, called nodes, can be activated at various levels of strength. If nodes are activated at a high level, we are conscious of what is activated. Even if nodes are activated at a low level, outside of "consciousness," behavior is still affected. Second, nodes are connected. Two nodes are linked either by connections resulting in simultaneous excitation of the nodes (if one is excited, the other is) or by connections inhibiting joint excitement (if one is excited, excitation of the other unit cannot occur). Third, learning is the creation of connections and changing the strength of connections. Connections are strengthened by simultaneous activation of nodes in a fashion analogous to strengthening of connections between neurons in the brain (Hebb, 1949).

Consider a sample neural network dealing with some knowledge that all adults possess, knowledge of the letters of the alphabet (Selfridge, 1959). The nodes in this case correspond to features of the letters, such as a horizontal bar, a vertical bar, an acute angle, a curve bulging to the right, and a diagonal bar. Suppose a letter is presented to the system, in this case a letter activating the vertical bar and rightward bulge features. Since adults have seen many *P*s and *R*s in their lifetime, each of these features is strongly connected to the capital letters *P* and *R*. Each exposure to these letters strengthens the connection between these two features and these capital letters. Thus, the nodes representing both letters are activated. The decision that this is a *P* is reached, however, because a clear signal that the letter is an *R* requires that another feature be activated, a diagonal bar in the lower half of the letter. When the features add up to a *P*, inhibitory signals are sent out from the P node to the R node and to all other letter nodes.

As children learn letters, they build up connections between features and letters. Preschoolers often know the names of the letters before they ever have any idea what the letters look like (Adams, 1990). For example, because of listening to the alphabet song, watching *Sesame Street*, playing with magnetic letters on the refrigerator, and reading books on Daddy's or Mommy's lap, a preschooler has many exposures to the name and shape of the letter *P*. With each of these exposures, the connections between the features of the letter *P* and the name of the letter strengthen. Eventually, features defining the letter automatically activate the letter's name.

Strengthening of connections also explains word recognition (McClelland & Rumelhart, 1981). Consider what happens when the word *EACH* is presented. Connections are activated between the individual features defining each letter and the letters themselves. Connections between each letter and its position in a word also are activated. That is, activating the *E* also partially activates connections with words beginning with *E*. Activating the *A* also partially activates connections with words having *A* in the second position and so on. For adults who have experienced the set of connections between *E, A, C,* and *H* in the first, second, third, and fourth position, respectively, many times before, there is activation of the word *EACH* and inhibition of other words (e.g., words sharing letters with *EACH*).

What are the implications of the neural network model for educators? In this perspective, knowledge boils down to patterns of connections. The patterns develop slowly as reflected by the incremental nature of learning in that learners

Young children strengthen connections between nodes of letter features through frequent exposure to letters.

must master lower-order knowledge before higher-order knowledge. Thus, knowledge of particular letters, associations between patterns of feature activations and their corresponding letter names and sounds, must be well established before it is possible to learn to recognize words.

Practice is important for building and strengthening connections (Annett, 1989). Practice can take many forms. The young child who is learning letters is exposed to letters in a variety of formats. Teachers can help students build connections by providing multiple ways to practice in a variety of formats. For example, mental practice can be effective (Feltz, Landers, & Becker, 1988), and practice tests help strengthen connections (Glover, 1989). Whenever possible, teachers should provide feedback with practice (Lhyle & Kulhavy, 1987) so students have information on what they need to learn. Teachers can encourage students to space out their practice (**distributed practice**) rather than cram all their practice into one long episode (**massed practice**). Distributed practice is more effective than massed practice (Dempster, 1988).

Schemata

Some theories of knowledge representation focus on larger chunks of knowledge than the concepts, propositions, and neural networks we have already discussed. Specific units of information, such as concepts and propositions, that commonly co-occur in particular situations, are best described as **schemata.** Schemata are generalized knowledge about objects, situations, and events. For example, your knowledge of what you might expect to see when you go to a play is represented in a schema. You would expect scenery, costumes, actors, props, separate acts, and an intermission. Schemata are abstract knowledge representations that can be *instantiated* in a particular instance. In other words, the events and situations have skeletal structures that are relatively constant, although the particular way the skeleton ends up taking on flesh varies from instance to instance. Thus, every time you go to a play you instantiate your play schema with instances from that particular play (e.g., the particular scenery, props, actors, etc.).

Consider the following example (R. C. Anderson & Pearson, 1984) of a schema for christening a ship. The schema for a ship's christening includes its purpose, which is the blessing of the ship. It includes information about where it is done (i.e., in dry dock), by whom (i.e., a celebrity), and when it occurs (i.e., just before launching of a new ship). The christening action is also represented (i.e., breaking a bottle of champagne that is suspended from a rope). These parts of a schema are referred to as *variables,* or *slots.* At any particular christening, these slots are instantiated with particular instances (e.g., New Haven, with the president of the United States breaking a bottle of California-produced champagne on a new submarine). There are clear constraints on the instances that can occur in these slots. The celebrity is usually from government and would never be a person of ill-repute (e.g., a publisher of smut or a famous criminal). There are constraints on the champagne as well, with a bottle of expensive French champagne acceptable but a bottle of $3.99 sparking wine unlikely. Once instantiated, the schema is represented as a series of propositions capturing that it was the president who christened the ship. The ship was in the New Haven Shipyard. The champagne was produced in California, and so on.

Activation of schema can dramatically affect comprehension, inferences, attention allocation, and memory of what is read (R. C. Anderson & Pearson, 1984). For example, try to make sense of the following passage (Bransford & Johnson, 1972, p. 722):

> The procedure is actually quite simple. First, you arrange the items into different groups. Of course one pile may be sufficient depending on how much there is to do. If you have to go somewhere else due to lack of facilities that is the next step; otherwise you are pretty well set. It is important not to overdo things. That is, it is better to do too few things at once than too many. In the short run this may not seem important but complications can easily arise. A mistake can be expensive as well. At first, the whole procedure will seem complicated. Soon, however, it will become just another facet of life. It is difficult to foresee any end to the necessity for this task in the immediate future, but then, one can never tell. After the procedure is completed one arranges the materials into different groups again. Then they can be put into their appropriate places. Eventually they will be used once more and the whole cycle will then have to be repeated. However, this is part of life.

Did you experience more than a little frustration with this passage? The details of the procedure seem so disconnected and arbitrary. Perhaps we should have told you before you began reading that the title of the passage is "Washing Clothes." When a title is provided before this passage is read, comprehension is better than when there is no title. The title *activates a schema* that makes the passage sensible.

Sometimes a schema affects subsequent inferences made about the text. Read the following text, which was used by R. C. Anderson, Reynolds, Schallert, and Goetz (1977):

> Every Saturday night, four good friends get together. When Jerry, Mike, and Pat arrived, Karen was sitting in her living room writing some notes. She quickly gathered the cards and stood up to greet her friends at the door. They followed her into the living room but as usual they couldn't agree on exactly what to play. Jerry eventually took a stand and set things up. Finally, they began to play. Karen's recorder

filled the room with soft and pleasant music. Early in the evening, Mike noticed Pat's hand and the many diamonds. As the night progressed the tempo of play increased. Finally, a lull in the activities occurred. Taking advantage of this, Jerry pondered the arrangement in front of him. Mike interrupted Jerry's reverie and said, "Let's hear the score." They listened carefully and commented on their performance. When the comments were all heard, exhausted but happy, Karen's friends went home. (p. 372)

Did you infer that the story was about playing cards or music? Either fits. If you believed it was about cards, it is likely you made inferences consistent with card playing as you read the rest of the passage. For instance, participants in the study who thought the passage was about cards made inferences such as, "She is playing with a deck of cards" and "Mike sees that Pat's hand has a lot of diamonds." Those who concluded the passage was about music made inferences such as, "Mike brought out the stand and began to set things up" and "As usual they couldn't decide on the piece of music to play." An activated schema affects the *inferences* made.

An activated schema also influences *attention*. For instance, read the following passage as if you were a burglar making plans to rob the house described:

The two boys ran until they came to the driveway. "See, I told you today was good for skipping school," said Mark. "Mom is never home on Thursday," he added. Tall hedges hid the house from the road so the pair strolled across the finely landscaped yard. "I never knew your place was so big," said Pete. "Yeah, but it's nicer now than it used to be since Dad had the new stone siding put on and added the fireplace." There were front and back doors and a side door which led to the garage, which was empty except for three parked 10-speed bikes. They went in the side door, Mark explaining that it was always open in case his younger sister got home earlier than their mother. Pete wanted to see the house so Mark started with the living room. It, like the rest of the downstairs, was newly painted. Mark turned on the stereo, the noise of which worried Pete. "Don't worry, the nearest house is a quarter of a mile away," Mark shouted. Pete felt more comfortable observing that no houses could be seen in any direction beyond the huge yard. . . . (Pichert & Anderson, 1977, p. 310)

Now reread the passage as if you were a potential home buyer. What should be apparent during this second reading is that you attend to different parts of the passage when the schema for a burglar is activated than when a schema for a home buyer is activated (see Table 3.1).

The schema activated during recall also can have a powerful impact on what is remembered. R. C. Anderson and Pichert (1978) asked adults who originally read and recalled the selection from the perspective of a burglar to later recall it from the perspective of a home buyer. Likewise, those who had read and recalled the selection originally from the perspective of a home buyer attempted to recall it from the perspective of a burglar. Following the direction to switch perspectives, these adults recalled additional information consistent with the new perspective. To illustrate how an activated schema guides retrieval, consider the example cited by R. C. Anderson and Pearson (1984) of this study participant's attempt to recall the passage from a burglar's perspective:

I just thought of myself as a burglar walking through the house. So I had a different point of view, a different objective point of view for different details, you know. I

Table 3.1

Some of the Salient Information from the Perspectives of a Home Buyer and a Burglar

Home Buyer
- Landscaped yard
- New fireplace
- New stone siding
- Garage
- Newly painted
- Huge yard

Burglar
- Hidden from the road
- Mom not home on Thursday
- Three 10-speed bikes in garage
- Open side door
- Stereo

noticed the door was open, and where would I go here, go there, take this, take that, what rooms would I go to and what rooms wouldn't I go to. Like, you know, who cares about the outside and stuff? You can't steal a wall or nothing. . . . I remember [the color TV] in the second one, but not in the first one. I was thinking about things to steal, things you could take and steal. In the den was the money. China, jewelry, other stuff in other places. [Q: Why do you think you remembered the color TV the second time and not the first time?] Because I was thinking of things to steal, I guess. (p. 283)

Sometimes errors in retrieval are the result of faulty inference. Remember the passage on washing clothes? If the schema for washing clothes is guiding recall, some learners might incorrectly infer that the passage mentioned the use of detergent and recall that detergent was used. Such distortions are common, reflecting **reconstruction** of the information to be learned based on prior knowledge during recall. We often use schemata to help us reconstruct unclear memories. Think back to your birthday celebration two years ago. Maybe you remember the celebration clearly. It is more likely that you use your schema of birthday celebrations to help you reconstruct your memory.

Children's Use of Schemata

Do children store knowledge in schemata, and, if they do, how do schemata affect their processing of new material? Not surprisingly, the schemata that children possess are determined by events that recur in their lives. Thus, children have schemata representing events such as dinner, bedtime, making cookies, and going to a museum (J. A. Hudson & Nelson, 1983; J. A. Hudson & Shapiro, 1991; K. A. McCarthy & Nelson, 1981; K. Nelson, 1978; K. Nelson & Gruendel, 1981). If children listen to a brief story pertaining to one of their schemata, they can answer inferential questions about the story. These questions require knowledge about the situation described in the text that is over and above the information specified in the text. Consider the following short story:

Johnny and his mom and dad were going to McDonald's. Johnny's father told him he could have dessert if he ate all his dinner. They waited in line. They ate their hamburgers. And they had ice cream. (J. A. Hudson & Slackman, 1990, p. 378)

When presented with the question "Why did they stand in line?" the 4- to 7-year-olds had no difficulty responding since the schema for McDonald's contains this information, even though the story did not.

The powerful effect of schemata on children's comprehension and memory is evident when children listen to stories that include information inconsistent with schemata stored by most children. Consider this story that J. A. Hudson and Nelson (1983) presented to 4- to 7-year-olds:

One day it was Sally's birthday and Sally had a birthday party.

Sally's friends all came to her house.

Sally opened her presents and found lots of new toys.

Everybody played pin the tail on the donkey.

Then Sally and her friends ate the cake.

They had some chocolate and vanilla ice cream.

Everybody had peppermint candy, too.

Sally blew out all the candles on the cake.

Sally's friends brought presents with them.

Then it was time for Sally's friends to go home. (p. 628)

Is there anything wrong with this story? You probably realized that Sally opened the presents before the friends brought them. In addition, the children ate the cake before the candles were blown out.

It was apparent that the children used schema to comprehend and remember this story. Some children repaired the story during recall by not mentioning either one or both of the misordered elements. Others reported the misordered acts in the schematically correct order rather than as specified in the story. In short, recall

Children develop schemata for recurring events such as birthday parties.

of the story was consistent with the schema for a birthday party, even though the original presentation of the story was not.

Schemata for Text Structure

Students develop schemata for recurring intellectual tasks. For instance, texts have conventional structures that are familiar to readers (Kintsch & Greene, 1978). Both **narrative text structures** (i.e., the structures of fictional stories) and **expository text structures** (i.e., the structures of factual texts) have been identified.

Narrative Text Structures. Perhaps an English teacher once asked you to think about the key parts of a story. You and your classmates were able to generate and agree on a list. According to Jean Mandler (1978, 1987), a story grammar structure, or story structure, consists of a *setting* and an *event structure,* which is composed of *episodes.* Each episode has a *beginning,* which is an event that initiates a complex reaction; a *complex reaction,* which is composed of an emotional or cognitive response and a state the protagonist wishes to achieve; a *goal path,* which involves a plan of action by the character and the consequence of setting the plan of action in motion; and an *ending,* which is a reaction. Here is a simple two-episode story adapted from Mandler (1978):

> Once there were twins, Tom and Jennifer, who had so much trouble their parents called them the unlucky twins (*setting*). One day, Jennifer's parents gave her a dollar bill to buy a turtle she wanted, but on the way to the pet store she lost it (*beginning* of first episode). Jennifer was worried that her parents would be angry with her so she decided to search every bit of the sidewalk where she had walked (*reaction*). She looked in all the cracks and in the grass along the way (plan of action, part of the *goal path*). She finally found the dollar bill in the grass (consequence, part of the *goal path*). But when Jennifer got to the store, the pet store man told her that someone else had just bought the last turtle, and he didn't have any more (first *ending*). The same day, Tom fell off a swing and broke his leg (*beginning* of second episode). He wanted to run and play with the other kids (*reaction*). So he got the kids to pull him around in his wagon (plan of action, part of the *goal path*). While they were playing, Tom fell out of his wagon and broke his arm (consequence, part of the *goal path*). Tom's parents said he was even unluckier than Jennifer and made him sit in bed until he got well (second *ending*). (p. 22)

How does knowledge of story grammar influence story recall? First, stories that do not conform to the story grammar structure are difficult to remember (and are processed more slowly) compared to stories that do. This is true for children and adults (Kintsch, Mandel, & Kozminsky, 1977; Mandler, 1978; Mandler & Johnson, 1977; Stein & Nezworski, 1978). It also applies to stories presented on television (W. A. Collins, Wellman, Keniston, & Westby, 1978). Second, when story information is presented in an order that is inconsistent with conventional story grammar, both children and adults tend to fix up the story at recall, remembering the elements of the story in an order that adheres to conventional story grammar (Mandler & DeForest, 1979; Stein & Glenn, 1979). Third, the probability that an element will be recalled from a story depends on the role it plays in the story as defined by story grammar (Mandler, 1984; Mandler & Johnson, 1977; Stein & Glenn, 1979). Fourth, reading times for material at the beginning of episodes are greater than for material in the middle of episodes, and content at the end of episodes is processed especially quickly (Haberlandt, 1980; Mandler & Goodman, 1982).

Expository Text Structures. Perhaps an English teacher once asked you to write an expository text designed to achieve a specific purpose. For example, maybe you were asked to write a descriptive text, a text that compares and contrasts two perspectives, or a text that illustrates a general principle. These types of text are examples of expository text structures (Kintsch, 1982).

Kintsch and Yarbrough (1982) asked university students to read texts that were examples of classification, illustration, comparison and contrast, and procedural description. The texts were presented in either a well-organized or a poorly organized expository form. Readers were much better able to state the main idea and recall ideas from well-organized passages than from poorly organized ones. Thus, the well-organized texts triggered the appropriate schema for expository text in the reader.

One way to make the organization of the text more explicit is to provide **signals,** text conventions that flag the structure of the text (Meyer, 1975). For example, a cause-and-effect relationship can be signaled with an introductory clause such as "The cause of X is . . ." Sequences of events can be signaled with the words *first, second,* and *third* or with *(1), (2),* and *(3).* Signals make expository text more comprehensible (B. J. F. Meyer, Brandt, & Bluth, 1980).

Schemata for Mathematics Problems

Most of the mathematics problems presented in school textbooks have typical structures. For instance, Mayer (1981) analyzed high school algebra texts and identified about a hundred common types of problem material. For example, any first-year algebra textbook contains a problem such as this one:

If a car travels 10 hours at 30 miles per hour, how far will it go?

For many, this problem activates their schema for problems that involve the following relationship: "Distance = rate × time."

Students who have successfully completed high school math and science courses have developed schemata for the problem types presented in these courses and can classify problems into types (Hinsley, Hayes, & Simon, 1977). In addition, students use their problem-solving schemata as they identify the critical information in the problems (Hayes, Waterman, & Robinson, 1977; Mayer, 1982; Robinson & Hayes, 1978). This may be one reason that students who possess greater knowledge of problem schemata (and hence are more proficient at problem classification) also are better at problem solving (Silver, 1987). See Table 3.2 for the problem-solving schemata associated with simple math and science problems.

What are the implications of schemata theory for educators? Schemata have a powerful effect on the comprehension and recall of information in learners of all ages. As we have seen, schemata focus students' attention, influence the infer-

Table 3.2

Sample Math and Science Problems and the Associated Problem-Solving Schemata

- If a machine can produce 10 units per hour, how many units can be produced in an 8-hour day? (output = rate × time)
- If pencils cost 5 cents apiece, how much will a dozen pencils cost? (total cost = unit cost × number of units)
- How much will be earned if $1000 is invested at 8 percent interest for 1 year? (interest = interest rate × principal)
- If a TV set costs the seller $300 and the markup is 20 percent, how much profit will be made? (profit = markup rate × cost)
- John's living room is 9 feet long and 12 feet wide. How many square feet of carpet is required to cover the floor? (area = length × width)
- If the voltage of a dry cell is 1.5 volts, find the current that cell will produce in a single-cell flashlight bulb having a resistance of 10 ohms. (current = voltage/resistance) (Mayer, Larkin, & Kadane, 1984, pp. 246–247)

ences students make, and have a bearing on students' recall of the information. When teachers introduce new lessons, they need to try to activate schemata that will facilitate students' understanding of the new material. (See the "What Do I Do on Monday Morning?" feature on making use of connections that appears later in this chapter.) Some students, however, may not have developed the schemata for text structure or mathematics that they need to succeed. As described in Chapter 4, teachers can explicitly teach the appropriate schemata. For example, poor readers taught a schema for narrative text greatly improved their comprehension and recall of narrative texts (Nolte & Singer, 1985; Short & Ryan, 1984).

Images

Could you describe where you live to your classmates? As you try to do this, you would likely access mental pictures, or **images,** in your long-term memory store. How is knowledge in the form of images represented? Allan Paivio proposed the **dual coding model** (J. M. Clark & Paivio, 1991; Paivio, 1971, 1986) to articulate the difference between images and the other forms of knowledge described earlier in this chapter. This model describes knowledge as associative networks of verbal and imaginal representations. The verbal system contains wordlike codes for objects, events, and abstract ideas that, like propositions, are only arbitrarily related to what they represent. For instance, the word *book* has no physical resemblance to an actual book.

The imagery system, on the other hand, contains nonverbal representations that resemble the perceptions that give rise to them. It includes visual images (e.g., a bell), auditory images (e.g., the sound of a bell), actions (e.g., a ringing motion),

Contrast this picture of a classroom with the following verbal representation: The room has desks, aisles, and chalkboards. The desks are arranged in rows. Assignments are written on the chalkboards in white chalk. The students' work is posted on the walls. The room smells like glue and chalk and on and on. Is an image worth 1000 words?

sensations related to emotion (e.g., a racing heart), and other nonverbal representations. Thus, an image of a book shares visual and tactile qualities with the perception of an actual book.

Items in the imagery system are connected to items in the verbal system. For example, the connections between your image and a verbal representation of a book permit you to make mental images in response to words or to generate the names of items depicted in pictures. There are also connections within both the verbal and nonverbal systems. In the verbal system, words are associated with other words, so that some students associate the word *school* with *friends, work,* and *challenge.* Categories and their instances are connected within the verbal system, so that *tree* is associated with *maple, oak,* and *pine.* In the nonverbal system, there are associative connections between images within or across sensory modalities. Thus, an image of your grandmother may be associated with the warm feeling of a hug and the smell of chocolate-chip cookies in the oven.

Is there research support for Paivio's (1986) dual-coding theory? Concrete materials, which more readily elicit images, are more memorable than abstract materials, and pictures are learned better than words. Words can be read faster than pictures can be named, which suggests that words access the verbal code directly, while pictures access the verbal code only through the image. There is also neuropsychological evidence supporting a dual-coding theory in that left-hemisphere damage to the brain disrupts verbal processing more than nonverbal processing. Right-hemisphere damage has the opposite effect. As described in Chapter 4, mental imagery can have a powerful effect on recall. Material that is easy to image is also recalled easily. Readers who construct mental images as they read facilitate their understanding of what they read (Sadoski, 1983; 1985).

● "What Do I Do on Monday Morning?"

Making Use of Connections

Making connections between units of information in our knowledge base is critical. Connections are important in semantic networks based on concepts, in propositional networks, and in forming schemata, and they are the major components of knowledge in neural networks. How can teachers encourage students to make these connections and to make them work for them?

The Use of Reaction Time to Determine the Psychological Reality of Images

Roger Shepard and his colleagues (e.g., Shepard & Metzler, 1971) conducted a series of experiments that provide additional support for the psychological reality of images. They presented adults with a complex geometric figure and a second figure, which was either the same figure (but rotated 0 to 180 degrees) or a mirror image (also rotated some number of degrees). The task was to decide whether the original figure and the rotated figure were the "same" or "different." The amount of time needed to recognize the same figure as same was a linear function of the number of degrees of rotation required to make the figure parallel the original figure.

Since the time required for mental rotation corresponds to the physical process of rotation, this sug-

It takes 4-year-olds longer to decide that the figure on the left is an *R* than to decide the figure on the right is an *R*, thus indicating that children can rotate images in their heads.

gested that the participants were "flipping" the figures in their heads, using some kind of image. Even 4-year-olds seem to rotate figures in their heads. It takes longer for a 4-year-old to decide that a capital *R* and an upside-down *R* (i.e., an *R* flipped 180 degrees) are the same letter than that the *R* and an *R* on its side (i.e., an *R* flipped 90 degrees) are the same letter (Marmor, 1975).

Additional support for the psychological reality of images comes from people's descriptions of having and using mental images. For instance, people report flipping the complex figures in their heads in the Shepard and Metzler (1971) task. People report images more often when learning concrete materials than when learning abstract materials. They also report relying on their images during recall of concrete materials.

Think back to Chapter 1. How was triangulation achieved for the reality of mental images using objective and subjective measures? (Objective measures include data on reaction time. Subjective measures include self-reported information. Also, the experimental results were replicated in multiple age groups.)

How do students make connections between new content and their knowledge base? Recall that priming, via spreading activation, helps students understand related material. Teachers can prime knowledge they know students already have. For example, teachers can introduce lessons by saying something like "Yesterday, we discussed. . . . Today, we will discuss . . . which is related to yesterday's topic in the following ways."

Teachers can also encourage students to make connections by asking why questions and by fostering students' self-questioning (King, 1989, 1990, 1992, 1994). Learners often fail to relate what they already know to new material unless they are prompted to do so, such as when they are asked to answer why questions pertaining to the material (e.g., "Why would the largest percentage of unionized workers be in British Columbia?"). Activating prior knowledge through the use of why questions improves the learning of facts that are presented in lists and in paragraphs (Bransford et al., 1982; Martin & Pressley, 1991; Woloshyn, Pressley, & Schneider, 1992).

Another way to facilitate activation of prior knowledge is through the provision of **advance organizers.** Advance organizers, originally proposed by David Ausubel (1960), are processed before the new material and are at a "higher level of abstraction, generality, and inclusiveness" (Ausubel, 1960, p. 148) than the information to be learned. This rather vague definition has been reformulated from the perspective of schema theory. Basically, an effective advance organizer activates prior knowledge (i.e., schemata), which increases the likelihood that the learner will be able to understand new information by relating it to prior knowledge (Mayer, 1979). For instance, students learning Greek mythology benefit from an advance organizer contrasting themes of Greek mythology with familiar biblical themes (Derry, 1984).

Other methods of accessing and using prior knowledge, including using story schemata, imagery, and analogies, are discussed in Chapters 4, 11, and 12.

Productions

Up to now we have focused on knowledge about things, knowledge *that* something is the case. This is **declarative knowledge.** Declarative knowledge is represented in knowledge structures already discussed, such as concepts and propositions. We also know *how* to do things, which is called **procedural knowledge.** There are many distinctions between procedural and declarative knowledge (Tulving, 1983). For example, procedural knowledge can be demonstrated only by performing the procedure. Evidence of declarative knowledge can come in a variety of forms (e.g., recall, recognition, application, and association to other knowledge). Procedural knowledge is neither true nor false, whereas the truth value of much of declarative knowledge can be determined. Procedural knowledge is often acquired only after extensive practice. Much declarative knowledge is acquired after a single exposure. See Table 3.3 for examples of declarative and procedural knowledge.

Procedural knowledge is represented in action sequences called **productions.** A production specifies some action and when the action should occur. Typically, productions are represented in if-then form:

If I get good grades in high school
and I score high on the SAT
then I can apply to the college of my choice.

Table 3.3

Examples of Declarative and Procedural Knowledge

Declarative Knowledge
- Knowing what the Declaration of Independence is
- Knowing the states and the capitals
- Knowing the formula for computing area
- Knowing what a circle is
- Knowing who wrote *War and Peace*
- Knowing the genus and species of a spider
- Knowing the Pythagorean Theorem

Procedural Knowledge
- Knowing how to use a computer program
- Knowing how to perform mathematical operations
- Knowing how to play basketball
- Knowing how to write
- Knowing how to study
- Knowing how to look up information in the library
- Knowing how to perform a laboratory procedure
- Knowing how to dissect an animal

Some productions allow us to recognize and classify information, such as the following production used to solve a mathematical equation:

> If an equation has the form $y = ax^2 + bx + c$,
> then classify the equation as a quadratic.

These **pattern-recognition productions** are important because a situation must be recognized before it is possible to determine whether the conditions are met for other actions. For instance, pattern-recognition productions are used to identify a problem before a solution is attempted. In the following math example, a quadratic equation must be recognized before application of a production to solve the problem:

> If equation is quadratic,
> and the goal is to know the value of x,
> then apply formula of $x = (-b \pm \sqrt{(b^2 - 4ac)})/2a$.

In general, the "if" information in action-sequence productions must be recognized via pattern-recognition productions before it can be determined whether or not the conditions for the action sequence are met. Whenever the "if" conditions are met, then the action associated with the "if" information occurs. For example, in mathematical problem solving, the type of problem must be recognized via pattern-recognition productions before the action sequence for solving the problem can occur. How productions operate in thinking can be illustrated by considering briefly the ACT* model of thinking.

ACT*

ACT* is a knowledge system that includes both procedural knowledge encoded into productions and declarative knowledge encoded in the following three ways (J. R. Anderson, 1983): First, *temporal strings* code the order of a set of items—which of a set of items occurs first, which second, third, and so on. A whole event that is comprised of a sequence of steps, such as a schema, can be captured by such a representation. Second, *spatial images* code the spatial configuration of elements in an array (i.e., which items are above others, below others, to the left of others, and to the right of others). Third, *propositional representations* operate as discussed earlier; that is, they encode meaningful relationships between elements.

Thus, the declarative memory of the ACT* system includes many of the types of representations discussed in this chapter—from concepts, to images, to propositional relations, to schemata. This declarative knowledge is used in conjunction with procedural knowledge. For instance, some declarative knowledge is activated when pattern-recognition productions identify an example of a category member. Thus, when encountering a four-legged animal with a characteristic elliptical head, sharp claws, and a meow, the pattern recognition productions identify a cat. This information is used to determine which action procedures to activate. If your goal is to make the animal happy and the animal is a cat (two conditionals), you give it some milk (an action).

Acquisition of Procedural Knowledge. According to Anderson's theory (Neves & Anderson, 1981), all procedural knowledge starts as declarative knowledge. How to do something starts as a verbal characterization of the procedure.

When a sequence of cognitive actions is represented declaratively, it is carried out slowly and requires more of the limited capacity of the working memory (as described in Chapter 1). When first learning an action sequence, we have to interpret each step one at a time. Such interpretation and step-by-step consideration require cognitive capacity. With practice, the procedure can be executed automatically (quickly and easily as described in Chapter 1). The movement from declarative representation of a sequence of actions to a single procedure is known as **proceduralization.**

An example can illustrate proceduralization. Let's say you acquire new word processing software. The first time you use it, you read every line of the directions and spend a lot of time making certain you understand each line. Then you struggle to use the program. Initially, you need to cue yourself to use the right commands. For instance, you may say to yourself, "When I want to save a file, I press the function key F10. If I press F7, I will exit, and I better make sure I save the file." Gradually, you will need less and less verbal cuing. Eventually, you can write an entire paper without thinking about the word processing commands. At this point, you are no longer using much short-term capacity when you use the word processing program and can think more about what you are writing.

■ Building Your Expertise

Constructing Knowledge You Can Use

We may develop understandings of concepts or build connections between propositions, but can we really use our knowledge to construct understandings or solve problems in learning situations? For instance, many students do not completely understand the concepts they encounter in science classes. They can define concepts on a test but cannot apply them in the everyday world. Many students who can state the processes involved in photosynthesis fail to realize that the tree in their front yard is manufacturing food in its leaves, rather than getting food from the soil (K. J. Roth, 1990). Concepts can be known well enough so that they can be defined and instances separated from noninstances, but a person may still not be able to use the concept to solve a problem.

Students can also master procedures that they later use without understanding (Schoenfeld, 1988). For example, consider the following problem: "An army bus holds 36 soldiers. If 1128 soldiers are being bused to their training site, how many buses are needed?" Although 70 percent of the 13-year-olds given this problem performed the steps for long division accurately, only 23 percent actually gave the correct answer of 32 buses (Carpenter, Lindquist, Matthews, & Silver, 1983). Some students said the number of buses needed was "31 remainder 12"; others said, "31." Clearly, both of these incorrect answers would result in transportation problems! These students did not correctly apply their procedural knowledge to real-life situations.

One explanation for this discrepancy between knowledge we know and knowledge we can use in various situations is related to the setting in which we learned the knowledge. **Situated cognition** or **situated knowledge** cannot be separated from the actions that give rise to it or from the culture in which those actions occur (J. S. Brown, Collins, & Duguid, 1989). Actions undertaken in a cultural setting largely determine the meaning of a concept rather than some abstract features. Consider the knowledge about teaching that a student possesses before

What is the food source for this tree? Do you really know the concept of *photosynthesis?*

working as a student teacher. This knowledge was developed in the culture of school through the actions required to pass examinations in college courses. During student teaching, however, the student has many interactions with master teachers and acquires the understandings held by experienced teachers. The development of teaching ability occurs through observation of skilled teaching, followed by opportunities to teach.

According to this framework, knowledge is implicit, and it is obtained by acting in authentic situations, such as the student teacher's instructing real students in a real classroom. Knowledge is built up through real problem solving and real dilemmas. It is constructed rather than given. The master teacher does not offer precise rules but rather brainstorms with the student teacher about the options. Moreover, after ten years of practice, the former student teacher, now an experienced teacher, is still learning.

■ Building Your Expertise

Episodic Versus Semantic Memory

Tulving (1972) distinguished between two types of declarative knowledge, which he called **episodic memory** and **semantic memory.** Episodic memory is memory of personally experienced events. Semantic memory is organized knowledge of the world that is independent of specific experiences. Thus, your semantic memory contains an image of a cat, or a prototype of the concept of cat, or a propositional network about cats. You may also have episodic memories of specific cats, including one that was in your neighborhood, two that were the pets of friends, and so on. You may have semantic knowledge of baseball games and episodic knowledge of specific games.

Table 3.4		

Different Representations of Knowledge

Types of Knowledge	Description	Classroom Example
Concepts	Mental representation of a category. Concepts are connected in hierarchical semantic networks.	Animal phylum, types of rocks.
Propositions	Relationship between things and properties of things specified by a subject (or object) and a verb and/or preposition. Propositions are connected in propositional networks. Meaning of text in macropropositions is derived from micropropositions.	The propositions "Concepts are connected in semantic networks" and "Propositions are connected in propositional networks" yield the macroproposition "Knowledge is connected."
Neural networks	Connected nodes. Knowledge is in connections.	Features of letters associated with letter names.
Schemata	Generalized knowledge about objects, situations, and events.	What goes into an essay? (expository schema) What kind of math problem is this? (mathematics problem schema)
Images	Nonverbal representations that resemble perceptual experience.	Imaging swinging a bat, imaging performing a dance movement.
Productions	Specified action and when the action should occur.	"If I want to find a word processing file, then I press F5."

There are five distinctions between semantic and episodic memory (Tulving, 1983): First, the point of reference for semantic knowledge is the world. Is the knowledge true about the world? The point of reference for episodic knowledge is the self. Did this event happen to me? Is this what really happened on that occasion? Second, semantic memory is not coded with respect to *when* the information was acquired. Episodic information often is. Third, semantic information is unlikely to be forgotten; episodic information is easily forgotten. Fourth, semantic knowledge is *known;* episodic knowledge is *remembered.* Fifth, educators are typically more concerned with the development of high-quality semantic knowledge than with the development of episodic knowledge.

Chapter Summary

- A variety of different types of representations function in thinking (see Table 3.4). Features of stimuli are critical to classification in both feature comparison and prototype theories of concept formation. Prototype theories can better explain how nondefinitive features contribute to classification (e.g., such as grandmothers having gray hair) and how people classify instances of fuzzy concepts.
- Concepts are related to each other in hierarchically organized semantic networks. Although some of children's knowledge probably is in categorical hierarchies like

those of adults, many concepts held by children differ from those held by adults. Moreover, children are less likely than adults to rely on hierarchical concept knowledge.

- Propositions are the smallest unit of knowledge that can be judged true or false. They are linked together in propositional networks. Readers process text into its micropropositions and then combine these idea units into macropropositions, or the gist of the text. Macropropositions are integrated with prior knowledge in situation models.
- Connections between units of information are best represented in neural networks. Nodes in neural networks are linked by either simultaneous excitation or inhibition. Learning is the creation and the strengthening between nodes.
- Adults and children have schemata for familiar events, and these schemata determine how new information is processed, interpreted, and retrieved. The availability of this generalized representation from a very young age suggests that schematic representation is a fundamental human competency.
- Images are nonverbal representations that resemble perceptual experience. According to Paivio's dual-coding model, items in the imagery system are connected to items in the nonverbal system. Evidence for the psychological reality of images is found in self-reports and studies of mental rotation.
- Knowing how to do something, procedural knowledge, is represented in productions. Productions are in an if-then form that specifies conditions under which actions should occur. ACT*, a model of complex thinking, includes both procedural knowledge encoded into productions and declarative knowledge encoded in a variety of ways.
- Adults have complex networks of procedural and declarative knowledge built up through experience. Procedures develop from declarative representations through repeated practice. Connections between procedures are strengthened when a sequence of procedures is executed with success.

Return to the Classroom Predicament

Has reading this chapter helped you understand Jason's situation? Jason had generalized knowledge, a schema, about how to be a student. Although the school was new to him, there were enough similarities to his old school to help him activate his schema for student so he was able to instantiate the schema and behave appropriately in the class. Jason didn't understand the discussion because he didn't have the needed declarative knowledge. Since he was missing the required conceptual or propositional nodes or neural network, he did not experience spreading activation to related knowledge and was completely lost.

Chapter Outline

Chapter 4

Strategies and Metacognitive Regulation of Strategies

Classroom Predicament

Isaac has difficulty remembering information he is taught in school. His teacher asks him, "What do you do to try to remember information?" Isaac replies, "I read it over and over." The teacher says "I know how to help you. I can teach you some good ways to learn information. These methods have always helped me." So the teacher takes some time to teach Isaac ways to go about learning new information. The teacher makes sure that Isaac practices the methods, and Isaac does remember more than usual during the practice session. To the teacher's surprise, however, Isaac's remembering of new classroom information in the weeks after the instruction does not improve. When the teacher asks Isaac how he studied, Isaac replies, "I read it over and over." The teacher can't help but ask, "Why didn't you study the way I showed you?" Isaac shrugs his shoulders.

Why didn't Isaac use the methods the teacher taught him when he had to study on his own? He was able to use them during the practice sessions. Reflecting on the information presented in this chapter will help you formulate a response to this question.

In addition to being motivated and having a knowledge base, good thinking, as described in Chapter 1, requires a rich repertoire of strategies and the ability to use them. The main focus of the first part of this chapter is memory strategies and the development of their use. Strategies such as rehearsal, organization, and elaboration help students make connections between even arbitrarily associated items. Then, we describe strategies even more directly applicable to educational settings. Some of these strategies, such as imagery and story schema training, are based on the knowledge representations presented in Chapter 3. Other, more familiar study strategies, such as note taking and outlining, are also analyzed. Then, we discuss important considerations for the teaching of strategies. As the classroom predicament indicates, teaching strategies is not just a matter of showing students how to use the strategy. In order for students to use strategies on their own, teachers must help students develop metacognition for monitoring and regulating strategy use. Finally, we explore the relationship of memory to strategy use.

What Is a Strategy?

Consider first a formal definition of strategies:

> [Strategies] . . . are composed of cognitive operations over and above the processes that are a natural consequence of carrying out [a] task. . . . Strategies achieve cognitive purposes (e.g., memorizing) and are potentially conscious and controllable activities. (Pressley, Forrest-Pressley, Elliott-Faust, & Miller, 1985, p. 4)

An example may help you understand this definition better. Suppose you have to read a chapter for a class. What are the cognitive processes you must carry out? Of course, you must decode the words, normally by reading the chapter from front to back. This is not a strategic activity, however, since decoding is a natural consequence of carrying out the task of reading.

What could you do that would go beyond front-to-back reading? You could employ many strategies. For example, before reading the chapter, you could skim the title, pictures, and headings to get a general idea of what the chapter is about. This might lead you to make predictions about what you will be learning. During reading, you might monitor carefully whether your predictions were correct and whether what you are reading makes sense. If it did not make sense, you might reread. Finally, after one reading of the text, you might self-test your understanding of the content by trying to recall the chapter material. After doing this, you might look through the chapter, construct a summary, and note which parts of the chapter you did not remember during the self-test.

In short, there are many different ways of processing text, beyond simple reading, that facilitate understanding and memory of text information. These are strategies. Often readers execute strategies consciously and intentionally. Sometimes, however, very good readers carry out some of these processes automatically, with great ease and little awareness. However, these readers could consciously control their strategies if they chose to do so.

Memory Strategies

What do you do to remember a telephone number you have just looked up in the phone book? Perhaps you repeat the number over and over until you can dial it.

This strategy of repeating information to be remembered is called **rehearsal.** What if you need to remember a few items to pick up at the grocery store and you don't have a pen or pencil to write them down? You can rehearse the grocery list as you did the telephone number, or you can use **organization** (i.e., grouping items on some characteristic) to facilitate your recall. "Ok, I need a lot of groceries. But I really only need two categories of supplies—stuff to make tuna melts and stuff to make brownies." How do you remember the names of people you meet at a party? This problem requires you to make associations between names and faces. Perhaps you use elaboration to make a connection. **Elaboration** is the construction of a meaningful context, which can be either verbal or visual. A verbal elaboration might be, "Ok, she looks a lot like Orphan Annie and her name is Frannie." A visual elaboration might be, "His name is Robin, I'll just picture a robin sitting on his shoulder."

Although rehearsal, organization, and elaboration have been frequently studied for the task of learning arbitrarily related items such as word lists and word pairs, students often employ these strategies in classroom contexts. For example, a student who studies for a science test by reading the chapters over and over is using rehearsal. Drill and practice used for learning multiplication tables is another example of rehearsal in a classroom context. Some college students study for midterms by copying over their lecture notes, another form of rehearsal. Simple rehearsal, however, is usually less effective than other strategies that require students to process the material more actively by organizing related ideas or elaborating new ideas by making connections to prior knowledge.

Students often use organization strategies as well. As students study for a test, they may group like ideas together to help them remember them. For example, a student may categorize countries together that share similar characteristics, such as location, climate, or governments. Common uses of elaboration include connecting events from history to events occurring in a novel or picturing what it might be like to live during a particular event in history. When do children first begin using memory strategies like these?

Strategy Use by Preschoolers

Preschoolers exhibit memory strategies for familiar tasks in naturalistic settings. For example, with children watching and aware that later they would have to retrieve the hidden object, DeLoache, Cassidy, and Brown (1985) hid an object (usually a familiar toy such as Bugs Bunny or Big Bird) in a living room. In this situation, even 2-year-olds are strategic. Although they will play in the living room during the retention interval (i.e., the time between when the object is hidden and when they must retrieve it), preschoolers frequently look at the place where the object was hidden. Sometimes they even point to the location and say the name of the hidden object. These checking-back and simple rehearsal strategies are, in fact, memory strategies.

Sometimes preschoolers exhibit memory strategies that are not yet useful to them (Lange, MacKinnon, & Nida, 1989). Baker-Ward, Ornstein, and Holden (1984) presented preschool children with sets of toys. In both conditions of the study, children played with the toys. In one of the conditions, the directions given to the children only mentioned playing with the toys. In the other condition, the children were asked to remember some of the toys. The

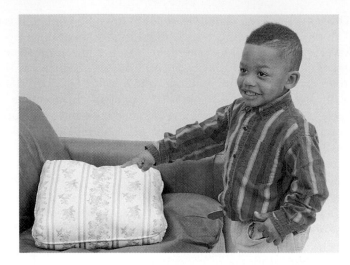

This child is using a pointing strategy to help remember that an object is hidden under the pillow. Preschoolers exhibit strategies for familiar tasks in naturalistic settings.

addition of this memory demand changed the processing of the preschoolers dramatically. The children given the memory instruction played with the toys less. Instead, they looked more intensely at the toys to be remembered and named them. Even though these children engaged in strategic behavior more than the children who only played with the toys, they did not remember more of the toys.

Preschoolers can also elect strategies that actually hinder their memory performances. L. S. Newman (1990) found that children who were given a memory demand actually remembered *less* than children in a play condition. What was going on in the play condition? The children were creating verbal stories and constructing interactions between the toys. Taking unrelated objects and placing them in a meaningful context, such as a story that sensibly relates them or a picture that integrates them, facilitates memory. Such stories and pictures are examples of elaborations. The children who were asked to remember the items rehearsed the items or repeatedly looked at them, which is less effective than using elaboration (Levin, 1976; Rohwer, 1973).

Thus, preschoolers sometimes are strategic, although their efforts to **encode,** to create durable memory traces, are not always successful. Even if preschoolers have a memory trace, however, that does not mean they will **retrieve,** or access, the memory trace later. For example, children who learned associations or elaborations between pairs of items, such as *rock* and *turkey*, through interactive pictures (e.g., a picture of a turkey sitting on a rock) did not recall more pairs unless the children also were given a retrieval cue, such as, "Think back to the pictures you saw. . . ." This retrieval deficiency in preschoolers is surmounted shortly with development. Pressley and MacFadyen (1983) found that unlike preschoolers, kindergarten children do not need retrieval cues to make use of elaborated pictures that are presented to study. Since preschoolers experience retrieval difficulties that do not occur with older children (Ritter, 1978; Sodian & Schneider, 1990), teachers working with these young children need to provide retrieval cues for optimal memory performance.

Development of Strategy Use in School-age Children

School-age children develop sophisticated rehearsal strategies. Many studies of school-age children's memory investigated rehearsal of lists of items. In a typical **serial recall task,** a researcher would present a child some items to remember—perhaps a row of picture cards, one picture to a card, with the faces turned down. After informing the child that the task was to remember the picture cards in order, the researcher would turn each card face up for a few seconds.

One strategy that learners can apply to this task is known as **cumulative rehearsal-fast finish** (Barclay, 1979; Butterfield & Belmont, 1977). In this strategy, the learner says the early- and middle-list items over and over in order of presentation. Suppose the pictures are of, from left to right, a chair, a dog, a cup, a car, a radio, a book, and a tree. After seeing the chair, the learner says "chair" several times. Then, when a picture of a chair is turned face down and a picture of a dog revealed, the learner says, "Chair, dog" several times. By the time a picture of a radio is presented, the rehearsal includes saying, "chair, dog, cup, car, and radio" as many times as time permits. This add-on of rehearsed items, the cumulative-rehearsal part of the strategy of cumulative rehearsal-fast finish, continues during the presentation of the entire list. The fast-finish part is obvious when the learner recalls the list. The learner immediately "dumps out" the last item or two (*book* and *tree* in our example) and then recalls the earlier items in order.

The use of the strategy of cumulative rehearsal-fast finish develops slowly (Schneider & Pressley, 1989). Preschoolers and early-elementary-age students do not exhibit anything that looks like the fully developed strategy. Their most typical strategy is simply to say the name of the picture as it is displayed. This is a **labeling** strategy (Flavell, Beach, & Chinsky, 1966). Children commonly use cumulative rehearsal by the end of the elementary school years (Flavell, Beach, & Chinsky, 1966; P. A. Ornstein, Naus, & Liberty, 1975). Learners typically do not add the fast-finish component until late adolescence (Barclay, 1979).

▶ **Diversity**

Cultural Influences on Strategy Development

Is the increased use of rehearsal strategies that comes with age due to biological factors related to age (i.e., brain maturation) or experience? Cross-cultural research helps to answer this question. One important approach is to compare Western-schooled students with other members of a culture who have not received Western schooling. Schooling does make a difference. Use of strategies (and hence increased performance) on basic memory tasks and school experience are related. Students who had experienced several years of Western-style schooling exhibited greater use of strategies than students in the culture who had not attended Western-type schools (D. Sharp, Cole, & Lave, 1979; H. W. Stevenson, Parker, Wilkinson, Bonnevaux, & Gonzalez, 1978; Wagner, 1974, 1978).

Of course, not all Western countries are alike. Parents in distinct Western cultures provide differing amounts of support for use of memory strategies, and these differences in parental encouragement of memory strategies are reflected in children's use of strategies (Kurtz, 1990). For example, in one study (M. Carr, Kurtz, Schneider, Turner, & Borkowski, 1989), German parents reported more instruction

Parents influence strategy development in their children.

of memory strategies at home than did American parents. German children also perform differently from American children on recall tasks. In particular, when German students learn lists of items with the items selected from several different categories (e.g., furniture, animals, foods), they are more likely to make use of the categories in the list during study than are American children of the same age (Schneider, Borkowski, Kurtz, & Kerwin, 1986). Cross-cultural research provides compelling evidence that life experiences help determine the use of strategies by children (Wagner & Spratt, 1987).

Prolonged Development of Strategic Competence

Students as young as third graders can discover strategies on their own if they have experiences that support the discoveries (Best, 1993; Best & Ornstein, 1986). For example, if students practice learning lists made up of items that are clearly related (e.g., tiger, bus, carrot, giraffe, celery, van, beans, car, and camel), they learn to use an organizational strategy of grouping the items into categories (e.g., zoo animals, vehicles, and vegetables). The students are then likely to use this organizational strategy on lists that are not as clearly categorizable.

Although use of some strategies, especially rehearsal, clearly increases during the elementary school years, use of other and often more effective strategies develops slowly. Consider, for example, how elementary school children tackle paired-associate learning, that is, learning associations between two items such as a vocabulary word and its definition, states and their capitals, names and inventions, and cities and their products. Some of the most effective strategies for learning paired associates involve elaborations. The elaboration to learn a paired associate (e.g., *turkey* paired with *rock*) could be either a verbal elaboration in the form of a meaningful sentence containing both pair members (e.g., *Turkeys* have *rocks* in their gizzards) or a meaningful interactive image (e.g., a *turkey* scratching at *rocks* in the barnyard). Elementary-age children do not use elaboration strategies on their own (Pressley & Levin, 1977a, 1977b); even many adults fail to elaborate (Bower, 1972; Kliegl, Smith, & Baltes, 1990; Rohwer, 1980; Rohwer & Litrownik, 1983).

Making meaningful associations for effective elaboration requires an extensive

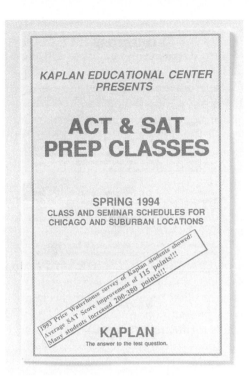

Many college students do not study effectively and can benefit from a course in study skills and test-taking strategies (see Chapter 15).

knowledge base, knowledge which tends to increase with development. Chan, Burtis, Scardamalia, and Bereiter (1992) asked elementary school children to think aloud as they read texts about dinosaurs and gems. As age increased, the students were less likely to rely on superficial understandings and to make irrelevant associations and were more likely to relate ideas to each other and to their own prior knowledge.

Even university students, however, often do not study effectively (Mathews, 1966). They fail to use effective memory strategies as well as effective procedures for reading comprehension, writing, and problem solving. As a result, many college campuses now offer courses in study skills, which focus on strategy instruction. Later in this chapter, we review some study strategies often taught in these courses (Devine, 1987).

Strategy Interventions Inspired by Theories of Knowledge

The theories of knowledge representation described in Chapter 3 inspired many strategies for understanding and remembering, particularly material presented in text formats. The success of these strategies highlights the importance of understanding the nature of knowledge. By understanding the nature of knowledge, educational psychologists have been able to create ways of improving students' learning from text.

Summarization Strategies

According to propositional theories (Kintsch & van Dijk, 1978; van Dijk & Kintsch, 1983), good readers store the main ideas presented in text in macropropositions.

In contrast, novice readers, such as children, are much less likely to store the main ideas of what they read (A. L. Brown & Day, 1983; A. L. Brown, Day, & Jones, 1983). If children are taught to extract the main ideas and summarize text, their comprehension and memory of text should improve.

For example, A. L. Brown and Day (1983) devised an intervention based on the summarization strategies used by skilled readers. The summarization rules are to (1) delete trivial information, (2) delete redundant information, (3) substitute more inclusive terms, (4) combine a series of events with a more inclusive action term, (5) select a topic sentence, and (6) invent a topic sentence if there is none. Instruction in these summarization rules improves the reading performance of elementary school students (Bean & Steenwyk, 1984; Rinehart, Stahl, & Erickson, 1986).

Other summarization interventions have also improved the comprehension and memory of elementary school students. For example, Taylor and her associates (Taylor, 1982; Taylor & Beach, 1984) taught students to outline text using text headings and subheadings. The students generated main-idea statements for every paragraph and used them in the outline. Berkowitz (1986) taught students to construct maps of passages. First, they identified the main ideas in the passage and placed them in boxes surrounding the title. Then, they filled in each of the boxes with supporting details for the main idea placed in it. Both of these successful summarization strategies focus students' attention on the organization of text.

Story Grammar Training

Schema theory, particularly text schemata, has also inspired the development of strategies. Since some children do not possess knowledge of story schemata, Short and Ryan (1984) reasoned that teaching such children the elements of a story and having them use these elements to understand text would improve their comprehension and memory of stories. The researchers taught poor readers in the fourth grade to ask themselves five questions corresponding to the elements of story grammar as they read stories:

- Who is the main character?
- Where and when did the story take place?
- What did the main characters do?
- How did the story end?
- How did the main character feel?

Students who received this training could recall more of stories they read than students who did not receive training. The facilitation was very large, great enough to improve the reading of the poor readers to the level of skilled fourth-grade readers.

Other research has supported the merit of teaching students to use story schemata. Idol (1987; Idol & Croll, 1987) taught 9- to 12-year-old poor readers to construct a story map as they read stories. The map was to contain the elements of story grammar: setting, problem, goal, action, and outcome. Memory of stories improved following this training. Nolte and Singer (1985) taught students to ask themselves questions as they read, questions focusing attention on the story grammar elements of stories, such as the setting, the main characters, the goals of the characters, and the obstacles encountered on the way to these goals. This instruction improved students' ability to complete short-answer questions about the text.

Explicitly teaching students text schemata is effective for learning expository text as well. Armbruster, Anderson, and Ostertag (1987) taught students the problem/solution structure that is characteristic of many social studies texts. The students learned to summarize the problem covered by a passage and the actions taken to resolve the problem.

Mental Imagery

For about two thousand years (Yates, 1966), there have been reports of magnificent feats of memory when people have used imagery to assist their learning. At least since the thirteenth century (Desrochers & Begg, 1987), performers have made a living by using imagery to perform feats of memory. Scientific analysis of imagery has been undertaken only in the last 30 years or so, however, stimulated in part by Paivio's dual-coding theory of knowledge representation described in Chapter 3.

Researchers concerned with the educational utilities of imagery have made a distinction between representational and transformational, or mnemonic, imagery (Levin, 1982). A **representational image** is a mental picture of material to be learned that involves no intentional transformation of the content. Thus, for example, when reading a fairy tale about a king and elves, if the story says, "The king led the elves through the driving rain storm," the learner constructs an internal representation of a king leading the little guys while they all get soaked by a torrential downpour. In contrast, a **transformational image** involves recoding some part of the original message into something concrete that is then embedded in an image with images of other information. The keyword method, useful when the task is to learn an association between two items, is an example of transformational imagery. If an unfamiliar item sounds like a familiar word (the keyword), then the keyword is linked, via an image (or a sentence), with the other items of information. For example, to learn that the Old English word *carlin* means "old woman," the learner transforms the unfamiliar word *carlin* into the more familiar, acoustically similar keyword (*car*) and then generates an image of the keyword in interaction with the definition. Thus, the learner might imagine an old woman driving a car.

Representational Imagery. In general, by the middle-elementary school years, instructions to generate representational images facilitate learning of textual material (Gambrell & Bales, 1986; Pressley, Borkowski, & Johnson, 1987; Pressley, Symons, McDaniel, Snyder, & Turnure, 1988). Most students reading this text read novels. Do novels stimulate interpretative, personal, and vivid images for you, the reader? Literary response theorists argue that one of the principal ways that good readers respond to text is to construct images of the meanings conveyed by the text (Rosenblatt, 1978).

Unfortunately, not all readers respond to text by constructing visual images. The result is that they miss the major themes in text. Mark Sadoski (1983, 1985) studied the consequences for readers who do not construct images in reaction to text. Students in the middle-elementary grades read stories, each of which had a climax. For example, one story, "Freddie Miller, Scientist," was about the plight of a boy scientist whose frequent home experiments go awry and get him into trouble. In the end, the boy becomes the family hero when he aids his sister, who has become locked in a closet, by constructing a homemade flashlight and lowering it to her through the transom vent above the closet door. About half of the children reported images at the point of climax in the story, and these students were much more likely than students who did not report a climax image to recall the theme of the story. Thus, representational images promote a deep understanding of what we read.

Sadoski and Quast (1990) also found that college students who read articles in popular magazines remembered the parts of the texts that were most easy to image more than other sections of the text, even if they were the most important sections. Text that evokes images is memorable.

The role of representational imagery in thinking is probably not confined to reading. Famous scientists, such as Albert Einstein and Neils Bohr, and mathematicians, such as Jules-Henri Poincaré, reported vivid images as part of their thinking processes while working on cutting edge problems (John-Steiner, 1985; A. I. Miller, 1984). Moreover, facilitative images are not confined to a specific modality. Mozart reported auditory images of works that he had not yet written (Ghiselin, 1952). When we consider such reports in combination with the well-known descriptions of imagery facilitating memory, it is not surprising that there is considerable interest in nonverbal representations, such as visual and auditory images, that can depict wholes.

Transformational Imagery. The most extensively studied transformational imagery strategy is the keyword method. The keyword method is effective for school learning when students have to remember linkages between one type of information and another (Levin, 1982, 1983, 1985, 1986). Students can remember the states and capitals more easily with the keyword method. For example, to

What do Einstein and Mozart have in common? They both reported use of vivid images as they worked.

remember that Madison is the capital of Wisconsin, imagine a *maid* using a *whisk* broom. Students can remember artist and painting associations using the keyword method. For example, imagine those huge *Campbell Soup cans* in a *war* to remember that these pieces of art were created by Andy Warhol. Students can also learn facts about American presidents more easily using the keyword method. For example, many facts can be related to a mnemonic image of a *ray gun,* a keyword for *Reagan,* to remember information about the fortieth president.

Some of the most impressive effects of the keyword method have involved learning from prose (McCormick & Levin, 1987). For instance, in one study (Woloshyn, Willoughby, Wood, & Pressley, 1990), Canadian university students were given paragraphs containing facts about particular Canadian universities, such as the following:

> The land on which McGill University stands was donated by a fur trader. The university's first faculty was a medical faculty. The university is also recognized for establishing the first medical faculty in Canada. The psychology department at the school is internationally acclaimed. The school has an extensive puppet collection. Many students consider the university's athletic facilities to be old and small. (p. 523)

The students in the transformational imagery condition of the study were instructed to learn each fact about McGill by imagining the fact occurring in the school's geographical location. Thus, for McGill, the students related information about McGill to McGill's geography, which is Montreal. Students who were given this imagery instruction recalled considerably more of the facts for each school than control students not given imagery instructions.

Mastropieri and Scruggs (1989) have developed transformational imagery instructions for teaching social studies content that requires the learner to engage in what they call *mimetic reconstruction* after retrieving the transformational image. Thus, a piece of factual information, such as, "Early bridges often rotted and washed away," might be accompanied by a drawing of a rickety bridge with a woman in settler's clothing watching as the bridge beneath her feet is swept away by the rushing water of a stream. Later, by remembering the picture, the learner can reconstruct the more abstract fact—that bridges in the days of the settlers often did not hold up and were swept away by water. Another type of transformational imagery devised by Mastropieri and Scruggs involves *symbolic reconstruction* at recall. Thus, an illustration accompanying text about American isolationism prior to World War I might involve Uncle Sam standing on a depiction of North America and looking toward fighting on a depiction of Europe. Uncle Sam could be saying, "It's not my fight." Recalling this image later would permit reconstruction of the fact that the United States stayed out of the conflict in Europe for some time. Embellishing texts with such mimetic and symbolic transformational pictures increases learning of content.

Other Strategy Interventions for Studying

Other strategies besides summarization, story grammar, and imagery strategies improve reading comprehension (Alvermann & Moore, 1991; Weinstein & Mayer, 1986). You might recognize some of these as strategies you use while studying.

Many students use the strategy of **note taking** to study course material, although most students receive little or no direct instruction in note taking. Note taking serves two primary purposes. First, the act of taking notes encourages the student to transform the material. The student selects important information and may make connections between the text and prior knowledge. This is called the *process* function of note taking (DiVesta & Gray, 1972). Second, the notes themselves are valuable for reviewing. This is the *product* function of note taking (DiVesta & Gray, 1972). There is evidence that both note taking functions are important (Kiewra, 1989).

In taking notes, at the very least the student rehearses the material. Students remember correctly copied material more than material not copied (M. J. A. Howe, 1970). The most effective note taking, however, must go beyond simple rehearsal. Note takers should also organize and elaborate on the material. When instructed to reorganize text (Shimmerlik & Nolan, 1976) or to write summary (or paraphrase) notes instead of verbatim notes (Bretzing & Kulhavy, 1981), students perform better. In general, when note takers are more active, they process the material more deeply and learn more material.

What about note taking during lectures? Note taking can hinder recall of lecture material if the lecture presentation is fast and the density of information in the lecture is high. However, if the rate of presentation is reasonable, note taking enhances the learning of lecture content (Cook & Mayer, 1983). Students also can be trained to produce better notes resulting in better recall of lectures (Carrier & Titus, 1981).

How much note taking helps students learn depends on both the quality and the quantity of the notes students take (Kiewra, 1989). Even the format of the notes influences lecture recall. Kiewra and his associates (Kiewra, DuBois, Christian, & McShane, 1988; Kiewra et al., 1991) investigated three different note taking formats: conventional, outline, and matrix. Conventional notes are the ones that students typically take when left to their own devices. These are usually brief, often disorganized, typically verbatim accounts of the lecture. In the outline format, the lecturer's major topics and subtopics are listed in a linear fashion and the note taker takes notes in the spaces between topics on the list. Matrix notes are in a two-dimensional format with the lecturer's topics listed across the top of the page and subtopics listed along the left margin. Notes taken are listed in the intersecting cells. Usually notes taken in the outline and matrix format are more detailed and more organized and lead to better lecture recall than those taken in a conventional format.

Another common strategy used by students is **outlining,** which is essentially a way of summarizing text. While outlining, students organize and summarize the material they read. Traditional outlines are linear; that is, specific points are grouped under general ideas. Alternative outlines, such as text maps, are two dimensional. For example, in text mapping, students diagram relationships among ideas in the text (Dansereau et al., 1979). These text maps spatially organize the links between the ideas in the text. Since there may be many different ways to map a given text, it might be a good idea for students to compare their maps (see also the discussion of concept maps in Chapter 12).

In studies in which students are told to outline but not taught outlining techniques, outlining is not very effective (Armbruster & Anderson, 1981). In general, students can be taught to benefit from outlining if given substantial instruction in how to do it. In particular, students can be trained to identify text structures, such as those described in Chapter 3 (Cook, 1982).

Self-questioning can also improve learning from text. Students can be instructed to use self-questions designed to prompt them to look for main ideas and elaborate on them. They learn to ask themselves questions such as, "What is important here?" or "What must I remember?" They can also learn to formulate questions in reaction to content that is confusing or might be clarified by subsequent text, such as, "I wonder whether this Oz place is real?" Students taught to generate and respond to inferential questions requiring explanatory responses understand and remember text better than students not taught to do so (King, 1989, 1990, 1992, 1994). Students can also learn to construct questions to self-test, with even just the creation of testlike questions probably improving learning of the text (Dole, Duffy, Roehler, & Pearson, 1991; Davey & McBride, 1986). Although low-ability students may benefit even more than high-ability students from self-questioning, they need training to use it effectively (Andre & Anderson, 1978–1979).

Some strategies used extensively by college students and often recommended in study skills courses are not very effective.

Rehearsal of complex materials (e.g., copying a passage) can be effective, but it requires a great deal of time. Also, if a student only rehearses, more meaningful, conceptual analyses of text may actually be reduced. In general, although rehearsal in the form of rereading of text is common, it is not particularly effective.

Underlining of text produces small, inconsistent improvements in learning at best. Under some circumstances, underlining can be beneficial in comparison to reading text without underlining (Rickards & August, 1975). Benefits from underlining are more likely if students limit how much they underline and look for the organization and connections in the text as they underline. Unfortunately, students often tend to underline everything that seems remotely important and wind up underlining most of the text, which does little good.

Some study strategies recommended in many studies skills courses (e.g., *SQ3R*-Survey, *Q*uestion, *R*ead, *R*ecite, *R*eview) are not very effective (Forrest-Pressley & Gilles, 1983). A study strategy called *PQ4R* (*P*review, *Q*uestion, *R*ead, *R*eflect, *R*ecite, *R*eview) has had some success. For example, fifth graders who used PQ4R recalled more on both immediate and delayed tests than those who used their own methods (Adams, Carnine, & Gersten, 1982). The steps of the PQ4R method are as follows:

1. *Preview.* Survey headings to get an idea of the overall topics and organization of the material.
2. *Question.* Ask yourself questions about the material as you read.
3. *Read.* Read the material.
4. *Reflect.* Make the material more understandable and meaningful by making connections to your prior knowledge.
5. *Recite.* Test your memory of the information by asking yourself questions.
6. *Review.* Reread portions of the material you do not understand or remember.

The extra *R* for reflection in *PQ4R* (compared to *SQ3R*) prompts readers to elaborate, think of examples, invoke images, and make connections. That is, students are urged to do more than just rehearse text, which is the primary focus of SQ3R.

A generalization emerging from the research on study strategies is that less effective techniques largely involve simple rehearsal of material rather than extensive recoding and relating of new content to other knowledge. More effective procedures require the learner to process the meaning of the text actively. The

Long-Term Effects of Early Science Instruction Building on Students' Knowledge

The most effective strategies require learners to process actively the meaning of the text, often relating it to prior knowledge. Novak and Musonda (1991) designed an audiotutorial science instruction program that first built upon common knowledge held by the students and then in later lessons built on the knowledge learned in earlier lessons. In a typical lesson, the key ideas of the lesson were introduced. Related ideas presented in previous lessons were reviewed, and students were given some indication of how the new materials related to the previously learned ideas. In this way, the researchers tried to develop *advance organizers* to facilitate students' learning. As introduced in Chapter 3, advance organizers are introductory materials that serve as a bridge between what the learner already knows and what the teacher is trying to teach (Ausubel, 1968).

Students who received this science instruction during first and second grade were interviewed periodically about science concepts until the twelfth grade. A comparison group of students who did not experience the instructional program but who were students from the same schools and had equivalent SAT scores in the twelfth grade were also interviewed.

The researchers transformed the interviews into **concept maps,** which represented the students' knowledge structure (see also Chapter 12). A concept map is a diagram depicting concepts (typically identified by circles) and the relationships among them (typically designated by lines and by words indicating the nature of the relationship). The concept maps were scored in terms of the relevance of the concepts expressed, the interlinkages between concepts, and misconceptions revealed. The students who received the instruction developed more valid understandings of science concepts and displayed fewer misconceptions than the comparison group. Examples of the growth in science concepts expressed by a single child are provided in the three concept maps shown here. When Amy was

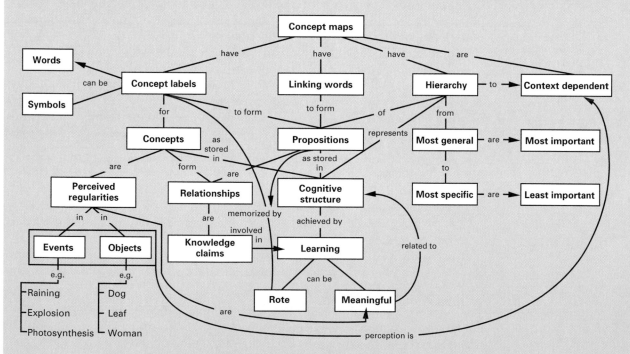

A concept map showing the key ideas underlying the study's use of concept maps.

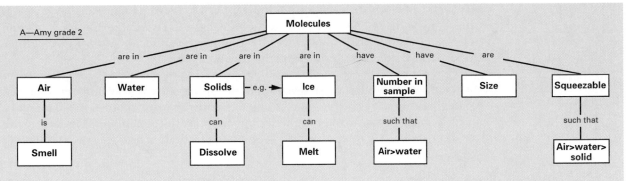

Concept map for Amy, grade 2.

a second grader, she correctly recognized that all substances are made of molecules, although she had the misconception that substances differ in the "squeezability" of their molecules. When Amy was a twelfth grader, she correctly believed that atoms in solids have space between them but she had a new misconception about density.

Think back to the types of developmental research described in Chapter 1. What kind of developmental study is this, cross-sectional or longitudinal? (It is longitudinal, since the researchers observed the same students over time in order to see the growth in knowledge.) Is this research qualitative or quantitative? (They used qualitative methodology but quantified some of the results, such as the scoring of concepts maps.) How did the researchers try to establish equivalency of the instructed and comparison groups? (The students attended the same school and had similar SAT scores.)

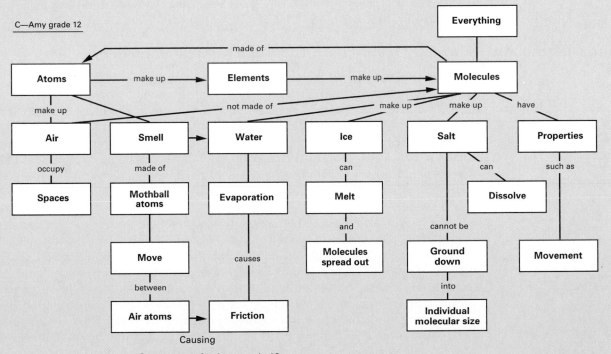

Concept map for Amy, grade 12.

Source: Concept maps from "A Twelve-Year Longitudinal Study of Science Concept Learning" by J. D. Novak and D. Musonda, 1991, *American Educational Research Journal, 281(l)*, pp. 117–153. Copyright 1991 by the American Educational Research Association. Reprinted by permission of the publisher.

learner works with the text content, analyzing connections between the text and other knowledge the learner possesses and elaborating on the text to integrate the new material with prior knowledge. In summary, whether or not a study strategy works depends on the type of effort the learner applies.

Educators are becoming increasingly aware that they must do more than teach the content; they also must teach students strategies for learning the content. Strategies uniquely suited to specific content domains are examined in Chapters 11 and 12. Strategies particularly effective for students with exceptional characteristics are discussed in Chapter 16. Still other strategies designed to increase test-taking skills are presented in Chapter 15.

The Teaching of Strategies

As discussed earlier in this chapter, young children often fail to use effective rehearsal strategies when learning lists. It takes only brief instructions, however, to teach 6- and 7-year-olds how to rehearse lists so they remember them later (Keeney, Cannizzo, & Flavell, 1967). Children in the early school years (kindergarten through third grade) also often fail to make use of organizational properties of lists, such as categories, that can aid memory. Again, it is easy to teach children to sort lists into categories (Moely, Olson, Hawles, & Flavell, 1969). There have been many demonstrations of teaching children to use memory strategies that they did not exhibit prior to instruction (Pressley, Heisel, McCormick, & Nakamura, 1982). Instruction in strategy use, however, is not always enough to turn nonstrategic students into strategy users.

Age Differences in Strategy Instruction: The Case of Mental Imagery

Children do not benefit from all types of strategy instruction. One example is instruction in mental imagery. Preschoolers instructed to construct interactive images to remember paired associates perform no better than children who are simply asked to try to remember the pairings (Levin, McCabe, & Bender, 1975). If preschoolers are asked to generate a sentence linking paired items, however, they can do so easily, and the verbal elaboration facilitates memory. Thus, the failure to benefit from elaborative imagery instructions is not due to inability to think of linking relationships but instead due to difficulty in generating an interactive image.

The ability to generate interactive images develops during the elementary school years. For example, second-grade children can make up linking images when given paired items with obvious linking relationships, such as a needle and a balloon. They do not benefit, however, from imagery instructions when trying to learn pairs that are less obviously related to one another, such as a turkey and a rock. Children up to 8 years of age also experience difficulties generating images representing the content of information presented in paragraphs (Guttmann, Levin, & Pressley, 1977; Shimron, 1975). Slightly older children, however, do benefit from instructions to construct images of information presented in paragraphs (Gambrell & Bales, 1986; Pressley, 1976). In general, the strategy of generating images is teachable by the middle of the elementary school years. Children in the early-elementary school years, however, typically do not benefit from instruction on generating imagery.

Continued Use of Strategies Following Instruction

Teaching students how to execute a strategy does not guarantee they will use the strategy in appropriate situations. Students sometimes fail to continue using strategies in situations *almost identical* to the ones in which they first learned the strategies. This is a failure to **maintain** strategies. Failure to **transfer** occurs when students do not apply strategies they have learned to *new* situations and tasks where they could be appropriate.

Why are there maintenance and transfer failures? Sometimes students simply do not recognize that they could apply a strategy they have learned in a new situation. They can, however, apply the strategy if given gentle hints to do so (Gick & Holyoak, 1980, 1983; Ross, 1984).

On other occasions, students recognize that a strategy they know is applicable, but their use of it in the particular situation is so jumbled that the strategy is neither recognizable nor effective (Harris, 1988). Still other times students do not use a strategy because they do not enjoy carrying it out or do not feel that the gains produced by the strategy are worth the effort (Rabinowitz, Freeman, & Cohen, 1992). Thus, simply instructing a student about how to carry out a strategy in no way assures maintenance or generalization of the strategy.

Metacognition and Regulation of Strategy Use

One explanation for transfer and maintenance failures is deficiencies in metacognitive knowledge (Borkowski, 1985; A. L. Brown, Bransford, Ferrara, & Campione, 1983). Metacognitive knowledge about strategies refers to understanding when and where to apply strategies and the gains produced by strategies when used. Simply teaching a student how to carry out a strategy does not assure that the student understands how the strategy would benefit performance. Understanding strategy benefits, however, is critical if the student is to continue to use the strategy following instruction. Students informed about the **utility** of the strategy, that is, the potential beneficial effects of using the strategy, are more likely to maintain the strategy than students not provided with the utility information (Pressley, Borkowski, & O'Sullivan, 1984, 1985).

Although understanding utility might increase persistent use of a strategy in a situation extremely similar to the original instructional situation (maintenance), it is likely that learners need more support to transfer instructed strategies. For instance, increased transfer of a strategy results when strategy instruction is embellished with information about when and where the strategy might apply, which is sometimes called **conditional knowledge** about a strategy (Paris, Lipson, & Wixson, 1983). For example, J. T. O'Sullivan and Pressley (1984) taught children in the fifth and sixth grades to use the keyword method, described earlier in this chapter, to learn associations between cities and the products produced in those cities. For example, to remember the manufacturing of *submarines* in *Long Beach,* the students imagined a submarine running ashore on a very long beach. The conditions of the study varied in terms of the amount of information provided to students about when and where to use the keyword strategy. Students in the most complete instructional condition were taught to apply the strategy whenever there were pairings to learn and when it was possible to think of something that could serve as a keyword for the less familiar of the paired items.

The transfer task in J. T. O'Sullivan and Pressley's (1984) study required students to learn Latin words and their meanings. To use the keyword method to learn a vocabulary-definition linkage, the first step is to identify a part of the foreign word that sounds like a familiar English word, the keyword. The second is to generate an interaction between the keyword and the definition of the word. None of the students, however, were explicitly taught how to apply the keyword method to learning foreign vocabulary.

Did students transfer use of the keyword strategy to the foreign-language task? Only students provided information about when and where to apply the keyword strategy during instruction for its use in learning the cities and their products transferred the keyword strategy to the Latin-vocabulary task. Therefore, providing metacognitive information about when strategies are effective increases transfer of strategies (Weed, Ryan, & Day, 1990).

Durable use of strategies might be especially likely if strategies are taught using what A. L. Brown and her colleagues (Brown, Bransford, Ferrara, & Campione, 1983) called **self-controlled training.** Such instruction involves teaching a strategy, encouraging the student to evaluate the gains produced by the strategy (attend to utility information), and instructing students to remind themselves to use the strategy using self-verbalizations.

For example, Asarnow and Meichenbaum (1979) used a self-controlled training approach to teach kindergarten students to use cumulative rehearsal for serial recall tasks, remembering items in order. The experimenter first modeled cumulative rehearsal for the students. Then the children attempted to use the strategy, with the experimenter offering support and additional instruction as needed. The experimenter explicitly taught the students to use a question-and-answer routine to support their application of the cumulative rehearsal strategy to serial recall. Here is what the experimenter modeled for the children:

> Now what is it I have to do? I have to find a way to remember the order in which the pictures are pointed to. How can I do that? Hmm. I know I can keep saying the names of the pictures over and over again until it is time to point to the pictures. Let me try it now. I have to remember three pictures. . . . That's right. . . . I just keep saying the names of the pictures in the right order. I won't forget the order of the pictures if I keep saying their names in the right order. [The model covered the pictures and continued to repeat the names of the pictures, saying good after each complete series.] Good. I knew I could do it. All you have to do is keep saying the names of the pictures—remembering which picture came first, second, etc. (Meichenbaum & Asarnow, 1979, pp. 21–22)

Notice how much is in this instruction. The kindergarten children are taught explicitly to evaluate whether the learning task was one requiring serial recall. If it was, they are taught to use cumulative rehearsal procedures including a self-testing procedure. The steps involved in rehearsal are repeated several times. The utility of the rehearsal procedure is also emphasized. In short, there were multiple components in this instruction. Students were taught not only the strategy but also how to use it—how to regulate it—as well as metacognitive information about the effects of the strategy on performance.

Did all of this training in self-control make a difference? Self-controlled instruction of cumulative rehearsal was compared with more conventional cumulative rehearsal instruction, which consisted only of teaching the children to say the names of the pictures to be remembered over and over. Immediately following training, students who were given self-control training and those who were a conventionally instructed outperformed the control groups. Two weeks later, however, on a test of strategy maintenance, only the students who received self-control training used the strategy of cumulative rehearsal.

Monitoring a Strategy's Effectiveness

How do students monitor a strategy's effectiveness? When do they become aware that a strategy is affecting their performance positively? What difference does such awareness make? Suppose that you learn a new strategy and try it out. How can you know whether the strategy has worked for you, whether it has improved your performance in comparison to what it would have been if you had done the task as usual before you learned the new strategy? If you do recognize the value of the strategy, does it affect your decision to use the strategy in the future?

Pressley, Levin, and Ghatala (1984) asked adults as well as fifth- and sixth-grade children to learn some foreign vocabulary words. All participants learned the keyword method and used it for half of the words on the vocabulary list. For the remaining words on the list, they used rehearsal, saying the word and its meaning over and over. As expected, both the adults and the children learned the items studied using the keyword method better than those studied using rehearsal. When asked immediately after they studied the words *but before a memory test* to estimate how many vocabulary words they had learned with keyword versus the rehearsal method, neither the adults nor the children recognized that they had learned the keyword-studied items better. The learners were not monitoring the effectiveness of the two strategies as they used them. After they were given a test over the vocabulary items they had studied, the adults realized that they had learned the items they studied using the keyword method better than the ones they studied using rehearsal. Although the children also recognized there was a difference in learning that favored the keyword method, they were not aware of just how great the advantage was. Learners often fail to monitor how a strategy is affecting them as they use it, but they can come to realize that a strategy is effective in promoting learning by being tested on what they had learned with one strategy versus another (Ghatala, 1986; Pressley & Ghatala, 1990).

What influence did awareness of strategy effectiveness have on decisions to use the more effective keyword strategy for future learning? After the test, the adults and children had to choose one of the two strategies to use to learn a new list of vocabulary words. Both the adults and the children overwhelmingly chose the keyword method, reporting that they were doing so because it was more effective than the rehearsal method. The adults' confidence in the effectiveness of the keyword method was stronger than that of the children. Once having seen for themselves on the test that they had learned more with the keyword method, adults adamantly resisted a suggestion by the experimenter that the rehearsal method was better. With the children, however, it was a different story. The experimenter could talk the children into using the rehearsal strategy instead of the keyword strategy even after the children had figured out on the test that they had performed better with the keyword method. Children can resist the experimenter's suggestion only when given explicit feedback about how many they had correct on the first list. An example of explicit feedback is "You had seven items right when you used the keyword method and two items right when you used the rehearsal method."

In conclusion, opportunities for comparison of strategies can lead to better understanding of the utility of a strategy, which in turn leads to continued use of the procedure, at least for young adults. Such clear effects are not so certain with either children or older adults.

Younger Versus Older Children. Are there differences in children's metacognitive understandings of strategy use? In Pressley, Ross, Levin, and Ghatala (1984), 10- to 13-year-old students practiced learning vocabulary definitions with two strategies. One was the keyword method and the other was a familiar, less effective method, which required using the new vocabulary words correctly in a sentence (the sentence method) (Pressley, Levin, & McDaniel, 1987). After studying practice lists using the two methods, the students took a test of the vocabulary they had studied with the two procedures. As expected, the keyword method produced more learning than the sentence method.

However, after recalling more vocabulary words learned with the keyword method than with the sentence method, only 42 percent of the students selected the keyword method for learning another vocabulary list. This was despite the fact that 3 out of 4 of the students knew they had recalled more items using the keyword method.

Prompting the students to consider their relative performances had some effect. Pressley, Ross, Levin, and Ghatala (1984) prompted some students just before they made their strategy selection to consider how they had performed on the practice list and test.

> I want you to think back to the words you just remembered. Did you remember more of the words when you used [the keyword method], or did you remember more words when you made up a sentence using the word correctly? Which type of words did you remember more of, the ones you [used the keyword method for] or the words that you made a sentence [with] using the word correctly? (p. 497)

When given this prompt before strategy selection, the students selected the keyword strategy 89 percent of the time. Thus, it might be necessary to prompt children in the middle-elementary grades to have them make use of their knowledge of strategy utility in making strategy selections, because they won't use what they know about the effectiveness of a strategy unless they are reminded to do so.

Younger elementary school children require even more prompting (Ghatala, 1986). For example, Ghatala, Levin, Pressley, and Goodwin (1986) asked second-grade students to choose between two different strategies—one effective, one not. The children did not select the effective strategy unless specifically instructed to assess how they were doing with the two strategies, to attribute performance differences to the use of the different strategies, and to use the knowledge they had gained about the relative utility of the two strategies in making their future strategy selections.

Younger Versus Older Adults. What about older adults' metacognitive understanding of strategy use? Brigham and Pressley (1988) asked younger (24 to 39 years of age) and older (60 to 88 years of age) adults to practice learning vocabulary words with two strategies. Once again, one strategy was the keyword method and the other was the less powerful sentence strategy. The younger adults behaved just as the younger adults in the study by Pressley, Levin, and Ghatala (1984) did. They recognized during the test that they had learned many more words using the keyword method, and when presented another list of vocabulary to learn, they selected the keyword method. They based their decision on the greater utility of the keyword method relative to the sentence method.

The behavior of the older participants, however, was very different. Although they recognized during testing that they had learned more using the keyword method than the sentence method, they were not as aware as the younger subjects of just how great an edge the keyword method provided. In addition, the greater utility of the keyword method was much less of a determinant of subsequent strategy selections for the older participants than it was for the younger ones. Although 93 percent of the younger participants made their choices on the basis of relative utility of the two strategies, only 47 percent of the older adults did. The older adults often chose the sentence method either because they perceived it to be easier to carry out than the keyword method or because it was more familiar.

The Role of Memory in Strategy Use

There are many different explanations for how knowledge is represented in long-term memory (see Chapter 3). Which of these knowledge representations best explains how strategies are stored? There are important similarities between strategies and productions, as described in ACT* theory (J. R. Anderson, 1983). As defined in Chapter 3, a production specifies some action and when the action should occur. Typically, productions are represented in if-then form.

Consider the following:

> If the task is to learn an association between two items, and if one of the items is unfamiliar, and if the unfamiliar item has some part that is familiar, then it is appropriate to use the keyword method.

The "if" information can be thought of as metacognitive information about when and where the action in question applies. The "if" information is conditional knowledge because it encodes the conditions that must hold for the action specified in the "then" portion to occur. With productions, whenever the "if" conditions are met, then the action associated with the "if" information occurs. In contrast, use of strategies is not automatic.

The action portion of productions is sometimes referred to as procedural knowledge. As described in Chapter 3, procedural knowledge is knowledge of how to do things. Procedural knowledge is knowing *how;* declarative knowledge is knowing *that.* For example, a student may know the rules for basketball (declarative knowledge) but may not be able to dribble a ball down a court (procedural knowledge). Both procedural knowledge and declarative knowledge are stored in long-term memory.

When people use what they know (i.e., their procedural and declarative knowledge), it is activated into short-term memory, a memory store of limited capacity and duration (see Chapter 1). Short-term memory, also called working memory, is often thought of as active consciousness or active memory. It is the information that you are holding in your head at this very moment as you try to understand this paragraph.

The capacity of human short-term memory is extremely limited (Miller, 1956), so if as you read you are distracted by noise in the next room or by thoughts of what you are going to do later today, it will be more difficult for you to understand this paragraph.

A brief exercise will demonstrate the capacity limitations of short-term memory. Read the following list of digits one time, attempting to remember them. Then turn away from the page, and try to recall them in order.

1, 8, 1, 2, 9, 8, 5, 8, 3

How did you do? A good bet is that you did not remember all nine digits. You were certainly conscious of the numbers as you processed them (i.e., they were in short-term memory), but memory of each one faded quickly. That is what working memory is like. All of human thinking has to deal with this limitation in cognitive capacity.

How do procedural and declarative knowledge work together during strategy execution? What is the role of long-term and short-term memory? Suppose a student who learned the keyword method is studying a list of vocabulary words. Consider the first word on the list, *carlin,* meaning "elderly lady." *Carlin—elderly lady* would be in active memory, that is, in short-term memory. The task is to learn the association between items. One of the items is unfamiliar (in this case, an Old English word), and the unfamiliar item sounds like a familiar word (i.e., a keyword of *car*). Therefore, because the conditions required for use of the keyword method are met, the procedure of using the keyword method is activated into short-term memory.

Long-term declarative memory also plays a role in strategy use, however. For example, application of the keyword method involves noting the keyword for an item and then searching long-term declarative memory for images of the keyword and definition and for a relationship linking them. The learner possesses images in long-term memory of cars and elderly ladies. One of each is activated into short-term memory. In addition, declarative knowledge includes a specification of how cars and elderly ladies can be related. For example, elderly ladies can drive cars. Application of the keyword method results in the learner's creating an image of an elderly lady driving a car.

In summary, strategies are like the productions of ACT* theory in that both specify cognitive actions and both are regulated by conditional specifications. Both are carried out in short-term memory, operating on external input and on declarative knowledge activated from long-term memory. In ACT* theory, if the conditions associated with a procedure are met (i.e., if the "ifs" occur), the procedure is executed. For strategies, it isn't nearly so certain. Strategies sometimes fail to transfer, even on occasions when students know when and where a strategy applies.

Acquisition of Procedural Knowledge: A Strategy Example

As discussed in Chapter 3, all procedural knowledge starts as declarative knowledge (Neves & Anderson, 1981). For instance, when learners first learn to use the keyword method, they may have it represented as follows: First, look to see whether you have to remember that two things go together. If that is the case, then look to

When you first learned to drive, it was an effort to remember each step. With practice, driving becomes easier and more automatic.

see whether the less familiar term has some part that is familiar. Take that familiar part, and make an image between it and the information to be learned.

When learners are first using the keyword method, they are very conscious of each of the steps. Perhaps they even say them aloud. Often they make errors during this stage. With practice, errors become less frequent. There is less and less need to verbalize overtly. Execution of the entire sequence becomes smoother until the strategy is no longer a sequence of declarative directions but now one smooth procedure.

As discussed in Chapter 3, when a sequence is represented declaratively, it is carried out slowly and with a high cost in terms of short-term memory capacity. For instance, when first learning an action sequence, students have to interpret each step as they do it (e.g., "Can I find something in this unfamiliar word that sounds or looks like a word I know? I wonder how close it has to be? What if it sounds like a word I know but looks a little different . . . ?"). Such interpretation and step-by-step consideration require cognitive capacity. With practice, the sequence can be executed automatically.

■ **Building Your Expertise**

Short-Term Memory Capacity and Strategy Instruction

How does the capacity limitation of short-term memory influence strategy instruction? Strategies, like all procedures, are always executed in short-term memory. Thus, people with larger short-term memory capacities are more likely to execute capacity-demanding strategies.

Think about all that had to be done at one time to apply the keyword method to the vocabulary item *carlin.* Once the learner retrieved images of the keyword referent (an image of a car) and the definition (an image of an elderly lady) from declarative memory, a linking relationship had to be retrieved as well, with the images and linking relationships then combined into an image of an elderly lady driving a car.

The ability to carry out imagery instructions is linked to differences in working-memory capacity (Cariglia-Bull & Pressley, 1990; Pressley, Cariglia-Bull, Deane, & Schneider, 1987). These researchers asked 6- to 12-year-old children who varied in terms of their short-term memory capacities and general verbal competence to learn sentences, such as the following:

The angry bird shouted at the white dog.

The toothless man sat on the orange couch.

The fat boy ran with the grey balloon.

(Cariglia-Bull & Pressley, 1990, p. 396)

In the imagery condition, children were told to visualize in their heads the meaning of each sentence. In the control condition, children were instructed to try really hard to learn the sentences. After presentation of ten of these sentences, the researchers cued recall of each by presenting the subject of the sentence. For example, the researchers prompted, "Tell me about the boy sentence. Tell me about the bird sentence."

The results were very clear. General verbal competence predicted performance on this task. In the imagery condition, however, short-term memory capacity predicted performance even after verbal competence and age of the learner were taken into account. Short-term memory capacity, however, did not predict performance in the control condition. The benefits of instruction in the capacity-demanding imagery strategy were greater for students with relatively large short-term memory capacity than for students with less capacity.

Capacity differences may affect use of strategies in other ways, however. To demonstrate this, we would like you to try another digit-span task. You will be reading four rows of digits. Once you have read each row, turn away from the book and try to recall the digits in order. Here are the rows:

5,4,8,5,7,3,8,5,7,0,3,5,1,7,6,7

4,8,7,3,5,6,7,3,4,5,2,9,3,5,9,8,6,8,5,6,8,5,0

9,2,4,7,5,9,2,3,8,7,4,2,9,8,4,1,3,0,9,4,8,4,1,3,8,4,5,7,1

4,6,4,3,8,7,9,4,5,7,8,5,4,3,3,5,6,7,8,6,8,9,3,2,6,5,7

Did you try to remember all four rows? Was it fun having such a heavy demand placed on your capacity? Would you want to continue with more rows? If you are like many students, the answer is no. It is not fun doing a capacity-demanding task and you certainly don't want to do any more such lists! One of the reasons children may not use more strategies than they do is because the strategies are capacity demanding for them and thus somewhat unpleasant to carry out (Guttentag, 1984; Guttentag, Ornstein, & Siemens, 1987).

Thus, low short-term memory capacity has the potential to undermine strategic competence in several ways. Some strategies require more capacity than some students possess. For some students who have sufficient capacity to carry out particular capacity-demanding strategies, the strain associated with doing so may be so great that they simply will not use the strategy if they are in a situation in which they are free to choose.

● "What Do I Do on Monday Morning?"

Guidelines for Strategy Instruction

- Keep in mind effective instructional techniques such as direct explanation and modeling (described in Chapters 1 and 10), scaffolding (described in Chapters 1 and 8), and self-controlled training (described earlier in this chapter). All of these techniques include teacher modeling of the strategy during which the teacher is certain to verbalize the steps of the strategy overtly, followed by practice of the strategy by students. The students' practice is guided by the teacher's support and feedback until the student can execute the strategy independently.
- Be sure to inform students of the *utility* of the new strategy. Describe the potential benefits.
- Be sure students have *conditional knowledge* about the strategy. Describe when and where the strategy is most effective.
- Simply having students practice the new method is not enough for maintenance and transfer. Be sure students *monitor* the effectiveness of the new method relative to their old methods by comparing their performance on tests. "Try it, you'll like it" is not enough; instead "Try it and compare."
- If working with students younger than middle school children, prompt them to think back to their performances using the new strategy compared to the old. Young children often require explicit feedback on their performance using the different strategies. Help the students attribute increased performance to strategy use.
- If working with older adults, encourage them to use the more effective method even if it is unfamiliar and seems more difficult. Be sure to point out how effective the method is.
- Always be aware that strategy use is capacity demanding. Students will need to use a strategy over and over again until it becomes more automatic and uses less capacity.

Chapter Summary

- Whether children use a memory strategy depends on the children's age and the strategy in question. Preschoolers routinely use some simple strategies, such as looking at a spot where an item to be remembered is hidden. Familiarity of setting, materials, and task combine to permit greater strategic competence by preschoolers. Rehearsal strategies develop during the early-elementary school years, and elaboration strategies emerge later in elementary school and high school. Many complex strategies are not always common even among university-age students.
- Some cultures, including traditional Western educational culture, encourage the use of strategies more than other cultures. Whether parents and educators encourage strategy use in children is an important determinant of whether or not children will use strategies.

- Learners do not always construct as complete representations of text as they could. Instruction that encourages students to construct summaries of what they read, to attend to story grammar elements, and to construct both representational and transformational images often produces dramatic increases in comprehension and memory. A key to understanding these and other strategy interventions is the conceptions of knowledge summarized in Chapter 3.

- If given a small amount of instruction, students can often successfully apply strategies they do not use on their own. Unfortunately, not all strategies can be taught to all students. For example, young children cannot effectively use mental imagery. Even when students receive instructions to carry out strategic processes effectively, there is no guarantee that they will maintain and transfer use of the strategy.

- Metacognitive knowledge, such as knowledge about where and when to use a strategy (conditional knowledge) and the gains produced by a strategy (utility knowledge), increases maintenance and transfer of a strategy. Unfortunately, students do not always develop metacognitive knowledge on their own. Compared to both children and older adults, young adults more accurately monitor how great an advantage an effective strategy provides on a test in comparison to a less effective strategy. Moreover, young adults are more likely to use their perceptions of strategy utility to make decisions about later use of strategies than do children or older adults.

- Acquisition of procedural knowledge, such as strategies, often takes a while. At first, execution is slow and often guided and supported by verbal representations of the sequence of actions comprising the procedure. With experience, strategies are executed faster, with less explicit verbal mediation, and with less demand on short-term capacity.

- Educational interventions must be designed so that the procedures can be carried out given the short-term capacities of targeted students. Strategies that require more capacity than students possess will not facilitate performance because the students will not be able to execute them. Strategies that are within a student's capacity but are stressful to carry out because they require much of the available capacity may not be used.

- Whether a learner executes a strategy when it would benefit performance depends on several factors. Of course, the learner has to have the procedure in long-term memory. The learner also must have conditional knowledge about strategies (the "ifs" in a production system) to use them appropriately. Another determining factor is whether the learner possesses declarative knowledge to use with the strategy. The learner must also have sufficient short-term memory capacity to execute the strategy in question. Finally, the learner must be motivated to use the strategy (see Chapter 2).

Return to the Classroom Predicament

Has reading the chapter helped you understand better why Isaac did not use the methods his teacher taught him? Isaac is not maintaining and transferring strategy instruction. In addition to teaching Isaac the steps of the strategies, his teacher also needs to make sure that Isaac develops metacognitive understandings of strategies.

These include conditional information of when and where to apply strategies and utility information of how effective the strategies are. Isaac needs to be prompted to monitor his performance with and without the strategies. Think back to Chapter 2 for motivational explanations for Isaac's failure to use the strategies on his own. Think back to Chapter 3 for knowledge-based explanations of Isaac's failure to use the strategies on his own.

Chapter Outline

Chapter 5

The Role of Knowledge in Thinking

Classroom Predicament

Maria is in the initial month of her first teaching position. The first few weeks were pretty hectic, but now she feels she is getting into the swing of things. She has just given her first test, and she is pleased with her students' performance, so she is totally unprepared for her students' responses as she hands back their tests. All the students are complaining. Even if they received an *A* on the test, they want to argue about the points they lost. They keep criticizing the test and her grading of their responses. The class is quickly getting out of control. Shocked and upset, Maria loses her temper and angrily tells the class that she is the teacher and they are just going to have to live with their grades.

Later in the teachers' lounge, Maria tells an experienced teacher, Cloris, what happened and how disappointed she is in how she handled the whole episode. Cloris says, "Do you want to know what I do? Before I hand back a test, I explain the criteria I used for grading. I tell the students that I would be happy to reconsider an answer if they write down their rationale for why they believe their answer was correct. I give them some class time to do this. That way, I avoid the unseemly fighting over points, and the students learn from having to make cogent arguments for their perspectives. Some additional advantages are that I learn more about what they really understand and it forces those students who like to argue for argument's sake alone to put some effort into a written product." Maria tries this idea out the next time she gives a test and it works like a charm. "Why didn't I think of that?" Maria muses.

Why didn't Maria think of this solution to her problem or, for that matter, any solution better than losing her temper? Is Cloris more intelligent than Maria? How long do you think Cloris has been a teacher? Do you think Cloris would have solutions for other problems Maria will face? Why? Reflecting on the information conveyed in this chapter will help you formulate responses to these questions.

hat difference does a large, well-organized knowledge base make? What can a person with extensive knowledge about a particular domain (an expert) accomplish that a person lacking that knowledge base (a novice) cannot? The short answer to these questions is "Quite a bit." As outlined in Chapter 1, access to an extensive knowledge base is a critical component of good thinking, and, as described in Chapter 3, knowledge can take a variety of forms in memory. This chapter examines the considerable impact of knowledge upon cognitive performance.

Why should teachers know about the development of expertise? One of the goals of an effective teacher is to help students move along the continuum of novice to expert. Once again, the model of good thinking outlined in Chapter 1 is useful. Experts have profound knowledge bases, make exceptional use of strategies, and are incredibly motivated in their chosen fields. In this chapter we begin by demonstrating the power of knowledge to predict performance in different domains for learners of all ages. Then, we outline the characteristics of expert thinking in general. The nature of expert thinking in professional fields such as medicine and teaching is highlighted, followed by the development of exceptional talents. Finally, the interrelationships between knowledge and strategies are examined.

Knowledge as a Determinant of Performance

High prior knowledge often is associated with high cognitive performance. For example, suppose 10-year-olds and adults were trying to remember the placement of chess pieces on a chess board. Who would you bet on to perform better on this memory task? You would probably bet on the adults, since adults typically perform better than 10-year-olds on memory tasks. What if the 10-year-olds were chess masters and the adults were chess novices? Would you want to change your prediction? You would be wise to do so, since 10-year-old chess experts consistently outperform adult novices on this task (Chi, 1978).

Now, what if the adults and 10-year-olds were trying to recall a list of vocabulary words. Who do you think would do better on this memory task? In this case, the adults would outperform the children.

How can this phenomenon be explained? The children are experts in a particular domain of knowledge—chess. Their knowledge of the game permits them to categorize meaningful arrangements of chess pieces (e.g., a checkmate), so they

Children who are chess experts can remember more about the placement of chess pieces on the board than adults who are chess novices.

really only have to remember a few chunks of information for each chess board they see. To the adult chess novices, the relative positions of the chess pieces are meaningless. They have to learn the board on a piece-by-piece basis with little if any grouping together of pieces in a meaningful chunk. Those who possess **domain-specific knowledge,** that is, knowledge about a particular topic, process information from that domain very differently than domain novices.

Domain-specific knowledge also influences the learning of information from textual material. In studies by Chiesi and his colleagues (Chiesi, Spilich, & Voss, 1979; Spilich, Vesonder, Chiesi, & Voss, 1979; Voss, Vesonder, & Spilich, 1980), adults with varying degrees of knowledge about baseball were asked to read text about baseball games. The adults with high knowledge of baseball remembered more about the baseball game described in the text and had better organized memory of the game; that is, they remembered more critical information, rather than unimportant details, than the baseball novices. The baseball experts did not have better memories across the board, only better memories for baseball content. The novices and experts also differed in their recall errors. When baseball experts misrecalled, they misrecalled details. When novices misrecalled, they often reported illegal plays or impossible situations.

Children also tend to learn more from text about topics they know a great deal about (Pearson, Hansen, & Gordon, 1979). For example, Means and Voss (1985) analyzed the learning of a *Star Wars* text by students in grades 2, 3, 5, 7, 9, and college. Learning was better for experts of *Star Wars* at every grade level. Expert performance also increased with age, possibly due to qualitative differences in the sophistication of *Star Wars* knowledge in older compared to younger students. Younger children saw *Star Wars* as being about good guys and bad guys. In contrast, older experts constructed layers of meaning, including themes of morality and the appropriateness of militarism.

The Nature of Expert Thinking

Expert performances in a number of domains—including chess, typewriting, cab driving, memorizing restaurant orders, mental calculation, computer programming, judicial decision making, solving of poorly structured problems, medical diagnosis, and teaching—have been studied (for examples, see Chi, Glaser, & Farr, 1988). Some generalities have emerged from this research, despite the wide variety of expertise studied.

What are some important characteristics of expert thinking (R. Glaser & Chi, 1988)?

- *Experts excel mainly in their own domains.* When an expert political scientist solves a problem in political science, the result is a sophisticated analysis. When an expert chemist tries the same problem, the solution is simplistic (Voss, Blais, Menas, Greene, & Ahwesh, 1989). Expertise in one domain is not valuable in another domain.
- *Experts perceive large meaningful patterns in their domains.* A chess expert sees chunks of information on a chess board (Charness, 1989), and radiologists see organized patterns of shading, depth, and location in X rays that are merely patches of white and gray to the rest of us (Lesgold et al., 1988). Skilled lawyers and judges detect overarching principles in legal documents that novices do not notice (Lundeberg, 1987).
- *Experts are faster than novices at performing skills and at solving problems in their domains.* In a given domain, experts have many skills practiced to the point of

Focus on Research

Studies of Knowledge and Intelligence

Are the differences observed between experts and novices due to differences in knowledge or to differences in intelligence? Is high intelligence simply reflected by high knowledge across several domains (Garcia, 1981; R. J. Sternberg & Wagner, 1985)? How do domain-specific knowledge and general intellectual aptitude compare as predictors of performance?

Schneider, Körkel, and Weinert (1989) and Schneider and Körkel (1989) measured both the soccer expertise and the general intelligence of 8-, 10-, and 12-year-old children who read passages about soccer. The passages contained some contradictions, and there were several places where readers needed to make inferences to make sense of the texts. Performances, including the generation of appropriate inferences and detection of contradictions, improved with age. At every age, however, soccer experts exhibited high performance compared to the performance of soccer novices. For example, 8-year-olds high in soccer expertise detected about ten times as many contradictions as 8-year-olds low in knowledge of soccer. General intellectual aptitude was not a strong determinant of the children's performance, especially compared to the effect of soccer expertise.

Domain-specific knowledge is a better predictor of performance than general intellectual aptitude in adults as well as children. C. H. Walker (1987) demonstrated that adult baseball experts, with low general aptitude, can learn more from a baseball passage than adult baseball novices with high aptitude. In another demonstration, Ceci and Liker (1986) visited a racetrack and found expert handicappers who were able, based on a collection of statistics about the horses and jockeys in races, to pick the "top horse" at race time for nine out of ten races. In contrast, the nonexperts picked the top horse five times or less out of ten. The expert and nonexpert handicappers were otherwise comparable. The two groups had similar amounts of schooling, were similar in occupational prestige, and had comparable number of years of track experience.

Ceci and Liker asked these experts and nonexperts to handicap 50 two-horse races in which horses described by extensive statistics were pitted against a standard horse. The standard horse was an average horse on several measures pertinent to handicapping, such as speed, lifetime earnings, and the record of the jockey. The subjects computed the odds for each of the 50 races.

The reasoning of the experts with lower intelligence was more complex than the reasoning of highly intelligent nonexperts. The experts considered many variables in making decisions, simultaneously considering how these variables interacted. Thus, general intelligence did not determine expertise in this handicapping task. Knowledge relevant to the domain of a task is a more important determinant of performance on many tasks than general intelligence.

Think back to the discussion of manipulative and nonmanipulative research presented in Chapter 1. Were these studies manipulative or nonmanipulative? (They are nonmanipulative since researchers cannot randomly assign people to have a certain level of expertise or intelligence. These studies relate differences between people to differences in performance.)

automatization, which means they can be executed quickly, with great ease, and with little awareness. For them, many problems are no longer problems that require searching for a solution. Instead, they have stored a solution. Experts are also fast at identifying (or constructing) a schema that permits a good start on solving the problem (W. G. Chase & Simon, 1973; Lesgold, 1984).

- *Experts use their short-term memory more effectively than novices.* The biological capacity underlying short-term memory is no greater for experts than for novices. The difference is that experts have many skills and strategies automatized to the point at which their execution requires very little short-term capacity. Experts' vast knowledge of patterns and relationships in the domain also reduces the need for short-term processing. For example, chess novices may play out in their heads step-by-step how their opponents might react to a move they might make. In contrast, chess experts simply know the consequences of certain moves from years of experience.

- *Experts represent problems in their domain at a deep level; novices represent problems at a superficial level.* For example, physics experts (Chi, Feltovich, & Glaser, 1981) categorized problems conceptually, grouping together those that represented particular physics principles. The experts would classify a problem referring to a spring applied to a block with another problem involving a block sliding down an inclined plane, according to the principle of conservation of energy. Physics novices focused on surface features, and thus they grouped problems on the basis of low-level features. For example, the novices would group together problems involving objects sliding down planes.

- *Experts spend proportionately more time analyzing a problem qualitatively than novices do.* Experts size up problems and identify patterns before attempting solutions. Since experts often identify plans that permit efficient solution of a problem, much of the time they spend on a problem is devoted to planning rather than to the actual solving of the problem. For example, an expert might take 5 minutes to complete a task that a novice would take 10 minutes to complete. The expert might devote 60 percent of the time (3 minutes) to planning and 40 percent to task execution. In contrast, the novice might spend proportionately less of the total time planning (e.g., 40 percent) even though that might represent more planning time in absolute terms (i.e., 4 minutes).

- *Experts have strong self-monitoring skills.* Many students fail to monitor their performances (see Chapter 4). They often do not know how a strategy they are using is affecting their performance and may not, for example, know whether they are ready for a test or have comprehended the main idea of a passage. For experts in their areas of expertise, however, it is a different story. They are very well aware of how they are doing as they work on tasks in their domain of expertise. Moreover, experts test their approaches to determine whether they are making progress. They fine-tune solutions when they detect difficulties with solution attempts (Voss, Greene, Post, & Penner, 1983).

Table 5.1 summarizes the important characteristics of expert thinkers.

Table 5.1

Characteristics of Expert Thinkers

- Expertise is domain-specific.
- Experts see meaningful patterns.
- Experts perform skills and solve problems quickly.
- Experts make effective use of short-term memory.
- Experts represent problems at a deep, conceptual level.
- Experts emphasize analyzing problems and planning solutions.
- Experts self-monitor.

Expertise in Medical Diagnosis

Research describing medical expertise can help us understand expertise in general. For example, Alan Lesgold and his colleagues (Lesgold et al., 1988) have studied how expert and novice radiologists read X rays. The experts quickly get a general idea of what might be going on in the X ray and select a general schema for additional consideration that is consistent with certain characteristics of the X ray. This is called the schema invocation phase. As introduced in Chapter 3, a schema is a generalized body of knowledge. Once a general schema is invoked, the expert fine-tunes the evaluation by conducting a series of additional tests to reach a diagnosis and confirm it.

Here is how one expert responded to an X ray. He took a two-second look and began searching for a general schema that might fit the situation. The expert generated a schema for a collapsed lung and tested it: "There may be a collapse of the right lower lobe, but the diaphragm on the right side is well visualized and that's a feature against it. . . ." He continued to test this possibility, noticing clues that there had been a previous surgery. "I come back to the right chest. The ribs are crowded together. . . . The crowding of the rib cage can, on some occasions, be due to previous surgery. In fact . . . the third and fourth ribs are narrow and irregular, so he's probably had previous surgery. . . ." The expert then changed schemata and solved the problem. "He's probably had one of his lobes resected. . . ." He kept testing, however, especially for the possibility that what was needed was an explanation involving both a collapsed lung and a lobectomy. That is, he attempted to combine two schemata to build a unique mental representation of the situation (adapted from Lesgold et al., 1988, pp. 319–320).

In building their mental representations of the situation, the expert radiologists quickly generated a possible schema that might explain the data in the X rays. Once activated, the schema guided the processing of the experts. Sometimes the schema needed to be modified or changed if it did not fit the features of the data. Experts applied their knowledge of normal anatomy to the X rays but did not try to force pathological features into their normal schemata. Novices were much more likely to explain away pathological features as normal.

The novices often were willing to accept a general schema as the correct diagnosis without additional checking. Thus, when an X ray was presented that superficially suggested a lung tumor, the novices concluded lung tumor. Half the experts

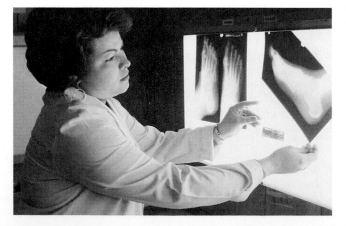

This expert radiologist exhibits thinking consistent with the general model of expert thinking discussed in this chapter.

in the study, however, detected features in the film suggesting a less obvious—but, as it turns out, correct—diagnosis. One possibility suggested by Lesgold is that the radiological novices may have had their short-term memory capacities full, using most of their capacity to discern just the gross features and come to an interpretation. If so, little capacity would have been left for the consideration of nuances. The experts' years of experience make salient these nuances with less effort and less strain on their short-term memory capacity. Since expert radiologists know what to expect of normal characteristics, their attentional resources can be directed toward abnormal features (Myles-Worsley, Johnston, & Simons, 1988).

Expertise in Teaching

Extensive knowledge can be a powerful determinant of professional competence in many fields, including teaching. Berliner and his colleagues (Berliner, 1986, 1988; Carter, Cushing, Sabers, Stein, & Berliner, 1988; Carter, Sabers, Cushing, Pinnegar, & Berliner, 1987) studied teachers early in their careers (novices) and teachers nominated by their schools (and then screened by outside observers) as expert teachers. Several studies examined the perceptions that expert and novice teachers have about classroom events.

Sabers, Cushing, and Berliner (1991) had teachers watch a videotaped lesson. Using a complex setup involving three screens, this videotape managed to capture the simultaneous events occurring in all parts of the room (left, center, and right). During part of the session, the participants talked aloud about what was happening in the classroom. They also answered questions about classroom events, including the routines in the lessons, the content covered, the motivation in the classroom, the students' attitudes, the teacher's expectations and roles, and the interactions between students and teacher.

In general, the expert teachers had very different understandings of the teaching they were watching than the inexperienced teachers did. Specifically, the experts and novices differed in their abilities to monitor and interpret the complex set of events occurring in the classroom. The experts were better at making sense of a panorama of events so complex that it required three screens to present it. They made proportionately more interpretations and evaluations of what they saw, and these interpretations and evaluations were more coherent than those made by novices. Here are sample interpretations and evaluations from the experts (Sabers, Cushing, & Berliner, 1991, pp. 72–73):

> On the left monitor, the students' note taking indicates that they have seen sheets like this and have had presentations like this before; it's fairly efficient at this point because they're used to the format they are using.

> I don't understand why the students can't be finding out this information on their own rather than listening to someone tell them because if you watch the faces of most of them, they start out for about the first two or three minutes sort of paying attention to what's going on and then just drift off.

> I think there is an indication here of the type of structure of this classroom. It's pretty loose. The kids come in and go out without checking with the teacher.

In contrast, the less experienced teachers do not see as much and do not perceive the overall structure of the classroom and the events taking place in it. A high proportion of the novice teachers' comments were simply descriptions of what was happening without interpretation or evaluations. Here are some of their comments (pp. 72–73):

> I can't tell what they're doing. They're getting ready for class, but I can't tell what they're doing.
>
> She's trying to communicate with them here about something, but I sure couldn't tell what it was.
>
> It's a lot to watch.

The experts were more able to classify the type of instruction they were watching. They also took in more of the room, distributing their attention between the left, center, and right portions of the room more evenly than the novice teachers did. Visual information captured the attention of the novices. In contrast, the experts processed both the visual and auditory input, using the language cues they picked up to aid in their interpretations of the classroom events.

Novices noticed students' misbehavior and were critical of it but did not make inferences about the underlying causes. The experts' perceptions of misbehavior were less evaluative and included explanations for the disruptions. In general, the experts explained the classroom behaviors rather than simply describing them or disapproving of the students.

The expert teachers in this study (Sabers et al., 1991) were able to discern patterns not apparent to novices. They were able to size up a classroom quickly and generate a possible general schema to explain classroom interactions. Differences between experts and novices are apparent even after a very brief exposure to classroom situations. For instance, Berliner (1988) noted differences between expert and novice descriptions of a classroom following a mere 1-second exposure to a slide of the classroom. The novices commented on superficial features of the class (p. 12):

> A blond-haired boy at the table, looking at papers. Girl to his left reaching in front of him for something.
>
> [A] classroom. Student with back to camera working at a table.
>
> A room full of students sitting at tables.

In contrast, the experts perceived structure and organization and focused on instructionally important characteristics of the scene (p. 12):

> It's a hands-on activity of some type. Group work with a male and female of maybe late junior high school age.
>
> It's a group of students maybe doing small group discussion on a project as the seats are not in rows.

One second of viewing was all that was needed for experts to perceive structure, whether it was a chalkboard activity, independent seat work, or a laboratory exercise.

Other researchers studying expert teaching have also produced results consistent with the general research on experts. Peterson and Comeaux (1987) studied how experienced and inexperienced high school teachers represented and remembered events that occur in classrooms. Their participants watched 4-minute videotapes of three classroom events, all involving misbehaviors common in classrooms. After watching each tape, the students described the behaviors and interactions

After viewing scenes like this for just 1 second, expert teachers were able to discern patterns of classroom interactions. Novice teachers were not.

depicted on the tape. Then, the participants watched the same tape again, this time to identify places in the sequence at which the teacher could have made different decisions. The participants generated alternative actions the teacher could have taken and specified the action that they would have taken. Even though the experienced and inexperienced teachers did not differ in general memory ability, as measured by a digit span task, the experienced teachers recalled many more of the behaviors depicted on the tapes than the novice teachers did.

In addition, the alternative courses of action recommended by the two groups differed. The more experienced teachers were more likely to offer principled suggestions, such as the following, than the novices:

> You can use the test as a learning experience rather than just to hand back.

> [H]e can stimulate a little interest without always leaning on the test. . . . [I]t's just not motivational enough . . . isn't decisive enough . . . isn't well organized enough.
> (p. 324)

In contrast, the comments of the novices focused on particular alternative behaviors to encourage rather than a conceptual analysis of the situation, as is evident in the following examples (p. 324):

> He probably should have told them to get their notebooks out and take notes or ask for general attention before he started going into what he was going to talk about.

> I'd have handed out the test after they had cleared their desks of all other materials.

Peterson and Comeaux concluded that the experienced teachers had more sophisticated schemata for encoding classroom events. These schemata permit more complete encoding and recall of the events and more principled interpretation of the classroom situation.

How do differences in knowledge about teaching translate into differences in teaching? Borko and Livingston (1989) highlighted the flexible use of schemata by expert compared with novice teachers. They studied three experienced mathematics teachers and the student teachers assigned to them. The teachers were interviewed before and after each day of classroom observation. The first interviews focused on planning for the lessons; the second interviews elicited reflections on the teaching of the lessons.

Borko and Livingston then described differences in the planning carried out by the expert and novice teachers. The experienced teachers planned more for the long term than the novices did. Although both experienced and novice teachers made detailed daily plans, the novice teachers' planning exclusively focused on the lesson for just that day. In contrast, the more experienced teachers continuously thought about upcoming sections in the text and the overall organization of the chapter. An even more striking difference was that much of the planning of the experienced teachers was done in the context of teaching. For example, experienced teachers did not concern themselves with determining which examples they would use. They were always able to come up with apt examples, either ones they knew from experience or ones that they could locate quickly in the text. The novices agonized over which examples to present and how to present them. Moreover, the novices were not very good at improvising, as one noted:

> This is all so new to me that thinking up, I have to do a lot of thinking ahead of time. I really do. I have to think out what kind of questions to ask. I have to think out the answers to the questions . . . so that my answers are theoretically correct and yet simple enough to make sense. And I have to really think in math. I love it. But I have to really think carefully about it. I can't ad-lib it too well. (Borko & Livingston, 1989, p. 487)

The schism between planning and what actually occurred in the classroom was much wider for the novices than it was for the more experienced teachers. In particular, the novices had difficulties with the students' questions and with making adjustments to the students' misunderstandings. The students' questions often got the presentation off track, and the novice teachers had difficulty getting it back on track. In contrast, the experienced teachers were expert in using the students' errors and questions to guide and shape instruction in meaningful ways.

What accounted for the teaching differences between the experienced and the inexperienced teachers? Undoubtedly, one difference was content knowledge. Here is how one of the more experienced teachers described the difference in content knowledge between the first and second year of doing a course:

> When I begin teaching a course, I do a thorough outline on each chapter. . . . I take out all the important words and define them . . . vocabulary words, examples, diagrams. If there's like a lot of information that I feel is important, I'll even copy that down right from the book . . . and emphasize certain things I want to emphasize. And then I do all the problems I assign. (Borko & Livingston, 1989, p. 490)

After the first year, she merely fine-tunes her notebook.

> It's a matter of rearranging it mentally and becoming more comfortable with it, have it become part of my knowledge, rather than just, you know, notes. (Borko & Livingston, 1989, p. 490)

This teacher also recognized that the difference in her knowledge of the content translated into quality of instruction:

> Last year I was much too rigid because I didn't see some of the relationships I'm seeing now . . . and I've shared a lot of this with the students, which I think has helped them because their viewpoint is the narrow viewpoint I had last year. (Borko & Livingston, 1989, p. 490)

Part of her increasing knowledge base comes from interaction with students as they attempt problems. In particular, there is an increase in understanding which parts of the content will pose difficulties for the students. This increased understanding permits preventive action by the teacher:

> As you see different types of mistakes the students make—they usually stay the same from year to year—you can pinpoint that out for the students ahead of time . . . but that kind of comes automatically. The more you teach in the class, the more you realize where the pitfalls are. (Borko & Livingston, 1989, p. 490)

Over the years, good teachers accumulate cogent explanations and examples. They also develop understanding of when extensive explanations and demonstrations are in order and when more rapid coverage is possible.

Expert teachers have extensive and connected teaching schemata, but they do not apply them rigidly. Instead, the teacher constructs an internal representation, called a *mental model,* of a teaching situation and flexibly combines and adjusts prior knowledge to fit the current situation. Borko and Livingston (1989) emphasized the ability of expert teachers to improvise. The ability to adjust to new situations is a mark of high competence.

What else have researchers learned about the nature of expert teaching? Expert teachers have definite routines that they use when teaching lessons (Leinhardt, 1986; Leinhardt & Greeno, 1986). These routines allow the experts to be more efficient in procedural activities (e.g., taking less time to pass out papers and to correct homework than novices) and in conveying important points (e.g., providing lessons that are more clear, accurate, and rich in examples than those of novices). Expert teachers also have extensive hierarchical classification structures for students' abilities and characteristics (Calderhead, 1983). With experience, teachers increase their understanding about how to be flexible in their thinking and how various teaching behaviors interrelate. Experienced teachers exhibit more complex thinking about teaching than inexperienced teachers do (Strahan, 1989).

Much of the knowledge that expert teachers have is derived from practice. They have built up coherent theories about and representations of good teaching through their personal experiences. Often, experienced teachers claim they have "images" of good teaching that have developed as a result of their experiences in teaching. Two such images are the "classroom as home" (Clandenin, 1986; Connelly & Clandenin, 1985) and the curriculum as a "conduit" (Russell & Johnston, 1988) through which the teacher leads the students. Teachers possess images of what ideal lessons look like (Morine-Dershimer, 1979) and of everyday situations in classrooms (Eraut, 1985). Many teachers claim that their images guide their practice (Calderhead & Robson, 1991). Experienced teachers have well-organized schemata for teaching, many of which are encoded as images.

■ Building Your Expertise

Knowledge Representation of Expert Teachers

The research on expert teachers points out the significance of the types of knowledge representations discussed in Chapter 3.

- Expert teachers have content knowledge of the fields they teach (represented in concepts and/or propositions). Expert teachers can classify types of instruction and exhibit hierarchical knowledge of students' abilities, ideas easily conveyed through concepts.
- Expert teachers readily perceive patterns in classroom interactions. Their knowledge is in the connections as best represented in neural networks.
- Expert teachers use metaphoric images to represent their understanding of teaching and to guide practices.
- Expert teachers possess generalized knowledge about teacher-student interactions. These schemata enable them to explain and predict classroom events better than novices.
- Expert teachers have developed a large number of productions applicable to the classroom situation. If they recognize a pattern, they know what action to take. Expert teachers can readily suggest alternative courses of action.
- Expert teachers have sufficient knowledge to form sophisticated mental models of educational environments, models that draw on knowledge that is based on experience (Schön, 1988; Strauss & Shilony, 1994). These mental models allow teachers to generate inferences and expectations, as well as solutions to problems. In any given situation, this knowledge can be modified to take into consideration new constraints in the environment. The result is a mental model that is unique and translates into a unique plan of action rather than simply a replication of a plan of action that worked in a different setting. Reflective educators (Schön, 1983, 1988) do not attempt to transfer unmodified schemata from one situation to another. Instead, they use their schemata and images as starting points, which are then transformed to produce new educational experiences and environments.

The Development of High Competence

What does it take to become an expert? How do we acquire the many procedures involved in expert performance? How long does it take to understand how the various concepts in a domain interrelate, and how long does it take to coordinate extensive procedural and declarative knowledge to solve new problems?

In most instances, expertise requires many years of education. The answer is the same whether archival data on the careers of the greatest geniuses in history are analyzed or analyses are made of the very competent professionals who remain among us. For example, expert chess players spend thousands of hours playing chess and studying the game; grand masters invariably have played for ten or more years (de Groot, 1965, 1966; Simon & Chase, 1973). The expert radiologists studied by Lesgold and his colleagues (1988) had read 200,000 X rays in their careers. The expert teachers in Berliner's research had more than five years of teaching experience.

The Development of Great Composers and Artists

Hayes (1985) analyzed the careers of some great musical composers and painters. He reasoned that if it takes a long time to become an expert, then the early works of great composers and artists might not be as good as the later works. Hayes made the additional assumption that better works of the composers would be recorded more often. To aid in his research, he used a publication known as *Schwann's Guide*, which provides listings of the recordings available for each composer. By graphing the number of recordings of pieces against the year when the piece was composed, Hayes compared the popularity of pieces produced early in a career with those produced later.

Consider the case of Mozart. His productivity increased during the first decade of his career (from ages 4 to 14) from zero to about two compositions per year. For the remaining years of his career, he published between one and four pieces a year. Although Mozart produced 12 percent of his compositions between 4 and 14 years of age, these are preserved in only 5 percent of the Mozart recordings. The ones recorded from this era were generally recorded as part of complete anthologies. Mozart composed the first piece preserved in as many as five recordings when he was 16 years old—fully 12 years after he had begun to compose. In all of the subsequent years of his life, Mozart composed pieces that are more popular than anything he composed during his first decade of productivity.

Hayes analyzed an additional 75 composers and found that their popularity curves were much like that of Mozart. The pieces produced during the first 10 to 12 years are much less popular than those pieces produced later in the career. Once composers achieved excellence, they maintained it for an average of 30 years, with decline in distinguished works typically only apparent by the fiftieth year of a career. Hayes and his colleagues found a similar pattern for artists.

Factors Influencing the Development of Talent

Benjamin S. Bloom (1985) and his colleagues investigated the role of parents, teachers, and other factors in the development of extraordinary talent. They sought out highly skilled concert pianists, sculptors, research mathematicians, research neurologists, Olympic swimmers, and tennis players. Most of the subjects were under the age of 35 at the time of the study. The talented individuals were interviewed about how they became interested in their vocation and how they learned it. In addition, they were asked to pinpoint factors that contributed to their extraordinary attainments. Parents and influential teachers also were interviewed.

Although there was some variability from talent area to talent area, there was also similarity across the talent areas. In general, these talented people liked their domain of expertise from their first exposure to it. In every case, there were years of study and practice. These people also had child-oriented parents who dedicated resources to the development of their children. The families in which they grew up stressed high achievement and striving for success. Good teaching in the area of expertise was available to them early in life. Initial success led to selection into even better educational environments. With success, these talented people invested more effort in their talent, and expert teachers played a greater role in the actual instruction and monitoring of practice. As their proficiency grew, their commitment grew stronger, with many hours per week devoted to the emerging vocation. Eventually the young talent was ready for the master teacher, with virtually all time spent on mastering the field. The typical time course for this education was 15 to 25 years.

Bloom's main message is that great accomplishment is the product of years of high-quality education. He didn't report any genuine child prodigies. Even when the talented individuals were ages 11 to 12, there was little suspicion by parents or teachers that they would become one of the top 25 people in the world in a field. In short, great accomplishment does not just happen. It is the result of years of preparation.

Extraordinary Abilities

Some people can perform extraordinary feats of memory or computation, but these abilities often are very specific. Thus, a person who can remember long lists of digits often proves to have ordinary memory abilities in other tasks, and a gifted square root calculator performs at an average level on many other numerical tasks. People who demonstrate such extraordinary competencies often have sophisticated procedures for performing the tasks in question accompanied by vast prior knowledge that facilitates execution of the strategies. Thus, extraordinary ability is often a matter of good strategies and extensive knowledge.

Memory for Digits. A research group at Carnegie Mellon University has worked with two people who have exceptional abilities to recall long lists of digits in order. One, S. F., was studied by W. G. Chase and Ericsson (1982). S. F. increased his digit span to more than 80 digits. This feat required about two years of practice.

How did S. F. do it (Ericsson & Staszewski, 1989)? It helped that he had extensive prior knowledge of track and field records, especially running times. What S. F. did was to chunk short groups of digits and then recode them as running times, dates, and ages:

> For instance, he would encode the sequence 3492 as "3 minutes, 49.2 seconds"—a near world record for the 1-mile run . . . 798 would be coded as a "79.8-year-old man" and dates (e.g., 1860, 1963) to accommodate digit sequences not easily encoded as running times. (Ericsson & Staszewski, 1989, p. 239)

In addition, S. F. devised mechanisms for keeping track of the order of these chunks. He would code several of the groups of digits encoded in terms of track times into a supergroup. This supergroup would be embedded in a hierarchical network. With practice, S. F.'s facility and speed in coding digit strings using prior knowledge elaborated into hierarchical networks increased dramatically, increasing his functional short-term memory capacity. S. F. used complex strategies that were possible because of extensive prior knowledge of track times, ages, and dates.

Another subject, D. D., who also had extensive knowledge of running times, dates, and ages, practiced the methods devised by S. F. for 4.5 years and eventually was able to code 106 digits (Staszewski, 1990). Consistent with other studies of expertise, S. F. and D. D. did not demonstrate better memory for tasks other than digit span. Thus, exceptional memory for digits in order does not imply exceptional memory for other materials in order (W. G. Chase & Ericsson, 1981, 1982).

Memory for Restaurant Orders. There is a waiter in Boulder, Colorado, who can remember the orders for 20 customers at once, an ability that pays off handsomely in large tips. Ericsson and Polson (1988) studied how this fellow, J. C., remembered material in a laboratory version of restaurant ordering. They compared the performance of J. C. with others who were not exceptionally proficient at remembering such lists. The participants in the study learned dinner orders consisting of an entrée (one of seven possibilities) prepared at a particular level of doneness (one of five choices). Each order included a salad complete with one of five dressings and either fries, baked potato, or rice.

J.C.'s thinking definitely was strategic. First, he dealt with orders in groups of four at a table by developing a memory structure that could be retrieved later. For each person in the group, he constructed a mnemonic image of the person's face in interaction with the entrée item. As part of this, he sized up the customer and included information in the image about the fit between the entrée and the type of person. For example, he might reason that the king-sized prime rib doesn't seem to fit that delicate, blond woman. Each salad dressing had a letter associated with it, such as *B* for "blue cheese," *O* for "oil and vinegar," *T* for "Thousand Island," and so on. If the four salad dressings at a table were blue cheese, oil and vinegar, oil and vinegar, and Thousand Island, they would be encoded into the word *BOOT*. For the meat orders, an internal graph would be formed in J. C.'s mind of the various levels of doneness requested. The ordinate would encode the level of doneness, with the lowest point representing rare, moving higher to medium rare, higher still to medium, up to well-done. For the first order, the leftmost point on the graph would be plotted. The rightmost point on the graph would correspond to the fourth person in the order pattern. Thus, if the first person wanted rare, the second well-

Good servers use their prior knowledge and develop suitable memory strategies to keep orders straight.

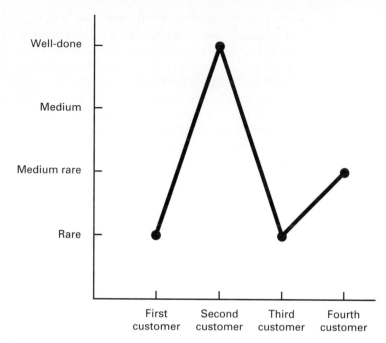

Figure 5.1

A depiction of an internal graph that might be used used by the waiter J. C. to help remember how the people at his tables wanted their steaks cooked.

done, the third rare, and the fourth medium rare, the internal image of a graph would start low, spike up, dip low, and then end halfway up the ordinate (see Figure 5.1). The starch order, since there were only three choices, was always rehearsed as a serial order—for example, rice, rice, fries, baked.

Not surprisingly, J. C. recalled much more in the formal studies of his memory than control subjects did. The inexperienced subjects performed few transformations on the incoming data, attempting instead to memorize the information exactly as given.

Consistent with what was found with S. F. and D. D., J. C. improved over the year he was studied, becoming even faster and more accurate. J. C. clearly had knowledge of the four categories of information that would occur in restaurant orders, and he used this knowledge to devise a memory plan. His memory plan included letter codes for salad dressing, an image of a graph for level of doneness, and serial rehearsal for the starches. He also had extensive prior knowledge about different people and their characteristics, information he used to construct interactive images and elaborations with information about the entrée. This waiter used strategies that were enabled by prior knowledge.

There was only one major difference in the general conclusions that followed from the study of J. C. and the study of D. D. and S. F.: J. C. was able to transfer his skill to other types of items, learning other materials that could be placed into categories, whereas digit-learning abilities did not seem to be transferable. Some obscure skills that require a lot of effort to acquire are more useful than others.

● **"What Do I Do on Monday Morning?"**

Classroom Practices That Promote Expertise

How can teachers help students develop expertise?

- Teachers can encourage their students to *practice* skills and procedures in different contexts. As described in Chapter 3, practice is required for proceduralization, which increases the automaticity of response. The more automatically students can use a sequence of procedures, the less short-term capacity is required to execute the procedures. This leaves more capacity for other activities. For example, when a child has automatized forming letters into words, more capacity is left over for composing sentences and paragraphs. Elite performers develop expertise through deliberate practice (Ericsson & Charness, 1994). Their practice sessions tend to last about 1 hour, followed by a period of rest, for an average total of 4 hours a day.
- Teachers can foster students' *interests*. Skilled performers initially displayed interest in their field of endeavor, an interest that was encouraged by their parents and that motivated them to practice (Ericsson & Charness, 1994). Teachers can help nurture students' interests by first noticing what individual students are interested in and then by giving the students the means and opportunity to learn more in their areas of interest. When students are learning about material they find interesting, they work harder and learn more. Specifically, material that is personally interesting stimulates pleasant emotions, more personal associative networks, and the use of imagery (Hidi, 1990; Tobias, 1994).
- Teachers can promote *self-regulation* in their students by encouraging them to take an active role in their own learning. Learners who are **self-regulated** keep themselves on task and guide their own thinking. As a result of their ability to take advantage of learning opportunities, self-regulated learners become even more powerful thinkers. For instance, when solving problems, self-regulated learners increase their domain knowledge as well as their knowledge of where and when to apply the strategies needed to complete the problems. When their prior knowledge does not fit the current situation, self-regulated learners make adjustments and inferences (i.e., create a new mental model of the situation), thereby building new knowledge that will be available in the future and developing expertise.

Performance Increases with Development: Increases in Knowledge or Strategies?

As children develop, their level of performance on many tasks increases. What is responsible for these increases in performance—increases in knowledge or more effective use of strategies? As we shall see, these two components of good thinking interact in complex ways.

Suppose children are given the task of learning a 30-item list. One-third of the list items are names of pieces of furniture (e.g., table, chair, piano), one-third are the names of fruits (e.g., cherries, orange, melon), and one-third are the names of zoo animals (e.g., lion, elephant, monkey). If first-grade, sixth-grade, and eleventh-grade students learn such a list presented in random order, it is apparent that memory performance increases with age. As their age increases, students are more likely to recall the pieces of furniture together, the fruit together, and the zoo animals together. Thus, the recall of the older students is more clustered; that is, similar pieces of information are grouped together.

One interpretation of why recall increases and becomes more organized with age is that older students are more likely to use strategies intentionally (Moely, 1977). That is, in the previous example, students either reorganized the list into categories as they studied or used the category labels (e.g., furniture, fruit, or zoo animals) to organize their recall. An alternative interpretation is that the increases in performance and organization are due to older children's expanding and ever more connected knowledge base (Bjorklund, 1985, 1987; Lange, 1973, 1978). With increases in size and connectedness, the knowledge base becomes more accessible (Rabinowitz & McAuley, 1990). Thus, presentation of a list that can be broken down by categories, such as the one in the previous example, results in automatic associations to the category labels of furniture, fruit, or zoo animals and associations between list items in the same category.

Recall of categorizable lists, however, can be interpreted in terms of *either* strategies or knowledge base. When recall is low, it is always possible that the poor performance reflects the failure to use strategies or the lack of a knowledge base. When recall is high, it could be due to intentional use of categorization as a strategy, automatic mediation by the knowledge base, or a combination of strategy and knowledge-base mediation. This third possibility may be closest to the truth for learning lists. With increasing knowledge and stronger associations between list items and category label, it becomes *easier* to apply a categorization strategy (Guttentag, 1984; Guttentag, Ornstein, & Siemens, 1987). The expanding knowledge base increases motivation to use categorization strategies by reducing the amount of effort required to apply them to lists.

Knowledge Can Replace Use of Strategies

Sometimes children use strategies because they do not yet possess a knowledge base. For example, experienced readers have knowledge of thousands of words they can use as they read, whereas beginning readers must rely much more on decoding strategies, such as sounding out words, than more experienced readers do. The trade-off between strategies and knowledge is most evident in the development of children's knowledge of simple addition facts.

Siegler and Shrager (1984) studied children's responses to simple addition problems such as $6 + 5 = 11$, $3 + 4 = 7$, and $2 + 5 = 7$. The younger participants (5- to 7-year-olds) solved such problems by using strategies. They used their fingers or other manipulative objects to represent the problem and generate a solution (e.g., four fingers up and then three more put up for $4 + 3$). Sometimes they used counting up strategies (e.g., saying "5, 6, 7" in response to $4 + 3$). In contrast, older children (7- to 9-year-olds) rarely displayed these strategies. Instead, they rapidly retrieved the answers to problems from long-term memory.

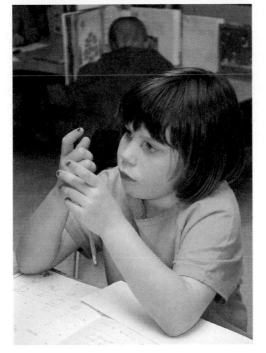

Some successful strategies such as counting on fingers disappear once a child acquires substantial knowledge.

Knowledge Can Enable Use of Strategies

Students simply cannot carry out some strategies successfully without appropriate prior knowledge. An obvious example of this is activation of prior knowledge as described in Chapters 3 and 4. When the content of a text is completely foreign to readers, there is little gain in asking them to relate the text to what they already know (Pritchard, 1990). Pressley and Brewster (1990) demonstrated that the ability to execute strategies can depend on certain knowledge. They asked Canadian middle school students to learn some facts about Canadian provinces, such as "Canada's first museum was in Ontario." Pressley and Brewster instructed some of the students in their study to construct images of the facts occurring in settings unique to those provinces. To do this, however, the students needed prior knowledge of unique images for each province.

Realizing that many students lacked unique images of the Canadian provinces in their long-term knowledge, Pressley and Brewster (1990) included a condition in which students learned a unique image for each province before attempting to learn the facts. For example, the image for the province of Saskatchewan was a wheat field. The researchers found that the imagery strategy was effective only if the student already possessed an image corresponding to the province in question.

Knowledge Can Interfere with New Learning

Not all prior knowledge possessed by students is accurate or consistent with new knowledge presented in school. Scientific misconceptions are a case in point. For example, students often believe that plants get food from soil and water. This misconception persists even after students learn about photosynthesis (K. J. Roth, 1990). What is even worse is that activation of errant prior knowledge can substantially interfere with acquiring any new information at all. Instructional techniques teachers can use to overcome students' misconceptions are discussed in Chapter 12.

Alvermann, Smith, and Readence (1985) examined the impact of errant prior knowledge. In their study, sixth-grade children either activated or did not activate knowledge relevant to a passage they read. Those who activated prior knowledge wrote down everything they knew about light and heat before they read a passage on that topic. These students activated numerous misconceptions during this exercise, and the passage contained information that clashed with these misconceptions.

After reading the passage, memory of its content was tested in several ways. When students activated prior knowledge, they recalled *less* of the information in the passage, specifically the information that was incompatible with their misconceptions. In addition, these students were less likely to respond correctly to multiple-choice items containing misconception foils. Thus, activation of prior knowledge can undermine learning of content that is incompatible with it.

Similarly, prior knowledge can affect students' observations, guiding the students to information consistent with their own perceptions. Students often are looking to confirm what they "know" already, and in doing so they selectively attend and distort information provided during instruction. Thus, classroom demonstrations intended to make one point can end up supporting an inaccurate alternative perspective already held by students (Duit, 1991).

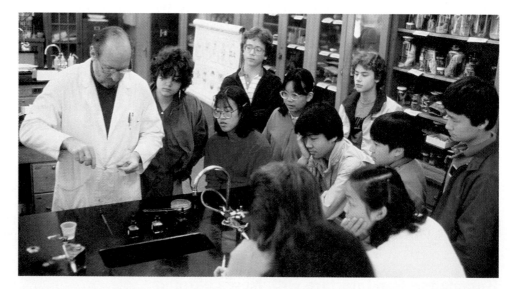

Students' misconceptions can affect their observations, so they confirm their mistaken ideas rather than learn the correct information.

▶ **Diversity**

What Is Cultural Literacy?

Proponents of cultural literacy believe that to participate in American society, it is necessary to have command of a certain core of knowledge essential to understanding American life and thinking (Hirsch, Kett, & Trefil, 1988). Hirsch is editing a series of books that specify what aspects of cultural literacy should be taught at each grade level. For instance, *What Your 2nd Grader Needs to Know: Fundamentals of a Good Second-Grade Education* (Hirsch, 1991) reports the language arts, social studies, fine arts, mathematics, and natural sciences that second grade should include. For example, a second-grade student should know the following in geography:

World geography
- Mediterranean Sea
- Aegean Sea

United States geography
- U.S. map of states
- The first states

Geography of Mexico, Central America, and South America
- Spanish, the main language
- Names of explorers

One problem with the movement for cultural literacy is the emphasis on traditional mainstream knowledge. Some believe that this knowledge created by "dead European males" is of decreasing relevance in today's multicultural society. J. A. Banks (1993) believes that all knowledge reflects the values and interests of its creators. He described five types of knowledge that should be included in schools:

- *Personal and cultural* knowledge is that which is derived from personal experiences in family and community cultures.
- *Popular* knowledge is that which is presented by mass media.
- *Mainstream academic* knowledge is traditional Western-centric knowledge.
- *Transformative academic* knowledge is that which challenges mainstream academic knowledge. Sometimes transformative academic knowledge replaces mainstream academic knowledge through scientific revolution.
- *School* knowledge is that which is presented in textbooks and lectures by teachers.

Banks suggested that the challenge to teachers is to utilize the personal and cultural knowledge of students while simultaneously helping them transcend cultural boundaries. He used a unit on the Westward movement to illustrate how teachers can incorporate all five forms of knowledge into a lesson.

When beginning the unit, teachers can draw upon the students' personal and cultural knowledge about the Westward Movement. They can ask the students to make a list of ideas that come to mind when they think of "the West." To enable the students to determine how the popular culture depicts the West, teachers can ask students to view and analyze the film, *How the West Was Won*. They can also ask them to view videos of more recently made films about the West and to make a list of [their] major themes and images. Teachers can summarize Turner's frontier theory to give students an idea of how an influential mainstream historian described and interpreted the West in the late 19th century and how this theory influenced generations of historians.

Teachers can present a transformative perspective on the West by showing the students the film *How the West Was Won and Honor Lost,* narrated by Marlon Brando. This film describes how the European Americans who went west, with the use of broken treaties and deceptions, invaded the land of the Indians and displaced them. Teachers may also ask the students to view segments of the popular film *Dances With Wolves* and to discuss how the depictions of Indians in this film reflects both mainstream and transformative perspectives on Indians in U.S. history and culture. Teachers can present the textbook account of the Westward Movement in the final part of the unit. (Banks, 1993, pp. 11–12)

The purpose of lessons like this one is to help students comprehend how knowledge reflects the culture in which it is created. The eventual goal is for students to develop the understandings needed to construct knowledge on their own.

Chapter Summary

- This chapter opened with the question, "What difference does a large, well-organized knowledge base make?" Knowledge is intellectual power. The knowledgeable 10-year-old is more than equal to the unknowledgeable adult. The person high in knowledge about horses wins at the betting window, and the soccer expert processes information about soccer more completely than a soccer novice, no matter how intelligent the novice is.
- Expertise is domain-specific. Experts can identify large and meaningful patterns in their domain of expertise that novices cannot identify. Experts process material in the domain of expertise efficiently and understand problems in the area of expertise at a more principled level than novices do. Their problem solving in the area of expertise is planful. They monitor their performances, analyzing progress toward task accomplishment.
- Experts have rich networks of concepts and associations. The schemata they possess are flexible, with experts modifying them as necessary to deal with new situations. Because experts are always modifying their schemata, their education never really stops. It takes long years of preparation to develop expertise. One to two decades of preparation is typical, with much of the second decade a period of immersion in the discipline. Chess masters have seen hundreds of thousands of chess boards, and expert radiologists have analyzed hundreds of thousands of X rays.
- Rich prior knowledge can empower learners, permitting them to complete some tasks more quickly than strategy use would and permitting them to carry out

some strategies that require certain prior knowledge. Unfortunately, not all knowledge that students acquire is correct. Students often have faith in and a commitment to misconceptions, and these misconceptions can hinder new learning.

Return to the Classroom Predicament

Has reading this chapter helped you understand why Cloris was able to help Maria so easily? Maria is a novice teacher, so she does not quickly identify a problem, nor does she have a store of possible solutions based on previous experience. Cloris is probably not any more intelligent than Maria, but she is an expert teacher who has probably been teaching for more than 10 years and has stored solutions that she can quickly access. Maria would be wise to consult Cloris frequently to avail herself of Cloris's expertise in the classroom.

Chapter Summary

Chapter 6

Biological Factors Affecting Learning and Development

Classroom Predicament

A teacher is thinking about the class she will meet for the first time tomorrow. There's a lot of information about some of these students in their files. One student has been identified as dyslexic. Another student suffered brain damage in a car accident and now has difficulty comprehending numbers. Still another experienced prenatal malnutrition. Several students have been identified as having attentional deficits and take medication. The teacher exclaims, "So many of these students have learning problems that are biologically based. There really is nothing a teacher can do about their school progress. The limitations on their abilities will always remain the same."

Do you agree with this teacher? Reflecting on the information presented in this chapter will help you formulate a response to this question. You will come to understand the biological foundations of learning and development better.

Educators have become increasingly aware that biological factors profoundly affect learning and development. Given the tremendous growth in our understanding of biological influences upon all aspects of our lives in recent years, it is reasonable to predict that biological explanations of learning and development will become even more prominent in the future. These new understandings may lead to alterations in accepted classroom practice. Therefore, it is important for future educators to have at least a rudimentary understanding of the biological foundations of learning and development.

We begin with the basics of neurological development and the milestones of normal development. Then, we outline possible disruptions of normal development. The importance of early intervention for fostering normal development and for overcoming the negative effects of disrupted development is emphasized. We then describe how human beings are biologically prepared to acquire certain kinds of learning, such as language. Next, we detail the biological foundations of academic competence and biologically based explanations for the failure to acquire reading and math skills. Finally, how we construct knowledge from our perceptions is introduced in an overview of perceptual learning theory.

Neurological Foundations

Human neurology begins in the developing fetus as a single layer of cells lining something called the neural tube (Goldman-Rakic, Isseroff, Schwartz, & Bugbee, 1983). These cells multiply through normal cell division at an extremely rapid rate. At some points during development, approximately 50,000 new nerve cells form every second (M. C. Diamond, 1992). Through processes not completely understood, neural cells move to destinations corresponding to the beginnings of various parts of the nervous system. Most neurons will be formed and will have migrated to their destinations by birth (Konner, 1991). Once this period of rapid cell growth, which is called **neurogenesis,** is concluded, there will be no new neurons. Any neurons lost due to disease, injury, or normal death will not be replaced.

Once neurons have migrated to appropriate locations, they develop axons and dendrites (see Figure 6.1). Each nerve cell normally has one **axon,** which conducts impulses away from the cell body. **Dendrites,** which are branchlike extensions of the cell body, transmit impulses toward the cell body from other cells. Eventually, **synaptic connections** between neurons are established. These connections involve an axon's meeting a dendrite, a cell body, or another axon. Once the physical connections are formed, the physical and chemical characteristics develop that permit the transmission of impulses (K. R. Gibson & Petersen, 1991). Then nerve cells can send these transmissions to other cells via the synapses (E. Gardner, 1975).

The basic structure of the human nervous system is in place by about 8 weeks following fertilization (E. Gardner, 1975). The first behaviors, which are basic reflexes, appear at this time as well. Although human newborns are neurologically immature compared to other mammals, there is substantial neurological development after birth (K. R. Gibson, 1991a, 1991b). In particular, the cerebral cortex, the part of the brain responsible for many of the complex thought processes carried out during human thinking, expands greatly after birth (see Figure 6.2).

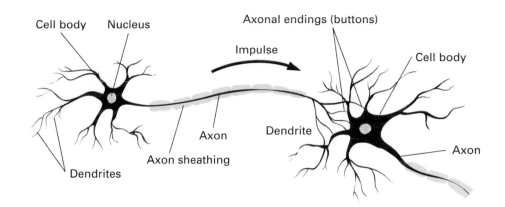

Figure 6.1

Axons and dendrites enable nerve cells to establish synaptic connections with other nerve cells.

Source: From *Cognition, Teaching, and Assessment* by M. Pressley and C. B. McCormick. Copyright 1995 by M. Pressley and C. B. McCormick. Reprinted by permission of HarperCollins College Publishers.

Neurological Development Following Birth

Three-fourths of brain development occurs following birth, even though all of the neurons a person will ever have have already been formed (Prechtl, 1986). Neurons take a long time to mature; some argue as long as 10 years, and others argue even as long as 18 years (K. R. Gibson & Petersen, 1991). With maturity, there are changes in the dendrites and the axons. Dendrites start out as short, tubular, and unbranched. With development, they become longer and have many branches. The longer and more numerous the branches, the more possible sources for connections resulting in transmissions to the nerve cell. As the dendrites branch, the axons acquire a layer of axon sheathing called **myelin.** Myelin is important because it permits more rapid firing of the axons by reducing both the stimulation needed and the recovery time required between firings.

There are some forms of experience that the brain is genetically programmed to expect. For example, some areas of specialization in the brain correspond to perceptual systems, such as visual or olfactory; others correspond to affective systems, cognitive capacities, or linguistic competencies (Anastasiow, 1990; Fodor, 1983; Panksepp, 1986). These areas of specialization are rich in **experience-expectant synapses,** which proliferate 2 to 3 months following birth (Greenough & Juraska, 1986). For example, experience-expectant synapses for the visual system are sensitive to light. When light stimulation is encountered, neurons activate, and their functioning results in the establishment of synaptic connections with other neurons. The experience-expectant synapses that do not make stable connections die off (Anastasiow, 1990, Black & Greenough, 1991; Crutcher, 1991).

In general, experience-expectant synapses either stabilize or die off during **critical periods.** These are time periods of great sensitivity to environmental input. For the sensory systems, these critical periods tend to be early in life (Greenough, Black, & Wallace, 1987). For example, if particular visual experiences do not occur early in development, visual perception is impaired for life, regardless of subsequent remediation efforts. Thus, kittens who are deprived of light for the first 8 weeks of their lives are blind once they are exposed to light (Hubel & Wiesel,

1970). Because experience-expectant synapses did not function during the critical period, they did not stabilize and eventually died off (Black & Greenough, 1991).

For human beings, the critical period for some visual capabilities is considerably longer than 8 weeks. For example, if strabismus (a disorder involving poor muscular control of the eyes) is treated before the age of 5, it produces no long-term impairment (Aslin, 1981). If it is left untreated, however, strabismus negatively affects the visual system (Anastasiow, 1990). This is because the sensory organs affected by the strabismus provide inaccurate information, which results in the faulty stabilization of the experience-expectant synapses.

Other synapses, **experience-dependent synapses,** are not genetically predetermined to be sensitive to particular types of information (Greenough & Juraska, 1986). Instead, they stabilize in reaction to whatever environmental stimulation an individual encounters. These types of synapses can be formed at any time during life and account for many of the synaptic connections made throughout life (Anastasiow, 1990).

Synaptic connections are established by repeated firing of one neuron near another (Hebb, 1949). The more often excitation of cell A results in the firing of cell B, the stronger the connection between the two and the more certain that B is fired whenever A is fired. If neuron A is never stimulated by the environment, it cannot fire and form a connection with B. In most learning, more than two neurons are involved. Then, **cell assemblies** are formed. Cell assemblies are closed paths that include a number of neurons synaptically connected to one another. For instance, human beings can process visual information the way they do because they have formed cell assemblies organizing neurons that are sensitive to visual input. These cell assemblies were formed as a result of visual experiences during the critical period, when the cells sensitive to visual input were particularly rich with experience-expectant synapses. If visual stimulation had not occurred within a particular period after the formation of the experience-expectant synapses, the synapses would have died off. (Cell assemblies are structurally similar to the neural networks described in the connectionist view of knowledge in Chapter 3.)

There is substantial death of neurons during this early period of life. In fact, half of the neurons generated before birth have already died by the time of birth. Up to half of the remaining neurons in some parts of the brain die within a few years after birth (Crutcher, 1991; M. C. Diamond, 1992; Shonkoff & Marshall, 1990). Most of this death is genetically preprogrammed in that the dying cells are not critical to later functioning (E. Gardner, 1975). In fact, it is likely that the elimination of excess synapses and nerve cells is necessary for cognitive development to proceed to maturity (Goldman-Rakic, 1987).

In addition to the physical growth of neurons, the formation of synapses, and the elimination of excess synapses and neurons, the central nervous system matures via three other mechanisms. These are myelination; physical growth of the brain; and the development of a particularly important region of the brain, the frontal lobe (see Figure 6.2).

Myelination. Myelination is the development of a fatty sheath that envelopes a neuron (Gibson, 1991b). Myelin insulates nerve fibers in mammals and permits rapid conduction of impulses (Konner, 1991). In human beings, myelination begins before birth and continues for many years. In general, myelination occurs first in the inner areas of the cortex and then occurs in the outer cortical areas. For example, some outer layers of the cortex involved in association learning will not myelinate until 4 to 8 years of age. The cortical areas of human beings continue to acquire myelin at least until adolescence and may do so until 30 years of age. Myelination occurs throughout the nervous system.

Loss of myelination due either to disease, such as amyotrophic lateral sclerosis (ALS, or Lou Gehrig's disease), or to an intentional experimental manipulation has important consequences due to the reduction of impulse speed (Konner, 1991). Since it takes longer for a nerve cell to recover after firing, the time between firings is greater and conduction failures are more frequent. When myelin is re-acquired, cell functioning returns to normal.

Physical Growth. There are striking changes in the brain's structure and function in the two years following birth (Konner, 1991). For instance, between birth and the age of 1, the brain doubles in volume. By the age of 1, it is a little more than half the size of an adult brain. The growth rate continues to be high during the second year.

Is the physical growth of the brain simply a preprogrammed unfolding, or is its development tied to experience? Research with rats (M. C. Diamond, 1991) suggests that experience can play a large role in the physical development of the brain. In these studies, rats (from pups to "elderly" rats) either received environmental enrichment, such as objects to explore, climb, and sniff, or they did not. In general, environmental enrichment increased the size of the rats' brains. Enrichment also increased the number of branches in the dendrites (M. C. Diamond, 1992; Greenough, 1993). In contrast, poor environments, such as isolation, retard neurological growth in animals.

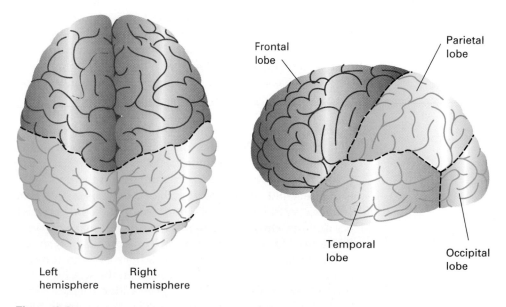

Left hemisphere   Right hemisphere

Frontal lobe   Parietal lobe

Temporal lobe   Occipital lobe

Figure 6.2
The human cerebral cortex is divided into left and right hemispheres, which in turn are divided into frontal, parietal, occipital, and temporal lobes.

Rats raised in a poor environment such as this one have smaller and less complex brains than rats raised in good environments in which there are many stimulating objects to explore.

Does environmental enrichment make a difference in learning? Yes. Research with laboratory animals indicates that the brain is **plastic.** This means that its fundamental physical properties, including size and number of synaptic connections, vary with environmental stimulation (M. C. Diamond, 1988, 1991).

Development of Frontal Lobes. The neurons in the frontal lobes mature following birth. Synaptic branching and connections in the frontal lobes of infants are not as extensive as they are in adults but become more complex by the end of the first year of life (Huttenlocher, 1979; Schade & van Groeningen, 1961). In addition, there is little myelin sheathing in the frontal lobes during the early months of life (Yakovlev & Lecours, 1967).

There also are changes in behaviors associated with the development of the frontal cortex during the first year of life. For example, the human infant's ability to find an object hidden at one of two locations (A or B) is an indicator of development of the frontal lobe (A. Diamond, 1990a, 1990b, 1991). In a typical test of this ability, an object is hidden in full view of the infant and there is a delay between the hiding and when the child can retrieve the object. The object is consistently hidden in one place (either A or B) until the child finds it, and then the object is hidden in the other place.

Infants who are less than 6 months old make a classic error called the "A, not B" error. This means they reach to the place where the object was hidden and retrieved the last time rather than where they saw it hidden this time. This error is more likely the longer the delay between the second hiding and when the child can retrieve the object. As children grow older, it takes a longer delay to produce the "A, not B" error (A. Diamond, 1985). For example, the "A, not B" error can be induced with delays of 2 to 5 seconds in 7½- to 9-month-old infants. By 12 months of

This infant is making the classic "A, not B" error by looking for an object where it was last found rather than where it was hidden this time.

age, the "A, not B" error does not occur even with delays of 10 seconds. This improvement in performance occurs during the period when the frontal lobe is developing (Fox & Bell, 1990).

Early Intervention

Sometimes neurological development goes terribly wrong. For instance, some children, known as PKU babies, are born with the inability to metabolize phenylalanine, an amino acid. This is a problem, because larger than normal amounts of phenylalanine can cause severe neurological damage. There is at least a partial cure, however. It is now routine to determine at birth whether infants lack the capacity to break down phenylalanine. Once PKU children are identified, their diets are strictly controlled so that they ingest only a very small amount of phenylalanine. With increasing age, dietary control can be eased (Scarr & Kidd, 1983). However, since high levels of phenylalanine can produce damage even in later childhood, dietary controls are only relaxed, not eliminated (Stern, 1985). When this intervention begins shortly after birth, general intelligence is impaired little. If PKU is not detected until 3 years of age, however, intervention has little effect and profound retardation results (Zigler & Hodapp, 1986).

Why so much damage if the disorder is not identified early? After all, diet control can be eased considerably for those who were treated as infants. The answer is that the myelinated nervous systems of older children are much more resistant to the biological assault from high levels of phenylalanine than nervous systems that are not yet myelinated. Because the first several years of life are characterized by enormous growth in the central nervous system, the lack of protection that myelin provides is especially critical during these early years.

Although PKU is the best known of such disorders, there are a number of biological disorders that can be countered with diet but that if left untreated result in mental retardation (Fernandez & Samuels, 1986). With treatment, usually a dietary supplement, the risks of retardation generally are reduced or eliminated. Unfortunately, not all biological risks are so easily managed through early intervention.

Biologically Determined Disruptions of Normal Development

Disease and injury are potential dangers from the moment of conception until old age. The timing of the trauma determines the extent of the effects of disease or injury. A critical period for adverse neurological events is during neurogenesis, when many new nerve cells are forming (during the first 2 to 3 months of life).

Teratogens

Teratogens are agents that can damage a developing brain. They are more dangerous during the first trimester of pregnancy than during the second and third trimesters. That is, there is a critical period early in prenatal development during which teratogens have the most serious effects. A large number of disease and chemical teratogens have been identified (Shonkoff & Marshall, 1990). In many cases, prenatal exposure to disease or chemicals does so much damage to the developing nervous system that normal learning and development can never occur. For example, exposure to rubella during pregnancy can produce extreme mental retardation as well as a host of other symptoms, such as growth retardation, hearing loss, and heart disease, in the developing infant (Shonkoff & Marshall, 1990). Maternal alcoholism can result in **fetal alcohol syndrome** (FAS). A child with fetal alcohol syndrome has experienced central nervous system damage that can result in learning difficulties and mental retardation. Children exposed to other chemical teratogens, such as lead and narcotics, experience a range of behavioral and cognitive disorders. See Chapter 16 for a more complete discussion of the learning difficulties experienced by children who are victims of chemical assaults.

Malnutrition

Prenatal and postnatal malnutrition can also reduce mental competency (H. Chase, 1973). Once again, the timing of malnutrition is important (Morgan & Gibson, 1991). Greater damage results when malnutrition occurs at critical periods corresponding to rapid development of the nervous system. Neurogenesis through the second year of life, when neural cell growth via the proliferation of dendritic synapses is rapid, is an especially vulnerable period (Dobbing, 1974). Because substantial myelination occurs during the middle preschool years (3 to 4 years of age), this is also a period of great sensitivity to the effects of malnutrition. The children who are most likely to suffer malnutrition are children in homes from low socioeconomic levels of society. In developing countries where long-term malnutrition is common, many children exhibit lower cognitive development and reduced capacity for attention (Sigman, Neumann, Jansen, & Bwibo, 1989). Making sure that all children are well nourished will increase their long-term mental competency.

Neurological Injury

Injury can also reduce mental competency. A common form of injury is **anoxia,** the reduction of the infant's air supply, during birth. Intracranial hemorrhage is also common, especially among premature infants. Fortunately, the incidence of these types of disorders is on the decline because of better fetal monitoring procedures and widespread dissemination of improved methods of delivery (Rosen, 1985).

For example, using ultrasound procedures, doctors can determine when a baby is in a breech position. A breech position is any position except head first and engaged in the birth canal. In this situation, delivery by cesarean section is easiest and safest for both child and mother. Not so long ago, the delivery team only discovered the breech presentation when the baby came into view. Such deliveries took a long time, with great risk of anoxia and hemorrhage due to injury involved in pulling the baby from the womb. Technology such as ultrasound is improving the mental health of many children.

Early Intervention

Children who are at biological risk at birth are more certain to thrive if they experience diverse and stimulating environments, environments with caregivers who are attentive and responsive to them (Anastasiow, 1990; Beckwirth & Parmelee, 1986; Goldberg & DeVitto, 1983; Morgan & Gibson, 1991; Sameroff & Fiese, 1990; Werner, 1990; Werner & Smith, 1982). What explains the benefits of high-quality early childhood environments for at-risk children? You'll recall that there is an overabundance of experience-expectant synapses during the early preschool years. This abundance permits greater plasticity in comparison to later stages of development (Anastasiow, 1990). In addition, there is a relationship between plasticity and myelination. Once myelination occurs, the nervous system is more mature and less open to change than before myelination. Clearly, there are advantages to providing treatment to at-risk children early in life. Waiting until the school years often means opportunity lost, since the critical periods for stimulation will have passed.

Biologically Determined Biases and Constraints

There are many similarities in the knowledge that all people acquire and in the things that people can do. The most likely explanation of these human similarities is that biology prepares human beings to attend to some information more than other information and to be able to do some things and not others. Experience-expectant synapses described earlier in this chapter most likely play a large role in the development of these similarities.

Sensation Preferences

Even very young babies prefer some forms of visual stimulation to others, although preferences change with development. For example, 1-month-old infants prefer stripes over a bull's-eye pattern, whereas slightly older children prefer the bull's-eye (Fantz & Nevis, 1967). With increasing age, there is increasing preference for more complex visual stimulation (Brennan, Ames, & Moore, 1966; Hershenson, Munsinger, & Kessen, 1965; Munsinger & Weir, 1967). From birth onward, there is a bias toward looking at contours or outlines of shapes, which is adaptive since the contour defines the shape (Banks & Salapatek, 1983). There are clear biases in

The Infant Health and Development Program: A Longitudinal Experiment

The Infant Health and Development Program (1990) is a compelling demonstration that a rich environment can help make up for initial biological disadvantage. The children in this study were infants with low birth weights, a group at substantial risk for later academic difficulties (D. T. Scott, 1987). These infants are more likely than peers to have perceptual problems and learning disabilities during school years (F. C. Bennett, 1987; Meisels & Plunkett, 1988). Approximately one-third of these children were randomly assigned to the treatment condition, and two-thirds to the control condition.

The treatment consisted of home visits during the child's first year of life. The visitor provided health and developmental information to the family as well as other forms of support as needed. Two curricula were introduced into the home during this first year. One was a cognitive, linguistic, and social development curriculum consisting of games and activities that encouraged parent-child interaction. The second curriculum provided child management information to parents, aimed specifically at problems parents often encounter with infants. At 1 year of age and continuing until 3 years of age, the children in the treatment group attended a child development center five days a week. The learning curriculum initiated at home was continued and extended at the center. There was an excellent adult-to-child ratio in these centers, with one adult for each three 1-year-olds and one adult for each four 2-year-olds. The parents of the children at the center met twice a month in groups to receive information about child rearing, safety, and health.

The effects produced by this treatment were dramatic. By the age of 3, the intelligence test scores of treated children were substantially higher than the intelligence test scores of children in the control group. Some of the children were functioning almost at the mean of the normal distribution of intelligence.

This is a dramatic demonstration of the effects of early environment on the intellectual development of biologically at-risk children. One question to ask is whether such services could be provided on a large scale. Another question is whether the treatment gains produced by the Infant Health and Development Program will persist and whether normal intelligence will translate into normal academic achievement when these children reach school age (Lazar, Darlington, Murray, Royce, & Sipper, 1982). Fortunately, the Infant Health and Development Program is collecting more longitudinal data to help answer these questions (Bradley, Whiteside, Mundfrom, Casey, Caldwell, & Barrett, 1994).

What makes this study a true experiment? Think back to the description of experiments provided in Chapter 1. Random assignment is a key characteristic of an experiment. Why is it so important to conduct a longitudinal study? Longitudinal studies allow researchers to observe the course of change over time. This is particularly important in an intervention study because questions are always raised about the long-term benefits of the intervention.

visual perception that result in human beings' processing some types of information more than others.

Preparedness for Language Acquisition

Biological preparedness is not limited to basic perceptual processing. Human beings are also biologically prepared to learn the complex systems of representation that comprise language (Chomsky, 1965, 1980a, 1980b). Chomsky claimed that human beings all have the competence to acquire language, that there is a genetically determined "language acquisition device" in the human mind.

Chomsky also claimed that language is "uniquely human." This claim is not consistent with what is known about genetics. Evolution is gradual, and differences between species in communications and symbolic skills tend to reflect this gradualness (Parker & Gibson, 1990). The language capacity of human beings is not completely different from the capacities of the great apes. Great apes have some understanding of number, use categories to some extent, can learn to use sign language with some sophistication, and may be able to invent rules of grammar (Boysen & Berntson, 1990; Greenfield & Savage-Rumbaugh, 1990; Matsuzawa, 1990; Miles, 1990). In human beings, the evolution of characteristics, such as human speech and neural-speech perception mechanisms, support language and the learning of language (Lieberman, 1984, 1989).

Biology is linked to language comprehension and learning (Maratsos, 1989). Children acquire languages in many different settings and in many different cultures. In fact, language learning proceeds uniformly across different cultures. First words appear around the first year, followed by two-word utterance at about the second year, leading to sentences during the third year of life (Gleitman, 1986). Moreover, the errors children make are systematic and suggest the use of an emerging grammar. For example, application of emerging rules of grammar is exemplified by a 4-year-old who said, "I runned in the backyard." This child is applying a rule of grammar (adding *ed* for the past tense) to create a verb construction that he or she has likely never heard from adults.

Language learning, however, is also diverse. Languages vary across cultures (Maratsos, 1989). For example, different parts of sentences receive focus in different languages. Also, sentence elements such as agents and objects are typically ordered in one way in some languages such as English and are not marked by order in other languages, thereby indicating that human beings have the innate capacity to acquire a range of language rules.

Great apes can learn to communicate with human beings by using American Sign Language.

▶ **Diversity**

Biology and the Acquisition of a Second Language

Many students entering schools do not speak or speak little of the primary language of the school (see also Chapter 16). Does biology constrain the age at which a learner can easily acquire a second language? Is there a critical period for second-language learning? On one hand, adults learn both syntax and pronunciation more rapidly than children in the early stages of language learning. On the other hand, those who begin a second language in early childhood are more likely to obtain eventual fluency in the foreign language (J. S. Johnson & Newport, 1989).

For example, when the English-speaking ability of native Korean and Chinese adults who immigrated to the United States is examined, there is a strong correlation between the age at which they immigrated and syntactical competence (Johnson & Newport, 1989). Those who arrived when younger (between 3 and 7 years of age) were more competent than those who arrived around adolescence (between 11 and 15), who in turn were more competent than those who arrived when even older. In general, language proficiency is more certain if acquisition of a language begins before puberty.

Hemispheric Specialization

The left and right hemispheres of the brain are specialized to perform different functions. The left hemisphere is specialized for processing of language and analytical information; the right hemisphere is specialized for nonverbal, visual-spatial content. Damage in the left hemisphere results in language disabilities, with particular sites associated with particular language difficulties (R. A. McCarthy & Warrington, 1990). The left hemisphere is specialized for processing of sequential and temporal content and is more logical, analytical, and rational than the right hemisphere (Springer & Deutsch, 1989). In contrast, the right hemisphere is better than the left in processing simultaneous, spatial, and analogical information, and its functioning is described by many as intuitive.

There are also differences in hemispheric functioning associated with particular talents (Hoptman & Davidson, 1994). English majors have more blood flow to the left hemisphere than do architecture majors, who have more blood flow to the right hemisphere (Dabbs, 1980). Eye movements consistent with left-hemispheric dominance are more common in English majors than in engineering majors, who display eye movements more indicative of right-hemispheric dominance (Bakan, 1969). It is possible that such differences have been shaped by years of processing more of one type of information than another. If these differences predict success in some endeavors more than others, however, they could be useful in making decisions about curricular emphasis for some students. Longitudinal research on the stability of individual differences in hemispheric specialization is needed.

Some argue that Western schooling focuses on developing only one side of the brain, the left hemisphere (Bogen, 1975; R. Ornstein, 1977, 1978). There have been many proposals in response to this perceived bias in education. Most approaches encourage more teaching of art, music, and intuitive interpretation in school. Other proposals, however, suggest short-term interventions aimed at developing one hemisphere over another through specific environmental stimulation that have not been demonstrated to be effective (Prince, 1978; Springer & Deutsch, 1989).

■ Building Your Expertise

Capacity Constraints

Short-term memory capacity increases with development (see also Chapters 1 and 4). This is most apparent in the increase with development of children's **attention span,** which is how much and how long they can attend at any one time. Preschool teachers are well aware of limits in young children's attention spans. One way to think about attentional capacity is to consider the number of pieces of information a student can have active at any one time while working toward some cognitive goal. Case (1985, 1991) called this **executive processing space.** Students can only perform tasks that do not require more executive processing space than they have (Case, 1985). Case argued that executive processing space increases during development because of neurological maturation and practice of familiar tasks. As a result of practice, children can automatically perform tasks that once were done only with considerable effort and attention. This frees up capacity for attention to tasks requiring more effort and attention.

The following are some ways for teachers to reduce the effects of their students' short-term memory constraints (Case, 1985; P. H. Miller, Woody-Ramsey, & Aloise, 1991). They reflect different ways to engineer materials and the learning environment.

- Analyze academic tasks for the capacity demands they place on students. One way to do this is to ask students to rate how hard they had to concentrate to accomplish the task. Ask them whether they were able to do other things, such as listen to music, watch TV, or talk to their mothers, while working on the task.
- Simplify tasks identified as complex. Break large tasks into more easily accomplished steps that do not tax short-term memory capacity. For example, let's suppose you have already determined that writing a ten-page term paper is a capacity-demanding task for your ninth-grade students since they rated this task high on a scale measuring capacity demands. To help your students accomplish this complex task, break the task of writing a term paper down into the following steps: selecting a topic, finding information on the topic, preparing an outline, writing a rough draft, revising, polishing the final draft.
- Coach and prompt students to help them complete complex tasks. Provide supportive materials (handouts, questions, prompts, hints) designed to reduce short-term memory load.

Some students have an attention disorder, **attention deficit–hyperactivity disorder (ADHD),** which makes learning in school difficult (see also Chapter 16). A number of biological explanations for this disorder have been suggested, including a developmental delay in the cerebral cortex and disruptions in neurotransmitters, which influence neuronal activity (Driscoll, 1994). Many of these students can be successfully treated with drugs that increase the release of these neurotransmitters. Students with ADHD can also benefit from behavioral interventions that teach them how to focus their attention (see the discussion of cognitive behavior modification in Chapter 7.)

Biological Foundations of Academic Competence

Biological studies offer a tremendous opportunity to expand understanding of important academic competencies. In particular, there has been progress in analyzing the biological foundations of reading.

Studies of Reading

Reading researchers are using biological methods such as brain imaging (see Chapter 14) to provide windows on reading processes. For example, Roberts and Kraft (1987) studied the electrical brain activity of primary-grade and middle-grade readers (6- to 8-year-olds and 10- to 12-year-olds, respectively) as they read material that was slightly challenging for them. For the younger students, most of the comprehension activity occurred in the left hemisphere. For the older students, the activity was more evenly divided between the two hemispheres. As a result of that study, Roberts and Kraft suggested that the predominantly left-hemispheric reading by the younger students reflected their nonstrategic reading. On the other hand, the older students used more diverse reading strategies, which resulted in the more balanced hemispheric patterns.

Reading familiar words stimulates processing in the back part of the brain, more in the right hemisphere than the left, in an area of the brain known to be involved in pattern recognition (Petersen, Fox, Posner, Mintun, & Raichle, 1988; Petersen, Fox, Snyder, & Raichle, 1990; Posner, Petersen, Fox, & Raichle, 1988). This makes sense since reading involves the recognition of visual patterns. Reading of real words also activates the left frontal lobe (known to be involved in associative memory), but reading of nonsense words does not. This also makes sense since there is a meaning to associate to a real word but not to a nonsense word.

Reading researchers also use computer simulations of neural networks to understand how word recognition occurs (McClelland & Rumelhart, 1988). Specifically, they study how connections are built up between features of letters and between letters to create long-term memories of words, memories that can be evoked given only part of the word. When a reader sees "M_ _ _L," the connections between the initial M and final L stimulate activation of all the words that the reader knows that start with M and end in L. Cues help to reduce the possibilities. Is the second letter fat or thin? If it is thin, connections to words such as MICHAEL and MINERAL are activated; if it is fat, there is additional activation of words such as METAL, MOTEL, and MATERIAL. (In this case, it's fat.) Length cues suggest that there are at most three letters between the M and L. Then, activation of METAL and MOTEL grows stronger. The brain scrutinizes the middle three positions, and it is observed that the letter just before the L is more squarish than triangular. This produces additional activation of MOTEL, rather than METAL. Eventually, there are enough cues to conclude that the word is MOTEL.

Academic Dysfunctions

Some students experience difficulties acquiring academic competencies. Sometimes these difficulties reflect biological differences between these students and other people.

Dyslexia. **Dyslexia,** the failure to learn to read despite substantial reading instruction, affects a fairly small proportion of readers—at most 1 to 2 percent (Farnham-Diggory, 1992). There are different types of dyslexia (Caplan, 1992; Rayner & Pollatsek, 1989). *Acquired dyslexia* results from some type of brain injury, and *developmental dyslexia* refers to otherwise normal children who experience difficulties in reading that are not due to obvious brain injury. There are also subcategories of both of these types of dyslexia. For example, acquired phonological dyslexics cannot sound out nonsense words but can read actual words they learned before they suffered brain injury. In contrast, acquired surface dyslexics can sound out nonsense words but cannot read words they knew before their injury. Acquired deep dyslexics sometimes misread a word by producing a semantically related item, for example, saying "table" when shown the word *chair*.

Educators encounter developmental dyslexia much more often than acquired dyslexia. There are a variety of symptoms of developmental dyslexia. These include eye-scan patterns that do not match the normal patterns; difficulties with spatial orientation, including confusing left and right; and better reading of upside-down text than right-side-up text. The particular symptoms differ from student to student. The most important characteristic is poor word recognition and decoding during childhood, persisting throughout life in most cases (Bruck, 1990).

As early as 2 years of age, dyslexic children experience language difficulties not seen in children who become normal readers (Scarborough, 1990). They produce relatively short utterances, and their pronunciations are less accurate. Their receptive vocabularies are not as well developed, and they have more difficulties providing labels for common objects. Thus, dyslexia is part of a general language-processing deficiency (Vellutino, 1979).

Some proposed explanations for dyslexia, such as dysfunctional eye movements and an underdeveloped left hemisphere, have not been supported (Vellutino, 1979). There is, however, evidence of physiological differences between developmental dyslexics and normal readers. Left-hemispheric activity is not as predictable in dyslexics as it is in normal readers. There is also abnormal tissue growth in the brain, especially in the left hemisphere (Galaburda, 1983). These findings are stimulating research to identify the genetic underpinnings of these brain differences.

Disorders in Mathematical Competency. As a result of head injury or disease, some people lose their capacity to calculate mathematical problems. This is called acquired **dyscalculia.** In order to calculate, people must be able both to comprehend numbers and produce them (McCloskey, 1992). There are a variety of ways in which comprehension and production can fail. For instance, a person may be able to understand that a number such as *70* involves "tens" quantities but cannot decide which of the tens quantities (e.g., . . . 40, 50, 60, 70, 80, etc.) it is. Some of this person's comprehension functions are intact; others are not.

Some otherwise normal people never acquire calculating competence. This developmental dyscalculia (analogous to developmental dyslexia) may be due to brain differences between those with dyscalculia and those who can calculate normally. Some students have problems that are mainly verbal. For instance, they cannot name numbers, symbols, or mathematical relationships. They cannot read math, or they cannot write mathematical symbols. Others have problems involving calculation (Keller & Sutton, 1991).

Certain brain structures contribute to mathematical competencies. Difficulties in reading and understanding word problems, as well as difficulties in understanding mathematical concepts and procedures, involve the higher association areas of the individual's dominant hemisphere (Keller & Sutton, 1991). Quick mental calculation ability, abstract conceptualization, and some problem-solving skills are linked to the functioning of the frontal lobes. Visual processing of mathematical symbols involves the occipital lobes, and auditory perception of numbers requires intact temporal lobes (see Figure 6.2).

Genetically Determined Modules in the Mind

The idea that the mind includes faculties specialized to deal with particular types of information has been around for a long time. It can be traced back at least as far as Descartes's doctrine of innate ideas. This idea of separate mental faculties is supported by evidence of different sensitive periods for some acquisitions compared to others. For instance, the sensitive period for organization of visual processing in human beings appears to be the first four or five years of life. In contrast, the sensitive period for acquisition of language may be longer, perhaps the entire prepubertal period (R. Goodman, 1987).

Such observations fuel the argument that there are distinct human capacities that are inherited. Fodor (1983) argued that human beings inherit **cognitive modules.** These are "cognitive systems that are domain specific, innately specified, hardwired, autonomous . . ." (p. 37). There are modules for each sensory/perceptual mode: hearing, sight, touch, taste, and smell. There are also modules for language. The modules interact, and there are many connections between them.

Howard Gardner's (1983) **multiple intelligences theory** (see also Chapter 13) is related to this idea of modularity. Gardner argued that people have a set of specific intelligences that are biologically determined. These include linguistic intelligence, musical intelligence, logic-mathematical intelligence, spatial intelligence, body-kinesthetic intelligence, interpersonal intelligence (the ability to notice and make distinctions among other individuals), and intrapersonal intelligence (access to one's own feelings). These seven abilities exist in the context of other abilities or knowledge that may be more general, such as common sense, originality, metaphorical abilities, and wisdom. One of the most critical features of this theory is that people vary in the strength of their particular faculties. From this perspective, it makes no sense to think of someone as smart or not smart in a general sense. Rather, people with musical intelligence would be expected to excel in music given appropriate stimulation; those who have superior capacity in mathematics would be expected to do well given appropriate exposure to mathematics.

Fodor's and Gardner's ideas of innate differences in particular capacities have important educational implications. One of the problems with contemporary schooling from Gardner's perspective is that linguistic, logic-mathematical, and intrapersonal intelligences are emphasized to the exclusion of the other intelligences. Moreover, there is little attempt to gauge the strengths and weaknesses of students with respect to the various intelligences.

Even if relative strengths and weaknesses were known, however, it would be difficult to know what to do. Should strengths be emphasized or should weaknesses be bolstered? Even when a person is favored biologically with respect to some ability, enormous educational resources must be expended to produce someone who is expert in that ability (B. S. Bloom, 1985; see also Chapter 5). When we talk about inheriting multiple intelligences, what we are referring to are potentials, potentials that will be fully realized only given extremely favorable long-term educational and environmental circumstances.

● "What Do I Do on Monday Morning?"

Biological Foundations and Classroom Practices

Principles that emerge from biological research have important implications for educators, and educators are becoming increasing aware of these implications (Cohen, 1995).

- *Plasticity.* The plasticity of neurological development argues strongly for the importance of educational intervention. The brain can learn to modify the function of structures and to create alternative pathways or compensatory mechanisms. Enriched educational environments are associated with superior cognitive development. Teachers need to stimulate their students' intellectual development by providing a wide range of challenging instructional materials and experiences.

- *Critical period.* Plasticity declines with age, and for certain acquisitions, those managed by experience-expectant synapses, the window of opportunity for educational intervention may be small. Therefore, early intervention is critical in the preschool years. Teachers of older students, however, must keep in mind that experience-dependent synapses can form all during life. It is never too late to teach an old dog certain new tricks.

- *Course of brain development.* There is considerable individual variation in the rate of development of working-brain systems. For example, poor performance in isolated literacy skills is fairly common in normal children. Yet, teachers tend to view learners as homogenous in skills and are unlikely to recognize that both low and high functioning occur in normal children (Berninger & Hart, 1992). Thus, the differences between "normal" and "disabled" children may not be as extreme as teachers believe.

- *Modularity of mind.* Learners likely possess differences in cognitive function that are biologically based. These may be reflected in processing differences or in differences in cognitive abilities. Teachers must develop a wide repertoire of instructional strategies using a variety of modes of instruction, experiences, and tasks. For example, in a social studies class, a teacher can present content visually (slide show), verbally (descriptions and books), rhythmically (rap songs for major products, chants as an exercise, or clapping), and tactilely (relief map).

- *Cautions.* Teachers must be cautioned to beware of questionable interventions supposedly based on biological research that are disseminated without research support. One example is the Doman-Delacato "patterning" technique for the treatment for mental retardation and brain damage (Doman, Spitz, Zucman, Delacato, & Doman, 1960). The treatment consists of several adults' manipulating the limbs and body of the child to mirror the movements that would have occurred in the absence of neurological injury. The assumption is that if the body is put in motion enough times, noninjured brain cells, ones ordinarily unused, will become programmed to perform the functions usually carried out by the injured region of the brain. The benefits of this technique have not been consistently supported by research (Neman, Roos, McCann, Menolascino, & Heal, 1974; Zigler & Hodapp, 1986). Another intervention rationalized in biological terms is vitamin therapy as a treatment for mental retardation. Harrell, Capp, Davis, Peerless, and Ravitz (1981) reported large gains in intelligence in retarded children who were treated with large doses of vitamins. A number of better controlled replication studies, however, failed to produce significant effects in favor of vitamin therapy (Smith, Spiker, Peterson, Cicchetti, & Justice, 1984; Zigler & Hodapp, 1986).

Perceptual Learning Theory

Eleanor Gibson's (1969) theory of perceptual learning highlights interactions between biologically determined potential and the environment. Babies enter this world active. From the beginning, babies have goals. They want to touch things, to see things, to begin to understand the world. They live in a world brimming with stimulation that contains information.

For example, a 4-month-old plays with a set of rubber alphabet letters, ones that float in the bathtub. These letters have features, such as curves, straight lines, diagonals, and color, that differentiate them. Although children may be able to tell that two letters are the same or different from an early age, they do not notice the features that differentiate one letter from another until quite a bit later. At first, children learn to spot particular letters such as Mommy's letter (*M*), Daddy's letter (*D*), or the letter for their own names. Still later, they can reliably spot all the letters of the alphabet and name them, although there may be occasional slipups, almost always involving letters that share features, such as *h* being mistaken for *n*.

The features that define letters (and other things) are always available. With experience, people discover the critical features that differentiate a set of items. Thus, when you were young, different models of cars may have looked pretty much the same. After years of experience, you can now differentiate different models. You have increased your knowledge of the **distinctive features** that differentiate car models.

What is necessary for perceptual learning to occur? Repeated exposure to a set of objects that differ in particular ways is essential. Thus, in order to figure out which letter is the one Mommy calls hers, a child has to grasp how Mommy's letter differs from other letters. With increasing practice, there is an increase in specificity of the objects classified as Mommy's letter. At first, any letter with verticals (e.g., *H, M, N, P, R, D*) is sufficient, then two verticals (e.g., *H, M, N*) are required,

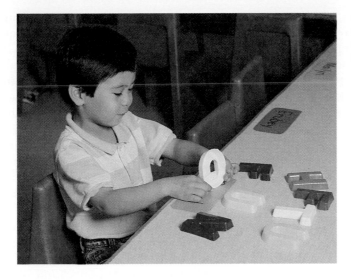

Children discover the distinctive features of letters through repeated exposure to letters such as these.

then two verticals and at least one diagonal (e.g., *M, N*), and finally only *M*s. When children classify any *M* as an *M* and never confuse it with another letter, they have acquired the distinctive features associated with *M*.

There are a few basic mechanisms of perceptual learning. One mechanism is *abstraction,* which is the finding of distinctive features or invariant relationships (i.e., relationships that remain constant for a class of events). For example, after experiencing many of Mommy's letter, a child can abstract the distinctive features for *M*. A second mechanism, *filtering,* involves ignoring the irrelevant dimensions. For example, a student may learn to classify maple and oak leaves by relying on shape and filtering out color and size, which do not reliably differentiate them. A third mechanism is *peripheral attention.* The processing of peripheral information is critical to determining where next to focus attention. Peripheral visual mechanisms "look ahead" and guide the movement of the eyeball from fixation at one point A to a next point B (Just & Carpenter, 1987). The selection of the next point B is not random. For example, if there is a noun and a function word (such as, *a* or *the*) to the right of the current focus of attention during reading of a sentence, the eyeball is much more likely to land on the noun than on the function word. Due to guidance provided by peripheral attention, the eye moves to highly informative parts of text, not to uninformative parts.

With increasing age and experience, children's attention to and processing of perceptual information become more efficient. Salient environmental stimuli irrelevant to the task at hand often capture younger children's attention. In contrast, older children can more often ignore stimulation irrelevant to a task (A. T. Higgins & Turnure, 1984). With increasing age, children are also much more likely to examine stimuli more systematically and completely (Vurpillot, 1968). For example, they become better at deciding whether two complex patterns are the same or different. In general, with increasing age, children focus on information that is pertinent to the task they are asked to perform. They are also more flexible in attending to features of objects, sometimes systematically examining them in one way and sometimes in another, depending on the task. They learn to know what to expect and thus are better at knowing what to look for.

According to Gibson's theory, the processes underlying perceptual learning are the same in adults and children. Adults are sometimes quicker at any given perceptual learning task because their previous experiences have produced understanding of what to look for. For example, it takes a child several years to learn to differentiate the letters of the alphabet. In contrast, an adult familiar with the English alphabet could acquire the distinctive features of the Cyrillic alphabet in a matter of days, largely because of prior knowledge about the types of features that can differentiate letters of an alphabet.

Eleanor Gibson's view is that people are inherently motivated to learn. They are biologically prepared to abstract particular types of information from the environment, yet learning is gradual and covaries with experience. High-quality perceptual learning depends on diverse perceptual experiences and many opportunities to interact with the world in meaningful ways.

The need for experiences that require processing of important distinctive features is critical. Deciding whether similar situations, patterns, or events are the same or different and how they are the same or different can have great impact on coming to understand which features are critical and distinctive. Many different types of educational contents require such discriminations, from learning forms of letters to recognizing particular plays in football or baseball. Perceptual learning continues well past childhood. Fighter pilots must learn to discriminate "our" planes from "their" planes; doctors must be able to differentiate a benign mole from a probable malignant skin growth; and baseball players must be able to see the difference between a slider and a curve ball. All of these skilled performances involve learning distinctive features.

Chapter Summary

- How learning occurs and what is learned are determined to some degree by neurology. With changes in neurological capacity, either due to experience or normal development, there are changes in cognitive capabilities.
- Experience-expectant synapses provide biological preparedness for learning from certain types of experiences during particular periods in life. The existence of critical periods for neural development makes it clear that it is often not possible to put off providing stimulation to a child until some later point in development. Other synapses are experience-dependent and can be formed at any time during life.
- Neurological development reaches maturity through a number of mechanisms, particularly myelination, physical growth of the brain, and the development of the frontal lobe.
- There is reason to be concerned about the environment a child encounters from the point of conception. Maternal malnutrition, chemical dependency, disease, or injury during a pregnancy can affect the biological development of a fetus. The result can range from mild mental handicap to severe retardation. The severity of disability at maturity can often be reduced or eliminated by responsive stimulation during infancy and the preschool years.
- Human beings are prepared better to learn some information at particular points in development. Human biology biases human beings to certain types of information over others, makes some learning more likely than others, determines that

some learning such as language acquisition will almost certainly occur given exposure to any part of the human family, and constrains other learning and performance demands to those not exceeding short-term capacity.

- Performance on academic tasks, such as reading and mathematics, can be linked to physiological differences among individuals. Some human beings are capable of learning contents that are much more difficult for others to acquire, possibly because of biologically based differences in faculty strengths.
- Perceptual learning theory emphasizes interactions between biologically determined potential and environmental stimulation. Environmental stimulation builds knowledge of distinctive features necessary for perceptual learning.

Return to the Classroom Predicament

Has reading this chapter helped you decide whether or not you agree with the teacher described in the classroom predicament? This teacher is making the mistake of believing that biologically based learner characteristics are immutable or unchangeable. On the contrary, biological perspectives support the idea of a certain amount of plasticity in development. Educational interventions can have tremendous impact. Moreover, biologically based arguments for the modularity in mind encourage multiple teaching approaches.

Chapter Outline

Chapter 7

Psychological Theories of Learning and Development

Classroom Predicament

Ms. Campbell has arranged the students in her class into groups and given them the following directions: "Here's a bushel of apples at the front of the classroom. Work in your groups to figure out how many apples you will have altogether if you start out with two apples and then get three more." Ms. Campbell listens to the groups as they work on this problem. The students seem to be having fun manipulating the apples. Some groups even get into small arguments about the best way to count the apples.

Mr. Sharp is teaching his students the rules for long division. The class is watching some of their classmates working at the board on a long division problem. Mr. Sharp asks the students at the board to explain the steps they are using. When they are correct, he praises them. When they are incorrect, he asks the class to give their classmates suggestions. Then all the students in the class work on more problems at their desks. The first problems are easy, but the later ones are hard because the numbers have many more digits. Some of the students seem to be talking to themselves as they work. Little by little, the students learn to apply the rules of long division.

Is it likely that both of these instructional approaches will be effective? What principles of learning and development theory are incorporated into these teaching practices? Reflecting on the information presented in this chapter will help you formulate responses to these questions.

This chapter features psychological theories of learning and development, each of which proposes explanations for how we acquire knowledge and construct understandings. A generalization that spans these psychological theories is that genetic inheritance provides potential, and appropriate experiences allow realization of the potential. Some of the theories in this chapter emphasize biology more than experience, and some emphasize experience more than biological determination.

We begin with Piaget's theory of cognitive development. Although Piaget emphasized the importance of biological maturation, he also stressed the active role of the learner in interaction with the environment. Next, we describe the behavioral perspective on learning. In this view, the learner also takes an active role and learns through patterns of reinforcement and punishment in interaction with the environment. Another perspective, social learning theory, emphasizes that learning can occur through observation of others. The group of theories introduced in this chapter focus on the individual learner in interaction with his or her environment. In Chapter 8, we present theories that place more emphasis on the social context of learning. The psychological perspective on learning and development conveyed by the information processing approach is not presented in this chapter since this approach is well represented by the good information processor model introduced in Chapter 1 and described more completely in Chapters 2, 3, 4, and 5. Indeed, the central role of knowledge, strategies, metacognition, and motivation in learning and development is articulated in many chapters of this book.

Piagetian Theory of Cognitive Development

No single individual has had as much impact on the study of children's mental capacities as Jean Piaget. Although there are some problems with his descriptions and explanations of development, Piaget defined many important issues in the development of mental capacities, and his theory inspired a philosophy that continues to influence education.

The Four Stages

Piaget (1983) described a sequence of four stages of cognitive development. Progress through the stages can occur at different rates, but it is always orderly, taking place in an invariant sequence. Each stage is characterized by the development of cognitive structures, or schemes. A **scheme** is a coordinated pattern of thought or action that organizes an individual's interaction with the environment. The schemes of infants are simple and action-oriented, such as a scheme of reaching-grasping-pulling an object close for careful examination. The following descriptions of Piaget's stages illustrate that schemes become more complex and sophisticated and that the ability to acquire knowledge from the environment increases.

Although Piaget warned against applying age norms to the stages, the first stage, the **sensorimotor stage,** is generally considered to include the first 2 years of life. According to Piaget, intelligence during this period is not yet in the mind as we normally think of it; instead, it is in the actions of the child on the environment. Piagetians called these actions **motor schemes.** How do infants acquire these first schemes? Young infants possess innate reflexes, such as sucking, crying, or grasping, and these reflexes serve as the basis for the first motor schemes. For example, infants initially suck their fingers instinctively. Eventually, sucking becomes a strategy for exploring new objects in the environment, a motor scheme. What are infants likely to do when handed a rattle? Their sucking response is their strategy for interacting with the rattle and other objects in their environment.

The motor schemes of infancy permit interactions with the environment that eventually lead to the development of object permanence. **Object permanence** refers to a child's understanding that objects continue to exist regardless of whether or not the child can see or touch them. Before acquisition of this scheme, children act as if objects that are out of their sight no longer exist. Once children acquire object permanence, however, they understand that objects have an existence independent of their perception of them. What do infants do if someone hides their rattle under a blanket? If they have object permanence, they will lift up the blanket to look for the rattle. If not, they will just look away, seeming undisturbed by the object's disappearance. This explains the attraction of peekaboo for young children. Once children have completely acquired object permanence, the game is not as interesting.

The next stage, the **preoperational stage,** roughly corresponds to the preschool years. Children in this stage have developed cognitive structures called **symbolic schemes,** which allow them to represent objects or events by means of symbols such as language, mental images, and gestures. The first evidence of this representational ability is often the display of **deferred imitation.** This means children are able to imitate behavior long after witnessing it. For example, a child who witnessed another child's tantrum at the grocery store last week is capable of imitating the tantrum today. Another example of representational ability occurs during **symbolic play.** To a child capable of symbolic representation, an empty box becomes a castle and a stick becomes a magic wand. The most powerful representational ability is demonstrated in children's use of language, arguably the most powerful symbol system for knowledge acquisition.

Despite these advances in children's thought due to increased use of symbolic schemes, descriptions of reasoning during the preoperational stage typically emphasize differences between the logic of younger children and that of older children. Preoperational children possess a logic of their own; it is just not the same logic as that found in older children and adults. According to Piaget, preschoolers exhibit **egocentrism,** a lack of awareness of the perspective of others. They view situations primarily from their own perspective and are unable to understand a situation from another person's point of view. For example, a little girl may have difficulty understanding that her grandma is her mother's mother. How can *her* mother be someone else's daughter? Another example is that preschoolers believe that others viewing a set of objects from a different angle than they do see the objects in the same way as they see them. This is why most preschoolers have to be reminded constantly during show-and-tell to hold the object so the other children in the class can see it. A high proportion of preschoolers' speech is described as egocentric since many of their utterances are not social in intent in that they frequently all talk at once, ignoring the speech of others. Preschoolers' egocentric utterances often do not communicate information to other people well. For instance, when preschoolers tell stories, they tend to leave out important information needed to understand the story fully.

Preschool children are also unable to solve conservation tasks. **Conservation tasks** typically involve children's watching the transformation of a substance that does not alter its basic characteristics but changes its appearance. An example of a conservation task is pouring liquid from a tall, slender glass to a short, wide glass. Preschoolers will claim that the amount of liquid changed, although nothing was added or subtracted. *Dominated by perception,* the children attend to misleading perceptual cues and argue that there is more liquid after pouring because the water is wider or that there is less liquid because the water is not as high in the glass. Several years later, when children understand conservation, they offer explanations about how height and width offset one another and about how the amount cannot change when nothing is added or subtracted. This does not mean that preschoolers are completely illogical. Preschoolers understand that it is the same water that is transferred from glass A to glass B. That is, they are beginning to understand that the **identity** of the water survives a perceptual transformation.

According to Piaget, preschoolers' thought lacks some of the logical **operational schemes** that underlie mature thought, which accounts for their errors in conservation tasks. These operations are cognitive rules. One is the identity function already described. When children completely understand identity, they realize that objects remain the same despite perceptual transformation. A second is **reversibility.** This refers to the understanding that an operation can be undone by reversing it, such as physically or mentally pouring the water back into the tall glass. A third is **compensation.** This is the recognition that change on one dimension can be compensated for by change on another dimension. For example, the same amount of water will be higher in a narrow glass than in a wide one.

Having these operational schemes permits conservation. Children with operational intelligence can reason that the amount of water in the wider glass is the same as that which is in the taller glass because they can mentally reverse the pouring. They can also point out the reciprocal relationship between height and width of the liquid. Children in either of the next stages of operational intelligence, concrete and formal, are more powerful thinkers than preoperational preschoolers.

During the **concrete operational stage,** which corresponds roughly to the elementary grade years, children can apply cognitive operations to problems involving concrete objects, but they cannot apply them to problems involving abstract manipulation or hypothetical situations. This means that concrete operators can solve conservation tasks. Thus, if shown two rows of seven buttons lined up evenly, conserving children believe the two rows contain the same number of buttons even when one of the rows is stretched out so that there is greater space between individual buttons. This is a conservation of number problem. If two balls of clay are the same weight as shown by a balanced scale, conserving children will predict that the scale will stay in balance even if one of the two balls is reshaped, perhaps flattened like a pancake or rolled into a snake. This is a conservation of mass problem.

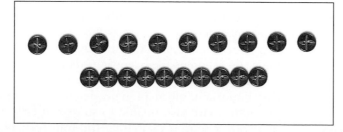

Concrete operators will know that these two rows have equal numbers of buttons, thus exhibiting conservation of number.

Concrete operations permit the performance of other tasks as well, such as **class inclusion problems.** In these problems, children view sets of objects, some of which are subsets of each other, and they answer questions about the subset relationships. For example, if given a set of pictures of five cardinals and four robins and asked, "Are there more cardinals or birds?" conserving children understand there are more birds than cardinals. Preoperational children, however, are more likely to respond that there are more cardinals, since there are more cardinals than robins in the pictures they are viewing. In addition, concrete operations permit children to **seriate** items. That is, they can order objects on some dimension, such as shortest to tallest or lightest to heaviest. For example, concrete operators can correctly arrange sticks in order of increasing length.

Students at the **formal operational stage** (beginning typically with early adolescence) are capable of even more complex problem solving. They can handle problems that involve more factors. Thus, although concrete operational children can seriate on only one dimension, formal operational children can seriate on several dimensions simultaneously. For example, they can correctly arrange sticks in order of color and increasing length. Formal operational thinkers are capable of *"thinking in possibilities."* This means that they can generate all combinations of possibilities for a given situation. For example, formal operational thinkers can infer "invisible forces" and thereby solve problems involving such forces. This allows them to solve problems such as how hydraulic presses work given some weights and several presses. Moreover, the thinking of the formal operational adolescent is not closely tied to the constraints of the real world. Whereas concrete operators often rely on concrete objects, called concrete manipulatives, to aid their reasoning, formal operators can discuss complex issues without the concrete props. In addition, the formal operational adolescent routinely utilizes planning and foresight, or *thinking ahead.* Probably the thinking ability most characteristic of formal operators is *thinking in hypotheses.* This means they can survey a problem, formulate all potential hypothetical outcomes, and go about testing the possibilities one at a time. Table 7.1 illustrates how these various characteristics interplay for those presented with a formal operational reasoning task.

Table 7.1

A Formal Operational Reasoning Task

How might everyday life be different if we all had tails? College students who were asked this question as a classroom exercise have generated a variety of responses, ranging from fashion and furniture to religious values and courting rituals.
- *Fashion comments*—tail jewelry, tail braiding, ribbons, cover-ups
- *Furniture*—differences in chairs and beds, hooks to hang by tails
- *Sports*—new ball games, new Olympic sports, tail workouts
- *Dating*—the question of whether your date is allowed to see your tail on the first date
- *Religion*—the questions of whether to display tails or not and whether there are differences for men and women
- *Political*—prejudice based on tail's length, color, or amount of hair

Scientific reasoning is a hallmark of formal operational thought.

This characteristic of thinking in hypotheses is a critical component of scientific reasoning. In one of the Piagetian tasks designed to elicit scientific reasoning, the pendulum problem, students are provided three lengths of string and three different weights that they can attach to the string. The students' task is to determine which factors determine the rate at which a pendulum swings. Usually, the students conduct one of the following two actions. They use one of the strings and try each weight in succession, or they use one of the weights and try each string in succession. What students notice is that the speed of swinging varies with the length of the string, not the weight. Good students also systematically vary how much force they use to set the pendulum in motion. They determine that force is not a critical factor in the speed of the pendulum swing. The students act like scientists in this situation, varying one factor at a time while holding other factors constant. Thus, they are thinking in hypotheses. In contrast, children who are not formal operators often proceed in a haphazard fashion, sometimes changing two features, such as the size of the weight and the length of the string, at once.

Progress Through the Stages. By training and by conviction, Piaget was a biologist who believed there was a biological inevitability to the stages, of cognitive development and hence a universality to them (Brainerd, 1978b; Piaget, 1967). The stages build upon one another, with each one a prerequisite for the next. Some individuals, however, move through the stages more rapidly than others, and some do not make it all the way to formal operations. Piaget suggested that individuals reach formal operations in "different areas according to their aptitudes and their professional socialization" (Piaget, 1972, p. 10). Thus, successful mechanics, carpenters, or composers may use formal operational reasoning in their particular specialties, but not necessarily in other areas.

Initially, Piaget argued that once in a stage, all thinking reflects the underlying competencies characteristic of the stage. Thus, a student who is concrete operational for one task should be concrete operational for all tasks. A later version of the theory permits "stage mixture" (Brainerd, 1978b, 1978c; Flavell, 1971, 1972), so that some students might be preoperational for some tasks and concrete operational for others. Other students might be able to attack some problems in a formal operational fashion but still require concrete manipulatives for others. **Horizontal décalage** is the term used to describe the fact that students do not master all problems requiring the same logical operations at the same time. For example, children typically acquire conservation of length (i.e., recognition that the length of a string does not vary no matter how the string is shaped) before conservation of liquid.

Table 7.2 presents a summary of Piaget's four stages of cognitive development.

Mechanisms of Cognitive Change. How did Piaget explain progression through the stages? Piaget (1983) recognized there are multiple determinants of developmental change. The first, *maturation*, is biological. As children mature physically, new possibilities for development evolve. Although biological development is necessary for cognitive growth, it is not sufficient for such growth to occur. *Experience* plays a role as well. As children practice new cognitive acquisitions, their experiences with the physical world permit them to learn important regularities. For example, one regularity might be as the amount of something increases, its weight increases. Another might be color and weight do not always covary. The *social environment* also plays a role in development. The quality of children's social environment at home and school affects the speed of movement through the stages. Environments that provide new experiences and permit practice of new skills facilitate the movement from one stage to the next.

At any given point of development, children understand the world in terms of the cognitive operations they have developed. That is, they assimilate new information. Children **assimilate** when they incorporate environmental stimuli into an existing scheme. For example, a child who sees a girl playing with a dog may be able to assimilate this observation into his or her existing scheme of household pets by thinking, "That girl's dog is her pet just like my collie, Cody, is my pet."

If this child walks by a training ground for guard dogs, this new information

Table 7.2

Summary of the Piagetian Stages

	Characteristic Schemes	Characteristic Accomplishments	Characteristic Limitations
Sensorimotor stage	•Motor	•Object permanence	•Thinking only by doing
Preoperational stage	•Motor •Symbolic	•Deferred imitation •Symbolic play •Language	•Dominated by perception •Lack of awareness of others' perspectives •Lack of reversibility •Lack of compensation
Concrete operational stage	•Motor •Symbolic •Operational—concrete	•Class inclusion •Seriation •Conservation	•Thinking only in concrete terms •Thinking only about two attributes simultaneously
Formal operational stage	•Motor •Symbolic •Operational—concrete and formal	•Thinking in possibilities •Thinking ahead •Thinking in hypotheses	

from the environment cannot simply be assimilated into an existing cognitive structure. Instead, the child must accommodate the new information. **Accommodation** refers to the modification of existing cognitive structures in response to environmental demands. Thus, the child needs to modify existing schemes about dogs to comprehend that some dogs are not pets but are trained to protect and attack. Every assimilation of a stimulus involves an accommodation of the learner to the stimulus. Even the girl's pet dog would not look and behave exactly like Cody at home.

Consider how a preoperational child, who does not have cognitive structures that permit understanding of compensation, responds to a conservation of weight problem. When an experimenter rolls a ball of clay into a sausage shape, the child thinks there is less clay than when the clay was in a ball, because the sausage is thinner. The cognitive structures a preoperational child possesses foster attention to only one dimension in making conservation judgments. If the experimenter continues to roll the sausage out, it gets longer and longer so that the length dimension becomes more salient and less easy to overlook. Some of the time the child responds on the basis of this increase in length, reporting that there is more clay when the clay is in the shape of a sausage than when it is in the shape of a ball. The child eventually notices the inconsistency in responding one way on the basis of length and another way on the basis of width. The result is **cognitive conflict.** There is increasingly obvious difficulty in making a conservation judgment based on only one dimension.

When the child experiences cognitive conflict (e.g., "If I just look at length, I answer one way. If I just look at width, I answer another way. Both answers can't be true.") and perceives that the cognitive structures are no longer adequate, there is disequilibrium. **Disequilibrium** is the realization that two contradictory ways of thinking about the world cannot both be true. This realization motivates the process of resolving the contradiction through the construction of new cognitive structures. Thus, the child accommodates to the environmental stimulus. Once accommodation occurs, there is a return to equilibrium, and Piaget called this important mechanism of cognitive change **equilibration.** In the case of conservation, the child constructs new cognitive structures that permit compensation to produce solutions to conservation problems. Cognitive development involves many cycles of equilibrium, disequilibrium, followed by equilibrium at a higher level of competence (Piaget, 1983).

● "What Do I Do on Monday Morning?"

Piaget in the Classroom

Piaget and his colleagues (Inhelder et al., 1974) argued that the only educational mechanisms that could produce legitimate conceptual change were ones that would mirror natural development via equilibration (cognitive conflict). How can educators design learning environments so that discovery via equilibration is likely (Brainerd, 1978a, 1978b; Kamii, 1985)?

- Diagnose students' current developmental stages so that developmentally appropriate assignments and instruction can be given. For example, it is possible for students in the formal operational stage to learn abstract scientific principles through a lecture. Students in the concrete operational stage, on the other hand, would have to see concrete applications of the scientific principles.

- Design instruction so that students are active participants in their own learning. Construct learning environments conducive to exploration by students. Provide concrete manipulables. For example, although formal operational students can learn from lectures, it is difficult to keep them active participants in their learning using the lecture format. Opportunities for exploration, especially with concrete manipulables, increase the likelihood of learning for both concrete and formal operational students. For example, if the objective is for students to understand the principle of compounding interest, ask them to demonstrate their understanding using Monopoly money.
- Make students aware of conflicts between their approaches to problems and the features of the problems. Probing questions, such as "What will happen if . . . ," should be asked. Present counterexamples, and point out inconsistencies that may lead to disequilibrium. For example, "I see you are thinking about the width of the clay sausage. What have you noticed about its length?"
- Reduce adult power as much as possible, with instruction that encourages the exchange of points of view between teachers and students and between students and students. Foster collaboration with peers who have mutual interests.
- Encourage children to think in their own ways rather than to produce the right answers in the right way as defined by a teacher. Analyze students' errors to gain a better understanding of their thought processes.

Evaluation of Piaget's Theory

Does Piaget's stage theory adequately explain what we know today about cognitive development? Research has produced many outcomes inconsistent with various aspects of Piaget's theory. Some Piagetian conceptual acquisitions, such as the ability to solve abstract logical problems, develop earlier than Piaget described (Brainerd, 1978a). Other acquisitions, such as the conservation of volume, come later than specified by the theory. Some behaviors reported by Piaget are never manifested in the way Piaget proposed. For example, Piaget's depiction of preschoolers' speech as extremely egocentric is not consistent with the many communicative competencies possessed by preschoolers. Piaget's theory is also limited in generalizability. It does not take into account cultural differences; only describes the development of normally functioning children; and only accounts for a fraction of life span development, rarely mentioning adult development.

Moreover, Piagetians have long held that acquisitions such as conservation could not be taught and that attempts to do so would invariably disrupt natural development. Researchers, however, have had little difficulty establishing conservation using conventional learning procedures such as the following (Brainerd, 1978a; T. L. Rosenthal & Zimmerman, 1978):

- *Simple correction.* Give nonconservers repeated trials on conservation tasks, and tell them whether their answers are right or wrong. For example, after pouring liquid from a tall glass into a wide glass, provide positive feedback if a child indicates that there is still the same amount of liquid in the wide glass as there had been in the tall glass. Provide negative feedback if a child indicates the liquid changes in quantity when it is poured from one glass to the other.

- *Rule learning.* Teach the child a rule. For example, when correcting a failure to conserve, tell the child, "I did not add or subtract anything."
- *Observational learning.* Expose the child to a model who performs conservation perfectly.

Although Piaget's theory is not completely consistent with our current understanding of cognitive development, many educators find the basic principles of Piagetian theory to be useful. In particular, the principle of cognitive conflict is prominent in current instructional models for science and math education (see Chapter 12).

Behavioral Perspective of Learning

Theorists who take the behavioral perspective focus on behavior rather than internal, unobservable explanatory variables such as Piaget's operations. Thus, behaviorists interested in reading focus on observable reading behaviors, from gazing at a book to turning pages to completing whole books. They are not concerned with cognitive structures such as the narrative and expository text structures described in Chapter 3.

Mechanisms of Classical and Operant Conditioning

Ivan Pavlov first explained **classical conditioning** in the late-nineteenth century (Bower & Hilgard, 1981). Pavlov observed that when meat powder is placed in a dog's mouth, the dog salivates. The food is an **unconditioned stimulus** that elicits an **unconditioned response,** salivation. Pairing a neutral stimulus, such as the sound of a bell, with the food powder results in conditioning dogs to salivate at the sound of the bell. The bell is a **conditioned stimulus** that has acquired the power to elicit what is now the **conditioned response** of salivation. Thus, neutral stimuli that accompany (usually precede) unconditioned stimuli often become conditioned stimuli (Bower & Hilgard, 1981).

Classical conditioning is not a very prominent part of what we typically think of as school learning, but human beings frequently do develop emotional responses through classical conditioning. For example, fearful reactions to stimuli associated with pain are easily learned via classical conditioning (Bandura, 1986; H. S. Hoffman, 1969). For instance, many people feel a rush of anxiety when they hear the sound of the dentist's drill. Others feel anxious as they approach an intersection where they previously had a car accident. In these cases, the sound of the drill and the sight of the intersection have become associated with an anxious response. Classical conditioning can also account for emotional responses learned in school environments. For example, a student who trips over a hurdle may become classically conditioned to fear gym class. A student who was embarrassed by knocking over a podium during a speech may become classically conditioned to fear public speaking.

Classically conditioned emotional responses often are not maintained. They are extinguished through the process of **extinction** when there is subsequent experience with the conditioned stimulus that is not followed by the unconditioned response. Thus, if future experiences in gym class or speaking in front of the class are pleasant, after a while the fear subsides.

Operant conditioning applies to more learning situations than classical conditioning. In classical conditioning the focus of learning is on the stimulus that elicits a response, typically an involuntary emotional response or reflex. In operant conditioning the focus is on an emitted response, a behavior the learner can control. Although B. F. Skinner is the psychologist most associated with operant conditioning (Skinner, 1953, 1987), E. L. Thorndike detailed its most fundamental principle in 1913. Thorndike's law of effect describes the following relationship: The likelihood of an operant response being emitted is increased when it is followed by a reinforcer.

Consider an example. Suppose you are thirsty. You put 75 cents in a soda machine and receive a soda. Receipt of the soda is reinforcement for depositing the 75 cents. When you are thirsty in the future, you will be more likely to put 75 cents in a soda machine as a result of this experience. The operant response of putting money in a soda machine can undergo the process of extinction, however. This process begins when you make a response and do not receive the expected reinforcement. If you put 75 cents in a soda machine and no soda comes, you will not put any more money in that machine. One trial of not receiving a soda may be enough to extinguish your response of putting money in the soda machine, at least with this particular soda machine at this particular time. Usually, extinction only occurs after several instances of unreinforced operant responses.

Putting money in a soft drink machine to receive a can of soda is an example of a conditioned response.

Receiving a soda is an **unconditioned reinforcer** in that it satisfies a biological deprivation, that of thirst. Other unconditioned reinforcers include food, sex, and exposure to aesthetically pleasing stimuli, such as the magnificent view from the top of a mountain after a hard day's climb. Most reinforcers that people receive are not unconditioned reinforcers, however, but **conditioned reinforcers.** Thus, for coming to work and doing your job, your employer gives you a check. No biological need is satiated by the check directly. The check allows you to purchase goods and services, however, that do fulfill basic needs such as those for food, beverages, or stimulation. Conditioned reinforcers acquire their reinforcement properties by being paired with unconditioned reinforcers. That is, money was not always valuable to you but became so because it allowed you to acquire unconditioned reinforcers. Conditioned reinforcers can lose their power through extinction as well. Consider companies in serious financial trouble that hand their employees bad checks. If the checks come on Friday, many employees will not show up on Monday, even if there are promises that the company will make good on the checks in the future. The conditioned reinforcement value of the company's checks has been extinguished.

There are two general categories of reinforcers, **positive reinforcers** and **negative reinforcers.** The occurrence of both of these types of reinforcers following a behavior increases the likelihood of that behavior. The difference between the two is in the type of consequence that causes the increase in the behavior. For example, you are positively reinforced for turning on the radio and hearing music that you like. If you turn off a radio that is blaring out music you dislike, however, you experience negative reinforcement. Positive reinforcement involves the presentation of a stimulus following a response; negative reinforcement involves the cessation of aversive stimulation following a response. That is, if polka music were aversive to you, you would be reinforced for the behavior of turning the radio off because cessation of the music occurs after you turn off the radio and you would likely turn the radio off again next time you hear polka music. In other words, you have been conditioned to escape the stimulus of polka music.

Negative reinforcement is often confused with punishment, even though negative reinforcement and punishment result in different outcomes. Negative reinforcement increases the likelihood of the behavior it follows; punishment decreases the likelihood of the behavior it follows. **Punishment** is the presentation of aversive stimulation following a response. Thus, if a preschooler darts into the parking lot, the teacher gives the child a stern reprimand, which serves as punishment. The response of darting away was followed by the aversive stimulation of adult disapproval. Consider this example of negative reinforcement: If the sound of a car's warning buzzer is aversive, a high school student taking behind-the-wheel instruction will buckle the seat belt. The behavior of buckling the seat belt is negatively reinforced, and the probability of this behavior's occurring increases. In the example of negative reinforcement, the response (buckling the seat belt) resulted in the cessation of the aversive stimulus (buzzer). In the example of punishment, the aversive stimulus (the reprimand) was not present until after the response.

Students often have great difficulty with these two terms. The difficulty is made worse by the fact that these terms are often misused in everyday use by teachers, principals, and almost everybody in the media. Even some textbook authors mistakenly present negative reinforcement and punishment as synonymous. Check your understanding with the examples in Table 7.3.

Table 7.3

Examples of Negative Reinforcement and Punishment

Classify each of the following as an example of negative reinforcement or punishment.

- Taking an aspirin relieves a headache. Taking an aspirin is . . .
- Being spanked after talking back decreases future talking back. Talking back is . . .
- Receiving a ticket after speeding decreases future speeding. Speeding is . . .
- Pretending to be ill to avoid going to school increases future pretend sick days. Pretending to be ill is . . .

Answers (respectively): Negatively reinforced; punished; punished; negatively reinforced.

How can teachers get students to exhibit the behaviors they want using principles of operant conditioning? If sometimes the desired behavior is exhibited by the students, then teachers can increase frequency through positive or negative reinforcement. How can teachers get students to exhibit behaviors they have not yet exhibited? Teachers can **shape** the students' responses gradually. Thus, when students first learn to write, teachers must reinforce whatever they can do and keep at them to write more. Then the demands of the teachers increase. Initially, students are reinforced for forming letters correctly, but later they are only reinforced if their groups of letters form words, and eventually they are only reinforced for writing complete sentences. Finally, they have to put sentences together in coherent paragraphs. The demands increase as schooling continues. Ultimately, college students only receive reinforcement for an accurate and clearly written 15-page paper. Many patterns of response are learned through shaping.

Teachers can also vary the delivery of reinforcements. Typically, reinforcements occur intermittently rather than after every response. Learning that occurs via **intermittent reinforcement** is more resistant to extinction than learning that occurs under continuous reinforcement. For example, perhaps one in three football games is really exciting. Nevertheless, people keep coming back for more despite the high likelihood of a boring game. Although Skinner did not use the term *expectation,* other behaviorists have in their explanations of such behavior (Rotter, 1954). Continuous reinforcement produces an expectation of reinforcement every time, which increases vulnerability to extinction whenever a reinforcement fails to occur. In contrast, intermittent reinforcement creates an expectation that reinforcement is a sometime occurrence and that if a person persists, reinforcement eventually occurs.

There are two ways that reinforcement can be intermittent. In a **ratio reinforcement schedule,** reinforcement follows a certain number of desired responses. Thus, children in a class who receive stickers for completing ten worksheets are on a ratio schedule of reinforcement. Alternatively, reinforcement can be delivered at certain time intervals, or on an **interval reinforcement schedule.** For example, some teachers reinforce a class on Fridays with extra time to talk to friends if the class has been able to get weekly work in on time. The two types of schedules lead to different patterns of response. The ratio schedule tends to produce high rates of responding that do not vary much, except perhaps for a small reduction in responding immediately after payoff. The interval schedule tends to produce a rapid decline in performance immediately after payoff that only gradually increases until it reaches a maximum just before the next payoff. Thus, for the teacher with the Friday reinforcement schedule, there would be fewer assignments coming in on Monday, Tuesday, and Wednesday, compared with Thursday and Friday.

● "What Do I Do on Monday Morning?"

Skinner in the Classroom

Using the principles of operant conditioning in the classroom is not as simple as it may seem. A general rule of thumb is to emphasize the use of reinforcement and to limit the use of punishment. Unfortunately, it is often difficult for teachers to select reinforcers since choosing what is reinforcing is subjective; that is, it varies from student to student and especially changes as students mature. Teachers must keep in mind that if the reinforced behavior does not increase, then the reinforcer the teacher selected was not really reinforcing for the students in question. Praise, smiles, attention, and stickers from the teacher are reinforcing for many elementary school children. In middle school and high school, however, these teacher-oriented reinforcers are not likely to be effective. Well-intentioned teacher praise may even backfire because it may be perceived as singling out a middle school student as a teacher's pet, thus leading to peer disapproval and ultimately to decreases in the supposedly reinforced behavior. Alternatively, teacher ridicule or sarcasm intended as punishment may result in attention from peers that actually reinforces the targeted behavior. As a result, some teachers become discouraged and abandon reinforcement, often resorting to punishment.

One way to discover potential reinforcers is to use the Premack (1965) principle of making high-frequency behavior contingent on low-frequency behavior. In other words, observe students' behavior to determine preferred activities, and then use these preferred activities (e.g., conversing, reading magazines, reading comics, resting, playing a game on a computer) as reinforcers for targeted behavior. For example, after students have participated intelligently in a class discussion, demonstrating they have read the assignment, a teacher may then allow the students to take a 10-minute break to discuss any issue they would like among themselves. (Talking to peers is a high-frequency behavior among middle school and high school students.) Teachers need to develop a variety of potential reinforcers. Raschke (1981) suggests giving students a list and allowing them to pick their own reinforcement or making a game of reinforcement, such as earning the right to spin a dial to win a reinforcer. Ultimately, the goal is to shift control of reinforcement to the students themselves, that is, to have to have success itself becomes reinforcing. This shift needs to be fostered as early as elementary school so students are not working exclusively for teachers' reinforcement but rather for their own satisfaction. For example, teachers can encourage self-testing by students during study, a practice which not only gives students information about what they still need to study but also reinforces study behavior.

Behaviorism in Educational Settings

In the 1960s, educators explored how to use principles of operant psychology in school. Three applications were devised. The first, programmed instruction, is no longer widely employed, but it was the forerunner of the current generation of educational software. The second, behavior modification and token economies, is now used more in educational settings serving special populations than in settings serving normally achieving students. Many teachers, however, still use some components of behavior modification. The third application, classroom management, is essential knowledge for any teacher and is discussed in Chapter 10. One aspect of classroom management, the use of punishment in schools, is discussed here.

Programmed Instruction and Teaching Machines. The idea of programmed instruction was that if learning could be broken down into small enough segments and presented in sequence, then exercises could be devised in which students would learn a little bit at a time with few misunderstandings (Pressey, 1926; Skinner, 1961). For each little bit of knowledge, students would be given an opportunity to respond. A correct response would be reinforced by showing the students that they were correct. Because learning occurs one little bit at a time, most responses would be correct and reinforced.

As an example, consider this sequence of frames from the Holland and Skinner (1961, pp. 52–56) program (an example that also reviews the difficult concept of negative reinforcement):

> Reinforcement which consists of presenting stimuli (e.g., food) is called positive reinforcement. In contrast, reinforcement which consists of terminating stimuli (e.g., painful stimuli) is called _____ reinforcement. [*Answer:* negative]

> Turning off a television commercial is reinforced by the termination of a(n) (1) _____ reinforcer; turning on a very funny program is reinforced by the presentation of a(n) (2) _____ reinforcer. [*Answers:* (1) negative, (2) positive]

Immediately after producing a response, students could check their responses, perhaps by opening an answer window on a teaching machine or turning the page in a printed program. Determining that their responses match the ones provided by the program is reinforcing. Such reinforcement keeps motivation high so that the students stick to it and answer many such questions.

Much of today's computer-assisted instruction is constructed on similar principles. One example is the *Reader Rabbit* program. This program has four different games (each with a number of variations) appropriate for children first learning to read words. One game presents an array of 12 "cards," each of which can be illuminated one at a time to reveal a word or a picture. The goal is to illuminate pairs of cards that go together, a word (e.g., *bike*) and its referent (e.g., a picture of a bike). Each time a match is made, there is positive reinforcement in that the two cards disappear and a bell sounds. If the child makes all six matches quickly, Reader Rabbit appears and does a little dance. Because there are different levels of each game, it is possible to find a level for most children that results in a high rate of correct responding and thus, high positive reinforcement.

Behavior Modification and Token Economies. In some classrooms or other settings, systematic **behavior modification** is used. The behavior management procedures used in these programs are based on the principles of reinforcement and punishment that you have already learned. The main idea of behavior modification is to reinforce behaviors that are valued. If students are not capable of those behaviors at present, teachers should reinforce behaviors they are capable of performing that are in the direction of the desired response. Gradually, teachers increase the criteria for reinforcement until the students can produce the desired behavior. In other words, teachers shape the response. In some classrooms, children are reinforced for completing homework by receiving stickers. The stickers are a form of **token reinforcement.** Other token reinforcements sometimes include chips that can be accumulated and eventually traded in for treats or privileges.

Teachers typically use reinforcement systems on an intermittent basis, since it is hard for a classroom teacher to monitor and reinforce every appropriate response by all of the students in a classroom and also so the student responses are less susceptible to extinction. An important goal of any token economy is to increase the ratio, or interval, between reinforcements until the desired behaviors are occurring with only typical classroom reinforcements, such as praise. The gradual reduction in the use of reinforcement is known as **fading.**

Good behavior modification environments often have other features as well. For example, correct and preferred behaviors are consistently modeled by teachers. Adult attention, which is a powerful reinforcement for many children, is provided for appropriate action rather than inappropriate action. Thus, if the teacher wishes to reduce a student's talking out of turn, the student does not get the teacher's attention when engaged in that behavior. Instead, the teacher responds to the student only when the student raises his or her hand and waits for acknowledgment before speaking.

Behavioral contracting is another behavior modification option. The student makes an agreement with the teacher to attempt to reach a particular goal (see Table 7.4). Usually the contract is negotiated, with students helping to decide what the goal will be, what reinforcement might be earned, and how much progress toward the goal is required before there is any reinforcement. Often, parent training complements classroom behavioral programs. Parents learn how they can use behavioral principles to provide reinforcement consistent with the school's program. Thus, a teacher who is reinforcing a student for bringing homework into school also trains the parent to reinforce the student at home for doing homework.

Table 7.4

Example of a Behavioral Contract

Goal: To hand in assignments regularly on time.

When I,_____, hand in all of my assignments on time for five days in a row, I will be able to (read a magazine, play a computer game, or put my head down to rest) for 10 minutes during class time.

This contract will be in effect during the month of October. For every month that passes, two days are added to the number of days of on-time assignments necessary before I receive my reward (e.g., November—7 days, December—9 days, etc.).

Student:_____

Parent:_____

This child is placed in time-out, a form of punishment sometimes used in behavior modification programs.

Some forms of punishments are widely accepted in behavior modification programs. For example, one form of punishment used in a token economy for engaging in inappropriate behavior is **response cost.** In this technique, students are first given a number of tokens. If they engage in the unwanted behavior, they must forfeit some of these tokens. The students refrain from the unwanted behavior in order to keep the tokens.

An alternative punishment acceptable in many settings is **time-out,** in which a student is physically removed from the other students or activities for a short period of time. Time-out can involve moving a student to an isolated corner of the classroom or to an empty room. Time-out is punishing because of the lack of reinforcers. For time-out to be effective, the area left must contain reinforcers and the time-out area must not have any reinforcers. Teachers must take care that the amount of time spent in time-out is appropriate. For elementary school children, only a few minutes in time-out may be required.

Special educators, in particular, are interested in the application of behavioral principles to education (Kiernan, 1985). For example, behavioral principles have been used to teach everything from clearly academic tasks, such as the basic arithmetic facts (Dunlap & Dunlap, 1989; Van Houten & Rolider, 1989), to life skills tasks, such as banking (McDonnell & Ferguson, 1989), and acting in socially appropriate ways in employment settings (Park & Gaylord-Ross, 1989). There are also important applications to regular education. For instance, behaviorists have developed effective procedures for teaching children how to fend off potential sexual abuse and abduction (Miltenberger & Thiesse-Duffy, 1988; Poche, Yoder, & Miltenberger, 1988).

▶ **Diversity**

Token Economies and Special Populations

Behavior modification and token economies of various sorts enjoy a long track record of success (Hobbs & Lahey, 1983), especially for special populations in institutional settings. For example, Achievement Place was established in the late 1960s and early 1970s by faculty at the University of Kansas as a residential-style halfway house for juvenile delinquents (Phillips, 1968; Phillips, Phillips, Fixsen, & Wolf, 1971). A main assumption of the developers of Achievement Place was that their delinquent clients had not acquired many of the constructive social behaviors needed to function in society as productive, nondelinquent citizens. In an Achievement Place home, residents were reinforced for doing all those little things that are simply part of normal life for most people, but which were never learned by these youth.

At first, the residents received points for everything from making their beds to arriving at a meal clean to reading the newspaper, with more points earned for more demanding tasks. There were also response costs—and very hefty ones at that—for socially inappropriate behaviors, such as being late or lying. The points could be traded in for privileges and tangible rewards, including particular snack foods and telephone privileges. With the passage of time and the acquisition of increasingly sophisticated social behaviors, the daily point system was faded and replaced by a weekly point system, which also eventually was faded, until the resident functioned without a point system. Eventually, the resident exited the setting in a program of transition to home. Fading is possible when the previously reinforced behaviors become reinforcing themselves. For instance, reading newspapers and listening to the news really became enjoyable. Moreover, the more appropriate the resident's social behavior, the greater the freedom at Achievement Place. Freedom is very reinforcing, especially if you have lost your freedom via court action, as was the case for Achievement Place residents.

Did Achievement Place work? There were multiple indicators that it did. Compared to otherwise comparable delinquents treated in other settings (e.g., more restrictive environments) or in other ways (e.g., probation), Achievement Place graduates attended school more regularly following release from Achievement Place, were in trouble with the law less, and did better academically (Fixsen, Phillips, & Wolf, 1973). It really is not surprising that this intervention was effective. With everyone being reinforced for prosocial behaviors, there is a great deal of modeling of prosocial and appropriate conduct by peers (that is, everyone is trying to be good). Exposure to such modeling is a powerful learning opportunity. In addition, the treatment had many components, including caring house parents and a transition mechanism that permitted the homeward-bound resident to come back from time to time to consult and talk with Achievement Place staff.

Punishment in Schools. In Skinner's view, behaviorism is a very positive approach to students' learning and development. The emphasis is on catching the students doing well and reinforcing them for it. If the students cannot do well given current competencies, then they need to be reinforced for behaviors in the right direction and the appropriate response gradually shaped. Skinner (1953) suggested that when teachers use punishment, they should also provide an alternative behavior that will be reinforced. For example, if a student is talking during a quiet study time, the teacher should remind the student firmly that this is the time to study quietly but should also make sure the student has something interesting to work on. Skinner also argued that reductions in the frequency of undesirable behaviors using punishment were short-lived and that punishment led to undesirable by-products, such as emotional responses of anxiety or anger.

Other researchers have found that punishment can have enduring effects on the elimination of undesirable behaviors without enduring side effects (Walters &

Grusec, 1977). For example, supplementing punishment with rationales for obeying can make punishment more effective (Cheyne & Walters, 1969; LaVoie, 1973, 1974; Parke, 1969, 1974). In many cases, however, rationales alone are as effective or more effective than punishments, and they may also help students internalize prohibitions, thus making it more likely they will behave appropriately in the future (M. L. Hoffman, 1970; Kanfer & Zich, 1974). Rationales presented to young children (e.g., preschoolers) need to be concrete (e.g., "You might break this toy if you play with it because it is fragile"). Abstract rationales that focus on the rights and feelings of others (e.g., "The owner of this toy will feel bad if you play with it"), however, are increasingly effective with advancing age during childhood (LaVoie, 1974; Parke, 1974; Walters & Grusec, 1977). Thus, undesirable behaviors can often be suppressed without resorting to punishment.

Nevertheless, punishment still exists in schools. Effective school punishments are ones that have a reasonable connection to the infraction. In Blackwood (1970), junior high students who had misbehaved copied essays as punishment. Some students copied an essay emphasizing the negative effects of classroom disobedience, while others copied an essay about steam engines. The students who copied an essay emphasizing why misbehavior was problematic were less likely to misbehave following the punishment than were those who copied the essay on steam engines. MacPherson, Candee, and Hohman (1974) conducted a similar study with elementary school students who had misbehaved in a cafeteria. Again, postpunishment behavior was more effective for students who had copied essays providing rationales for obeying school rules.

Although there is little evidence that corporal punishment leads to better behaved students (R. Edwards & Edwards, 1987), it is still used in some schools (Hyman, 1990; Hyman & Wise, 1977). This practice would not meet with Skinner's approval, since he was generally opposed to corporal punishment (Skinner, 1977). He believed that corporal punishment teaches that might makes right: "The punishing teacher who punishes teaches students that punishment is a way of solving problems" (p. 336).

Social Learning Theory

We learn many behaviors without benefit of reinforcement. We learn many things by observing others. That is, other people serve as **behavioral models.** This is the main principle of **social learning theory** proposed by Albert Bandura and his colleagues (Bandura & Walters, 1963). There have been studies of observational learning of aggression, altruism, sex-typed behaviors, attachment behaviors, and social independence (Mussen, 1983).

Observational Learning of Behaviors and Expectancies

In observational learning, people learn through **vicarious experiences.** That is, when they see others experience reinforcements and punishments, they form expectations about the reinforcements or punishments they might receive for their own behaviors. For example, Albert Bandura (1965) had young children view a film in which a child exhibited some very novel physical and verbal aggressive behaviors toward a set of toys. At the completion of the film, the child model was either punished for the aggression (spanked and verbally rebuked), reinforced for it (given soft drinks, candy, and praise), or provided no consequences. After watching the film, the children were left alone in the room where the film was made with an opportunity to play with the toys seen in the film. Children who had watched the film in which the child model was spanked for aggression were much less likely to exhibit the aggressive behaviors when interacting with the toys than if they had watched the film depicting reward or no consequences for the aggression. Then, all children in the experiment were offered stickers and fruit juice if they would show the experimenter the aggressive behaviors that the film model had exhibited. The children had little difficulty reproducing the behaviors.

What was going on in this situation? The children had clearly learned the aggressive behaviors in question because they could reproduce those behaviors when given an incentive to do so. However, they were less likely to perform the aggressive behaviors after viewing the film in which the child model had been punished because they had learned to expect punishment for aggressive behavior from the film. Performance of a behavior depends on knowing a response as well as the expectation of reinforcements that are valued by the performer. When punishments are expected, performance often will not occur unless there are offsetting reinforcements. For many children in the Bandura (1965) study, the fun of playing with the toys aggressively was not worth the risk of getting spanked or verbally rebuked.

Consider another example. Although you have seen many high-speed car chases on television or at the movies, they are statistically rare. Why? People know that if they speed away from a traffic stop, they may be caught and punished. This *expectancy* has been established through years of observing the villains on television or in the movies being punished for their wicked deeds. Moreover, the punishments are usually very aversive (i.e, they have negative *value*), ranging from personal remorse and guilt to imprisonment. Whether a person executes a given behavior depends on expectations of rewards or punishments for performing the behavior and the value of the rewards and punishments. In other words, the probability of performing behavior X is a function of the expectancy of reward or punishment for X *and* the value of the reward or punishment (Rotter, 1954).

Try this little test of your understanding if you are not sure whether you understand expectancy-value theory:

People build up stores of knowledge by watching movies and television. As described in social learning theory, some knowledge gained through observation may never be used.

1. You expect that studying for a test will make it likely you will pass a test. The test does not count in your grades and is on material that is boring. Will you study or not?
2. You expect that studying for a test will not increase the likelihood you will pass or earn a better grade. Your entire semester's grade depends on this test. Will you study or not?
3. You expect that studying for a test will increase your grade, you like the content, and the grade in this course is important to you. Will you study or not?

For situation 1, you probably will not study because the value of reinforcement is low and there is a negative value (boredom) associated with studying. For situation 2, you probably will not study because your expectation of reinforcement following studying is low. For situation 3, you will study since the expectation of reward is high and there are two sources of positively valued reinforcement (i.e., the pleasure of processing this material and an important course grade).

Cognitive Mechanisms Mediating Social Learning

Social learning theory stresses not only principles of behavioral learning theory, such as reinforcement and punishment, but also many aspects of cognitive theory as well. Bandura (1986) described the following four processes of social cognitive theory: attentional processes, retention processes, motor reproduction processes, and motivational processes.

Attentional Processes. What the learner observes or attends to depends on characteristics of the model and characteristics of the observer. For example, not everyone has equal access to the same types of models. Children who are reared in environments with gentle people have more opportunities to view gentle behaviors than children who are raised in environments filled with aggressive people. To some extent, all of us, with the exception of very young children, have some control as to the social models available to us. Thus, people who elect to attend college select surroundings where there are models of studious behavior. People who elect gang life select themselves into situations where aggression is modeled. In both the college and the gang situation, some of the people will command greater attention than others. Thus, the president of a fraternity is more likely to be observed and imitated than a pledge. The leader of a gang is much more likely to be watched and imitated than someone who is not as respected by gang members.

Retention Processes. Once a person attends to a behavior, it must be remembered if it is to affect future behaviors. Thus processes, such as imagery and rehearsal, that enhance memory are mediators of observational learning (Bandura, Grusec, & Menlove, 1966; Bandura & Jeffery, 1973; Bandura, Jeffery, & Bachicha, 1974). For example, imaging speaking in public may improve public speaking performances and visualizing leaping over hurdles may improve performance in a race.

Motor Reproduction Processes. Not only must learners perceive and remember a behavioral sequence, but they also must be able to produce it themselves. In some cases, the observed sequence is readily reproducible. In other cases, the

Electing to join a gang results in exposure to aggressive models.

observer can carry out components but not the entire action. Sometimes individual components must be acquired before the entire sequence can be executed. For example, a very skilled gymnast can watch another gymnast's routine (e.g., on the balance beam) and copy most or all of it immediately. A less skilled gymnast would have to break the routine into segments (e.g., practicing the mount over and over again, practicing a particular type of handstand over and over, practicing the dismount over and over) before attempting to integrate the segments. For some of us, it would never be possible to execute a routine on a balance beam.

Motivational Processes. People can see an action, one that they are capable of doing, remember it, and still not perform it. One example is the group of children who failed to perform the aggressive actions after seeing the aggressive model punished in Bandura's (1965) study. Performance depends on motivation, which in turn follows from an expectation of a valued reward if the behavior in question is performed. Sometimes this expectation follows from observing reinforcement of others who perform the behavior (i.e., vicarious reinforcement). Sometimes the expectation follows from a personal history of reinforcement for performing the behavior, as when a person continues to run in marathons simply to experience the runner's high and the congratulations at the finish line. Sometimes the reward is expected because the person will self-reinforce himself or herself for performing the action. For example, some writers only permit themselves to relax in the evening once they have completed a certain number of pages for the day.

■ Building Your Expertise

Observational Learning of Language

Can social learning theory explain how we acquire our most important tool—language? Chomsky's nativist position for language learning is discussed briefly in Chapter 6. The major assumption of this theory is that human beings have biologically determined language capacities. Thus, from the nativist perspective, learning mechanisms simply do not play much of a role in language acquisition (R. Brown, 1973).

There is evidence, however, that many grammatical rules can be learned via imitation (I. Brown, 1979; T. L. Rosenthal & Zimmerman, 1978). Imitation involves inducing rules from multiple exposures to examples of a phenomenon and using these rules to guide future behavior (Bandura, 1977b). I. Brown (1976) established that nursery school children could induce the grammatical rules governing the production of passive sentence constructions if they were presented a sample of passive sentences accompanied by enactments of the actions specified by the sentences. For instance, the passive sentence "The car was hit by the truck" would be accompanied by an enactment of a toy truck hitting a toy car. Moreover, imitation is apparently innate. Within hours of birth, infants who observe an adult opening his or her mouth or sticking out his or her tongue respond by opening their mouths or sticking out their tongues (Meltzoff, 1985; Meltzoff & Gopnik, 1989; Metlzoff & Moore, 1977, 1983).

Cognitive Behavior Modification

Language serves an important role in learning and behavior (see also Chapter 8). Arguing that self-speech could be used to organize behavior, Donald Meichenbaum (1977, p. 19) cited the following example of a child's speech that directed the construction of a Tinkertoy car:

> The wheels go here, the wheels go here. Oh, we need to start it all over again. We have to close it up. See it closes up. We're starting it all over again. Do you know why we wanted to do that? Because I needed it to go a different way. Isn't it pretty clever, don't you think? But we have to cover up the motor just like a real car. (Kohlberg, Yaeger, & Hjertholm, 1968, p. 695)

Although young children often use such self-instructional speech on their own (Kohlberg, Yaeger, & Hjertholm, 1968), they also benefit from explicit instructions to self-verbalize (Patterson & Mischel, 1976; Wozniak, 1972). Instructional approaches that focus on self-verbalizations, called **cognitive behavior modification,** combine key components of other learning theories. These include reinforcement and fading from the behavioral perspective and modeling from social learning theory. Self-verbalization, itself, is clearly a cognitive concept.

For example, Meichenbaum and Goodman (1971) reduced the impulsive responding of hyperactive second graders by teaching them to instruct themselves to go slowly and reflect before responding. Using teacher modeling, guided practice, and the gradual fading of teacher cuing, they taught students to make self-verbalizations such as the following:

> Okay, what is it I have to do? You want me to copy the picture with the different lines. I have to go slowly and carefully. Okay, draw the line down, down, good; then to the right, that's it; now down some more and to the left. Good, I'm doing fine so far. Remember, go slowly. Now back up again. No, I was supposed to go down. That's okay. Just erase the line carefully. . . . Good. Even if I make an error I can go on slowly and carefully. I have to go down now. Finished. I did it! (Meichenbaum & Goodman, 1971, p. 117)

First the teacher described and modeled self-verbalization. Then the teacher provided external support and guidance as students attempted to apply the approach

Self-Instruction in a Variety of Contexts

Educational researchers have found self-instruction to be effective in a variety of contexts, under a number of instructional conditions, and with very different types of research methodologies. Consider the following examples:

- Patterson and Mischel (1976) taught preschoolers to resist a temptation by training them to tell themselves not to pay any attention to the distraction.
- Manning (1988) randomly assigned the most behaviorally inappropriate first- and third-grade children in a school to either a self-instructional treatment group or a control condition that received additional instruction and attention, but no self-instruction. For example, when the students in the experimental condition saw a teacher self-instruct to inhibit inappropriate behaviors, control students received additional explicit instruction in the school rules prohibiting the inappropriate behaviors. Both experimental and control students received 8 hours of instruction, and the classroom teachers did not know the condition assignment of the children involved in the study. The results were compelling, both immediately following training and three months later. The students receiving self-instructional training were perceived as more self-controlled by their teachers, were more often on task (working when they should), and believed themselves to be more in control of their behaviors.
- Manning (1990) used cognitive self-instruction to increase the on-task behavior of a fourth grader. At the beginning of the intervention, Jill (the student) was on task during school assignments only 15 percent of the time. Following training in self-instruction, Jill was on task 80 percent of the time, with high on-task behavior still evident 3 months after the self-instructional training.

- Zentall (1989) reported that self-instructional training is more effective than behavioral training alone for increasing self-control and reducing impulsivity in hyperactive and impulsive children.
- Graham and Harris (1989) combined strategy instruction with self-instruction to teach writing skills to learning disabled fifth- and sixth-grade students (see Chapter 11). They taught teachers to provide explanations of rationale and the potential benefits of a writing strategy focused on defining, identifying, and generating story grammar elements (see Chapter 4). The students learned to ask themselves questions such as, "Who is the main character? When does the story take place? What does the main character want to do? What happens when he or she tries do it? How does the story end? How does the main character feel?" The students also learned the following self-statements designed to support and guide the execution of strategy:

    Problem definition: "What is it I have to do?"

    Planning: "Now I'd better write down my story-parts reminder."

    Self-evaluation: "Am I using all my parts so far?"

    Self-reinforcement: "Good, I like these parts."

Graham and Harris (1989) found that the quality of the students' stories increased and the students' self-efficacy became more positive.

Think back to the discussion in Chapter 1 of the importance of replicating research results in multiple settings, in diverse samples, and with various research methods. Self-instruction has proved to be effective in research using case study approaches (e.g., Manning, 1990) as well as experimental approaches (e.g., Manning, 1988). These studies also provide evidence that self-instruction can be generalized to diverse populations (preschoolers, hyperactive students, and learning disabled students).

to problems. The teacher encouraged the students to internalize the self-verbalizations by guiding the students to whisper rather than talk aloud and then eventually only to think about the problem definition, the task-focusing and guiding directions, and the self-reinforcement as they performed the task.

An important component in the self-instructional approach is a teacher who consistently models self-control using self-instruction (Manning, 1991). Anyone who has ever taught knows the frustration of trying to figure out what is wrong with the overhead projector. A self-instructing teacher might cope by first defining the problem verbally, followed by self-verbalizations to direct appropriate actions:

> "Why won't this overhead turn on? Let me see. I'll try all the switches again. This arrow points to the right. Did I turn left or right? Try again." When frustrated, the teacher models coping via self-instruction: "It's easy to get frustrated. Take a deep breath and relax. There must be a solution." Once a solution is found, the teacher self-reinforces: "Hey! I stuck with it and found the outlet is faulty. I'll try this other outlet. Yay! It works." If there is no success, the teacher models more coping and adapting: "I've tried all I know. I'll either show you this information by putting it on the board or call the media specialist to help fix the machine. Which would be fastest?" (Manning, 1991, p. 134)

The self-instructing teacher also models for students how to cope with problems and temptations to behave impulsively or inappropriately. Thus, the teacher might model the following sequence for a student who is unprepared and caught attempting to cheat. Again, the teacher starts with a verbalization of the problem and then models self-direction and self-coping until a solution is achieved that can be self-reinforced:

> "I forgot to study for my test. Should I look at my friend's test? I can see her paper easily. But, is that right? Just do my best. I'll feel better about myself if I don't look. This is hard. I know my answers are wrong. That's okay. I've done the best I can. Next time I won't leave my book at school. I'm glad I didn't take answers that didn't belong to me. I feel good about that!" (Manning, 1991, p. 135)

Some specific components of self-instruction supported by research are teaching students (1) to recognize when they are at risk for behaving in a noncontrolled fashion, (2) to realize that there are more appropriate behaviors than the ones they are using to solve problems, (3) to interrupt impulsive responding by making comments such as, "What am I supposed to do here?" (4) to set standards that define effective performance of the task, (5) to self-monitor, (6) to cope, and (7) to self-reinforce (Zentall, 1989).

Chapter Summary

- Piaget described four stages of cognitive development, each characterized by the schemes used to learn about the world. In the sensorimotor stage, infants use motor schemes to interact with the environment. One major accomplishment of this stage is the development of object permanence. Children in the preoperational stage use symbolic schemes. The mental representations and language of this stage promote deferred imitation and symbolic play. In the concrete opera-

- tional stage, students develop operational schemes, which allow them to solve logical tasks such as class inclusion and conservation. The success of concrete operators is limited to concrete tasks with only two dimensions. Finally, students in the formal operational stage are capable of scientific thought.

- Schemes change and develop through the process of equilibration. Equilibration involves both assimilation and accommodation. Assimilation is the interpretation of new situations in terms of existing cognitive structures. Accommodation is the adaptation of cognitive structures so that they correspond to what actually occurs in the world.

- The behavioral perspective focuses on observable behaviors. In classical conditioning, a neutral stimulus becomes conditioned to a reflexive response. In operant conditioning, whether or not a behavior occurs depends on consequences. Reinforcers increase the likelihood of behavior; punishment decreases the likelihood of behavior.

- Principles of behaviorism are often applied to classroom settings. Programmed instruction and computer-assisted instruction positively reinforce correct responses. Behavior modification programs and token economies systematically employ the principles of reinforcement and punishment. Specific techniques include the gradual reduction of reinforcement (fading), behavioral contracting, loss of tokens due to engaging in unwanted behavior (response cost), and removal from sources of reinforcement (time-out). In general, since the possible benefits of punishment are short-lived and since punishment is often accompanied by undesirable side effects such as anxiety and anger, the emphasis is placed on reinforcement in many classroom applications of behavioral principles.

- All of us are constantly being exposed to behaviors, ones that we could learn and imitate. Of course, only some of the behaviors that are observed are learned and few that are learned, are performed. Social learning theory describes this process. For a behavior to be observationally learned and performed requires attention to the behavior, retention of the behavior in memory, the ability to perform the behavior, and the motivation to perform the behavior.

- The motivation to carry out an action depends on the expectancies of the learner about reinforcements for performing the action. The probability of any behavior, including observationally learned behaviors, is a function of the expectancy of reinforcement and the value of the reinforcement to the performer.

- In self-instructional approaches to education, students learn to make self-verbalizations that direct and guide their learning activities.

Return to the Classroom Predicament

Has reading about the theories of learning and development presented in this chapter helped you understand the instructional approaches used by Ms. Campbell and Mr. Sharp in the classroom predicament? Ms. Campbell is trying to teach number concepts through the use of concrete manipulables. Her students are actively experimenting on their own in small groups, and apparently some of the students in the groups are experiencing cognitive conflict as their understandings are challenged. Some of these ideas are derived from Piaget's theory of development.

Mr. Sharp is incorporating some of the characteristics of social learning theory into his teaching techniques. He is reinforcing the student models who are working on problems at the board for the correct use of the rules of long division. Thus, the rest of the students can engage in observational learning. In addition, some of the students working on problems at their desks are using self-instruction to help themselves perform the steps accurately. By increasing the difficulty of the students' problems, Mr. Sharp is shaping his students' ability to solve any long division problem, no matter how difficult.

Chapter Outline

Chapter 8

Social Interactional Theories of Learning and Development

Classroom Predicament

The teacher is leading a discussion on World War II.

Teacher: Who were Germany's allies during the war?

Manuel: Japan.

Teacher: That's one of the allies. Can anyone think of another ally?

Pamela: Switzerland?

Teacher: No. Switzerland was neutral. Anyone else?

Tara: Italy.

Teacher: Good. Who was the leader of Italy at the time?

Andrew: The pope?

Teacher: No, not quite. I mean the political leader. Does anyone know? OK, have you heard of Benito Mussolini? He was the leader of the Italian Fascist Party. Now, what did these three countries have in common?

Millie: They hated Jews.

Teacher: Does anyone have another idea?

Anita: Their leaders respected and liked one another.

Teacher: Well, maybe that was true to some extent, but their relationships were complicated. What else did they have in common? Did anyone read the chapter assigned for today?

Evaluate this classroom dialogue. Is there anything the teacher could do to foster more meaningful instructional conversations? Reflecting on the information presented in this chapter will help you formulate responses to this question.

Peaple learn from other people. This is certainly not a new idea. For example, social learning theorists argue for the powerful roles of imitation and modeling in learning (see Chapter 7). The theories of knowledge construction described in Chapter 7, however, focus on the learner as an individual in interaction with the surrounding environment. In contrast, the emphasis of social interactional theories of knowledge is on the role of the social environment in learning and development. In this view, development of the individual cannot be understood without understanding the social environment. Perhaps the major contribution of these theories is the investigation of types of human interaction that foster learning and development.

These theories propose ideas that are relevant to classroom interactions. Many important classroom interactions are essentially conversations between teachers and students. How do these classroom conversations foster learning? This chapter begins with a discussion of the ideas of two important theorists, Lev Vygotsky and M. M. Bakhtin, who emphasized the role of language and social interactions in cognitive development. Then we introduce instructional techniques derived from these theoretical ideas. The chapter concludes with an analysis of typical instructional conversations, followed by ideas for promoting more effective academic conversations.

Sociocultural Approaches to the Mind: Vygotsky and Bakhtin

Perhaps the most influential theorist emphasizing social interaction as a determinant of the qualities of the mind is Lev Vygotsky (1962, 1978). Although Vygotsky lived in the first half of the twentieth century in what was then the Soviet Union, English translations of his works did not appear until the 1960s and 1970s. In recent years, no theorist has commanded as much attention from psychologists interested in instruction as Vygotsky (A. L. Brown & French, 1979; Das & Gindis, 1995; Wertsch, 1985, 1991).

The main theme of Vygotsky's theory is that it is impossible to understand development without considering the social environment in which development occurs. Development is influenced by the social institutions of a culture, such as its schools and government. The tools developed by a culture, such as language and technology, also greatly influence the development of cognitive abilities in each new generation.

The Developmental Relationship Between Thought and Speech

According to Vygotsky (1978), the relationship of thought to speech is different for adults than it is for children. In all stages of development, however, language plays an important role.

Thought and Speech in Adults. Vygotsky (1962) believed that inner speech plays an important role in adults' thought. Inner speech is very different from outer speech. Outer speech should be readily understood by others. In contrast, **inner speech** is an internal dialogue that is abbreviated and fragmentary, with the meaning of complex thoughts captured in very few words.

What is the relationship between thought and speech? Consider a complicated task, one that requires some thinking. For example, let's say that you are trying to research the topic of language at the library and that you are inexperienced in using computer search techniques. Your inner speech will guide the search process. Perhaps you begin by saying to yourself something such as, "Now, how do I use this computer to access the right database? That's it, I first find the menu list and search for the one I need." Then you may mumble to yourself an abbreviated, "Pick this one," as you select the Psychlit database instead of ERIC. As you gain more experience using the database, you learn to access it without any awareness of additional inner speech. Inner speech is no longer necessary since you are solving a familiar problem.

Thought and Speech in Children. Inner speech also has an important role in the development of thinking. Vygotsky's theory of the development of thought and speech in children specifies four stages. During the first two years of life, thought is nonverbal and speech is nonconceptual with no relationship between thought and speech. With the development of language, beginning at about the age of 2, thought and speech begin to merge. The most obvious manifestations are labeling many objects by their names and developing verbal communications with others. However, children do not use self-speech in any sense to direct thinking during this second stage, although the speech of others often is directive (Luria, 1982). For example, while 2-year-olds often live up to their "terrible" reputation, many times they really will come when you ask them to. This is not likely in younger children unless there is nonverbal cueing about the appropriateness of coming, such as an adult's offering outstretched arms (Service, Lock, & Chandler, 1989).

The role of self-speech in directing thought and behavior begins to emerge in the third stage, which is characterized by **egocentric speech.** Egocentric speech refers to the tendency of preschoolers to talk to themselves about what they are doing. Piaget argued that this represented a deficit in preschoolers in that they could not communicate meaning to others (see Chapter 7).

In contrast to Piaget, Vygotsky viewed the emergence of egocentric speech as an advance because this speech influences what children think and do. Preschoolers will often say, "I'm going to play with the dog" or "I'm going to ride my tricycle" before they actually do so. Often, these utterances come when the children are trying to figure out what to do.

In one study, Vygotsky asked preschoolers to complete tasks that were complicated by some obstacle. For example, something the children needed to complete the task was missing. The amount of egocentric speech uttered by the preschoolers during the completion of these tasks was much greater than when they performed the same tasks without obstacles. As an example, consider this monologue produced by a preschooler faced with a difficult task: "Where is the pencil? I need a blue pencil now. Nothing. Instead of that I will color it red and put water on it— that will make it darker and more like blue" (Vygotsky, 1987, p. 70). This child is clearly using speech as part of thinking.

During the fourth stage, the egocentric speech that was overt becomes covert and abbreviated. For example, the egocentric speech described previously would become inner speech as follows: "Where's the pencil? Need blue. Will use red, add water." Actions are much more prominent in inner speech than in egocentric speech.

In Vygotsky's view, learning begins in the social world. Speech is originally external to children in that they speak in order to address others but not to talk to themselves. Only when speech becomes established for others can it then become internalized. Thus, children can have *monologues* with themselves only after they have developed the

Children use speech as part of their thinking. This child is telling himself, "I need to put a wheel here."

ability to hold *dialogues* with others. Internalized, or monological, speech is not egocentric in the Piagetian sense; rather it is social speech that has reached a higher stage, being for the self. It is how a person communicates with himself or herself.

■ Building Your Expertise

Vygotsky and Piaget

Although Vygotsky and Piaget were contemporaries, Piaget's theory arguably reached its peak of influence in the 1960s and 1970s. Vygotsky's theory became influential only in the last 15 to 20 years, when his works were more widely translated.

The theories of Piaget and Vygotsky share some similarities. Both are dialectical in that they view development as occurring because of interaction between the individual and society. Both perspectives view the individual learner as active, with active exploration the key to development. Development is viewed as a dynamic process, composed of upheaval and sudden change.

There are, however, some important differences between the two theoretical positions. In Piaget's view, influences of the social world are not central; the child acts as an individual. In contrast, according to Vygotsky, it is impossible to understand development without understanding the social environment. They also ascribed different roles to language. In Piaget's view, speech is symptomatic of ongoing mental activity, and egocentric speech disappears with maturity. In contrast, Vygotsky argued that such speech does not die out but rather goes underground, becoming inner speech, which plays a pivotal role in shaping thinking.

Development of Sophisticated Thought

Adults often assist children in thinking about problems they face. For example, they may help children solve a puzzle or help them figure out how many "big sleeps" until their next birthday. What goes on in these interactions is thinking,

thinking involving two heads. Children cannot possibly think through many problems without help, but with adult assistance they make fine progress. Years of participating in such interactions lead to internalization by children of the types of actions once carried out between children and adults. Vygotsky summarized this developmental progression as follows:

> Any function in the child's cultural development appears twice, or on two planes. First, it appears on the social plane, and then on the psychological plane. . . . Social relations or relations among people genetically underlie all higher functions and their relationships. . . . In their private sphere, human beings retain the functions of social interactions. (Vygotsky, 1981, pp. 163–164)

According to this perspective, cognitive development moves forward largely because the child is in a world that provides aid when the child needs it and can benefit from it. There are many things that 2-year-olds can do for themselves, and the responsive social world lets children do them independently. For example, a parent may allow a child to pick out a T-shirt to wear, especially when the child insists, "I can do it myself." There are other things that 2-year-olds could never do, no matter how much help they were given. The responsive social environment does not encourage children to do these sorts of things and, in fact, often discourages their attempts at overly difficult tasks. For example, a parent would physically remove a toddler who insists on trying to drive from the driver's seat of a car.

The responsive social world provides assistance on tasks that are within, what Vygotsky called the **zone of proximal development.** Tasks in the zone of proximal development are ones that children cannot accomplish independently but can accomplish with assistance (see Figure 8.1). Children learn how to perform tasks within their zone through interactions with responsive and more competent others who provide hints, prompts, and assistance to them on an as-needed basis. These hints and prompts encourage children to process a task appropriately, until they eventually can perform the task without assistance. For example, a kindergartner can write a story with help from a parent. This help may include the parent's printing out the story line as the kindergartner dictates it and showing the kindergartner where to copy the words onto the appropriate pages. Thus, the task of writing a story is within the kindergartner's zone of proximal development.

A concept based on the principles of Vygotsky's theory is scaffolding

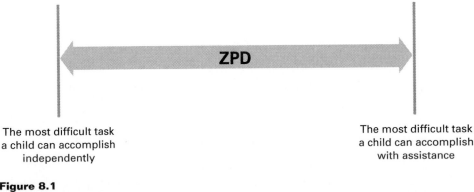

The most difficult task
a child can accomplish
independently

The most difficult task
a child can accomplish
with assistance

Figure 8.1
Zone of proximal development.

This child could not put this model airplane together without the help of the adult. The adult is working with the child within the child's zone of proximal development, since this task is one the child can accomplish with a little assistance.

(S. S. Wood, Bruner, & Ross, 1976), which is discussed in Chapter 1. Builders use a scaffold to erect a building, gradually removing it as the building becomes self-supporting. Likewise, adults or older children who are helping younger children with a task should gradually remove their prompts and hints. They should provide enough support and assistance so that the child does not fail but eventually remove the support as the child is capable of performing independently.

One example of scaffolded instruction is found in Reading Recovery (see also Chapter 11), which is a method for remediating the reading of elementary school children who are experiencing reading difficulties. A Reading Recovery teacher permits children to do as much as they can independently and only intervenes with hints and supports to lead children to process effectively when they stumble (Clay & Cazden, 1990). Thus, children in Reading Recovery work within their zones of proximal development. The following dialogue (Clay & Cazden, 1990, p. 214, adapted) illustrates how an adult tutor scaffolded the instruction of a tutee, Larry:

> **Larry:** The great big enormous turnip. Once an old man planted a turnip.
> **Teacher:** Good.
> **Larry:** He said grow, grow little turnip, grow . . . (pauses at the next word)
> **Teacher:** How does that word start? Can I help you start it off? How does it start? s_____ He tells it to grow sw____ sweet.
> **Larry:** Grow little turnip, grow s_____.
> **Teacher:** How else does he want it to grow? He wants it to grow sweet, and he wants it to grow str_____.

Larry: Strong.
Teacher: Good boy, that's lovely. Grow strong.
Larry: And the turnip grew up sweet and strong and . . .
Teacher: What's the other word that begins with *e*? Enor_____.
Larry: Enormous.
Teacher: Good.

And so it goes. The teacher continues to provide hints and support as needed. In this case, the hints encouraged the student to apply "word attack" skills to decode words. The teacher is scaffolding this instruction by providing input only when the child stumbles, never when the child can proceed on his own. During Reading Recovery, children reread a text until they are 90 percent successful in decoding. Less teacher input occurs on each rereading. The teacher supports independent functioning in the children by not intervening. Once a child can read a text at the 90 percent level, another text is selected, one that is within the child's zone of proximal development. The child will not be able to read this text fluently without support but can get through the text if provided hints and prompts.

Bakhtin's Theory

When you make a presentation in one of your classes, your speech is very different from what it is when you speak to your friends. Your voice is decidedly less casual.

Focus on Research

Children's Use of Private Speech

Berk (1986) observed first and third graders working on math seat work in the naturalistic setting of their own classrooms. She was interested in exploring the significance of thoughts spoken out loud, called **private speech,** to task performance. As predicted by Vygotskian theory, Berk noted developmental differences in the students' use of private speech for self-guidance. Private speech was more common in younger students, whereas the older students were more likely to have internalized their private speech in inner speech.

The focus of the private speech also varied with development. The speech changed from having task-irrelevant, self-stimulating content to task-relevant content that was, for example, descriptive or self-guiding. The final transformation was to barely audible task-relevant speech that was only discernible through inaudible muttering or lip movement. The type of private speech was related to performance, in that task-relevant private speech predicted greater attentional focus and fewer extraneous behaviors.

Berk also found that the relationship of private speech to intelligence shifted with age. The total amount of private speech was positively related to intelligence for the first graders ($r = 0.33$) but was negatively related to intelligence for the third graders ($r = -0.49$).

Think back to the discussion of correlation coefficients in Chapter 1. What do these correlation coefficients of 0.33 and −0.49 mean? When a correlation is positive, it means that high values on one variable (in this case, private speech) are associated with high values on another variable (in this case, intelligence test scores). Thus, in the first grade, high levels of private speech were associated with high intelligence test scores. When a correlation is negative, it means that high values on one variable (in this case, private speech) are associated with low values on another variable (in this case, intelligence test scores). Thus, in the third grade, high levels of private speech were associated with low intelligence test scores. The more intelligent third graders had internalized their private speech.

Your speech is probably still different on other occasions, such as when you speak to your parents. People typically use different **social languages** in different situations. They ventriloquate to use Bakhtin's (1981) term or are multivoiced to use Wertsch's (1991) vernacular.

M. M. Bakhtin, a Russian contemporary of Vygotsky, also emphasized the importance of culture on cognitive development and intellectual functioning (Wertsch, 1991). Bakhtin's view was that the voices we have show up in our expressions of ideas. Nothing we say or write is solely our own, but rather it reflects internalized social understandings. The speech of others shapes our ideas.

Whenever someone produces an utterance, the most obvious question from Bakhtin's perspective is "Who is doing the talking?" (Wertsch, 1991). The answer is always one's own voice and at least one other voice. Think back to the presentation of Skinner's theory in Chapter 7. Who is doing the talking? We are, but so are the many people who taught us Skinnerian theory, and, of course, Skinner's voice is also in the text.

The social voices we have internalized determine in part what we say and what we think. If you spend time in the culture of baseball, you will come to think on some occasions as baseball players do. If you spend some time in the culture of police officers, sometimes your thought will reflect the predominant thought patterns of police officers. If you live in a Quaker community, you may think as a Quaker does much of the time. If you spend time in a Quaker community, then a Catholic community, and then a Jewish community, your thought will reflect all three perspectives. Moreover, sometimes when you speak, you will speak as a Quaker would, sometimes as a Catholic would, and sometimes as a Jew would. **Multivoicedness** is inevitable, and the social environment surrounding a person colors consciousness and thought (Wertsch & Minick, 1990).

Apprenticeship

According to Vygotsky and Bakhtin, cultural factors have a much greater impact on mental functioning than other factors. Educators who adopt this view believe that a form of instruction that emphasizes social interactions between an apprentice student and an expert is superior to other instructional approaches. Apprentice carpenters learn to build houses by working with experienced builders. Airline captains learn how to fly planes from years of experience flying as first officers working with captains. Medical residencies are really apprenticeships in many ways. They are opportunities for young physicians to learn through direct contact with the senior physicians.

Barbara Rogoff (1990) argued that apprenticeship occurs in many cultures and may be a universal of human life. She believes it is the principal means for adults to pass on knowledge to children about the intellectual tools valuable in the culture, a truly Vygotskian idea. Typically, these tools are complex enough that years of apprenticeship are necessary. There are societies in which apprenticeships provide education in agriculture, hunting, fishing, weaving, and healing. Rogoff contends that there is great similarity across various types of apprenticeships.

During an apprenticeship, the master provides bridges from what is known by the apprentice to the unknown. The master translates the task into terms the apprentice can understand, and the master makes demands on the apprentice that the apprentice can meet. As the apprentice learns, the master gradually increases

Your "voice" reflects the many influences in your life.

the demands. Thus, there is guided participation of the apprentice, with the master providing the guidance. Gradually, the master transfers responsibility. Scaffolding is the key process here, with the master providing as much support as the apprentice needs to function until support is entirely withdrawn because the student can do it alone.

What do apprentices do (Collins, Brown, & Newman, 1989; Rogoff, 1990)? Apprentices *observe*. They receive *coaching* from their mentors. Apprentices *practice* the tasks required in the profession while being coached by their mentors. Good mentors scaffold their input, providing assistance as it is needed—not so much that the apprentices become dependent on it and not so little that they falter (S. S. Wood, Bruner, & Ross, 1976). Just as the scaffold of a building is removed as the building becomes freestanding, so it is with the mentor's scaffolding, with less and less of it provided as the apprentice is able to go it alone.

Apprenticeship results in the production of new members of the culture who possess important skills and who talk and think differently—not because they are

This glassblower is learning his craft through apprenticeship to a master.

acting, but because they have really changed (Lave & Wenger, 1991). For example, members of Alcoholics Anonymous learn how to talk as a member of that community (Jordan, 1989). Young repairers learn war stories that serve to change their thinking about how to do particular repairs (Orr, 1990). An important part of any apprenticeship is learning to talk as the master does, which leads to thinking in ways consistent with the community the apprentice is entering, a thoroughly Bakhtinian idea.

Given how common apprenticeship experiences are in professional training, it is surprising that educational researchers have only recently tried to understand the nature of learning in such situations. An important idea emerging from this research is that of **situated knowledge** or **situated cognition** (Brown et al., 1989), introduced in Chapter 3. When students learn how to read, write, and solve problems in school, their understandings of reading, writing, and problem solving are largely tied to school environments. This is a problem because school environments are very different from the places where the skills learned in school are put into practice. A real challenge is to make the school environment sufficiently like the real world so that the skills learned there are tied to important real-life situations. Many educators believe school should be reconstructed so students have the opportunity to serve as apprentices to people doing real reading of real books, doing real writing for real purposes, and doing real solving of real problems.

The apprenticeship model also requires that teachers be real readers, writers, mathematicians, scientists, and social scientists rather than people who just talk about reading, writing, mathematics, science, and social science. Some teachers are real readers and can let their students know about real reading. These teachers let their students know how excited they are about reading particular authors. They also provide their students with many insider hints about how to get the most out of books. Other teachers bring real writing to the classroom. They teach writing by having everyone write a lot, including the teacher. The best writing teachers identify themselves as writers. Since real writers publish, students also publish class books. The publishing activity is sometimes tied to introducing students to computers via word processing.

Successful teacher-student apprenticeships are hard work, and teachers must be motivated to do it. If teachers are going to be willing to work that hard, they have to care about their students. According to Noddings (1984), caring is at the center of teacher-student apprenticeships, and that this can be a wonderful and fulfilling situation for the teacher:

> The teacher works with the student. He becomes her apprentice and gradually assumes greater responsibility in the tasks they undertake. This working together, which produces both joy in the relation and increasing competence in the cared-for . . . needs the cooperative guidance of a fully caring adult. . . . The caring teacher . . . has two major tasks: to stretch the student's world by presenting an effective selection of that world with which she is in contact, and to work cooperatively with the student in his struggle toward competence in that world. (pp. 177–178)

Noddings also recognizes that teaching caring for students is difficult to foster. She is aware of the current classroom realities—many students, limited time, and numerous objectives to meet. However, she urges teachers to give up some of their control and to foster trust between them and their students. She argues that true dialogue promotes deep contact with the ideas presented in the curriculum and stimulates the development of an active thinker who is willing to take intellectual risks.

Apprenticeship in the Classroom. Is it sensible to think about teaching elementary school students within an apprentice relationship? Mark Lepper and his colleagues (Lepper, Aspinwall, Mumme, & Chabey, 1990) observed six expert tutors of elementary arithmetic as they worked with individual students in grades 2 through 5. What did the expert tutors do? They consistently let their students know that although the task they were trying was difficult, the students had the ability to succeed. There is a good reason for this. If students failed, it would be easy for them to blame their failure on the difficulty of the task. The attribution to task difficulty should not discourage efforts on future tasks (Weiner, 1979, see also Chapter 2). The tutors also fostered attributions that encourage future efforts. Thus, after a student successfully completed a problem, a tutor might say, "I guess we'll have to try to find an even harder one for you next time." This is a subtle way of making the point that even though the last problem was hard, the student succeeded on it.

There were many more subtleties in the tutors' interactions with their students. There was little overt corrective feedback and little in the way of overt diagnoses about what the student was doing wrong. Indeed, most of the time the tutors did not label the errors. There was little direct help, and the tutors rarely gave students the answers to the problems. When students made errors or were having difficulties, the tutors provided hints of three sorts: (1) questions or remarks implying that the previous move was an incorrect one; (2) suggestions, often in the form of questions, about a potential direction the student might take with the problem; and (3) hints, often in the form of questions, about the part of the problem the student might want to think about.

When the students were in trouble, these tutors asked them questions. For example, when a student added 36 and 36 and came up with 126, the tutor inquired, "Now how did you get that *6*?" When this did not work, hints in the form of questions became increasingly specific: "Which column do we start in? Where is the ones column?" Good tutors know when and where to provide hints, prompts, explanations, and modeling. They realize that this assistance is contingent on the need of the student.

● "What Do I Do on Monday Morning?"

Components of Apprenticeship

Collins, Brown, and Newman (1989) summarized the following components of apprenticeship:

- *Modeling.* Masters show their apprentices how to do tasks that are important, and they make their actions obvious to ensure that the apprentice sees the actions and hears a rationale for why the actions were taken.
- *Coaching.* Masters watch students attempt a task, and they offer hints, feedback, and guidance. As they coach, they sometimes offer additional modeling or explanation.
- *Scaffolding.* Masters offer support, guidance, and reminders. They do not offer too much support, however, and they pull away as their apprentices learn to function independently. Scaffolding requires experts to determine both when the apprentice needs help and how appropriate redirection should be offered. Experts must understand the many different types of errors that apprentices can make and know how to deal with such errors.
- *Articulation.* Articulation is a form of testing. Masters require their apprentices to explain what they are doing. Thus, an expert math teacher may ask students how they solved a problem and why they picked one particular solution method over others.
- *Reflection.* Masters encourage apprentices to compare their work with that of others, including the master and other apprentices (Schön, 1983, 1987). For example, young teachers often watch videotapes of themselves teaching and reflect on their work, perhaps discussing their teaching actions with more expert teachers or fellow apprentice teachers.
- *Exploration.* Apprentices cannot be mere copies of their mentors. The apprenticeship relationship permits safe exploration. Good mentors teach their apprentices how to explore, and they encourage them to do so.

Reciprocal Teaching

Reciprocal teaching is a form of instruction that is often showcased as being consistent with Vygotskian principles (A. L. Brown & Palincsar, 1989; Palincsar & Brown, 1984). It involves instruction of comprehension strategies in the context of a reading group. Students learn to make predictions when reading, to question themselves about the text, to seek clarification when confused, and to summarize content. The adult teacher initially explains and models these strategies for students, but very quickly students are leading the group. One student is assigned the role of group leader. The group leader supervises the groups' generation of predictions, questions, and summaries during reading. The group leader also solicits points that need to be clarified and either provides clarifications or elicits them from other group members. The group's interactions are cooperative. The teacher provides support on an as-needed basis, that is, scaffolded instruction.

During reciprocal teaching, the students experience multiple models of cognitive processing; that is, the teacher models and explains. Peers in the group are also continuously modeling reasoning about text as part of group participation. The discussions permit students to air their various points and require them to justify their claims. These discussions also allow students to review and comment about the strategies as well as the content they are learning. The teacher is progressively less involved as the students gain competence. The assumption is that by participating in the group, students will eventually internalize use of the strategies encouraged as part of reciprocal teaching. This is consistent with the Vygotskian perspective that individual cognitive development develops from participation in social groups.

Dialogue from a sample lesson should help clarify what occurs during a reciprocal teaching reading group. The dialogue that follows is from a discussion by a group of low-achieving middle school students after 13 days of experience with the method (A. L. Brown & Palincsar, 1989). The students had just read the following brief text:

> In the United States salt is produced by three basic methods: solar (sun) evaporation, mining, and artificial heat evaporation. For salt to be extracted by solar evaporation, the weather must be hot and dry. Thus, solar salt is harvested in the tropic-like areas along our southern ocean coasts and at Great Salt Lake.

Student Leader (Student C): Name three different basic methods of how salt is produced.
Student A: Evaporation, mining, evaporation . . . artificial heat evaporation.
Student Leader C: Correct, very good. My summary on this paragraph is about ways that salt is produced.
Teacher: Very good. Could you select the next teacher. (Student C does so, selecting Student L, with the reading continuing.)

> The second oldest form of salt production is mining. Unlike early methods that made the work extremely dangerous and difficult, today's methods use special machinery, and salt mining is easier and safer. The old expression "back to the salt mine" no longer applies.

Student Leader (Student L): Name two words that often describe mining salt in the old days.
Student K: Back to the salt mines?
Student Leader L: No. Angela?
Student A: Dangerous and difficult.
Student Leader L: Correct. This paragraph is about comparing the old mining of salt and today's mining of salt.
Teacher: Beautiful!
Student Leader L: I have a prediction to make.
Teacher: Good.
Student Leader L: I think it might tell when salt was first discovered, well, it might tell what salt is made of and how it's made.
Teacher: OK. Can we have another teacher?

Table salt is made by the third method—artificial evaporation. Pumping water into an underground salt bed dissolves the salt to make a brine that is brought to the surface. After purification at high temperatures, the salt is ready for our tables.

Student Leader K: After purification at high temperatures the salt is ready for what?
Student C: Our tables.
Student Leader K: That's correct. To summarize: After its purification, the salt is put on our tables.
Teacher: That was a fine job, Ken, and I appreciate all the work, but I think there might be something else to add to our summary. There is more important information that I think we need to include. This paragraph is mostly about what?
Student A: The third method of evaporation.
Student B: It mainly tells about pumping water from an underground salt bed that dissolves the salt to make a brine that is brought to the surface.
Teacher: Angela hit it right on the money. The paragraph is mostly about the method of artificial evaporation and then everything else in the paragraph is telling us about the process. OK. Next teacher. . . . (pp. 421–422)

In this lesson, all students were participating, and there was an obvious structure to the participation. Even so, after 13 days of reciprocal teaching, there were no requests for clarification, although some of the students were having trouble understanding the text. They did not monitor when they understood and when they did not. In addition, the questions generated by the student leaders were all literal questions, requiring only low-level responses. Such questions do not stimulate thinking, either to formulate the question or to answer it, beyond the surface structure of the text. In addition, there was little scaffolding of the processing by the teacher. The teacher primarily monitored whether the students were understanding the passage and provided clarification of the content as needed. Finally, because reciprocal teaching emphasizes the teacher's fading support, there were often long pauses in lessons, with students fumbling because the teacher was uncertain whether to enter into the conversation and provide input.

Even with these drawbacks, however, there is research evidence to support reciprocal teaching. Rosenshine and Meister (1994) reviewed studies to compare reciprocal teaching with other forms of instruction. Most of these interventions were brief, a little more than 1 to 6 weeks of instruction, but the studies varied in other ways. First, some studies involved only reciprocal teaching in that the children learned to dialogue as just described and the comprehension strategies were introduced during the dialogue. In other studies, students received explicit instruction on how to execute the comprehension strategies before they began reciprocal teaching. Second, some investigations focused on students who had reading problems; other studies involved students who had no decoding difficulties but who experienced comprehension problems; still others involved students of all abilities. Finally, some studies included standardized tests; some used experimenter-generated tests, which typically tapped the processes encouraged by the four strategies; and some included both types of measures.

In general, the effects of reciprocal teaching were greater when explicit teaching of the comprehension strategies occurred before participation in the study. Although the benefits of reciprocal teaching were very modest on standardized tests (effect size of 0.32; see Chapter 1), the effects of reciprocal teaching were quite striking on the experimenter-constructed measures tapping the processes stimulated by the strategies (effect size of 0.88; see Chapter 1). Finally, students of various ages and abilities benefited similarly from reciprocal teaching.

If a reciprocal teaching group is doing well, the adult teacher's presence should hardly be noticeable. Student control of the interactions in the group is an important part of the eventual internalization by the students of the strategies being taught. In addition, the students construct content knowledge for themselves in the group. The knowledge they construct from making predictions, generating questions, seeking clarifications when confused, and summarizing text is more meaningful to them than if the teacher intervenes and provides information about the text.

Research Validating Sociocultural Positions

Are the instructional models derived from sociocultural theories generally observed? Do adults provide children with instruction for behaviors that are in their zone of proximal development? Do adults assume the more demanding roles in such interactions in order to reduce the workload for the child? Do adults eventually cede control of tasks to their students?

On the positive side of the ledger, consistent with Vygotsky's ideas, adults do regularly provide instruction to children in a way that is supportive but not overly so (W. Gardner & Rogoff, 1982). Adults also reduce the workload for children. For example, academic tutors provide more support to younger students, such as 7-year-olds, than to older, 11-year-olds (Ludeke & Hartup, 1983). When expert weavers teach their craft, they intervene more with younger and less experienced learners (Greenfield, 1984). In addition, adults are more likely to intervene when children are having trouble with a task than at other times (Greenfield, 1984; McNamee, 1979). Also, adults control an instructional situation less as a student becomes more and more capable of doing a task independently (Childs & Greenfield, 1980; Wertsch, 1979). Thus, there is support for the Vygotskian perspective, at least when observing naturally occurring adult-child tutoring.

Supporters of Vygotskian theory, however, have made very strong claims about the superiority of scaffolding compared to other forms of instruction. Jeanne D. Day and her colleagues (1983; Day, Cordon, & Kerwin, 1989; Kerwin & Day, 1985) have examined the research supporting sociocultural instructional recommendations and believe there is a negative side of the ledger. Day has not found that children who receive scaffolded instruction from a parent learn any faster than children who receive instruction from a parent who is less attentive to the child's competence and pattern of difficulties. Summarizing across studies, Day suggests that children probably receive a mix of different types of instruction. Some is scaffolded; some is not. This is not particularly surprising, since scaffolding is extremely time-consuming and difficult to do (Day, Cordon, Kerwin, 1989).

Gelman, Massey, and McManus (1991) also recognized limits to the adult scaffolding in their study of the types of instruction that parents provide to their children during museum visits. There were several different approaches to parent-child teaching in museum settings besides scaffolding. First, the types of interactions between parents and children varied with the type of exhibit. For example, in an interactive grocery store exhibit, parents prompted, requested, and ordered their children to do things. In this setting the adults provided support for their children, although there was little indication that the parents adjusted the support according to the level of competence of the child. In contrast, even though an exhibit intended to develop number skills was designed as a parent-child interactive activity, adults rarely helped their children with this exhibit. Gelman and her colleagues (1991) speculated that the adults may have felt more competent to help their children in the more familiar grocery setting than in a math exhibit, since math is an area in which many adults do not have statable knowledge of many basic concepts. Finally, even when Gelman and her colleagues themselves designed an exhibit intended to stimulate experimentation, they observed little scaffolded interaction between parents and children.

In summary, while many demonstrations of adult-child apprenticeships exist (Rogoff, 1990), parent-child and teacher-child scaffolding is anything but universal. Moreover, although there are effective forms of instruction involving scaffolding, it has not yet been demonstrated that scaffolding is far superior to other forms of instruction.

■ Building Your Expertise

The Uniqueness of Sociocultural Ideas

Some of the most important sociocultural ideas about instruction are not conceptually unique. For example, scaffolding resembles what the behaviorists call fading (see Chapter 7). Fading involves provision of reinforcement and modeling as needed, with both reinforcement and modeling withdrawn as the learner becomes more adept. With scaffolding, what is withdrawn is modeling, hints, and prompts, some of which arguably serve as feedback that functions as reinforcement.

Another example is the concept of the zone of proximal development. Vygotskians believe instruction will be most successful if it aims at acquisitions that are in the zone of proximal development but just a bit beyond where the learner now is. Concepts and behaviors in the zone are in their formation stage, and thus additional instructional input aimed at zone items will be more successful than instruction aimed at concepts and behaviors that are beyond the zone. This principle of teaching just beyond the current competency of the student is also supported by Piaget's ideas about disequilibrium and cognitive conflict (see Chapter 7).

Instructional Conversations

Conversation is probably the most common form of human interaction both inside and outside of classrooms. What is the nature of classroom conversations?

Typical School Conversations: Initiate-Response-Evaluation Cycles

Conversations structured such as the following occur every day in school:

> **Teacher:** Where is the Tomb of the Unknown Soldier? (Initiation)
> **Student 1:** In Arlington Cemetery? (Response)
> **Teacher:** That's right. (Evaluation) And what might you see at that tomb? (Initiation)
> **Student 1:** There's always a guard of honor there. (Response)
> **Teacher:** Yes. (Evaluation) Do you remember what is interesting about this guard? (Initiation)

Student 1: Uh, uh, no. (Failed response)
Teacher: Someone else? (Implied evaluation, initiation)
Student 2: He's a member of the Old Guard. Really hard to get into the Old Guard. (Response)
Teacher: Correct. What else is at Arlington Cemetery? (Initiation)
Student 1: President Kennedy's grave. (Response)
Teacher: Anything else? (Implied acceptance, initiation)
Student 1: President Kennedy's brother's grave. It's over the hill a little bit down from the turning flame. (Response)
Teacher: Eternal flame. (Implied evaluation) Yes, near President Kennedy's grave. (Evaluation)

The teacher initiates an interaction, often with a question; the student responds; and the teacher evaluates the response before making another initiation. Teachers and students know how to interact with each other in this way. For example, teachers send clear nonverbal signals to students that a sequence of questioning is about to begin and they expect student responses (Cazden, 1988). Cazden sees such interactions as part of classroom management. If students are familiar with initiation-response-evaluation (IRE) cycles, they can direct their attention to the content of the academic conversation. Moreover, teachers can conduct lessons in an orderly fashion and make certain that the points they consider important are covered.

There are negatives aspects of IRE cycles, however (Cazden, 1988). For example, questioning is often low-level, filled with literal, factual questions. In addition, because only one student can be active at a time, this is a passive approach to learning for many students (Bowers & Flinders, 1990). Finally, if the goal is for students to learn to control their thinking, IRE cycles are particularly unattractive since they are almost completely teacher controlled. The students are powerless to do anything except answer questions they had no part in formulating (Bowers & Flinders, 1990). Students get the message that education is receiving knowledge from an authority rather than working with knowledge to understand it in ways that are personally meaningful and that create new knowledge.

True Dialogues in School

In natural conversations, there are evolving meanings and real attempts to inform and persuade as participants try to understand what is going on. Consider the following conversation between two high school students about an upcoming school dance:

Shawn: Um . . . Are you going to the school dance? (From this Nicole infers that Shawn may be working up to asking her to go with him. She knows that he is a little shy.)
Nicole: I don't know. . . . Alex just asked me to go but . . . I'm not sure. (From this Shawn infers that Nicole doesn't really want to go with Alex and is waiting for someone else to ask her.)
Shawn: Is Maria going? (Change of topic while Shawn gathers up the courage to ask Nicole.)
Nicole: Yes, she is going with Luis. She wants to know whether I want to double with them. . . . I have to let her know soon whether I'm going. (Nicole brings the conversation back to the issue and lets Shawn know that she is not going to be available for long.)

Shawn: I like Maria and Luis. Do you want to go to the dance together? (Shawn picks up the hint but is vague in his invitation.)
Nicole: Are you asking me to be your date? (Nicole wants a real invitation from Shawn.)
Shawn: Yes, will you go with me?

A lot is going on here! Each of these two people makes inferences based on prior knowledge, going well beyond the surface level of the conversation, and each leaves the conversation with more knowledge than is apparent from the surface comments in the conversation. People learn a lot in conversations.

Educators believe that conversations more natural than IRE cycles might promote learning in school. There are four important structural differences, however, between "natural" classroom conversations and other types of natural conversations (Cazden, 1988). First, classroom conversations typically involve more people. Second, although students and teachers often know each other well, many of the relationships in the group are not close. Third, one of the players in the classroom conversation, the teacher, is often someone who is much more knowledgeable and has the resources to exert control. Fourth, the topic of discussion shifts within narrower boundaries in instructional conversations. So, if the discussion of the day is about dinosaurs, it stays on dinosaurs rather than switching to how the local baseball team is doing. Natural conversations are much more free-ranging, jumping from topic to topic.

An Example of a Naturalistic Academic Conversation. Students and teachers can create conversations in which the teacher is much less in control, with the comments of students stimulating other students to participate in real interactions. Consider this example of conversation generated as kindergarten students and a teacher discuss the story, "Tico and the Golden Wings" by Leo Lionni:

Teacher: I don't think it's fair that Tico has to give up his golden wings.
Lisa: It is fair. See, he was nicer when he didn't have any wings. They didn't like him when he had gold.
Wally: He thinks he's better if he has golden wings.
Eddie: He is better.
Jill: But he's not supposed to be better. The wishing bird was wrong to give him those wings.
Deanna: She has to give him his wish. He's the one who shouldn't have asked for golden wings.
Wally: He could put black wings on top of the golden wings and try to trick them.
Deanna: They'd sneak up and see the gold. He should give every bird one golden feather and keep one for himself.
Teacher: Why can't he decide for himself what kind of wings he wants?
Wally: He has to decide to have black wings. (Cazden, 1988, p. 55, from a lesson taught in Vivian Paley's kindergarten class)

What a difference from IRE cycles! The students did not raise their hands to participate. The teacher did not evaluate their responses and decide who would next get a turn to answer a question. Instead these children applied their prior knowledge to this story and interpreted it. There were many elaborations of student knowledge and inferences in this few minutes of conversation. It is a good bet that the individual students reading alone would not have come up with many of the interpretations that emerged during the discussion and a certain bet that no one reader would have thought of all the counterarguments.

The Distributed Nature of Cognition in Naturalistic Classroom Conversations. Naturalistic instructional conversations are excellent examples of **distributed cognition.** That is, the cognition—the thinking—that goes on here is not a product of one student but a product of *several students in interaction* with one another (Hutchins, 1991). Powerful interpretations and understandings will likely emerge from students putting their heads together. There are a couple of reasons for this. First, different students have different prior knowledge. Second, different students attend to different aspects of the information. As the talk in the group proceeds, the students make connections. For example, something Carmen says connects with knowledge activated in Malcolm who in turn responds. Malcolm may combine some of what he knows with something Carmen said that he did not know before to produce a new inference. This inference might trigger something in Tommy, and so it goes.

What does the teacher do in all of this? The teacher provides conversational starters and perhaps nudges the group one way or another with questions, as the kindergarten teacher did in the example. A powerful figure in a group can do much to shape the group's opinion (Hutchins, 1991). One of the challenges for the teacher is to shape the group's opinion enough to get some important messages across to students but not so much as to stifle constructive and appropriate interpretations. This may be difficult for many teachers, especially those accustomed to IRE cycles in which they are in control of what happens in the group as well as the information that will receive positive evaluation. Choosing to conduct real dialogues means giving up some of what has been a teacher's traditional power.

Effects of Naturalistic Academic Conversations on Individual Students. A group of students interacting might understand a problem at a high level as a group. Hatano and Inagaki (1991) wondered whether the processing carried out by the group would transform the thinking of the individuals in the group. That is, would the students internalize some of the processes experienced in the group? Hatano and Inagaki explored an instructional procedure called hypothesis-experiment-instruction (Itakura, 1967). In this method, students answer a question that has several alternative responses. Each of the students selects an answer, followed by a show of hands to see how the other members of the group think. The students then explain and discuss their choices, followed by another opportunity for each student to select the correct answer. Students then can test the alternatives by observing an experiment about the problem posed or by reading a passage about the problem. Here is how one teacher began such a sequence:

> Mr. Shoji started the lesson with a question: "Suppose that you have a clay ball on one end of a spring. You hold the other end of the spring and put half of the clay ball in water. Will the spring (a) become shorter, (b) become longer, or (c) retain its length?" (Hatano & Inagaki, 1991, p. 337, based on an example from Inagaki, 1981)

Before the discussion, 12 students in the group selected option (a), 8 chose option (b), and 14 favored option (c). After a discussion and a second attempt at the problem, 21 students selected the correct alternative, option (a). Clearly, the arguments during discussion influenced individual understanding of the students, who shifted to the correct response. Consider the following arguments students made in support of the correct response, option (a):

[To a student who had selected (c)]: Your opinion is strange to me. You said, "The weight of the clay will not change because it is only half immersed in water." But you know, when a person's head is above the water, his weight is lighter in water. I don't agree with the idea that the clay ball is as heavy in water as in air. I think that water has the power to make things float. If the clay is a very small lump, I think the water can make it float. (Hatano & Inagaki, 1991, p. 338, based on an example from Inagaki, 1981)

Thus, there was a shift in individual students' reasoning as a result of participation in group discussions. Can these students explain why they changed their opinions? In Inagaki and Hatano (1989), fifth graders read a passage about animal characteristics and lifestyles. Then the students responded to a multiple-choice problem about the characteristics of a monkey, such as the following:

Do the thumbs of monkeys' forefeet oppose the other "fingers" (like in human hands) or extend in parallel to other "fingers" (like in human feet)? How about the thumbs of their hind feet?: (a) the thumbs are never opposing; (b) the thumbs are opposing only in the forefeet; or (c) the thumbs are opposing in both the fore and hind feet [the correct response]. (pp. 341–342)

The students in a group discussion condition first made a choice individually, followed by group discussion, followed by a second opportunity to respond to the problem. The students then read a passage that provided the correct answer but did not provide an explanation about why the answer was correct. Students in the control condition made an initial choice of an answer and then read the passage containing the answer.

Students in the group discussion condition provided more complex defenses of their answers than control students. Moreover, those students who had talked more during the discussion provided more detailed answers than students who had talked less. In short, participating in the group discussions promoted learning by the individual participants in the group.

Other researchers have also found that when students in groups construct explanations about information they are learning, their acquisition and understanding of information is more certain. For example, N. M. Webb (1989) conducted several studies in which students solved problems as a group. The students who explained in the groups learned more (as determined by measures of individual achievement) than students who were content to listen. Although there are alternative explanations for this effect (e.g., more able students might be more likely to lead group discussions), such alternative explanations do not apply to experiments conducted by Alison King (1990) and her colleagues.

In King's research, students talked in groups about content to be learned. In some conditions, students learned how to generate thought-provoking questions by using question frames with open slots such as the following:

How would you use _____ to _____?

What is a new example of _____?

Explain why _____.

How does _____ affect _____?

Do you agree or disagree with this statement?

These question frames stimulated discussions with more interaction and genera-tion of new ideas than unstructured discussion of content. In addition, the students learned more when they used the question frames to structure discussion.

In summary, group discussions can result in the generation of ideas related to the content that would not have occurred to individual group members working alone. Students learn the content better through group interaction, particularly if the situation is structured so each group member participates (Hatano & Inagaki, 1991; King, 1989).

Factors Promoting Effective Academic Discussions

Haroutunian-Gordon (1991) suggested factors that can inhibit and promote pro-ductive classroom conversations. One way to stifle interaction is for the teacher to believe there are certain issues, perspectives, or opinions that must emerge during the discussion. Haroutunian-Gordon refers to conversations in which the teacher tries too hard to control the discussion as "phony" conversations. Although it is appropriate for teachers to steer conversations gently so students stay on topic, interpretive discussions at their best probably involve issues that the students value and ideas that the students find intriguing. Students are more likely to per-ceive discussions around such issues as "genuine" discussions (Haroutunian-Gordon, 1991).

Often, a real tension develops. Interpretations that the teacher feels are impor-tant do not get out on the floor, and others that the teacher might consider to be misinterpretations are embraced by the group. Consider a discussion between Haroutunian-Gordon and Ms. Spring about the progress of a discussion group they are "leading" on Shakespeare's *Romeo and Juliet:*

> **S:** What is to be done if the students leave this classroom with an erroneous vision of the play and Shakespeare's message? What have they learned in such a class?
> **H-G:** Well, one thing we can say is that they have begun to do the job that they are sup-posed to do when reading the play, right? They have begun to construct a story that allows them to connect the events in the play to one another in a meaningful way. That means they will remember those events, that the story they use to connect them will allow them to bring the events up so as to, perhaps at some point, connect them to their lives.
> **S:** Yes, but that story about Benvolio was all wrong . . .
> **H-G:** Wrong? By what criteria? It is not your story . . .
> **S:** It is not Shakespeare's story!
> **H-G:** Well perhaps not, I agree. But is yours Shakespeare's story?
> **S:** Look, I don't claim to have any corner on his views. What I do know is that those two girls have made an interpretation of Benvolio that cannot really stand up to the text in its entirety.
> **H-G:** You may well be right about that. But don't they now have a view to modify at least? And won't there be another class tomorrow?
> **S:** Yes, but the question is, what should I do then? I can't tell them the truth, as we said a long time ago. They won't hear it. And they won't entertain conflicting evidence—that much we have seen. They even resist the questions I ask to get them to rethink their per-spectives.
> **H-G:** Maybe you ought to forget about Edna and Abby. Maybe things will straighten out.

S: Maybe. But what they need is a new perspective on Benvolio, another way of looking at him. (Haroutunian-Gordon, 1991, pp. 162–163)

Many interesting points emerge in this conversation. Haroutunian-Gordon clearly felt the students were getting a lot from the class discussions by learning to interpret and think critically about plays. Discussions have high potential for increasing students' understanding. Interpretive class discussions, however, will be difficult for teachers if they fail to accept that there are alternative interpretations and that their own interpretations may be inadequate. Once such discussions get going, many students will find it difficult to accept standard interpretations, since they will have discovered alternative ways of looking at the content.

Another important factor in classroom conversations is that because of years of participating in IRE cycles it takes a while for a group of students to be able to engage in interpretive discussion (Haroutunian-Gordon, 1991). In addition, it may take a while for students to make really interesting inferences about new content. Thus, it was several sessions before the students in Ms. Spring's and Haroutunian-Gordon's *Romeo and Juliet* discussion group were making sophisticated comments about the play, ones reflecting deep understanding about the characters and their situation.

Organizational psychologists, who study how committees of people function and how productive collaborations proceed, have described the characteristics of successful interpretive discussions (Schrage, 1990). The group must foster cooperation, rather than competition. Discussion is fruitful when members can take risks and when there are possible alternatives instead of one correct answer. Discussion is not for deciding who has the best idea but for the group to take ideas that are on the floor and to pick and choose strengths and weaknesses until a consensual point of view begins to emerge. Successful discussion groups value candor more than politeness. Such candor is possible because there is trust, trust that nonsupportive comments are not personal insults but simply directed at the ideas under consideration. These are academic arguments rather than personal disputes.

Finally, as obvious as it may seem, some physical environments are more conducive to collaborative dialogue than others. Productive classroom discussions take place around a table or with students in a circle. This setup makes it easy to watch and listen to the speaker who has the floor as well as to monitor reactions from others. Straight rows of chairs or chairs bolted to the floor do not foster high attention to the ideas being discussed or to monitoring reactions of others to the ideas that are being presented.

Potential Problems with Real Classroom Dialogues

There are difficulties with collaborative dialogues. First, teachers have to give up some control, which is a problem for teachers who are schooled in the tradition of not smiling until Thanksgiving. Some teachers also believe deeply in IRE structures, especially since these structures assure that the teacher's interpretations and concerns will get a hearing. Second, some teachers and administrators are concerned that collaborative dialogues do not force individual students to think on their own. Third, many forms of standardized testing tap standard interpretations and understandings (see Chapter 14). Schooling that emphasizes discussion does not guarantee coverage of sanctioned perspectives and factual knowledge and may undermine students' achievement on standardized tests. Fourth, parents are often concerned that cooperative, collabora-

Which of these two physical environments is more conducive to collaborative dialogue?

tive discussions hold back the "best" students in the class. These parents believe their talented children are getting little from their interactions with weaker students.

Given the current educational accountability system, these are sensible concerns. Most student achievement is measured by testing individual students working alone. Nevertheless, assessments of collaborative thinking can be developed. Indeed, some of the new performance assessments incorporate students' collaboration into the assessment (see Chapter 14).

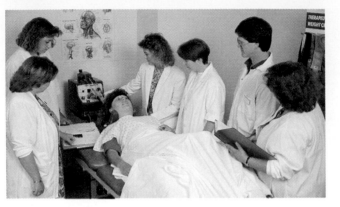

These medical professionals collaborate as they perform their jobs.

There are many arguments to counter these concerns. First, from a Vygotskian perspective, the opportunities to participate in groups that dialogue about important content should have profound long-term effects on cognitive development. Opportunities to engage in interpersonal problem solving and thinking stimulate the development of personal problem-solving and thinking skills. Many of the processes that the group carry out together eventually are internalized by individual members of the group. Group participation also develops the habits of elaborating good ideas and dismissing bad ones.

Second, much of mature thinking is collaborative thinking (Resnick, Levine, & Teasley, 1991; Schrage, 1990). Flying an airliner requires several minds in collaboration to produce a safe flight. Controlling a large ship requires even more minds in interaction. Surgeons, anesthesiologists, and nurses think together to perform a complicated surgery. Innovative new products are not the inventions of individuals but the result of teamwork, groups of people reflecting and thinking together to create an idea that is better than any one of them could have produced on their own. Because of the value of collaborative thinking in the modern world, it makes sense to foster such thinking in schools.

Finally, there are clear advantages that derive from opportunities to explain to others. When stronger and weaker students interact with one another, as during tutoring, both tutor and tutee benefit (V. L. Allen, 1976). In fact, stronger students often get more out of the interaction than weaker students because the stronger students do so much of the explaining (see also Chapter 10).

▶ **Diversity**

Cultural Differences in Conversational Style

Although we are just beginning to learn about differences in conversational style across cultures and gender, there are some indications that teachers who foster academic conversations in the classroom will need to be sensitive to these individual differences. For example, Heath (1989) studied African American communities in rural southeastern communities and found that older adults do not censor or simplify talk around children. Instead, they expect the young to adapt to changing contexts and speakers. Adults in these communities only ask children "real" questions, not questions the adults already know the answers to. For example, these adults would not ask a child, "What color is your shirt?" since the adult already knows the answer to that question. In some cultures, it is considered inappropriate for students to show off what they know. For example, teachers' calling on individual students to answer questions is ineffective instruction for native Hawaiian students who function better under different classroom participation structures (Carlsen, 1991). Thus, the traditional initiate-respond-evaluate cycle with its pattern of factual level (what everyone should know), teacher-controlled questions are a particularly poor instructional tactic for students of some cultural backgrounds.

What do we know about the differences in the conversational styles of males and females? Tannen (1990) described gender differences in communication style as being based on two different views of the world. Males engage a hierarchical world in which they are constantly jockeying for position. To them, conversations are negotiations in which they try to achieve and maintain the upper hand if they can. Their goal is to attain status and preserve independence. Females, on the other hand, engage the world as individuals in a network of connections. To them, conversations are negotiations for closeness and intimacy. E. E. Maccoby (1988) reported speech patterns in boys and girls during play that were similar to these patterns observed in adults. The boys issued more commands and threats, and they interrupted each other more. The girls were more likely to take turns talking and to use the talk for social binding.

How do these gender differences emerge in the classroom (H. Grossman & Grossman, 1994; Tannen, 1990)? Since female students are more likely to tag on questions such as "Don't you think?" or "Isn't it?" to engage their listeners, they sound less decisive and certain of themselves than the male students. The female students are also more likely to let the male students choose topics, interrupt, and hold the floor, although there are some indications that African American females are less likely to let the males dominate.

Who interrupts more during a classroom discussion? It depends on the nature of the interruptions. Female students are more likely to display cooperative overlappings, in which they show support and anticipate where the speaker is heading. Male students are more likely to interrupt to change the direction of topic. There are also regional and cultural differences in the rate of interruptions. New Yorkers talk without pauses between speakers; southerners pause between speakers; and Navajo pause at length between speakers.

Chapter Summary

- Theorists such as Vygotsky and Bakhtin suggest that the quality of thought varies as a function of social experience. Human beings internalize cognitive processes first experienced in a social situation. Eventually, the ways of thinking of our surrounding culture become our own way of thinking. Inner speech plays an important role in this process.

- Tasks that are in the zone of proximal development are ones that can be accomplished through interactions with more competent others who provide scaffolding until the task can be accomplished independently.
- What happens when children can be apprentices to avid readers, real writers, and capable mathematicians? They come to think like real readers, real writers, and real mathematicians. That is, the apprentice attacks academic tasks in ways similar to the expert, talks like the expert, and adopts the intellectual attitudes and preferences of the expert.
- One advantage of reciprocal teaching, a technique in which students in reading groups predict, question text, seek clarifications when confused, and generate summaries, is that eventually the individual members of the group predict, question, seek clarification, and summarize when they read.
- There are several different social interactional approaches to instruction. In some of these (e.g., initiate-response-evaluate cycles), if there is scaffolding of learning, little attention is paid to the scaffolding that occurs. In contrast, scaffolding is at the center of apprenticeship and reciprocal teaching models. Scaffolding is difficult conceptually, requiring understanding of students and their potential understandings and misconceptions about the instructed domain. Scaffolding is also hard work, and teachers must be motivated to do it.
- Group discussions can result in content-related ideas that would not have occurred to individual group members working alone. Students learn the content better through group interaction, particularly if the situation is structured so each group member participates.
- Student participation in interpretive discussions probably encourages general thinking skills and often increases learning of the specific content covered in such discussions. How to conduct such groups, however, is not understood. Moreover, students may not learn particular content as intended.

Return to the Classroom Predicament

Has reading this chapter helped you evaluate the classroom dialogue presented at the beginning of this chapter? This is clearly an example of an initiate-respond-evaluate (IRE) cycle. The questioning was entirely under the teacher's control, most of the questions asked were factual, only one student participated at a time, and the discussion was not very interesting. No true dialogue emerged, the students just stuck to answering the questions, and there is little evidence that the interaction shifted the students' understandings. The teacher asked questions, and when the students gave the correct responses, the teacher praised them. When no one knew the correct answer, the teacher provided it and expressed some frustration with the lack of participation by the students. This type of instructional conversation is a familiar sight in classrooms.

What could the teacher do differently? The teacher could encourage the students to collaborate on the responses to high-level questions that require reflection and discussion. The teacher could support the students in their development of understanding by providing scaffolding through hints and prompts. The teacher could teach the students to use reciprocal teaching techniques as they read the assignment. In adopting these strategies, however, the teacher would have to accept that the more naturalistic academic conversations promoted by these classroom practices might not lead exactly where the teacher would want them to go. According to the social interactional theories of learning and development, true instructional conversations as described in this chapter promote students' construction of knowledge.

Chapter Outline

Chapter 9

Social Influences in the Classroom

Classroom Predicament

Near the end of a parent-teacher conference, a parent says, "I know only one of my children is in your class, but maybe you can help me understand both of my children a little better. My oldest seems to be changing every day. She comes home with a new hairstyle almost every week. She also changes the way she dresses and even the way she talks—I heard her and one of her friends speaking with English accents last week. It seems as though she spends all her time with her friends, and when she isn't with them, she is talking to them on the phone. I've even had to learn how to discipline her differently. She used to do whatever I said just because I said so. She still obeys me, but now I have to explain why she should do what I say. I guess that's good because she usually agrees with my reasoning. Now, her younger sister is a different story. She still does what I say without question, but I'm a little worried about her understanding of schoolwork. She seems to think that working hard is the same as doing well. She'll say, 'I worked on this assignment for an hour, and it is neat, so I'll get an *A.*' Now, she does do well in school, but I'm a little worried that she is not learning that the quality of her work matters, not just how neat it is and how long she worked on it. She has friends at school, and they play well together, but they just don't seem to talk to each other very much. Will she learn how to develop deeper friendships?"

Are these differences between the two girls normal? How would you explain these developmental differences? Reflecting on the information presented in this chapter will help you formulate responses to these questions.

There are many specific activities teachers can use to help students develop a positive self-concept. Canfield and Wells (1994) described 100 ways to enhance self-concept in the classroom. Some examples follow:

- *Student journal.* Students keep a record of their feelings, thoughts, and behaviors. Teachers can ask students to record what they have learned about themselves as a result of classroom activities. The journal is a cumulative account of those reactions.
- *Ten questions.* Students write down a list of positive personal characteristics. They ask other students to guess the positive qualities on their list. The teacher makes sure the students understand their guesses must be positive. If a guess is not on the list, the student responds, "Yes, I am _____, but that wasn't what I was thinking of." Teachers can help young children develop their lists by providing a list of positive qualities they may possess.
- *Collage of self.* Each student puts together a collage (pictures and words) representing things he or she likes and enjoys doing. The other students in the class try to guess which collage belongs to which student.
- *Success recall.* The teacher asks students to think back to times they have been successful. Students are asked to remember how they became successful and how the achievement made them feel.

● "What Do I Do on Monday Morning?"

Self-Reference as a Memory Strategy

Schemas refer to generalized knowledge about events or things (see Chapter 3). You'll recall that we possess schemas about typical events in stories and about characteristics of mathematical problems, which we access when we read stories and attempt to solve problems, respectively. We also possess schemas about ourselves called self-schemas. **Self-schemas** are knowledge structures about the self that organize our interpretations of our experiences and guide our behavior (Markus, 1977).

Our knowledge about ourselves is a rich and powerful knowledge base that we can use to help us interpret new information. Often we begin to understand new information by relating it to ourselves. For example, if you take a course about personality development and read about a personality disorder, you may reflect on the new information by examining your own behavior for evidence of this personality disorder. Accessing knowledge about yourself helps you learn this new material. If you read a newspaper article about symptoms of a newly discovered malady, comparing these symptoms to those you have noticed in yourself will help you remember this information. The increased recall of new information when it is related to self-schema is called the **self-reference effect.** The potency of the self-reference effect has been demonstrated in children as well as adults for a variety of tasks, from learning lists of words (T. B. Rogers, Kuiper, & Kirker, 1977) to remembering information from texts (Reeder, McCormick, & Essleman, 1987).

Teachers can encourage students to self-reference through assignments, teacher-generated questioning, and student role-playing as in the following examples:

- In social studies, ask students to reflect on what it might be like to live in a different culture. For example, get them to consider, "How would my life be different if I were a Muslim woman living in Iran?" or "What would my life be like if I were a Protestant growing up in a Catholic community in Belfast?"
- In literature class, assign students to play the roles of the main characters in a scene that takes place one year after the last event in the play, novel, or short story. Ask students to answer questions modeled after the following examples:

> What if you were orphaned and living on the street like Oliver Twist? How would you feel? What choices would you make? Defend and or critique the choices Oliver Twist made. Pretend you are Romeo or Juliet and your family has forbidden you to date your beloved. How would you feel? How would you act? How would your parents respond? Explain the actions of Romeo or Juliet.

- In history class, ask students to enact a significant event in history. Ask students questions that require them to take the perspectives of important groups in history, such as the colonists loyal to England versus the patriots.

Erikson's Theory of Identity Development

Development of a sense of self has also been described in psychological theories of personal and social development. Erik Erikson's theory (1968) focused on the development of ego identity in social contexts. He proposed that over the course of life people pass through eight developmental stages. Each stage involves a central conflict, which is resolved either positively or negatively. The way in which each conflict is resolved has a lasting effect on an individual's development, although sometimes the ramifications of negative outcomes can be resolved later in development. These conflicts, and the approximate time of life when they happen, are as follows:

- *Trust versus mistrust.* During infancy, children can form a trusting relationship with an adult. Lack of interaction with an adult who can be trusted to meet the infant's needs can result in long-term mistrust. This is a time when affectionate, physical contact and consistent caregiving are crucial to future development.
- *Autonomy versus shame and doubt.* During the early preschool years, children begin to do things on their own, such as feeding or dressing themselves, thereby establishing some autonomy from others. This is a time when preschoolers are struggling to stand on their own two feet, with the battle cry of "I can do it myself!" Part of autonomy is self-control, and during the early preschool years self-control centers around toilet training. If children have difficulties establishing self-control and autonomy, the result may be shame in not being more independent and doubt about whether autonomy is possible. Preschool teachers and parents must be careful not to suffocate or punish this struggle for autonomy.

- *Initiative versus guilt.* As the preschool years proceed, there are many more initiations into the world and trying on of new roles. Many of these initiatives occur during play. If children are overly punished for acting without thinking or are not allowed to explore their burgeoning initiative, feelings of guilt can result.

- *Industry versus inferiority.* With the school years, children are expected to begin to master the skills of the culture. The classroom is the arena for much of this growth. For example, in Western culture, children are expected to develop fundamental literacy and numeracy skills. Success leads to a sense of industry; failure can lead to a sense of inferiority. Since students can readily compare their performance on classroom tasks with that of their peers, teachers must guide students in the development of a sense of competence and not of failure.

- *Identity versus identity confusion.* During adolescence and early adulthood, the central crisis is one of identity. Young people struggle with determining who they are, what they believe in, and what they want to become. Successful identity achievement requires trying various possible identities and struggling with them before making a commitment. Failure to achieve an identity results in confusion.

- *Intimacy versus isolation.* After youth, a person either achieves intimacy with others, usually a marital partner or the equivalent, or is at risk for feeling psychological isolation.

- *Generativity versus stagnation.* Adulthood is either a period of contributing to society and to the development of the next generation, or there is a risk of stagnating.

- *Integrity versus despair.* The person who resolves all of life's crises in a positive fashion is likely to be able to look back and feel a sense of integrity. Those who fail to resolve positively one or more life crisis are at risk for disgust and despair.

The most prominent crisis in Erikson's theory is the identity crisis. Marcia (1966) identified four different identity statuses, differing in terms of the experience of crisis and commitment to an identity. Most people can easily think of friends and acquaintances who fit into each of the following four identity statuses:

- People in **moratorium** are in ongoing crisis, actively exploring potential identities. This is a healthy and appropriate status for adolescents. Adolescents in moratorium are perceived by others as introspective, anxious, and valuing independence (Mallory, 1989).

- Those who are **identity achieved** have gone through crises and have made commitments. These who have achieved identities are perceived by others as productive, consistent, and valuing independence.

- People in **diffusion** have not experienced either crisis or commitment. They have not tried out, nor are they trying out, new roles and have made no commitments. Youth in diffusion often appear to be living lives without personal meaning. They are reluctant to make commitments to positions, they avoid close relationships, and they are unpredictable and changeable (Mallory, 1989).

- Youth in **foreclosure** have come to commitments without experiencing any crises. Young people who follow a plan of life devised by their parents are one example. The plan may be as follows: go to a prestigious college followed by law school, accept a place in the family firm, and settle down in the same commu-

Adolescents often try on different identities when they are in moratorium.

nity as the parents. Those with foreclosed identities often have conservative values; are moralistic; exhibit conventional, sex-appropriate behaviors; and are satisfied with themselves (Mallory, 1989).

In a healthy progression of identity achievement, moratorium should be experienced before identity is eventually achieved. According to Erikson's theory, identity crises arise during adolescence in part because of the quantum leap in intellectual sophistication that occurs with the onset of formal operations. As described by Piaget (see also Chapter 7), formal operational thought permits introspection and reflection on alternative possibilities, which is at the heart of the identity crisis. Adolescents with formal operational thought are capable of thinking in possibilities, thinking in hypotheses, and considering multiple factors simultaneously. Armed with the intellectual power provided by formal operations, adolescents struggle with what they believe about sexual orientation, intellectual interests, a philosophy of life, vocations, religion, and so on. The power to think about hypothetical situations often increases doubt in long-held beliefs (Boyes & Chandler, 1992).

Is there also movement toward identity achievement during college years? College is a setting that introduces students to diverse possibilities, and there are correlations between changes in identity status and exposure to diverse students (Komarovsky, 1985; Madison, 1969; P. Newman & Newman, 1978). Pascarella and Terenzini (1991) found that commitments to vocation, lifestyle, and philosophy develop during the college years. Identity achievement, however, is certainly not assured by the end of the college years. For example, Waterman and Goldman (1976) observed that only a little more than half of the college seniors they studied had achieved identity with respect to religious or political philosophies.

Focus on Research

A Longitudinal Study of Dualistic and Relativistic Thinking

Identity is often defined by what you believe in. However, knowing what you truly believe in requires exploring alternative views. William G. Perry (1970) explored fundamental changes during the college years in the ways that students think about issues. Specifically, he studied transitions from dualistic thinking to relativistic thinking. **Dualistic thinking** refers to the belief that one and only one perspective is right; all others are wrong. **Relativistic thinking** refers to the belief that the appropriateness of a perspective often depends on the context. A relativistic thinker does not think that right versus wrong is the way to evaluate issues. For example, dualistic thinking may direct absolute statements such as "War is wrong." A position reflecting relativistic thinking might be "Is war wrong? Well, it depends on the situation. Certainly, peaceful attempts to appease Hitler failed, and war was inevitable."

Perry's study began with his observations that students reacted differently to the relativism they encountered at Harvard University. Some students were shocked as their favored perspectives were presented as one viewpoint among many legitimate perspectives; others were much more comfortable with the idea of multiple positions.

Perry then administered a questionnaire to a large sample of first-year students at Harvard. The questionnaire was designed to determine where a student fell on a continuum from dualistic thinking (engaging in "right-wrong" thinking) to relativistic thinking (accepting a multiplicity of views and recognizing that the appropriateness of perspectives depends on the situation). At the end of each of their four undergraduate years, some of these students were interviewed. The initial question in each year's interview was "Why don't you start with whatever stands out for you this year?" Interviewers sometimes asked students to explain their thoughts by role-playing what they would advise other students to expect, such as, "If you had a cousin, say, who was coming here next year and he asked you what to expect and so on, how do you think you might answer?" After the interview, students were shown the written questionnaire responses they had produced in their first year and were asked to indicate if now there were any differences in their thinking. The interviewers were instructed to do everything possible not to suggest potential responses to the students.

Think back to the discussion of the different

▷ Diversity

Ethnic Differences in Identity Development

Ethnicity shapes students' exploration and commitment to identity (Rotheram-Borus & Wyche, 1994; Spencer & Markstrom-Adams, 1990). An important component of personal identity for ethnic students is **ethnic identity,** which encompasses the feelings, perceptions, and behavior due to membership in an ethnic group. The experience of prejudice shared by members of a minority group fosters ethnic identity in students and motivates a desire to understand their own culture.

At the same time, these students are also members of the majority culture. It may be difficult for ethnic minorities to become bicultural due to conflicting values between the minority and majority culture (Spencer & Markstrom-Adams, 1990). For example, Native American students may be torn between school attendance and the threat of rejection by the tribe if they do not participate in lengthy religious ceremonies. African American students may be torn between the pursuit of academic achievement and rejection by their peers for "acting white." The higher rate of approaches to studying developmental differences described in Chapter 1. Since the purpose of Perry's study was to examine changes in students' thinking as a function of college experience, this was a longitudinal study. Do you think the instruction to the interviewers helped increase the internal validity of this study?

The students in this study provided information about their views of knowledge, how they studied, beliefs about social relationships, and their moral values. In these responses, Perry observed a general movement during the undergraduate years from dualism to relativism—an increasing recognition of a variety of legitimate perspectives in the world. For example, one freshman on the initial questionnaire indicated that it was easy to disagree strongly with the following claim: "One thing is certain: even if there is an absolute truth, man will never know about it and therefore must learn to choose and venture in uncertainty" (W. Perry, 1970, p. 69). By the end of the year, this same participant agreed with this item. Immersion in a college world with many opinions reduces confidence in the righteousness of one perspective.

Some students begin to make commitments, tentatively in the beginning and advancing eventually to more complete commitments. Others become intent on avoiding commitments, recognizing the multiplicity of perspectives but unwilling to identify with any of them. Perry (1970) reported that about three-fourths of the students he studied were making commitments by the end of their undergraduate years. For instance, a student may be committed to going to law school, practicing Catholicism, and staying single, while at the same time feel perfectly comfortable and accepting of a friend who has decided on investment banking, has converted to Judaism, and is marrying the girl back home, or of another acquaintance who is going to teach grade school and continue to be an agnostic. Arguing that college students make commitments does not imply that their growth is concluded, since the possibility of changing commitments and making new commitments is present across the life span (Pascarella & Terenzini, 1991; W. Perry, 1981).

foreclosure among ethnic minority adolescents may be due to cultural pressures limiting exploration of alternative identities. For example, Chinese American adolescents live in a culture that emphasizes group identity, and parental pressure limits Japanese American students' options to explore. Those ethnic youth who do explore alternative identities in the majority culture may experience conflict with members of the older generation. Foreclosure may be adaptive for minority youths, however, since social roles are clearly defined by the minority community and their place in the culture is clear.

How can teachers integrate the issues of ethnic identity into school curriculum? Understanding the influence of ethnic identity upon students is daunting, especially given the diversity within ethnic classifications. For example, Native Americans belong to distinct tribes with vastly different values. The term *Hispanic* refers to a vast range of peoples with varying histories and cultures. The same applies to the generic terms *Asian American* and *African American*. The experience of all minorities in the past has been either a sense of invisibility in school materials or negative imagery as in the portrayal of Native Americans as an impediment to overcome during the westward expansion. The following are some suggested school-based interventions for identity development (J. A. Banks, 1994; Markstrom-Adams & Spencer, 1994; Rotheram-Borus & Wyche, 1994):

Although both of these students could be described as Asian American, their ethnic identity may be influenced by very different Asian traditions.

- Highlight the value of different cultures through a variety of vehicles, such as languages, novels, poetry, folktales, films, art, and architecture.
- Discuss explicitly the impact of discrimination and prejudice, particularly in history and literature.
- Train students in perspective taking, a process by which they learn to see the world from another's perspective, by creating situations in which students compare the similarities and differences between themselves and other groups.
- Present diverse role models by inviting members of minority communities to the classroom to discuss their viewpoints and experiences.
- Develop apprenticeship programs in the community that enhance future educational and employment opportunities.

Self in Interpersonal Relationships: Influences on Academic Achievement

How do others in our social world influence our development? Operant conditioning theory (see Chapter 7) suggests that others influence our behavior by serving as sources of reinforcement and punishment. You'll recall that reinforcers occur following behavior and increase the likelihood of that behavior in the future; punishment decreases the likelihood of that behavior in the future. Social learning theory (see Chapter 7) suggests that others influence our behavior by serving as models for us to imitate. You'll remember that the likelihood of imitating a model's behavior is greater if we observe the model's being reinforced for the behavior, which is called vicarious reinforcement. Two important sources of reinforcement, punishment, and modeled behaviors are our parents and peers.

Relationship with Parents

Parents can serve as models and sources of reinforcement and punishment. General patterns of parenting styles have been described in terms of how *demanding* parents are of their children and how *responsive* they are to their children (Baumrind, 1980, 1983; Maccoby & Martin, 1983).

- **Authoritarian parents** are demanding and unresponsive. They make demands of their children and are unresponsive to their children's point of view. They use power-assertive discipline, meaning that they are likely to correct their children's behavior through coercion such as by saying, "This is the way you must behave, because I said so." Such power-assertive discipline does not lead to the internalization of behavioral standards and controls.
- **Authoritative parents** are demanding and responsive. They make demands of their children but are responsive to their children's point of view. They use inductive discipline, meaning that they are likely to correct their children's behavior through appeals to reason such as by saying, "This is the way you should behave, because otherwise you disturb others and that isn't fair to them." Inductive discipline can foster the internalization of behavioral standards and controls.
- **Indulgent/permissive parents** are undemanding and responsive. These parents are responsive to their children but make few demands of them and set few limits on their behavior.
- **Neglecting parents** are undemanding and unresponsive. These parents pay little attention to their children at all.

How are these parenting styles associated with academic achievement? According to Darling and Steinberg (1993), the effects of parenting style depend on the social context. Authoritative parenting is most strongly associated with academic achievement among European American adolescents but is less associated with academic success in Asian American and African American youth. Apparently, the influence of parenting style on academic achievement is moderated by peer support for academic endeavors. Steinberg, Dornbush, and Brown (1992) found that while authoritative parenting and peer support for academic achievement both facilitated academic endeavors in European American adolescents, in African American adolescents the absence of peer support for academic achievement undermined the beneficial effects of authoritative parenting. These researchers also found that although authoritarian parenting and low peer support for academic achievement both negatively affected academic achievement for Hispanics, peer support for academic achievement among Asian Americans offset the negative impact of authoritarian parenting.

Relationship with Peers

Peers are influential models and sources of reinforcement and punishment. Descriptions and expectations of friendship change substantially from preschool through adolescence (Elkind, 1994; Hartup, 1989). The expectations of sharing and reciprocity in friendship appear early in development. For example, the friendships of preschoolers are focused on common activities, proximity, and the sharing of toys. Later in the middle childhood years and in adolescence, friendships begin to focus on mutual understanding, loyalty, and intimacy. Cross-sex friendships are relatively rare, most likely as a result of natural sex segregation based on common play interests.

Understanding peer interactions is important to educators since these interactions are crucial to several models of good teaching. It is helpful to recall Vygotsky's zone of proximal development (see Chapter 7), which refers to the range of behaviors between what a student can accomplish independently and what the student can accomplish with the assistance of an adult or a more capable peer. In addition, successful implementation of cooperative learning (see Chapters 2 and 10) requires students to possess at least rudimentary interpersonal skills.

In his theory of peer relations, Selman (Yeates & Selman, 1989) described four levels of social competence. These levels reflect students' increasing capability to distinguish the perspectives of others from their own and to integrate their own perspectives with those of others. The levels are as follows:

- *Impulsive.* Students, usually preschoolers, cannot distinguish between action and feeling. They do not realize that others may interpret the same behavior differently than they do, and they resolve conflict by force (fighting, grabbing) or withdrawal (whining, hiding).
- *Unilateral.* Students, usually in early-elementary school, know others have a different point of view but cannot simultaneously consider their own perspective and that of others. They resolve conflict either by controlling others (commanding, bullying) or by appeasing others (giving in, waiting for help).
- *Reciprocal.* Students, usually in middle-elementary school, can take others' points of view, but they cannot integrate them with their own. They resolve conflict by attempting to satisfy the needs of others through negotiating trades and making deals.
- *Collaborative.* Students, usually in late-elementary school, are able to coordinate two perspectives in order to meet mutual goals. Demonstrating concern for the continuation of relationships, they resolve conflicts by trying to negotiate compromises.

What are the implications of these stages of social competence for peer collaboration in the classroom? Students in the impulsive and unilateral stages are likely to experience considerable conflict during cooperative tasks, and these conflicts are unlikely to be resolved in ways that benefit the intellectual development of the students. Students in the reciprocal and collaborative stages, however, are more skilled in cooperative learning tasks, with those students in the collaborative stage able to integrate multiple perspectives.

Self in Society: The Development and Education of Moral Judgment

Perhaps the most influential theorist of moral reasoning was Lawrence Kohlberg. Kohlberg not only described different stages of moral reasoning, he also proposed a theory about how to advance moral reasoning through the stages, a theory of moral education. Kohlberg's theory of moral reasoning was heavily influenced by Jean Piaget's perspective of moral judgement.

Piaget's Theory of the Development of Moral Judgment

Jean Piaget's (1965) observations of children playing games by the rules, cheating, and changing rules helped him formulate hypotheses about children's moral understandings. He then tested these hypotheses by asking children to reason about social dilemmas that he presented to them as short stories ending in a question. For example, one of these dilemmas posed to children was whether a child who accidentally broke fifteen cups was naughtier than one who intentionally broke one cup. Piaget proposed two stages of morality, one stage reflecting the conceptions about rules held by preschoolers and children in the early-primary school years (*stage of heteronomous morality*) and the other stage reflecting the thinking of older children about rules (*stage of autonomous morality*).

Children at the stage of heteronomous morality focus on the objective consequences of an action. Therefore, those in Piaget's study exhibiting heteronomous morality concluded that the child who broke fifteen cups was naughtier than the child who intentionally broke only one cup since more cups were destroyed. In contrast, children at the stage of autonomous morality make decisions on the basis of the intentions of the actors. Therefore, the children in Piaget's study exhibiting autonomous morality concluded that breaking one cup intentionally was much worse than accidentally destroying fifteen. The heteronomously moral child views rules as sacred, as if they were written by the hand of God, never to be reconsidered. In contrast, the autonomously moral child recognizes that rules are inventions of people and can be changed if people will it. For example, children who learn to play games such as Monopoly at home may learn when they play Monopoly at someone else's house that other families may have different Monopoly conventions, such as whether or not money accumulates in free parking, what deals property owners can make, or even whether or not properties are dealt out at the beginning to make the game shorter. A heteronomously moral child would view such alterations of the official Monopoly rules as almost a sacrilege.

As in Piagetian stages of cognitive development (see Chapter 7), there is an

These children are playing according to the rules of the game. Heteronomously moral children believe that rules are absolute; autonomously moral children realize that rules are social contracts agreed upon by the players.

invariant order of development, meaning a child must display heteronomous morality before autonomous morality. As in the Piagetian view of cognitive development, equilibration (cognitive conflict) is the main mechanism of cognitive change, facilitating movement from heteronomous to autonomous morality. Conflicts with peers that stimulate cognitive conflict, such as arguments about the rules of marbles, are especially helpful. Such conflicts can move the child from viewing rules as God-given and inalterable to seeing them as agreements that the children playing marbles can change by mutual consent.

■ Building Your Expertise

Social Learning Theory and Moral Reasoning

Social learning theorists emphasize the role of imitation in learning (see Chapter 7). Can children with immature moral judgment learn to make more mature judgments using social learning principles? Yes, they can. Bandura and McDonald (1963) initially assessed children to determine how they made judgments about stories similar to the one involving the broken cups. Those children who could clearly be classified as making judgments based on consequences (i.e., the amount of damage done) and as making judgments based on intentions (i.e., why the damage occurred) were assigned to one of three conditions.

Children in the first condition of the study (*modeling and reinforcement*) saw a model who made moral judgments that were always opposite to the type of judgment favored by each child during the preexperiment assessment. The children also observed the model's receiving reinforcement for these judgments. The children were then presented with moral problems and reinforced for making judgments opposite in type to those they had made during the preexperimental assessment. Thus, in this condition, children who focused on intentions during the assessment viewed a model who made judgments based on objective consequences and was reinforced for doing so; then the children were reinforced for making judgments based on objective consequences. In contrast, children who had focused on objective consequences during the assessment saw and were reinforced for judgments based on intentions.

In the second condition (*modeling*), the children observed a model making judgments and receiving reinforcements for choices that were opposite to those favored by the children in the preexperiment assessment. This was identical to what was done in the first condition. When the children attempted the problems, however, they were not given any reinforcement, which was unlike the first condition. In a third condition (*reinforcement control*), the children did not see a model but were reinforced for making judgments opposite to those they favored in the preexperiment assessment.

What did the researchers find? The two conditions with modeling produced dramatic shifts in the children's moral judgments that were much more striking than that which occurred in the third condition where the children only received reinforcement. Other research supports the conclusion that moral judgments can be shifted through social learning principles (T. L. Rosenthal & Zimmerman, 1978).

Kohlberg's Stage Theory of Moral Reasoning

Kohlberg (1969, 1981, 1984) described the development of moral reasoning as progression through an invariant sequence of six stages. Kohlberg developed the stages based on a research tactic similar to that of Piaget. He presented moral dilemmas in the form of stories to adolescent boys. One of these dilemmas involved a character named Heinz:

> In Europe, a woman was near death from a special kind of cancer. There was one drug that the doctors thought might save her. It was a form of radium that the druggist in the same town had recently discovered. The drug was expensive to make. He paid $400 for the radium and charged $4000 for a small dose of the drug. The sick woman's husband, Heinz, went to everyone he knew to borrow the money and tried every legal means, but he could only get together about $2000, which is half of what it cost. He told the druggist that his wife was dying, and asked him to sell it cheaper or let him pay later. But the druggist said, "No, I discovered the drug and I'm going to make money from it." So having tried every legal means, Heinz gets desperate and considers breaking into the man's store to steal the drug for his wife. (Kohlberg, 1984, p. 640)

The boys were asked to respond to questions, such as the following, about the moral dilemmas posed by the story.

1. Should Heinz steal the drug? Why or why not?
2. Is it actually right or wrong for him to steal the drug? Why is it right or wrong?
3. Does Heinz have a duty or obligation to steal the drug? Why or why not?
4. Is it important for people to do everything they can to save another's life? Why or why not?
5. It is against the law for Heinz to steal. Does that make it morally wrong? Why or why not?
6. In thinking back over the dilemma, what would you say is the most responsible thing for Heinz to do? Why? (Kohlberg, 1984, pp. 640–641)

What mattered in the interview was not whether the boys felt Heinz should steal the drug but the *reasons* they gave for Heinz's actions. These reasons varied from stage to stage (all quotes from Kohlberg, 1984, pp. 49–53, based on Rest, 1968).

The stages of **preconventional morality,** stages 1 and 2, focus on self-interest in decision making. The reasons given by the boys in stage 1 centered on obedience and avoiding punishment, as exemplified in this rationale in favor of stealing the drug: "If you let your wife die, you will get in trouble. You'll be blamed for not spending the money to save her and there'll be an investigation of you and the druggist for your wife's death." Of course, a case can also be made that the best way to stay out of trouble is not to steal the drug: "You shouldn't steal the drug because you'll be caught and sent to jail if you do. If you do get away, your conscience would bother you thinking how the police would catch up with you at any minute."

The stage-2 thinker is only concerned about his or her own pleasures. What is right is what brings pleasure to the self. Consider this stage-2 justification for stealing the drug: "If you do happen to get caught, you could give the drug back and wouldn't get much of a sentence. It wouldn't bother you much to serve a little jail term, if you have your wife when you get out." Self-interest can be used to justify not stealing as well: "He may not get much of a jail term if he steals the drug, but his wife will probably die before he gets out, so it wouldn't do him much good. If his wife dies, he shouldn't blame himself; it isn't his fault she has cancer."

The stages of **conventional morality,** stages 3 and 4, focus on maintaining the social order. The stage-3 thinker is sometimes thought of as displaying "good boy-good girl" thinking, which is concerned with helping and pleasing others. This is conformist thinking in the sense of wanting to go along with the majority. Consider this example in favor of stealing the drug: "No one will think you're bad if you steal the drug but your family will think you are an inhuman husband if you don't. If you let your wife die, you'll never be able to look anyone in the face again." The concern for the opinion of others comes through in this justification for not stealing the drug as well: "It isn't just the druggist who will think you're a criminal, everyone else will, too. After you steal it, you'll feel bad thinking how you've brought dishonor on your family and yourself; you won't be able to face anyone again."

The stage-4 thinker is concerned with being in synchronization with the standards of his or her society. Those in stage 4 have a deep respect for law and order. This rationalization in favor of stealing the drug is based on the perception of duty to family members that is expected by society: "If you have any sense of honor, you won't let your wife die because you're afraid to do the only thing that will save her. You'll always feel guilty that you caused her death if you don't do your duty to her." Consistency with the laws of society comes through in this opposition to stealing the drug offered by another stage-4 thinker: "You're desperate and you may not know you're doing wrong when you steal the drug. But you'll know you did wrong after you're punished and sent to jail. You'll always feel guilty for your dishonesty and lawbreaking."

The stages of **postconventional morality,** stages 5 and 6, are characterized by shared or potentially sharable principles and standards. The stage-5 thinker views rules and laws in terms of a contract, which is intended to protect the will and rights of others. After entering a contract, rules are obeyed as part of a social understanding rather than because of fear of retribution, respect for authority, or a sense of duty. If the social purpose for the rules cannot be fulfilled by obeying them, it is all right to dispense with the rules, as reflected in this opinion, which favors Heinz's stealing the drug: "The law wasn't set up for these circumstances. Taking the drug in this situation isn't really right, but it's justified to do it." The social contract orientation also comes through in this stage-5 opinion against stealing the drug: "You can't have everyone stealing when they get desperate. The end may be good, but the ends don't justify the means."

Finally, the stage-6 thinker does not compromise in respecting the sanctity of life and human freedom. This type of thinker might say, "Heinz should steal the drug because the sanctity of human life must take precedence over all other considerations." The stage-6 thinker can rationally make decisions without taking self-interest into account. Thus, Kohlberg embraced rationally determined justice as the highest of moral ideals. A summary of Kohlberg's six stages of moral reasoning is shown in Table 9.1.

Kohlberg argued that a person's moral stage affects thinking about many types of social problems, not just hypothetical dilemmas. Carol Gilligan and her colleagues identified Kohlbergian stagelike differences in the reasoning of high

Table 9.1

Summary of Kohlberg's Stages of Moral Reasoning

Preconventional Morality (focus on self-interest)
- Stage 1—focus on obedience and avoiding punishment
- Stage 2—focus on obtaining rewards or pleasure

Conventional Morality (focus on maintaining social order)
- Stage 3—focus on being a good boy or a good girl
- Stage 4—focus on law and order

Postconventional Morality (focus on shared standards and principles)
- Stage 5—focus on social contract
- Stage 6—focus on principle

school juniors in their reactions to dilemmas faced by most young people such as the following (Gilligan, Kohlberg, Lerner, & Belensky, 1971; all quotes based on selections made by Lickona, 1976, pp. 39–42):

> A high school girl's parents are away for the weekend and she's alone in the house. Unexpectedly, on Friday evening, her boyfriend comes over. They spend the evening together in the house and after awhile they start necking and petting: (1) Is this right or wrong? Why? Are there circumstances that would make it right or wrong? (2) What if they had sexual intercourse? Is that right or wrong? Why? (3) Does the way they feel about each other make a difference in the rightness or wrongness of having sexual intercourse? Why? What if they are in love? What does love mean and what is its relation to sex? (Gilligan, Kohlberg, Lerner, & Belensky, 1971, p. 151)

Some reactions reflected preconventional morality, with its emphasis on rewards and avoidance of punishment: "There's nothing wrong with intercourse because I think people can do whatever they want" and "It would be wrong if they had intercourse without thinking about pregnancy—a child can cause a lot of trouble to high school kids." There were good boy–good girl responses, reflecting stage-3 thinking: "It's OK as long as you do it as an act of love rather than as an act of sex—if you do it with an emotional tie" and "It's someone you like to be with no matter what you do" and "Sex is part of showing you care. It should be for a special relationship." One stage-3 reason for abstaining from sex was "You can get away with it, but you're not, like, clean anymore." The respect for authority, laws, and order that refects stage-4 thinking comes through in this rationalization: "It would be wrong in our society—how will they fit in?" The social contract orientation of stage 5 was reflected in the following response: "Sex is OK if they are honest with each other, if they know each other's motives."

Sex and Cultural Differences in Moral Reasoning

Kohlberg (1969) based his theory on a study that included only midwestern boys, and he claimed universality of the stages based on this sample. Some theorists suggested that Kohlberg's theory neglected themes particularly important to women. For example, Carol Gilligan (1982) argued that females were much more likely than males to consider issues of interpersonal caring and connections as they reasoned about moral dilemmas. Female responses to the dilemma faced by Heinz are much more likely than male responses to include arguments such as, "I . . . think he [the druggist] had the moral obligation to show compassion in this case . . ." (p. 54) and "You have to love someone else, because you are inseparable from them. . . . That other person is part of that giant collection of everybody" (p. 57), and "Who is going to be hurt more, the druggist who loses some money or the person who loses her life?" (p. 95).

In Kohlberg's traditional scoring scheme, such concerns about caring and connection result in a lower score since the scoring scheme was sensitive to a masculine strategy based on rationality and justice but insensitive to thinking strategies in which dilemmas are analyzed in terms of the human, interpersonal consequences of the various possible actions by the actors in a dilemma. Gilligan contended that, at a minimum, the traditional analyses of moral judgment missed the rich diversity of thinking about moral issues. Atlhough there has been some research evidence supporting Gilligan's point of view (Gilligan & Attannucci, 1988; D. K. Johnson, 1988), other studies suggest that the thinking of males and females about moral issues is much more similar than it is different (Galotti, 1989; Galotti, Kozberg, & Farmer, 1991; Gibbs, Arnold, & Burkhart, 1984; Rest et al., 1986; L. Walker, 1984).

Challenges to Kohlberg's thinking about the universality of moral reasoning are not all concerned with issues of gender. Others focus on investigating potential cross-cultural differences (Gates, 1990; Iwasa, 1992; Luhmer, 1990; Maosen, 1990; Thomas, 1990; Tzuriel, 1992). In general, although the general Kohlbergian pattern of development is observed, there are often differences in moral thinking that reflect the socialization pressures of the culture. For example, people in cultures that emphasize benefits for the collective good rather than focus on individual rights (e.g., Chinese) endorse practices such as capital punishment more readily than do many Westerners (L. J. Walker & Moran, 1991).

Moral Education

Can students learn to be more sophisticated in their moral reasoning? Can moral education be successful? Enright, Lapsley, and Levy (1983) summarized research on two popular approaches to moral education. The first approach is to offer a philosophy course in ethics to students. Learning how philosophers think about the topic of ethics, however, does not have a lasting effect on moral reasoning. Courses in social studies dealing with topics such as civil rights and overcoming prejudice do little for moral reasoning either. In summary, direct instruction about moral behavior does not seem to affect the ability to reason about moral issues.

The second approach is to have students argue about moral dilemmas, that is, for them to experience cognitive conflict as part of discussions about moral issues. This is sometimes referred to as the **plus-one approach** because it results in each student's being exposed to information from a stage beyond his or her current level of reasoning about moral dilemmas. This discrepancy is likely to induce cognitive conflict, which motivates reflection on the new information, reflection that often results in coming to understand the more advanced position (see Chapter 7).

For example, Blatt and Kohlberg (1975) had teachers present moral dilemmas to junior and senior high school students, who debated the pros and cons of various resolutions. Although the teachers sometimes clarified and summarized argu-

These prisoners in a Japanese jail for motorists are bowing before a monument of atonement. Kohlberg's theory of moral development may be culturally bound in its emphasis on individual rights and freedoms. Other cultures emphasize benefits for the group instead of the individual.

ments and challenged low-level reasoning, the teachers did not provide resolutions to the dilemmas. The moral discussions included a mixture of opinions, with some at a higher stage than others, so that most students were exposed to thinking at least a bit beyond them. Students who participated in discussions of moral dilemmas reasoned at higher levels during moral judgment interviews than they did before experiencing the moral conflict discussions. Positive effects of plus-one moral reasoning discussions have been obtained consistently both with short interventions (a single session) and long ones (full-semester courses) (Enright, Lapsley, & Levy, 1983).

Kohlberg envisioned community environments that would stimulate moral reflection. He believed that there was the potential for moral growth from community participation in a setting similar to the traditional New England town meeting. Schools and other institutions dedicated to improving their clients' thinking and morality could encourage such participation. To prove his point, Kohlberg created "just communities" within the boundaries of institutional settings (Power, Higgins, & Kohlberg, 1989).

For example, Kohlberg, Kauffman, Sharf, and Hickey (1974) took over part of a women's prison. The just-community way of doing business was for decisions, including the development of rules for the prison community, to be made in town meetings. Instead of discipline being overseen by guards, juries that were composed of both staff and inmates considered offenses against the community and reached decisions on the basis of discussion and reflection. Instead of letting the community slip into a lull of satisfaction with the rules as established by the community, there was continuous review of rules. Did living in this community increase moral judgment skills as defined by Kohlberg's interview measures? Yes, a little.

Just communities were also set up in both elementary and secondary schools.

These schools were structured according to town meetings and used self-enforced discipline via reflective discussion. Did attending a just-community school increase moral judgment skills as defined by Kohlberg's interview measures? Yes, a little.

In addition to collecting evidence of moral-judgment abilities with the standard Kohlbergian interviews, students in eight just-community high schools were also asked to reason about dilemmas that occur in school settings. Topics included drugs in school, stealing, and group consequences for harmful actions by particular members of the school community (Power, Higgins, & Kohlberg, 1989). Just-community students tended to give more thoughtful responses to such dilemmas than students in conventional high schools did. In particular, the responses of the just-community students reflected more concern for meeting the needs of others and thinking about the consequences of one's own actions on others. Just communities have been created in a variety of institutions including schools (Higgins, 1987; Power & Power, 1992; Rulon, 1992), institutions serving emotionally disturbed adolescents (Blakenay & Blakenay, 1990), and prisons (R. E. Powell, Locke, & Sprinthall, 1991).

It is not easy, however, to carry out Kohlbergian type of programs of moral instruction, especially for elementary school students. For example, A. M. Sharp (1987) argued that the types of discussions required in just communities demand much of students. Students must be capable of all of the following: willing acceptance of corrections by peers, open and attentive listening to others, revision of views in light of ideas from others, development of ideas without fear of rebuff or humiliation from peers, detection of underlying assumptions, the ability to ask relevant questions, sensitivity to context when discussing moral conduct, and impartial discussion of issues. Given the complexity of plus-one exchanges, it is easy to understand why moral discussions have been less successful with younger students than with older ones (Enright, Lapsley, & Levy, 1983).

Thomas Lickona's Integrative Approach to Moral Education

Both Piaget and Kohlberg offered theories of thinking about moral issues rather than theories of moral behavior. Behavior is determined by more than just moral considerations, and there is a low correspondence between the stage of moral thinking and moral behavior (Kohlberg & Candee, 1984). For example, whether people steal depends in part on their expectations of gratification if they steal the desired object as well as their expectations about consequences if they are caught (Pearl, Bryan, & Herzog, 1990). These expectations develop through past reinforcements and punishments they have either received or witnessed (Rotter, 1954). For educators who are concerned at least as much with affecting moral behavior as moral thought, interventions, such as cognitive conflict, that affect thinking alone are not enough. More pragmatic moral educators, such as Thomas Lickona, have designed interventions blending behavioral interventions aimed at improving moral action and more cognitive interventions aimed at influencing moral thinking.

Lickona (1991) has compiled a comprehensive sourcebook on techniques for moral education including the following:

- *Modeling of moral behavior and reasoning by teachers.* Teachers who model moral behavior and reasoning are more likely to have students who act in moral ways and can reason in a sophisticated fashion about moral issues. Moral behavior and reasoning are affected by observational learning experiences (Bandura &

McDonald, 1963; T. L. Rosenthal & Zimmerman, 1978). Thus, teachers must model the themes of justice and caring in their daily interactions with students.

- *Guest speakers.* Consistent with the social learning perspective that people learn how to be better than they are by exposure to people who are exemplary, teachers should expose students to real ethical models whenever possible. For example, the teacher could invite to class a whistle-blower who exposed wrongdoing at some personal cost.

- *Use of storytelling and literature.* People can learn from symbolic models, such as characters in books (Bandura, 1969, 1977b). Stories, such as those in *Aesop's Fables*, have survived for more than two millennia in part because they increase moral understanding.

- *Use television viewing.* Social learning researchers established that both antisocial and prosocial behaviors can be learned from television (Comstock & Paik, 1991). Teachers can encourage viewing of television in which positive behaviors are featured, through specific assignments, parent conferences, and so on.

- *Discussion of controversial issues that concern society.* Students can learn that controversial issues are many sided and complex by being encouraged to discuss them in class. For example, debates considering alternative perspectives can fit into a social studies class on the views of rival political candidates or into a science class on the ethics of genetic engineering.

- *Use of the curriculum to encourage moral growth.* Teachers should take advantage of any opportunities that arise to teach responsibility. For example, the class's pet rabbit or hamster can be used in many ways for lessons in caring and responsibility. When class lessons permit opportunities to relate the issues of respect, care, and justice to the lives of the students, teachers should help students to see the linkages. Ethics should be made an important theme in the school day.

- *Asking students to be more ethical in their conduct and explaining why.* Receiving explanations about why antisocial behavior is unacceptable compared to prosocial behavior increases socially acceptable behavior. Children who may not think about the consequences of their unethical behaviors on their own can come to understand the effects of their behavior on others when an adult explains them (M. L. Hoffman, 1970).

- *The institution of negative consequences for unethical conduct and positive consequences for ethical, fair, and altruistic behavior.* Punishment and reinforcement affect the acquisition of many behaviors (see Chapter 7). Teachers should use them to promote the development of positive behaviors and to discourage immoral, antisocial behaviors. A variety of behavioral techniques can be helpful, including encouraging students to chart their misbehaviors in order to increase their awareness of how salient their unwanted conduct is and to provide them with tangible evidence of improvement when positive change occurs.

- *High expectations.* Effective schools have high expectations for their students (see Chapter 10). Teachers should send the message that there are high expectations about the moral, ethical, and civic development of students in the school and the corresponding responsibility.

- *The fostering of cooperative learning and cooperation in general.* Evidence is growing that the ethical and mental-health components in a cooperative environment are better than those in a competitive environments (Davidson & Worsham, 1992; see also Chapters 2 and 10).

- *Mentoring and individual guidance.* Development of close relationships between teachers and students can have a tremendous influence on the latter's moral and ethical development.
- *The rejection of ethics as simply a matter of personal opinion.* One movement in moral education, *values clarification,* encourages teachers not to make value judgments about the stances students take on ethical issues. Lickona rejects this thinking, believing there are some unequivocally moral and immoral stances. The teacher should challenge students when they voice ethical positions that are contrary to stances that are acceptable in society.

In summary, Lickona (1991) believes that there are multiple mechanisms for producing advancement in moral thinking and the effective moral educator constructs an environment that incorporates many of them. Although the whole of moral education may be greater than the sum of the parts, the parts are generally recognizable as variations on observational learning, cooperative learning, direct explanation, the plus-one strategy, and so on.

Classrooms That Promote Students' Thoughtfulness

Adolescence and young adulthood are periods of great importance in the development of moral reasoning and reflection on values and beliefs. Successful passage through these periods requires thoughtfulness of students in response to social influences. Can classrooms be designed to promote such thoughtfulness? Some researchers have been examining whether high school social studies classrooms in particular are thoughtful learning environments (Newmann, 1988, 1990a, 1990b, 1991a, 1991b, 1991d; Newmann, Onosko, & Stevenson, 1990; Onosko, 1989, 1991, 1992; Onosko & Newmann, 1994).

Newmann and Onosko proposed a model of cognitive components that contribute to in-depth understandings of social studies issues. This model includes all four of the main components of good thinking described in this book: (1) To think about social studies issues, students must have *knowledge* of content (e.g., historical facts plus sociological, economic, and political science concepts). (2) Excellent social studies instruction promotes the development of *strategies,* including identification of problems; formulation of hypotheses; recognition of hypotheses when they are presented; and the detection of biases, logical consistencies, and inconsistencies. (3) *Motivation* to engage in hard thinking is necessary as well. Students with a disposition for thoughtfulness are curious, consistently want arguments to be supported by reasons, and enjoy reflecting on new information in light of what they already know. (4) *Metacognition* is also part of the components described by Newmann and Onosko, including the disposition to monitor thinking, knowing when and where to use skills, and important beliefs about the mind. Some of these beliefs might be that knowledge is socially constructed, that knowledge can be revised in light of new data, and that hard thinking often leads to solutions of problems.

The following are characteristics of effective classrooms identified by Newmann and Onosko:

- Lessons are substantive, coherent, and built on previous knowledge in sufficient depth for students to develop deep and connected knowledge.
- Students are allowed time to think. For example, they are given time to formulate answers before responding to questions. (See also the discussion of wait time in Chapter 10.)

- Teachers pose challenging questions to students and give them challenging tasks. (See also the discussion of questioning by teachers in Chapter 10.)
- Teachers model thoughtfulness and flexibility in thinking. Teachers let students know how they are thinking about a problem, and they make it clear that the thinking process that precedes a final decision is important. (See also the discussion of social learning theory in Chapter 7 and the discussion of direct explanation and modeling in Chapters 1 and 10.)
- Students explain their thinking and provide reasons for their conclusions. The message is sent consistently to students that the validity of a solution depends on being able to support it in a well-reasoned fashion.

Newmann (1990b, 1991c, 1991d) observed teaching and interviewed teachers in 56 high school social studies classrooms across the nation. He found that schools that promoted thinking skills as a priority tended to have classrooms that were thoughtful. Although there was more thoughtfulness in classrooms with high-ability students than in those with low-ability students, thoughtful instruction was offered to students at all ability levels in schools committed to stimulating the thinking abilities of its students. Teachers who presided over thoughtful classrooms tended to be committed to the promotion of thinking as an important goal of social studies instruction; they tended to be less committed than other teachers to having great breadth in their coverage. Schools with leaders (i.e., principals, department heads) who were committed to the promotion of thinking in the curriculum tended to have more thoughtful classrooms than those without such committed leaders. (See also the discussion of leadership in effective schools in Chapter 10.) Perhaps most importantly, thoughtful classrooms were more engaging for students than those that were less thoughtful (Newmann, 1991a). That is, students really did spend more of their time thinking about the content in more thoughtful ways compared to less thoughtful classrooms; students viewed such classes as more challenging, engaging, worthwhile, and interesting. Unfortunately, relatively few American classrooms stimulate students to think deeply about issues (R. G. Brown, 1991; Cuban, 1984; Goodlad, 1984; A. G. Powell, Farrar, & Cohen, 1985; Sizer, 1984).

Is it likely that there will be movement toward the development of many more thoughtful classrooms in thoughtful schools? It is difficult to create a social environment in school that stimulates academic growth. Newmann and Onosko and others (R. G. Brown, 1991; Voss, 1991) are realistic in recognizing that there are many challenges to the development of thoughtful classrooms. The barriers to thoughtful education include the following:

- Critical discussion is hard work for students but also requires hard mental work by teachers. Often it is easier for students to memorize and reproduce; often it is easier for teachers to present material and oversee examinations that only require recall than ones that require reflective understanding and interpretation.
- Teachers often lack the in-depth knowledge required to be effective facilitators of classroom discussions of real-life problems. They also do not know how to conduct thoughtful education. They never saw it when they were in school, and they were not taught it in their teacher education programs. Moreover, many educators have low expectations for their students and believe that their students are not intelligent enough to participate in a thoughtful classroom.
- In thoughtful classrooms, knowledge is constructed as part of active problem solving, discussion, and writing. Such construction takes time, with partial understandings and corrections along the way. Construction of knowledge involves

taking intellectual risks and advancing ideas that sometimes conflict with conventional thinking. This conflicts with the many forces in education favoring breadth of coverage, and it is painful for many to contemplate cutting out some content to permit greater attention to fewer topics, which is essential for thoughtfulness.

● "What Do I Do on Monday Morning?"

Criteria for Whether Classrooms Promote Thoughtfulness

How can teachers determine whether their classrooms promote thoughtfulness? They can roughly estimate by observing a class and responding to the six items that follow. The class should be rated on each question from 1 to 5, with a 1 given if the class is not at all like the stated criterion and a 5 if it definitely meets the criterion.

1. A few topics are examined in depth, rather than many topics covered superficially.
2. The teacher asks challenging questions and/or presents structured, challenging tasks (given the ability level and preparation of the students).
3. The students offer explanations and reasons for their conclusions.
4. The teacher carefully considers explanations and reasons for conclusions.
5. The students assume the roles of questioner and critic.
6. The students generate original and unconventional ideas, explanations, hypotheses, or solutions to problems. (Newmann, 1991a, p. 395)

All six scores should be added together and then divided by 6 to find the average. An average of 4 or higher is consistent with the best 25 percent of the classrooms in Newmann's studies.

Chapter Summary

- Students' self-concepts, that is, their perceptions of themselves, become increasingly abstract and differentiated as students develop. By the middle to end of the elementary school years, students distinguish academic from social competence and their perceptions of academic competence are influenced by task difficulty and changes in schooling practices.
- Erik Erikson's theory of social development describes eight life stages between infancy and death, each of which involves a central conflict. The conflicts during the four stages of childhood are developing a sense of trust instead of mistrust, a sense of autonomy instead of shame and doubt, a sense of initiative instead of guilt, and a sense of industry over inferiority. The central conflict of adolescence is the achievement of identity instead of role confusion. Ethnic identity and cultural differences influence identity achievement. Adults struggle to achieve intimacy, generativity, and integrity.
- Students' relationships with parents and peers influence academic achievement. Parenting styles differ in terms of how demanding parents are of their children and how responsive they are to their children. The effect of parenting style upon academic achievement is moderated by peer influences and ethnicity.

- Kohlberg's theory of moral reasoning includes three levels: (1) the preconventional level, at which moral judgments are based on self-interest; (2) the conventional level, at which judgments are based on maintaining social order; and (3) the postconventional level, at which judgments are based on shared standards and principles. Critics argue that Kohlberg's view does not account for possible sex and cultural differences in the basis for moral judgments.
- Approaches to moral education based on Kohlberg's theory emphasize creating cognitive conflict about moral reasoning through student debates about moral dilemmas. Lickona's approach to moral education combines behavioral interventions aimed at improving moral action with cognitive interventions affecting moral reasoning.

Return to the Classroom Predicament

Has reading this chapter helped you formulate responses to the questions about the parent-teacher conference? The oldest daughter is apparently an adolescent, trying out new identities and developing intimate friendships. Moratorium is a healthy and appropriate state for her to be in at this stage of her life. Her younger sister is obviously in early-elementary school, since she doesn't perceive the difference between ability and effort and work habits. Moreover, she has the typical early-elementary school pattern of friendship in which the focus is on doing things together, rather than on intimacy and mutual understanding. These students are at vastly different stages of social development but are behaving in ways appropriate for their age group. The parent, who has noticed that authoritarian parenting is not effective with the adolescent daughter, should be encouraged to use authoritative parenting for both daughters in order to achieve the goal of internalization of standards.

Chapter Outline

Chapter 10

Schooling Practices

Classroom Predicament

A student teacher addresses a few colleagues in the teacher's lounge. "I'd like advice on some problems I am having in class. How do I get my students more involved in class discussions? Many times I'll ask a question, and no one responds. My students say they are bored because we do the same thing every day. What do they mean? I just teach them every day. I also have a few students whose records indicate they have never done well in school, and, as I expected, they are not doing well in my class. What can I do to help them? My students also complain about the homework I give them. They say it really doesn't help them learn. Is homework beneficial? I have established rules and procedures, but one of my students isn't following them very well. How do I handle him?"

What would you say to this student teacher? Reflecting on the information presented in this chapter will help you formulate a response to this question.

We begin this chapter with a discussion of the general characteristics of effective schools—ones that lead to student engagement and ultimately produce good thinkers. This is followed by an examination of general classroom practices, ones not associated with a particular instructional model, and how variations in these practices influence students' achievement. Examples of the general classroom practices discussed are classroom questioning, classroom expectancies, peer tutoring, ability grouping, homework, and students' activities. Then, we analyze specific instructional methods in terms of their unique characteristics and strengths. Some teachers explicitly prefer one of these methods over another. Other teachers select the method that best suits particular learning tasks. Most of these methods, such as direct instruction, direct explanation and teacher modeling, reciprocal teaching, discovery learning, and cooperative learning, have already been introduced in other chapters.

Finally, although sound instructional practices go a long way toward keeping students engaged and classrooms functioning smoothly, we address methods for establishing good classroom management. We take a proactive approach, focusing our discussion on how to avoid problems. Given the realities of everyday classroom life, however, we also provide general guidelines for dealing with disruptive behavior.

Schools That Promote Good Thinking

What are the characteristics of schools in which achievement of students is high? Many studies have described differences in school environments that produce achievement differences (Firestone, 1991). The following are characteristics of exceptionally effective elementary schools (based on Edmonds, 1979; and supported by Bryk & Thum, 1989; Good & Brophy, 1986; Mortimore, 1991; Rutter, 1983; Stedman, 1988)):

- Strong administrative leadership
- High expectations for all children
- A safe, orderly but not rigid environment
- Top priority given to students' acquisition of basic school skills
- Frequent monitoring of pupils' progress

Studies of effective secondary schools produced a similar list of characteristics (based on Newmann, 1991b):

- Strong leadership that actively recognizes problems in the school and seeks to solve them
- High expectations for learning by students
- Orderly school environment, with fair discipline
- Academic curriculum for all students, with homework assignments
- Recognition of students' accomplishments
- Recognition of good teaching
- High involvement by parents and the community in school affairs
- Teachers and administrators who believe they are in control of the school and teaching
- Staff collegiality

In both lists, academic leadership, high expectations for all students, and an orderly school environment emerge as important characteristics of effective schools. These characteristics permit and foster a high degree of pupil **engagement** in learning (Newmann, 1991b). Engaged students are highly invested in and committed to learning, understanding, and mastering what is presented in school. Engaged students concentrate on their work, are enthusiastic about it, and are deeply interested in academic content. They care about whether they are doing well in school (Strong, Silver, & Robinson, 1995).

According to Newmann, engaging educational environments present students with tasks that seem real to them. The pace and methods of teaching are flexible. There are many opportunities for students to ask questions that are important to them, frequent occasions to pursue issues that students see as important, and many demands that students create new understandings rather than simply parrot back what the teacher has said. Engagement is fostered by academic environments that encourage risk taking. In other words, there is no shame for trying and failing. Rather there is great respect for making an effort and support for making new attempts following a failure. Engagement is fostered by environments that respect students' dignity and project a message that young people are important. Not the least of all, engaging environments are fun.

Classroom Practices and Achievement by Students

Practices that occur daily in the classroom influence students' achievement. Most of these practices are not associated with a specific instructional mode. Some of these are practices that individual teachers can control; others are controlled more at the level of the school or the district.

Classroom Questioning

Do you recall classes that were little more than one question by the teacher after another? The most common classroom interaction involves the teacher's initiating a question, students' attempting to respond, followed by the teacher's evaluation. Interactions such as these are called initiate-response-evaluation (IRE) cycles (Mehan, 1979; see also Chapter 8 for a description of more naturalistic classroom conversations). Do the thousands of questions that students experience in their years of school make a difference in learning?

There are two main types of classroom questions. **Higher-order questions** require manipulation of information and reflection, and **lower-order questions** require simple recall of information. For example, a history teacher could ask a question such as, "How would a Confederate soldier explain to our class why he decided to take up arms against the federal government?" rather than "What does your textbook say are the causes of the Civil War?" Some researchers have found that high proportions of higher-order questions are especially important in classes with high-ability students (Brophy & Evertson, 1976). In contrast, predominantly lower-order questioning may lead to higher gains in achievement for low-ability students. Presumably, lower-order questions increase the likelihood that weaker students will at least learn the facts; higher-order questions stimulate those students who acquire the facts with less effort and are able to go beyond the information given—to reflect and relate the new content to prior knowledge. What about "typical" classrooms that have a mix of abilities? Redfield and Rousseau (1981) found a moderate-sized effect favoring higher-order questioning in their meta-analysis of studies of the effects of questioning in classrooms. (See Chapter 1 for a description of meta-analysis and effect size.)

Even though lower-order questions may promote the learning of weaker students, classrooms in which teachers mainly ask lower-order, factually oriented questions are filled with less interesting conversations than classrooms in which teachers encourage more natural discussion (Almasi, 1993; Dillon, 1985, 1991; Wong, 1991). When asked for the facts, students tend to give just the facts. When asked for opinions and examples and when encouraged to follow up on peer comments, students are capable of far-reaching discussions (Almasi, 1993).

Whether teachers give students a long enough time to respond after they pose a question makes a difference in students' achievement. When teachers give students enough time to respond, in other words, when they provide **wait time,** they give the students a chance to think before responding. This wait time is associated with increases in achievement (Tobin, 1987). The wait does not have to be very long in order to have an effect on learning. A teacher's waiting as little as 3 seconds provides a learning advantage for students compared with a teacher's demand for an immediate response before providing the answer or moving on to another student.

It is also important for teachers to keep in mind the issues of cultural diversity in communication raised in Chapter 8. Cultures vary in how they teach children to answer questions. For example, Heath (1989) found that adults in African American communities in the rural Southeast only asked children *real* questions, ones the adults needed to have answered, not ones the adults could answer themselves. Imagine a student from such a community wondering whether the teacher was stupid and that is why such simple questions were being asked. Students from still other cultures, such as some Native American cultures, are reluctant to "perform" before the rest of the class by responding to questions.

Teachers can answer questions as well as ask them, and when they do, it often helps students understand new material (Fishbein, Eckart, Lauver, Van Leeuwen, & Langmeyer, 1990; H. S. Ross & Balzer, 1975; H. S. Ross & Killey, 1977). The catch is that some of the students most in need of assistance will not seek it out, wanting to be independent or believing that their efforts to seek help may be perceived as a reflection of low ability (L. S. Newman, 1990; R. S. Newman & Goldin, 1990; van der Meij, 1988). This is why many educators encourage students to ask questions when they are not sure of the material and why they send many messages to their students that asking questions is not a sign of low ability, but something smart people do whenever they need assistance.

Is it possible to teach children how to ask questions about academic content? Yes, even preschoolers can learn how to ask for information (Courage, 1989). Lyman (1992) taught elementary school students to ask questions about text, questions that helped them understand cause-and-effect relationships, time sequences, and similarities and differences between ideas covered. Children can learn to be good questioners.

● **"What Do I Do on Monday Morning?"**

Advice for Questioning in the Classroom

Lively class discussions can be sparked by skillful questioning. Some teachers are uncomfortable planning and conducting such classroom interactions because of their concerns about loss of control, increased time requirements resulting in less coverage, and unprepared students. Here are some guidelines to facilitate teacher questioning in the classroom:

- Prepare the questions in advance.
- Ask students to repeat the question before answering.
- Allow students to talk to each other as they try to answer.
- Wait for students to think about their answers.

Suggestions for responses by the teacher to students' answers include:

- Provide feedback so everyone knows the correct answer.
- Affirm the correct portion of partially correct responses. For example, "Well, you've answered one part of the question, but what about . . ."
- State or pose a relationship between a previous response and what was just said. For instance, "Luis just said that the Civil War resulted from a disagreement about state's rights, and Glenda said earlier that slavery was the reason for the war. How are these two answers related?"
- Prompt responses from other students. "I see, any further ideas? What do you think of this?"

Teachers can be tempted to ask students questions they are certain will be quickly answered, because teachers can be uncomfortable with long pauses before responses. Remember, it takes time for students to respond to questions that are high level, those requiring reflection and integration of knowledge. Quick responses are more likely if questions are low level, those only requiring parroting back of information. The following can help teachers determine the level of the questions they ask in the classroom:

- Can this question be answered in a word or two (more likely to be low level), or does the response take at least a sentence or two (more likely to be high level)?
- Do students' hands go up immediately (more likely to be low level), or do they seem to be thinking before they raise their hands (more likely to be high level)?
- Are students rattling off answers (more likely to be low level), or do they seem to work through their answers as they talk (more likely to be high level)?

Classroom Expectancies

If a teacher expects a student to do well in school, will that student excel academically? Will the teacher's expectations be fulfilled—perhaps because the teacher acts differently toward the student because of this belief in the student's ability? In *Pygmalion in the Classroom*, R. Rosenthal and Jacobson (1968) reported a study suggesting that teacher expectancies about students' achievement alone were a powerful determinant of actual achievement.

What happened in this study? Early in the school year, all students in one school were administered a standardized test that was represented to their teachers as identifying students who were likely to exhibit substantial intellectual growth in the next year. When the tests results were reported to the teachers, 20 percent of the students in each classroom were identified as likely to make larger than typical gains during the current school year. In reality, these students had been selected at random, so there was no reason to believe these students would gain any more or less during the upcoming year than other students in the class. However, when the students were tested at the end of the school year, the students who had been identified to their teachers as likely to make large gains *had made larger gains* than the rest of the students.

Have the results of R. Rosenthal and Jacobson (1968) been replicated in follow-up research? Researchers have not consistently obtained significant teacher-expectancy effects, and sometimes those expected to do poorly did well and those students expected to do well did poorly (Goldenberg, 1992). R. Rosenthal (1985) reported that significant effects were obtained in a little more than one-third of the teacher-expectancy studies. Using meta-analysis (see Chapter 1 for a description of this procedure), R. Rosenthal (1985) argued that Pygmalion effects were real, although they tended to be small.

Although there are many doubts about whether teacher expectancies alone can affect achievement, there are far fewer doubts that teachers do behave differently as a result of their expectancies about students based on previous experiences with those students (V. C. Hall & Merkel, 1985). That is, even if teachers do not react differently to students on the basis of test reports about the students' abilities, they do react differently when they see evidence of high and low ability in their daily interactions with students.

Based on observations of teacher-student interactions in classrooms, Brophy and Good (1970, 1974; Brophy, 1985) compiled a list of ways in which classroom environments are different for low-ability students than for high-ability students:

- Teachers demand less from low-ability students.
- Teachers are less likely to wait for a low-ability student to respond to questions than for a high-ability student.
- Teachers give briefer responses that are not as informative to the questions of low-ability students than to those of high-ability students.
- Low-ability students are criticized more often, such as in response to their failures, and receive less praise than high-ability students.
- Teachers' reinforcements are less likely to be contingent on correct responding for low-ability students compared to high-ability students.
- Teachers are less friendly in their interactions with low-ability students.
- Teachers call on low-ability students less often than they do high-ability students.
- Teachers seat low-ability students further away from the teacher's desk than they do high-ability students.
- Teachers are less likely to give low-ability students the benefit of the doubt on close calls in grading than they are high-ability students. (The list is based on Brophy, 1985, pp. 309–310.)

What is more, these differences in how low-ability and high-ability students are treated are easily detected by other teachers and students (Babad, Bernieri, & Rosenthal, 1991). It is easy for others to spot which students a teacher expects to do well and which students the teacher believes will be slow. Brophy and Good (1970, 1974; Brophy, 1985) believe that differential treatment affects students' perceptions of themselves and their own abilities. Low-ability students come to perceive very clearly that they are less likely to succeed than high-ability students. They form a negative academic self-concept, which in turn reduces their motivation for school and learning and their level of aspiration.

One reason why effective schools have high expectancies for students is to take advantage of the phenomenon of a **self-fulfilling prophecy.** For instance, when

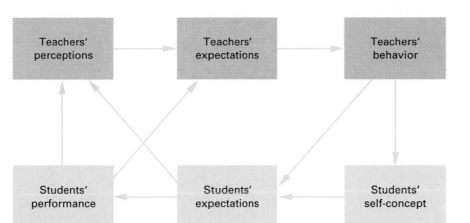

Figure 10.1
This figure depicts the complex interactive relationship between a teacher's perceptions, expectations, and behavior and their influence upon students' expectations, academic self-concept, and performance.

teachers expect much of their students, the teachers' positive expectations can influence their own teaching behaviors so that their interactions with students are more favorable. In turn, the academic self-concepts of students can be improved when taught by teachers who believe in them. Students' motivational beliefs and, ultimately, their long-term academic performances probably can be affected by teachers' expectancies as well. Fortunately, with support, teachers can learn to raise their expectations of students (Weinstein, Madison, & Kuklinski, 1995).

Expectancy effects in classrooms are not just one-way—that is, teachers' reacting to students—but can also be influenced by students' reactions to teachers. Jamieson, Lydon, Stewart, and Zanna (1987) convinced two classes of eleventh-grade students that they were being taught by a very able English teacher. These students outperformed students in control English classes who had not been led to believe that the very same teacher was exceptionally able. A number of interacting effects may have contributed to the overall difference: Students in the positive-expectancy classes talked more, which affected the teacher's perceptions, which in turn affected the teacher's behavior, and so on. See Figure 10.1 for an illustration of this kind of circular relationship generated by expectancies.

Peer Tutoring

In classrooms, often one student can be found tutoring another. Both the tutor and the tutee (the student being tutored) benefit from this interaction (V. L. Allen, 1976). If anything, peer tutoring is an even more positive educational opportunity for the tutor than the tutee since learning of course material is probably improved more by being a tutor than a tutee (Semb, Ellis, & Araujo, 1993).

Peer tutoring also clearly benefits the tutee. Greenwood, Delquadri, and Hall (1989) compared a group of students with a low socioeconomic status who had been in classrooms that emphasized peer tutoring all through grades 1 to 4 with a similar group of students in more conventional classrooms. At the end of fourth grade, the students who experienced peer tutoring achieved at higher levels than the control students in reading, math, and language arts. There were other benefits of tutoring as well. The peer-tutored students were better behaved in class and spent more class time engaged in academic activities. The students themselves also readily accepted peer tutoring and considered it to be fair (Thorkildsen, 1993).

Peers are not the only source of potential tutors; some children also have brothers and sisters. Older siblings may be especially effective as tutors, with younger tutees more attentive to and willing to interact actively with older siblings than with other child tutors (Azmitia & Hesser, 1993). In recent years, volunteer tutoring has become one important way adults in a community can contribute to schools. This type of tutoring also increases the achievement of the tutees (Michael, 1990). College students also often volunteer in schools, and their efforts clearly promote the achievement of students they tutor (Reisner, Petry, & Armitage, 1989). Many teacher education programs require potential teachers to gain hands-on experience in real schools by participating in tutoring programs during teacher preparation.

Peer tutoring can also be successful for college students. Fantuzzo, Riggio, Connelly, and Dimeff (1989) used a peer-tutoring intervention called *reciprocal peer tutoring* in a university-level psychology course. First, students were paired with one another for most of the term. Before each unit exam, each partner constructed multiple-choice questions on the material in the unit. Then, the partners met and administered the exams to one another. This was followed by a discussion in which the partner writing the exam questions explained to the partner taking the exam the answer for each item answered incorrectly. It is easy to understand why this treatment might be effective:

- Students generate questions over academic content, which increases learning (Rosenshine & Trapman, 1992).
- Students take practice tests, which also increases learning (Glover, 1989).
- Students explain the material to another person, which also increases learning (N. M. Webb, 1989).

Peer tutoring benefits both the student tutor and the student being tutored.

Ability Grouping

Ability grouping, or **tracking,** for instruction has been common in schools. It may begin with three different groups for reading in first grade (good readers, average readers, weak readers) and continues through the end of high school, with advanced placement courses for the best students and vocational education options for students who have not fared well academically in junior high school and the early years of high school.

In the last two decades, the practice of ability grouping, or tracking, has come under attack since it does not promote academic achievement (Oakes, 1987; Slavin, 1987a, 1990). Putting a student in the middle or slower group guarantees that student will receive different instruction than those in the high group receive. The materials read are different, the pace is slower, and members of the group are less capable (Juel, 1990). Another reason why tracking may have a negative effect on the achievement of students in the low tracks is that their teachers' expectations about their potential for achievement are low (Brophy, 1985).

Oakes (1985) examined tracking in 25 high schools across the United States. Students in the high tracks were exposed to much more important content than the students in the low tracks. Consider the following answers from students in high-track classes to the question, "What is the most important thing you have learned or done so far in this class?" (All examples are from Oakes, 1985, pp. 67–72.)

> Things in nature are not always what they appear to be or what seems to be happening is not what is really happening.

> To infer or apply the past ideas to my ideas and finally to the future's ideas.

> We have learned the basics of the law of relativity, and basics in electronics. The teacher applies these lessons to practical situations.

Now consider answers to the same question from low-track students:

> To be honest, nothing.

> How to blow up light bulbs.

> Spelling, worksheets.

In addition to finding that low-track students are exposed to less knowledge and knowledge that is not as valued in our culture, Oakes (1985) demonstrated that less of the total class time in low-track classes is devoted to instruction. Students in low-track classes spend more time fooling around, and they are assigned much less homework. Despite the fact that it is known that it takes longer for low-ability students to learn content than high-ability students (Carroll, 1963), low-track classrooms are structured so that low-ability students spend even less time on learning than high-ability students do. In addition, the quality of school life was worse for low-ability than for high-ability students. Teachers were less enthusiastic about teaching them. The high-track classes seemed better planned and organized than the low-track ones. The teachers were more respectful toward high-track students; they were more punitive of low-track ones. They were more open to questions from high-track than low-track students. Even peer relations were warmer and friendlier for high-track students than low-track students, who seemed to take their frustrations out on each other.

▶ **Diversity**

Special Education and Mainstreaming

Special education has sometimes been offered as an extreme form of tracking, with placements in "special" schools, special classrooms, and "resource room" given to students identified as learning disabled or mildly retarded (see also the discussion in Chapter 16). The law (in particular, *U.S. Public Law 94–142*) now requires that special education students be placed in minimally restrictive environments or environments that are as much as possible like a normal school. This often means placement in a regular classroom environment. Many efforts are now underway to identify ways to maximize the learning of special education students in regular classrooms (Schloss, 1992).

Research supports the intent of PL 94–142. When special education students are isolated for instruction, the instruction often is not very good. Even assignment to resource rooms for part of a day, which is a much less extreme form of special placement than assignment to a separate school or a special classroom for the entire day, has a negative impact on the quality of instruction offered to students. When students receive instruction in the resource room, they actually receive less total instruction. At the very least, the time that might have been used for instruction is eaten up shuttling from the regular classroom to the resource room. In addition, the instruction in the resource room does not typically address the content and skills these students are expected to acquire in the regular classroom. Indeed, rather than make these students' lives better, resource room instruction can make special education students' lives worse, fragmenting their day and their instruction and providing less opportunity for them to learn the material on which they are evaluated than they would have had without the resource room instruction (Allington, 1983, 1991a, 1991b; Allington & McGill-Franzen, 1989, 1991; McGill-Franzen, 1987; Meyers, Gelzheiser, Yelich, & Gallagher, 1990; P. J. O'Sullivan, Ysseldyke, Christenson, & Thurlow, 1990).

Homework

For most students, homework is a fact of life from the middle-elementary school grades through the remainder of school. Does this pervasive educational "intervention" actually improve academic achievement? Harris Cooper (1989b) summarized the research on homework and reached the following conclusions:

- Doing homework promotes learning.
- The positive effects of homework are very small in the upper-elementary school years and gradually increase until they are moderate in magnitude during the high school years.
- The effects of homework on math, reading, and English are probably greater than the effects of homework on social studies and science achievement.
- Homework benefits simple skills that require practice and repetition more than complex skills that require integration and reflection.

Does homework improve academic achievement? Yes, but how much depends on the age of the student and the academic content of the homework. Parental supervision of homework also increases its effectiveness.

- For junior high school students, 1 to 2 hours of homework per night seems optimal. High school students benefit from more homework, although it is not clear what a reasonable maximum might be.

Homework may also elicit parental involvement in school, a fact that promotes academic achievement (D. L. Stevenson & Baker, 1987). Although well-educated parents are most likely to be involved with school, any parent can be. Parents' working with their children on homework tasks clearly improves the academic performances of their children in school (Goldenberg, 1989).

▶ Diversity

After-School Tutoring in Japan

Students who are slower to learn might benefit from additional instructional time after school. After-school tutoring, however, is not common in Western cultures, but it is common in Japan (Rowan & Guthrie, 1989). *Juku* instruction is commonly sought out by the brightest of Japanese students who participate for years in after-school tutoring to prepare for difficult university entrance examinations (White, 1987). In Japan, there is a clear perception that after-school tutoring makes a substantial difference in the ultimate achievement levels of Japanese students.

The dynamics of after-school tutoring are probably very different from the dynamics operating in school. The following description of one *juku* tutor, Sagara, illustrates the extremely social and motivating nature of this type of instruction compared to normal schooling:

> The students see him as on their side, as uncompromisingly working *with* them, and sometimes even as an ally against their parents. He constantly rewards them, and provides nurturance in the form of treats and surprises, such as getting them ice cream on a hot day or buying them

In Japan, after-school tutoring, or *juku*, often plays a significant role in the student's academic life.

books or special gifts. [One student] even received several comic books from Sagara when the young student was sick, and Sagara offered him a whole set of them if he'd promise to study hard for his high school entrance exam. Sagara's relationship with his students is of the kidding, big-brother sort. Sagara once bet his students on the answer to a very hard problem and said that if he were wrong, he'd cut his hair very short. He was and he did. He is boyish and dresses casually, and the intensity of *juku* study is mitigated by Sagara's cheerful liveliness. . . . For the graduates, the *juku* experience seems to have been more meaningful than their time in regular schools, for they say "after I graduated from *juku* . . ." instead of "after I graduated from junior high. . . ." They all say Sagara is one of the most important people in their lives. (White, 1987, pp. 148–149)

This tutoring relationship is likely to be more personal and supportive than the relationships typically developed in schools.

Students' Activities

Does playing sports, cheerleading, participating in drama or debate, or playing in the band affect students' achievement? If these extracurricular activities take time away from schoolwork, they might interfere with achievement (Coleman, 1961). Alternatively, they might be enriching experiences. Using data collected by the federal government in more than 1000 high schools, Marsh (1992) determined that there were small but consistently positive correlations between extracurricular participation and a variety of academic outcomes. In addition, students who participated in extracurricular activities tended to have slightly better academic self-concepts. Of course, since this is correlational evidence, it is impossible to determine whether participation in extracurricular activities increases academic ability or more capable students elect to participate in extracurricular activities.

A. Holland and Andre (1987) offered an especially optimistic appraisal of extracurricular activities. They claimed that participation in extracurricular activities was correlated with higher self-esteem; better racial relations; more political

What is the relationship between extracurricular activities and achievement? What about between working and achievement? In general, extracurricular activities tend to support academic achievement, and extensive employment does not.

and social involvement; feelings of greater control; lower delinquency; and higher grades, academic achievement, and aspirations. In addition, A. Holland and Andre found that students enrolled in small schools were more likely to partake of extracurricular activities and enjoy the benefits of such experiences.

How does after-school employment affect students' achievement? Although many believe in the benefits of after-school work, such as increased self-reliance, work orientation, and self-esteem, there is little evidence that working students receive these advantages (Steinberg & Dornbusch, 1991). In fact, extensive after-school employment is associated with poor school performance, psychological distress, substance abuse, and delinquency (Steinberg & Dornbusch, 1991; Steinberg, Fegley, & Dornbusch, 1993). If economic realities require students to work, they should try to limit their work hours so the job does not interfere with schoolwork. Unfortunately, students who are already having difficulty in school are most likely to elect outside work, which results in even lower in-school achievement (Steinberg, Fegley, & Dornbusch, 1993).

Instructional Methods

Because school learning includes many different types of information, one instructional approach is not appropriate for all types of content and all types of learning goals. Furthermore, teachers develop instructional preferences and, perhaps, instructional habits. A variety of instructional techniques are described in other

Focus on Research

Quantitative and Qualitative Research on Class Size

The typical elementary school teacher in the United States has between 20 and 30 children in his or her classroom, with the average in the mid–20s. The typical secondary school teacher faces sections with between 25 and 30 students, with the average in the upper–20s; five or more sections per day is common (National Center for Education Statistics, 1992). Virtually all reviewers of research on class size conclude that small classes boost achievement, particularly for weak students (H. M. Cooper, 1989; Educational Research Service, 1978; Glass & Smith, 1979; Hedges & Stock, 1983; Slavin, 1984). How small must classes be before there are worthwhile gains in achievement? Some argue that reducing classes to 15 pupils makes a difference (Glass & Smith, 1979), and others believe that gains are not large until class size is reduced to numbers typical of small-group tutoring, such as 3 students per teacher (Slavin, 1984) or even 1-to-1 tutoring (Slavin, 1989).

The issue of class size has been addressed in true experimental studies, which permit cause-and-effect conclusions. Think back to Chapter 1, and review the characteristics of a true experiment. Using 76 schools in Tennessee, Finn and Achilles (1990) randomly assigned kindergarten students either to small classes (i.e., 13–17 students) or large classes (i.e., 22–25), with the presence or absence of an aide systematically manipulated in the larger classes. These class sizes and class assignments were held intact through the first grade. At the end of first grade, the students in the smaller classes displayed greater achievement in mathematics and reading. The advantages of the smaller class were especially striking for minority students. Although the presence of an aide helped, especially in first grade, the students in the smaller classes generally outperformed those in larger classes taught by a teacher and an aide.

What kinds of questions about the effects of class size could qualitative research methods begin to answer? Think back to the discussion of the strengths of qualitative methods in Chapter 1. Qualitative investigations could examine much more completely the diversity and types of learning opportunities occurring in small versus large classes. For instance, Morrow and Smith (1990) found differences in the interactions, that is, the process of instruction, when reading instruction occurred in small groups rather than in whole classes. Qualitative research methods could also examine whether the curriculum really is more individualized with fewer students and how small classes must be before it is possible to monitor and reinforce individual student growth with sensitivity.

chapters of this book (see especially Chapters 1, 2, 8, 11, and 12). Keep in mind, the goal of education is to develop good thinking in students and to facilitate their construction of knowledge as described in Chapter 1.

Direct Instruction

Teachers who employ **direct instruction** as the primary instructional method create classrooms that are academically focused and teacher-directed (Rosenshine, 1979). These teachers present academic content in a sequenced and structured fashion. Direct instruction also involves clear specification of goals to students, with detailed explanations and extensive coverage of content. Teachers ask questions that students can handle, typically directing low-level, literal questions to weak students and more demanding questions to better students. Teachers monitor students' performance, providing immediate corrective feedback. Even with all of this academic work going on, the most effective classrooms that use direct instruction are warm, democratic, and cooperative.

Direct instruction can be summarized in the following six fundamental instructional functions (Rosenshine & Stevens, 1986, p. 379):

1. Review
   - Check homework
   - Review relevant past learning (perhaps include questioning)
   - Reteach, if necessary
2. Presentation
   - State lesson objectives and goals, providing an overview
   - Proceed in small steps but at a rapid pace
   - Intersperse questions to check for understanding
   - Provide demonstrations, illustrations, and concrete examples
   - Highlight main ideas
3. Guided student practice
   - Check for understanding by evaluating student responses
   - Question frequently
   - Give additional explanation, when necessary
   - Provide prompts, when appropriate
   - Continue until students can work independently (approximately 80 percent correct)
4. Correctives and feedback
   - Acknowledge correctness of quick and firm correct responses
   - Provide process feedback to hesitant correct responses ("Yes, that is correct because . . .")
   - Monitor students for systematic errors, which may reveal misunderstanding
   - Provide sustaining feedback to incorrect responses (simplify question, give clues, review steps, etc.)
5. Independent student practice
   - Allow for sufficient practice for overlearning, when responses are quick, firm, and automatic (approximately 95 percent correct)
   - Actively supervise independent practice, when possible
6. Weekly and monthly reviews
   - Review previously learned material systematically
   - Test frequently
   - Reteach information missed in tests

Proponents of direct instruction argue that it produces the best learning (Rosenshine, 1979; Rosenshine & Stevens, 1984). They emphasize the teacher (rather than the student) as decision maker and embrace orderliness in the classroom. Since direct instruction endorses asking questions that students can answer rather than questions that challenge them and require reflection, proponents of direct instruction believe that drill and overlearning are important in school learning.

Direct Explanation and Teacher Modeling

An alternative method of instruction is **direct explanation and teacher modeling** (see also Chapter 1). In this method, the teacher begins with explanations and modeling. Then the teacher monitors students' practice, providing additional explanations and modeling as needed. As the student becomes more and more independent, the teacher reduces the feedback and instruction. Thus, the teacher scaffolds instruction. As described in Chapters 1 and 8, in **scaffolded instruction** the teacher provides help to students on an as-needed basis. The teacher monitors the progress of students toward a goal and provides only enough support for the student to accomplish the goal.

Classrooms that use direct instruction and those that use direct explanation and teacher modeling are similar in several ways. They are more teacher-directed than student-directed. Since they are well structured with clearly articulated lesson goals, they use the students' time well. The tasks (including questions) given to students are ones they can handle, at least with some support from the teacher. Teachers also provide immediate academic feedback to students.

There are also differences between the two instructional methods. Teachers who use direct explanation focus on processing by students, which is often revealed by students' thinking aloud. They are concerned that students develop a deep understanding of the strategies they are learning as well as about when and how to use them. In contrast, direct instruction emphasizes academic performance rather than how students achieve that academic performance.

Any strategy can be taught with direct explanation and teacher modeling (see also Chapter 4). A very important part of this instruction is what Duffy and Roehler (1989) call mental modeling. **Mental modeling** refers to the teacher's showing the students how to apply a strategy simply by thinking aloud as he or she uses the strategy. Another extremely important idea in this approach to instruction is **responsive elaboration.** With this instructional technique, the teacher provides additional input and elaborations that are responsive to the needs of particular learners and dependent on the particular problems the students encounter. Reinstruction and reexplanations as well as follow-up mental modeling are responsive to student needs and usually are an elaboration of students' understandings up until that point.

Is direct explanation and teacher modeling effective for strategy instruction? Duffy et al. (1987) taught third-grade teachers to explain reading strategies directly. (One example is the prefix pronunciation strategy described in the "What Do I Do on Monday Morning?" feature.) The teachers learned first to explain a strategy and then to model the use of the strategy mentally for students. The mental modeling showed students how good readers apply the strategy when they read. Then came guided student practice, with the students' initially carrying out the processing overtly so that the teacher could monitor their use of the new strategy. At first, there was substantial assistance, but it was reduced as students became more proficient.

Teachers encouraged transfer of the strategies taught by going over when and where the students might use the strategies. Teachers cued students to use the new strategies when they encountered situations in which they might be applied profitably, regardless of when these occasions arose during the school day. Teachers continued the cuing and prompting until students autonomously applied the strategies they were taught.

After a year of this type of instruction, students who were instructed using direct explanation and teacher modeling were more aware of lesson content and the strategic nature of reading at the end of the year than control students who did not receive direct explanations about reading strategies were. In addition, the students who were taught with direct explanation outperformed the control students on a number of measures of reading. In short, a full year of direct explanation of reading strategies made a substantial difference in the reading achievement of third-grade students.

● "What Do I Do on Monday Morning?"

Sample Dialogue for Direct Explanation and Modeling

What would a direct explanation and modeling lesson be like? Consider the following dialogue from part of a third-grade lesson on a prefix-pronunciation strategy:

Introducing the basal text lesson: "Today we are going to read a story about a monkey that lived in the zoo. How many of you have been in the zoo? What do you see in the zoo? . . . Now in this story there are some hard words that you have never had before. Here's one right here (shows students). Here's another. I'm going to teach you a strategy for figuring out these words and others like them so that, when you come to them in the story, you will be able to figure them out yourselves and go right on finding out about what happens to the monkey."

Introducing the strategy: "Sometimes when you are reading, you run into a word you don't recognize. . . . So we need to stop and figure out the word. . . . This strategy will help you figure out the pronunciation of prefixed words so you can continue getting the author's meaning despite these hard words. In order to do this, you need to look for the root word, then look for the *dis-* or the *un-*. Then you separate the two, pronounce each one separately, then say the prefix and the root word together."

Mental modeling: "I'll explain how I figure out words like these. You'll do this in a moment, so pay attention to the way I figure these words out. [Mental modeling follows.] Let's say that I'm reading along in my basal story and I run into the word *unhappy*. If I've never seen this word before, I say to myself, 'Oh, oh. I need to figure this word out if I'm going to continue getting the author's meaning.' So I stop, look at the word and think about what strategy I can use to make sense out of this word. I see that it is a prefixed word, so I think about a prefix strategy. I find the root [circles it]. I separate the root from the prefix [draws a line between them]. Then I pronounce the prefix—*un-*. Then I pronounce the root—*happy*. Then I say the two parts together—*unhappy*. Then I put the word back into the sentence in the story to make sure it makes sense. Now let's review what I did. You tell me the steps I followed, and I'll list them up here on the board. Susie, what did I do first? Yes, first I [writes on board] . . . then I . . . [writes on board] . . . [etc.]."

Mediating students' initial attempts to apply the strategy using directives and cues: "Can you use my strategy to figure out unrecognized words? . . . You have . . . things to help you: the steps in the strategy listed on the board here [points]. . . . Mary, show me how you use the strategy to figure out this word. [Mary does so successfully—that is, she mentally models her use of the strategy.]"

Interaction with questions and faded cues: "Now let's see if you can do the same thing when I give you less help. I'm going to erase from the board the steps of my strategy, and you see if you can use a strategy of your own that is like mine. . . . [Teacher is attempting to fade support here. Puts new word on board.] Now, Sam, what would you do first to figure out this word? Can you show me how you'd figure out the word? [Sam responds by just pronouncing the word.] . . . [The teacher responds with responsive elaborations, ones tailored to the teacher's perceptions of Sam's needs.] You said the word correctly, Sam, but I don't know whether you were doing the thinking correctly. What did you do first? [Teacher cues the student to model mentally what follows.] Talk out loud so I can hear how you figured that word out. [Sam responds, stating the steps he used.] That's good, Sam. You stated the steps you used to figure out the word correctly. This strategy doesn't work all the time, because some of our words look like words with prefixes but really aren't. [Illustrates the word *under.*] See if this word can be pronounced using our prefix strategy. [Leads students through the process showing them where the strategy doesn't work and why. Scaffolding occurs in that the interaction that follows involves fewer cues; eventually there is interaction with supportive feedback but no cues.]"

Setting purposes for reading the basal selection: "Now we are going to read the story about the monkey named Clyde. . . . There are some hard words in this story, which you haven't seen before. [Mental modeling follows.] When you come to these words, say to yourself, 'Oh, oh. I'm going to have to figure this word out.' Then see if your prefix strategy will work, and, if the hard word does have a prefix, use what we learned about figuring out prefixed words to figure out the word in the story. [Silent or oral reading follows.]"

Discussion: [Leads discussion in which questions are posed about both the content and the application of the prefix strategy while reading the story. The intent is to assess whether students understand the content and the application of the prefix strategy.]

Lesson closure: [Closes the lesson by having students summarize what happened in the story and how the prefix strategy was used to help understand the story.] "All right. Now that you have successfully used the prefix strategy to figure out hard words in the basal text story, we have to be sure to use it in other things you read. [Teacher is providing some metacognitive information about the strategy—that is, information about when and where to use the strategy.] What other things do you read where you could use this strategy? What if you ran into an unknown word when reading in . . . (another) book? Could you use this strategy in this situation? Can you tell me how you would use the prefix strategy in reading a newspaper?" (Adapted with permission from Duffy & Roehler, 1989, Example 13.1, pp. 228–229.)

Reciprocal Teaching

In Chapter 8, **reciprocal teaching,** a form of instruction consistent with Vygotskian principles, was introduced. This method involves instruction of comprehension strategies in the context of a reading group. Students learn to make prèdictions when reading, to question themselves about the text, to seek clarification when confused, and to summarize content. The teacher initially explains and models these strategies for students, but very quickly students are leading the group. One student is assigned the role of group leader. The group leader supervises the groups' generation of predictions, questions, and summaries during reading. The group leader also solicits points that need to be clarified and either provides clarifications or elicits them from other group members. The teacher provides support on an as-needed basis. In other words, the instruction is scaffolded. (See Chapter 8 for an extended example of reciprocal teaching.)

Reciprocal teaching and direct explanation are similar (Pressley, Snyder, &

Cariglia-Bull, 1987). Both involve teaching cognitive processes for coming to terms with text. Both involve modeling and explanation of strategies. During both, students can see multiple models of cognitive processing since some students use the cognitive processes that are being taught. Both involve teacher scaffolding of instruction. The teacher monitors what is going on and offers supportive instruction on an as-needed basis. In both approaches, the teacher is progressively less involved as instruction proceeds.

There are also differences between reciprocal teaching and direct explanation. The most important difference is the saliency of the teacher. In reciprocal teaching, the teacher reduces control quickly. The belief is that if students are to internalize decision making for cognitive processes, they need to control their cognitive processes. In contrast, the teacher remains more visibly in charge in direct explanation, although the goal is always to reduce the teacher's input.

Discovery Learning

In **discovery learning,** teachers present tasks that offer opportunities for students to construct understandings (Bruner, 1961; Gagné, 1965; Wittrock, 1966). Students interact with objects in the classroom, exploring, manipulating, and performing experiments. For instance, if a teacher wishes students to learn about magnetism, the teacher provides magnets and objects made of all different kinds of materials and allows the students to discover which materials are attracted by magnets and which are not. This approach is student-directed, and the teacher's input is often limited to answering students' questions and monitoring for incorrect conclusions (Suchman, 1960; see also Chapters 1 and 12). The basic idea behind discovery learning is that students will learn if teachers cultivate their natural curiosity. Theoretical support for this view can be found in Piaget's concept of the learner as naturally active, learning through experimentation and manipulation (see Chapter 7).

Discovery learning is most effective when teachers make sure students have the necessary knowledge to allow discovery, when the appropriate materials are available, and when students are interested. Discovery learning, however, can be inefficient and can even lead to incorrect conclusions (Schauble, 1990; see the discussion in Chapters 1 and 12). For example, students discover on their own many subtraction rules that are wrong (van Lehn, 1990). This is why some educators favor a structured modification of pure discover learning called **guided discovery.**

In guided discovery, the teacher's role is more explicit than in pure discovery learning. The teacher typically poses questions to students. The intent of these questions is to lead students to "discover" knowledge about the task at hand. For instance, in the magnetism example, the teacher would ask questions such as, "What are the characteristics of objects that are not attracted by the magnets?" and "What characteristics are shared by the objects that are attracted by magnets? " Not surprising, guided discovery leads to more certain and efficient learning than pure discovery learning (Gagné & Brown, 1961; Kersh, 1958).

In both of these discovery approaches, the role of the teacher is more limited than in either direct instruction or direct explanation. Discovery learning approaches are clearly student-centered.

Cooperative Learning

Students can often learn a great deal by working together. Sometimes one student tutors another (see discussion of peer tutoring in this chapter). Other times students work together in groups toward a common goal. **Cooperative learning** has four essential characteristics (Johnson & Johnson, 1985; see also Chapters 2 and 12). First, learning should be *interdependent* in that task completion requires all students to work. Second, there should be *face-to-face interactions among the students in small learning groups*. Third, each student must be *individually accountable*. Fourth, students need to learn *interpersonal skills*. In cooperative learning approaches, students work together to learn and are responsible for one another's learning (Slavin, 1991).

In his synthesis of the research on cooperative learning, Slavin (1991) found that cooperative learning facilitated learning at all grade levels, for all subjects, and for all achievement levels (high, medium, and low). There are also social effects associated with cooperative learning, including increases in self-esteem, positive attitudes toward school, and acceptance of the handicapped. More research on cooperative learning has been conducted in elementary schools than in high schools.

How can teachers implement cooperative learning in their classrooms? Student Teams-Achievement Divisions (STAD) is a cooperative learning approach that is adaptable to most subjects and grade levels (Slavin, 1991). Students are assigned to four-member teams that are mixed in terms of performance level, sex, and ethnicity. The teacher presents the lesson, and the teams work together to make sure all students master the lesson. The students take individual quizzes, without the assistance of team members, to assess what they have learned. The teacher compares students' quiz scores with their own past averages and computes a team average based on the students' improvement. Perfect performances always receive a maximum score regardless of the previous performance.

In this approach, every student must know the material. Thus, there is *individual accountability*. The teams can also earn *team rewards* if they achieve at or above a designated criterion. The teams are not in competition with each other; all teams could earn a team reward. Since team averages are computed in consideration of students' past averages, all students have an *equal opportunity for success* and can contribute to the team's performance by improving on past performances.

Another cooperative learning approach, Team Assisted Instruction (TAI), was originally designed for mathematics learning (Slavin, 1985a, 1985b). TAI combines cooperative learning with individualized instruction. A class is divided into four- to five-member teams that are mixed in terms of performance level, sex, and ethnicity. Although individual members may be working on different instructional units, students remain in their teams for 8 weeks or so at a time, changing teams at the end of this period.

Instructional sessions are divided into periods of individualized study and team study. During the individualized portion, each student works on self-instructional materials. Each assignment includes an instruction sheet that details the skill to be mastered, including step-by-step instructions about how to do assigned problems.

During the period of team study, students work in pairs or in triads with team members. The students try to solve work sheet problems, assisting one another with the instructions or with specific problems and checking each other's answers against the answer key for the work sheets. After working through all the work sheets, a student takes a practice test, which is then checked by a team member.

If a student works eight of the ten practice test problems correctly, the team certifies the student to proceed to the final test. If the practice test score is less than *8,* the adult teacher is called in to provide guidance, which usually means assigning the student to work on the worksheets more, leading up to a second practice test. Students monitor carefully whether fellow team members make the required score of *8* on the practice test before they are permitted to proceed to the final test.

At the end of each week, a team score is calculated based on the total number of units completed per team member, with additional points given for exceptionally high performances on final tests. The teams that do exceptionally well receive certificates denoting their accomplishment. The teacher does not disappear completely in this process but rather provides daily tutorials to small groups of students, ones who are at about the same point in the various units, bringing students together from different teams in order to form tutoring groups of three to four students.

Third- through sixth-grade students who experienced TIA displayed math achievement that was superior to that of students receiving conventional instruction (Slavin, 1985a, 1985b). In addition, students' attitudes toward mathematics improved following participation in TAI.

Slavin (Stevens, Madden, Slavin, & Farnish, 1987) has also developed an effective program for reading, the Cooperative Integrated Reading and Composition program (CIRC). The group arrangements are similar to those used in TAI. The teacher provides instruction in reading and composition strategies to the class as a whole. Activities in small groups follow reading of a basal reader selection. These exercises include reading, analysis of narrative structures of stories, writing, word mastery and learning of definitions, story retelling, and spelling. All of this work is done with partners, who also monitor each other's progress in preparation for formal tests of stories and story-related activities.

● **"What Do I Do on Monday Morning?"**

Suggestions for Creating Cooperative Learning Groups

- Be sure to use both *group rewards and individual accountability* (e.g., R. Slavin, 1985). Individual accountability helps to eliminate freeloading, and a group reward provides incentive for the students to work together. A group reward is very different from a group grade, which is giving the same grade to everyone. Group grades undermine individual accountability and can be blatantly unfair (S. Kagan, 1995).
- Make sure the students in each cooperative group represent a *range of ability* but cooperative learning seems to work better if groups do not include the full range of ability (N. M. Webb, 1992, 1989). For example, place high-ability and medium-ability students together. Similarly, place medium-ability and low-ability students together. As in peer tutoring (see earlier discussion), students who do the explaining often learn the most, so it is important to structure groups so that a high percentage of students participate.

- Make sure the groups are *gender balanced* as well. Girls are more likely to be interactive and have higher achievement in cooperative learning groups if there are equal numbers of boys and girls (N. M. Webb, 1984). If there's a majority of boys, girls are more likely to be ignored. If there's a majority of girls, proportionately more interactions are directed at the few boys. If it all possible, try to make the groups racially or ethnically balanced as well.
- As much as possible, *monitor* group interactions. Make sure groups stay on task and that all students have equal opportunities for learning. If needed, teach students appropriate social skills, such as techniques for compromise and respectful disagreements. For example, N. M. Webb and Farivar (1994) found that seventh graders benefit from training in communication skills and academic helping skills.

Mastery Learning

Mastery learning (B. S. Bloom, 1968) typically involves breaking course content up into manageable units, with students studying and taking quizzes on a unit until they pass the test at a high level of mastery, such as 80 to 100 percent. The course consists of the student's proceeding through units, mastering each along the way. The small, discrete units are presented in logical sequence and build upon one another. For example, a student would master concepts of addition before the introduction of multiplication.

The assumption of mastery learning is that some students need to study more than others, and some require more instruction than others. All students, however, can end up mastering the material and earning an *A*. Mastery learning is very different from conventional instruction, which involves all students' receiving a fixed amount of instruction and a fixed number of quizzes. With conventional instruction, some students learn more than others and, thus, make better grades than others. Mastery learning is consistent with the task-oriented, noncompetitive models of classroom motivation described in Chapter 2. In addition, programmed instruction and computer-based instruction often use a mastery learning approach (see Chapter 7).

Although mastery learning can and has been implemented in elementary and secondary schools, it is used much more frequently in higher education. When students' achievement as measured on final exams in mastery courses is compared with learning and achievement in traditional courses, mastery learning boosts performance on teacher- or experimenter-constructed tests about a half standard deviation (Kulik, Kulik, & Bangert-Drowns, 1990), a moderate-sized effect (see the discussion of meta-analysis in Chapter 1). Students also tend to like mastery courses better than traditional courses.

Classroom Management

Effective schools are safe and orderly environments for learning. Before it is possible to teach anything academic, the teacher must take control of the class. For generations of teachers, conventional wisdom dictated, "Don't smile until November" or "Spare the rod and spoil the child." These maxims are clearly inadequate. If nothing else, acting upon these old sayings makes school a dreary and threatening world and sets the teacher up as an adversary. Principles of classroom management provide teachers with guidance about how to maintain order in the classroom without creating an unpleasant environment (Doyle, 1986; Evertson, 1989). Of course, it is impossible to provide prospective teachers step-by-step directions guaranteed to establish sound classroom management. Individual teachers are comfortable with only some techniques, and classrooms may respond differently to procedures the teacher uses. Instead, the beginning teacher must develop understanding of general classroom principles and, through experience, learn to apply them flexibly in the classroom.

The first step to classroom management is to create a classroom environment that facilitates student engagement. Suggestions for fostering student engagement appear in this chapter as well as in other chapters throughout the book. Motivated students are more likely to be engaged in schooling, and suggestions for creating motivated students are detailed in Chapter 2. There are other steps classroom managers can take, however, to help establish good classroom management. Logical physical arrangements of classrooms, reasonable rules and procedures, and effective communication skills set the stage for good classroom management. Good classroom managers also know multiple ways to intervene when the behavior of students is inappropriate.

Arrangement of the Classroom Environment

Classroom management starts before the year begins. Teachers should arrange the physical classroom so that they can maintain order, secure smooth transitions between classroom activities, and monitor students easily. The following guidelines for classroom arrangement are adapted from Emmer, Evertson, Clements, and Worsham (1994) and from Evertson, Emmer, Clements and Worsham (1994):

- Keep high-traffic areas, such as the water fountain, pencil sharpener, and supply areas, free of congestion. If students have plenty of room to maneuver in these high-traffic areas, there will be fewer opportunities for distraction and disruption. Large disruptions in classrooms often begin with students' jostling each other in cramped areas.
- Be sure the teacher can easily observe students. Arrange desks, tables, and other pieces of furniture so the teacher can see all students at all times. For example, in many elementary school classrooms, small reading groups meet with the teacher in one section of the room while the rest of the class does seat work. The classroom furnishings must be arranged so the teacher can conduct the reading group and easily look up to scan the rest of the classroom. Teachers who wish to encourage discussion among students should arrange classrooms so students can see and hear each other as well.
- Keep frequently used teaching materials and supplies for students readily accessible. This reduces the opportunities for distraction and disruption by allowing smooth, brief transitions between classroom activities.
- Arrange seating so the students can easily see instructional presentations. If students do not have to lean into the aisle, tap their neighbor's shoulder so their neighbor will move aside, or crane their heads over their neighbor's shoulder, they are more likely to pay attention.

Establishment of Rules and Procedures

An orderly classroom is one in which students know how they are expected to behave. This is why it is important to establish classroom rules and procedures. **Classroom rules** are general standards of behavior (Emmer et al., 1994; Evertson et al., 1994). Some rules, such as no running in the halls, no smoking in school, or needing a hall pass, are established for the entire school. Teachers develop other rules that apply only to their own class. Usually a set of five to eight rules is sufficient to cover most important behaviors. For example, some rules absolutely essential for many teachers are "Show respect to others," "Respect others' property," "Listen carefully to others when they are speaking," "Come to class prepared," and "Obey all school rules." Students understand rules better if the teacher provides specific examples. For instance, a class rule of "showing respect to others" is more understandable if the teacher gives examples of being polite, not making fun of other students, not talking while others are talking, and not engaging in name calling.

In contrast to rules, **classroom procedures** are directed at a specific activity (Emmer et al., 1994; Evertson et al., 1994). For example, there may be classroom procedures, such as how to get the teacher's attention or whether some talking is allowed during seat work. There may be procedures for transition. Do students leave at the bell or wait until they are dismissed? Do they leave all at once or in order of rows? The point of movement procedures is not just quiet and orderly transition but also rapid transition. Time spent in transition is time lost, and students' achievement in school very much depends on the amount of time they are engaged in instruction.

The teacher must clearly communicate all rules and procedures. The teacher must remind students of the rules and procedures as much as possible, via oral instructions or bulletin board displays, until the students internalize them. This is particularly important for young elementary school students, who are being initiated into the classroom culture.

Students can participate in the formation of rules and procedures in a variety of ways. At the very least, the class can discuss the rationale for rules and procedures. Older elementary and high school students can even influence the decision-making process. The teacher and the students together can establish the reasonableness of the rules through class discussion. Teachers should make sure, however, that the rules the teacher absolutely needs are adopted and that classroom rules do not contradict school rules.

Effective Communication

Another important aspect of classroom management is good communication (Emmer et al., 1994; Evertson et al., 1994). In particular, teachers must communicate effectively when students violate rules and procedures. *Constructive assertiveness* and *empathic responding* are two vital communication skills.

Teachers who are constructively assertive stand up for their rights without attacking students. They identify problematic behavior engaged in by students, describe its effects, insist on corrections, and resist manipulation. They are careful to focus on the behavior and not the personality, which reduces student defensiveness and potential conflict. In general, they are clear and calm, not hostile or timid. They are consistent in their dealings with students. For example, a teacher who

Well-managed classrooms have explicit rules that are known by all students.

says, "Talking out of turn infringes on the rights of other students to participate" is first identifying the offending behavior and then describing its effects.

There is a vast difference between being assertive and being hostile. Assertive teachers make eye contact; hostile teachers glare. Assertive teachers face the students in an alert, but not threatening, posture; hostile teachers physically intimidate students by making threatening gestures. Assertive teachers use firm voices at an appropriate volume; hostile teachers shout.

Teachers who are effective communicators also empathically respond to their students and listen to their perspectives. They exhibit good listening skills, such as letting students know they are listening by nodding, making eye contact, or saying things such as, "I see," "I hear you," or "Tell me more." They reflectively listen by repeating what a student says, for example, "So you feel . . ." In general, they make it clear that they hear the students and respect their feelings. It is possible to do this and still not agree with the students. Even though the students will know they haven't changed their teachers' minds, they will feel that they have been heard.

Interventions for Problematic Behavior

Good classroom managers signal when they are concerned about classroom misconduct well before the misconduct accelerates into a situation that requires sanctions. They display what Kounin (1970) called *"with-it-ness";* that is, they are aware of and constantly monitoring the classroom and the activities of students. When sanctions are necessary, good classroom managers deal with the situation quickly and as unobtrusively as possible.

The following suggested interventions for dealing with misbehavior by students are adapted from Emmer et al. (1994) and from Evertson et al. (1994):

- The teacher focuses on getting the academic activity moving, thereby reducing the transition time when misbehavior is more likely to occur.
- The teacher gives nonverbal signals, such as making eye contact, shaking his or her head, or moving closer to the offending student. Teachers must be sure to be sensitive to cultural differences in their students. For example, although most teachers interpret students' making eye contact with the teacher as an indication of attention and respect, in some cultures seeking eye contact with an authority figure is considered a sign of defiance.
- The teacher redirects students' attention, reminding them of what they are supposed to be doing. For example, the teacher might say, "Sonya, now's the time to be working on math problems." The teacher monitors to make sure the student remains on task.
- The teacher alerts students to models of good behavior by praising the students who are following directions with comments such as, "Row 2 has really been working hard this morning—way to go!" This is more effective with younger, rather than older, students.
- The teacher explicitly asks or tells a student to stop an inappropriate behavior.
- The teacher gives a student a choice either to behave appropriately or to continue to misbehave and receive the consequence of rule violation. Stating the consequence emphasizes that it is up to the student to take responsibility for self-control.
- The teacher uses an "I-message," which describes the problem and how it affects the teacher. "When you (state the problem), then (describe the effect), and it makes me feel (state the emotion)." For example, a teacher might say "When you talk to one another while I am talking, then I know you are not paying attention to me, and that makes me feel annoyed.

If these interventions are ineffective and the misbehavior continues, the teacher increases the level of intervention as follows:

- The teacher imposes some sort of punishment such as staying in class a few minutes after the bell or giving detention. The teacher may also withhold a privilege or favorite activity, such as sitting near friends or being able to walk around the classroom.
- The teacher isolates or removes a student to some place separate from the other students, in other words, the teacher puts the student in **time-out** (see also Chapter 7.) By using time-out, the teacher essentially withholds the student's privilege of taking part in the classroom activities.
- The teacher meets with the student individually, and they agree on a **behavioral contract.** This contract specifies goals for the student's behavior and a schedule of reinforcements for reaching the goals (see also Chapter 7.)
- The teacher arranges a conference with a parent or parents. During this conference, the teacher must use effective communication skills. This means the teacher clearly identifies the problem with the student's behavior, without implying the parent is at fault, and asks for parental support. The teacher is careful to listen to the parent to make sure the parent feels that he or she is being heard.

■ Building Your Expertise

The Theme of Classroom Management Throughout the Text

Issues central to the theme of classroom management have been discussed in several other chapters of this text. Reviewing some of the most important ideas will help you build your classroom management expertise.

- Understanding the principle of *reinforcement* is one aspect of successful classroom management (see Chapter 7). A reinforcer increases the likelihood of the behavior that precedes. Let's say a teacher reinforces a middle school student's polite behavior to another student by praising it highly in front of the entire class. The teacher is surprised to see that same student behave rudely to another student later that same day. What is going on here? Was the teacher's reinforcer really reinforcing the desired behavioral response? You'll recall from Chapter 7 how difficult it is for teachers to select reinforcers since what is reinforcing varies from student to student and especially changes as students mature. Whereas a young elementary school student may have responded positively to the teacher's praise, this middle school student is more oriented to approval from peers rather than the teacher. The teacher's well-meaning public praise singled out the student as a teacher's pet. What can a teacher do? One tactic is to observe students to determine what they like to do and to use these preferred activities as reinforcers (the Premack [1959] principle described in Chapter 7).

- When their attempts at reinforcement are ineffective, teachers often rely on *punishment* to manage their students behavior. A punishment reduces the likelihood of the behavior that precedes it. A few punishment techniques used in behavior modification programs, including time-out, are discussed in Chapter 7. As a general rule, it is helpful to suggest an alternative behavior that will be reinforced when using punishment and to select a punishment that fits the misbehavior. Teachers should always keep in mind the possible side effects of punishment, such as inducing anxiety or anger in students.

- Another technique for reducing the likelihood of a behavior is *extinction* (see also Chapter 7). A behavior that does not receive reinforcement will eventually disappear. Unfortunately, sometimes a teacher's attention, even in the form of scoldings, is reinforcing, especially if peers giggle during the scolding. Eliminating the reinforcement by ignoring the misbehavior may actually extinguish the misbehavior. It is important is keep in mind that behaviors that are intermittently reinforced are particularly resistant to extinction.

- Sometimes a behavior that a teacher wishes to reinforce does not often occur. In this case, a teacher may chose to use *shaping* to obtain the desired behavior (see also Chapter 7). For example, suppose a teacher wants a first grader to stay in his seat during a 15 to 20 minute lesson. Because the teacher knows the student is incapable of sitting still for that long, the teacher begins by reinforcing the student's staying seated for a few minutes at a time. Gradually, the teacher increase the time the student must remain seated before reinforcement. Eventually, the student learns to sit for the required length of time; the behavior of sitting in the seat has been shaped.

- Teachers often make good use in the classroom of the social learning principles introduced in Chapter 7. Students learn by watching others. Thus, pointing out models of desired behavior and reinforcing these models can result in other students' learning the appropriate behavior. As Lickona argued in his suggestions for moral education in Chapter 9, teachers are significant models as well.

- A major goal of classroom management is to foster student internalization of appropriate standards of conduct. Cognitive behavior modification, introduced in Chapter 7, can help teachers achieve that goal. Teachers can instruct students to observe their behavior, to use self-verbalizations to direct appropriate behaviors, and to reinforce themselves for appropriate behavior.

- The discussion of parenting styles in Chapter 9 revealed that *authoritative* parenting (that is, parenting that is demanding but responsive) is associated with students' internalization of standards of conduct. Obviously, teachers can be authoritative as well. They can establish firm rules and be consistent in implementing them, but they can also be responsive to students by explaining the rationales for the rules.

- Expert teachers, as described in Chapter 5, are better able to make sense of a complex classroom scene, give more coherent explanations for students' misbehaviors, and make recommendations based on principles of classroom management more often than teachers who are novice. Thus, expert teachers exhibit "with-it-ness." They are also more efficient at completing classroom procedures, which reduces the total time students are in transition, a period particularly conducive to misbehavior. As we have learned, expertise develops with classroom experience.

Chapter Summary

- Some of the characteristics shared by effective schools are academic leadership, safe and orderly environments, and high expectations for students' achievement.

- The following specific classroom practices facilitate student achievement: higher-order questioning and wait time during questioning; tutoring by peers and volunteers; small classes; and homework, especially after the elementary school years. A teacher's expectancies about achievement may affect his or her behavior, which in turn affects students' achievement.

- Other classroom practices have clear negative effects on students' achievement. For instance, students in low-ability tracks are provided instruction that is less rich and that undermines their achievement. Although the influence of extracurricular activities on student achievement is uncertain, after-school employment negatively effects achievement.

- No single instructional approach is appropriate for all content and contexts. Direct instruction is characterized by structured teacher-directed presentation of content, with clearly specified learning goals. The focus is on the student's academic performance. Direct explanation and teacher modeling begins with explanations and teacher modeling. As students practice, the teacher gradually withdraws support; instruction is scaffolded. The focus is on processing by students. Like direct explanation and teacher modeling, reciprocal teaching is scaffolded instruction involving teacher modeling and explanation of strategies, but the teacher's role is less salient in reciprocal teaching than in direct explanation and modeling.

- Discovery learning is student-directed. The teacher's role is to allow opportunities for students' construction of understanding. Discovery learning can be inefficient and may lead to incorrect conclusions. In guided discovery, the teacher guides students' discovery through questioning.

- Two other instructional approaches are cooperative learning and mastery learning. In cooperative learning, students work together in groups toward a common goal. In mastery learning, students demonstrate understanding of each instructional unit before moving on to the next unit.

- Classroom management begins with a logical physical arrangement that facilitates monitoring of students' activities. Order is maintained through students' awareness of the classroom rules and procedures. Good classroom managers exhibit two vital communication skills—constructive assertiveness and empathic responding.

- Good classroom managers have a repertoire of effective interventions to deal with misbehavior by students. Typical interventions may include nonverbal signals, redirection of students' attention, highlighting models of good behavior, and explicit directives. Continued misbehavior by students may be countered with punishment or withholding of a desired activity, time-out, collaboration with students on a behavioral contract, and parent conferences.

Return to the Classroom Predicament

Has reading this chapter helped you formulate responses to the questions raised by the student teacher? The student teacher should be sure to increase wait time to allow the students time to formulate responses to his questions. In addition, the student teacher should plan the questions ahead of time to increase the likelihood that some of his questions are thought-provoking and more likely to engage the students. Although it is difficult to be sure what the student teacher means by "I just teach," it is most likely that he employs direct instruction as his teaching method. He should be encouraged to include other instructional methods and techniques in his teaching repertoire, including guided discovery learning, peer tutoring, and cooperative learning. The student teacher also should be reminded of the powerful influence of teachers' expectations on the behavior of teachers and probably that of students. In addition, the student teacher should be encouraged to reassess his use of homework, considering the age of students (whether elementary or high school) and the subject content (simple skills or complex skills). Finally, the student teacher is apparently aware of the need to establish rules and procedures but needs to be encouraged to review his communication style and planned interventions for problematic behaviors.

Chapter Outline

Chapter 11

Reading and Writing Instruction

Classroom Predicament

Mrs. Jackson has many questions for her child's teacher at the parent-teacher conference. "I not only want to learn about my child in your class, but I also have a lot of questions to ask you about my other children. I want my children to read and write well, and to enjoy reading and writing. I think that is the key for a successful future. I have a preschooler who is beginning to show an interest in words. How do I encourage this? My child in elementary school seems to be getting a different kind of reading instruction than her cousin who lives in a different town. I don't understand this. My child in high school never seems to do well on term papers, and that really worries me. Is there any way to help students become better writers?"

How would you answer this parent's questions about literary instruction? Reflecting on the information presented in this chapter will help you formulate responses to these questions.

The literacy skills of reading and writing are the basis of much of school learning. Students must be able to comprehend the texts in all school domains and frequently demonstrate their understandings through written responses to questions, in projects and in term papers. One goal of teachers in all content domains is to help students become skilled readers and writers. In this chapter, we explore what is known about the acquisition of skilled reading and writing. The good information processing model introduced in the first chapter applies to these two important competencies. The components of the good information processing model—strategies, metacognition, world knowledge, and motivation—are critical to skilled reading and writing. There are many opportunities for teachers to foster the development of these skills.

Reading

A student who has excellent reading skills can excel in all academic endeavors. What are the characteristics of a skilled reader?

The Nature of Skilled Reading

How do skilled readers construct meaning from a text? One way to study this is to use a technique known as **thinking aloud**. In this technique, capable readers talk as they read, relating to the researcher what they are doing and thinking as they read (Pressley & Afflerbach, 1995; D. Wyatt et al., 1993). Skilled readers do and think a lot! Their activities and cognitions exemplify the characteristics of good thinking described throughout this text (see especially Chapter 1).

Before reading, good readers sometimes overview the text, trying to discern important themes. Once they begin to read, they formulate tentative hypotheses about what the text will be about. They sometimes predict what will be in the text. The good reader frequently looks ahead for information and sometimes backtracks or rereads, revising incorrect predictions and constructing an interpretation of the text consistent with the points made in the text. Sometimes good readers construct mental images portraying the messages related in the text. Sometimes they construct summaries of what has happened. Good readers might underline or make notes to themselves. In short, good readers *use a variety of strategies* as they figure out the story in a work of fiction or the messages in a factual piece.

Capable readers do not use strategies haphazardly; they coordinate them to respond to the content and demands of the text being read. Good readers know when it is appropriate to skim versus read slowly and carefully. They know when to take notes and when to look back. That is, they *possess metacognitive knowledge* (knowledge about thinking, described in Chapter 4) pertaining to the appropriate use of reading strategies.

Good readers also *monitor* their reading (see Chapter 4). This metacognitive process refers to their awareness of whether what they are reading makes sense; whether the text is difficult or easy to understand; and whether what they are reading is relevant to their reading goal, such as finding material for a term paper. Such monitoring is also critical to the regulation of strategies: For example, when readers sense that they are confused, they change reading tactics. If they perceive the text as easy to comprehend, they speed up. If a portion of the text is especially relevant to a reading goal, such as enabling the students to answer a teacher's questions, they slow up at that point. Good readers either skip over or skim text content that they believe is irrelevant to their current reading goals. Because monitoring produces knowledge about how reading is going, monitoring is a metacognitive process that is important in comprehension and memory of what is read.

Good readers *relate their knowledge of the world* to what they read (see Chapters 3 and 5). Thus, when reading about marine life, it is natural for people who live near the ocean to relate their experiences at the shore to the text's content. When reading about baseball, the avid fan makes associations to information in the text. The more extensive a reader's knowledge, the richer his or her associations to the text will be, and the more the reader will understand and appreciate the text at a deep level.

Good readers are evaluative as they read, basing their evaluations on prior knowledge. Good readers react to opinions represented in a text that differ from their own. They also evaluate the style of writing. Good readers draw conclusions about whether the ideas in the text are interesting and new or dull and commonplace. Sometimes these reactions can be pronounced and easy to spot, such as when the person in the seat next to you responds to a newspaper article by exclaiming, "Nobody would believe this article!"

Good readers are also extremely *motivated to read* (see Chapter 2). You may have professors who avidly seek out new articles in their fields of specialization. You may have friends who regularly devour publications such as the *New Yorker, Outside Magazine,* and *Sports Illustrated.* One of the reasons good readers are proficient readers is that they read so much. A great deal of reading permits practice of reading strategies to the point of automaticity. As they use reading strategies, readers come to understand when and where they work and when and where it is appropriate to use particular procedures. In other words, their metacognition expands. Readers also build up world knowledge through reading. This ever expanding knowledge increases the quantity and quality of potential connections between what the reader knows already and what is presented in a text. And as one reads, the motivation to read increases, for there is expanding understanding of the power gained by knowledge of the printed word.

One way to become proficient at reading is to read a great deal. Avid reading is essential for a person to become an expert reader.

Good information processing during reading is not common in college-age readers (Pressley, El-Dinary, & Brown, 1992). Many college readers use unsophisticated reading strategies. For example, they read text over and over in order to learn it. Often students do not monitor well so they are not aware of whether they have understood the main ideas in the text or not (Pressley, Woloshyn, & Pirie, 1990). In part, this may be because students often lack extensive background knowledge that can be related to the text's content as it is read.

As students specialize, they learn the strategies that are effective in the domains in which they work (see Chapter 5). Prior knowledge that can be related to newly encountered materials does not simply accumulate but is increasingly organized in the reader's head. Motivated by their interests, readers decide to specialize and focus their attention on the fields they choose to enter. They read many articles and books in their areas of interest. This explains why professional-level adults often are good information processors as they read material in domains of interest in comparison to college students, who are just beginning to build their expertise.

■ Building Your Expertise

Good Reading as an Example of Expert Performance

Good readers display many of the characteristics of expertise described in Chapter 5. Good readers *recognize letters and words automatically*. They have knowledge of many specific words built up from their reading experiences. In addition, good readers' knowledge of syntax is complete and used automatically, so they quickly understand even the most difficult syntactic constructions.

Good readers use their prior knowledge extensively, *recognizing large patterns of meaning in text and making strong connections* between ideas in text and their previous experiences (D. Wyatt et al., 1993). The considerable background knowledge of good readers permits inferences that elaborate on the stated meanings in the text and permits linkages between ideas in the text (R. C. Anderson & Ortony, 1975). The knowledge of good readers includes knowledge of text structures, the typical elements in narratives and expositions described in Chapter 3, which permits them to abstract main points and important details from text.

Good readers *respond to challenging sections of texts strategically,* with the result that their reading is extremely active. They anticipate what might be in text, attempt to figure out the intended messages in confusing text, and reflect on and summarize what they have read.

Good readers have *sufficient working memory* to be able to "hold in mind" some of what they have read previously as they take in new information. They also understand a text's meaning by integrating in working memory what they are reading with what they have already read. Finally, good readers *monitor* whether they are understanding what they read. Reading expertise *takes a long time to develop.*

Development of Reading

How does skilled reading develop? What can we do to create more adults who are good information processors as they read? Fortunately, there are many opportunities for teachers and parents to increase literacy from early childhood to late adulthood.

Emergent Literacy. **Emergent literacy** refers to the reading and writing behaviors from infancy through the preschool years that precede and develop into conven-

Focus on Research

Thinking Aloud: An Important Qualitative Methodology

Think back to Chapter 1 to the introduction to qualitative methods, approaches that capture hard-to-quantify information. One important qualitative method used by cognitive psychologists is thinking aloud. Shearer, Coballes-Vega, and Lundeberg (1993) asked teachers to read articles in professional journals pertaining to teaching. These teachers selected articles that were particularly interesting to them. As the teachers read the articles, they thought aloud, reporting what they were thinking and doing as they read. Here are some strategies they used, along with examples of comments reflecting the use of the strategy:

- *Overviewing:* "I'm looking at different headings and where they're going with it; how they set up the article."
- *Predicting:* "They mention things like case studies, empirical research and research synthesis. That tells me they're probably going to be talking about the different kinds of research, funding, publication, getting started."
- *Looking for information relevant to reading goal:* "This is the kind of thing I look for . . . information examples of what other districts are doing."
- *Backtracking:* "The part here about the LPE Form I find myself going back and rereading because I didn't get it the first time through."

The teachers often related information in the text to prior knowledge and experiences, such as in the following examples:

- *Knowledge of students:* "For my students, I think I would have to teach them that."
- *Prior knowledge:* "Often articles in the *Journal of English* don't contain that large a bibliography."
- *Professional practice and experience:* "There are some examples that we could do"; "This field research . . . is a type of research that I have people in business communications do."

The teachers monitored as they read as well, and their awareness of reading affected their subsequent reading. For example, at one point a teacher related, "I'm rereading this because I lost my train of thought," indicating an awareness of a comprehension difficulty and an adjustment made in response to that awareness.

The teachers also reacted and evaluated what they encountered in the readings. Examples included a teacher's reacting to the way participants were selected for a study: "How did they determine who was gifted?" The teachers signaled results they found surprising by self-reports such as, "I wouldn't expect such differences in just two years." Predictable results received reactions such as, "Maybe I was looking for something new, but I didn't find it, you know."

In summary, these teachers were engaging in good information processing when they read. The sophisticated type of reading observed in this study requires years of practice and extensive prior knowledge. Having them think aloud provided the researchers with a good window on the qualitative characteristics of how professionals read articles in their area of expertise, permitting researchers to identify the many strategies used.

---

tional literacy (Morrow, 1983; Sulzby, 1988). Environments that support emergent literacy involve exposure to literacy materials ranging from magnetic plastic letters used on a refrigerator to storybooks to writing materials, along with the display of a high regard for literacy by family members and important others (Morrow, 1989). An important emergent literacy experience during the preschool years is **storybook reading.** Children who experience frequent, high-quality storybook reading during the preschool years are more likely to be interested in reading later and to experience success in early reading (Sulzby & Teale, 1991).

What do we know about storybook interactions? Whether storybook reading occurs at home or at school, there are rich discussions and animated conversations between the reader and the child. The adult and child work out the meaning of the text, and they have a lot of fun doing it (Morrow, 1989). There is questioning, both by the adult and the child; there is modeling of dialogue by adults, with children sometimes participating; adults praise the children's efforts to get meaning from the pictures and print; and both adults and children relate what is happening in the text to their lives and the world around them (Applebee & Langer, 1983; Pellegrini, Perlmutter, Galda, & Brody, 1990).

Consistent with the Vygotskian ideas about scaffolding described in Chapter 8, many parents encourage children to participate as much as possible in storybook interactions, provide support as children need it, and contribute input that children can understand (DeLoache & DeMendoza, 1987). A lot is learned in these interactions largely because parents help the child as needed and up the ante when the child is ready for it. For example, the parent might read longer sequences to a child or urge a child to sit still for longer periods of time. Of course, all of this is consistent with Vygotsky's general claim that thinking abilities develop as a result of interactions with cognitively more capable people, such as parents.

Interventions can improve interactions between parents and children during storybook reading (Whitehurst et al., 1988). Parents can learn how to ask better questions about text as they read to their children, how to respond appropriately to their children's comments during story reading, and how to expand on what the children say. As a result, the quality of interactions between the children and parents increases, which is reflected in higher scores on tests of language ability (Valdez-Menchaca & Whitehurst, 1992).

There are many ways to structure children's worlds in order to increase their emergent literacy experiences. For example, more emergent literacy experiences are observed when children's play areas include props that encourage literacy. Thus, labeling of objects in the child's world can stimulate interaction with print and words. The world of play can include paper, pencils, and pens; "stores" and "offices" in play settings can include "order forms" and letters, appointment books, and message pads; and children's attempts at drawing and writing can be displayed. The presence of magazines and books as well as cozy corners in which to read them

Years of emergent literacy experiences like this one result in vast knowledge about literacy—even before children begin formal reading and writing instruction.

Preschoolers learn a great deal about reading and writing from their friends on *Sesame Street*. Still, *Sesame Street* cannot take the place of reading, writing letters to Grandma, and other more active experiences that occur in homes rich in emergent literacy experiences.

also stimulate emergent reading and writing activities (Morrow, 1990; Morrow & Weinstein, 1986; Neuman & Roskos, 1992).

Even television can play a role in the development of preschoolers' literacy skills. Since the fall of 1969, American preschoolers have had *Sesame Street* in their living rooms, with a typical audience of about 10 million homes (Palmer, 1984). Evaluators of *Sesame Street* have concluded that children learn about the alphabet and language from watching the program, much more so than from watching entertainment television (D. R. Anderson & Collins, 1988). Watching Ernie, Bert, and Big Bird can stimulate some fundamental literacy understandings (Rice, Huston, Truglio, & Wright, 1990).

● "What Do I Do on Monday Morning?"

Stimulating Preschoolers' Development

Preschoolers learn a great deal about literacy when adults read to them. From storybook interactions with adults, preschoolers come to understand what words are and how they function (B. Roberts, 1992). Not surprisingly, 5-year-olds who show well-developed emergent literacy—reflected by competence in reenacting stories, writing individual words, "writing" stories, and "reading"—tend to outperform other 5-year-olds in reading during the elementary school years (Barnhart, 1991). Researchers have identified a numbers of ways to improve emergent literacy experiences, whether those experiences occur in parents' laps, on *Sesame Street*, or in classroom literacy centers. Important ways to stimulate a preschooler's literacy development include the following:

- Help children act out stories.
- Encourage children to retell stories they have heard before.
- Assist children as they try to write stories and letters.

- Teach them letters and sounds whenever there is an opportunity to do so, from letter-shaped refrigerator magnets to monograms on a snowsuit.
- Answer children's questions.
- Ask them questions. Talk with them about events and ideas that they find important and interesting.
- Praise children's efforts to read.
- Respond to children's reactions to a text. For example, discuss with them the relative merits of Goldilock's perspective and that of the Three Bears.
- Provide lots of books, pencils, paper, and trips to libraries and bookstores.

The Elementary School Years. Both decoding of words and comprehension of text are taught throughout the elementary grades. There is greater emphasis on decoding and word identification in the earlier grades, however, with increasing emphasis on comprehension at the upper grade levels.

Emergent literacy experiences do not produce all of the competencies that are essential for success at reading during the elementary school years. One such critical competency is **phonemic awareness,** which is awareness that words are composed of separable sounds (i.e., phonemes) and that phonemes are combined to create words. For example, the sound of *s*, short *a*, and *d* combine in the word *sad*. Phonemic awareness is one of the best predictors of success in early reading in school (M. J. Adams, 1990). Children who fail to learn to read during the first several years of schooling often lack phonemic awareness. Children who lack phonemic awareness also have a difficult time learning to spell and developing an understanding of the relationships between letters and sounds. Poor readers at all age levels often are less phonemically aware than good readers of the same age (M. J. Adams, 1990).

In order for phonemic awareness to develop in normal readers, formal instruction in reading is often essential. Bradley and Bryant (1983) found that providing instruction to children about how to categorize words on the basis of their sounds increased phonemic awareness and long-term reading achievement. This instruction emphasized that the same word can be categorized in different ways on the basis of sound when it is in different sets of words. Thus, if *hen* is in a group of words that include *hat, hill, hair,* and *hand,* it would make sense to categorize all of these words as starting with *h*, especially in contrast to other words starting with another letter (e.g., *b* words such as *bag, band, bat,* etc.). If *hen* were on a list with *men* and *sun,* however, these three words could be categorized as ones ending in *n*. If *hen* were on a list of words that included *bed* and *leg*, it would be possible to categorize the words as ones with a short *e* in the middle. Young children given this training displayed substantial gains (about a year's advantage) in standardized reading performance relative to control conditions; these gains were still evident five years later.

How do beginning and skilled readers decode words? Decoding is extremely complicated, involving a number of different strategies (Ehri, 1991). Children read logos, sound out words, use rules of phonics, and build up their knowledge of words and parts of words they know by sight. Each of these processes is described in what follows.

When children decode words by **logographic reading,** sometimes referred to as visual cue reading (Ehri, 1991), they rely only on the salient visual characteristics of a word. For example, children often can read the word *Apple* on a computer or the same word on television when it is accompanied by the company's multicolored apple with a bite out of it; some children can read *STOP* correctly as long as it is in the middle of a red hexagon; many 5-year-olds can read the words *SCHOOL BUS* on the back of a large yellow vehicle; and what 4- or 5-year-old has trouble reading Disney's signature, even though it is written in script?

However, there is much more to reading than recognizing logos. Traditional decoding instruction emphasizes sounding out words using letter-sound relationships (Ehri & Wilce, 1985; Huba, 1984; Scott & Ehri, 1990). When readers know some letter-sound relationships, they are capable of doing what Ehri (1991) refers to as **phonetic cue reading.** For example, whereas logographic readers might recognize *yellow* as the word with the "two sticks" in the middle, phonetic cue readers might recognize the two *l*'s in *yellow* and know their sound, using this information to recall the entire word from memory (Seymour & Elder, 1986). Phonetic cue reading, however, has its hazards. If the same letter cues are used for several words or a cue used to decode

Preschoolers can often read logographs such as these, although they may not be able to read any other words.

some word is experienced in a new word, there may be mix-ups. For example, it is not uncommon for a child to misread a word, referring to it as another word the child knows that is similar in length and shares common letters (e.g., *yellow* read for *pillow*).

Eventually, young readers learn all of the letter-sound relationships. They acquire the **cipher,** which is a code that maps all the sounds of their language (i.e., phonemes) onto its alphabet (Gough, Juel, & Griffith, 1992). There are a number of specific letter-sound relationships that must be acquired as part of cipher learning. Some are easy, for they require only one piece of information; for example, the letter *b* is pronounced the same regardless of context; the same is true for *d, f, l, n, r, v,* and *z.* Others are hard, because some letters sound differently, depending on other letters in the word. For example, vowels are long if there is a final *e* in a syllable and short if there is not. Acquiring the cipher and using it increases speed and accuracy in reading unfamiliar words, permitting students to sound out words and to blend the sounds represented by the letters in words to say the words.

Traditional early reading instruction also often includes **phonics rules.** Students in phonics-based programs are taught rules such as, "When two vowels go walking, the first does the talking" and "When there is an *e* at the end of a syllable, the vowel is long." There are a manageable number of such rules. Clymer (1963) produced a list of 45 of them. Although termed rules, phonics generalizations never hold 100 percent of the time. For example, "When two vowels go walking . . ." works about 66 percent of the time.

Instruction in phonics rules helps many children learn to read (Adams, 1990; R. C. Anderson, Hiebert, Scott, & Wilkinson, 1985; Ehri, 1991). Sounding out of words is more likely among children receiving explicit phonics instruction than among children receiving no such instruction (R. C. Barr, 1974–1975). The value of phonics instruction is in giving students a good start. Although the rules and letter-sound associations do not always work, they work enough of the time to be useful.

We doubt that anyone reading this text has had to sound out a single word in this chapter, except perhaps for unfamiliar proper names such as *Ehri.* Every word in the chapter is in our readers' sight vocabularies. There was a time for every reader of this book, however, when most words in this chapter would have been sounded out. Many trials of successfully sounding out a word, however, increase the connections between the letter pattern defining the word and the word in memory (M. J. Adams, 1990). Thus, on initial exposure to a word such as *frog,* the word is sounded out. Eventually the spelling is represented in memory as a unit (*frog*) that is automatically recognized when encountered.

With decoding experience, young readers learn the common **orthographic patterns** (Stanovich & West, 1989), that is, meaningful strings of letters that can be processed as wholes. Prefixes (e.g., *re-, mis-, pro-*) and suffixes (e.g., *-ing, -ed*) are obvious examples of orthographic patterns, but there are other recurring combinations, many of which are root words (e.g., *take, mal, ben, rog, do*). Once orthographic patterns are learned, it is not necessary to decode the orthograph alphabetically. Instead, there is a direct connection with the sound sequence in memory and probably direct connections with meaning as well. For example, a beginning chemistry student may have no idea what *maleic acid* is but might be certain at first glance—based on the *mal* part—that there was something bad about it! (There is, by the way—it stinks!)*

---

*Actually *maleic* is derived from the Latin word for apple, *malum,* not from *malus* (bad).

■ Building Your Expertise

Automaticity Theory and Short-Term Memory

There are tremendous advantages when words can be read by sight and orthographic chunks can be processed as wholes as described by what is called **automaticity theory** (LaBerge & Samuels, 1974; S. J. Samuels, Schermer, & Reinking, 1992). Two tasks are required to get the meaning out of a word: (1) It must be decoded. (2) What is decoded must be comprehended. Both require use of short-term memory, that extremely limited resource that can be thought of as attentional capacity (see Chapters 1, 4, and 7).

The application of alphabetic decoding or phonics rules requires a great deal of attention on the part of the reader. If all of the attentional capacity is consumed by decoding, there is nothing left over for comprehension and, thus, words may be pronounced but not understood. One solution for the slow alphabetic decoder might be to decode first and then comprehend. The cost of this method is enormous: It is extremely slow. Because decoding and comprehending are done in sequence, the phonological representation of the word must be held in short-term memory, which involves reduction of capacity that is needed for comprehension. No matter how the alphabetic reader approaches the task, there is strain on short-term capacity.

In contrast, automatic sight word reading and automatic recognition of orthographic chunks require little effort or attention. Thus, there is substantial mental capacity left over for comprehension when decoding is automatic. Indeed, for many sight words and orthographic chunks, there are probably automatic connections between the sight words and the chunks, the phonological representations of the word and the chunks, and the meanings of the words and the chunks (Baron, 1977). With experience and development, the result is faster, more accurate, and less effortful reading (C. C Horn & Manis, 1987). A paradox of slow, high-effort alphabetic reading is that it is less certain to result in accurate decoding than fast, low-effort automatic decoding via sight words and orthographic chunks. The reader who automatically recognizes orthographic regularities is especially advantaged when words are encountered in isolation, that is, when there are no external context cues about the word or its meaning (Barker, Torgesen, & Wagner, 1992).

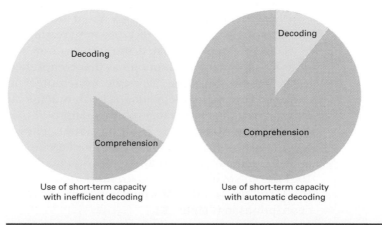

Use of short-term capacity with inefficient decoding

Use of short-term capacity with automatic decoding

Just as readers can become familiar with orthographs, they can become familiar with the overall visual and sound pattern of a word, permitting reading of other words by visual and sound **analogy** to it. Thus, a child who knows how to pronounce *beak* could make a good guess at *peak* the first time it is encountered simply through analogy (i.e., "This is like beak only it starts with a *p*"). Using the analogy strategy, that same child would also have a fighting chance with *bean, bead,* and *beat.* There is increasing evidence that even very young readers sometimes decode by analogy (Goswami & Bryant, 1992). Of course, decoding by analogy can result in errors, such as using *beak* to decode *break.*

In summary, except for the youngest of readers who might only know some logographs, readers do not use only one approach to decode words. With increasing experience, students use a greater variety of decoding strategies and *do so with increasing flexibility* (Rayner, 1988). When really good readers read text that is easy for them, much of it is sight word reading. On other occasions, skilled reading involves other strategies. Thus, when an adult sees a Russian can of Pepsi (which looks remarkably like an American Pepsi can), there is logographic reading of the word *Pepsi,* even though the word is written in the Cyrillic alphabet. When teachers read the roll the first day, much of the reading of unfamiliar last names involves alphabetic reading and sometimes reading by analogy. For example, a teacher might guess the pronunciation of *Baser* given its resemblance to *laser.* The full repertoire of decoding strategies taken up in this section is available to good readers.

That is not the case with young readers. It takes the young reader a while to build up a sight vocabulary. It also takes a while to build up sufficient knowledge of orthography to use analogy strategies to the full extent. Most of the first three years of formal reading instruction has typically been dedicated more to decoding instruction than anything else; decoding instruction continues through the grade school years and, in many cases, into the middle school years. Good information processing—even with respect to the limited skill of reading single words—takes time to develop.

The long-term goal of reading instruction is not the training of readers so they can say words, however. It is the development of readers who can construct meaning, that is, who can comprehend. Dolores Durkin (1978–1979) observed that elementary reading instruction included very little teaching aimed at fostering comprehension. Instead of teaching comprehension, teachers seemed to be testing it all of the time, asking lots of question about what had been in the text, with little information provided to students about how they might prepare themselves to answer questions about the text they were reading.

Durkin's study motivated research on how to increase reading comprehension. An important assumption was that comprehension could be increased if students were encouraged to create coherent representations of the meanings conveyed by the text. Elementary school students can be taught a number of strategies for creating memorable representations of the text they read (Pressley, Johnson, Symons, McGoldrick, & Kurita, 1989). These include strategies that can be applied before (e.g., making predictions based on prior knowledge), during (e.g., imagery generation), and after (e.g., summarization) reading (Levin & Pressley, 1981). Some of the strategies best supported by research are included in the "What Do I Do on Monday Morning?" feature below. (See more complete strategy descriptions in Chapter 4.)

● "What Do I Do on Monday Morning?"

Reading Comprehension Strategies

- *Summarization.* Teach students to extract the main ideas from factual text. For example, students can be taught to outline text using text headings and subheadings. They generate main idea statements, which are placed in an outline. Alternatively, students can be taught to construct maps of passages. They can learn to write the title of a passage in the middle of a page and then identify a half dozen or so main ideas in the passage (Berkowitz, 1986). Students place these ideas in boxes surrounding the title. They then fill the boxes with supporting details for the main idea placed in it.
- *Story grammar training.* Teach children the elements of a story and how to use these elements to understand text. This will improve comprehension and memory of stories (Short & Ryan, 1984). As they read stories, readers in elementary school can learn to ask themselves five questions that correspond to the elements of story grammar. (1) Who is the main character? (2) Where and when did the story take place? (3) What did the main character do? (4) How did the story end? (5) How did the main character feel?
- *Representational imagery.* Instruct children to create images depicting what they have read. This works for children who are at least more than 8 years of age (Gambrell & Bales, 1986; Pressley, 1976; Pressley, Borkowski, & Johnson, 1987).
- *Mnemonic imagery.* Teach students to construct images that transform text meaning in some way in order to make it more memorable. For example, when reading a biography of Charles Dickens, image each of the events occurring to one of Dickens most memorable characters, such as Scrooge, Tiny Tim, or Oliver Twist.
- *Generation of questions.* Teach students to think of questions about the meaning of text as reading proceeds (Rosenshine & Chapman, 1992).
- *Activation of prior knowledge.* Teach students to relate what they already know to information encountered or expected in the text (Dole, Valencia, Greer, & Wardrop, 1991).
- *Prediction.* Teach students to predict what might happen in the text. This is actually a form of activating prior knowledge, since predictions are based on prior knowledge.

Good readers who are good information processors, however, do not use just one particular strategy to understand a text. Instead, they coordinate a number of strategies. Thus, when educators teach their students to use comprehension strategies, they teach students to use several strategies.

For example, students in some programs learned to predict, question, seek clarifications, visualize, activate prior knowledge, and summarize as they read (Pressley, El-Dinary, Gaskins et al., 1992; Pressley, Schuder, Students Achieving Independent Learning Program Faculty and Administration, Bergman, & El-Dinary, 1992). Generally, such programs stimulate active processing by having the students think aloud during reading instruction and by encouraging associations to background knowledge as they do so. Such thinking aloud reduces impulsive responding and encourages planning prior to and during reading. The teachers in these programs use outstanding children's literature from trade books, magazines, or basal reader anthologies as they teach strategies.

A lesson might begin with the teacher's reading first, thinking aloud about how the text ought to serve her or his purposes, and then thinking aloud about how the text's content and structure might relate to prior knowledge. The teacher might make predictions; report images stimulated by the text; or note consistencies and inconsistencies between the content of the text, the structure of the text, and the expectations of the reader. Then the teacher might invite students to try using the strategic procedures with the text. Members of the reading group might take turns reading aloud. Throughout the process, students are encouraged to interpret the text, which exposes reading group participants to a variety of interpretations of text and the processes for constructing and evaluating those interpretations.

Pressley, El-Dinary, Gaskins et al. (1992) referred to this type of instruction as **transactional strategies instruction,** so dubbed because what happens during reading group is codetermined by a teacher and the students in interaction with a text (Bell, 1968; Bjorklund, 1989, Sameroff, 1975). In particular, the interpretations of text are codetermined by teacher-student-text interactions (Rosenblatt, 1978). Years of such transactions involving predictions, questions, clarifications, visualizations, associations, and summaries are intended to produce independent, successful readers who engage in such processes on their own. As the strategies are practiced by students, metacognition that permits their informed use develops. That is, students discover when the strategies help them and when they do not. By using the strategies, students learn more content than they would have otherwise, so that their knowledge of the world increases. Motivation develops as students come to understand the utility of strategies in an instructional environment that sends the message that students can become better learners, especially if they acquire the strategies and other knowledge taught in school. In short, when comprehension strategies are taught well, they are taught in such a way as to stimulate the development of all aspects of good information processing as first outlined in Chapter 1.

Whole Language: An Alternative Approach. Elementary school reading education, especially beginning reading education, has fueled enormous controversies for decades (Chall, 1967). In the 1990s there are debates about the merits of an approach to reading instruction known as whole language, which emphasizes comprehension to the exclusion of explicit decoding instruction (K. S. Goodman & Goodman, 1979; Symons, Woloshyn, & Pressley, 1994).

Whole language is difficult to define (see Watson, 1989, for an entire article on the challenges of defining it). Educators who use whole language believe that the integrity of language should be preserved during literacy education and that children should be presented with "whole" language rather than language skills instruction. There is reading of "whole" texts and writing of "whole" texts as well. Language instruction occurs within the context of the "whole" life of the child.

Some of the tenets of whole language include the following (adapted from Weaver, 1990, p. 6):

- Children learn to read and write as they learned to talk, which means as a gradual and natural process, one in which instruction is downplayed. The teaching role is that of someone who assists rather than instructs the child.

- Children are encouraged as they work with language. For example, creative, inventive spellings that reflect the sounds of the language are praised.
- Children read real stories, poems, and books every day.
- Children write something for a real audience every day. For example, they might write a story that will be read to classmates.
- Reading and writing occur across the school day as part of art, social studies, science, and so on.

Can children learn to read without explicit decoding instruction? The evidence is simply overwhelming that explicit decoding instruction benefits most children and might be essential for many students, especially those with special needs, if they are to make rapid progress in becoming readers during the elementary school years (M. J. Adams, 1990). Researchers who compared approaches that use whole language with other approaches to literacy instruction that include more explicit decoding instruction found that both seem to produce equivalent outcomes for average and strong readers (Stahl & Miller, 1989). The use of whole language, however, may negatively affect the reading progress of weak students. In contrast, there is substantial evidence that explicit attempts to increase phonemic awareness and explicit teaching of phonics benefit students who are at risk for reading difficulties (M. J. Adams, 1990).

Even so, there is still much that is very attractive about using whole language as an approach. Who could argue that reading fine literature is not a good thing for children to do? Who could argue with daily writing? Such experiences have profound effects on children, ones that may not be captured readily by standardized tests such as those used in evaluations to date.

Reading Recovery. Many first-grade students make little progress in learning how to read. Such students are at long-term risk for academic difficulties. An important program aimed at such children was developed by New Zealand educator Marie Clay (1985). Reading Recovery, which was introduced in Chapter 8, involves daily one-teacher, one-child sessions for 10 to 20 weeks, with each session lasting approximately 30 to 40 minutes. The goal is to help the student catch up with peers. The starting assumption is that students may be learning too narrow a range of strategies for dealing with print and may not be flexible in their use of the strategies they have acquired. For example, students may attempt to sound out every word, when in fact a variety of strategies (see the earlier discussion in this chapter) can be applied during the identification of words in texts.

Much of Reading Recovery is teaching students strategies, which are defined by Clay (1985; Pinnell, 1989) as the processes required to read. This is consistent with the good information processing framework emphasized in this book. The strategies taught in Reading Recovery include the following:

- Monitoring whether what is being read makes sense.
- Using cross-checks on meaning-making processes. For example, a reader might use one kind of information to predict a word but will check that prediction by using another source of information. Suppose, in glancing at a picture of the Billy Goats Gruff going across a bridge, a young reader predicts the use of the word *water* in the text. Checking the print, however, the reader might notice that the word *stream* is not visually consistent with that prediction. This cross-checking may lead to a self-correction or other indication from the child of an awareness of a discrepancy (Pinnell, 1989, p. 166).

- Searching for cues to meaning from pictures, language structures, and visual cues in print.
- Rereading when meaning is unclear.
- Self-correction rather than waiting for teacher correction of errors.

There is a common structure to each Reading Recovery lesson: (1) The child rereads two or more short, familiar books. (2) Then the child reads a book introduced the day before, with the teacher keeping track of errors that are made. The goal of the child is to read the book eventually with 90 percent accuracy. (3) There is a letter identification exercise involving plastic letters that attach to a metal board. Once children know letters, teaching of decoding strategies occurs. (4) The child composes and writes out a story. (5) The child reassembles the story after the teacher cuts it up into pieces. (6) A new book is introduced and read by the child.

This interaction between student and teacher is definitely scaffolded instruction (see Chapters 1, 7, and 10), with the student receiving hints and support as needed (Clay & Cazden, 1990). For example, when the student writes, the teacher calls attention to the sounds and spelling patterns of words by urging the student to listen carefully to words that will be written, prompting the student to write out a new word several times so that it will be memorable, praising progress, and so on. Consistent with Clay's (1991) perspective that reading instruction should help the student develop internalized use of strategies taught to him or her, such support is faded as the student is able to function independently, with additional support provided as more challenging texts and tasks are presented following success with easier ones.

Does Reading Recovery work? Most Reading Recovery students catch up with their classmates and two or three years later they are still reading on about the same levels as other students (Pinnell, 1989). Although not all outcomes are as impressive (Center, Wheldall, Freeman, Outhred, & McNaught, 1995), many educators are as excited about Reading Recovery as an intervention as they are about other one-on-one tutoring programs that seem to be effective in improving beginning reading (Wasik & Slavin, 1993). In a potentially important development,

One-on-one tutoring, such as occurs in Reading Recovery, is sometimes needed to jump-start first-grade students who experience difficulty learning to read in the classroom program.

Iversen and Tumner (1993) produced quicker improvement when Reading Recovery was complemented with more explicit phonics instruction than usually occurs in Reading Recovery lessons. This is one more piece of evidence favoring the explicit teaching of decoding to beginning readers.

The Secondary School and College Years. There has been little study of literacy and literacy instruction during middle school, high school, college, and beyond. This is regrettable because it is clear that there is still a great need for reading and writing instruction after elementary school. Far too many students receive high school diplomas even though their literacy skills are very weak compared to what they should be or could have been. Far too many students arrive at universities ill prepared for the demanding reading and writing expected of college students (Royer, Marchant, Sinatra, & Lovejoy, 1990). Increasingly, as technology changes and the economy shifts, adults need to learn new literacy skills in order to keep pace with employment demands.

What do we know about literacy and literacy instruction after childhood? There is substantial evidence that secondary school students can learn a variety of comprehension strategies that enhance their understanding and memory of text (Alvermann & Moore, 1991; Weinstein & Mayer, 1986). Many of these strategies are the same ones that can be taught to elementary school students, which means that some students arrive at high school not having learned efficient comprehension strategies during the elementary years. Beneficial strategies that can be taught at the secondary level include the following (see also Chapter 4):

- Using and analyzing the text structure to abstract main ideas.
- Summarizing, outlining, and mapping of text, if substantial instruction is provided about how to do it.
- Note taking.
- Self-questioning, with the benefits greater for low-ability students. This can include self-questions designed to prompt students to look for main ideas and elaborate on them.
- Elaborating text in various ways, including representational imagery, relating to prior knowledge, and thinking about why the relationships specified in text are valid (Pressley, Wood et al., 1992).

These clearly effective procedures require more of the learner than simple rehearsal. The learner works with the text's content, analyzing relationships between elements of the text as given and considering the text that is given in light of other knowledge already possessed by the learner.

The most frequent method of instruction in comprehension strategies used in the secondary school and college years is to teach a large number of strategies in a relatively short period of time, such as in the context of a study skills course. There are few evaluations of such courses, and the ones that do exist suggest small to inconsistent effects. These traditional study skills courses provide too much, too fast. High school and college students need to receive systematic instruction in ways that complement rather than threaten the content-driven curricula of secondary and postsecondary education.

Adult Literacy. In recent years much has been written about an adult literacy crisis (Northcutt, 1975; U.S. Department of Education, National Commission on

Excellence in Education, 1983). The literacy deficiencies of the nation have been apparent in the "nation's report card," the National Assessment of Educational Progress (Kirsch & Jungeblut, 1986). Put simply, many American adults lack fundamental literacy skills.

On the positive side of the ledger, by the age of 17, virtually 100 percent of current American students can perform the most simple of literacy tasks: they can locate a single piece of information in a newspaper article of moderate length, or they can select words, phrases, or sentences to describe a simple picture (Kirsch & Jungeblut, 1986). The problem, of course, is that much more is demanded in our increasingly complex society, and only a small proportion of students seems to be able to carry out literacy tasks equal to these new demands (Mikulecky, 1987). For example, less than 5 percent of 17-year-olds can work with ideas in a specialized, complex text. That is, most students have a tough time with demanding scientific materials, critical essays, historical source documents, and technical materials such as those encountered in the workplace. They have trouble linking ideas in complex essays and are not facile at making generalizations based on such texts.

Fortunately, adults of all ages can learn to read better than they do now. Most adults are faced with the need to obtain information from expository materials, but many are not armed with the strategies to extract such information efficiently. Bonnie Meyer and her colleagues (B. J. F. Meyer, Young, & Bartlett, 1989) were interested in whether adults could be taught to identify the common structures in expository text and to use this information to increase learning from text.

They taught younger and older adults the Plan Strategy. This strategy involves identifying the writing plan of the author of an expository piece. For each type of expository structure (for example, description, a comparison, a cause-and-effect sequence, or a problem-solution structure), participants learn the words in a text that could signal its use. For example, they learn that descriptive text is signaled by phrases such as *for instance, this particular, for example, specifically, such as, attributes of, that is, namely, properties of, characteristics are,* and *in describing.*

Knowledge of such signals is a form of metacognition, tipping off the reader about the type of text the author composed. Other metacognition about strategies was developed as well, including providing instruction about when the Plan Strategy works. For example, this strategy is effective when readers want to be able to recall the most important information in a text. It is not a useful strategy, however, when the goal is to find some particular piece of information in a text.

Strategy training increased recall of passage ideas both in the elderly and in the young. Importantly, the strategy-trained subjects recalled more higher-order information than did control subjects not receiving the training. They were also better at identifying the main ideas in passages.

In short, adults who are able to decode may not comprehend as well as they could. High school students, college students, and adults of all ages often fail to use powerful comprehension strategies. Fortunately, comprehension can be improved in older readers by teaching them comprehension strategies.

Writing

Literacy requires skills in writing as well as reading. Unfortunately, if poor reading is common, poor writing is epidemic. Nevertheless, there has been a great deal of progress in the development of writings instruction that promotes composition skills.

The essentials of excellent writing are (1) planning, (2) composing a draft, and (3) editing and revising. This is not a strictly linear process, however, but rather recursive: Writers plan a little, write a little, plan some more, and write some more. Perhaps as they revise some of what they have already written, they realize they need to plan more, write more, and so on (Flower & Hayes, 1980).

Planning

Good writers spend a lot more time planning than weak writers do. Their planning activities focus on the meaning that the composition is intended to convey (Bereiter & Scardamalia, 1987). There are three subprocesses to such planning, with these occurring recursively. First, writers *generate the information* that might go in the composition. Writers accomplish this by retrieving information from long-term memory or from seeking information in the environment, such as when a reporter interviews witnesses to an accident or a student searches a library for material that might go in a paper. Second, writers *set writing goals.* Occasionally a goal is provided, such as when a teacher assigns an essay topic such as, "What I Did on My Summer Vacation." More often, however, it is up to the writer to decide on the topic of the composition and what effect the writer wishes to have on readers. For example, an essay on a condemned killer could be written to elicit sympathy from readers, acceptance of capital punishment as necessary, or political action from readers in the form of protest to the governor. Third, writers *organize the information* retrieved. A significant part of organization is selecting information that is relevant to the writing goals that emerged during the planning phase.

There are clear individual differences in the planning of student writers. For example, J. Nelson and Hayes (1988) studied how college students search for material for term papers. They found that some students go to the library shortly before the due date for the paper and complete their search in one afternoon and evening, with their selection of books anything but exhaustively systematic. Other students head to the library well in advance of the deadline and are extremely systematic and selective in their choice of references.

Suppose that a student is far enough along with a writing project to have a fairly clear goal and has photocopies of some relevant articles. Will the student find the information needed even if he or she has retrieved, photocopied, and read the article? Document search is not a linear process, but one that is recursive. Thus, a writer reading one section of an article he or she categorized as potentially relevant may discover that it is not relevant at all. This stimulates the writer to reconsider other sections of the text. In addition, some information found in a later section of the text might make clear that something read earlier was relevant, stimulating a search for material the writer had dismissed previously.

Finding information in a text is difficult even for bright high school and university students. Student writers often fail to identify the information they are seeking in a text even though it is there (Guthrie & Dreher, 1990). Students can even read the information that they are trying to find and not recognize that it is what they have been looking for (Symons & Pressley, 1993). Perhaps most readers would not be surprised to learn that the college students who went to the library just prior to the paper deadline in the study by J. Nelson and Hayes (1988) were also ineffective when it came to searching in the texts they located. They tended to do a lot of copying of quotes from sources without reflecting much on the appropriateness of the quotes. In short, document search is a challenging but essential part of planning, and it is less straightforward than it may seem.

Researchers in writing have documented a number of other difficulties during planning (Harris & Graham, 1992): A common one is that some student writers do not plan but rather simply write. For example, they may simply pour out what they did on their summer vacation trip, without planning the essay so that it makes sense to someone who was not on the trip. This is what Bereiter and Scardamalia (1987) refer to as **knowledge telling.** Some writers have a great deal of difficulty generating ideas for compositions and cannot zero in on an appropriate topic (Morocco & Neuman, 1986). Others have a lot of information in their heads about their writing topic but seem not to be able to access it or may do so inefficiently (Englert & Raphael, 1988; Graham & Harris, 1989).

Composing

The composing phase involves transforming the sketch of a paper that emerged from the planning stage into standard English sentences that go together reasonably well to form paragraphs and represent the arguments intended by the writing plan.

Sometimes deficiencies in the plan become evident during the composing phase, in which case more planning occurs. Although good writers plan before they write, they also do a lot of planning once writing has begun (Humes, 1983). They may alter their plan in light of what they discover as they write; this may even include changing their writing goal (Flower & Hayes, 1980). Often, additional planning is required because a gap in knowledge becomes evident as the author tries to craft a coherent essay.

A trip to any bookstore will confirm that there are many available writing style manuals. Most of these are filled with technical rules, detailing everything from when to use a semicolon to how to cite a reference. It is easy to get the impression from these books that good writing only requires application of such rules. Knowledge of such rules, however, does not produce people who can write. In fact, overconcern with such rules might actually interfere with the construction of text that conveys what the author wants to say (Bereiter & Scardamalia, 1987). The real challenge in writing is to express the author's intended meaning. That is what good writers can do and poor writers cannot do! Thus, there has been increasing emphasis in recent years on developing writers who can write what they mean.

One important difficulty in creating texts that convey meaning is that authors must respect what Nystrand (1986) refers to as the **reciprocity principle.** In constructing a text that makes sense, the writer must be aware of what the potential reader knows already. Good writers keep their audience in mind as they construct text. Because the reader is not there to ask questions of the author as the composition is created, the author must anticipate the questions the readers might have and answer these questions as part of constructing the text (McCutchan & Perfetti, 1983; Scardamalia & Bereiter, 1986).

Editing and Revising

Fitzgerald (1992) summarized that good revisers approach the task on two levels. First, they keep the overall meaning and what the reader needs to get out of the text in mind. Good revisers concentrate more on the overall organization of the text than on the construction of individual sentences. Second, although attention to higher-order meaning takes precedence, expert revisers also evaluate grammar and spelling and some writing maxims, such as the use of parallel constructions and the avoidance of wordiness. In short, expert revisers have a repertoire of strategies that they apply while they are revising, from ones that are directed at the main messages of the text to others that are directed at details of grammar, spelling, and punctuation.

If revision is so important, why does it sometimes fail to occur? First, writers might not detect there is a problem with their texts. When other people point out problems, however, writers often can fix the difficulty that they did not notice on their own (Beal, 1987, 1989). Second, writers may fail to identify problems because they lack adequate criteria for what makes a piece of writing appropriately communicative (McCormick, Busching, & Potter, 1992). For instance, some younger students think that only neatness counts and, thus, if the writing appears neat, they are content with their compositions. Alternatively, they may believe the text is communicative because they like their choice of examples such as anecdotes about favorite pets, even though the anecdotes are not good illustrations of the main messages of the text. Third, writers may not know how to revise to express meaning. Some students do not know how to make additions, deletions, substitutions, and text rearrangements as revisions (Fitzgerald & Markham, 1987).

Consistent with Nystrand's (1986) reciprocity principle, good revisers are aware of the needs of the reader. This is one reason why a popular instructional option is for students to revise in small groups, with peers reading one another's work and reacting with constructive criticism. According to Vygotskian theory, participating in such group discussions may lead to long-term internalization of the revision processing carried out in the group (DiPardo & Freedman, 1988; see also Chapter 8). Often these groups are as small as two or three students working together. As helpful as the groups are, however, revision input from teachers is also invaluable. Although peers can provide a lot of input about when a composition is unclear, even the most skillful peers do not know all of the tricks of the writing trade that excellent writing teachers know. Good writing teachers scaffold their comments to students, making certain that students are really active in the revision process, not simply doing as the teacher directs. In classrooms that support excellence in writing, both peers and teachers are helpful sources during the revision process.

■ Building Your Expertise

Good Writing as an Example of Expert Performance

Like good readers, good writers exhibit the qualities of expert performance described in Chapter 5. For instance, good writers view writing as a task requiring analysis at a *deep, principled level.* That is, they focus on the development of text that conveys meaning. They tend not to worry about the more superficial, mechanical aspects of their writing, largely because they have extensive vocabularies, excellent spelling skills, and well-developed knowledge of writing conventions. The good writer's application of writing rules and conventions is *automatic,* largely because they are so well practiced, thereby freeing more of limited *working memory capacity* for other more important writing considerations. Writing expertise *takes a long time to develop,* and good writers write a lot (Applebee, 1984; Applebee, Langer, & Mullis, 1986)!

Good writers *spend a good deal of their total writing time in planning*. They spend a significant amount of time gathering and organizing their ideas and information that might be included in text. Good writers *monitor their writing* as they proceed. For instance, they may determine that they need to plan more if they experience difficulties during writing. Also, good writers explicitly revise texts to communicate their meaning better (Beal, 1989). Yes, spelling, punctuation, and grammar are attended to and improved during revision, but the most important goal in revision, as it is for all aspects of writing, is to make certain the writing communicates well.

Development of Writing

How does skilled writing develop? What can we do to create more adults who are able to communicate in writing? Fortunately, just as was the case with reading, learners of all ages can learn to improve their writing.

Emergent Writing. There is a clear developmental progression in writing during the preschool years for children who live in environments supportive of writing (Sulzby, 1985). Drawing and then scribbling are significant precursors to conventional writing. Eventually, children produce letterlike features, both in drawings and scribblings. They learn to draw some letters, such as the ones in their names, although often the letters are far from perfect. With time and experience, children can write many more words, often inventing spellings based on the sounds of the word (Bissex, 1980). For example, a child might invent the spelling of *GNYS* for *GENIUS*. Invented spellings gradually approximate conventional spellings, until there comes a time that spelling is completely conventional. It is not unusual to see all types of writing in any given kindergarten, from drawings and scribblings to completely invented words to short sentences and phrases written with conventional spelling (J. B. Allen et al., 1989; Sulzby & Teale 1991).

Writing During the Elementary School Years. Elementary writing instruction frequently occurs in the context of **writers' workshops.** In this instructional method, students often choose their own topics for writing rather than have to address some teacher-prescribed topic. Students control the length of their essays and their revisions. As part of the writing process, students receive feedback from their peers and teacher, with a great deal of sharing of writing among students. When students reach the end of this process, many writers' workshops provide for "publishing" the work, perhaps in a class book or for display on a bulletin board.

There are five potential problems that elementary school students have with writing (Harris & Graham, 1992). They can fail to do the following:

- Establish a writing goal. They may not establish whether the task is to persuade or to tell a tale, or they fail to identify their audience.
- Generate enough content. They may fail to search their memories or environments completely for information that could be put in an essay.
- Organize what they write. They may not plan enough, often relying only on knowledge telling, which is simply writing without planning or organizing.
- Perform the mechanics of writing efficiently. Their writing, spelling, or sentence construction may be weak, or they may get so hung up on the mechanics that they pay little attention to the meaning and organization of what is being written.
- Revise.

Daily composing is now common in elementary schools, with the increased emphasis on writing instruction largely stimulated by the research on writing summarized in this chapter. For instance, this student planned before he began to write.

In short, writing by elementary school student is often very deficient with respect to the most important processes associated with good writing. Fortunately, writing instruction in the elementary school years is an area in which there have been many successes. Students can learn to write well. Much contemporary writing instruction is guided by the plan-write-revise model considered earlier in this chapter (Flower & Hayes, 1980). Effective writing instruction typically includes direct explanation and modeling of writing strategies, followed by scaffolded practice until the student is ready for independent performance (see also Chapters 1 and 10). Although it is possible to observe some benefits after a few weeks or months of some specific type of strategy instruction (Harris & Graham, 1992), writing instruction is a long-term prospect.

Harris and Graham (1992) recommend one set of strategies that predominantly addresses the planning stage. These include teaching students to use question prompts that stimulate systematic search of their memories for relevant content. Some useful question prompts include the following: What happened first? What happened next? Next? What happened last? When did it happen? Where did it happen? Whom did it happen to? Having students use sentence openers can have a similar effect, such as, "One reason . . . ," "Even though . . . ," "For example, . . . ," and "I think . . ." (Bereiter & Scardamalia, 1982). Perhaps the most intuitively appealing approach to stimulate student writers to search their memories for more content, however, is simply to tell the student who writes a very short essay, "Write some more!" (Graham, 1990; Scardamalia & Bereiter, 1986).

Harris and Graham proposed another set of strategies for the writing phase. Students can learn to instruct themselves to respond to a series of probes that are matched to the information contained in essays in a particular genre. Thus, to write a short persuasive essay, students can be taught to respond to the following four prompts in order: (1) Generate a topic sentence. (2) Note reasons. (3) Examine the reasons, and ask whether readers will buy each reason. (4) Come up with an ending (Graham & Harris, 1988). To write a narrative with conventional story grammar, they can be taught to use the following set of questions (Harris & Graham, 1992): (1) Who is the main character? (2) Who else is in the story? (3) When does the story take place? (4) Where does the story take place? (5) What does the main character do or want to do? (6) What do other characters do? (7) What happens when the main character does or tries to do it? (8) What happens with other characters? (9) How does the story end? (10) How does the main character feel? (11) How do the other characters feel?

There are also revision strategies that elementary students can learn (Graham & MacArthur, 1988). Students can revise by cycling through six steps: (1) Read the essay. (2) Find a specific sentence that tells what the student believes and wants to say. (3) Add two reasons to the essay for the belief. (4) Scan each sentence of the essay. (5) Make changes on the computer (or paper, if handwritten). (6) Reread and make final changes. Peers can give feedback on the content and the structure of a paper as well (MacArthur, Schwartz, & Graham, 1991).

Writing After the Elementary School Years. Does research on writing provide insights about the writing that college students must do, for example, term papers? Linda Flower and her colleagues (Flower et al., 1990) have been studying how college students read several different pieces of information in preparation for writing, a process akin to what college students do when they write term papers: (1) Some students did what Flower and her colleagues (1990) referred to as *gist and list* when they read. They simply listed the big ideas in the text in preparation for writing. (2) Others were more selective and evaluative, deciding whether the information being processed was true, important, or something with which they agreed. That is, they used the *true–important–I agree* strategy—TIA for short. This strategy has a lot of power, providing the student with ideas that are appealing and worth putting in an essay. The problem, of course is that the student's perspective can predominate rather than the messages that the writer or writers of the text originally intended. (3) The third strategy, the *dialogue strategy,* involved the student interacting actively with the text. The student may compare the texts being read, generate examples that are counter to information in the text, imagine occasions when the point made in the text might hold, and synthesize claims from different texts.

Once the students finished reading, it was time to plan the essay. Students differed in how they approached this task. Some hardly planned at all, simply writing an essay that reflected the ideas they had come up as they gisted and listed, used TIA, or dialogued during reading. Others, although they relied almost exclusively on the ideas generated during reading, did more planning, in the sense of carefully classifying and organizing the content. The difficulty with both approaches, however, is that they really are *knowledge-telling strategies,* a dumping out of what one knows. This is the strategy of an elementary school-aged student. Since much more is expected of writers in high school or college, such as interpretive reflection and creative insights, knowledge telling is not a very good strategy. Unfortunately, it was the strategy of choice for the majority of the first-year college students in the study conducted by Flower and her colleagues (1990).

A better approach, used by about 40 percent of those studied by Flower and her colleagues (1990) is *constructive planning.* Constructive planners

> spent time thinking about not only the content, as did everyone, but about the goals for the paper, about criteria for judging it, about problems in designing it, and/or alternative ways to handle the task. They became reflective, strategic thinkers, looking at their writing as a rhetorical problem and a constructive act. . . . Constructive planning . . . often came as a response to a problem. (p. 240)

College students differ enormously in the efficiency and effectiveness of their writing strategies.

Yes, the constructive planner uses the knowledge gained from the texts that were read, but the constructive planner tries to go beyond those texts, creating elaborations that permit a more creative essay. One of the subjects in the study (Flower et al., 1990) provided the following think-aloud protocol, which is representative of constructive planning:

> Unless I just restate a lot of this stuff, talk about the fact that, you know, it is important . . . but that's not what they want. They want me to assimilate this, come up with some conclusions, they [should] be related to something. . . . [He rereads his assignment and appears to conceive a new goal.] I guess I'm gonna have to deal with how, how to attack the problem of time management. It sounds good, write this down and attack problem. Yeah! Great! Things I can think of off hand, you got to put in there about . . . [At this point he begins to review notes, to search the text and to rethink his response. . . . A few minutes later he returns to his plan.] I guess I can do a little bit more than restate what they have in the text. I can relate to my situation as a college student. It would be easier to relate to a college student! Well, wonderful. (p. 241)

It is encouraging that some students used such a sophisticated approach. Unfortunately, however, the majority of university students sampled are prone to uncreative reading-writing strategies, such as gist and list and knowledge telling. We need to learn more about how to increase the reading and writing competence of university students and other adults.

▶ Diversity

Benchmark School and the Education of Bright Underachievers

Benchmark School, which is near Philadelphia, serves intelligent elementary school-age children who experience difficulties in learning to read and write in conventional schooling. Irene Gaskins, the founder, and her colleagues have developed a strategies-based curriculum for teaching students to decode and comprehend text and to create their own compositions (Gaskins & Elliot, 1991). Virtually all of the reading and writing strategies described in this chapter are taught in the school using the transactional strategies instruction model outlined earlier in this chapter.

Does the instruction at Benchmark work? On average, children begin at Benchmark after two years of school failure, usually entering the school at 8 years of age. Most of these students would continue to fail if they remained in conventional schooling. In contrast, at Benchmark they succeed. After several years at the school, four on average, but sometimes as long as seven years, the students return to regular schooling, empowered with reading and writing strategies similar to those used by outstanding readers and writers. Virtually all former Benchmark students subsequently graduate from high school. Most go on to college.

The Benchmark curriculum is a model of how powerful an elementary school curriculum can be when intelligent educators apply what is now known about the teaching and learning of reading and writing. Strategies are taught in the school. Metacognition about those strategies develops as students apply them to challenging academic tasks. The strategies are used to learn and work with important academic content, so that students' world knowledge is increased as they practice and master these strategies. The Benchmark teachers do everything possible to provide a highly motivating environment, especially emphasizing improvement and the understanding that academic achievement is under the control of the students. Benchmark School is a place where all aspects of good information processing are fostered.

Chapter Summary

- Decoding, comprehension, and composition strategies are acquired over years of effective teaching. The education and development of literacy begins with the emergent literacy experiences of the preschool years. The child who is immersed in high-quality verbal interactions, such as those that occur during storybook reading, is better prepared for formal literacy instruction offered at school.

- The good reader has a repertoire of decoding and comprehension strategies. These include sounding words out and using orthographic clues for decoding, as well as using imagery, summarization, and predicting for comprehension. The good reader uses the various strategies flexibly and appropriately. Although most students can decode by grade 6, not all do so with efficiency.

- Excellent writing involves planning, composing, and revising. Each of these components can be taught, but all three are coordinated and meshed by the skilled writer.

- Many students do not learn the comprehension and composing strategies necessary to read advanced texts with high comprehension and to create new texts that convey information well. Fortunately, both comprehension and writing strategies can be taught to high school and college students. It is important to continue identifying effective comprehension and composing instruction for adults.

Return to the Classroom Predicament

Has reading this chapter helped you formulate your responses to Mrs. Jackson's questions posed at the beginning of this chapter? The ideas presented in this chapter provide many possible responses. Mrs. Jackson should be encouraged to employ emergent literacy practices at home, especially storybook reading. The teacher could also reassure Mrs. Jackson that there are different approaches to teaching students to decode and comprehend and that as long as her child is learning to read, the particular method used should not be a concern. Of course, if her child has learning difficulties, an approach emphasizing explicit decoding would likely be the best option. Finally, Mrs. Jackson should be reassured that many high school students can benefit from instruction in the planning, composing, and revising stages of writing.

Chapter Outline

Chapter 12

Mathematics and Science Instruction

Classroom Predicament

Mr. Vargas is talking to another teacher about his class. "My students just don't seem to know how to think, reason, and solve problems. They really seem to have no idea how to go about working math problems. I have also noticed that they have misconceptions about scientific concepts that I can't seem to teach out of them. Is there anything I can do to increase their math and science skills in particular, and their reasoning and problem-solving skills in general?

What would you say to Mr. Vargas? Reflecting on the ideas presented in this chapter will help you formulate responses to this question.

dvances in mathematics and science education emphasize the creation of good thinkers as outlined in Chapter 1 and featured throughout this book. Moreover, the skills emphasized in mathematics and science curricula apply to other school content domains as well. For example, the reasoning skills that characterize good problem solving are important in many different contexts. Therefore, the understandings gained from mathematics education research about general problem-solving skills have broad implications. In addition, effective mathematics instruction provides insights into productive use of cooperative learning techniques and the educational use of technology such as computers, interactive videodiscs, and even television programming.

The ideas emerging from science education research have broader implications as well. The kinds of misconceptions especially evident in science classrooms are also found in other content domains. Teaching for conceptual change utilizes conceptual conflict, analogies, and multiple representations gained through collaboration. These are instructional techniques that can be readily applied to other disciplines.

Mathematics Teaching and Learning

We begin this chapter with a review of a well-known set of recommendations about problem solving.

Polya's Model and General Problem-Solving Strategies

In his legendary book on mathematics education, *How to Solve It,* mathematician George Polya recommended a set of general strategies for problem solving (adapted from Polya, 1957):

1. Understand the problem. Example approaches for doing so:
   Ask yourself, "What am I looking for?"
   Ask yourself, "What information is given in the problem?"
2. Devise a plan for solving the problem. Example approaches for doing so:
   Ask yourself, "Do I know a similar problem?"
   Ask yourself, "Can I restate the problem?"
3. Carry out the plan.
4. Look back. Example approaches for doing so:
   Check the calculations and result.
   Try to get the same result using a different method.

By now you may recognize some of the strengths of Polya's approach in terms of the good information processing model emphasized in this text. For example, formulating a plan and carrying it out are consistent with the good information perspective that tasks should be approached strategically. In addition, looking back, in good information processing terms, is equivalent to the metacognitive process of monitoring.

As we have learned, however, the most powerful problem solving in any domain is completed by individuals with a great deal of domain knowledge, since domain knowledge often includes knowledge of extremely efficient strategies for accomplishing specific common problems in the domain (Owen & Sweller, 1989; see also Chapter 5). Therefore, using a general problem-solving approach may be less efficient than applying well-known approaches that are almost rules of thumb. Nonetheless, there is a great deal of recent evidence supporting the usefulness of Polya's four-step approach for many problem solvers.

For instance, Burkell, Schneider, and Pressley (1990) analyzed studies in which elementary school-age students had been taught successfully how to solve problems. They found in every one of the successful studies that Polya's four steps were taught, although the researchers did not always use Polya's terms. Most importantly, Burkell and her colleagues (1990) concluded that effective problem solving involves a fleshed-out version of Polya's general model, one that specifies various ways in which the general Polya strategies can be carried out. This expanded version of Polya's approach is detailed in the "What Do I Do on Monday Morning?" feature below.

Hembree (1992) analyzed hundreds of studies evaluating general processes in skilled problem solving and found clear associations between each of the Polya strategies and problem-solving performance. For example, the correlation between comprehending a problem and performance was 0.54; between selecting the correct problem-solving operations and performance was 0.72; and between checking work and performance was 0.25. The most interesting relationship identified by Hembree, however, was that Polya's four general strategies had a greater impact with increasing grade level. The overall correlation between teaching Polya's strategies and math performance was only 0.17 for children in grades 4 to 5, increasing to 0.26 at grades 6 to 8, and increasing much more to 0.72 at grades 9 to 12.

● "What Do I Do on Monday Morning?"

An Expanded Version of Polya's General Model for Problem Solving

George Polya's four problem-solving steps are a good place to begin to understand problem solving, but students need to be taught how to carry out each of the general steps specified by Polya. Here is a revision of Polya's model including specific problem-solving procedures that can be taught to students as early as elementary school (Burkell, Schneider, & Pressley 1990):

1. *Understand the problem.*
   a. Read the problem slowly and carefully, identifying exactly what is being asked.
   b. Identify the important information in the problem, perhaps making a list or table to do so.
   c. Define the terms in the problem.
   d. Paraphrase the problem.
   e. Create a representation of the problem by using objects or by making a diagram or drawing.
2. *Devise a plan for solving the problem.*
   a. Relate the problem to other problems you may have encountered.
   b. Identify a familiar pattern in the problem, one that you have seen in a previous problem.
   c. Construct a hypothesis about the problem and possible solutions.

     d. Try to solve part of the problem.

     e. Try to solve a related problem.

3. *Carry out the plan.*

4. *Look back.*

     a. Check your answer, including all calculations.

     b. Compare the answer obtained through problem solving with an estimated answer.

     c. Solve the problem another way.

     d. Summarize what you did to solve the problem (and try to remember the solution for future reference).

     e. Construct a problem similar to this one, one that would be solved similarly.

Schoenfeld's Model of Mathematical Cognition

Alan Schoenfeld (1992) has offered a model of mathematics problem solving that includes four information processing components, which overlap considerably with the ingredients of good information processing (knowledge, strategies, metacognition, and motivation) considered throughout this book. This model includes (1) a knowledge base about mathematical concepts, (2) problem-solving strategies, (3) monitoring and control, (4) beliefs about mathematics that affect attitudes toward and motivation to do mathematics, and (5) instructional practices that foster effective mathematical thinking.

The information processing hardware, especially short-term memory, also figures in Schoenfeld's formulation, although it is not singled out as a component by him. Specifically, Schoenfeld recognizes that problem solving depends on short-term capacity, which is limited. The long-term knowledge of mathematics is well organized and "chunkable" for the expert problem solver, which does much to reduce demands on short-term capacity. Thus, good problem solvers are able to juggle more using the limited capacity they have than weak problem solvers can. In part, this is because the chunks of mathematical knowledge that good problem solvers handle are bigger, better organized, and more readily applicable to math problems (Cooney & Swanson, 1990; Dark & Benbow, 1990)

Schoenfeld's (1985, 1992) conception of mathematical thinking begins with *knowledge of mathematical concepts,* including both the declarative knowledge ("what," or factual, knowledge, such as knowledge about the characteristics of a sphere; see Chapter 3) and procedural knowledge ("how" knowledge, such as how to do addition, subtraction, and multiplication; see Chapter 3) required to do mathematics. The good thinker articulates declarative knowledge of mathematical concepts and procedural knowledge when solving problems. For example, the good thinker uses the single-digit addition facts that are stored as declarative knowledge (e.g., $2 + 2 = 4$, $5 + 4 = 9$) in solving a problem that requires application of the quadratic formula, which is a piece of procedural knowledge.

At the center of Schoenfeld's second component, *problem-solving strategies,* are Polya's strategies. Schoenfeld believes that these work only if the thinker is armed with a great deal of mathematical conceptual knowledge.

The third component, *monitoring and control,* is an aspect of metacognition that Schoenfeld highlighted. Schoenfeld focused on how monitoring contributes to self-regulated use of knowledge, including the procedural knowledge of strategies. Schoenfeld is aware that students often have misconceptions and misunderstandings about when and where to use the mathematical procedures they know (Confrey, 1990; Putnam, Lampert, & Peterson, 1990). Sometimes their execution of strategies is systematically flawed as well, as in the case of errors consistently made during subtraction (van Lehn, 1990). If students are to become aware of errors in metacognitive and procedural knowledge and correct them, it is essential that they monitor whether the strategies they are using are effective.

The fourth component, *motivational beliefs,* often is based on the experiences students have as part of mathematics instruction. Sometimes, the beliefs they develop in mathematics classes undermine the development of sophisticated mathematical behaviors. For example, the common beliefs that mathematics problems have one and only one right answer and that there is only one correct way to solve any mathematics problem (usually the rule the teacher has most recently demonstrated to the class) are likely to have high potential for discouraging reflective problem solving, including the generation of alternative ways to tackle particular problems. Also discouraging is the belief that when the teacher asks a question in math class, the students who understand only need a few seconds to answer correctly. In light of such beliefs, some students conclude that math learned in schools is mostly facts and procedures that have to be memorized. Many students come to believe more in memorization as a process underlying achievement in mathematics than in reflection. These students are more likely to believe such statements as "The best way to do well in math is to memorize all the formulas" and "You have to memorize how to do geometry constructions." By high school, students make attributions that clearly undermine their efforts when they are having difficulty with mathematics, often attributing achievement in mathematics to uncontrollable factors such as ability (see Chapter 2). Thus the argument develops that some people are good at math and some just are not.

The experiences that shape these beliefs include many nights of homework for which there is only one final answer, as well as years of taking tests that require quick responses. Some teachers even discourage reflective problem solving by emphasizing a speedy response, thereby sending the message that if a student cannot do a problem in a few minutes, it is probably beyond his or her capabilities. In short, much of conventional mathematics teaching seems to promote beliefs that can reduce motivation to learn and do mathematics. In contrast, an effective problem solver understands that problems can be solved in different ways, that understanding mathematical ideas is more important than memorizing formulas and definitions, and that mathematical competence is largely a function of learning and doing mathematics rather than something that is determined by innate factors.

This leads us to the fifth component of Schoenfeld's model—*instructional practices.* Schoenfeld believes that the good math instructor can do much to foster understanding of where and when particular mathematics strategies work, as well as to nurture a general tendency in students to monitor their progress during problem solving. The good mathematics teacher coaches his or her students during their problem-solving attempts, posing questions such as the following: "What (exactly) are you doing? Can you describe it precisely? Why are you doing it? How does it fit into your solution? How does it help you? What will you do with the outcome when you obtain it?" (Schoenfeld, 1992, p. 356).

Such questions, when posed consistently as part of mathematics instruction, sensitize students to monitor their problem solving and to become aware of the effects of the strategies they are using as well as where and when positive effects can be obtained.

Schoenfeld (1979) evaluated his model in a university course designed to stimulate the development of the four information processing components of his model. Teaching in the course was consistent with his vision of effective mathematics instruction, as reflected in the fifth component of his model. Students practiced doing the college-level problems in the course using the Polya strategies and then reflectively discussed how the Polya strategies were applied to the practice items, consistent not only with Schoenfeld's teaching model but also with recommendations about instruction coming from Vygotsky's theory (see Chapter 8).

Comparisons of problem solving before and after the course, as well as comparisons to students enrolled in another mathematics-oriented course, revealed that Schoenfeld's course had a substantial impact on students (Schoenfeld, 1985). There were clear differences favoring trained students, both on problems similar to ones covered in the course and on problems quite different from those practiced and discussed as part of the class requirements. The students made extensive use of the general Polya-type problem-solving strategies featured in Schoenfeld's course to organize the application of specific mathematical concepts and procedures learned in the course.

Schoenfeld's instruction can be termed direct explanation and modeling (see Chapters 1 and 10), in that the teacher provided the students with a good start on the processes that comprise effective problem solving through modeling and explaining, but students and teachers then worked together to develop a much fuller understanding of the problem-solving strategies. The teacher provided scaffolding to students as needed. Schoenfeld's students worked very hard to figure out how to adapt and elaborate the strategic scheme Schoenfeld provided them. The result was an internalization of a flexible approach to problem solving, one which the students constructed for themselves.

Natural Development of Mathematical Understanding

Mathematics educators described advances in mathematical understanding during the preschool years (Baroody, 1987; Fuson, 1988, 1992; Romberg & Carpenter, 1986). Children learn a great deal about mathematics in the first six years of life.

For example, many 2-year-olds can report to their parent when there are two toys, and 3- to 4-year-olds also can point out three cookies or four people. Recognition of such small sets seems to be based more on perceptual differences between one, two, three, and four items than on a deep conceptual understanding of the amounts represented by the numbers *1* through *4*. Young children's abilities to identify the number for small sets of objects is termed **subitizing.** Identification of larger sets of objects by number is infrequent for 2- to 4-year-olds.

Preschoolers sometimes perform addition and subtraction operations on small numbers, in the sense that they can "get some more" and "lose some." Preschoolers also can conserve in the Piagetian sense when small numbers of objects are involved (Piaget, 1965; see also Chapter 7): Suppose a row of three objects is shown to a child and then the row is covered with the middle object surreptitiously removed. When the cover is lifted, the child will definitely notice that the number of objects in the row has changed. The child is not fooled for an instant by the fact that the row of two mice spans the same distance as the row of three mice did (Gelman & Gallistel, 1978).

Many preschoolers learn the whole number sequence from 1 to 10, and some even acquire the sequence from 1 to 20. It is common for a child to arrive at kindergarten able to write the whole numbers to 20. Some kindergarten children learn to count to 100 or 200 as well as by 10s.

Preschoolers' counting is more than their just being able to rattle off the numbers from 1 to 100, however. Preschoolers can also use numbers to count objects, recognizing that they need to arrange items so that each item is counted once and only once, using the whole number sequence they have learned. Even so, preschoolers sometimes do not arrange relatively large numbers of objects, and they sometimes point to an object and fail to count it or point to an object and say two numbers. By 5 years of age, it is not unusual for children to be able to count up to 20 or more objects, although it takes a lot of effort and results in frequent errors. For the 5-year-old, because counting the objects is not automatic, the activity makes demands on short-term memory capacity.

An important acquisition for children is the development of understanding that the last number uttered in a count is the number of objects in the set counted. This is known as the **cardinal number.** The development of understanding of cardinality as it relates to counting is known as the **count-to-cardinal transition.** Many 5-year-olds recognize that if the count of two sets of objects ends in the same number, then the two sets have the same number of objects. That is, 1, 2, 3, 4, 5 apples in this row is equal to 1, 2, 3, 4, 5 apples in that row. This is an important understanding since a cognitive prerequisite for learning simple addition and subtraction is the ability to note equivalence of two sets. Beyond having this prerequisite knowledge, students in kindergarten and those entering first grade often know much more, including how to add and subtract, at least in some situations.

What mathematical concepts do preschoolers possess? What can their fingers reveal about their abilities to carry out mathematical procedures?

Addition and Subtraction. In a three-year longitudinal study of children's addition and subtraction, Carpenter and Moser (1982) and their colleagues (Carpenter, Hiebert, & Moser, 1981) evaluated how young children just entering school solved two types of addition problems:

- *Joining* problems involve putting together two quantities as in: "Connie had 5 marbles. Jim gave her 8 more marbles. How many marbles did Connie have altogether?" Joining problems involve a dynamic, changing relationship.
- *Part-part-whole* problems require analyzing an existing quantity and breaking it down into its components, such as, "There are 6 boys and 8 girls on the soccer team. How many children are on the team altogether?" Part-part-whole problems involve a static, descriptive relationship.

Children beginning school use several different strategies to solve these problems. Some used their fingers or other concrete objects to solve addition problems. For example, they represented the addends (the numbers in addition problems) with concrete objects and then counted the objects. Sometimes children relied on number facts they had learned. For example, if a child "knew" 8 + 5 = 13 based on prior experience, there was no need to use fingers or counting to solve the problem. Another strategy was **counting on from first.** Children would start from the addend mentioned first (e.g., 3 for 3 + 4) and count up by the number represented by the second addend (e.g., "3," "4," "5," "6," "7" for 3 + 4). Another strategy was **counting on from larger.** This strategy involves starting with the larger addend (e.g., 4 for 3 + 4) and counting up the number specified by the smaller addend (e.g., "4," "5," "6," "7" for 3 + 4). Counting on from larger is often referred to as the MIN strategy (G. J. Groen & Parkman, 1972), because it minimizes the number of counts required to solve an addition problem when using a counting strategy.

Just as children entering primary school can do several types of addition problems, Carpenter and Moser observed that they can also solve different types of subtraction problems. Moreover, preschoolers develop strategies for solving subtraction problems. For example, the strategy of **counting down from given** involves counting down from the larger number mentioned in the problem by the smaller number, one number at a time. For example, when given the problem 4 − 3, the child counts down "4," "3," "2," and "1." The **adding on** strategy begins with the smaller number of objects mentioned in the problem and involves counting the number of counts to reach the larger number. For example, for 4 − 3, the child would start with "3" and counting up 1 count to "4," so the answer is 1. For 5 − 2, the child would start with "2" and count "3," "4," and "5," which is 3 counts, so the answer is 3.

Development of Knowledge of Math Addition and Subtraction Facts.

Most children eventually abandon the counting strategies and come to rely on knowledge of math facts when presented simple problems. For example, if children are given 2 + 5 = ? they retrieve the answer of 7 from long-term memory. Siegler's (1989) theory is that as children use counting strategies to work addition and subtraction problems, they develop associations between the problem statements (e.g., 2 + 5) and the answers they generate. For example, the association between 2 + 5 and 7 is strengthened when a child solves 2 + 5 by using fingers or by counting. When the associative strength between the problem and the correct answer is sufficiently strong because of repeated practice, the math fact comes to elicit the correct answer reliably. The students no longer need to solve the problem using concrete aids or counting; they can simply "look it up" in long-term memory. Nevertheless, some students continue to count or use other strategies in order to "just make certain" they are reporting the correct answer (Siegler, 1988). What Siegler is describing is a shift from reliance on problem-solving strategies to reliance on the knowledge base (see Chapter 5).

By the middle-elementary school grades, many students rely on the retrieval of answers from long-term memory over any other strategy in generating answers to single-digit addition problems. With practice in performing other operations, such as subtraction and multiplication, there is a strengthening of associations between subtraction and multiplication problems and their correct answers as well. By the end of the middle-to-late elementary school grades, many students rely on retrieval from long-term memory to respond to basic subtraction and multiplication problems as well as addition problems. There are individual differences, however, in students' use of the retrieval strategy. For example, even some adults continue to rely on counting strategies to solve single-digit arithmetic problems (Widaman, Little, Geary, & Cormier, 1992).

Effective Mathematics Instruction

Unfortunately, many children do not naturally develop effective elementary problem-solving strategies. For example, some would not know to count up from the subtracted number to the larger number in order to determine a difference and would not be able to count up from 8 to establish that 6 digits intervene between 14 and 8 (the answer to $14 - 8$). More optimistically, Fuson and her colleagues (Fuson & Fuson, 1991; Fuson & Willis, 1988) have been able to teach primary school students the strategy of adding on by using direct explanation that emphasizes subtraction conceptualized as adding on. Direct explanation of elementary problem solving can result in students who are more adept at representing the world with mathematical expressions and better able to solve math problems that are presented to them. Thus, natural development of mathematical strategies is powerful, but it is not the only way to develop strategies. Instruction is effective, as well. Mathematics educators are on the cutting edge of new instructional approaches. What follows are some instructional and technological innovations currently advocated by mathematics educators and researchers.

Cooperative Learning. Cooperative learning (see Chapters 2 and 10) is used for many content areas but is especially appropriate for mathematics education, since contemporary mathematics educators emphasize social collaboration in problem solving. Many studies have demonstrated that students become better problem solvers as a function of participating in cooperative learning experiences (Davidson, 1985)

Neil Davidson and his colleagues (Bassarear & Davidson, 1992; Davidson & Kroll, 1991) have been at the vanguard in developing cooperative learning techniques for mathematics instruction. They believe that cooperatively interacting to solve problems can be a transformative experience for many students, with advantages that include the following:

- Students come to value the process of problem solving rather than production of a correct answer.
- Mathematics anxiety is reduced when students work in cooperative groups.

- Cooperative instruction permits more challenging and less conventional problems to be presented to students.
- Cooperation fosters students' explanations and reexplanations to one another, which is important since explaining difficult ideas to others is a very effective method of forcing people to understand the ideas fully (N. M. Webb, 1989, 1991). The discussions bring to light misconceptions, which can sometimes be resolved via discussion. Students make connections to other knowledge as they discuss a problem, with different students offering varying insights about how the mathematics being learned connects to the world.
- Multiple representations of problem situations are offered in discussions, which is very important, since good mathematicians and problem solvers realize that any situation can be represented in a variety of ways.

Cooperative learning researchers are analyzing the dynamics and structures of cooperative groups. For example, N. M. Webb (1989, 1991) has established both the positive effects of generating explanations in cooperative groups and the negative effects on achievement of only being told correct answers when seeking assistance. The students who do the explaining in cooperative groups learn the most. When all factors are considered, mixed-ability grouping representing less than the full range of abilities (i.e., students with high and medium ability together, and students with medium and low ability together) seems to be the arrangement that results in active participation by most of the group members.

N. M. Webb (1984) has also studied the effects of gender balance in cooperative groups. She reported that girls were more likely to be interactive in cooperative groups that were gender balanced, with equal numbers of boys and girls. Groups where boys were in the majority resulted in girls' being ignored, and groups where girls were in the majority resulted in disproportionate interactions directed at the boys. Achievement was greater for girls when they participated in gender-balanced groups.

Research on the dynamics of cooperative groups is very important, for it is becoming apparent that group problem solving sometimes goes awry. Stacey (1992), for instance, collected verbal protocols of students in grades 7 to 9 while they attempted challenging problems in small groups. What was disturbing was that the group members were often willing to go along with a simple and wrong method of problem solution that was put on the floor by one member of the group. Sometimes very good solutions were rejected. We need to learn more about when cooperative groups work and what can be done so that they work better.

Learning from Examples. Although social interactions can increase mathematical understandings, there are also nonsocial ways of increasing knowledge of mathematical problem-solving procedures. Working sample problems is important in learning how to solve problems (G. Cooper & Sweller, 1987; Sweller & Cooper, 1985). For example, as part of their work in high school mathematics instruction, Zhu and Simon (1987) found that students acquired the problem-solving procedures more quickly and with greater competence when they were provided worked example problems. It is likely that these students developed representations of specific problem-solving cases that they could then apply to other situations. Thus, they were building their case knowledge of mathematics problem solving.

Is there evidence that knowledge of individual cases produces generalizable knowledge? Ahn (1987) and his colleagues (Ahn & Brewer, 1988; Ahn, Mooney,

Brewer, & DeJong, 1987) presented adults with anecdotes about how a particular problem was solved, such as the following:

> Tom, Sue, Jane, and Joe were all friends and each wanted to make a large purchase as soon as possible. Tom wanted a VCR, Sue wanted a microwave, Joe wanted a car stereo, and Jane wanted a compact disk player. However, they each only had $50 left at the end of each month after paying their expenses. Tom, Sue, Jane, and Joe all got together to solve the problem. They made four slips of paper with the numbers 1, 2, 3, and 4 written on them. They put them in a hat and each drew out one slip. Jane got the slip with the 4 written on it, and said, "Oh darn, I have to wait to get my CD player." Joe got the slip with the 1 written on it and said, "Great, I can get my car stereo right away!" Sue got the number 2, and Tom got number 3. In January, they each contributed the $50 they had left. Joe took the whole $200 and bought a Pioneer car stereo. In February, they each contributed their $50 again. This time, Sue used the $200 to buy a Sharp 600 watt 1.5 cubic foot microwave. In March, all four again contributed $50. Tom took the money and bought a Sanyo Beta VCR with wired remote. In April, Jane got the $200 and bought a Technics CD player. (Mooney, 1990, p. 502)

The adults in this research either produced a summary of the problem-solving approach illustrated by the story, wrote another anecdote illustrating the application of the problem-solving approach, or answered questions about the problem-solving approach. In general, they could perform as well on these tasks after exposure to a single example as other adults presented with a formal summary of the problem-solving tactic. People often engage in case-based reasoning. Today's problem can remind a person of a situation encountered previously, permitting creation of a solution that is similar to the one used to solve the previous problem.

Calculators. Cognitive psychologists believe that the tools one uses to think can affect the way one thinks. Thus, students who use an abacus (an ancient type of calculating machine developed by the Chinese) to calculate come to perform mental calculations differently than students who use nonabacus methods do. Long-term use of an abacus results in an internal abacus, an image of an abacus that the students use to make mental calculations (Hatano, Amaiwa, & Shimuzu, 1987; Stigler, 1984)

Use of more up-to-date calculating machines, such as electronic calculators, can increase mathematical conceptual understandings, problem-solving abilities, and attitudes toward mathematics (Demana & Leitzel, 1988; Hembree & Dessart, 1986). For example, Russow and Pressley (1993) explored the effects when college-level students used graphing calculators in a basic mathematics course covering mathematical functions. Compared to control students who graphed functions by hand, students who used graphing calculators came to understand the concept of

Long-term use of an abacus to solve problems results in thinking that is abacuslike. Abacus users come to flip over beads in their head as part of problem solving!

Graphing calculators such as this one are powerful tools that permit students to explore mathematical functions and their properties. Such devices make a difference in students' understanding of mathematics.

function much more completely than those in the control group. The students who used the graphing calculator solved more problems on final exams that required understanding the relationship between mathematical functions and their graphs than the control students did.

Interactive Videodiscs. Interactive videodisc technology offers opportunities to present richly contexted problems to students. Students can be presented a complex set of relationships in a movielike presentation, with realistic depiction of the many features that define the complex contexts in which realistic problems can occur. It is a format that permits easy review of a section of the presentation. Thus, students can interact with the presentation, reexamining the images and screenplay to gather information needed to make a decision. Interactive videodisc presentations can be prepared that provide challenging and interesting problem-solving opportunities for students. The "Focus on Research" feature discusses the best-known research program evaluating problem-solving instruction via interactive videodisc technology.

Educational Television Programming. A fairly recent addition to public television is Children's Television Workshop's *Square One,* which was designed specifically for 8- to 12-year-olds. Its goals are to stimulate positive attitudes and enthusiasm for mathematics, to encourage development of problem-solving processes, and to present important mathematical content. Mathematical concepts are conveyed via a mathematized version of the police drama *Dragnet,* with the detectives encountering many problems that can be solved using math.

There is evidence for the effectiveness of *Square One* television. E. R. Hall, Esty, and Fisch (1990) pretested fifth-grade students on their mathematical problem-solving abilities. Some of the students then watched 30 episodes of *Square One,* while others in the control group were not exposed to the program at all. Careful

An Evaluation of an Educational Intervention Using Interactive Videodiscs

The Cognition and Technology Group at Vanderbilt University (1992) is investigating applications of videodisc technology to teaching and learning mathematical problem solving. For example, they have produced their own series of shows, dubbed the *Jasper* series, about the adventures of a character named Jasper Woodbury. The first tape in the series is a 17-minute adventure ending in a problem. For example, the plot of "The Journey to Cedar Creek" is as follows:

> [A] person named Jasper Woodbury takes a river trip to see an old cabin cruiser he is considering purchasing. Jasper and the cruiser's owner, a woman named Sal, test-run the cruiser, after which Jasper decides to purchase the boat. As the boat's running lights are inoperative, Jasper must determine if he can get the boat to his home dock before sunset. Two major questions that form the basis of Jasper's decision are presented at the end of the disc: Does Jasper have enough time to return home before sunset, and is there enough fuel in the boat's gas tank for the return trip? The story indicates that Jasper decides he can get home before sunset. (Van Haneghan et al., 1992, p. 22)

The students must attempt to solve the problems Jasper had to solve in reaching his conclusion, discussing and reviewing information in the videotape in order to do so. Just as real-life problems are often complex and the essential facts may be buried in many irrelevant details, so are the facts in the *Jasper* stories. Just as there are alternative ways of figuring out solutions to the com-plex problems that fill the real world, so there are alternative routes to finding a solution in the *Jasper* problems. Thus, this educational research is very realistic in its evaluation of a state-of-the-art curriculum product.

A study of learning with the *Jasper* series was conducted by Van Haneghan and his colleagues (1992). They found no important differences in the problem-solving performances of those in the interactive videodisc group and conventional instruction control participants at the start of the study. Following problem-solving experiences with the *Jasper* series, however, students in the experimental group performed better on a transfer task involving watching a short video and solving a problem. The think-aloud protocols of students using *Jasper* reflected more sophisticated problem solving, too. In addition, the overall solution rate of students using *Jasper* was twice that of control participants. The students using *Jasper* also performed better on written word problems, despite the fact that the students in the control group had practiced solving word problems and the students using *Jasper* had not. In short, this test of the *Jasper* program provided support for its efficacy in promoting problem-solving performances. The program is now being exported to classrooms in many school districts, with similar results observed whenever the videodisc-based technology is used to teach problem solving to middle school students (Cognition and Technology Group at Vanderbilt University, 1992). This research is particularly supportive of the effectiveness of *Jasper* because its effects were apparent on a number of different dependent measures, such as problem solving on the transfer task, think-aloud procedures, and performance on written word problems.

matching on the basis of pretest scores assured that the *Square One* viewers and controls were equal in problem-solving competence at the outset of the study. At posttesting, the students who watched the episodes outperformed the control students on a number of measures of problem solving.

Complementary Methods. The methods for enriching mathematics instruction just described are complementary, rather than competing, approaches. For example, interventions such as problem solving in reaction to interactive videodisc presentations naturally fit into the context of cooperative learning, since a group's sifting through and selecting information from videodisc adventures is a natural part of coming up with a solution plan. Although individuals can use calculators, groups of students can explore mathematics with them, too.

All of these interventions require students to solve real problems, which is always going to require taking what one knows and constructing innovative solution plans. The new media products and technologies do not just give information; rather they encourage students to use ideas that are new to them in ways that really require flexibility in application and reflection before and during problem solving. At its best, this technology permits alternative ways of examining mathematics and encourages active interaction with and thinking about important mathematical concepts and procedures.

▶ Diversity

Mathematics Achievement in Asian Schools

In international comparisons of mathematics achievement, American students do not do as well as students in many other countries, notably Japan and China (National Center for Education Statistics, 1992). After studying the differences between the American and Asian educational systems, H. W. Stevenson (1990, 1992) eliminated some potential explanations, such as differences in innate ability, and produced a list of likely contributors to the Asian-American achievement gap. They include the following factors:

Curriculum

- The Asian curricula are more difficult, with more advanced concepts being introduced earlier.
- There are national mathematics curricula in Asian countries, while in the United States there is localized decision making and hence greater variability in curricular expectations.

Amount of Time/Quality of Time Spent on Mathematics Instruction

- Many more hours are spent on mathematics in Asian classrooms than in American classrooms.
- Asian students are on task for a greater proportion of classroom time than Americans are. This may be due to differences in the scheduling of the school day in Asia, where students have more breaks for play during an overall longer school day. It is easier to be attentive during class time when there are periods of relaxation during the school day.
- Asian teachers are more energetic in class, perhaps because they teach fewer hours per day than American teachers and have much greater opportunity for preparation.
- Asian children spend more time on homework than Americans do.
- Mathematics instruction in Asian schools involves high-level interactions and teachers' monitoring students to determine whether and how well they understand. In contrast, the extensive seat work given in the United States compared to that in Asian schools does not promote teacher-student interactions.

The superior performance of Asians in mathematics can be traced to many factors, including values and beliefs about the importance of mathematics, the difficulty of the mathematics curriculum, and the time spent on mathematics instruction.

- Asian teachers do more to relate mathematics to the lives of their students than American teachers do.
- Asian teachers question their students more about mathematical concepts and the mathematics strategies that might be used to solve problems (M. Perry, VanderStoep, & Yu, 1993). Such questioning probably stimulates deeper thinking about mathematics in Asian classrooms (see also Chapter 10).

Values and Beliefs

- American students and parents are satisfied with lower levels of mathematics achievement than Asians are.
- Asians attribute successes and failures to effort, a factor under the control of students; Americans are much more likely to attribute successes and failures to ability, which does not motivate effort since ability is out of the learner's control (Hess, Chih-Mei, & McDevitt, 1987; Holloway, 1988; see also Chapter 2).
- Achievement in school is much more valued in Asia than it is in the United States.

In short, it is impossible to single out a single factor as the cause of superior mathematics achievement in Asian schools. The most likely explanation is that there are many ways that Asian instruction differs from American instruction, with the Asian curriculum filled with components that promote mathematics achievement.

Gender, Race, and Socioeconomic Differences in Mathematics Achievement

U.S. females historically have not achieved at the same level as U.S. males on standardized mathematics assessments. American minorities perform more poorly in mathematics than members of the majority culture do. Poor children do not perform as well in mathematics as children from middle- and upper-income families. The result is that females, racial minorities, and people with lower-income origins are underrepresented in the pool of mathematics majors and in professions that require mathematics competency (Maple & Stage, 1991; see also the discussion of motivational differences in Chapter 2).

On the positive side, male-female differences in U.S. mathematics achievement are not large and have declined in recent years (Friedman, 1989; Hyde, Fennema, Lamon, 1990). As far as classroom grades are concerned, females do better than males, with male advantages confined to math achievement as defined by standardized tests (Kimball, 1989). In addition, international comparisons are making it obvious that there is no inherent biological reason for female underachievement, for there are cultures in which males and females perform comparably on mathematics assessments (Walberg, Harnisch, & Tsai, 1986). There also has been some closing of the achievement gap between whites and American minorities in recent years (Dorsey, Mullis, Lindquist, & Chambers, 1988; Jones, 1984)

There is reason to be hopeful that it might be possible to produce large achievement gains for some groups. For example, Cardelle-Elawar (1990) taught sixth-grade Hispanic students who were experiencing difficulties in mathematics to apply a variation of Polya's model described earlier in this chapter to the solution of problems. First, the students learned to understand a problem, translating it into questions that could be answered. Essential knowledge and strategies needed to solve the problem were then identified and a solution plan devised. Students learned to monitor their execution of the problem-solving plan. Control students in this study received more conventional instruction, emphasizing feedback about the correctness of answers to problems. This intervention facilitated the students' problem-solving performance on a mathematics achievement posttest, with both boys and girls benefiting from the intervention. Thus, improved mathematics achievement is possible for economically disadvantaged groups, when they are provided with high-quality instruction (see also Chapter 2).

Situated Knowing About Mathematics

As described in Chapters 3 and 8, knowledge is not separable from the actions that give rise to it or from the culture in which those actions occur; knowledge is situated. Mathematical thinking often depends on the social situation in which it occurs (Greeno, 1991, 1992). For example, Carraher, Carraher, and Schliemann (1985) identified young Brazilians who make a living as entrepreneurs in city streets. As part of their business operations, these children perform complex calculations efficiently. When given problems in a formal testing situation, however, these children falter. Their mathematical competence is situated, tied to the world in which the mathematical operations typically are carried out. People often develop nonstandard ways of doing the math they need to function adequately in everyday life (Saxe, 1988). Of course, knowing only street mathematics is not adaptive to functioning in the multifaceted world of the twenty-first century. There are

Although this young Indian girl selling cosmetic dyes may falter in classroom mathematics, she can perform the calculations required to complete a sale successfully. This is an example of situated knowledge.

very good reasons for devising instruction that promotes the ability to use mathematics in diverse situations.

■ Building Your Expertise

A Return to Polya

We return now to the theorist whose ideas opened the chapter, George Polya (1954a, 1954b, 1957, 1981). His description of how highly effective mathematicians think is wholly consistent with the good information processing model.

Strategies are central to Polya's ideas. There are general problem-solving strategies, such as attempting to understand, solve, and check a problem, with understanding, solving, and checking processes applied recursively. In addition, there are particular strategies, such as focusing attention on the conditions of a problem, drawing figures to enhance problem comprehension, looking for analogies with other problems, and decomposing a problem into subproblems.

Polya also understood the importance of metacognition, such as the criticality of knowledge about where and when to use particular strategies. In particular, Polya emphasized that students should always attempt to increase their understanding of when and where particular problem solutions can be applied. Another aspect of metacognition that is important in good information processing is monitoring. Polya recognized very well that such awareness of cognitive actions and how they effect problem solving is salient in the thinking of good problem solvers. Here is how Polya on one occasion described what is referred to in this book as monitoring: "You keenly feel the pace of your progress. . . . Whatever comes to your mind is quickly sized up: 'It looks good,' 'It could help,' or 'No good,' 'No help'. . . . [S]uch judgments are important to you personally, they guide your effort" (Polya, 1954b, pp. 145–146).

Polya also understood how declarative knowledge can be critical to problem solving and how such knowledge must be used in conjunction with procedural competence in order to solve problems. For example, Polya (1981, p. 37) explained how it would be impossible to solve a problem about iron spheres floating in mercury without a great deal of knowledge about both iron and mercury. Motivation is in Polya's thinking, too. He believed that good problem solvers really get into problem solving, to use a contemporary expression.

All of the elements of good information processing have been present in Polya's writings for more than 40 years, just as they are clearly evident in Schoenfeld's more contemporary approach. The expanding database in mathematical cognition documents that strategies, metacognition, nonstrategic knowledge, and motivation are key determinants of success in mathematical problem solving.

Science Teaching and Learning

We are making substantial progress in understanding how to structure science education so that it is more effective than it has been historically. Contemporary science education is informed by the nature and representation of knowledge (see Chapter 3), Vygotskian theories (see Chapter 8), principles of motivation (see Chapter 2), and other psychological perspectives.

Misconceptions

One of Piaget's (1929) most important insights was that people often have ideas about the world that clash with scientific viewpoints. For example, young children can believe that inanimate objects, such as the sun, the stars, or a computer, are alive! Piaget believed that such **animism** is a characteristic symptom of preoperational intelligence. Piaget thought that with the development of concrete and formal operations, children's ideas about what is alive versus what is not alive would reflect generally agreed upon scientific understandings. Piaget was wrong. Animism can persist throughout adulthood (Brainerd, 1978b)

For years the discovery that nonscientific thinking, such as animism, was sometimes found in adults was largely forgotten. Then scientists and science educators noted that often people have important misconceptions about physical and biological relationships. "Intuitive physics" is a set of different laws than the laws of actual physics. For example, when a discus thrower spins around in a 360-degree motion, what is the trajectory of the discus from the point of release? Intuitive physics puts a curve on the trajectory, although the actual trajectory is a straight line, consistent with Newton's first law that in the absence of a force being applied to it, an object in motion travels in a straight line. What forces operate on a baseball after it is hit into the air? According to intuitive physics upward forces and gravity are responsible; in fact, gravity is the only force applied to the ball in flight (examples based on McCloskey, 1983).

Although scientific misconceptions in physics have been studied more than other misconceptions (Pfundt & Duit, 1991), people seem to have misconceptions about every scientific arena imaginable. Scientific misconceptions can have a range of consequences, including ones that are tragic. For example, consider the pain that has been inflicted on victims of AIDS by the following misconceptions (DiClemente, et al., 1989; DiClemente, Zorn, & Temoshok, 1986, 1987; Price, Desmond, & Kukulka, 1985): (1) A person can get AIDS by touching someone with the disease. (2) All homosexual men have AIDS. (3) AIDS can be spread by any object used by an AIDS victim. (4) A person can contact AIDS by being around someone with the disease. (5) All homosexual women have AIDS. (6) It is very easy

What forces are acting on the ball right now? Even students with formal instruction in physics sometimes believe that both a horizontal force and gravity are affecting the ball. This is a misconception. Once released by the pitcher, the only force acting on the ball is gravity.

to detect a person with AIDS. (7) All persons exposed to the AIDS virus will get the disease. (8) A person can get AIDS by attending school with a student who has AIDS. (9) It is unsafe for a person with AIDS to work near children. All of these statements are, of course, incorrect.

Even after completing science courses covering scientific concepts and passing tests on them, misconceptions persist. For example, C. W. Anderson, Sheldon, and Dubay (1990) studied college students' conceptions of respiration (which is the chemical and physical processes by which oxygen and carbohydrates are used to produce energy for an organism) and photosynthesis (which is the production of food by plants, a part of the energy production cycle for plants) at the beginning and at the end of a year-long biology course. At the beginning of the course, students offered grossly deficient answers, even though most students had had one or more years of biology previously. When asked on the pretest for a definition of *respiration,* few students mentioned energy, offering, in many cases, simplistic definitions such as the following: "Exhaling CO_2 for humans, exhaling O_2 for plants"; "breathing"; "has lungs to breath with"; and "air in, air out."

The same held for pretest definitions of photosynthesis, another chemical process producing energy conversion. A minority of students mentioned food or energy in their definitions, which included the following: "Plants take in CO_2 and change it to O_2"; "I remember needing to know a formula for it in high school"; "keeps plants green"; and "green plants turn sun and CO_2 into chlorophyll." Students offered the following as explanations of "food for a bean plant": "Food for a bean plant is what is necessary for it to grow—water, soil, minerals, and sunlight"; "the chemicals it receives from the sunlight, soil, and fertilizer"; "sunlight, water, soil"; and "The nutrients in the soil. The sun, the water, other animals that died and their body becomes part of the soil." In short, these students did not appear to understand that plants manufacture their own food through photosynthesis.

What is much more disturbing than the pretest performances, however, is that at the end of the course, many students still had misconceptions: Almost 25 percent had little idea about the nature of respiration; 20 percent did not understand that the essence of food is that it provides energy for metabolism and materials for growth; 40 percent did not completely understand that plants make their own food; and more than 50 percent failed to understand that animals obtain energy from food and plants obtain energy from sunlight.

The research on scientific misconceptions makes it clear that students do not arrive in the science classrooms as blank slates. Instead, they often possess prior knowledge that is inconsistent with the content they will be asked to learn in the science course. Errant prior knowledge often is so deeply entrenched that students continue to apply misconceptions even after learning new science content that is inconsistent with the prior knowledge.

There is reason for optimism, however, even when students are left on their own to process science content. Some students chose to wrestle with science content, for example, attempting to understand the meaning and significance of science text-book presentations and actively seeking to accommodate (to use the Piagetian term) their beliefs about a phenomenon with the information in text. K. J. Roth (1991) reported how some of the middle school students in her studies reacted to text:

> They recognized the conflicts between what the text said and their own personal theories and puzzled about these inconsistencies until they could resolve the conflict. Often, this meant changing their personal theories to accommodate scientific explanations. . . . The conceptual change readers:
>
> 1. Made efforts to link text ideas with their experiential knowledge.
> 2. Recognized and thought about central text statements that conflicted with personally held ideas.
> 3. Distinguished between main ideas and supporting details, often minimizing the importance of big words.
> 4. Experienced and recognized conceptual confusion while reading.
> 5. Worked to resolve this conceptual confusion.
> 6. Were aware that their own ideas about real world phenomena were changing.
> 7. Used concepts presented in the text to explain real world phenomena. (K. J. Roth, 1991, p. 52)

In short, some students activated prior knowledge related to the text but recognized that their prior knowledge was not entirely congruent with meaning presented in text. These students worked at understanding the discrepancy so that their own thinking could be refined. The result is knowledge that can be applied, as exemplified by one student who used this **conceptual change strategy:**

> **Interviewer:** If I were to cover up all but one leaf of this plant, do you think the way it grows would change?
> **Susan:** Yeah, it would, because there's only one leaf that can change the materials to food and regularly you have much more—and I don't think it could feed the whole plant. I just don't believe it.

Teaching for Conceptual Change

A variety of instructional techniques have been suggested as methods for increasing students' understanding, memory, and use of scientific content, especially content that conflicts with everyday knowledge. At the heart of some of these interventions is the conceptual change strategy.

Conceptual Conflict and Accommodation Model. Nussbaum and Novick (1982) proposed that to overcome a misconception, students first need to be aware of their belief. Once aware, exposure to an event that cannot be explained by their belief or is inconsistent with it has the potential for producing cognitive conflict. You'll recall from the discussion of Piaget in Chapter 7 that such cognitive conflict motivates efforts toward conflict resolution and, in particular, motivates efforts to understand the scientific concept explaining the observed event. That is, conflict motivates efforts toward accommodation, setting up the possibility of modification of current cognitive structures or beliefs and the creation of new ones.

In Nussbaum and Novick's (1982) study, primary school children were given a lesson on the particle theory of gases, which states that there is empty space between molecules of air. As part of the lesson, air was sucked from a flask with a hand pump. Students' awareness of their beliefs about air was induced by having them draw pictures of the flask and its contents before and after the air was removed. Some of the student drawings and explanations were discussed by the instructor, as was the scientifically correct position that the flask contained particles of air with empty space between the particles before and only empty space after pumping. Of course, many of the students did not understand that the air molecules had empty space between them before the pumping began, believing all of the space in the flask must have been occupied by air.

Then the instructor introduced a discrepant event. Students were shown two syringes with equal volumes of air and water in them. The teacher attempted to compress the water in one syringe by moving the syringe plunger. No movement was possible. Then, the teacher succeeded in compressing the air in other syringe. If there was no space between air molecules, such compression should not have been possible. Discussion followed about how the models of the flask situation might explain or be inconsistent with the compressibility of air but not water. The instructor's job was to help students see that the only model that could explain the evacuation of air from the flask and the compressibility of air in the syringe was the empty-space theory. The students accepted the empty-space theory after such instruction, despite having no conception of empty space between air particles at the beginning of the lesson. Thus, conceptual conflict was created when errant beliefs were activated and confronted by an event inconsistent with the preexisting beliefs. This motivated cognitive accommodation, apparent in the attention and openness to the scientifically correct conception. In general, conceptual conflict instruction is effective in promoting understanding of scientific ideas that are not consistent with prior knowledge (Guzzetti, Snyder, Glass, & Gamas, 1993).

Analogies. Making analogies involves finding similarities between a new concept and a familiar one in order to make the new concept more understandable. One reason it is good to teach students to think analogously is that scientists do so (Glynn, 1991). For example, Kepler explained planetary motion with analogies to clockwork; Priestley explained electrical force using analogies to gravitational force; and the physicist Campbell argued that particles of kinetic gases behave something like billiard balls. Powerful analogies can help teachers communicate to young minds as well and may be especially compelling when some scientific fact is difficult to comprehend to the point of being unbelievable.

Sometimes students find it difficult to accept that static objects exert force, so that it is somewhat unbelievable to many young students that the chair they are sitting on is exerting an upward force equal to their weight or that a table is exerting

What properties of gases are captured by drawing an analogy between kinetic gases and billiard balls colliding? How does this analogy break down, as all analogies ultimately do? If you cannot answer this question, that should tell you something about the shortcomings of analogies.

a force equal to the weight of the centerpiece, place settings, and food on top of it. Clement and his colleagues (Clement, Brown, & Zeitsman, 1989) had the insight that there were other physical situations analogous to static objects' exerting force that are understood and accepted by many students and that these situations could be used as analogies to explain more unbelievable ideas. They referred to the understandable situations as anchoring intuitions or bridging analogies.

In the study by Clement and his colleagues (1987), high school physics students received instruction about forces exerted by static objects, frictional forces, and Newton's third law of collisions (i.e., if one object exerts a force on a second object, the second exerts an equal and opposite force on the first). Students in the treatment classes were presented anchoring intuitions, which were discussed. For the example of a rigid table's exerting force on a book that was lying on it (i.e., of a force exerted by a static object), students considered how a book might cause a piece of foam rubber to sag if placed on it, or how a book might bend a "table" made of a flexible board (with the bending becoming less and less apparent as the board is thickened until the point when it is the thickness of a conventional table board). Students also reflected on how a spring would compress if a book were on it, and they experienced the force they exerted to hold a book in the palm of their hand. Although it took a number of discussions and bridging analogies to make the point, students in the classes using these analogies were better able to solve posttest problems involving forces exerted by static objects than were students receiving conventional instruction, with this advantage apparent even two months after instruction.

Caution in the use of analogies in science instruction, however, is justified for several reasons. First, analogies only work if learners understand them. Second, sometimes students have a difficult time mapping the relationship specified by the analogy to the material they are processing. For example, Kloster and Winne's (1989) students had difficulty relating an analogical advance organizer about abuses involving office photocopiers to a passage about computer crime, even though the designers of the analogous advance organizer built in a one-to-one relationship between the elements of the photocopier example and the information about computer crime presented in the text. A third caution is that analogies can produce misconceptions. For example, B. J. Walker and Wilson (1991) found the following analogy in a fourth-grade science textbook, which induces the misconception that for raindrops to appear, a cloud must be squeezed, which is not consistent at all with the scientific explanation for why the molecules come closer together:

> You might think of the air as a sponge. A sponge holds water until it is squeezed. Cooled air is like a sponge being squeezed. As air is cooled, its molecules lose energy and slow down. They come closer together. Some of the water molecules in the air are squeezed out. (E. Cooper, Blackwood, Bolschen, Giddings, & Carin, 1985, p. 169)

Fourth, even the best analogies break down at some point. Thus, even though water flow is a very good analogy for electrical flow, when an electrical wire breaks, the electricity does not flow out of it as water flows out of a broken pipe (Glynn, 1991). One solution to the inadequacy of single analogies may be to present multiple analogies. Although each analogy may break down in some way, in that it is incomplete, misleading, or fails to focus attention on important information (Spiro, Feltovich, Coulson, & Anderson, 1989), several analogies can cover all of the important information pertaining to the concept to be acquired.

Refutation Text. One possible way to deal with misconceptions is simply to alert students to potential misconceptions and to show how the misconceptions differ from the scientific concept that is being taught. Consider the following example of text that includes a refutation of potential misconceptions (italicized here):

> A central point to be made is that the medieval impetus theory is incompatible with Newtonian mechanics in several fundamental ways. . . . To get a sense of some of the motion studies mentioned, imagine the following situation. A person is holding a stone at shoulder height while walking forward at a brisk pace. What kind of path will the stone follow as it falls? *Many people to whom this problem is presented answer that the stone will drop straight down, striking the ground directly under the point where it was dropped. A few people are even convinced that the falling stone will travel backward and land behind the point of its release. In reality,* the stone will move forward as it falls, landing a few feet ahead of the release point. Newtonian mechanics explains that when the stone is dropped, it continues to move forward at the same speed as the walking person, because (ignoring air resistance) no force is acting to change its horizontal velocity. (C. R. Hynd & Alvermann, 1986, p. 444)

Adding refutations to text improved learning for low-achieving college students (Alvermann & Hague, 1989; Hynd & Alvermann, 1986). Similar positive effects of refutation text for average-achieving college students have not been obtained in studies to date (Alvermann & Hynd, 1991). Perhaps less able students cling less tenaciously to their misconceptions because they are less certain of them, lacking confidence in their knowledge and abilities in general (Alvermann & Hynd, 1991).

Multiple and Alternative Representations. Distinguished scientists (Ben-Zvi, Eylon, & Silberstein, 1987; A. I. Miller, 1984) and good science students (Bowen, 1990) report constructing alternative representations as they think about scientific problems. The skilled chemist can represent a reaction with an equation, imagine the molecules interacting in his or her mind's eye, and imagine what the reaction looks like (e.g., memories of water drops on the sides of the beakers used in classroom demonstrations of hydrogen and oxygen reacting). In contrast, many typical students do not construct multiple or alternative representations on their own (Ben-Zvi, Eylon, & Silberstein, 1987; Wandersee, 1988; Yarroch, 1985). For example, many do not think beyond the symbols in a chemical equation—so much so that the symbols are more like elements in a mathematical equation than symbols for chemicals with physical characteristics.

One possibility is that if students could only be taught and persuaded to construct multiple representations, their scientific learning and thinking would be improved. This hypothesis is particularly interesting because science educators have held it for so long. For example, generations of students have constructed ball and stick models in chemistry classes, mapping changes in the physical models to chemical reactions represented in equations. Tens of millions of frogs have been dissected in hopes of increasing understanding of anatomy beyond insights produced by text and pictures. When dissection is not possible, such as in introductory courses in human anatomy, students have been presented many different depictions of the same anatomical features.

Some of the multiple and alternative representational hypotheses currently being explored in formal science education research mirror ones discussed in earlier chapters (Chapters 3, 4, and 11). For example, in order to increase the comprehension and recall of science, a student should (1) read for main ideas and construct summaries capturing the important points in a piece of science text; (2) create verbal and imaginal (pictorial) representations of the same concept, for concepts dually coded are more memorable than those coded verbally only or imaginably only; and (3) write about science in order to learn science (Santa & Havens, 1991; Vasu & Howe, 1989; Walker & Wilson, 1991).

Other multiple and alternative representational hypotheses are more unique to science education, such as graphing of data as they are collected, which increases the understanding of the data's significance. For example, graphing the speed of an object as a function of time since it was thrown is a striking way to understand acceleration, especially if it can be done soon after the data pertaining to the physical event have been collected (Beichner, 1990; Brasell, 1987; Krajcik, 1991; Mokros & Tinker, 1987). Microcomputer technologies now exist that permit graphing of acceleration and velocity functions shortly after a movement occurs. A radar gun type of device directly feeds data into a microcomputer.

Videodisc and microcomputer presentations of scientific events (e.g., chemical reactions) when combined with more conventional symbolic representational activities (e.g., writing and balancing equations) also increase understanding of scientific concepts so represented (Krajcik, 1991; S. G. Smith & Jones, 1988). For example, videodisc visuals that illustrate the particulate nature of matter are known to be effective (Krajcik & Peters, 1989). Many such scientific microworlds are being created at present (Pea & Kurland, 1984; Simmons, 1991). They afford the possibility of watching and rewatching scientific phenomena (e.g., chemical reactions) at various levels of analysis and from various perspectives (e.g., a time-lapse presentation of a plow rusting as well as a molecular-level animation of the molecules reacting).

Scientific ideas can be rendered more understandable if students create conceptual maps that focus on the more important concepts and specify relationships between more and less important terms and ideas (see also Chapter 4). Science

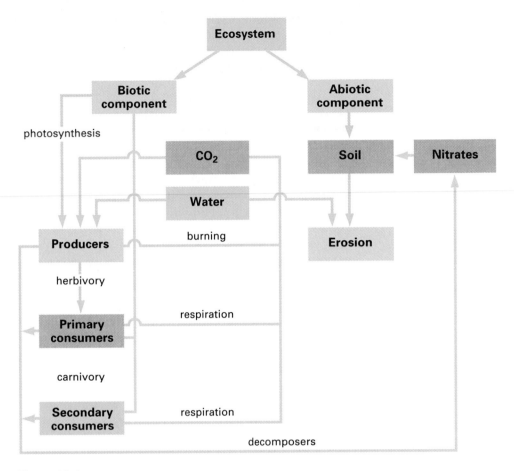

Figure 12.1
Concept maps, such as this one, increase scientific understanding.
Source: From "Attaining Meaningful Learning of Concepts in Genetics and Ecology: An Examination of the Potency of the Concept Mapping Technique" by P. A. Okebukola, 1990, *Journal of Research in Science Teaching, 27*, pp. 493–504. Copyright 1990 by National Association for Research in Science Teaching. Reprinted by permission of John Wiley & Sons, Inc.

educators such as Novak (Novak & Gowin, 1984) recommend conceptual mapping as a means of organizing scientific content that is presented initially in a poorly organized fashion. Once a decision has been made to map some content area, mapping proceeds as follows (Ault, 1985; Novak & Gowin, 1984; Okebukola, 1990):

- Key words and phrases are identified.
- Key concepts are ordered from the most general (i.e., most abstract and inclusive) to the most specific.
- The concepts are then clustered using two criteria. Concepts that interrelate are put together and classified with respect to their level of abstraction. All of the concepts are then arranged loosely in a two-dimensional array with abstractness as one dimension and main ideas as the other.
- Related concepts are then linked with lines that are labeled to specify the relationship between the concepts.

Uncertainties of Discovery Learning. Although discovery learning is commonly used in science classrooms, Schauble (1990) provided recent evidence of difficulties with discovery learning (see Chapters 1 and 10). Fifth-grade and sixth-grade students worked with a racing game that was run on a microcomputer. Children planned, carried out, and evaluated experiments aimed at determining the variables affecting the speed of the racing cars. The game permitted the construction of 48 different racing cars by selecting one value for each of five features: (1) engine: large or small? (2) fin: on or off? (3) wheels: large, medium, or small? (4) color: red or blue? and (5) muffler: on or off?

Over the course of the 8 weeks, there were improvements in discovering the variables affecting the speed of the cars. Nonetheless, the students were not very efficient in generating information, sometimes figuring out a causal relation in one session and then forgetting about it by the next session. Schauble's students also were not adept at monitoring their progress in understanding the causal variables in the microworld. Some students consistently made uninterpretable comparisons. For example, they tried to interpret a comparison when two variables varied at once, as in a race between a large-engined, finless, medium-wheeled, red, mufflerless car with a large-engined, finless, medium-wheeled, blue, mufflered car. Sometimes the students distorted evidence to fit their preferred theories about factors affecting speed.

Inefficiencies during discovery learning are not restricted to children. For example, Hardiman, Pollatsek, and Weil (1986) presented college students with Piaget's balance beam problems, which require the participants to determine the rule for placing weights on a beam so that the beam balances on a fulcrum at the midpoint of the beam. The college students required a mean of 49 problems before they figured out the principle for balancing the beam, with the most efficient student needing 30 trials. Even after inducing the rule, the students sometimes reverted to solving subsequent balance beam problems with an incorrect procedure. Learning from discovery experiences is often tentative at best.

Socially Supported Collaborative Construction of Science Concepts.
Despite demonstrations of inefficiencies in discovery learning, many science educators would like students to engage in pure discovery learning. Discovery is consistent with Piagetian notions of learning, specifically since natural cognitive conflict, which is viewed as a powerful mechanism for cognitive change, often accompanies discovery. These educators believe that discovery learning produces especially deep understanding of science and improves students' attitudes toward science (Ajewole, 1991; Dewey, 1933). Since there are so many misconceptions about science among students who have acquired scientific knowledge on their own, it is obvious that pure discovery learning alone is not always a good idea. Rather than abandon entirely the ideal of discovery, many science educators are exploring a number of socially mediated types of instruction that permit guided discovery and scaffolded student exploration of science concepts.

Consistent with this direction, social support is consistently observed in analyses of outstanding science teaching (Tobin & Fraser, 1990). Excellent science teachers are concerned with improving students' understanding of science content. Concrete examples and analogies are used to explain abstract ideas. Exemplary science teachers use management strategies that encourage high student engagement, especially in scientific problem solving, with adequate materials and support for problem-solving activities. Most critically, these teachers monitor students' understanding and react when there is misunderstanding, posing questions to students that stimulate thinking in particular directions. That is, instruction is scaffolded, consistent with Vygotsky-based instructional recommendations (see Chapters 8 and 10).

Glynn, Yeany, and Britton (1991) provided a summary of *socially interactive instruction* that captures all of its most important features:

> Teachers should require students to reason scientifically. One way they can do this is by modeling scientific reasoning for their students. In effect, teachers and students should become collaborators in the process of scientific reasoning. Together, students and teachers should construct interesting questions about scientific phenomena; simply telling students the answers has little lasting value. Teachers and students should guess, or hypothesize, about the underlying causes of science phenomena. Teachers and students should collect data and design scientific tests of their hypotheses. And, finally, teachers and students should construct theories and models to explain the phenomena in question. Throughout all stages of this collaboration, teachers and students should be constantly "thinking out loud" (Glynn, Muth, & Britton, 1990). By means of the "thinking out loud" technique, teachers can help students to reflect on their own scientific reasoning processes (that is, to think metacognitively) and to refine these processes. (p. 4)

Teachers' modeling and explaining processing to students as they carry out academic tasks in interaction with other students should be a familiar scenario by now. This is how sophisticated cognitively based instruction is occurring across the curriculum. No teacher could possibly explain or model all of the knowledge, or know-how, that is part of understanding any scientific concept (or any other concept for that matter). Students can acquire much knowledge, however, as they work on scientific problems with a little help from their classmates and their teachers (Champagne & Bunce, 1991).

It is very easy, however, for socially interactive instruction and problem solving to go awry. For example, in many cooperative science-instruction groups, one person does most or all of the work. Not surprisingly, many members of such groups learn little (Gayford, 1992). Students often lack critical prior knowledge that cannot be remediated effectively by group cooperative discussion (Basili & Sanford, 1991). Some children are helped some of the time by cooperation, but some also are harmed with little basis for predicting when to expect facilitation or interference (M. Perlmutter, Behrend, Kuo, & Muller, 1989). Implementation of cooperative learning alone guarantees nothing (Sherman, 1988; Tingle & Good, 1990).

What is required is not social interaction per se but social interaction in which all students participate and learn without fear or intimidation; the presence of a science expert who can detect a variety of misunderstandings that students may possess and intervene to provide remediation may be necessary for instruction in advanced conceptual areas, which includes most of science. Just as there is a need in mathematics education to understand the dynamics of cooperative groups better, there is a need to do so in science education.

Chapter Summary

- Both mathematics educators and science educators mix old theories and methods with new theories and methods, with some measure of success. In mathematics, Polya's ideas are being combined with new insights about problem solving based on modern research, with the result being a rejuvenation of Polya's theory and variations of it. Dewey's ideas about discovery and Piaget's insights about scientific misconceptions are both powerful building blocks in the reinvention of science education that is currently occurring.

- Although researchers have identified many ways that mathematical understandings develop naturally, such as the development of basic addition and subtraction strategies during the preschool years, there is still much room for improvement in areas that go beyond those that are discovered through interactions with the social and natural worlds of childhood. Mathematics instruction can make an important difference.

- Mathematics educators are exploring the impact of instructional approaches such as cooperative learning and learning from examples. Although technology has always played a role in mathematics instruction (e.g., the abacus has been in use since ancient times in China), new developments such as graphing calculators and interactive videodiscs provide important new opportunities for improving instruction of mathematics and problem solving. Researchers are developing powerful ways to incorporate these technologies into the curriculum. Old technologies, such as television programming, are also being exploited in new ways to educate children about mathematics, such as the innovative and effective TV production of *Square One*.

- There is no absolute answer for improving mathematics education, although some had hoped one would be found by studying cultures, such as Japan, where mathematics educational achievement is high. Instead, high mathematical achievement is a product of outstanding curriculum, many hours of high-quality instructional interactions around problem solving, and educational and cultural practices that foster the development of mathematical competence. There is every reason to believe that diverse students can become competent mathematicians if they are provided with substantial high-quality instruction and mathematical experiences.

- Consistent with Piaget, science educators recognize that the conceptual understandings students bring to a situation play a large role in determining their comprehension of it. If new information is inconsistent with the views already held by a student, there is a danger that the student's misconceptions will prevail even though the student can memorize the new information for a test. More positively, however, there also is the possibility for cognitive conflict, which motivates efforts by the student to comprehend the new input. Such conflict opens the possibility that the student will accommodate his or her current views to the new input, resulting in a new conceptualization of the situation by the student.

- A number of instructional methods can facilitate conceptual changes. For example, analogies can aid in the process by connecting new information with understandings already possessed, but not activated, by the student naturally. Refutation text and socially interactive instruction can stimulate students to activate simultaneously newly presented science concepts and erroneous prior knowledge. These interventions increase the likelihood that the student will exert cognitive effort to attempt to understand the scientific conception. Science educators believe that analogies, texts, and social interaction advance scientific understanding by stimulating cognitive conflict, which results in reflection and, ultimately, in a student's construction of new knowledge.

Return to the Classroom Predicament

Has the information presented in this chapter helped you formulate a response to the question posed by Mr. Vargas? Mr. Vargas faces the problem that many mathematics and science educators face—how to create successful problem solvers. His students could benefit from instruction in Polya's general problem-solving strategies. Of course, domain knowledge is also a very important component of problem solving. Often, teachers like Mr. Vargas are confronted with students' misconceptions that are difficult to change. Instructional techniques, such as creating multiple representations, analogies, and refutation text, can be very effective in creating conceptual conflict and eventual conceptual change.

Chapter Outline

Chapter 13

Traditional Perspectives on Intelligence and Academic Competence

Classroom Predicament

Mr. and Mrs. Skenadore are meeting with Ms. Fuentes, their child's teacher. The two parents are obviously concerned about planned assessments of their son's intelligence. They ask, "Why does Samuel have to be tested by the school psychologist?" "What kind of information will these tests give us? What will they mean for Sammy's future?" Ms. Fuentes tells them not to worry, that school personnel administer tests to students all the time and that they will be informed of the test results. The parents persist, "Why do children have to take so many tests today? Our daughter is already preparing for some test she has to take in order to get into state university. We're taxpayers. She's gotten good grades in high school, so why does she have to take a test, made up by people living in some other state, to get into our university? It just doesn't seem fair." Ms. Fuentes suggests that the Skenadores make an appointment with the high school counselor.

Can you make recommendations for how Ms. Fuentes could have handled this parent-teacher conference in order to address these parents' concerns more directly? Reflecting on the information presented in this chapter will help you formulate responses to this question.

People are different in ways that influence their academic competence. Some of these differences are discussed in earlier chapters of this book. People comprehend and remember information differently depending on the strategies they know and use (Chapter 4); differences in metacognition predict differences in strategy use (Chapter 4); differences in knowledge about a specific topic influence the ability to solve problems and to learn more about that topic (Chapters 3 and 5); and differences in motivational beliefs affect the willingness to attempt academic tasks (Chapter 2).

Traditionally, however, educators have focused on individual differences that are measured by standardized testing instruments such as intelligence tests or achievement tests. **Standardized tests** are given under controlled conditions so that every student taking the test has the same examination experience. Developers of standardized tests also provide test norms. A **norm** is the typical level of performance for a clearly defined reference group. For example, norms might be provided for students of various ages or in different grades. An individual score can then be interpreted by comparing it to the norm (that is, the typical performance) for the group to which the individual belongs. It is important for norms to be up-to-date and truly representative of the reference group. For example, a norm obtained in 1975 from a white, middle-class suburban population is not appropriate for interpreting scores obtained in 1996 from a culturally diverse urban school.

This chapter begins with a discussion of a standardized test that many students have taken recently—a college entrance examination. Discussion of this test leads to the consideration of two important characteristics of tests—reliability and validity. This is followed by an extended discussion of various conceptualizations and assessments of intelligence. Intelligence testing can be controversial. Some of the controversies raised in this chapter include the roles of heredity in intelligence and bias in mental testing. The chapter ends with an investigation of interventions designed to increase intelligence.

Higher Education Admissions Tests

It is very likely you have taken a standardized test, and perhaps your performance on the test influenced decisions about your future. Admission to college or graduate school often involves standardized testing of academic achievement. One of the most commonly used standardized college admissions test is the Scholastic Assessment Test.

Scholastic Assessment Test

Many readers of this book have taken the Scholastic Aptitude Test (SAT), which was revised in 1994 and renamed the Scholastic Assessment Test I: Reasoning Test (Viadero, 1994). Others have taken the American College Test (ACT), which is similar to the SAT. Performance on the SAT is reported in two scores—math and verbal. Most of the questions in the SAT are multiple choice, but in the revised version of the SAT mathematics section, students are also asked to supply the responses for ten questions and can use handheld calculators. The revised verbal section taps knowledge of vocabulary and reading comprehension. For example, students are asked to answer multiple-choice questions comparing two passages with contrasting points of view.

Scores on the verbal and math scores can range from 200 to 800. For more than 50 years, SAT scores were figured in terms of how students performed relative to a 1941 sample. A score of 500 in 1991 meant the same as it did 50 years earlier—the student was exactly in the middle of the range of 1941 performances. A score of 700 placed the student at about the 98th percentile of the 1941 distribution of performances. Because of declines in overall performance on the SAT, however, a 500 score in 1993 was well above the average for students taking the test in that year (the mean verbal score was 424, and the mean math score was 478; Lawton, 1993). Beginning with the high school graduating class of 1996, the SAT scores will be calibrated differently so the average score for both math and verbal sections will be 500 (Diegmueller, 1994). Why were standardized admissions tests, like the SAT, developed? Before the creation of these tests, many colleges devised their own tests based on expectations about what students should have learned in high school. This practice resulted in many difficulties for schools and students. How could high schools prepare their students for entrance examinations based on different expectations? Also, how could applicants prepare for different admissions test for each college they were interested in?

There are clear practical advantages to an admissions test like the SAT. First, students can apply to more than one school without taking multiple admissions tests. Second, what is tested is not based on a particular high school curriculum. Third, the primarily multiple-choice format allows computerized scoring so the SAT can be administered economically and efficiently to the more than two million students who take it annually.

Perhaps the most important characteristics of the SAT are that it has **reliability** and **validity.** A reliable test measures consistently, and a valid test measures what it is supposed to measure. The SAT is reliable in that if a student takes one form of the SAT today and a second form of it tomorrow, there is a very good chance that the scores for the two sittings will be within 30 points of one another. The SAT is valid because it generally predicts academic performance in college. SAT scores combined with high school grades predict grades for first-year college students better than when either is used alone (Anastasi, 1988). Other factors such as students' motivation, maturity, and course selection also influence college grades, but these factors are difficult to assess, so admissions tests such as the SAT and high school grades are the best predictors available.

With so many advantages, what are the disadvantages of the SAT? First, some groups consistently do better on the test than other groups. White students do better than minorities; men do better than women, (although the gap between males and females is narrowing; Lawton, 1993). For example, white students enjoyed at least a 40-point advantage on both verbal and math SAT scores in 1993 over Native Americans, African Americans, and Hispanic students (Lawton, 1993). The SAT, however, is a good predictor of college success for all groups (Reynolds & Kaiser, 1990a, 1990b). For instance, when only African Americans are considered, those African Americans who score well on the SAT are more likely to do well in college than the African Americans who score poorly. So the SAT is a valid predictor of college success for African American students, just as it is a valid predictor of college success for white students. Using SAT scores to make comparisons between these groups, however, is not valid. (See the discussion of bias later in this chapter.)

Second, some critics argue that the test does not provide enough of an increase in predictability over high school grades to justify its use. Countering this claim are arguments that standardized tests are great equalizers. That is, the SAT is the one hurdle faced by all applicants, giving students from little-known high schools a chance to distinguish themselves (Jensen, 1981). In addition, some national scholarship agencies use the SAT to identify talented youth, many of whom would be overlooked in other types of talent searches.

Important Qualities of Tests

Reliability and validity are important characteristics for all tests, not just the SAT. The first requirement, reliability means that a test must measure consistently; without reliability, it cannot possibly be valid and measure what it is presumed to measure (Anastasi, 1988; Cronbach, 1990; Sattler, 1992). These two characteristics are the very reason why the SAT has survived so long. It measures what admissions committees need to know—likelihood of academic success in college.

Reliability

The first step in understanding reliability is to grasp that any *observed score* on a test is comprised of two scores, the *true score* and *error*. Thus, *observed score = true score + error*.

Error represents the part of the score that is due to irrelevant and chance factors. On some occasions performance is higher than it typically would be, such as when the tester is lucky guessing between two responses; on other occasions it is lower than it typically would be. Some typical sources of testing error that may lower the scores of students taking the SAT are lack of sleep, illness, and an unusual level of anxiety. The greater the error, the lower the reliability.

One way to reduce error and to increase the reliability of a test is to make testing conditions as consistent as possible for all people taking the test. In other words, standard procedures must be followed. For instance, reliability of the SAT was calculated with group administration of the test; under particular time constraints; and when students were not permitted to interact with one another, consult notes, or open textbooks. If a student took the SAT with notes and open books, the reported reliability and validity would not hold under these circumstances.

How is reliability estimated? One method of establishing a test's reliability, **test-retest reliability,** is simply to administer the same test twice to a group of test takers. The correlation between the two scores earned by the test takers on each testing occasion indicates whether or not the test is measuring consistently (see the discussion of correlation in Chapter 1). If the students' relative performance on one test occasion is highly correlated with their relative performance on another testing occasion, the test is reliable.

Another form of reliability, **alternate-forms reliability,** measures the consistency of performance between two, supposedly equivalent, forms of the test. In this method of estimating reliability, students take two forms of the measurement. The correlation between performances on one form of the test and the other form measures the reliability of the test. The more similar the alternative forms of a test, the higher the reliability. Similar alternative forms cover the same content with the same number of roughly equally difficult items for each topic. Standardized tests, such as the SAT, often have multiple forms.

It is possible to estimate the reliability of a test even if the test is administered only once. This type of reliability measures the internal consistency of the items on the test. To calculate **split-half reliability,** a test is literally split in half. For example, scores for the odd and even items on the test are computed, and the correlation between the score on the odd items with the score on the even items is the estimate of reliability. The problem with this approach is that the reliability estimate will vary depending on how the items are split. In most cases the correlation between odd-even halves would differ from a correlation based on halves produced by randomly assigning items to half-test scores. One solution to this problem is **coefficient alpha,** which is the average of all possible split-half reliabilities (Cronbach, 1951).

Factors Influencing Test Reliability. A variety of factors influence the reliability of a test. These include:

- *Test length.* In general, the more items on a test, the more reliable it is.
- *Time between testing occasions.* Reliabilities computed using the test-retest method are generally greater if the retests are close in time.
- *Scoring methods.* Tests that can be scored objectively, with little opportunity for bias, are more reliable. The more subjective or open to interpretation the scoring of the test items is, the lower the reliability.
- *Question wording.* Poorly worded or vague questions that suggest answers to other questions reduce reliability.
- *Test-taker characteristics.* If the test takers are tired, anxious, excited, sick, or do not care about the test, the reliability is lower.

Validity

The reliability of a measurement is not enough. The measurement must also be valid for its purpose. Thus, although we can measure the circumferences of children's heads with high reliability, head circumference is not a valid measure of intelligence (Gould, 1981). A measurement can be no more valid than it is reliable, however, so test developers must consider issues of validity and reliability simultaneously.

Does this test measure what it is supposed to measure? That is the main validity question. More specific validity questions depend somewhat on what is being assessed. Three common types of validity are construct, content, and criterion validity.

Construct Validity. The question addressed by **construct validity** is, Does this test measure the construct it is intended to measure? To understand this question, it is first necessary to define *construct.* Most psychological variables of constructs are abstract rather than concrete (Nunnally, 1978). For example, ability cannot be observed directly, nor can intelligence. Such constructs must be inferred from behavioral observations. Thus, mathematical ability is inferred from consistent, exceptional mathematics performance. Anxious personality is inferred when an individual exhibits anxiety in situations that do not provoke anxiety in others. Intelligence is inferred from performances on academic tasks.

If a test developer is attempting to create a new test for a construct measured by existing instruments, construct validation requires demonstrating that the new test correlates with the accepted tests measuring the construct. For example, if test developers were trying to create a short intelligence test that could be given in groups, they would need to demonstrate high correlations between their new measure and standard measures of intelligence.

Content Validity. The question addressed by **content validity** is, Does this test include the content it is supposed to cover? Suppose a national testing agency wishes to devise a test of high school mathematics achievement. What should the test include? An assessment with content validity would include items from general mathematics, algebra, geometry, trigonometry, and calculus. Depending on the test's purpose, the proportions of these items might vary. If the purpose is to discriminate whether students have obtained basic numerical competencies, the test might consist primarily of general math items. If the purpose is to decide who should be selected as a finalist for scholarship consideration in mathematics, there would be a much greater proportion of calculus and trigonometry items than general math items.

Content validity is an important concern for an educational achievement test. When test developers are devising a subject area test to assess knowledge in some undergraduate area of specialization, they first must decide what should be covered and in what proportions. For example, developers of the Graduate Record Examination (GRE) in psychology might lay out all of the subfields of psychology that they wish to cover, such as social, clinical, physiological, educational, experimental, and so on. Then, they decide the proportions of items for each subfield, based on their conception about which areas deserve emphasis relative to others. For example, areas that all psychology majors would have studied receive more emphasis than areas that are completely elective.

Criterion Validity. The question addressed by **criterion validity** is, Does this test make the distinctions it is suppose to make? Does it predict performance on some criterion measure? For example, does the SAT discriminate between students who will be successful in college and those who will not be successful? It does. There is a positive correlation between SAT performance and grades in college. When the criterion is in the future, as it is when the SAT is used to predict college grades, the criterion-related validity is referred to as *predictive validity*. When both a measure and its criterion can be collected close in time, criterion-related validity is sometimes referred to as *concurrent validity*. For example, when the extent of brain damage evident from using medical technology such as a CAT scan correlates highly with a behavioral measure of neurological damage, this is evidence of concurrent validity for the two measures.

● "What Do I Do on Monday Morning?"

Questions to Ask Yourself About Any Test

Teachers have access to standardized test results in students' files. Parents receive reports of their child's performance on standardized tests. Older students request that reports of their test performance be sent to college degree programs for admission. What should these test consumers ask themselves about any test?

1. Is this test reliable?
    a. Does it measure consistently, and how was this determined? Test-retest? Alternate forms? Split-half?

    b. Does the test have many questions?
    c. Is the scoring objective?
    d. Are the test takers prepared?
2. Is this test valid?
    a. Does it measure what the test developers indicate?
    b. How are the test results being used?
    c. What is the evidence of test validity? Construct validity? Content validity? Criterion validity?
3. Are the norms appropriate?
    a. Is the norming group representative?
    b. Is the norming up-to-date?
4. Are standardized testing procedures followed?

These questions can be answered by seeking out information provided in testing manuals for the tests in question. In addition, test consumers can consult publications found in reference libraries, such as the *Mental Measurements Yearbook* and *Tests in Print,* which review published tests and how well they perform their purposes.

Conceptions of Intelligence

Traditionally, those who studied individual differences in intellectual functioning focused on the conceptualization and measurement of intelligence. The history of intelligence assessment has been charged with controversy from its beginning, and the controversies continue today (Block & Dworkin, 1976; N. Brody, 1992; Gould, 1981; Herrnstein & Murray, 1994; Kaufman, 1990; Plomin, DeFries, & McClearn, 1990; Sattler, 1992). As early as 1869, Francis Galton argued that blood relationships between geniuses are much closer than would be expected by chance. Galton concluded from these probabilities that genius is inherited. Galton's strong claims about the heritability of genius (see the discussion of heritability of intelligence later in this chapter) stimulated interest in individual differences in intellectual abilities.

One of the early intelligence theorists, Spearman (1904), conceptualized intelligence as consisting of multiple factors, one general factor (*g*) and the others more specific (*s*), such as mathematical abilities or verbal competence. Every item on an intelligence assessment was assumed somehow to be related to general intelligence. Spearman also argued that every measure of intelligence also tapped specific functions that were independent of the general factor.

In contrast, Thurstone (1938, 1947) emphasized the importance of the specific factors underlying intelligence. He suggested that there were at least nine **primary mental abilities:** inductive reasoning, deductive reasoning, practical problem reasoning, verbal comprehension, associative short-term memory, spatial abilities, perceptual speed, numerical competence, and word fluency. Others have continued to examine the many specific factors of intelligence; some have hypothesized more than one hundred primary mental abilities (Guilford, 1967).

Cattell and Horn's Factors of Intelligence

Some of the thinking processes examined by researchers studying intelligence correspond well to aspects of the good information processing model outlined in

Chapter 1 and developed throughout this text. For example, Cattell and Horn (1978; Horn & Cattell, 1967; Horn & Hofer, 1992; Horn & Stankov, 1982) describe nine factors implicated in intelligence. Two of these factors distinguish between the reasoning ability that allows the acquisition of knowledge, **fluid intelligence,** and the knowledge acquired, which is **crystallized intelligence.** Fluid intelligence is measured in tasks requiring reasoning abilities (e.g., inductive and deductive) to understand relations among stimuli, to comprehend implications, and to draw inferences. Crystallized intelligence is measured in tasks indicating breadth and depth of cultural knowledge (e.g., vocabulary knowledge). A third factor, **quantitative intelligence,** is measured in tasks requiring understanding and application of the concepts and skills of mathematics.

Two of the factors are memory processes, short term and long term. As described in earlier chapters, **short-term memory** is the awareness of events of the last minute or so and **long-term memory** is the retrieval of information stored for minutes, hours, weeks, or years.

There are also two processing factors, **visual processing** and **auditory processing.** Visual processing refers to the skills required in tasks involving visualization such as imaging the way objects appear in space as they are rotated and flip-flopped in various ways. Auditory processing is measured in tasks that require perception of sound patterns under distraction or distortion, maintaining awareness of order and rhythm among sounds, and comprehending elements of groups of sounds, such as chords.

The final two factors emphasize speed in the thinking process. One of these, **processing speed,** although involved in almost all intellectual tasks (Hertzog, 1989), is measured most purely in responses to intellectually simple tasks. These tasks are ones that almost all people could get correct if the task were not highly speeded. The other, **correct decision speed,** is the quickness of response in more complicated tasks that require more thinking.

According to this perspective, intelligence is the result of the coordinated use of the nine processes, not simply the sum of the products of the nine processes. Performance on standard intelligence tests has been found to be related to individual differences in these processes, particularly speed of information processing (L. A. Baker, Vernon, & Ho, 1991; Jensen, 1982; Vernon, 1983, 1985, 1987) and differences in working memory (Necka, 1992; Tomporowski & Simpson, 1990).

Triarchic Theory of Intelligence

Robert Sternberg (1985) proposed another process-oriented theory of intelligence called the **triarchic theory.** The triarchic theory is composed of three subtheories— *contextual, experiential,* and *componential.* The contextual subtheory highlights the sociocultural context of an individual's life. Intelligent individuals adapt in order to maximize the fit between themselves and their environment. They may also shape their environment to increase the fit or, if a satisfactory fit is not possible, select an alternative environment. According to this perspective, what is intelligent behavior depends on the cultural context.

The second subtheory, the experiential subtheory, emphasizes the role of experience in intelligent behavior. Sternberg argues that intelligent behavior sometimes reflects the ability to deal with novel experiences by drawing upon past experiences but it also refers to the ability to deal with familiar situations quickly and efficiently.

Thus, intelligent behavior involves accessing prior knowledge and developing automaticity, themes developed throughout this book (see especially the discussion of expertise in Chapter 5).

The third subtheory, the componential subtheory, specifies the mental structures that underlie intelligent behavior. These components correspond well to the characteristics of information processing described in Chapter 1 and throughout this text. "*Metacomponents* are higher-order executive processes used in planning, monitoring, and decision making in task performance" (R. J. Sternberg, 1985, p. 99). These include processes such as deciding what the problem is, selecting a strategy, and monitoring a solution.

"*Performance components* are processes used in the execution of a task" (R. J. Sternberg, 1985, p. 99). These include recall of new information, integrating and comparing pieces of information, and outputting solutions once they are determined.

"*Knowledge-acquisition components* are processes used in gaining new knowledge" (R. J. Sternberg, 1985, p. 107). These include distinguishing relevant from irrelevant information, combining encoded information into a coherent whole, and comparing new information with information acquired in the past.

Gardner's Multiple Intelligences

In his **theory of multiple intelligences,** Howard Gardner (1983) argued that people have a set of specific intelligences that are biologically determined (see also Chapter 6). These include linguistic intelligence, musical intelligence, logic-mathematical intelligence, spatial intelligence, body-kinesthetic intelligence, interpersonal intelligence (i.e., the ability to notice and make distinctions among other individuals), and intrapersonal intelligence (i.e., access to one's own feelings). People with strong linguistic abilities may excel in fields requiring verbal skills, such as journalism or politics. People with strong musical intelligence may excel as musicians or composers. Strong logic-mathematical intelligence would predict success as a mathematician or computer programmer. Those high in spatial intelligence may excel in fields such as sculpting or architecture. Body-kinesthetic intelligence is necessary for athletes and mimes. Interpersonal intelligence is a key characteristic of salespersons and therapists, and intrapersonal intelligence is important for successful actors. Almost every human endeavor, of course, requires more than one type of intelligence. For instance, dancers would need to be strong in musical intelligence as well as body-kinesthetic intelligence. Trial attorneys would need to be strong in linguistic intelligence and interpersonal intelligence. Engineers would need spatial intelligence as well as logic-mathematical intelligence.

One of the most critical features of this theory is that people vary in the strength of their particular faculties. Gardner argued that it makes no sense to think of someone in general terms as smart or not so smart, as is implied in traditional views of intelligence. Rather, people with musical intelligence would be expected to excel in music given appropriate stimulation; those who have superior capacity in mathematics would be expected to do well given appropriate exposure to mathematics.

Gardner believes that one of the problems with contemporary schooling is that linguistic, logic-mathematical, and intrapersonal intelligences are emphasized to the exclusion of others. There is little attempt in schools to gauge the strengths and weaknesses of students in terms of all of the various intelligences. He argued that educators should realize the multiple nature of abilities. This awareness would lead them to help students discover their own patterns of strengths and weaknesses. Then, teachers could encourage students to accentuate their strengths and help students to compensate for their weaknesses or even teach them ways of remediating their weaknesses.

● "What Do I Do On Monday Morning?"

Different Perspectives on Intelligence

A group of teachers is discussing students in the teachers' lounge. Can you match a teacher's description of a student with a particular theory of intelligence?

1. Mr. Cruz describes Yu-ling, who "excels in all academic subjects and skills. She can do everything well."
2. Mrs. Johnston describes Perry, who "knows how to go about acquiring knowledge. I just tell him what he needs to learn, and he takes it from there."
3. Mr. Cobb describes Sophia, who "does extremely well in mathematics but is really struggling in English."
4. Ms. Slotky describes Drew, who "seems to always understand what the other students are thinking and feeling. He is really smart that way."

Answers: Mr. Cruz: general *g* factor of intelligence; Mrs. Johnson: knowledge acquisition component of Sternberg's theory; Mr. Cobb: specific factors of intelligence (e.g., math and verbal); Ms. Slotky: interpersonal intelligence of Gardner's theory.

Intelligence Tests

The early years of the twentieth century witnessed the proliferation of measures of intelligence (Binet & Simon, 1905a, 1905b, 1905c; Terman & Childs, 1912; Yoakum & Yerkes, 1920). Why were intelligence tests developed in the first place? Alfred Binet was trying to find a way to discriminate between normal children and children with mental retardation. Terman believed the tests could also be useful in identifying feebleminded adults. Slightly later, Yoakum and Yerkes designed tests to select men for officers' training from the pool of army recruits. In general, these early tests focused on measuring general intelligence (*g*) and were able to make discriminations in ability.

Why are intelligence tests useful today? What do they reveal about academic competence? The intelligence quotient, or IQ score, produced by common measures of intelligence predicts important outcomes in a person's life. For example, the correlation between IQ score and school performance is estimated to be about 0.50 (N. Brody, 1992). The amount of schooling completed also varies with IQ score (Reynolds, Chastain, Kaufman, & McLean, 1987). College graduates have higher mean IQ scores than those who only graduated from high school, and high school graduates have higher mean IQ scores than nongraduates.

Although there are high-ability individuals in every one of the categories of educational completion, low-ability individuals are very rare at the college completion level. This suggests that there is a minimum amount of intelligence required

The athlete, musician, sculptor, and actor are in fields of expertise requiring demonstration of a type of intelligence described in Gardner's multiple intelligences theory.

to complete each level of education, with the minimum increasing with more advanced educational level. Overall, the correlation between IQ score and level of education completed is estimated to be about 0.60 (Kaufman, 1990).

IQ scores predict the achievement of occupational status as well. As the status of a job and the years of education required to perform a job decline, the lower the overall intelligence of all the people in the occupation (T. W. Harrell & Harrell, 1945). High intelligence, however, does not guarantee a high-status occupation in that there are people with high intelligence performing all types of jobs. Occupational success, based on measures such as supervisor ratings, correlates substantially (0.53) with intelligence (Hunter & Hunter, 1984). Thus, the smarter you are according to intelligence tests, the more likely you are to do well at your job.

Today, there are many different tests that are marketed as measures of intelligence. Some of these are individual assessments; others are administered to groups. What follows is a description of perhaps the most widely used individual assessments.

Wechlser Adult Intelligence Scale-III

David Wechsler began work on his intelligence test, the Wechsler Adult Intelligence Scale (WAIS), in the 1930s (Wechsler, 1939). Since that time, the test has been revised three times, most recently in 1991 as the Wechsler Adult Intelligence Scale-III (WAIS-III). Since Wechsler considered verbal and performance abilities as two different "languages" through which the underlying general competency (g) expresses itself (Kamphaus, 1993), the test is composed of both verbal scales and performance scales (see Table 13.1).

One of the strengths of the WAIS-III is that it has extremely high reliability (0.97). The concurrent validity (and to some extent the construct validity as well) of the WAIS-III is supported by high correlations of the WAIS-III IQ with IQ scores obtained with other tests (Thorndike, Hagen, & Sattler, 1986).

Differences in scores between males and females, urban and rural dwellers, and people living in different regions of the United States are fairly small. There are, however, differences in performance based on race. For example, white Americans on average score 15 points higher than African Americans. We discuss the interpretation of this race-correlated difference in IQ scores later in this chapter.

Wechsler Intelligence Scale for Children-III

The WAIS-III is an adult scale and not appropriate to administer to school-age children. However, the Wechsler Intelligence Scale for Children (WISC), originally published in 1949 (Wechsler, 1949) with a revision, the WISC-III, published in 1991, is appropriate for children ages 6½ to 16½. It has verbal and performance scales that are similar to the WAIS-III. The test-retest reliability is high (0.96) as is the concurrent validity, and the test correlates well with other standardized measures of intelligence.

Wechsler Preschool and Primary Scale of Intelligence-Revised

Because many decisions must be made about children during the preschool years, Wechsler (1967) developed a test for children ages 4 to 6½. It is called the WPPSI (Sattler, 1992; Wechsler, 1967; pronounced "whipsey" by users), with a revision, the

Table 13.1

Verbal and Performance Scales of the WAIS-III

Verbal Scales of the WAIS-III
- *Information*—questions tapping general knowledge from such fields as literature, history, and geography
- *Digit span*—lists of digits to recall either in order of presentation (forward span) or in reverse order of presentation (backward span)
- *Vocabulary*—words to define
- *Arithmetic*—problems to solve
- *Comprehension*—questions dealing with everyday problems requiring understanding of social rules and concepts
- *Similarities*—pairs of words, with the examinee asked to explain the similarity between the words in each pair

Performance Scales of the WAIS-III
- *Picture completion*—drawings of common objects, each of which is missing some essential component, with the examinee asked to indicate the missing part (timed)
- *Picture arrangement*—series of pictures to place in a logical sequence (timed)
- *Block design*—red-and-white pictures of designs, with the examinee asked to construct a matching design with red-and-white plastic blocks (timed)
- *Object assembly*—jigsaw puzzles to solve that produce pictures of well-known objects (timed)
- *Digit symbol*—number-symbol pairings to remember, with the examinee asked to copy the appropriate symbol when presented with numbers alone (timed)

WPPSI-R, published in 1991. The test-retest reliability is 0.91, and the test also has good concurrent validity, correlating highly with other intelligence scales used with children.

Stanford-Binet

The Stanford-Binet, fourth edition, published in 1986, can be used for a wide age range (norms are available for 2- to 23-year-olds). It provides a general score (g), along with scores in four areas, verbal reasoning, quantitative reasoning, abstract/visual reasoning, and short-term memory. This fourth edition of the Stanford-Binet is based on the conceptualization of intelligence described by Cattell, particularly fluid and crystallized intelligence, as well as others of Cattell's nine factors of intelligence outlined earlier (Kamphaus, 1993). Test-retest reliability for the composite score is 0.90, and concurrent validity for the composite score is fairly high with correlations with other intelligence tests ranging from 0.71 to 0.91.

Kaufman Assessment Battery for Children

Although the Weschler scales are the most commonly used measures of intelligence, a relatively new measurement tool, the Kaufman Assessment Battery for Children (K-ABC) (Kaufman & Kaufman, 1983) is also widely used (Kamphaus, 1993). Based on the processing-oriented theories of intelligence, this scale focuses on measuring mental processes, that is, how children tackle intellectual problems rather than simply whether they are successful or not. The K-ABC scales differentiate between simultaneous and sequential processing. Simultaneous processing refers to the ability to integrate information all at once to solve a problem correctly. Sequential processing refers to the ability to arrange information in sequential or serial order for successful problem solving. The K-ABC has good test-retest reliability and predictive validity for school achievement, and the test items were carefully designed to provide a fair assessment of minorities, bilinguals, and children with language difficulties (Anastasi, 1988; Kamphaus, Kaufman, & Harrison, 1990).

▶ **Diversity**

Measuring Intelligence in Special Populations

There are also many useful and well-validated measures that are designed for particular populations and purposes (Sattler, 1992). Some tests, such as the following, assess the intelligence of infants.

- *Brazleton Neonatal Behavioral Assessment Scale.* This scale can be administered to newborns to evaluate reflexes and responsivity to the environment. It predicts differences in mental and motor development many months later (Francis, Self, & Horowitz, 1987) but does not predict intelligence later in life very well.
- *Bayley Scales of Infant Development.* This is a test of motor skills and mental abilities, which can be administered to children 2 months to 2½ years of age. It does not correlate highly with intelligence in later childhood (J. F. Goodman, 1990).
- *Visual Habituation Paradigm.* This is one measure of infant intelligence that does correlate with later intelligence. In this approach, the susceptibility of infants to **habituation** is measured (Fagan, 1991; Fagan & McGrath, 1981). For example, an infant is shown two identical visual stimuli, such as two copies of the same face. Then, two more pictures of faces are shown, one identical to the original faces and one a new face. Habituation to the familiar faces is measured by the degree of preference for the new face, which is determined by the amount of time the infant gazes at the new face. Infant habituation and later intelligence are correlated, which suggests that children who are able to form and remember mental representations during early childhood (as reflected by preference for novel rather than familiar faces) are more efficient processors of information in later childhood.

Other tests, such as the following, assess the intelligence of individuals with wide-ranging special characteristics.

- *Blind Learning Aptitude Test.* This is a nonverbal test to assess the learning abilities of blind children.
- *Hiskey-Nebraska Test of Learning Aptitude.* This test assesses the cognitive abilities of deaf children and deaf adolescents.
- *K-ABC Nonverbal Scale.* This test is a subset of the K-ABC scales designed for use with populations with communication disorders

- *Raven's Progressive Matrices.* This nonverbal test can be used to measure the nonverbal abilities of culturally diverse individuals, as well as language- and hearing-impaired children and children with cerebral palsy (Naglieri & Prewett, 1990).

Group Measures of Intelligence

All intelligence tests with excellent reliability and validity are individually administered, although there are some tests of mental ability with acceptable reliability and validity that can be administered to groups of children. Since group measures are not as reliable as individual measures of intelligence, they are not used for placing children in special programs. Tests such as the Otis-Lennon School Ability Test (OLSAT), the Cognitive Abilities Test (CogAT), the Detroit Tests of Learning Aptitude (DTLA), and School and College Ability Tests (SCAT) provide helpful information to teachers and school personnel at low cost (Sattler, 1992). Typically, students are provided a response book or answer sheet and mark their answers in the booklet or on the sheet. The directions for these tests have been carefully prepared so that most students can understand them. Items on these tests call for students to make classifications and to solve analogies, number series, and problems (Anastasi, 1988). Educators should take care to read manuals and supporting materials carefully before they administer such tests or attempt to interpret the scores.

■ Building Your Expertise

The *g* Factor in Intelligence

Sometimes tests assess more than one process or knowledge domain. How do test makers determine which items on the test are assessing the same construct? When items test the same construct, performances on these items correlate more highly with one another than performances on other items (see the discussion of correlation in Chapter 1). **Factor analysis** is a way of making sense of the correlations between items. The starting point for factor analysis is identifying how performance on each item of a test correlates with performance on each other item on the test. For example, if every time a student is correct on item 12, he or she is correct on item 16, and every time a student is wrong on item 12, he or she is wrong on item 16, the correlation between the two items would be 1. If this is the case, performance on item 16 can be predicted perfectly from performance on item 12. If there is a 50–50 chance a person who gets item 12 right will get item 16 right and a 50–50 chance that a person who gets item 12 wrong will get item 16 right, the correlation between the two items would be 0. If this is the case, it is impossible to predict performance on item 16 from knowing performance on item 12. If there are 50 items on a test, there will be more than a thousand correlations to review, a difficult task made easier through factor analysis.

Factor analysis identifies clusters of items, or factors, that correlate with one another. Then the investigator examines items in each factor to identify what might be causing the correlations. When intelligence test data are factor analyzed, most or all of the items or subtests frequently cluster in one common factor, which has become known as *g* for general intelligence.

Interpreting Standardized Test Scores

Simply reporting the number of items a student got correct on a standardized test gives little information about the student's performance. In contrast, comparing a raw score to a measure of central tendency for the distribution of scores provides more information about the student's performance in relationship to the performance of others. The most commonly used measure of central tendency in reporting standardized test results is the mean.

The **mean** of a distribution of scores is the average score. The mean is computed by adding up the scores and dividing the sum of scores by the number of scores. For example:

> If there are raw scores of 2, 4, 5, 7, 1, 3, 8, 9, 1, and 10,
> The sum of scores = 50, and the number of scores = 10.
> Therefore, the mean is 5.

In this set of scores, six of the students (those scoring 2, 4, 5, 1, 3, and 1) scored at or below the mean. The other students (those scoring 7, 8, 9, and 10) scored above the mean. Measures of variation, such as the **standard deviation,** provide still more information. The standard deviation is a measure of how widely scores vary from the mean. The larger the standard deviation is, the more spread out from the mean the scores are. The smaller the standard deviation, the more the scores are clustered around the mean.

The norms for standardized tests are typically normally distributed. In a **normal distribution,** most of the scores fall near the mean and fewer scores are further away from the mean (see Figure 13.1). Using the mean and the standard deviation, the normal distribution can be divided into parts. Approximately two-thirds of the scores (68 percent) fall within 1 standard deviation of the mean. Fewer scores (28 percent) fall between 1 and 2 standard deviations from the mean and very few scores (slightly more than 4 percent) are more than 2 standard deviations from the mean. For example, scores on the SAT are normally distributed with a mean of 500 and a standard deviation of 100. In all the WAIS intelligence scales, the mean performance is set at 100 with a standard deviation of 15.

Scores on standardized tests are often expressed in **standard scores.** A very common standard score, the **z-score,** tells how many standard deviations above or below the mean a raw score is (see Figure 13.1).

> z-score = $X - M$/SD

> where X = any raw score
> M = the mean of the raw scores
>   SD = the standard deviation of the raw scores

Scores on standardized tests are also often expressed in terms of stanines. **Stanines** are standard scores with only nine possible categories corresponding to ordered regions of the normal distribution. The mean is 5, and the standard deviation is 2. As you can see from Figure 13.1, each stanine corresponds to a band of raw scores the width of half a standard deviation except for stanines 1 and 9, which include the ends of the distribution. Although stanines are less precise measures for the extreme scores, one advantage of this method of scoring is that performance can expressed in only one digit, from a low of 1 to a high of 9.

Finally, perhaps the most easily communicated method of expressing standardized test scores is in terms of percentile ranks. **Percentile ranks** are expressed in

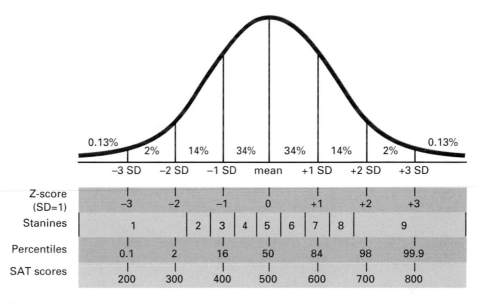

Figure 13.1
Normal distribution, with percentiles, z-scores, stanines, and SAT scores.

terms of relative position within a norm group. The percentile rank shows the percentage of students in the norming sample who scored at or below a particular raw score. For example, a percentile rank of 75 means the student scored the same or better than 75 percent of the other students in the norm group. Percentile ranks are often more easily understood by parents and teachers than the other methods of reporting standardized test scores.

Intellectual Competencies Across the Life Span

Does intellectual functioning change much across the life span? Do IQ scores at childhood correlate with scores at adulthood? Yes, IQ scores at the age of 7 correlate at least 0.6 with IQ scores at the age of 18 (E. B. Brody & Brody, 1978). (Scores generated earlier, however, typically do not predict adult intelligence very well.)

Do IQ scores change across the adult life span? For many years, psychologists reported that intelligence test scores decrease with increasing age during adulthood. After the age of 20, it was all downhill! This conclusion, however, was generated in cross-sectional studies. That is, different people provided the intelligence data at each age level. Cross-sectional studies confound age level and the cohort of people providing the data. This confounding is particularly important in this case because of the differences in educational and cultural experiences found in older and younger adults that influence their performance on intelligence tests (Baltes, 1968; Baltes, Reese, & Nesselroade, 1977; Kaufman, 1990; Schaie & Labouvie-Vief, 1974; Schaie, 1980). Intelligence data collected longitudinally, however, suggest that the decline in IQ is less dramatic than it seems when cross-sectional data are examined (Schaie, 1990).

Aging affects some aspects of intelligence differently. Many intelligence tests have items that can be thought of as tapping either knowledge or ability to process quickly and adeptly. Knowledge and the ability to process correspond to Cattell's (1987; also J. L. Horn, 1985) two factors of intelligence, fluid intelligence and crystallized intelligence, described earlier in this chapter.

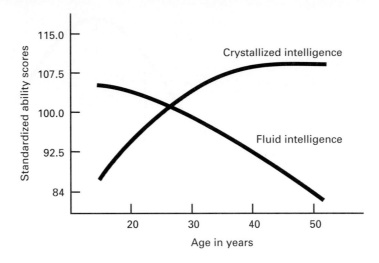

Figure 13.2
Fluid and crystallized intelligence.
Source: From " Major Abilities and Development in the Adult Period" by J. L. Horn and S. M. Hofer, 1992. In R. J. Sternberg and C. A. Berg (Eds.), *Intellectual Development,* New York: Cambridge University Press. Copyright 1992 by Cambridge University Press. Reprinted with permission of Cambridge University Press.

During the childhood and adolescent years, both fluid and crystallized intelligence increase (Sattler, 1992). During adulthood, however, there are important differences in their course (see Figure 13.2). Why? You'll recall from Chapter 6 that adults lose something like 50,000 neurons a day during adulthood! Thus, fluid intelligence, which is strongly dependent on biological wholeness, declines with advancing age (N. Brody, 1992; Kaufman, 1990). This means dramatic reductions in the ability to execute steps in problem solving quickly (Salthouse, 1982, 1985, 1988, 1992). On the other hand, life experiences accumulate with advancing age. Thus, knowledge continues to grow through most of the adult life span. Not surprisingly, crystallized intelligence, which is determined by knowledge, increases with advancing years. When individual differences in the speed of processing (fluid intelligence) and in the amount of education are taken into account, there is evidence for increases in crystallized abilities until the age of 70 (Hertzog, 1989; Kaufman, 1990; Kaufman, Reynolds, & McLean, 1989; Schaie & Labouvie-Vief, 1974).

Are there changes in the cognitive processes described in the good information processing model that can be related to changes in intellectual functioning with age? Some aspects of processing do decline with advancing age (Salthouse, 1992), all of which can be related to fluid abilities at least indirectly. There seems to be increasing difficulties with retrieval of information from memory with advancing age. In addition, many aspects of information processing are performed more slowly with advancing age. Since many perceptual and reasoning components are performed more slowly, these processes consume more capacity (Case, 1985). Therefore, functional processing capacity (i.e., short-term, or working, memory) declines with advancing age. For instance, additional task demands are consistently more disruptive to efficient task completion for older compared to younger adults.

More positively, some cognitive processes probably are not affected by aging (Salthouse, 1992). For example, there probably are not life span changes in the way knowledge is represented, either in long-term or short-term memory (see Chapter

3). There also probably are not life span declines in the ability to monitor adequacy of performance (Devolder, Brigham, & Pressley, 1990).

Individual Differences in Intelligence: Heredity and the Environment

No one is much surprised if two intelligent people marry and produce intelligent offspring. Have the children inherited their parents' intelligence? This is difficult to determine. Intellectually gifted and talented people provide environmental opportunities to their children not available to other children. Perhaps environmental richness, not heredity, is the critical factor in stimulating the intelligence or talents of offspring. Research on twins and adopted children can help us understand the influences of environment and heredity on intelligence.

Twin Studies

Identical twins have the same genes because the two children were produced by a division of the same fertilized egg. When identical twins are reared together in the same family, their environments also are very similar, perhaps as similar as any two person's environments could be. Thus, the very high correlations in intelligence between identical twins (i.e., usually 0.80 to 0.90 or higher) are due to both genetic and environmental determinants of intelligence. Sometimes, however, identical twins are reared apart. In that case, their genes are identical but their environments differ. Although the average IQ correlation (around 0.70) for identical twins reared apart is a little less than that for identical twins raised together, it is still a strong correlation.

Another important comparison is fraternal twins reared together. Since fraternal twins are the product of two different fertilized eggs, they share one-half of their genes. They also have roughly comparable environments, since they are reared in the same family at the same time. The correlation of IQ scores for frater-

The IQ scores of identical twins such as these are more highly correlated than those of fraternal twins.

nal twins (around 0.60) is less than that reported for identical twins (Bouchard & McGue, 1981; Loehlin & Nichols, 1976).

Researchers use data such as these to calculate the **heritability** of intelligence, or the variation in intelligence that is due to genetic variability (Plomin, DeFries, & McClearn, 1990). The general conclusion is that roughly half of the variability in intelligence is due to genes. The importance of genes is obvious from the higher correlations for identical than for fraternal twins. The importance of environment is obvious as well. The IQ scores of identical twins reared together are more similar than the IQ scores of identical twins reared apart. (This issue is controversial as seen in the response to the 1994 publication of a book detailing a strong view of the heritability of intelligence, *The Bell Curve: Intelligence and Class Structure in American Life*, by Herrnstein and Murray.)

Adoption Studies

What have we learned about the role of heredity and the environment from adoption studies? There is research that supports heredity as a determinant of individual differences in IQ (Bouchard & McGue, 1981). For example, the IQ correlation for parents and their biological children reared in their homes is 0.42. This is higher than the 0.19 correlation between parents and their adopted children, who do not have a genetic relationship to each other. In addition, the IQ correlation for biological siblings (who share 50 percent of their genes) reared together is 0.47. This is higher than the IQ correlation for biological half-siblings (who share 25 percent of their genes) reared together and the IQ correlation for nonbiological siblings.

On the other hand, there are also research results supporting the importance of the environment (Bouchard & McGue, 1981). For example, the IQ correlation of 0.47 for biological siblings reared together is larger than the IQ correlation of 0.24 for biological siblings reared apart. In addition, the IQ correlation of 0.42 between biological parents and their children when they live together is larger than the correlation of 0.22 when they do not live together. In general, consistent with the twin data, the adoption data indicate that about half of the variability in IQ scores is due to heredity (Chipeur, Rovine, & Plomin, 1990).

The adoption data also provide support for the effects of long-term exposure to a stimulating environment. First, the longer adoptive families are together, the greater the correlations in intelligence (Plomin, DeFries, & Fulker, 1988). Second, when adopted children are raised in families in which the family level of intelligence is higher than that of the biological family, the intelligence of the adoptees tends to be higher than what would have been expected if they had been raised by their biological parents. This is especially likely when the adoption occurs at an early age for the child (Scarr & Weinberg, 1976, 1983; Storfer, 1990; Weinberg, Scarr, & Waldman, 1992).

Bias in Mental Testing

Many Americans are aware that the IQ scores of African Americans are on average approximately 15 points lower than the IQ scores of whites. In both white and black groups, however, socioeconomic status is correlated with IQ scores. Specifically, those from socioeconomically inferior environments score lower (Jensen, 1973; Mensh & Mensh, 1991; Sattler, 1992). Socioeconomic differences between

Focus on Research

Methodological Issues for Twin and Adoption Studies

There have been methodological criticisms of both twin and adoption studies (Lewontin, Rose, & Kamin, 1984; Locurto, 1990; Plomin, DeFries, & McLearn, 1990). For example, two key assumptions in twin studies are that identical twins reared apart experience very different environments, while fraternal twins reared together experience very similar environments (Goldberger, 1977; Grayson, 1989; Wilson, 1982). Do these assumptions hold across most cases? Adopting families of separated identical twins often are similar in socioeconomic status to the biological families. Moreover, fraternal twins may lead very different lives, even during childhood. Factors such as sex, size, and physical appearance profoundly affect environmental interactions. In addition, estimates of what the IQ scores of an adopted child might have been if the child had been reared in the birth environment are often based on incomplete knowledge of the intelligence of biological parents. As we learned in Chapter 1, researchers must consider alternative explanations for the patterns they find. Despite the methodological limitations of particular studies, however, there are enough replications of twin and adoption studies with similar results to support broad conclusions.

blacks and whites almost certainly account for some of the difference (perhaps a third) in intelligence scores between blacks and whites (Jensen, 1973).

Other minority groups, such as Hispanics, are also disproportionately represented at the poverty levels of American society, which is reflected by lower scores on IQ tests. Since the Hispanic population of the United States has increased dramatically in size in the last 15 years and is projected to continue increasing in size, the appropriateness of standardized testing with Spanish-speaking Americans is being examined (Geisinger, 1992).

Minorities have every right to be concerned about how they are assessed and how assessments are used to determine their futures. There has been a historic tendency in the United States to denigrate the intelligence of minorities and to conclude that their minds are somehow biologically inferior. For example, intelligence

Immigrants to the United States often have been characterized as being substandard in intelligence. This is an argument for the presence of bias in intelligence tests.

data collected during World War I were used to prove that recent immigrants (Irish and Italian) were not as intelligent as people born in the United States.

Although some of the difference in intelligence test scores between whites and minorities is due to socioeconomic differences between the populations, not all of it is. What might account for IQ score discrepancies that cannot be explained by socioeconomic-mediated differences? Are IQ tests biased against various ethnic and racial groups?

Potential Sources of Test Bias

Bias can be introduced in tests in a number of ways (Reynolds & Kaiser, 1990a, 1990b). (Alternative measures that are perhaps less sensitive to bias are discussed in Chapter 14.) First, the content of items can tap concepts and experiences more familiar to some groups than others. For example, the vocabulary used to test a concept may be unfamiliar to some people taking the test. Although test constructors attempt to eliminate content bias, even experts in a culture cannot reliably identify items that will pose difficulty for children in their culture (Jensen, 1976; Sandoval & Mille, 1980). Fortunately, in well-constructed intelligence tests, there are high correlations in the difficulty level of items across populations (Reynolds & Kaiser, 1990b), reducing the likelihood that some items are particularly difficult for minority groups.

A second possible bias is in the predictive validity of the tests. Some tests may predict educational or other types of successes better for some groups than others. Well-constructed tests, however, predict equally well across racial and cultural groups. For example, if it is asked "Will this person do well in this college?," the test is unbiased if the answer it generates is "right" the same proportion of times for all groups.

A third potential source of bias is in the samples (e.g., predominantly white, English speaking) used to norm standardized tests. In particular, there may be sociocultural differences in understanding what it means to take a test and what the long-term implications of tests are (Rodriguez, 1992). Producers of well-constructed tests are aware of the need for representative national norming samples, however, and they generate such samples (Sattler, 1992).

A fourth potential source of bias is a mismatch between the test language and the primary language of the test taker. This is particularly important for Hispanic students. Until recently, there were laws in some parts of the United States requiring that all children be tested in English and that decisions about school placement into special education or giftedness classes be based on these tests (Donlon, 1992; Rodriguez, 1992). Disproportionately high numbers of Spanish-speaking children end up in special education and disproportionately low numbers of Spanish-speaking children experience accelerated offerings (Donlon, 1992; Pennock-Román, 1992; Schmeiser, 1992). Ability tests administered in English to Spanish-speaking students sometimes do not correlate at all with ability tests administered in Spanish (Pennock-Román, 1992) and may grossly underestimate intelligence. In one court case, retesting determined that seven of the nine students who had brought the case were much more intelligent than originally assessed (Constantino, 1992).

A fifth potential source of bias is a mismatch between the race and/or culture of the examiner and the test taker. There is little evidence, however, that the race of an examiner makes a difference in the test score earned by a person being examined (Graziano, Varca, & Levy, 1982). What does seem to matter is familiarity between the examiner and the person being tested, with personal familiarity between them boosting the performance of the examinee slightly. The familiarity effect seems to be especially large for lower socioeconomic populations (D. Fuchs & Fuchs, 1986).

Arguments that there are very real sources of test bias have appeared in the nation's court system. In *Larry P. v. Riles* (1979), a federal judge ruled that California's mandated use of IQ tests to decide special education placements for minorities was inappropriate. Tests that have been normed without sufficient samples of minorities are rejected as a reasonable basis for making decisions about minorities (e.g., *Rivera v. City of Wichita Falls*, 1982).

Despite all the concerns with potential test bias, when tests are reliable and valid and are not being used intentionally to discriminate, they are being upheld as appropriate, even if disproportionate numbers of minorities fail the test, such as the National Teacher Examination (*United States of America v. State of South Carolina*, 1978). The courts are not rejecting the use of tests wholesale. There is clear court support for tests that clearly tap competencies that are relevant to the selection process, such as competencies clearly required to do a job (*Washington v. Davis*, 1978). Still, there is more sensitivity now than ever before about how IQ tests and other standardized measures can be misused in their application with minorities, and there is greater legal protection for minorities than ever before.

Can Intervention Increase Intelligence?

Evidence from twin and adoption studies suggest that individual differences in intelligence are determined in part by genetic factors. Each of us is born with a genetic heritage. The genes we possess comprise our **genotype.** The genotype specifies a potential range of possible outcomes. These outcomes, or how the genes are expressed, are called **phenotypes.** Where we end up in the **reaction range** of possible phenotypes is highly dependent on the environment. According to this concept of reaction range, intelligence should be affected by the provision of high-quality environments. Let's examine these ideas in more detail.

Genotypes and Phenotypes

Any given set of genes specifies a variety of outcomes that depend on the environment. For example, you'll recall the case of PKU discussed in Chapter 6. A child with PKU has the genetically determined inability to metabolize phenylalanine. If a child with PKU experiences a nutritional environment rich in phenylalanine, the result is severe retardation. If the child experiences a nutritional environment in which phenylalanine has been eliminated, normal intelligence is the outcome. Consider a second example. Heart disease has a reasonably high heritability. Suppose someone has the misfortune to be born of parents who both suffer from heart disease. Whether this person actually develops coronary problems, however, depends largely on environmental factors such as diet, exercise, and lifestyle. That is, genes and environment interact to determine outcomes: there is a reaction range of phenotypes associated with each genotype (Gottesman, 1963; Lewontin, 1974; Scarr & Kidd, 1983).

The concept of reaction range is an important one for interventionists. The goal of the interventionist should be to do all possible to ensure their students, patients, or clients end up on the favorable end of the reaction range. Thus, educators should be doing all things possible to make certain that their students are as close as possible to the top of their reaction range for intelligence. There has been substantial progress in understanding how to accomplish this goal.

High-Quality Environments

Although there are critics of the research, (Jensen, 1969, 1972, 1973, 1980, 1992; Locurto, 1988, 1991a, 1991b, 1991c; Spitz, 1986a, 1986b, 1991a, 1991b, 1992) high-quality environmental manipulations at home and in preschool generally produce increases in measured intelligence (Storfer, 1990). These interventions include teaching parents how to read with and stimulate their children and introducing academically oriented day care to children from economically disadvantaged homes. Gains in IQ scores are most likely to be observed at the immediate conclusion of an intervention. Often, several years after the special intervention has ceased, the IQ scores of children participating in the intervention are no different than the IQ scores of children who did not participate, leading some to conclude that intervention programs are of little benefit. Others believe it is unreasonable to expect maintenance of intelligence advantages if children return to an environment that does not stimulate additional intellectual development. This is often the case for children targeted for preschool intervention. Educational and environmental interventions promoting academic competence are long-term affairs (Storfer, 1990).

If intervention advantages provided during the preschool years are continued into the schooling years, intelligence gains are more likely to be maintained and school achievement increased. Some of the strongest evidence in favor of continuing interventions initiated in the preschool years is provided by the Carolina Abecedarian Project (Ramey & Campbell, 1987). This project is aimed at increasing the intellectual competence of children who are at risk for intellectual deficiency because they come from economically and intellectually impoverished environments. Children in the Abecedarian Project began their participation shortly after birth. Both those in the intervention program and those in the control group were provided nutritional support, family-counseling contacts, and medical care. The children in the intervention, however, attended a high-quality preschool environment for the entire day throughout the year. Meetings were held with parents as part of this preschool program to increase parental awareness of how to stimulate their children's development and use community opportunities.

Is this program successful? In general, the more treatment received through the Abecedarian Project, the lower the failure rate and the higher the IQ at the age of 12 (Ramey, 1992). The message is clear: Children's intelligence and academic achievement that are at risk can be improved through intensive, long-term, academically oriented intervention.

Chapter Summary

- It is difficult to grow up in America without experiencing standardized achievement tests, such as the SAT. These tests were normed on large, nationally representative samples. They are reliable and valid in predicting future academic achievement.

- Reliability and validity are two basic requirements of all useful tests. Consumers of information generated by tests must always verify whether the test measures consistently (reliability) and whether the test measures what it claims to measure (validity).

- Intelligent functioning is described in a variety of ways. Initial theories differ in the degree to which they emphasize general and specific factors in intelligence. Other more recent theories focus on individual differences in information processing. The theory of multiple intelligences expands the definition of intelligence to include nonacademic competencies. Finally, distinguishing fluid from crystallized intelligence helps us understand the influence of biological and cultural factors upon intellectual competence at different points in the life span.

- Shifts in the nature of thinking abilities across the life span are illuminated from analyses of IQ data. The quick and somewhat contentless reasoning skills that are the endowment of the young give way with advancing age to content-filled knowledge acquired throughout the life span.

- Twin and adoption studies shed light on the relative roles of heredity and environment in development. About half of the variability in intelligence is due to genes. Minorities often perform at lower levels than members of the majority population on intelligence tests. Much of this lower performance, however, can be traced to a number of factors, including socioeconomic status and potential sources of test bias.

- Genes provide potential; whether a person's intelligence is at the high or low end of that range of potential depends on the environments encountered during development. There is substantial support for the conclusion that intelligence can be increased through environmental manipulations. Rather than accept low levels of achievement, it makes good sense to provide educational environments that encourage students to function nearer the upper boundary of their reaction range than they would in conventional environments.

Return to the Classroom Predicament

Has reading this chapter helped you formulate recommendations for what Ms. Fuentes could have said to address more directly the concerns Mr. and Mrs. Skenadore had about standardized tests? She could assure the parents that tests are given for many reasons, perhaps to assess special needs or to consider admission to an accelerated program. Then, she could explain what kind of test Samuel was taking and why he was taking it. She should offer to help the parents interpret the test results, whether they are expressed in standard scores or percentile ranks.

Any educator should be able to explain to parents the rationale behind standardized achievement tests such as college admissions tests. Ms. Fuentes could explain that universities use these tests because they need a way to compare students from different high schools, and admissions tests, in combination with high school grades, predict college achievement. She could assure the parents that the tests are standardized, reliable, and valid. She could also explain that although every attempt is made to make standardized tests fair, they may underestimate achievement in minority groups.

Chapter Outline

Chapter 14

Alternative Assessments of Academic Competence

Classroom Predicament

At the PTA meeting, a group of parents voice their displeasure with the school's state-mandated assessment program. The parents are especially concerned because of the large stakes involved: State funding and teacher salaries are tied to students' performance as measured by the assessment program. The test in question is primarily in a multiple-choice format. The parents wish to know, "How does my child benefit from the time and effort spent on this assessment, and is there any other way to evaluate my child?"

How would you respond to these concerns? Reflecting on the information presented in this chapter will help you formulate a response to this question.

The traditional assessments of intelligence and academic achievement presented in the preceding chapter are ones that most readers of this book have probably heard of before taking a course in educational psychology. SAT and IQ scores have been part of American life for most of the twentieth century. Educators, however, are rethinking how to measure academic competence and are developing many new measurements that are providing new conceptualizations of learning, thinking, and intelligence.

This chapter begins with a description of national and state achievement testing programs, which have great impact on public policy and public perceptions about education. Although many of these programs utilize traditional testing formats, some experiment with alternative testing formats, such as performance assessment and portfolio assessment, and the feasibility of using these alternative assessment techniques for large-scale assessment is explored. Other alternative techniques for assessing academic capabilities and academic achievement, dynamic assessment and curriculum-based assessment, are also discussed. Finally, this chapter concludes with an introduction to biologically based measures of academic competence, which may well become the assessment techniques of the future.

National and State Assessments

Given the great alarm about eroding educational standards articulated in publications such as *A Nation at Risk* (which was published in 1983) and an increasing emphasis on public accountability for tax dollars spent, federal and state governments are interested in determining how well schools are doing. Thus, many U.S. states and Canadian provinces conduct statewide or provincewide assessments of students' competence. The best known of the national testing efforts is the National Assessment of Educational Progress (NAEP).

National Assessment of Educational Progress (NAEP)

The NAEP is billed as the nation's report card by its administrator, the Educational Testing Service (ETS). The NAEP is a tremendous force in education. Based on its conclusions, elected and appointed government officials at both the federal and state level have designed new federal and state policies that have changed what is taught in school. Reports of the most recent NAEP data are prominently displayed in newspapers across the nation and are often relayed on radio and television broadcasts. Since there is every indication that this assessment will assume even greater importance in future decision making about education (Haertel, 1991; G. W. Phillips, 1991), educators and parents need to familiarize themselves with this assessment instrument.

The NAEP is administered biannually to students in fourth, eighth, and twelfth grades. Exactly which subject areas are tested varies from assessment to assessment. Over the years, reading, writing, mathematics, science, social studies, literature, art, music, citizenship, computer skills, and career development have been evaluated. ETS assures content validity of the exam by using a broad base of experts to generate and evaluate items before the test is used. The goal is to test content that students should know or processes they should be able to carry out without having to use a particular textbook or experience a particular curriculum. Items are reviewed to make certain they are not offensive to different cultural groups. In addition, there also are questions asking students about their educational experiences,

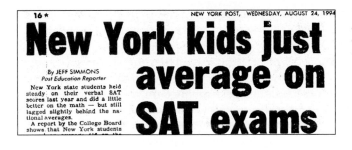

Large-scale student assessments such as the NAEP greatly influence public perceptions of public education.

including how much and what type of instruction they have received in the content area (L. Anderson et al., 1990; Mitchell, 1992).

Once the NAEP test in a subject area is constructed, great efforts are made to identify and test a nationally representative sample. For example, the 1988 civics assessment (L. Anderson et al., 1990) was administered to 11,000 students in more than 1,000 public and private schools across the country. Although most of the items on the civics NAEP were multiple choice in format, students at grades 8 and 12 also responded to an essay question requiring them to name the president of the United States and to take 15 minutes to write a description of his responsibilities. To get an idea of the types of multiple-choice items on this civics test, look at Table 14.1.

Table 14.1

Sample Items from the 1988 NAEP Civics Test

One of the easiest items (passing rate = 71 percent at grade 4, 94 percent at grade 8, and 99 percent at grade 12) is the following:

  Who would become President of the United States if the President dies?
    A. The Secretary of State
    B. The Speaker of the House
    C. The Chief Justice of the Supreme Court
    D. The Vice-President

The next item is more difficult (passing rate = 10 percent at grade 4, 61 percent at grade 8, 89 percent at grade 12):

  In the United States, an individual citizen has the right to:
    A. Impeach the President
    B. Vote for government officials
    C. Make new laws
    D. Collect taxes

The following is one of the most difficult items on the test (passing rate = 1 percent at grades 4 and 8, 6 percent at grade 12):

  In the execution of its responsibilities, which of the following is LEAST likely to be influenced by lobbying?
    A. The Supreme Court
    B. The House of Representatives
    C. The Senate
    D. A state governor

(L. Anderson et al., 1990, p. 39; answers to questions: [D], [B], and [A])

NAEP Test Outcomes. Beginning in 1992, students' performance on the NAEP was described according to three levels: basic, proficient, and advanced. To establish these benchmarks of performance, expert judges were asked to envision a particular level of performance. Then they reviewed each test item to determine the probability that a student at each level of proficiency could answer it correctly. For example, students' performance on the 1992 NAEP for reading revealed that the majority of students—59 to 75 percent across the three grade levels—were able to read at the "basic" level or better (Viadero, 1993b). The "basic" level for fourth graders meant being able to understand simple narratives. Only 25 percent of the fourth graders, 28 percent of the eighth graders, and 37 percent of the twelfth graders were judged able to read at the "proficient" level. Reading proficiently for fourth graders meant understanding and interpreting stories in context; for eighth graders, reading proficiently meant making inferences, comparing themes, and using a document to solve problems.

Students taking the 1992 NAEP for writing completed either two 25-minute or one 50-minute writing task, which were scored at one of six levels ranging from minimally responsive to extensively elaborated. The results revealed that even the best students who can write narrative and informative pieces have trouble preparing and organizing arguments to write persuasively (Olson, 1994). An example of an informative writing task for fourth graders was to describe a favorite object and why they valued it; a persuasive writing task for twelfth graders was to write about whether high school students should be required to perform community service to graduate.

The average student performance on the 1992 NAEP for mathematics increased from 1990 (Rothman, 1993a). About two-fifths of the students at each grade level, however, failed to achieve the "basic" level (which meant demonstrating some understanding of math concepts and procedures), and few demonstrated "proficient" achievement (which meant consistently being able to apply integrated knowledge).

Analysis of the NAEP data revealed that some aspects of the home environment were determinants of achievement. Students who watched more television and read less at home scored lower on the NAEP assessments. Also, the higher the educational level of the parent or parents, the higher the performance on the NAEP measures (Applebee, Langer, & Mullis, 1986, 1988; Educational Testing Service, 1985; Pikulski, 1991).

The NAEP was also informative about curriculum. In general, for all NAEP tests, more instruction in the area tested increased achievement on the test (Dorsey, Mullis, Lindquist, & Chambers, 1988). There were also reported links between students' reading achievement and type of instruction as follows:

- Students in programs emphasizing literature-based approaches to reading tended to perform better on the 1992 reading NAEP than other students (Viadero, 1993b).
- More than half of the variation in writing proficiency between the best- and worst-performing schools on the 1992 writing NAEP could be explained by instructional resources and practices (Olson, 1994). Teachers in top-performing schools were more likely to give longer writing assignments that required analysis and interpretation. Students in top-performing schools reported they were asked to plan writing, to write more than one draft, and to focus on the mechanics of writing, but they felt teachers graded their writing as much for quality and creativity of ideas as for spelling, punctuation, and grammar.

- The increase in the 1992 math NAEP scores was related to teachers' addressing more ambitious, complex math (concepts of algebra and geometry), rather than focusing on basic mathematics such as numbers and operations (Viadero, 1993a).

▶ **Diversity**

Differences in the NAEP Performance

The NAEP is useful not only for tracking general trends in students' academic achievement but also for revealing population differences in students' performance. What are some of these differences?

- Girls outperformed boys on reading and writing achievement. Although boys outperformed girls on math achievement, the gender gap in math achievement has narrowed in recent years. On the 1992 NAEP for mathematics, there was no difference between girls and boys in the fourth and eighth grades, but boys outperformed girls in twelfth grade (Rothman, 1993b).
- Whites and Asian Americans typically outperform African Americans and Hispanics on the NAEP tests. The gap in black-white performance has been narrowing over the years (Jaynes & Williams, 1989; Mullis, Owens, & Phillips, 1990), but not everyone is optimistic about its actually closing (Darling-Hammond & Snyder, 1992; Secada, 1992). Much of the performance improvement among African Americans is on lower-level competencies rather than the more advanced competencies tapped by the test (Jaynes & Williams, 1989; Kirsch & Jungeblut, 1986). For example, even though the gap in reading achievement between blacks and whites has narrowed, the percentage of black high school seniors performing at proficient level was less than half that of white students on the 1992 NAEP. Only 16 percent of African Americans were judged to be proficient readers compared with 43 percent of whites, 39 percent of Asian Americans, and 21 percent of Hispanics (Viadero, 1993b). Since African Americans and Hispanics were underrepresented at the top performing schools in most states, education is still failing to be effective with many more minority than white majority children. Some of these differences in performances may be explained by differences in educational opportunities and economic advantages, since students from advantaged environments outperform those from disadvantaged backgrounds on the NAEP tests.

Criticisms of the NAEP. The NAEP tests may have become increasingly prominent in educational and political circles but not without their share of criticisms. Here are some of the most common criticisms:

1. *The NAEP provides an overly pessimistic outlook on the current generation compared with past generations.* A consistent trend over the years has been for students to perform at lower levels on NAEP assessments than educators and public officials expect. Some prominent policy makers have used this information in stinging criticisms of American students and the schools that are educating them (W. L. Bennett, 1984; Cheney, 1987; Ravitch & Finn, 1987). They argue that schools are not preparing students as well as in the past (B. S. Bloom, 1987; Hirsch, 1987). In response to

such claims, Whittington (1991) examined students' performance on American history tests going back to 1915 (Tryon, 1927) and found that students' knowledge of history then and now was not all that different. In addition, M. Wyatt (1992) documented claims throughout the last two centuries about underprepared college students who were not able to read college-level texts or write college-level essays.

2. *Standards in the 1992 NAEP (basic, proficient, and advanced) may have been set too high.* Critics have compared some NAEP data with teachers' ratings of students, independent measures of students' ability, and SAT scores and have found that more students performed at basic, proficient, and advanced levels than identified by the NAEP (Viadero, 1993b).

3. *Because the NAEP tests basic skills much more than higher-order thinking skills, educational curriculum is driven toward drill and practice in order to ensure that students can perform the competencies tapped by the test (Squire, 1991).* Many of the content items require only superficial acquaintance with the material (e.g., knowing who wrote what) rather than the deep understanding that comes from critical reading, reflecting, discussing, and acting on important content (Rosenblatt, 1991). In response to this criticism, the NAEP test developers are experimenting with modifications of the NAEP, which are discussed in the next sections.

4. *The NAEP should not be used to compare students' performance across schools and across states.* Most (89 percent) of the variation among state average test scores on the 1992 NAEP math assessment could be explained by four factors beyond the control of school: the number of parents living at home, the parents' level of education, the community type, and the state poverty rate. Critics argue that it is unfair to compare the achievement of states with large numbers of poor and minority students with that of states that have relatively homogeneous and affluent populations (Olson, 1994). Moreover, even if differences in programs are related to differences in performance on the NAEP, it is impossible to determine which program differences are responsible for the performance differences (Koretz, 1991).

5. *There are some important sampling problems with the NAEP.* Only children who are enrolled in school are measured. Because minorities and members of economically disadvantaged groups tend to drop out from school in large proportions, they may be underrepresented in the high school data especially (Secada, 1992). In addition, students whom school officials believe would have difficulty with a standardized test because of language proficiency problems sometimes do not take the test (Secada, 1992). Thus, the NAEP may be substantially overestimating how well minorities and the poor are doing in academic achievement, because many of the most disadvantaged are not tested.

Performance Assessments

Tests designed to measure academic competencies have traditionally focused on whether or not students get the right answers instead of on *how* students arrive at their answers. In contrast to conventional (content-based) assessments, performance assessments require students to demonstrate knowledge or skills, focusing on processing abilities that are valuable in and of themselves (O'Neil, 1992). For example, performance assessments for writing require students to demonstrate how they plan, write, and revise essays. Performance assessments for science require students to demonstrate their ability to conduct scientific experiments, from hypothesis formation to actual experimentation to write-up of the outcomes of the experiment. Since many performance assessments focus on real-life prob-

Focus on Research

Politics and National Assessments

It is important for educators to realize that test results can be used for many purposes, often those not originally intended by the test developers. Educators, policy makers, and politicians can use the results of large-scale assessments such as the NAEP to achieve their own ends. For example, school officials can use test data to make the case that their particular schools are doing well. They can carefully select tests and the norms used to interpret them as well as continue to use the same standardized tests year after year so teachers learn to focus their teaching on the information covered by the tests. Smart administrators have no difficulty juggling their test scores to convince others (and perhaps themselves) that their students are more than OK—that their students are above the national average. As John Cannell (1987, 1989) pointed out, although it is impossible for all students in the nation to display above average performances, it often seems that most school districts report their students as doing better than average.

Policy makers can use test data such as that from the NAEP as leverage for reforms consistent with their agendas (Darling-Hammond & Snyder, 1992; Early, 1991; Farr & Beck, 1991; Ruth, 1991; Simmons, 1991). For example, some conservative political groups push for a common curriculum, one based on what they perceive to be the great Western ideas (Finn, 1991; Hirsch, 1987). The focus of this agenda seems to be on lower-order skills, such as memorization and rote learning, rather than the higher-order reading, writing, and problem-solving skills that educators believe are important and are learning how to promote better. Another conservative agenda fueled by NAEP results is the push for the advancement of private schools, including Catholic schools, because of the consistently higher scores on standardized tests achieved by private compared with public school students (Finn, 1991). The higher test scores can be used to lobby for federal dollars to benefit private schools. Of course, no mention is made of the private school's opportunity to select students from a pool of applicants or the differences in family factors, such as socioeconomic status or the emphasis placed on education.

lems and have meaning and value in and of themselves, they are considered more authentic than traditional assessments. **Authentic assessments** are directly linked to the goals of instruction. Notice how this emphasis on process corresponds to the model of good thinking described throughout this text and to the new conceptualizations of intelligence described in Chapter 13.

Educators interested in the possibilities of performance assessment for statewide testing programs are working on paper-and-pencil versions of performance assessments. These assessments require students to reveal their understanding of process. Consider the following example (Szetala & Nicol, 1992, p. 44), which involves presentation of a problem in mathematics and the solution attempted by another student:

> A bowl contains 10 pieces of fruit (apples and oranges). Apples cost 5 cents each and oranges cost 10 cents each. All together the fruit is worth 70 cents. We want to find out how many apples are in the bowl. Kelly tried to solve the problem this way:
>
> | | |
> |---|---|
> | $10 \times 5 = 50$ | $8 \times 5 = 40$ |
> | $2 \times 10 = \underline{20}$ | $3 \times 10 = 30$ |
> | 70 | $4 \times 10 = 40$ |
> | | $6 \times 5 = 30$ |
>
> There were 30 apples in the bowl.

The student taking the assessment is then asked to evaluate the Kelly's performance by responding to the following questions (Szetala & Nicol, 1992, p. 44):

1. Is Kelly's way of solving the problem a good one? Tell why you think it is or is not a good way.
2. Did Kelly get the right answer? Explain why she did or did not.

Most readers figure out that Kelly's solution contains serious errors. For example, 30 apples as an answer makes no sense when there are only 10 pieces of fruit total in the bowl. The correct solution is 6 apples. Kelly's mistakes were copying the wrong piece of information from her computations and failing to check her answer against the reality of the situation. The questions posed about Kelly's solution require that students reveal their thinking about the problem.

Those developing performance assessments for mathematics and science have considered a number of different ways to encourage students to communicate their thinking (adapted from Szetala & Nicol, 1992, p. 44).

- Present a problem and part of its solution, and have the student complete the solution.
- Present a problem that includes some irrelevant facts. Have students evaluate the quality of the problem and remove the incongruous information.
- Have students explain using only words how they solved a problem.
- After solving a problem, have students create a new problem using the same problem structure but a different context.

There are also various methods for scoring students' responses, ranging from (1) no credit for a response that misses the point of the problem completely to (2) partial credit for showing some appropriate reflection and progress toward the solution to (3) full credit for a fully reflective answer with detailed commentary on the processes required to respond to the request made by the test item (Szetala & Nicol, 1992).

Statewide Performance Assessments: An Example from Maryland. A number of states are piloting performance-based assessment approaches. In one of these, the Maryland State Performance Assessment Project (MSPAP), the assessments require integrated reading and writing. Consider an assessment used for eighth graders (R. Mitchell, 1992, pp. 47–49). The students are asked to read Jack London's classic story, "To Build a Fire." They are first asked to think about when they have been cold and are given 10 minutes to write about their experiences in a response journal. Then they read London's story and respond to a series of comprehension questions. Some questions can be answered by constructing drawings; most require written responses. The students also report how difficult the reading was for them and write about the reading strategies they used while reading the story. That is day 1 of the assessment.

The test continues on day 2. First, students write a 5-minute letter to the dying man in "To Build a Fire," advising him what to do to save his life. Then there is a class discussion of this topic, with the teacher's recording the students' ideas on the board. Students then read a short excerpt from a book about hypothermia and respond in writing to comprehension questions.

Day 3 is concerned with integrating the information from the two pieces that were read. Students are required to write one of three types of responses:

- An essay informing friends about what they need to do to be safe on a weekend trip.
- A poem, a story, or a play that captures the feelings associated with conditions such as extreme heat, cold, hunger, or fatigue.
- A speech attempting to persuade people not to travel to the Yukon.

Although the teachers know the students will be required to construct one of these three types of responses, they do not know which one the students will end up having to do. The idea, of course, is to encourage teachers to teach students how to compose essays, poems, stories, plays, and persuasive speeches.

As they construct their writing on day 3, students are required to show their process. They list words they have brainstormed in planning the essay or record in their journal the ideas used in planning the essay. Then, they write a rough draft, which they revise. The exam concludes with their using a proofreading guide sheet to check their final copy.

NAEP and Performance Assessment

The NAEP has modified its instruments so students can demonstrate what they can do through performance tasks in addition to multiple-choice items. In the 1994 NAEP, approximately half of the assessment time was devoted to a variety of performance assessments, typically open-ended responses. For example, in mathematics, students were required to explain their reasoning as they worked through an extended problem. In science, each student was given a science kit and asked to perform an experiment, make observations, and evaluate the results. In history, students analyzed primary source documents and submitted written analysis.

The development of good performance assessments takes a great deal of time, effort, and expense. There are high administration costs, and the tests require days of precious school time. Moreover, the scoring is very labor-intensive compared with the rapid machine scoring permitted by multiple-choice formats. R. Mitchell (1992) estimated that performance assessments may be ten times more costly than conventional assessments.

In addition, the problems on these performance assessments often are simplistic or contrived compared with the types of problems educators really would like students to be able to solve. For example, the essays that emanate from the writing assessments are often short and do not display the complexity of thought and feeling that educators want to see in their students' work. In short, performance assessments may not be authentic enough!

Portfolios: A Form of Long-Term Performance Assessment

How is a photographer hired? Several candidates are usually interviewed, each bringing his or her portfolio to the meeting. A photographer's portfolio consists of samples of his or her best work assembled over a long period of time. Potential future employers use the portfolio to make evaluations and hiring decisions. One form of performance assessment uses students' portfolios, much like photographers' portfolios, to evaluate students' progress (Bird, 1990).

Educational portfolios provide information so that inferences can be made about students' knowledge, ability, and attitudes. The portfolio is a collection of objects, often a file of completed projects. Some portfolios are more specific than others. For example, A. Collins (1992) suggests that physics students develop portfolios of evidence to verify their understanding of some physics concept. Such a portfolio might be created with examples of how physics impacts everyday life. Some portfolios show how much an individual student has learned by including examples of work that show improvement over time. Other portfolios are designed

Photographers bring portfolios of their work to job interviews. Potential employers use these portfolios to help make hiring decisions. In a similar manner, educational portfolios can provide the basis for academic judgments.

to evaluate teachers more than students and might include such things as summaries about how a school year was spent, complete with examples of outstanding student performances such as essays and projects. In short, **portfolios** are collections of objects assembled for a specific purpose (Bird, 1990; A. Collins, 1992). The purpose of the portfolio depends on a number of factors, including whether the portfolio is being used for large-stakes assessment, classroom assessment, or instructional purposes (see Chapter 15). Whatever the purpose, it must be clearly articulated at the outset.

NAEP and Portfolio Assessment. The NAEP has explored the possibility of a national portfolio assessment of writing. The 1990 NAEP portfolio writing pilot study involved fourth- and eighth-grade students who had participated in the regular NAEP writing assessment. The teachers of these students were contacted and asked to assist the students in selecting one piece of their *best* writing from the current school year. More than 1000 students participated at each age level.

The NAEP devised reliable ways of scoring the various types of writing to reflect the characteristics of good versus poor writing. Did the students score differently on this portfolio assessment compared with the more traditional NAEP writing assessment? As many as 77 percent of the fourth graders, but only 55 percent of the eighth graders, performed equally well on both assessments. When there was a discrepancy in students' performance at either grade level, the score was more likely to be better on the portfolio assessment than on the conventional assessment.

State Portfolio Assessments. A number of states are now developing portfolio assessments to measure students' achievement. In Vermont (R. Mitchell, 1992), the students not only take standardized writing and math tests but also construct portfolios, which include a "best" piece of work for each student. Statewide committees of teachers developed, piloted, and grade these portfolio approaches.

The amount and quality of information generated in the Vermont assessments can be appreciated by considering the various ways that mathematics portfolio products are scored. Evaluations of students' performance are made on the following dimensions (R. Mitchell, 1992, pp. 118–120):

- Ability to separate relevant from irrelevant information
- Quality of strategies used to solve problems
- Reasons for student decision making as problems are solved
- Quality and extent of decisions, findings, conclusions, observations, and generalizations made
- Use of mathematical language
- Use of mathematical representations: graphs, charts, tables, diagrams, manipulatives, and so on
- Clarity of presentation

■ Building Your Expertise

Reliability and Validity of Performance Assessments

It is important never to lose track of the basics of assessment. As described in Chapter 13, two important qualities of any assessment instrument are reliability and validity. Reliable tests measure consistently; valid tests measure what they purport to measure. It is necessary always to ask whether a test is valid for the purpose for which it is being used. One strength of performance assessments and other assessments described in this chapter is that their purpose is immediately obvious. For example, math portfolios are obviously related to math achievement. Some researchers caution, however, that knowledge of the quality and validity of performance assessments is low (E. L. Baker, O'Neil, & Linn, 1993). One strong rationale that proponents of performance-based assessments offer for continued efforts to develop them is the belief that the consequences for education of using performance assessments will be much more positive that those of traditional standardized tests (Linn, 1994).

Although proponents of performance assessment argue that validity is the most important consideration in the evaluation and use of assessment instruments, others argue that assessments with low reliability cannot be valid. Since reliability increases with the number of test items (see Chapter 13), performance assessments that have only one, two, or three unreliable items cannot be valid (Shavelson, Baxter, & Pine, 1992). One solution for low reliability is simply to increase the number of items. However, this is a problem for performance assessments because many of the individual items on these assessments take a long time to complete.

Shavelson and his associates (Shavelson, Baxter, & Pine, 1992) evaluated the reliability and validity of performance assessments for fifth- and sixth-grade science. Were these tests reliable? It was easy to get agreement between raters on the scoring of individual assessment tasks, but it was difficult to produce consistent results across performance tasks. Some students performed better on one task than another. This means that in order to assess performance reliably, a number of performance tasks have to be included in an assessment.

Were these tests that Shavelson and his colleagues looked at valid? The performance assessments were sensitive to an instructional difference. As expected, students enrolled in hands-on science courses that taught process outperformed students in traditional textbook-oriented courses. Traditional measures, however, did not differentiate students with hands-on science instruction from those receiving traditional instruction.

● **"What Do I Do on Monday Morning?"**

Considerations About Large-Scale Assessments for Classroom Teachers

Large-scale testing at the state and national levels has become a very real factor in many classrooms. Decisions about school funding, programs, and teacher salaries often are tied to students' performance on these measures. Such high-stakes testing brings out behaviors in many educators that perhaps would not occur otherwise. Some of these behaviors, such as teaching test-taking skills, checking answer sheets to make certain students have filled them out correctly, and attempting to increase student motivation to do their best on the test, are ethical. Other behaviors, such as teaching to the test, making certain low achievers are absent on the day of the test, and telling the students the test items before they take the test, are clearly unethical (Haladyna, Nolen, & Haas, 1991; M. L. Smith, 1991a, 1991b). Since teachers are powerful figures in students' social learning, observing a teacher resorting to unethical practices sends a powerful message that cheating is OK and that any means of beating the system is legitimate.

What follows are the most common concerns teachers have about national testing (Haney, 1991; Perrone, 1991):

- It puts unneeded pressure on students.
- Too much class time is spent preparing students for tests and administering them.
- The tests place too much emphasis on a specific curriculum.
- Since test scores correlate with the socioeconomic status of the students, most testing guarantees that schools serving the least advantaged students will be criticized one more time.
- These tests may have unintended motivational effects. They are more likely to undermine students' effort than to increase their academic motivation (Paris, Lawton, Turner, & Roth, 1991). In addition, teachers who consistently receive negative feedback may start to feel helpless and no longer even try to improve their teaching (see also Chapter 2).
- The resources being used to develop assessments could be used to develop more effective instruction. After all, the goal of school is to teach children well, not to test them well.

Dynamic Assessment (Learning Potential Assessment)

Because traditional intelligence tests such as those described in Chapter 13 tend to measure skills and knowledge already acquired, they may underestimate the competencies of many children. In essence, these tests measure static intelligence. Not everyone, however, has equal opportunity to acquire the skills and knowledge that these measures test. For example, children living in poverty do not have the same opportunities for exposure to the type of information tapped on IQ tests as other children do (Budoff, 1987).

Intelligence researchers such as Milton Budoff (Budoff & Friedman, 1964) have argued that a fairer test of intelligence would be dynamic and would measure speed of learning more directly. High intelligence would be defined as being able to benefit from experience readily, and low intelligence would be reflected by the inability to benefit from environmental experiences. In this general approach to dynamic assessment, students are tested, taught, and then retested. For example, a student might be given a mathematical word problem to solve. After failing to solve it, the student would receive instruction in problem solving. Then the student would be retested on the problem. If the student benefits from the short period of training, the inference is made that the student profits from experience.

Budoff and Friedman (1964) demonstrated that students with mental retardation benefited from the training they provided. Regardless of IQ score, however, some students benefit more from training than other students do. In addition, those who gain the most from training achieve at a higher level in school than low gainers do (Babad & Budoff, 1974; Budoff, Gimon, & Corman, 1974). In general, susceptibility to instruction, which is what learning potential is, predicts academic achievement.

Intelligence theorists working in other cultures have also explored dynamic assessment. Feuerstein (1979) found that posttraining performance of socioculturally deprived Israeli children often approaches the level of performance of mainstream children (Rand & Kaniel, 1987). This supports the claim that static measures of intelligence underestimate the competencies of socioculturally deprived populations. Moreover, Feuerstein and colleagues (Tzuriel & Feuerstein, 1992) contend that children who initially test poorly can improve dramatically if given intense, responsive teaching that emphasizes strategies and principles.

A great deal of work needs to be done before firm claims can be made about the value of dynamic assessment. First, little attention has been given to issues of reliability in dynamic assessment (Laughton, 1990; M. Samuels, Tzuriel, & Malloy-Miller, 1989). Second, more work needs to be done on the predictive validity of dynamic assessment relative to conventional assessment. One of the reasons traditional intelligence tests have endured is that they do have predictive validity in that they predict well who will succeed in school. Any alternative measure should have equal or greater predictive validity.

There is some evidence, however, that dynamic measures are better predictors of achievement than static measures. For example, Luther and Wyatt (1989) reported that dynamic assessments predicted the school success of students who speak English as a second language better than traditional IQ scores. In another study, dynamic assessments predicted better than conventional intelligence tests which preschool handicapped students would do well enough in school so that two years later they would be in regular classrooms rather than in special education placements (M. Samuels, Killip, MacKenzie, & Fagan, 1992). Guthke and Wingenfeld (1992) reported that among disadvantaged children in particular, dynamic assessments did a better job of predicting academic achievement longitudinally than static tests. Why might dynamic measures be better assessments than static measures? One possibility is that the intense social interaction between tester and the person being assessed during dynamic assessment might permit more complete understanding of how students process information (Delclos, Burns, & Kulewicz, 1987; Tzuriel & Haywood, 1992). Also, the tester-examinee interactions can provide insight into the emotional difficulties that might interfere with academic achievement; the degree to which students organize, plan, and are flexible in their processing of academic content; and problems with students' motivations that might dampen academic performances (P. Barr & Samuels, 1988; Kaniel & Tzuriel, 1992; M. Samuels, Lamb, & Oberholtzer, 1992).

Dynamic assessment is also appealing to those who believe that disadvantaged

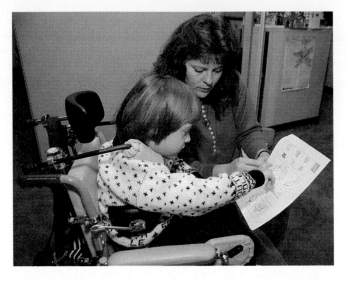

In dynamic assessment, the intense social interaction between tester and student allows more complete understanding of the student's information processing.

students are discriminated against by conventional assessments and that these conventional assessments are biased. For example, some of those fighting legal battles to prevent standardized assessment from being used to assign minority children to special education view dynamic assessment as potentially fairer to minority children, permitting more certain identification of students who would benefit from particular types of educational interventions (Elliott, 1992; Utley, Haywood, & Masters, 1992).

Dynamic assessment also could be used to facilitate instruction. The assessor could try a variety of teaching methods during the teaching phase of the test-teach-retest cycle, until he or she zeroes in on the methods that work with a particular student. If dynamic assessors can succeed in reliably identifying methods that work for some students but not others, this would be a tremendous accomplishment (Utley, Haywood, & Masters, 1992).

Curriculum-Based Assessment

Most of the assessments detailed in Chapter 13 and this chapter involve tasks and materials not typically found in actual classrooms. Therefore, it is not surprising that these assessments often are not helpful in instructional decision making. In contrast, curriculum-based assessment uses materials that are classroom authentic and generates recommendations relevant to the curriculum that the student is experiencing. There are four different models of curriculum-based assessment (Deno, 1987; Shinn, Rosenfeld, & Knutson, 1989).

1. *Curriculum-based assessment for curriculum design.* In this model, the key is to test students to find out where they are in the curriculum and to determine which tasks they can do with little challenge, which they can do only with hesitation or with assistance, and which are completely beyond them (Gickling, Shane, & Croskery, 1989). For example, students are in the appropriate reading level if they can do the skill and drill exercises for the level with 70 to 85 percent correct responses and recognize 93 to 97 percent of the words in the reading. These levels of correctness permit a student to do well much of the time, although there is still some learning required of the student to master the level.

The assessments to determine level of placement are constructed from course materials. Once the initial placement is made, based on determining which part of the curriculum offers optimum challenge, there is ongoing assessment to determine whether the student is making progress. If the student masters the current level, he or she moves on in the curriculum. If not, the teacher considers alternative instruction. In short, the assessment is for instructional planning. Because the assessment is grounded in the curriculum for which the student is accountable and because the focus is on whether and how the student can learn, it is a form of dynamic assessment (Haywood, Tzuriel, & Vaught, 1992.)

2. *Curriculum-based measurement.* This approach involves assessing students continuously with respect to a long-term goal (Deno, 1986; Fuchs & Fuchs, 1990). For example, suppose the goal is for a student to be able to read at a second-grade, second-semester level in a year. Throughout the intervention, the teacher measures the student's reading of second-grade, second-semester materials, perhaps including responses to comprehension questions, ability to retell what has been read, and oral fluency. The teacher often graphs the student's progress so that the student can have visual evidence of improvement when it occurs. If improvement is not occurring, it is a signal to the teacher to make some changes in the instruction. The goal is for the student to be able to perform capably in the future the tasks that are frustrating today.

3. *Criterion-referenced models (also known as the mastery learning approach).* In this approach, students are tested on the content that they are learning, with large chunks of content often broken down into smaller units (Fuchs & Fuchs, 1990). If the students meet some predetermined criterion for a unit test (e.g., 80 percent of the comprehension questions correct), they can move on in the curriculum to the next unit. If the students fall below the criterion on the mastery test, there is additional teaching and retesting.

4. *Curriculum-based evaluation.* Those favoring this approach (Howell & More-head, 1987) emphasize breaking tasks down into their subskills. During the initial assessment, students are asked to perform a certain task for the assessor. Analysis of the students' errors generates hypotheses about what students might be doing wrong while working the problems. Assessments are then designed that tap the presumed problems a student is experiencing. For example, for the task of subtraction of multidigit numbers, errors may reveal that a student cannot regroup during subtraction. The student's performance on problems requiring regrouping might then be compared to otherwise similar problems that do not require regrouping. Finally, the teacher plans appropriate instruction to remediate the student's shortcomings.

In summary, curriculum-based assessment is actually a family of procedures that have certain similarities. The assessments are based on the curriculum and are used to plan instruction. They also tend to be brief and inexpensive. All of these approaches are sensitive to students' improvement, and when students fail to improve, it is a signal that there is a need for change in instruction or, at least, for additional instruction. In general, the evidence is growing that students progress more if they experience curriculum-based assessment as an integral part of instruction than if they do not (Deno & Fuchs, 1987; Fuchs, Fuchs, & Maxwell, 1988; Marston & Magnusson, 1985).

Unlike standardized assessments, curriculum-based assessment is tied to actual classroom curricula. Thus, these assessments are content valid. Unfortunately, other reliability and validity issues have been neglected in the development of curriculum-based measurements.

Biologically Based Assessments

Scientific exploration of the brain and its relationship to intelligence and other psychological functions has expanded enormously with the development of new technologies and has led to the development of biologically based assessments of academic competence. Increasingly, educators are becoming aware of the connections between biology, particularly brain functioning, and intelligence. It is likely that biological assessment procedures will become more influential in classrooms in the future.

Brain researchers make an important distinction between *structure* and *function*. A diagnosis of a brain disorder or injury includes information about the parts of the brain involved (i.e., brain structure) and the processing (i.e., functioning) that is disrupted. There is not a one-to-one relationship, however, between brain structures and functions. Often, especially in young children, functions normally accomplished by one structure in the brain sometimes can be taken up by another region of the brain.

Neuropsychological Test Batteries

Neuropsychological test batteries are routinely administered to students suspected to have brain injury or to suffer from some serious brain disorders such as language disorders, epilepsy, dyslexia, and short-term memory deficiency (Golden, Zillmer, & Spiers, 1992). Two test batteries originally developed for adults have been adapted for use with children (Sattler, 1992). The Halstead-Reitan Neuropsychological Test Battery (Halstead, 1947) consists of a series of cognitive (e.g., concept formation, expressive and receptive language, memory) and perceptual-motor (e.g., finger tapping, marching, rhythm, tactile form recognition) tests. The Luria-Nebraska Neuropsychological Battery also includes basic cognitive and perceptual-motor tasks as well as others that are recognizably academic tests, such as reading, writing, and arithmetic scales. In addition to these batteries, there are large numbers of neuropsychological tests designed to tap very specific functions (Spreen & Strauss, 1991).

There are many children who require neuropsychological assessments. Some children suffer possible brain damage prenatally (see Chapter 6), whereas others contract disease, experience physical trauma, or are exposed to hazardous environmental agents including some illicit drugs. By examining the patterns of performances on the various subtests, the neuropsychologist often can make credible predictions about brain damage and functioning. Because specific brain injuries and disorders are related to important academic competencies such as reading, writing, calculation, and problem solving (R. A. McCarthy & Warrington, 1990), such knowledge is invaluable in educational planning and it should increase teachers' awareness of the potential limitations of brain-injured students. More importantly, this knowledge should also increase awareness of functions that are unimpaired, including those that teachers might capitalize on to compensate for functions that are dysfunctional. For example, knowing that the ability to read sight words is intact for a child even if the ability to decode using letter-sound rules is missing might be extremely helpful in planning reading instruction for the student.

Imaging the Brain

There have been many technological advances in producing brain images useful for medical diagnosis and research on brain functioning. Although these brain imaging techniques are currently used primarily for research, they have great potential for diagnosing differences in intellectual functioning. One of these new technologies, **positron-emission tomography (PET),** is an important tool in studies of cognitive processing. In PET scans the subject first is either injected with or inhales a substance that emits radiation. When neurons are active, they metabolize glucose; radioactive fluorine (a substance that emits radiation) can bind with one of the products of metabolized glucose that accumulate in the active brain cells. Thus, when a portion of the brain is active after taking in radioactive fluorine, the PET scan detects the radiation being emitted from the active sites. The result is an image that literally glows.

Researchers have found clear correlations between brain activity measured by PET scans and performance on intelligence tests (Haier et al, 1988; Parks et al., 1988). The subjects who performed better on the intelligence measures metabolized less glucose. This means that smarter subjects needed to exert less intellectual effort to do the items on the tests. Studies using PET scans have also established which parts of the brain are affected by listening to complex auditory input, such as a story, and which parts of the brain are affected by various types of dementia (Phelps, Mazziotta, & Huang, 1982; Risberg, 1986; Vernon, 1991).

Another new technology, **magnetic resonance imaging (MRI),** permits exploration of brain structure with higher resolution than that permitted by PET scans. In this method, a person lies in the machine for about 15 minutes, placing his or her brain in strong magnetic fields. Changes in the orientations of atomic nuclei are induced and measured (Churchland & Sejnowski, 1992). The precise measurement provided by MRI permits psychologists to resolve some old debates about intelligence. For example, there have been debates for more than a century about whether brain size correlates with intelligence. Before MRI, brain size could only be determined through primitive means, such as by measuring the girth of the head, and these primitive measurements correlated very little with differences in

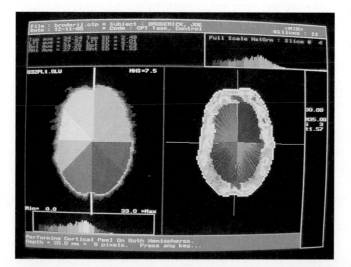

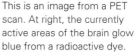
This is an image from a PET scan. At right, the currently active areas of the brain glow blue from a radioactive dye.

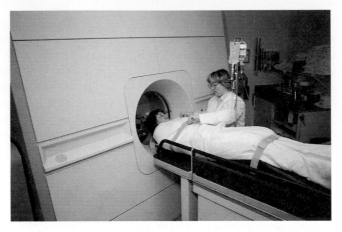

The image produced by the MRI process provides the most accurate measure of brain size currently available.

intelligence. In fact, brain size as measured by MRI correlates moderately (0.41) with measured intelligence (Willerman, Schultz, Rutledge, & Bigler, 1991).

Psychophysiological Measures

Psychophysiological measures are already being used to identify individual differences in basic functioning that may relate to general intellectual functioning. One is a simple form of *choice reaction time.* The subject sits in front of a panel with an array of lights (one, two, four, or eight lights, depending on the particular study). Below each light is a button. At the beginning of the test, the subject's finger is pushing down a home button, which is located at the bottom and center of the array. When one of the lights in the array goes on, the subject is to move as quickly as possible from the home button to the button corresponding to that light. Mean reaction time on this task is moderately correlated (0.40) with intelligence in that people with higher IQ scores react more quickly (Jensen, 1982).

A more complex version of this choice reaction time task involves three lights being illuminated. Two of the lights are closer together than the third "odd-man-out" light. The subject's task is to hit the button under the odd-man-out light. This choice reaction time task produces correlations with intelligence measures in the 0.6 range (Frearson & Eysenck, 1986).

How could being quicker influence intelligence? Jensen's answer (see also Vernon, 1987) is the *neural efficiency theory.* You'll recall that all conscious processing occurs in limited-capacity short-term memory. Slow processes consume more capacity than fast processes do. Thus, those who process more quickly have greater functional capacity, since they can perform more processes given the limited capacity they have.

Other reaction time data corroborate neural efficiency theory by demonstrating correlations between speed of information processing and intelligence measures. For example, there are individual differences in nerve conduction velocity that correlate 0.4 and higher with intelligence measures (Vernon, 1991). More intelligent people also scan their short-term memories more rapidly than less intelligent people (Keating & Bobbitt, 1978; Vernon, 1990). Highly intelligent subjects retrieve information more quickly from long-term memory than those of lower intelligence (Posner, 1969).

There are also important developmental differences in the speed of processing. There is a great increase in processing speed with development (Kail, 1991,

1992). One of the reasons that adults are smarter than children is that they process more quickly. This results in more processing of to-be-learned content given the same amount of time, which results in greater total learning.

Chapter Summary

- Some tests provide information about the promise of individual students based on what they have learned so far. These include conventional intelligence assessments, such as those described in Chapter 13. Individual differences, however, are assessed in different ways for other purposes, and a number of alternative measurement approaches are considered in this chapter.
- Some assessments, such as the NAEP and statewide assessments, are designed to measure the achievement of individual students as well as to summarize how well schools are educating their students. National and state assessment programs are increasingly attempting to capture through performance assessment whether students have acquired important processes, such as those needed for reading, writing, and scientific and mathematical problem solving. One specific approach to performance assessment, portfolio assessment, uses collections of objects to make inferences about students' expertise.
- Some tests provide information about differences in students' susceptibility to instruction and different types of instruction. Both dynamic assessments and curriculum-based assessments are suited to this purpose.
- Technological advances are illuminating the biological foundations of human competence. For instance, new brain imaging techniques such as MRI and PET scans directly measure the relationship of brain size and brain activity with intelligence. There are also psychophysiological indicators pointing to individual differences in the efficiency of basic information processing, which are related to general intelligence. Moreover, there are developmental differences in the speed of processing; specifically, children process more slowly than adults.

Return to the Classroom Predicament

Has reading this chapter helped you decide how the teacher should respond to the concerns about large-scale, high-stakes assessment raised by the parents in the scenario described at the beginning of the chapter? Although the test is primarily multiple choice, the teacher could assure the parents that some of the test questions do assess the processes their children use to solve problems. The teacher could then describe a specific example of performance assessment used in the test. The teacher could also remind the parents that the test results provide information about effective instruction, which has potential benefits for all students. If the state also uses portfolio assessment, the teacher could inform the parents that the state is collecting samples of their children's work as an additional source of evaluation. In response to the parents' question about alternative measures, the teacher could also describe dynamic assessment and curriculum-based assessment. The teacher should caution the parents that many of the alternative measures take even more time from classroom activities, cost even more money, and have not been systematically evaluated for reliability and validity.

Chapter Outline

Chapter 15

Teacher-Designed Assessments: Traditional and Alternative

Classroom Predicament

A classroom teacher planning a test thinks about the following issues: "Why am I giving this test? There are a number of possible reasons to test students. Do I want to be able to determine who in the class is doing the best? Do I want to see whether the students have learned what I set out to teach them? Do I just want feedback for the students on what they know and what we still need to work on? I know I want to be sure this test addresses all the ideas I want the students to learn, but what kind of questions should I ask to make sure they understand the ideas? I want to see whether they have acquired the basic facts, but I also want to make sure they can apply their knowledge. Also, I have to consider how much time I have to grade these tests. Can I do a good job with the amount of time I have available? Sometimes classroom tests just don't seem to give me enough information about my students' competencies. Are there any other methods I can use to assess my students' understandings?"

What recommendations would you make to this teacher? Reflecting on the information presented in this chapter will help you formulate responses to this question.

How does a teacher assess students' understanding of concepts taught in the classroom? In your career as a student, you have encountered many different types of classroom tests. You most certainly have taken essay examinations, multiple-choice tests, and a mixture of both, with maybe even a few true/false, matching, and completion items thrown in the question mix. Some of your teachers may have even used alternative methods other than the traditional paper-and-pencil tests to assess your acquisition of course content. Perhaps in speech class or a computer skills class you exhibited your acquisition of skills through performance tests. For example, you may have given a persuasive speech or keyboarded a letter. Perhaps you collected samples of your work in an art class or English composition class into an educational portfolio.

Assessment plays many roles in the learning process, including providing feedback to students on their progress, offering students an opportunity to demonstrate what they have learned, providing teachers an analysis of what students haven't learned, serving as a concrete referent of accountability to parents and principals, and preparing students for the types of national and state assessments described in Chapters 13 and 14. In this chapter, we begin with probably the most important question teachers ask themselves: "What do I want to measure?" We describe the variety of instructional objectives a teacher may hold. We then analyze the strengths and weaknesses of both traditional and alternative methods of student assessment in the classroom. There is no formula, recipe, or step-by-step procedure for student assessment; instead there are only guidelines and recommendations upon which teachers can base their own decisions. Finally, we conclude the chapter with a discussion of some key considerations in grading practices.

Purpose of Classroom Assessment

One critical testing decision is whether the test is norm-referenced or criterion-referenced. In **norm-referenced tests,** a student's performance is compared to the performance of other students in the class (Airasian, 1994). A high grade means a student performed better than his or her classmates; a low grade means a student performed relatively worse than his or her classmates. How well a student does in terms of mastering the content doesn't matter. What matters is how the student does in comparison to the rest of the class. Even if a student earns only half of the points on the test, if this was the highest score in the class, then the student receives a high grade. Sometimes a norm-referenced approach to grading is called "grading on a curve." This means that teachers decide the percentage of students who can receive each possible grade. Norm-referenced tests are appropriate in certain situations. For example, tests that measure students' achievement for the purpose of evaluating local standing in comparison to a state or national norm are appropriately norm-referenced tests (see Chapters 13 and 14). A norm-referenced test also makes sense if the instructional goal is to select a few students from a large pool such as in officer's training courses or in training courses for other high-level positions. In these cases, the purpose of the norm-referenced test is to predict future success.

In contrast, **criterion-referenced tests** compare students' performance to a predefined performance standard of what should be learned. Each student is graded on the basis of his or her performance relative to the standard, regardless of the performances of other students. Sometimes the performance standard spells out in detail what specific behaviors must be accomplished to receive a particular grade. At other times performance standards are specified in terms of cutoff scores based on the percentage of items answered correctly. For example, a 50 percent score on a test, even if it is the highest score in the class, may still represent a failure if the passing criterion is set at 75 percent. A criterion-referenced test makes sense if the instructional goal is to assess students' acquisition of the subject content in comparison to a legitimate standard. Licensure tests, such as those devised for assessing minimal competency in prospective teachers, are criterion-referenced tests.

Tests can also be classified in terms of whether they are formative or summative. **Formative evaluation** serves as a check on students' progress during instruction, providing feedback to students on how much they know and to teachers on what students need to review. Administration of formative tests, such as practice tests, is often informal, with students sometimes grading their own papers. In contrast, **summative evaluation** is a formal evaluation of what students have learned and is an important component of grade assignment. Teachers often use both formats. For example, formative evaluations give both students and teachers information to use for future instruction and studying, which is likely to improve students' subsequent performance on a summative evaluation.

■ Building Your Expertise

Tests and Motivation

How do norm-referenced and criterion-referenced tests influence students' motivation (see Chapter 2)? In norm-referenced tests, an individual score is interpreted by comparing it to the scores of others. Since one student's success decreases other students' chances for success, norm-referenced grading encourages a competitive classroom environment. Competition fosters **ego involvement** and a *performance orientation* in students (Ames & Ames, 1981; Nicholls, 1989; see also Chapter 2). Students who are ego-involved feel successful only by comparing themselves to others. Performance-oriented students focus on doing well rather than on how much they have learned. Since not all students can do well and come out on top of the grading curve, norm-referenced test feedback can undermine the learning and effort of students who continually score in the bottom of the class.

On the other hand, in criterion-referenced tests, individual scores are interpreted by comparing them to a specified standard or learning goal. Use of criterion-reference tests may foster **task involvement** and a *mastery orientation* in students (Ames & Ames, 1981; Nicholls, 1989; and see Chapter 2). Students who are task-involved concentrate on personal improvement. Mastery-oriented students focus on mastering the material presented in class. Feedback from criterion-referenced tests provides these students information to use in directing their efforts toward increasing their abilities.

Thinking back to your own classroom experiences, which testing situation has promoted better learning for you? Although some students enjoy competition (usually the ones who consistently win the competition), testing situations that promote mastery orientation facilitate lifelong learning.

Instructional Objectives

Assessment is an integral part of teaching and should be matched to instruction. One way to do this is to make sure that tests are tied to instructional goals or objectives. How does a teacher decide what to put on a test? The first step is made when the teacher considers the following questions: "What am I planning to teach? What is it that I want my students to know or be able to do when we finish this unit?" **Instructional objectives** are simple statements of desired student change that indicate the behaviors and skills students should exhibit after instruction (Ory & Ryan, 1993). For example, one instructional objective for this chapter might be that students will be able to articulate the differences between norm-referenced and criterion-referenced testing. Another instructional objective might be that when given a classroom situation, students will be able to determine whether the teacher is using a norm-referenced or a criterion-referenced approach. Teachers plan their instructional objectives before they begin to teach. The objectives guide instruction and the design of appropriate classroom assessment after instruction.

Objectives can describe different levels of learning. One classification scheme of educational objectives was developed by Bloom and his colleagues. In this taxonomy, learning is viewed as a hierarchy in that students can only get to the top of the hierarchy by completing the lower levels. The six levels in what has become known as Bloom's taxonomy (B. S. Bloom, 1986) begin with simple knowledge and increase in complexity.

1. *Knowledge.* The ability to know specific facts, common terms, basic concepts, principles, and theories. Examples:
   - Students can identify the characteristics of a sphere.
   - Students can list the qualities of a short story.
2. *Comprehension.* The ability to understand, to explain, and to interpret. Examples:
   - Students can interpret a graph showing supply and demand.
   - Students can explain the method used to compute a correlation.
3. *Application.* The ability to apply facts and concepts to new situations and to solve problems. Examples:
   - Students can construct a graph showing a distribution of test scores.
   - Students can apply principles of reinforcement to a classroom situation.
4. *Analysis.* The ability to break down a situation into its component parts, to distinguish between facts and inferences, and to identify the organizational structure of the whole. Examples:
   - Students can identify the organization of a persuasive essay.
   - Students can identify the flaw in a geometry proof.
5. *Synthesis.* The ability to integrate many ideas into a solution, a conclusion, or a generalization. Examples:
   - Students can create a well-organized theme.
   - Students can propose an idea for an experiment.
6. *Evaluation.* The ability to judge the quality of something based on criteria and standards. Examples:
   - Students can critique a piece of art.
   - Students can evaluate the validity of a conclusion based on data.

Traditional Classroom Assessment Techniques

Traditional classroom assessments are usually paper-and-pencil examinations that test knowledge of course content. Typical kinds of test questions are essay questions, multiple-choice questions, matching items, true/false items, and completion items. What follows are some guidelines for writing test questions that will likely increase the reliability and validity of classroom tests. As you may recall from Chapter 13, reliable tests measure consistently; that is, a test taker would be at about the same relative standing in the group each time the test is administered. Valid tests measure what they are planned to measure.

Essay Questions

Essay questions are designed to assess students' ability to express ideas, to organize ideas, and to integrate knowledge from different domains. Since the wording of essay questions profoundly influences the nature of students' responses, it is important to heed recommendations for writing effective essay questions (Mehrens & Lehmann, 1991; Ory & Ryan, 1993). When writing essay questions, try to use simple, clear, and specific language. This will reduce any ambiguity in the question. Avoid the use of vague and broad question stems such as "Discuss . . ." or "Tell what you know about . . ." Also, avoid the use of wording, such as "List . . ." or "What is . . ." that may encourage students to parrot back factual information. Examples of good stems for essay questions are given in Table 15.1.

Make sure students understand the ground rules of essay tests (Ory & Ryan, 1993). Explain the general criteria for grading the responses. Indicate the point value and an approximate time limit and length of response for each question. This will help students make the best use of the time allowed for the test. Avoid the use of optional questions. On the one hand, some students may spend too much of their limited time trying to figure out which essay question is "easier," with the result that the irrelevant characteristic of decisiveness becomes part of what the test is measuring. On the other hand, students who choose to challenge themselves by selecting more difficult or more complex questions might be penalized for their choice. It is generally better to use several short essay questions than one or two questions requiring extended responses.

Scoring of essay responses can be unreliable (Hopkins & Stanley, 1981;

Table 15.1

Examples of Stems for Essay Questions

Educational Objective	Wording of Stem
Application	"Describe a situation in which . . ."
Comparison	"Compare two methods of . . ."
	"Describe similarities and/or differences of . . ."
Analysis	"Explain how . . ."
Integration	"Combine these two theories . . ."
Evaluation	"Evaluate the position taken by . . ."

McDaniel, 1994). Two different graders can score the same essay response quite differently. Even the same grader may rate the same essay differently on two different occasions, and grading is influenced by the quality of the preceding essay. Other influences on essay scoring include the expectations the reader has of the writer's achievement, the writer's penmanship and the sex and race of the writer (C. I. Chase, 1986). Fortunately, there are some recommended techniques that may increase reliability when grading essays (McDaniel, 1994; Ory & Ryan, 1993). If **analytic grading** is used as a method, prepare in advance an outline of a model essay response and assign points to key components of it. Students' responses can then be compared with the model, and points may be awarded for the key components contained in the students' responses. The analytic grading method is especially appropriate for essay questions that focus on specific issues and restrict the nature and length of students' responses. For essay questions that do not restrict students' responses, **holistic grading** may be more appropriate. If this rating method is used, compare the essay response as a whole to some type of general standard of what an "A," "B," or "C" paper is. One way to do this is to review the papers briefly to divide them into three stacks of the best group of papers, the average group of papers, and the poorest group of papers. Then reread each stack, further dividing each into two or three smaller stacks until there are enough stacks to correspond to the teacher's grading scheme.

Teachers must decide how to handle surface features of the essay response such as neatness, handwriting, spelling, and punctuation. How heavily should the surface features of the response be weighted in the grade? Also, a decision must be made about how to deal with inaccuracies in the response. Should actual mistakes be weighted more heavily than missing ideas? It is a common practice of teachers to give both a "content" and a "form" grade to students' essays (Baker, Freeman, & Clayton, 1991). The content grade reflects the accuracy of the ideas in the response; the form grade reflects how well the ideas are expressed (Airasian, 1994; Ory & Ryan, 1993).

There are other essay grading techniques that can increase reliability. For example, grading all the responses to one question first avoids a shift of standards. It also reduces the likelihood of a halo effect in which an exceptional response to the first essay question influences the scoring of the second response on any one test. After reading all the responses to one question, shuffle the papers so they are in a different order when the responses to the next question are read. Grading answers without looking at students' names will limit unintended bias in grading. It is easy to read more into the answer of a strong student than that of a weak student, even if it is unintentional. Grading as many test papers as possible at one sitting makes it easier to keep a grading standard in mind. When this is not possible, read over a few already graded responses before beginning to grade again. When the papers are graded, skim through them once more to verify consistency in grading. If possible, ask a colleague to read a few of the papers to verify the reliability of the grading.

In addition to the difficulties of scoring outlined in the preceding paragraphs, another major weakness with essay tests is that, due to the time required for students to write responses and for teachers to grade them, essay tests sample only a small percentage of instructional material. See Table 15.2 for a brief guide to essay questions.

Table 15.2

A Brief Guide to Essay Questions

Advantages
- Easy and quick to write.
- Allows teacher to judge students' abilities to organize and integrate knowledge.

Disadvantages
- Scoring is time-consuming and difficult.
- Scoring can be biased and unreliable.
- Samples only a few content areas.

Guidelines
- Make the questions simple, specific, and clear.
- State the value and time limit for each question.
- Decide to use either analytic or holistic grading.
- Grade all responses to one question at same time.
- Ignore students' names when grading.

Multiple-Choice Questions

The problem of inadequate coverage of material as well as difficulties in reliably grading essays often leads teachers to develop **objective test questions** such as those in a multiple-choice format. Questions are objective to the degree that evaluation of the responses is less open to different interpretations.

Multiple-choice questions are composed of two parts, the stem and the alternative responses. Typically, the stem presents the problem in a question or incomplete sentence. Sometimes, however, information in other types of formats such as pictures, graphs, and diagrams is included in the multiple-choice question stem. The alternative responses include the correct answer and a number of distractors. The more distractors there are, the less likely students will be able to guess the correct answer. For example, with three distractors, the guessing rate is 1 in 4 (0.25), and with four distractors, the guessing rate is reduced to 1 in 5 (0.20). See Figure 15.1 for an example of a multiple-choice question that uses pictures.

Many multiple-choice questions only ask students to perform low-level reasoning, such as questions requiring students to recognize a definition that was presented in class or in the textbook. (See the first question presented in Table 15.3.) However, teachers can design multiple-choice questions that assess higher-order thinking skills, questions written at higher levels of Bloom's taxonomy. (See the second question presented in Table 15.3.) For instance, multiple-choice questions can require students to compare and contrast, make an inference, analyze an application, make a prediction (cause and effect), and recognize patterns. In some content areas such as mathematics and science, students solve a problem or complete a computation presented in the stem and then choose the correct answer from among the alternatives.

Circle the clock face that shows the time you usually eat lunch at school.

Figure 15.1
An example of a multiple-choice question using pictorial information This question can be read to very young students. Why do you think this multiple-choice question has only three alternatives? Read on to check your reasoning.

Writing Multiple-Choice Questions. The creation of easily understood and useful multiple-choice questions takes time and effort. The following are some tips for writing multiple-choice questions (Haladyna, 1994; Ory & Ryan, 1993).

- Be sure to use simple, clear language. Make the stem as simple as possible. Eliminate wordiness by not repeating words in the alternatives if they can be put in the stem.
- Avoid tricky and ambiguous questions. When in doubt, ask fellow teachers to review your questions.

Table 15.3

Examples of Multiple-Choice Questions That Test Recall and Application

The following multiple-choice question requires students to recognize a definition given earlier in the chapter:
    Individual performance is compared to the performance of others in a
        1. Norm-referenced test
        2. Criterion-referenced test
        3. Formative evaluation
        4. Performance assessment
The following multiple-choice question asks students to apply a definition given earlier in the chapter to a real-life scenario:
    Every year a large business administers a promotion examination to all employees. The employees in the top 10 percent of the test scorers are selected for further consideration for promotion. Those employees in the bottom 10 percent of the test scorers are put on probation, and their job performance is scrutinized closely. The promotion examination is used as a
        1. Norm-referenced test
        2. Criterion-referenced test
        3. Formative evaluation
        4. Performance assessment
Both of these multiple-choice questions assess students' understanding of norm- and criterion-referenced tests, but the first requires only recognition of a definition whereas the second requires students to apply the concept to a real-life situation. (Answers: 1,1)

Table 15.4

Example of Poorly Worded Multiple-Choice Question

Identify the problems in the following multiple-choice question:

Which one of the following is not a recommendation for writing multiple-choice questions?

1. Don't be tricky.
2. Use plausible distractors.
3. Avoid the use of negatives.
4. Common misconceptions are effective distractors and will attract students who know just a little about the tested concept.
5. None of the above.

Some problems you may have noticed:

- The stem is stated negatively, which is especially confusing with negatively stated alternative 1 and alternative 4.
- Alternative 4 is not like the other alternatives in length and grammatical form (and it overlaps with alternative 2).

- Avoid negatively stated stems. If unavoidable, increase the likelihood that students will notice the negative phrasing by using all-capital letters, underlining, or boldface for the word *NOT* in the stem.
- Make sure all distractors are plausible. Common misconceptions are effective distractors. Limit the use of "none of the above" as an alternative. If used, make sure it is sometimes the correct answer so it is a plausible distractor in all cases.
- Make sure all alternative responses are grammatically correct in relation to the stem. Make sure all alternative responses are as similar as possible and are approximately the same length.
- Make sure each question is independent and that one question does not give the answer to another.

Table 15.4 illustrates a poorly worded multiple-choice question.

Clearly worded multiple-choice questions that assess high-level thinking are difficult to write. Table 15.5 offers a brief guide to multiple-choice questions. A team of specialists at professional test preparation organizations may spend their entire workday developing, refining, and perfecting just a handful of questions. It is unlikely that a classroom teacher can sit down one evening at home and generate the number of good multiple-choice questions that are required for a unit test. Just like the professional test makers, teachers need to develop a pool of test questions that they are continually revising based on information obtained from each use. Obviously, teachers need to maintain the security of these test questions. This means that although the students can review the test and their responses in class, the students should not leave the classroom with a copy of the test.

Determining the Effectiveness of Multiple-Choice Questions. How can teachers determine when a question needs to be revised? How do they determine whether a question is working well? One way is through a procedure called item analysis. The purpose of **item analysis** is to determine item difficulty, to test for item discrimination, and to analyze distractors. There are commercially available soft-

Table 15.5

A Brief Guide to Multiple-Choice Questions

Advantages
- Scoring is efficient, reliable, and objective.
- Samples a wide range of course content.

Disadvantages
- Difficult and time-consuming to write.

Guidelines
- Test for major ideas.
- Don't be tricky.
- Write simply.
- Avoid negatives.
- Make distractors as plausible and as similar as possible.
- Conduct an item analysis to guide revision.

ware programs that perform item analysis quickly and easily. In addition, there are low-cost scanners that schools can purchase to score and tally students' responses on answer sheets. Even without these tools, classroom teachers can perform a rudimentary item analysis by hand. Table 15.6 provides an analysis of test items.

One important test item characteristic determined through item analysis is **item difficulty.** One way to determine item difficulty is to compute the percentage of students who answered an item correctly. What is considered "good" item difficulty? There's no simple answer to this question, since it depends on the goals of the teacher using the test. Obviously, an item difficulty of 0.10 indicates that an item is very difficult since only 10 percent of the students selected the right response. Likewise, an item difficulty of 0.90 indicates that an item is very easy since 90 percent of the students selected the correct response. If a test is norm-referenced, the goal is to have items fall somewhere in the middle, ones that are neither too easy nor too hard. If a test is criterion-referenced, the difficulty of items can range widely. It might be appropriate for all of the students to get some items correct and all of them to miss a few. Many of the items on a criterion-referenced test, however, should have a difficulty level of 0.80 and higher.

Another important test item characteristic determined through item analysis is item discrimination. **Item discrimination** refers to the ability of a test question to distinguish between more and less knowledgeable students. That is, the students who scored the highest on the test should answer an item correctly, and the students who scored the lowest on the test should answer an item incorrectly. The following paragraph explains a procedure that teachers can use to compute item discrimination (Hopkins & Stanley, 1981; Popham, 1995).

First, order the tests from high to low by total score. Then, beginning from the top, divide the tests into four groups, each with equal numbers of papers. For each test item, compute the percentage of students in the top quarter of papers and the percentage of students in the bottom quarter of papers who got the item correct.

Subtract the percentage of students in the upper quarter who got the item correct from that of those in the lower quarter who got the item correct.

(Percentage correct from students in upper quarter) − (percentage correct from students in lower quarter)

For example, if 90 percent of the students in the top quarter of performers on the test answered item 1 correctly and 20 percent of the students in the bottom quarter of performers on the test answered item 1 correctly, then the item discrimination would be 0.70. This would mean that the test question successfully discriminates high performers from low performers. Any test item with a discrimination index of 0.40 or higher discriminates very well between the students who did well on the entire test and those students who did not do well on the entire test. On the other hand, if 25 percent of the students in the top quarter and 20 percent of students in the bottom quarter answered item 1 correctly, then the item discrimination index would be 0.05. This would mean that the question does not discriminate high performers from low performers and accordingly should be revised. Finally, if 20 percent of the students in the top quarter and 70 percent of the students in the bottom quarter answered item 1 correctly, then the item discrimination index would be

Table 15.6

Analysis of Test Items

Analyze the following information obtained from an item analysis:
- Question 1, correct response is A.
  - A. Item difficulty (0.50); item discrimination (0.60)
  - B. Twenty percent selected, tended to be low performers
  - C. Ten percent selected, tended to be low performers
  - D. Twenty percent selected, tended to be low performers

Question 1 is fairly difficult (half of the students answered it correctly), but this may be an appropriate difficulty level, especially if this is a question on a norm-referenced test. The discriminability of this item is fairly high. All of the distractors are attracting some students, mainly low performers.
- Question 2, correct response is C.
  - A. Sixty percent selected, both high and low performers
  - B. Five percent selected, tended to be low performers
  - C. Item difficulty (0.30); item discrimination (0.10)
  - D. Five percent selected, tended to be low performers

Twice as many students selected incorrect option A than selected correct option C. Selection of option C does not discriminate well between high and low performers. Check to see whether option A is also a correct answer.
- Question 3, correct response is A.
  - A. Item difficulty (0.95); item discrimination (0.05)
  - B. Three percent selected, tended to be low performers
  - C. Two percent selected, tended to be low performers
  - D. No one selected

Almost all of the students selected the correct option A, so this is an easy item. If this question is on a norm-referenced test, it should be revised to be more discriminating. Also, make distractor D more attractive so some students, hopefully low performers, select it. On a criterion-referenced test, the question can remain as is.

−0.50. This would mean that although low performers are discriminated from high performers, the item is easier for the low performers. Items with negative discrimination indices should be revised after checking to make sure the item is not simply keyed incorrectly. It is important to keep in mind that item discrimination is related to item difficulty in that questions that are either very easy or very difficult will not discriminate between low performers and high performers.

Another question to ask about any multiple-choice item is whether or not the distractors are working as planned. In **item distractor analysis,** the teacher evaluates whether any one distractor is selected consistently by high performers on the test. If one is, check the distractor for possible correctness, and revise the item. If a distractor is not selected by any students, it should be revised or replaced.

Another way to find out how well test items are working is simply to ask students. Teachers can learn why a distractor attracted many students by asking the students when the class is reviewing the test what they were thinking when they chose that answer. Teachers may also allow students to earn extra points by handing in reasonable written arguments for why they chose the distractor and not the correct answer. These arguments are not only good opportunities for students to display what they do know, but they also have the potential for reducing students' frustration and for providing insight into how the test item is working. Requiring that the arguments be written (and the points well supported) reduces the number of frivolous gripes from students.

Matching Items

In matching items (Mehrens & Lehmann, 1991; Ory & Ryan, 1993), another type of objective test question, students match a list of premises (usually words or phrases in a column on the left) with a list of responses (words or phrases in a column on the right). Students need directions about the basis on which to match the premises with the responses. They also need to know whether some responses can be used more than once. Matching items are a reliable, objective, and efficient way to assess certain kinds of factual knowledge (e.g., persons and their accomplishments, dates and historical events, categories and examples), but they cannot be applied widely to other types of knowledge. Following are some recommendations for writing matching items that will reduce search time for the students and the likelihood of guessing:

- Put the responses and premises in a logical order, such as alphabetical or chronological.
- Do not have more than 10 or 12 responses or premises.
- Provide more premises than responses.

True/False Items

In another type of objective test question, the true/false item, the student decides whether a declarative statement is true or false (right or wrong, yes or no). Following are some general guidelines for writing true/false items (Mehrens & Lehmann, 1991; Ory & Ryan, 1993):

- Keep the language simple.
- Make sure there is only one idea per question.
- State the item positively when possible.
- Keep the number of true responses and the number of false responses approximately equal.

- Avoid the use of specific determiners, words such as *always, never,* or *every,* which hint that the item is false since few things in life are absolute.

The main advantages of true/false items are that they are fairly easy to write, are easy to score, and can sample a lot of course material efficiently (Ory & Ryan, 1993). This question format can be particularly useful in formative pop quizzes. The overwhelming disadvantage is that since few general principles are always true or false, teachers are more likely to focus true/false items on detailed low-level facts. In addition, there is a 50 percent guessing rate, so a true/false test may not be measuring what students know as much as how lucky they are at guessing. Sometimes teachers ask students to write down why the item is false, but then the true/false item becomes more difficult and time-consuming to score.

Completion, or Fill-in-the-Blank, Items

Completion, or fill-in-the-blank, items require students to supply a word, a phrase, or even a complete sentence in response to a short question or an incomplete statement (one with a blank). Some teachers use completion items to test vocabulary knowledge or in formative quizzes to generate good multiple-choice distractors for the summative evaluation. Definite and brief correct responses make completion items easy to score reliably. Unfortunately, as is the case with true/false items, this also means completion items often only tap low-level ideas.

Following are some recommendations for writing completion items (Airasian, 1994):

- Use only one blank per item, preferably at end of sentence.
- Make blanks the same length so size does not suggest length of correct response.

Stages in Test Preparation and Administration

The first stage in test preparation is the determination of the *purpose* of the test. What content will be tested? What kinds of performance do students need to display? How closely does the test match the instructional objectives? Is this a formative or summative examination? Is this test norm-referenced or criterion-referenced?

The next stage is the *selection and preparation* of test questions. What type of test question taps the information or skills desired? A test blueprint of some type can guide these decisions. One strategy is to prepare a **table of specifications.** The table of specifications is a concise way to represent the content of instruction, the types of cognitive performance expected from students, and the number and type of questions expected to elicit such performance. For example, the table of specifications shown in Table 15.7 lists the content areas down the left side and expected cognitive performance, using Bloom's taxonomy, across the top. This table should reflect the weight and importance of course content and should provide an estimate of content validity. Sharing the table of specifications with students allows them to know what is expected of them on the test, which can guide their study time.

How many total test questions are needed? The test needs to have enough items to be reliable but not to have so many questions that students run out of time to answer. How should the test questions be arranged? Some suggestions are to begin the test with easy items, to group together items that have similar content, to

Table 15.7

Sample Table of Specifications

Taxonomy of Objectives

Course Content	Knowledge	Comprehension	Application	Analysis	Synthesis	Evaluation
Purposes of classroom tests		2 multiple-choice questions				1 essay question
Characteristics of essay questions			2 multiple-choice questions	1 essay question		
Characteristics of multiple-choice questions			2 multiple-choice questions	1 essay question		
Characteristics of matching items		1 multiple-choice question	1 multiple-choice question			
Characteristics of true/false items		1 multiple-choice question	1 multiple-choice question			
Characteristics of completion items		1 multiple-choice question	1 multiple-choice question			

group together items by question type, and to place the more time-consuming items at the end (Ory & Ryan, 1993).

The next stage is test *administration*. Be sure to eliminate potential distractions to the students by placing a sign on the outside of the classroom door indicating, "Test in Progress." Make sure students are aware of the test directions, including the time allotted for the test, how to record answers, whether or not to show work, point totals for each question, whether or not there are penalties for guessing, and whether supporting materials such as notes or calculators can be used.

Another important component of test administration is reducing the likelihood and opportunity for cheating (Airasian, 1994). Some strategies to use before testing include announcing the test ahead of time and informing the students of the general nature and content of the test so students can adequately prepare without resorting to cheating. Strategies during testing include monitoring students' behaviors, making sure all books and papers are out of students' reach, arranging seating so students cannot easily look on each others' test papers, forbidding sharing of materials such as erasers and calculators, and using alternative test forms. Students should be aware of the consequences for being caught cheating, and these rules must be consistently enforced.

During the *scoring* of the examinations, make every attempt to score objectively (without bias) and reliably (consistently). This is easy for objective tests and may be approximated for essay tests if suggestions described earlier are followed.

Then, give *feedback* to the students. For norm-referenced tests, show the students where they fit in the class distribution. For criterion-referenced tests, show the students how close they are to meeting the passing (or A level, B level, etc.) criterion. Talk to students about the questions they have missed so they know what they need to review. Make the test a learning experience.

Finally, *revise* the test after each administration. Item analysis and comments from students should guide each revision.

Summarizing Test Scores

What can a teacher do to summarize a class's performance on a test? One way is to create a **frequency distribution** of the test scores. To create a frequency distribution, list every score and the number of times that score appeared in the distribution of scores, as shown in Table 15.8. If there are a large number of scores, it is

Table 15.8

Creation of a Frequency Distributions

Thirty students received the following scores on a 20-item spelling test:

Student	Score	Student	Score
Chris	19	Cruz	16
Mike	9	Aaron	14
Lauren	14	Mary Beth	12
Jessica	13	Carla	18
Art	16	Antonio	15
Tawna	17	Marie	12
John	8	Sharon	11
Anita	18	Will	17
Malcolm	12	Shelby	15
Sabina	15	Marcus	13
Kim	13	Rachel	14
Darryle	17	Taji	17
Heather	16	Dylan	15
Sammi	14	Sophie	15
Kim	14	Huynh	14

A frequency distribution of these scores would look like this:

Score	Frequency
20	—
19	1
18	2
17	4
16	3
15	5
14	6
13	3
12	3
11	1
10	—
8	1
9	1

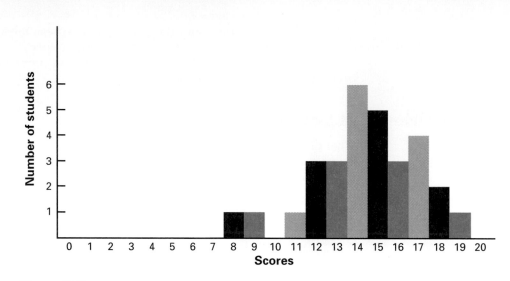

Figure 15.2

A histogram corresponding to the frequency distribution shown in Table 15.8.

often useful to group the scores in a way that makes sense (e.g., five-point intervals or grade ranges). The information from a frequency distribution can be displayed graphically in a **histogram.** In a histogram (or bar graph), the frequencies of the scores are represented by bars, as shown in Figure 15.2.

The mean, the measure of central tendency introduced in Chapter 13, can also help characterize students' performance. For the distribution of scores shown in Figure 15.3, the mean (the sum of the scores divided by the number of scores) is 433/30 = 14.43.

Distributions of scores on a test can approximate different shapes when displayed graphically. When the majority of students score in the middle of the distribution and approximately equal numbers of students score very high and very low, the class distribution approximates a **normal distribution,** the bell-shaped curve, described in Chapter 13. When a test is difficult, many students have low scores and the distribution is *positively skewed* as shown in Figure 15.3(*a*). The "tail" of a posi-

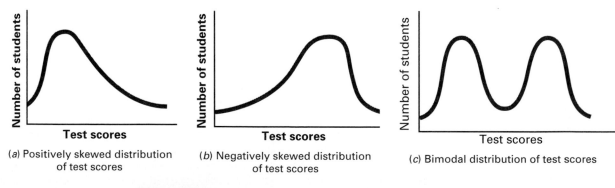

(*a*) Positively skewed distribution of test scores

(*b*) Negatively skewed distribution of test scores

(*c*) Bimodal distribution of test scores

Figure 15.3

Positively skewed (*a*), negatively skewed (*b*), and bimodal (*c*) distributions.

tively skewed distribution points to the right. (In this and following figures, the height of the curve indicates the frequency of scores at that point.) When a test is easy, many students have high scores and the distribution is *negatively skewed* as shown in Figure 15.3(*b*). The "tail" of a negatively skewed distribution points to the left. When a test is easy for half the students and hard for the other half, the distribution is *bimodal* as shown in Figure 15.3(*c*). A bimodal distribution may occur when the class is comprised of two groups with different levels of ability or when some of the students have prior knowledge of the content that has been taught and tested.

Good Test-Taking Skills

Some students are good test takers. Is it possible to teach these test-taking skills? Scruggs and Mastropieri (1992) describe good test-taking skills and how teachers can foster these skills in their students. They outline some general, all-purpose strategies that are useful to any test taker. These are (1) academic preparation strategies, (2) physical preparation strategies, (3) attitude-improving strategies, (4) anxiety-reducing strategies, and (5) motivational strategies.

Academic preparation strategies obviously include the strategies used to study the test material. Good test takers exhibit all the characteristics of good information processors as discussed throughout this textbook. They not only study hard, but they also study smart by using effective study strategies. They understand the material well enough to know what is important and what is peripheral. In addition, there are strategies particularly appropriate for test preparation. Good test takers learn what content is likely to be on the test and what type of questions will appear on the test. This information guides their selection of study strategies. Teachers can help students learn how to ask questions effectively about the test's content and form (Scruggs & Mastropieri, 1992).

The *physical preparation strategies* of good test takers include avoiding pulling all-nighters or cramming just before the test. They begin to study long before the day of the test, and they make sure they are alert on the test day by resting and eating properly beforehand (Scruggs & Mastropieri, 1992).

Good test takers exhibit *attitude-improving strategies*. They do not expect the worst ("I'll never pass."), and they do not have unreasonable expectations ("I'll get an *A* without even trying."). They have not given up ("How I do doesn't matter."). Instead, their attitude is positive, confident but realistic ("I can do well on this test if I pay attention, stay alert, and try my best.") (Scruggs & Mastropieri, 1992).

Good test takers possess *anxiety-reducing strategies*. Many students experience test anxiety occasionally. Perhaps they know they haven't prepared well for an examination, or they learn that a teacher makes a point of giving extremely difficult tests. Other students, however, experience test anxiety consistently. In comparison to other students, test-anxious students are more sensitive to failure, react more to adult evaluation, and are more focused on task-irrelevant thoughts while taking tests (K. T. Hill & Wigfield, 1984). The test performance of these test-anxious students is likely to be an underestimation of their skills and knowledge.

What can teachers do to reduce test anxiety in their students? Some suggestions center around empowering students with learning and metacognitive strategies. Mealy and Host (1988) advocate providing social support for test-anxious students through cooperative learning groups. In the learning groups, test-anxious students are exposed to strategy modeling and benefit from other students' estimations of what is important and what is not and of what is likely to appear on the test.

Scruggs and Mastropieri (1992) distinguish between teachers' comments that are helpful and those that are not. Helpful comments, such as, "You should be proud since you tried hard and used all the test-taking skills we practiced," encourage students to continue their efforts and to adopt effective strategies. Comments that are not helpful, such as, "You need an *A* on this test just to pass the course" or "This test is easy—everyone should do well," increase anxiety and discourage effort.

Scruggs and Mastropieri (1992) also recommend teaching students how to monitor their thinking so they realize when they are "off-task" and thinking of irrelevant things. For example, if students are surprised by something on the test or draw a blank, they can learn to calm themselves through self-instruction (see Chapter 7). Perhaps they learn to say, "OK, this is something I didn't expect. What do I know about this? I'm drawing a blank. OK, calm down. Relax. Take a few deep breaths. Wait, I remember something. Maybe that's the answer. I'll put that down for now and see whether any other question on the test helps me remember more." This internal dialogue is much more productive than the response of test-anxious students who might scream to themselves, "OH NO!! What does this mean? I just don't understand this stuff. I need an *A*! Everyone else seems to know the answer! I'm running out of time!"

Others advocate restructuring the entire climate of school. K. T. Hill and Wigfield (1984) recommended three major courses of action. First, change report cards and grades. To minimize comparisons, evaluate students on both achievement and progress and do not use letter grades until the end of elementary school. Second, change classroom tests. Reduce time pressure in testing and increase the information given about performance expectations during test instructions. Third, teach students how to deal with evaluative pressure. K. T. Hill and Wigfield (1984) described an intensive program in which students practice test taking, learn good test-taking strategies, and experience training designed to increase their motivation.

Motivational strategies are the last component of Scruggs & Mastropieri's (1992) general test-taking strategies. They recommend that teachers increase students' motivation by encouraging appropriate attributions (see Chapter 2). This means encouraging students to attribute success or failure to how well they have or have not applied their learned skills and strategies. Teachers should discourage attributions to forces outside students' control such as luck, difficulty, or bias.

Scruggs and Mastropieri (1992) also suggest specific strategies for taking classroom tests. Students with good test-taking skills *use time effectively*. They pace themselves throughout the test. They answer high-point gainers first and time-consuming items last. On essay tests, they read all the questions first, jotting down some ideas or an outline on how they will answer each question. Then if they run short of time and begin to get anxious, these jotted-down ideas help them remember what they had planned to say. They answer the specific essay questions and don't write down all they know about the general topics. On objective tests, they mark items about which they are uncertain for later review. So, if they begin to run short of time, they know to which items they should return.

Students with good test-taking skills *avoid errors*. They read directions carefully and ask questions if they are uncertain. On problem-solving tests requiring computation, they estimate answers before solving problems. On multiple-choice tests, they think of what the answer might be before looking at the alternative responses. They proof their work, especially when copying responses to answer sheets, and they change answers when they realize they've made a mistake in their reasoning. Many students feel they should never change an answer once they have selected one on multiple-choice tests. They believe they should always stick with their first reaction since they are more likely to notice the questions they changed and got wrong and not the ones they changed and got right. In general, if students have a good reason for changing an answer, then they should do so; otherwise, they should stay with their original response.

On multiple-choice tests, good test takers *eliminate incorrect alternatives*. They use deductive reasoning to figure out the correct response. They are cautious when alternatives use specific determiners such as *always* or *never*, since few things in life are absolute. On tests that penalize for guessing, good test takers *know when to guess*. If they can eliminate one alternative out of four, the likelihood of guessing correctly increases from 0.20 to 0.33. If they can eliminate two alternatives, the guessing rate increases to 0.50.

> ▶ **Diversity**

Developmental Considerations for Designing Tests

The test taker's age is an important consideration for a test's design (Mehrens & Lehmann, 1991). Switching from one kind of format to another on a test may seem to be a way to make the test more interesting and to access different skills, but it is likely to be confusing for young students. Also, since young students read, write, and think slowly and are likely to become restless during test taking, short tests are best for them. In the lower elementary grades, don't exceed 30 minutes; in the upper elementary grades, don't exceed 40 minutes. Tests for junior and senior high students can be as long as 90 minutes. If you are using multiple-choice questions, don't overwhelm young students with too many options. Three options is enough for second graders and younger, as demonstrated in Figure 15.1 presented earlier. Third and fourth graders can handle up to four items. Sixth graders and older can manage five choices.

The testing of older adults also requires special considerations (Hertzog & Schear, 1989). This is an issue of growing importance as more adults go back to school. Since the processing speed of older adults has slowed (see Chapter 6 and Chapter 13), avoid time limits for test taking. Older adults may be out of practice in taking tests, so allow practice with typical test questions and test formats. For example, make sure the older adults are familiar with the computer sheets often used in multiple-choice examinations. Watch for fatigue in older adults, and reduce the possibility of it by breaking up a long test over several sessions. Be aware of possible sensory deficits, since both visual and auditory acuity decrease with age. Therefore, make sure the test instructions are audible and the test materials can be easily read. If you are using norm-referenced tests, make sure the norms are appropriate for older adults, and intentionally select tests that provide life span norms. Finally, make sure the test questions are fair and do not include referents unfamiliar to older adults. In general, the performance of older adults may be assessed more accurately by alternative methods such as performance or portfolio assessment.

Alternative Classroom Assessment Techniques

Many educators report frustration with the disadvantages of the traditional types of assessments described in the first part of this chapter. They often feel that these assessments are not valid. For example, traditional assessments may not measure the instructional objectives selected by the teacher, and they certainly are not closely related to the kinds of performances expected of students outside of school, in the real world. These educators advocate assessments that are authentic. You may recall from Chapter 14 that authentic assessments are more directly linked to the goals of the instruction than the traditional classroom test. One of the most praised authentic assessments is the classroom portfolio.

Portfolios in the Classroom

As introduced in Chapter 14, portfolios are collections of objects collected for an identified purpose (Bird, 1990; A. Collins, 1992). Sometimes the purpose may be to impress prospective employers with competencies, as in an artist's or photographer's portfolio. In a classroom, students may keep a collection of most of their work in a *working portfolio* and at various points in the school year select pieces of work to include for evaluation in an *assessment portfolio.*

Characteristics of Classroom Portfolios. The three essential steps to the construction of an assessment portfolio are the following: Students (1) collect their work over a reasonable period of time; (2) review their work at some point, selecting some "best" work or most representative work for inclusion in the assessment portfolio; and (3) assemble the portfolio, including reflective, integrative commentary about the pieces selected and about the progress shown in their work.

Many teachers believe portfolio construction increases students' ability to reflect on their work, that is, to consider the processes required to produce the work. As an assessment device, it informs teachers about strengths and weaknesses of their instruction and curriculum and provides ongoing assessment of the efforts, progress, and achievements of students.

Having the students select the work to include in the portfolio is critical. The selection process encourages students to begin to take responsibility for their own work and to develop their own standards. They learn evaluation skills through the process of articulating why they have included each piece in their portfolio. These skills become fine-tuned through discussions with peers and teachers about their selections. Selection criteria tend to evolve through such collaborations. These criteria are often multidimensional and encourage different ways to evaluate learning. It is important not to expect students to accept preset teacher criteria on a routine basis. Some questions that will help to guide students' selections of writing pieces in a writing portfolio are (adapted from R. Mitchell, 1992, p. 112):

- Why did you select this particular piece of writing?
- What are the special strengths of this piece?
- What have you learned about writing from your work on this piece?
- If you could continue working on this piece, what would you do?

The pieces in the portfolio are not always the student's best work. Sometimes learning goals are enhanced by the student's analysis of "What I did earlier" in contrast to "What I can do now." This self-reflection and marking of progress encourages the development of goal setting and decision making in students and facilitates the growth of students as lifelong learners.

Assessments of classroom portfolios are provided by a variety of sources in a number of ways. Teachers can develop portfolio review sheets that list the strengths and weaknesses for each student. These sheets reflect the teachers' content knowledge and knowledge of the student. Portfolio review is time-consuming, so it is important for teachers to remind students to limit the number of items included in their portfolios. If teachers maintain a record of features and issues recurring across students' portfolios, they can use this information to inform their instructional practices.

Students and teachers meet in *portfolio conferences.* Teachers allow students to exert some control by asking them to present their portfolios and to articulate the strengths and weaknesses of their work. Together, the students and teachers create goals for the students. Teachers select one or two teaching points to stress during the conference. Typically, conferences last approximately 10 to 15 minutes. Teachers can also organize (and perhaps moderate) similar portfolio conferences between students and their peers and between students and their parents.

Difficulties with Classroom Portfolios. There is very little research directly measuring the impact of classroom portfolios on students' performance. Most published articles focus instead on detailing the grounds for using portfolios, illustrating ideas or models of portfolio construction, or recounting how portfolios were implemented in a particular classroom or school district (Herman & Winters, 1994). One difficulty in using portfolios for classroom assessment is obtaining reliability in portfolio evaluation (Herman & Winters, 1994; see Chapter 14). Reliable evaluation of portfolios is at least as difficult to achieve as reliable scoring of essay responses. Perhaps classroom portfolios function better as formative rather than summative evaluation methods. It is certain, however, that widespread utilization of classroom portfolios will encourage educators to reconsider traditional grading practices.

A second difficulty in using classroom portfolios is that it is more difficult to understand how to apply them to some content areas than others. It is especially difficult to see how portfolios can be used in situations in which instruction is focused on one right answer. Widespread use of classroom portfolios may encourage educators to reconsider instructional practices and goals. Let's consider some specific examples of portfolio use in a variety of content domains. A summary of the kinds of items that can be included in portfolios in various content areas is shown in Table 15.9.

Portfolio Examples for Literacy. Classroom portfolios used in reading and writing instruction vary widely. As part of Hansen's Literacy Portfolios Project in Manchester, New Hampshire, fourth-grade students prepared portfolios to document their literacy. Hansen (1992) believes these portfolios provided students as much opportunity to know themselves and how rich their literacy lives are as they provided opportunity for educators to get to know and understand students and their literacy better.

What might be in a fourth grader's literacy portfolio? Scott's is an example. It includes a drawing; a draft of some writing Scott had published as a "book" in the resource room; a piece of writing from the current year; a list of books he can read; his favorite book, *The Little Engine That Could;* his third-grade report card; a photo of his father; and a photo of grandparents (Hansen, 1992, p. 66). These objects are all critically important to Scott. They represent that he (1) can now draw, write, and

Table 15.9

Examples of Items Found in Portfolios for Selected Content Domains

Reading
- Descriptions of what has been read
- Drawings about what has been read
- Charts of reading
- Audiotapes of reading
- Reading goals
- Analysis of reading related to goals

Writing
- Selected writing pieces (drafts and finished samples)
- Descriptions of selection criteria
- Illustrations for writing
- Responses from writing audience (often peers)
- Writing goals
- Analysis of writing related to goals

Science
- Journal chronicling understandings
- Lab reports
- Observations of science in real world

Math
- Observations of math in real world
- Student-generated word problems
- Explanations of reasoning for problem set
- Analysis of graphic information

Physical Education
- Videotapes of performances of skills
- Charts of acquisition of skills
- Strategies for competition
- Practice journal
- Visualization exercises
- Analysis of team goals
- Newspaper clippings of athletic achievements
- Analysis of own progress and goals

Art
- Own artwork
- Pictures of own artwork
- Works in progress
- Analysis of own progress and goals
- Responses to "art show"
- Analysis of the art of others
- Examples of art encountered outside of school

read, whereas before he could not; (2) can now earn passing grades; and (3) has family members who are dear to him, including a father away from home whom he misses very much.

The purpose of the portfolios is not only to document reading and writing growth of the child but also to be an expression of who the child is, both as a literate person and as a person in a broader sense. Thus, one first-grade student's portfolio includes a book about a character who has trouble speaking, which is important to the child because he has a speech problem, too. One junior high student's portfolio includes a book about a juvenile who had stolen a car, went to prison, and reformed. This book meant something to the young reader because he had been thrown out of a previous school for misconduct and found the story inspirational as he attempted to make good in a new school.

Hansen (1992) and her colleagues believe it important that portfolios capture students' perspectives on their literacy, at least some of the reasons why reading and writing are important to them, and why some books they read and some things they write are more important to them than others. Such a literacy portfolio provides a great deal of information that can be used by new teachers the student will encounter to aid in planning a literacy curriculum that is sensitive to students' needs, concerns, and interests.

Portfolio Examples for Science. Science educators are exploring the use of portfolios in the science classroom. Describing potential fourth-grade science portfolios, A. Collins (1992) classified four types of objects: (1) *Artifacts* include such items as written reports of experiments and tests. (2) *Reproductions* refer to items such as a photo of a bulletin board display created by the student. (3) *Attestations* are appraisals of the student by someone other than the student and his or her teacher. Examples include letters of gratitude for something a student did (e.g., organized an environmental clean-up day) or a note from other members of the students' cooperative learning group praising a particular contribution made by the student. (4) *Productions* are objects prepared especially for inclusion in the portfolio. For example, this type of object might include goal statements from the

This student is sorting through a working portfolio to select items for an assessment portfolio.

teacher about the purpose of the portfolio, reflective statements by the student indicating the importance and relationship of the various documents in the portfolio, and captions attached to each document in the portfolio to describe what the object is and why it is significant.

One fourth-grade science teacher's goal was for students to document that they had acquired balanced science knowledge during the year (A. Collins, 1992). Thus, students were required to include documentation about their learning in the content area they liked best during the year of science instruction, two thinking skills they had mastered, and evidence that they had learned about some topic of public concern. These three categories corresponded to the particular instructional objectives the teacher had for the class during the year, which were to develop in-depth knowledge about a range of topics, to increase thinking skills, and to stimulate awareness of the social relevance of science.

The portfolios could include work sheets from problem-solving activities, diagrams or pictures that had been graded, and products from group work. The number of pieces of evidence was limited, and students were required to develop captions for each exhibit and a reflective statement summarizing how the various exhibits related to one another. The individual students consulted with their teacher about what ought to be included in their portfolios, with the construction of the portfolios viewed as a dynamic experience, permitting review of the year's work as well as increased self-understanding by the students.

The science portfolios provided a great deal of assessment information about what had been accomplished by the students that year. They were a valuable experience for the students, and for parents they were rich documentation of their children's progress. The portfolios together provided next year's teachers with a rich fund of evidence about the science coverage experienced in fourth grade.

Portfolio Examples for Mathematics. Portfolios are also used by mathematics educators. One example is Pam Knight, a middle-school mathematics teacher in California (Knight, 1992). Knight had her students keep exhaustive files of their work for the year, including some long-term projects, notes they had taken, tests, problems of the week, homework, and journal remarks about especially difficult exam problems. At the end of the year, she had them go through their folders to select some items that would represent their knowledge of math and the efforts they had expended during the year. The students attached a personal statement to each of these exhibits. Here are two examples:

> I chose three papers for my portfolio because they show my best work and my worst work. They portray both sides of my academic performance in math this last semester. The 45 percent math test is in my portfolio because it shows that I have some problems in math. It shows my bad work. It shows that sometimes I have a bad day. It shows also that I forgot to study (ha, ha, ha).

> I can sum up three papers in this paragraph. Those are the Personal Budget, the James project, and the $2000 lottery project. On all of these papers, I did really well. That shows I do much better on those projects, especially the creative ones. I have a bit more fun doing them rather than doing just normal take home math assignments. These papers definitely show me at my best. (Knight, 1992, p. 72)

One of the most immediately obvious effects of this new form of assessment for Ms. Knight was that it did what performance assessment is intended to do; it changed her teaching:

As a result of trying to implement portfolio assessment, my classroom has definitely changed. It became apparent early on that if I wanted variety in my children's portfolios, I had to provide variety in assignments. I have changed my curriculum to include more problem-solving opportunities with written explanations. I have also had my students do two long-term situational problems. In the past, although I knew my algebra classes found such problems entertaining, I had questioned their lasting value. Now I see that these problems are the ones the kids remember the most. (Knight, 1992, p. 72).

The portfolios were used as part of assessing students in the course, providing about 20 percent of the total grade. Ms. Knight felt that the portfolios provided her with increased understanding of students' maturity, self-esteem, and writing. She also believed that students' self-assessment was an important gain from construction of the portfolios, with the students having to review their strengths and weaknesses and what had been accomplished in the class.

▶ **Diversity**

Developmental Considerations for Classroom Portfolios

Portfolios can be constructed and discussed by even very young children. It is important, however, for teachers to recognize some developmental characteristics that may influence the effectiveness of portfolios for different age groups. Young children may require more guidance in their self-evaluations than older children do. Although children can look at their own work and make an evaluation (Hart & Goldin-Meadow, 1984), the standards they use to evaluate their performance shift from autonomous, idiosyncratic perspectives to social comparison (Veroff, 1969). During the early-elementary school grades, there is a sharp increase in children's tendency to rely on social comparison and evaluate themselves in comparison with their peers. During middle childhood years, children begin to develop their own standards, at first by incorporating external standards, such as those of the teacher, into their own. They also begin setting more realistic goals for what they can accomplish (Wigfield & Karpathian, 1991). Given these developmental characteristics, one danger is that self-assessment may become something the teacher does while pretending the student is actually doing it.

High school teachers encounter a different set of problems. Their students may find it difficult to be suddenly responsible for their own evaluation after years of responding (or not responding) to teachers' evaluations. Moreover, since high school teachers work with large numbers of students, the sheer number of portfolios may be overwhelming. High school teachers may wish to meet with students in small groups rather than in individual portfolio conferences. In addition, high school teachers can focus on facilitating effective peer portfolio conferences.

Performance Assessments in the Classroom

Teachers sometimes have instructional goals that are best assessed by requiring students to demonstrate their acquisition of knowledge and skills directly via performance assessment (Airasian, 1994; McDaniel, 1994; Stiggins, 1987; see also Chapter

14 for a discussion of large-scale performance assessment). For example, performance assessments for writing may call upon students to demonstrate how they plan, write, and revise essays as reflected in writing portfolios. Performance assessments for science may require students to demonstrate their ability to conduct scientific experiments, from hypothesis formation to actual experimentation. Other classroom examples of performance assessments include asking students to demonstrate their competencies by completing a musical or dramatic performance, executing a psychomotor routine, giving a speech, keyboarding a letter, or working effectively in cooperative groups.

Successful performance assessment requires careful planning and thoughtful evaluation. Guidelines for teachers using performance assessment include at the very least (Airasian, 1994):

- Identifying the steps or characteristics of the performance or task
- Listing the important criteria of the performance or product
- Communicating the criteria in terms of observable behavior by the student or specific product attributes

Observations of important classroom behaviors can be maintained by checklists or rating scales (Airasian, 1994). *Checklists* are simple listings of performance criteria. As the teacher observes the performance or reviews the product, whether or not the performance or product meets each criterion is noted by placing a check mark before the appropriate criterion on the checklist. For example, a checklist for a speech may include appropriate level of volume, good articulation, and eye contact, among other characteristics.

Rating scales or scoring rubrics are similar to checklists, but they allow the teacher to judge the performance or product along a continuum rather than as a dichotomy. That is, the teacher judges the extent to which each criterion is present in the performance or product. For example, students' papers can be evaluated in

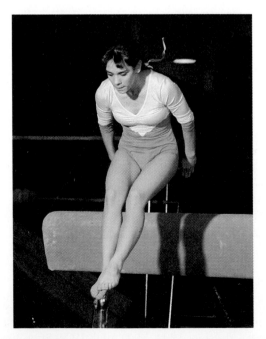

Acquisition of certain skills, such as vaulting, is best determined through performance assessment.

terms of organization, ideas and content, sentence fluency, and mechanics. Each of these dimensions would be rated on a scale. In one possible scale, a "5" in organization would mean that the ideas in the paper are presented in a logical and compelling manner, whereas a "l" in organization would mean that the paper lacks a coherent structure. One way to communicate the criteria to students is to discuss the checklist or rating scales before the assessment begins.

Grading Practices

Grading requires teachers to make judgments about students' performances, which many teachers find difficult and uncomfortable to do. Most classroom teachers grade their students because they are expected to and because they realize that grades provide information used to determine such things as suitability for promotion to the next level and to inform the community, including parents and students, of each student's progress. The following are some general principles or golden rules of grading (Ory & Ryan, 1993):

- *Fairness.* There should be equal opportunity for all students.
- *Accuracy.* Grades should be based on all available sources of evidence such as tests, papers, projects, and sometimes assignments.
- *Consistency.* Grading practices should be planned ahead of time and presented at the beginning of instruction. Any changes in the grading plan should be carefully thought out and communicated promptly.
- *Defensibility.* Grading practices should be easily explained and defended when asked by student, parents, or principal. For example, it should be easy to demonstrate why one student received an *A* and another a *B*. Students' personal characteristics such as ability or personality should not influence grade assignment.

Teachers must decide what components to consider in grading. For example, will attendance, mechanics, neatness, and timeliness of work affect grades? How will the components be weighted? What is the weight given to classroom participation relative to test performance? How does the final project compare to test performance? If the teacher uses both alternative and traditional assessment techniques, the relative weight of each type of assessment should be carefully considered. What if a student does poorly in traditional assessments but excels in alternative assessments, should the assessment techniques have equal weight in the grading scheme? Students' effort, participation, and behavior should not be major components of subject grades since these attributes are difficult to assess fairly and unrelated to the students' competence in a given subject (Airasian, 1994). Moreover, formative assignments should not be incorporated into summative grading practices.

Another issue is the standards used for comparison, specifically whether they are norm-referenced or criterion-referenced. If grading is normative, then grading standards may depend on who is in class, since one student's grade affects that of another. Norm-referenced grading makes it difficult for parents or other interested parties to interpret the grade outside of the class standard. If grading is criterion-related, then students' performance is compared to a predefined standard of mastery and one student's grade does not affect the grade of another. One way to

Focus on Research

A Study of Grading Practices

Do classroom teachers follow recommended grading practices? In a descriptive study reported in Stiggins and Conklin (1992), the grading practices of 15 high school teachers across core high school subjects, each with a minimum of 5 years experience, were examined. The researchers first identified recommended practices across a number of sources. In other words, they used multiple dependent measures (see Chapter 1). The extent of a teacher's adherence to each guideline was determined through observation; interviews; and document examination of grade books, assignments, and tests. The teachers followed some of the identified recommended practices, including:

- Communicating grading methods to students
- Not considering students' characteristics of attitude and personality in grading
- Using methods of obtaining grading data such as written tests or performance assessment and not using oral questioning
- Not using the normal distribution to determine cutoff scores

The teachers, however, did not follow other recommended practices. Instead, they reported:

- Incorporating student characteristics such as effort, motivation, and learning ability into grades
- Using formative daily assignments in summative grading
- Not determining quality (reliability and validity) of grading data
- Using arbitrary methods of setting cutoff scores that were not consistent throughout the high school for same course
- Deciding borderline cases in a subjective manner.

The researchers tried to analyze why the teachers followed some recommendations and ignored others. One explanation referred to differences in the values held by teachers and testing experts. Although experts discourage grading on effort, teachers feel that effort is an important student characteristic and that grading is an important feedback mechanism. Also, the realities of classroom life make it unlikely that teachers have the time or expertise to use more complicated methods of figuring grades. Some teachers were also unaware of recommended grading practices since they were not stressed in teacher education programs.

specify a criterion of mastery is to detail the specific criteria describing students' performance at various levels of proficiency in scoring rating scales or rubrics. These criteria provide the meaning behind the grade and have the additional benefit of helping students learn the characteristics of good work.

Another standard of comparison used in grading relies on the specification of cutoff scores in terms of the percentage of correctness across many individual assessments. Students who make the specified cutoff score receive the associated grade. One major difficulty with percentage-based criteria is that the cutoff set is typically arbitrary and may vary widely across teachers and grades within the same school.

Another standard of comparison is grading on the basis of improvement or effort. This approach may penalize those students who enter with high levels of knowledge and skills. It is also difficult to compare grades across students since the meaning of a given grade varies across students.

Chapter Summary

- Teachers must first consider the purpose of a test. If the test is meant to provide feedback to the student and the teacher on the progress of instruction, then the test is a formative evaluation. If the test is meant to assess what the students have learned and will be used in grade assignment, then the test is a summative evaluation. If an individual's score is compared to that of other students, then the test is norm-referenced. If an individuals' score is compared to a standard or criterion, then the test is criterion-referenced.

- Classroom assessment should be based on instructional objectives that are simple statements of the behaviors and skills students should exhibit after instruction.

- Traditional classroom tests employ a variety of question types including essay, multiple-choice, matching, true/false, and completion items. Essay questions can be designed to tap higher-order thinking but are difficult to grade reliably and objectively. Multiple-choice questions are reliable and objective, but it can be time-consuming to develop multiple-choice questions that tap higher-level reasoning. Multiple-choice questions can be evaluated and revised according to the information obtained in item analysis.

- Good test takers possess general test-taking strategies for academic preparation, physical preparation, improving attitudes, reducing anxiety, and increasing motivation. Specific test-taking strategies for traditional classroom tests include using time effectively, avoiding errors, eliminating incorrect alternatives, and knowing when to guess. Consideration of the developmental characteristics of test takers may influence length, time, and format of tests.

- An assessment portfolio is a collection of a student's work selected by the student for evaluation. The goal of portfolio assessment is to develop skills in self-assessment through the collaboration of students, teachers, and peers. Alternative assessment strategies include performance assessment through observations via checklists and rating scales.

- Grading practices should be fair, accurate, consistent, and defensible. Issues to consider are the components to be used in grading and the basis for making comparisons with other students.

Return to the Classroom Predicament

Has reading this chapter helped you formulate responses to the questions raised by the teacher planning a test at the beginning of the chapter? The teacher is considering a number of issues about testing. What is the purpose of the test? Is it a norm-referenced or a criterion-referenced test? Is it a formative or summative evaluation? The teacher is aware that the test should be tied to instructional objectives and that the test could have a variety of questions designed to assess different levels of learning. The time the teacher is willing and able to spend grading determines whether or not essay questions will be on the examination. The teacher might consider other forms of assessment such as classroom portfolios or performance assessment.

Chapter Outline

Chapter 16

Diversity of Learners

Classroom Predicament

The 25 students in this classroom are all working on an assignment. Let's look more closely at 5 of these students.

Jason, as usual, seems to have problems even staying seated. He keeps jumping up and moving around the classroom. Even when he is at his seat, he is more often kneeling on his chair than sitting on it. It doesn't look as if he is going to manage to complete this assignment. Even when he does manage to complete an assignment, he typically makes careless errors.

Keesha has quickly mastered the assignment. She is motivated to work and completes classroom tasks quickly and accurately. She already knows a lot and seems to know how to learn. Sometimes she makes points in classroom discussion that even her teacher had not thought about. Now she is looking around the classroom for something else to do.

Mateo is avoiding working on the assignment because it involves reading. He feels stupid because reading has always been very hard for him, and now he just hates to even try to read. Instead, he takes out his math problems and works on them because he finds equations easy to solve.

Amalia has little confidence in her ability to complete the assignment. She finds all of school difficult and she doesn't really know how to begin to tackle this assignment. She feels bad because she believes she is stupid, and asking the teacher for help would make her feel even more stupid.

Joseph is new at the school. Until recently he attended school on the Navajo reservation. He had some problems understanding the teacher's directions for the assignment since his English is not that good. He would like to work with another student, but everyone is supposed to work independently.

What are the special educational needs of each of these students? Is it typical to find such diverse learners in one classroom? What can a teacher do to meet their special needs? Reflecting on the information contained in this chapter will help you formulate responses to these questions.

C onsider the diversity among learners found in a classroom today. The student raising his hand may have learning disabilities. The student talking to her neighbor may belong to an economically disadvantaged minority. The student returning a book to the shelf may not speak the language of his teacher and classmates. The student looking out the window may be receiving treatment for a medical condition such as cancer. Another student may have mental retardation; yet another may be intellectually gifted. It is important to understand differences in learners found in today's classrooms.

The first part of this chapter reviews three classifications of exceptional learners: mental retardation, learning disabilities, and giftedness. Then there is an overview of students who exhibit general characteristics that make them at risk for difficulties in school. These include students living in poverty (especially economically disadvantaged minorities), students with a native language other than the majority language, students with a serious disease or medical condition, and victims of chemical assault (including those suffering from fetal alcohol syndrome, cocaine damage, and lead exposure). The chapter concludes with a discussion of two individual dimensions that affect all of us: sex differences in thinking abilities and cognitive changes during the adult years.

Diverse Learners in the Classroom

In the past, some students with disabilities were placed in regular classrooms where they received few if any special services. More students with disabilities, however, were placed in **self-contained classrooms** where they were taught by special education specialists and had little contact with regular instructional programs, or they attended separate schools designed for students with particular special needs (such as schools for the visually or hearing impaired and schools for students with mental retardation). Today, students with disabilities often take their place next to nondisabled students in regular education classrooms. Educational practices for students with disabilities have changed greatly in response to criticisms of the failure to maximize the educational opportunities for all students and the passage of a series of legislation beginning with Public Law 94–142 in 1975 (Hunt & Marshall, 1994). Public Law 94–142 stipulates that students with disabilities be provided a free, appropriate education in the **least restrictive environment.** The term *least restrictive environment* is interpreted as meaning that students with disabilities must be educated with their nondisabled peers to the maximum extent appropriate. This provision has led to **mainstreaming,** the practice of placing students with disabilities as often as possible in regular classrooms with their nondisabled peers, rather than in separate classrooms or schools. Implementation of the principle of least restrictive environment can range from **inclusion,** in which all instruction is received in the regular classroom (often including consultation or collaboration with special education teachers or other specialists), through temporary removal to a **resource room** for special services, to placement in a self-contained special education classroom.

Public Law 94–142 also calls for development of an **individualized education program (IEP).** The IEP describes a particular student's disability and outlines an educational plan to address the student's learning difficulties. The team that draws up the IEP is typically comprised of the special education teacher, the regular education teacher, the school principal, and the parent or parents. An IEP has the following components:

- A summary of the student's present level of educational performance, based on sources such as standardized tests and classroom observations.
- A listing of both long-term goals and short-term instructional objectives for the student. The short-term objectives build toward the long-term goals.
- A plan for support services the student needs to reach the goals and objectives. This plan also specifies the extent to which the student will participate in regular education programs.
- A method for evaluating whether or not the student attains the objectives and goals.

Thus, in today's classrooms, many educators work in teams to provide appropriate instruction for students with a wide range of special needs. These include physical and sensory disabilities, such as visual and hearing impairments; speech and communication disorders, such as articulation difficulties and stuttering; and emotional and behavioral problems, such as conduct disorders that include aggressiveness and withdrawal. Three common classifications of learning differences are discussed more completely in the following sections on mental retardation, learning disabilities, and giftedness.

Mental Retardation

The American Association on Mental Deficiency suggests three characteristics of individuals with mental retardation (H. J. Grossman, 1983):

- They have significantly below-average general intellect, usually defined as an IQ of 70 or lower, which is two standard deviations below the mean (see Chapter 13).
- They have deficits in adaptive behaviors, which means that their personal and social behaviors are atypical for their age and culture.
- Their retardation is apparent during the first 18 years of life.

In general, the long-term prospects for independent functioning vary with the degree of retardation. A common convention is to consider individuals with IQ scores between 50 and 70 to have *mild retardation* and those with IQ scores below 50 to have *severe retardation* (Richardson & Koller, 1985). Most individuals with severe retardation require substantial social services and support their entire lives. Many individuals with mild retardation manage to live reasonably independent lives as adults.

There is nothing magical about an IQ of 70 as a cutoff. In fact, there is a long history of considering people who have IQ scores of between 70 and 85 as borderline for retardation, with these students at greater risk for failure in school than students with average intelligence (IQ scores around 100). There are four times more people in this borderline group, with IQ scores between 70 and 85, than people with IQ scores of 70 or lower (Zetlin & Murtaugh, 1990).

An important distinction is between retardation caused by known organic causes and retardation due to social and cultural factors (Burack, 1990). There are a number of causes of organic retardation including the following:

- Chromosomal anomalies, including Down syndrome, which usually is due to an extra copy of chromosome 21. Other chromosomal abnormalities associated with mental retardation include recently identified abnormal genes and "fragile" sites on chromosomes (Evans & Hamerton, 1985).
- Prenatal factors, including disease and infection, such as syphilis and rubella; exposure to radiation; malnutrition; and exposure to alcohol and other drugs (Berg, 1985; Stern, 1985).
- Injury at birth, including oxygen deprivation (Berg, 1985).
- Premature birth, which results in greater susceptibility to injury such as brain hemorrhage (Berg, 1985).
- Neonatal hazards, including head injury, disease (e.g., meningitis), chemical assault (e.g., exposure to lead), and disorders caused by malnutrition (Berg, 1985; Stern, 1985).

Distinguishing retardation due to organic causes from that due to social or cultural causes is difficult. Social-cultural retardation tends to run in families, but explanations for this vary. One obvious possibility is heredity. Perhaps parents of below-average intelligence simply provide their children with a genetic endowment that places them at the low end of the range of intelligence. There is always the possibility, however, that social-cultural retardation is due to some inherited, but undetected, organic disorder. In addition, parents of low intelligence may provide less stimulating environments for their children than parents of high intelligence do. In short, it is likely that familial retardation is multiply determined.

Determining the prevalence of retardation is also extremely difficult (Richardson & Koller, 1985; Zigler & Hodapp, 1986). About 75 percent of all retardations are of the social-cultural type, which results in much less severe impairment than organic retardation. One good ballpark estimate is that at most 1 in 100 people have severe retardation, mostly organically caused. Another 2 to 3 people per hundred have mild retardation, with more of these having social-cultural retardation than organic retardation.

Information Processing by Students with Mental Retardation

What are the information processing abilities of students with mental retardation? It is useful to analyze these abilities in terms of the characteristics of good information processing described in Chapter 1 and emphasized throughout this text.

Strategies and Metacognition. Individuals with mental retardation are less likely to develop learning strategies than normally intelligent individuals are (Ellis, 1979). When given strategy instruction, however, students with mental retardation can learn to use a variety of strategies, such as rehearsal, categorization, and elaboration (Blackman & Lin, 1984; A. L. Brown, 1978).

Students with mental retardation, however, do not regulate their use of the strategies that they know (A. L. Brown, 1974; A. L. Brown & Campione, 1978). That is, although they can carry out strategies, they often do not do so on appropriate occasions. Fortunately, with more elaborate instruction, students with mental retardation can learn to regulate their use of strategies (Belmont, Butterfield, & Ferretti, 1982). One way they can learn to do so is through self-instruction (Meichenbaum, 1977; see Chapter 7). For example, these students can learn to self-instruct as follows (Belmont, Butterfield, & Ferretti, 1982):

1. Decide on a goal.
2. Make a plan to reach the goal.
3. Try the plan.
4. Ask themselves after their attempt, "Did the plan work?"
5. If yes, do nothing more; if no, ask, "Did I actually follow the plan?" If the answer is no, try to follow the plan. If the answer is yes, ask themselves, "What was wrong with the plan?" and devise a new plan and try it.

Why does this kind of self-instruction work? Students with mental retardation are often impulsive. **Impulsivity** refers to the tendency to respond quickly without considering alternatives. Self-instruction forces students to plan and reflect on their actions and the characteristics of the situation. When students check their performance following use of a strategy, they are attending to utility information, or how well the strategy works, which is important in promoting maintenance of strategy use (see Chapter 4). Attempting to devise a new plan when an old plan fails also forces attention to information about when and where strategies are helpful. Thus, self-instruction affects long-term self-regulation by increasing metacognition about strategies such as knowledge of when and where strategies work (Borkowski & Kurtz, 1987).

Motivation. Students with mental retardation often undermine their own learning by making attributions that reduce future effort (see Chapter 2; Merighi, Edison, & Zigler, 1990; Zigler & Hodapp, 1986). When students with retardation fail at tasks, they tend to blame themselves more than do normally intelligent students (MacMillan & Knopf, 1971). Their failures lead them to doubt whether they could possibly solve problems presented to them, which increases their dependency on others to provide solutions to them (Achenbach & Zigler, 1968; Zigler & Balla, 1982). Ironically, this dependency is particularly a problem for students with mental retardation since they tend to be more wary of helpful adults than other students (Merighi, Edison, & Zigler, 1990). Students with retardation often have little confidence in themselves as learners or problem solvers.

Fortunately, some motivational interventions work extremely well with the retarded (Kiernan, 1985). Behavior modification, which involves the provision of reinforcement (see Chapters 7 and 10) for appropriate behaviors, is often successful with retarded populations. Behavior modification can improve communication skills, increase attention span, decrease hyperactivity, decrease aggression, and increase social interaction. A variety of reinforcers, ranging from opportunities to interact with others to earning money, are powerful motivators for behavioral changes in individuals with mental retardation.

Motivation is critical if individuals with mental retardation are going to learn to self-regulate (Whitman, 1990). They need to understand that they can experience success if they exert effort by executing effective strategies and that failure often results from lack of effort and failure to use appropriate strategies. They need to acquire beliefs that are likely to motivate cognitive effort and strategy use, such as "I can do this if I try hard and use a plan," rather than to persist with beliefs that support passivity, such as "I am dumb, so why try?"

Processing Efficiency: Interactions Among Working Memory, Speed of Processing, and Knowledge. Working-memory capacity probably is more limited in students with mental retardation than in normal achievers (Hulme & MacKenzie, 1992). It is uncertain whether students with mental retardation really have less neurological capacity or if it only seems so because they use their capacity inefficiently (Brewer, 1987; Nettlebeck & Brewer, 1981; Torgesen, Kistner, & Morgan, 1987). Although students with mental retardation can learn to do many tasks faster with practice, they remain far slower than normally intelligent students given equivalent practice (Brewer, 1987). They are also often less attentive than normally achieving students to task-relevant information (L. E. Ross & Ross, 1984; Zeamon & House, 1979). In addition, students with mental retardation do not possess as much knowledge of the world and academic content areas as normally intelligent students. This means that they are less able than normally intelligent students to "chunk" information into larger units that are more easily held in working memory, such as recoding the sequence of numbers 7–4–7 as "747 jet" or 4–1–1 as "directory assistance." In summary, a variety of factors, such as working-memory capacity, knowledge, motivation, and strategies, combine to reduce the efficiency of processing by students with mental retardation compared to normally achieving students.

Interaction Between Genetics and Environment: Down Syndrome

Down syndrome is a genetic disorder caused by three copies of chromosome 21 rather than the usual two. It is the most common of the severe mental disabilities, with about 7000 children with Down syndrome born each year in the United States (Wishart, 1988). Children with Down syndrome are recognizable by distinctive facial features, including slanted eyes and a broad nose. Their posture and gait are distinctive as well, and their hands are often stubby with some apparent webbing. People with Down syndrome often have congenital heart difficulties, which are treatable.

We know a great deal more about people with Down syndrome than we did 20 years ago. Perhaps the most striking finding is that children with Down syndrome function at much higher levels when reared in supportive and rich home environments than when reared in institutions (J. Carr, 1975, 1985). Many students with Down syndrome can function in the range considered borderline for mental retardation when they are appropriately stimulated (Wisniewski, Miezejeski, & Hill, 1988). Unfortunately, adults tend not to stimulate these children as they would other children. For example, they use more verbal commands and engage in less interactive questioning when playing with a child with Down syndrome (Krasner, 1985). Adults often send the message to children with Down syndrome that they do not expect much of them and that they expect to provide more help for these children than normal children. This may contribute to a tendency of children with Down syndrome to avoid or ignore stimulation when it is more than minimally challenging in contrast to normal children who seek content that is just a bit beyond them (Wishart, 1988). Educators must always keep in mind the importance of providing a stimulating environment.

Individuals with Down syndrome have distinctive facial features. The range of behaviors exhibited by a child with Down syndrome depends on the amount of environmental stimulation the child receives.

Learning Disabilities

Debates over the definition of *learning disabilities* rage (Kavale & Forness, 1992; Torgesen, 1991). Learning disabled (LD) students perform below expected levels in some academic area but otherwise perform within expected levels of achievement for age and grade. Learning disabilities may be specific to one or two competencies or to a cluster of closely related competencies, such as reading and writing.

Many people think of dyslexia when they hear the term *learning disability.* **Dyslexia,** which is the inability to decode words well despite intensive educational efforts, accounts for only a small proportion of all learning disabilities (see also Chapter 6). Probably no more than 1 percent of all people suffer from dyslexia. Learning disabilities are more wide-ranging than dyslexia. They include difficulties in comprehension once decoding is accomplished, difficulties in remembering what has been read, as well as nonverbal disabilities such as extreme difficulty in calculating (see also Chapter 6).

It is difficult to determine how many students are learning disabled. The percentage of students classified as LD in schools is typically reported as between 4 and 5 percent of the population of children in school (Kavale & Forness, 1992). There are many reasons to suspect that too many students are being classified as learning disabled. For example, sometimes that is the only way to obtain needed services (and financial resources for the services) for some students. Moreover, parents are less likely to protest their child's being diagnosed as having learning disabilities than as having mental retardation. Since the federal government has increased pressure to identify no more than 2 percent of the total school-age population as learning disabled, the number of students classified as such has declined.

Attention Deficit–Hyperactivity Disorder (ADHD)

Students with specific learning disabilities quite often exhibit difficulty maintaining attention. Sometimes these attention deficits are paired with other behavioral symptoms (Lerner, Lowenthal, & Lerner, 1995). Students who display attention deficits, impulsivity, and hyperactivity are identified as having attention deficit–hyperactivity disorder (ADHD). The *attention deficit component* of ADHD refers to difficulty sustaining attention. Phrases used to describe ADHD students include "fails to finish tasks," "can't concentrate," and is "easily distracted." The *impulsivity component* of ADHD refers to the difficulty ADHD students experience inhibiting responses. These students respond without considering alternatives, are careless and inaccurate, and appear unable to suppress inappropriate behavior. The *hyper-activity component* of ADHD refers to frequent and excessive body movements and vocalizations. Descriptions of ADHD students relevant to this component are "squirmy and fidgety," "hums or talks incessantly," and "can't sit still." In an accurate diagnosis of ADHD, these symptoms are observed in different situations, such as both home and school, and appear early in life (typically by the age of 7). ADHD is more often identified in boys than in girls.

Many students identified as ADHD are treated with medications, most often stimulants such as Ritalin or Dexedrine (Lerner, Lowenthal, & Lerner, 1995). These medications stimulate areas of the brain that control attention and can improve performance in the classroom. Some students experience side effects such as insomnia and loss of appetite. Some also experience a "rebound effect," in which their behavior deteriorates later in the school day as the medication wears off (Lerner, Lowenthal, & Lerner, 1995).

Treatment with medications, however, does not teach students how to control their behavior or promote self-regulation. Teachers can employ a variety of techniques in the classroom that help ADHD students focus and sustain their attention. For example, teachers can make sure that the directions they give students are brief, clear, and simple. They can also limit the number of distractions in the student's work area. They can surround the ADHD student with good role models or place the student near the teacher's position. It is also important for teachers to prepare students for transition and reduce transition time by establishing routines. Recognizing that all students (especially ADHD students) have difficulty focusing attention for long periods of time, teachers can schedule frequent breaks between demanding tasks. Finally, teachers can promote self-regulation in students with ADHD through self-instruction techniques described in this chapter as well as in Chapter 7. These recommendations fit in well with the perspective that it is best to view ADHD behaviors as resulting from the interaction between the biological characteristics of the student and variables in the classroom (Pellegrini & Horvat, 1995).

Information Processing by Students with Learning Disabilities

Progress in understanding the information processing differences between students with learning disabilities and normal achievers has assisted the design of instructional interventions that increase the academic performance of learning disabled students (Larson & Gerber, 1992). It is useful to analyze the information processing skills of learning disabled students in terms of the characteristics of good information processors described in Chapter 1 and emphasized throughout this text.

Strategies and Metacognition. Learning disabled students are less likely than normally achieving students to use strategies for performing academic tasks (Bauer, 1977a; Torgesen & Goldman, 1977). Fortunately, learning disabled students are able to carry out strategies when instructed to do so (Bauer, 1977b; Tarver, Hallahan, Kauffman, & Ball, 1976; Torgesen, 1977). For example, students with reading disabilities benefit from learning prediction, questioning, clarification, and summarization strategies through reciprocal teaching as described in Chapter 10. Students who have difficulty in language arts can learn to use writing interventions such as the plan-write-revise approach to composition (Chapter 11).

Strategy instruction for learning disabled students includes extensive attention to metacognition, including efforts to increase students' awareness of when and where the strategies can be used, and many prompts that encourage students to monitor their performance. The reason for this is that weak students and learning disabled students often are not as aware as normally achieving students of their cognition (Larson & Gerber, 1992).

Motivation. Learning disabled students are more passive than other students (Torgesen, 1975, 1977). They often are caught in a terrible cycle. Because they have done poorly in school, they think of themselves as academic failures; that is, they begin to believe they are stupid. Such a belief does nothing to motivate academic effort. The result is additional failure, which in turn strengthens the perception of low ability (Borkowski, Carr, Rellinger, & Pressley, 1990; Licht, 1983, 1992; Torgesen, 1977; see Chapter 2). Consequently, compared to normally achieving children, learning disabled students lack academic self-esteem, and they expect to do poorly in school (Butkowski & Willows, 1980; H. Rogers & Saklofske, 1985; Winne, Woodlands, & Wong, 1982).

Conventional schooling often reinforces the negative academic self-esteem of children with learning disabilities. Classrooms are filled with reminders to students who are doing poorly that they are doing so. Their papers are not displayed with the "A" papers, their names are not displayed in the "Geographer of the Week" display, and they are not members of the reading group that includes all the smartest children in the class. The more the classroom publicly honors its high achievers, the worse the social comparison for the low achievers (Ames & Archer, 1988; Stipek & Daniels, 1988). This situation is worse for girls, since girls are more likely than boys to attribute their failures to ability (Licht, Kistner, Ozkaragoz, Shapiro, & Clausen, 1985; Winne, Woodlands, & Wong, 1982). Boys more readily explain away their failures as caused by factors other than their low ability, such as "The teacher doesn't like me" or "The tests aren't fair" (see also Chapter 2).

This situation is not hopeless. As students are taught strategies that improve their task-related performances, they can also learn to attribute their performances to use of the strategies (Borkowski, Carr, Rellinger, & Pressley, 1990; Licht, 1992). The long-term commitment of learning disabled students to the use of new strategies is increased when they understand that their performances improve because of their use (see Chapter 4).

There are also other instructional procedures that increase learning disabled students' sense of competence and control (Licht, 1992). Focusing students' attention on successful attainment of concrete and immediate goals, such as getting today's problems correct, increases student **self-efficacy.** You may recall that self-efficacy refers to students' beliefs that their performances are under their own control (Bandura & Schunk, 1981; see Chapter 2). In contrast, focusing students' attention on progress toward long-term goals, such as on how many more days it will take to cover the entire unit of material, has much less of an impact on self-efficacy. In addition, modeling can increase self-efficacy. When students see another student like themselves struggling with a task, but finally accomplishing it, their self-efficacy is likely to improve (Schunk, Hanson, & Cox, 1987). In addition, students seem to have greater self-efficacy, more positive feelings of competence, and better performance in classrooms that emphasize improvement rather than performance relative to peers (Nicholls, 1989).

Processing Efficiency: Interactions Among Working Memory, Speed of Processing, and Knowledge. Although processing inefficiencies in students with learning disabilities are not as pronounced as in students with mental retardation, learning disabled students make less efficient use of their limited-capacity working memory than normally achieving students (Hulme & Mackenzie, 1992; Swanson & Cooney, 1991). It is impossible, however, to be certain that there is really less capacity. Rather, it may only seem that way because of processing inefficiencies. Because many students with learning disabilities are easily distractible, so much of their attention may be diverted away from the task that little of the total capacity is used for the memory demand (Shaywitz & Shaywitz, 1992). Moreover, because learning disabled students lack prior knowledge possessed by normally achieving students, they are prohibited from forming meaningful "chunks," which are easier to hold in working memory. Also, learning disabled students do not readily use strategies such as taking notes to reduce capacity demands.

■ Building Your Expertise

Assessment of Learning Disabilities Using Alternative Methods

There has been progress in identifying neurological abnormalities, especially for reading disabilities. For example, using a variety of techniques—from studies of cerebral blood flow to autopsies—abnormal structures and dysfunctions of the left hemisphere have been detected in the reading disabled (Flowers, Wood, & Naylor, 1991; Galaburda, Sherman, Rosen, Aboitiz, & Geschwind, 1985; Hier, LeMay, Rosenberger, & Perlo, 1978). The use of brain imagery techniques, such as MRI technology (see Chapter 14), has revealed that regions of the brain implicated in language processing tend to be smaller in students with reading disabilities (G. W. Hynd & Semrud-Clikeman, 1989). MRI studies have also detected abnormal brain structures at the back of the left hemisphere of dyslexics (Jernigan, Hesselink, Sowell, & Tallal, 1991; Larsen, Hoien, Lundberg, & Ødegaard, 1990). In addition, there also are abnormalities of blood flow in the frontal lobes of attention deficit children (Lou, Henriksen, & Bruhn, 1984) which is not surprising since the frontal lobes are critical for self-control and self-regulation.

Giftedness

The intellectually gifted are a great societal resource. Some of the gifted become great writers, physicians, and national, business, academic, and industrial leaders. The gifted are a diverse group. One distinction is between **prodigies,** who are very talented in one particular domain, and people who are generally very intelligent but not exceptionally talented in any one area. Thus, the gifted include both specialists and generalists (Feldman, 1986).

Who is gifted? What defines a gifted student? One criterion is IQ, although many different IQ cutoff points have been used as the starting point for giftedness. Often scores of 130 to 140 are considered the lower part of the gifted range. In many school districts, however, scores as low as 115 are taken as the beginning of the gifted range, which means that approximately 10 percent of all children would be considered gifted (Grinder, 1985). Of course, a high IQ score alone does not define giftedness. For example, there are underachievers who perform well below what they are capable of based on their IQ scores. Some students are much stronger on some subscales of intelligence tests than on others, so their overall IQ scores do not adequately represent their giftedness. Not surprisingly, some have argued in favor of expanding the definition of giftedness beyond being a label for the upper end of the IQ distribution (Richert, 1991). You'll recall, for example, the discussion of Gardner's multiple intelligences theory in Chapters 6 and 13. A person can have much greater intelligence for music, math, or physical activities than for other competencies.

Prodigies

What is a prodigy? John Radford offers one definition (1990, p. 200): "Statistically, a prodigy comes at the extreme end of a distribution of achievement in a particular activity." For example, Wayne Gretsky is clearly the best of the best, a hockey prodigy if there ever was one, with his talent apparent since he first showed up at the neighborhood rinks in Brantford, Ontario. Liona Boyd received a guitar for Christmas when she was 12 and as a young adult had established herself as the first lady of classical guitar. Stevie Wonder was a successful songwriter and singer at the age of 12 and continues his distinguished career today.

A main question posed by many who study prodigious genius is how to foster the giftedness of such individuals. What environmental variables influence whether a person with a great talent becomes a leading figure in a field of specialization? If the talent is there, how can we increase the odds of producing a great mathematician, a scientist, or an artist? The following are mentioned often as important to the development of prodigious genius (B. S. Bloom, 1985; Feldhusen, 1986; Feldman, 1988; Pleiss & Feldhusen, 1995; Radford, 1990; Tannenbaum, 1986; see also Chapter 5):

- Instruction related to exceptional abilities. Often there is a series of teachers of increasing sophistication who coach the student in the area of giftedness.
- Parents who are generally nurturant and supportive, but also supportive of the development of the particular talent.
- Long-term motivation to develop the ability, often to the point of obsession where it is as much play as work.

- Multiple rewards for engaging in the activity such as attention, applause, evident progress, and the opportunity to distinguish themselves from their peers.
- A great deal of practice of the special ability or abilities.
- Confidence in the special ability.
- High ability in a field in which recognized accomplishment is possible. It helps if it is a developing field, not so advanced that it cannot be mastered in a reasonable period of time and not so developed that it is closed to new ideas. For example, a young genius in calculus will have a tougher time coming to a new insight than a burgeoning genius in computer programming will (Feldman, 1986).

This list makes it clear that prodigious talent is the happy coincidence of many factors. A child with the right genes is born into a supportive family; the child is excited by the special competency and dedicated to developing it; and the talent is one that is needed by society, in that it is matched to the needs of the world at the moment.

For the child who does not have parents who are committed to developing his or her talent, school usually is society's best shot at directing the talent appropriately. Emerging genius requires some creative linking of resources to educate well. For example, conventional educational options may not serve well the brilliant fifth-grade computer programmer. Perhaps a solution for such a student would be to match him or her with community members who are excellent programmers or at least interested in computing. Such individuals may be able to introduce an exceptional student to a much larger world of computing than anyone in the school could offer.

People Who Are Generally Highly Intelligent

Suppose that we accept an IQ of 130 as the cutoff for high general ability. Since that figure represents roughly only $2\frac{1}{2}$ percent of the population, it is obvious that general intelligence is a scarce resource, yet it is not so rare that most educators are not going to be dealing with it on a regular basis. If a person is teaching 125 students a day at a high school, 3 or 4 of that teacher's students would likely have IQs exceeding 130. Thus, all educators should have a working understanding of such students.

Terman's Study of the Gifted. Genius fascinated Lewis Terman, a professor at Stanford University. During the years when he was developing the Stanford-Binet test (see Chapter 13), Terman encountered a number of children with high IQ scores. He was absorbed by the tales their parents told of their sons and daughters reading and writing early. Terman knew of the stereotypes—that geniuses were quirky, eccentric, and even unhealthy. He also realized, however, that most of the geniuses he was meeting were well-adjusted and happy (Shurkin, 1992; Terman, 1925; Terman & Oden, 1947; Terman & Oden, 1959).

In the early 1920s he began a longitudinal study of very bright children. He administered intelligence tests and other assessments to a large number of children throughout California. Contrary to the stereotypes, Terman's gifted children were more healthy and slightly superior physically to the population as a whole. They excelled in school and often moved ahead in the curriculum. Half of the sample was able to read before they began school. They tended to graduate from high

Focus on Research

Sampling Methods in Terman's Study

How were children selected to participate in Terman's study? In other words, what sampling methods were used to select the study's participants? Many of the children who were subjects in Terman's study had been nominated by their teachers as exceptionally bright. Others were nominated in a haphazard fashion by those acquainted with the study; some were brothers and sisters of nominated children. In the end, a sample of 643 children was identified as gifted in the sense of having IQ scores of 135 or higher. Other children from outside the geographic areas searched were added to the sample, as was a group of children with special talents, so that the final sample comprised more than 1500 children.

Are there any problems with this sampling procedure? Is this sample of children representative of gifted children? Some have complained about the method of sampling used in this study. For example, teachers' nominations may have been biased in favor of well-adjusted children, those children doing well in a conventional school. There may very well have been bright kids who were not nominated because they did not do well in school. Although some precautions were supposedly taken to reduce bias due to language and cultural differences, the total sample included much lower proportions of minorities than were present in California in the 1920s. The initial sample was also biased in favor of boys and children from middle-class and upper-middle-class families.

school early and entered college at a young age. The kids in Terman's study excelled in college, and a high proportion were elected to Phi Beta Kappa. In addition to being academically successful, these gifted people were also socially adept and accepted by their peers.

As adults, those in Terman's study were more likely to earn doctorates and professional degrees than members of the general population, with the majority eventually earning graduate degrees. Quite a few earned fame in their fields, even if very few earned widespread recognition. Their incomes were also well above population averages. Given the era of the study, it was not surprising that the majority of the women became homemakers.

The majority were very satisfied with their life and life's work. Alcoholism was low for the group, as was criminality. In general, they reported that personal satisfaction was more important than occupational satisfaction. The adults in the study married other bright people and gave birth to children with IQs that were well above average. In the twilight of their lives, the surviving men and women appear happy and mentally active.

One interesting comparison made by Terman was between the very successful kids and the less successful ones. The successes had parents who really pushed them to achieve in school and to go to college. Thus, as with prodigies, parents seemed to play a guiding, shaping role in the lives of successful people with high intelligence. Ability alone does not guarantee great success.

Information Processing by the Gifted

Although Terman's study provided many measures of the participants' competence, it did not analyze specific aspects of information processing. Fortunately, other studies examine the very good information processing of gifted individuals compared with the population at large. The information processing skills of gifted students bear a resemblance to the characteristics of good information processors described in Chapter 1.

Strategies and Metacognition. The gifted use more advanced strategies than peers of average intelligence on memory and problem-solving tasks (Jackson & Butterfield, 1986; J. A. Robinson & Kingsley, 1977). They also have superior metacognition (R. J. Sternberg, 1981). Gifted children are more likely to transfer new strategies they have learned from one task to another in which the strategies will be useful (Borkowski & Peck, 1986; Jackson & Butterfield, 1986).

Motivation. The gifted have a strong commitment to excellent performance in one or more fields (Feldhusen, 1986; Feldman, 1979; Terman & Oden, 1959). They also have high self-concepts (Feldhusen,1986; Feldhusen & Kolloff, 1981; Ketcham & Snyder, 1977; Ringness, 1961).

Processing Efficiency: Interactions Among Working Memory, Speed of Processing, and Knowledge. Gifted people process information more efficiently than other people do. For example, they can scan a set of items being held in memory more rapidly than people of average intelligence can (Keating & Bobbitt, 1978; McCauley, Kellas, Dugas, & DeVillis, 1976). They also can retrieve information more rapidly than people of average intelligence can (Borkowski & Peck, 1986; E. Hunt, Lunneborg, & Lewis, 1975; Jackson & Myers, 1982; Keating & Bobbitt, 1978). Gifted students process information more efficiently than less talented people do, and this efficiency frees up more of their short-term capacity for consideration and manipulation of strategies and other knowledge.

The gifted also have great facility in combining information and working with knowledge to produce new ideas and products (Feldman, 1982; MacKinnon, 1978; R. J. Sternberg & Davidson, 1983). They acquire early mastery of knowledge in the field in which they are gifted, and their knowledge is deeper and broader than that of people with normal intelligence (Feldhusen, 1986; Gagné & Dick, 1983; Rabinowitz & Glaser, 1985; R. J. Sternberg, 1981; Tannenbaum, 1983).

Students at Risk for Difficulties and Failure in School

There are students other than those with identified learning disabilities or mental retardation who are at risk for failure in school. This group encompasses many different classifications, and within every one of these categories there are individual differences, with some students functioning much better than others. However, at-risk students are more likely than typical students to be noncompliant; they are also less likely to self-regulate their behaviors. This means they fail to attend to and process information as efficiently as normally functioning students, are less likely to be calm and organized, and are less likely to adapt to new situations. At-risk students are more likely to have language problems, experience difficulties in social relations, and be slow to acquire problem-solving and decision-making skills. Fortunately, functioning often can be improved through environmental (i.e., educational, medical, family, or community-based) interventions; the earlier the interventions are introduced, the better (L. J. Stevens & Price, 1992).

Students Living in Poverty

In America, 1 in 5 children lives in poverty; in Canada 1 in 10 does so. Economic conditions have not only increased the number of poor but have also made it more difficult to escape poverty through personal effort (Eitzen, 1992). The more successful programs for poor children, such as Head Start, only serve a fraction of the children who need the service. In past decades, doing well in school was a passport for many from poverty to the middle class. This route is much less certain in the 1990s.

Poor children fare worse in school than those who live well above the poverty line. Poor children are less likely than age-mates to master basic skills and to be orderly in the classroom. The traditional approach to these disadvantaged students has been to provide them more instruction in basic skills, which reduces the amount of instruction devoted to grade-level skills and knowledge (Allington, 1991a, 1991b). The current emphasis is to provide high-quality instruction aimed at developing higher-order competencies. For example, providing low-level computational practice to students experiencing difficulties in mathematics while their classmates receive high-order problem-solving skills is no longer recommended. Instead, the goal is to provide instruction that promotes new understandings a bit beyond current conceptions (Porter, 1991; Secada, 1991).

One in five American children lives in poverty. Children living in poverty are at risk for failure in school.

Economically Disadvantaged Minorities. On average, economically disadvantaged minorities do not fare as well in school as mainstream youngsters. Most researchers acknowledge the enormous contributions of the environment in producing achievement differences between groups who are poor and those who are well off. In addition, the school environment may be mismatched to the personal characteristics and proclivities of minorities in ways that reduce academic achievement and full participation in the schooling community. For example, the strategies and knowledge acquired by the majority population are often better matched to the demands of school than the strategies and knowledge acquired by minority children. In one case in point, Shade (1982) argued that schools require sequential, analytical, and object-oriented strategies, which are fostered in the majority culture. In contrast, African American students typically grow up in environments that foster intuitive and person-oriented strategies, ones typically not valued or valuable in school. For instance, the emphasis placed on community, rather than individual, advancement in some cultures does not promote success in classrooms emphasizing individual achievement.

Harry (1992) also documented mismatches between economically disadvantaged Spanish-speaking Puerto Rican American families and the schools where their children were enrolled in special education. She detected potential miscommunications between schools and the minority parents and noted that these miscommunications reduce the likelihood of positive relationships between schools and families. The results were quite striking:

- These Puerto Rican American families reported that the American school seemed impersonal and uncaring compared with schools they remembered in Puerto Rico.
- The schools often made errors in the classification of the students in these families, for example promoting students by mistake and then returning them to their previous grade level, and these errors reduced parental trust of the school.
- The written communications from the schools were off-putting to these parents, in part because the letters were in English, which required finding someone to interpret them. The letters were also filled with educational jargon and were written above the readability level of many parents.
- Many of the parents withdrew from interactions with the school and increasingly felt alienated.

These findings are especially distressing, given that the education of disadvantaged children is most likely to be successful when there are coordinated efforts between families and schools. Thankfully, educators are beginning to understand how to educate disadvantaged minorities. Franklin (1992) summarized a set of beliefs of many educators about how to be successful in educating students from diverse cultures. These include the following (pp. 116–117):

- Instruction should incorporate elements of the students' cultural environment. Instruction that relates to students' prior knowledge is more likely to be successful than instruction that cannot be understood in terms of prior knowledge. For example, students from cultures emphasizing oral traditions should have the opportunity to bring these skills in oral tradition to bear on classroom tasks.
- Good teachers accentuate students' strengths and interests. All students bring extensive knowledge to school, which is a starting point for building new and

more powerful understandings. The teacher should access students' knowledge that may be related to school information in nontraditional ways.

- Teachers need to be sensitive to the possibility of misunderstandings because of differences between the language used by educators and the dialects and language used by students.
- New skills and strategies should be taught in culturally sensitive ways. For example, reading and writing strategies can be used to interpret literature from the student's own culture and to create new literature reflecting the student's culture and interests.

Much more is needed to make a difference in the lives of disadvantaged cultural minorities. First of all, much of school is structured so that those who are behind are guaranteed to stay behind. For example, competitive grading practices all but assure that many minorities will receive poor marks in school. The evidence is overwhelming that such grading practices cause great pain to disadvantaged students and do much to discourage them (D. Hill, 1991). An educational system that maximizes the achievement and happiness of all students would abandon competitive grading in favor of reinforcement of improvements. This would give those who start at the bottom a chance to be rewarded. Second, the interventions that work with disadvantaged students—and indeed all students—such as high-quality strategy instruction often require a high degree of monitoring and instruction by the teacher directed at particular students. Such instruction is unlikely when teachers are confronted with classrooms of 25, 30, or more diverse students. Third, the way that schooling is financed in the United States, largely through local property taxes, assures that students living in the poorest communities will have the worst school buildings, the fewest and most dated materials, the least equipment, and the most poorly paid teachers (Kozol, 1991).

Students Whose Native Language Is Not the Majority Language

It is not unusual in major urban environments in the United States and Canada to have 20 to 40 different first languages in a school population. All of the points made about children in poverty also hold for many of the children with a first language that is different from English. In addition, these students are faced with the challenge of learning English as a second language (or French as in some parts of Canada).

Attitudes can influence second-language learning. For example, differences in attitudes about a second language are associated with differences in success in learning the second language (R. C. Gardner & Lambert, 1972; R. C. Gardner, 1980). Moreover, students who have a negative attitude about the second language come from families who foster negative feelings toward the second language and culture (R. C. Gardner, 1983).

There are many pressures for increased bilingual instruction, including legal ones. For example, in *Lau v. Nichols* (1974), the U.S. Supreme Court ruled that non-English-speaking children had to be provided instruction that permitted their participation in school, including the possibility of instruction in English or instruction in their native language. In addition, the Bilingual Education Act, originally passed in 1968, has been amended to increase the pressure on educators to provide bilingual education.

In most bilingual education programs, two languages are used in part or all of the school instruction.

In most bilingual education programs, two languages are used in part or all of the instruction in school. The primary goal is to teach students in the language they know best but also to reinforce learning through the use of the target language. English as a second language (ESL) programs differ from bilingual education in that the former emphasize the target language, English, in the classroom.

One type of bilingual instruction developed in Canada and adapted in the United States, **immersion programs,** has as its goal the development of proficiency in both languages. When immersion programs are used in the primary years, most of the school day is spent in the second (target) language. Beginning at about the third grade, the day is more evenly split between instruction in the second language and instruction in the first language. By high school, the majority of instruction is in the first language, although a significant proportion of the day (e.g., 40 percent) is spent in classes conducted in the second language. The immersion model stimulates the acquisition of both first and second languages.

Students with Medical Conditions

Some students who attend school are seriously ill. For some of these students, their illness is terminal; for others, there will be complete recovery; and some will live with lifelong disabilities caused by the childhood sickness or injury. Some diseases and injuries cause mental impairment, and some treatments produce side effects that affect participation and progress in school.

AIDS. Somewhere between 15,000 and 30,000 babies are born each year infected with HIV (human immunodeficiency virus), which may eventually lead to AIDS (L. J. Stevens & Price, 1992). A critically important effect of AIDS early in life is that it causes central nervous system damage, including, in many instances, mental retardation. Fortunately, cognitive stimulation programs can be effective with HIV-infected children. For example, Seidel (1992) reported that children with HIV who received a year of cognitive stimulation intervention displayed gains in cognitive and motor tasks.

Cancer. The most common childhood cancer is leukemia (Bartel & Thurman, 1992). Because of great advances in treatment, most childhood leukemia victims do survive. Brain tumors are the next most common form of childhood cancer, and although the survival probabilities are not as great as they are for leukemia, the chances of survival are increasing steadily with new understandings about effective treatments.

At a minimum, students with cancer are at risk for getting behind in school at the time they are treated. The illness and treatment dramatically disrupt normal life and school attendance. Often the treatment produces side effects, such as fatigue, that hamper normal academic activities.

The treatments also can negatively affect long-term cognitive development. For example, radiation to the brain to treat a brain tumor is likely to impair long-term functioning. How much impairment occurs depends on a number of factors, including the age of the child when the cancer occurs and how much radiation therapy he or she receives. Radiation during the preschool years, when the brain is developing rapidly, produces more impairment than radiation later in childhood (Bartel & Thurman, 1992).

Children Who Are Victims of Chemical Assaults

Parents who abuse chemical substances, especially mothers who drink or take drugs during pregnancy, create great risks for their children.

Alcohol. More people have mental retardation because of prenatal exposure to alcohol than for any other reason (Burgess & Streissguth, 1992). The child experiencing the full effects of **fetal alcohol syndrome (FAS)** (see Chapter 6 as well) has low birth weight (itself a risk factor), facial disfigurations, and damage to the central nervous system that can translate into behavioral disorders ranging from retardation to learning disabilities. The mean IQ for individuals with fetal alcohol syndrome is about 65 or 70, with a range of 30 to a little more than 100, which is significantly lower than the distribution of IQ scores in the normal population. In a school of 1000 students, approximately 3 of the students might be expected to have experienced fetal alcohol effects.

A common problem for FAS children throughout their years in school is inappropriate behavior, with lying, stealing, and acting out common. Students with FAS are often so impulsive, hyperactive, and out of control that the school will refer them for evaluation and treatment. These students display limited communication

One of the most common causes of mental retardation is prenatal exposure to alcohol. This child has fetal alcohol syndrome.

abilities, so it is possible that they often are inadequately communicating what happened rather than intentionally telling mistruths. Of course, such poor communication skills also negatively impact social relationships. If anything, the social problems worsen with advancing grade in school, with these dysfunctions producing an isolated and depressed adolescent in many cases (Burgess & Streissguth, 1992).

At present, educators understand little of how to intervene with FAS children, except for the general consensus that early intervention is better than later measures. In addition, there is recognition of the great need to improve the social and communications skills of FAS children.

Cocaine and Other Drugs. Firm conclusions about the effects of cocaine addiction, or addiction to any particular drug, on the developing fetus or child are difficult to produce because drug users rarely rely on one drug exclusively. Thus, this section is really about "cocaine/polydrug-exposed" children (Griffith, 1992). The effects of drug exposure are apparent during infancy with poor self-regulation. These children do not display the "quiet alert" state that permits information from the environment to be processed. Much more swaddling, rocking, and pacification is required to induce quiet alertness in these children than in normal children. Moreover, these children can be overstimulated easily, using disorganized crying and extended sleeping as ways of reacting to overstimulation. Great care must be taken to avoid overstimulation if drug-exposed babies are to be able to attend to their environments for prolonged periods of time, which is absolutely essential for cognitive growth (Griffith, 1992).

Little is known about the long-term effects on mental functioning of crack-

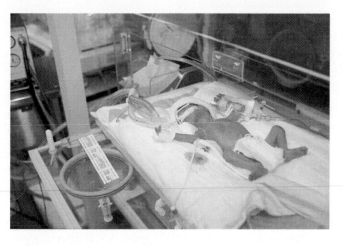

This child was born to a drug-addicted mother. The effects of prenatal drug exposure are often found in poor self-regulation.

cocaine exposure during the prenatal period. For some children whose mothers sought treatment during pregnancy and who experience appropriate levels of stimulation, the long-term effects may be much less than suggested by the sensationalistic accounts in the mass media. Still, 3-year-olds who were exposed to drugs prenatally have smaller heads on average than normal children. Also, even some children who receive the best treatments manifest communication and attentional problems at the age of 3. They are less likely to be able to control themselves and are easily overwhelmed by the environment, resulting in their withdrawal or going out of control when challenged. Although we do not yet know how to treat such symptoms, the best advice available is to adjust the environment as much as possible to eliminate overstimulation by reducing distractions and transition times. It is possible that the approaches that help to increase self-regulation, such as teaching students to self-instruct (see Chapter 7), that work with other students will also work with drug-exposed children.

Lead. Herbert L. Needleman (1992; Needleman & Bellinger, 1991) claims that even low levels of lead exposure pose a long-term risk to neurological functioning. Needleman argues that 16 percent of American children have lead levels in their blood that are reason for concern, with poor children much more likely to be exposed to dangerous levels. Lead exposure can reduce IQ, impair language, and decrease self-regulation and attention. Even low levels of exposure to lead in early childhood are associated with long-term risks, such as reading disabilities and increased likelihood of failing to graduate from high school.

What is the source of this lead? Flaking, chipping lead paint is common in the homes of poor children and common in the homes of children with high blood lead levels. Paint chips are nibbled, and flaking paint produces dust that is inhaled. Needleman and his colleagues argue that the cost of repairing homes with lead paint is quite small compared with the long-term medical and special education costs if the repairs are not made.

Sex Differences in Cognition

Are there differences between males and females in their abilities to perform cognitive tasks? Are there biological differences in the central nervous system that produce sex differences in the ability to perform particular intellectual tasks?

There is no overall difference in the intelligence of males and females as measured by intelligence tests (Halpern, 1992). The mean IQ scores for males and females are both about 100. Intelligence is normally distributed for both males and females, with the standard deviation for IQs equal to 15 for both sexes. When processing and abilities are examined more closely, however, there are small differences:

- *Verbal ability* refers to word fluency, grammatical competence, spelling skills, reading, vocabulary, and oral comprehension. When differences are found in verbal ability, females typically display a slight advantage. Dysfunctions in verbal abilities, such as stuttering and dyslexia, are identified much more frequently in males. Verbal impairment following stroke is also more likely for males than females.

- *Visual-spatial skills* refer to abilities such as being able to imagine figures and move them around "in the head" in order to understand relationships among them. In general, males are superior to females in visual-spatial ability but the magnitude of this sex difference has decreased in recent years (Voyer, Voyer, & Bryden, 1995).

- *Field independence* refers to the ability to perceive an object separate from its background (Witkin, Moore, Goodenough, & Cox, 1977). For example, if presented with a printed figure embedded in a more complex form, males are more certain to locate the figure quickly than females (see Figure 16.1). Females are more likely to perceive the pattern holistically than analytically and to have more difficulty separating intermingled items from each other. That is, they are more likely to be **field dependent.** Field independence may only reflect male superiority on visual-spatial tasks, since all tests that produce male-female differences in field independence have a large spatial component.

- *Quantitative skills* as measured by tests are typically stronger in males, when sex differences are detected. In particular, males are more likely than females to score high on tests such as the SAT mathematics sections. Among top SAT math scorers (those with a score of 700 or higher), there is a 17 to 1 ratio favoring males (Stanley & Benbow, 1982). There are clear developmental patterns showing differences between the sexes in mathematical ability. Females actually outperform males on math tasks in the elementary and middle school years, with male superiority appearing for the first time in high school. The difference favoring males seems to increase into the adult years (Hyde, Fennema, & Lamon, 1990). The female advantage during the elementary school years is in

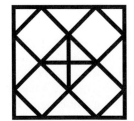

Figure 16.1

An example of a figure used on a test of field independence. People who are field independent can find such embedded figures easily.

Source: From "Field-Dependence and Field-Independence: Cognitive Styles and Their Educational Implications" by H. Witkin, C. Moore, D. Goodenough, and P. Cox, 1977, *Review of Educational Research, 47,* pp.1–64. Copyright 1977 by the American Educational Research Association. Reprinted by permission of the publisher.

computation skills; elementary school males do better on measures of problem solving than their female classmates do.

There are several striking aspects to this list of differences. For one, it is so short! There are many aspects of performance that produce no sex differences. Males and females are cognitively more similar than dissimilar (Halpern, 1992).

Are there sex differences in the use of cognitive strategies, metacognition about strategies, and other knowledge? The specific knowledge people possess can reflect differences in experiences between the sexes. Because prior knowledge does affect comprehension and interpretation, the reaction of males and females to different materials and events sometimes differs (Crawford & Chaffin, 1986). There is, however, no evidence of differences in the abilities of males and females to learn strategies or to acquire metacognition or other knowledge.

Chapter 2 considered some motivational differences between males and females, especially with respect to mathematics. In order to understand better why so few women choose careers in math and physics, Benbow and Lubinsk studied males and females who have the highest math SAT scores (see Raymond, 1992). They found that even females who are strong in mathematics are less likely to aspire to scientific careers. Females want more social contact than they perceive is permitted by work in mathematics and physical sciences, and so they elect alternative careers.

Potential Causes of Sex Differences

Some theorists argue that sex differences can be explained by biological differences between males and females. Others argue that sex differences represent differences in the experiences of males and females.

Biological Theories. The following are theories about how biology affects sex differences in cognition (Halpern, 1992):

- Sex hormones may operate in various ways. Prenatal sex hormones, especially testosterone, are critical to the determination of sex. Testosterone stimulates the development of male external genitalia. Its absence results in female sex organs. Testosterone also affects development of sex differences in the brain, as do the hormones secreted by the fetal ovaries. Manipulating the presence of such hormones at various points in the development of rats produces changes in brain structures. In humans, there is evidence that exceptionally high levels of androgen (a male hormone) during the fetal period increase spatial abilities in females. Some biological males do not respond to androgen and, thus, develop female characteristics including a pattern of higher verbal than spatial ability. Women with Turner's syndrome, who have low levels of both male and female hormones, also have strikingly reduced spatial skills relative to other females.

- For females, cognitive abilities vary somewhat with hormonal differences during the menstrual cycle. Menstruating women perform better on tasks typically performed better by males, such as map problems, mazes, and visual-spatial problems (Hampson, 1990a, 1990b; Hampson & Kimura, 1988). Female hormones are at the low ebb at this point in the monthly cycle. When female hormones are at the peak of their cycle (i.e., at midcycle), females do better on tasks that are typically performed better by females than males, such as speech articulation, verbal fluency, and manual dexterity.

- Males have more clearly lateralized brains than females do. For example, verbal skills are more of a left-hemisphere function for males than females. For females, verbal skills are carried out by both hemispheres, with spatial abilities confined to the right hemisphere. The result is that there is less right-hemisphere capacity in females dedicated to spatial abilities than in males and more overall capacity in females dedicated to verbal skills. Thus, Levy (1976) proposed that spatial skills get "squeezed out" of the right hemisphere in females to provide more verbal capacity.

- Some portions of the **corpus callosum**—the bundle of fibers connecting the two hemisphere—are larger in females than in males, supporting the possibility that greater verbal facility in females is due in part to greater interhemispheric communication in females than in males.

Psychosocial Theories. Males and females are treated differently from the moment the delivery room nurse reaches for a blue blanket for a boy or a pink one for a girl. These differences in treatment are not necessarily a problem. The problem is that the behaviors encouraged in females are often less positively regarded and rewarded than the behaviors encouraged in males. Moreover, societal stereotypes often ascribe less valued roles for females than for males. For example, doctors are males and nurses are females; lawyers are males and paralegals are females; and pilots are male and flight attendants are female. The pervasiveness of such sexism can affect behavior if internalized. Perhaps much of the reason girls have less interest in math and careers requiring mathematics is that they have internalized stereotypical beliefs such as, "Math is for boys," and "Engineers and scientists are men." Parents, television, teachers, and community members all contribute to the stereotyping (Halpern, 1992).

Furthermore, if being surrounded by sex-role stereotypes is not enough, more obvious and tangible rewards are given to boys when they do well in math and science than to girls who also do well (Stage & Karplus, 1981). Indeed, math and science classes foster boys more than girls in a number of ways. Boys ask more questions in these classes, and they get more answers, with males generally dominating science and math discussions in school (Morse & Handley, 1985). When volunteering is a main mechanism for determining who participates, when competitive grading is the norm, and when public recitation is a large part of the culture of the math and science classroom, male interactional patterns of aggression and competitiveness are favored more than female patterns of cooperation (Eccles & Blumenfeld, 1985). Moreover, males get more experience operating in competitive and publicly interactive activities from the preschool years on (Huston & Carpenter, 1985). When boys and girls work on problems together, boys dominate the interactions and the decisions that are reached (Lockheed, 1985). After several years of these interactions, males are better able to pose questions to other group members that produce assistance and are more likely to seek assistance when they need it (N. M. Webb & Kenderski, 1985). When males and females are in situations requiring negotiation, males dominate (Tannen, 1990).

What are some of the particular experiences that might contribute to the sex differences in cognition that have been observed (Halpern, 1992)? Sex differences in spatial abilities might be accounted for by greater male experience with games that require such skills, such as video games and billiards. Boys' toys and play activities in general may encourage development of spatial skills more than girls' toys do. Boys may be more curious about the environment than girls, a difference reinforced by adults who are more willing to allow boys than girls to roam the world in search of new possibilities (Lindow, Marrett, & Wilkinson, 1985). This greater exploration also would be expected to foster visual-spatial skills.

A number of socialization differences contribute to sex differences in mathematics (Halpern, 1992). Females take fewer mathematics courses, and there is much greater tolerance of high-ability girls' dropping out of mathematics sequences than of high-ability boys' doing so. The majority of math teachers expect more from boys than girls and are more responsive to male achievements in mathematics than female achievements. In addition, many adults who interact with children believe that math is harder for girls than for boys. This bias affects the messages sent to students about the possibility of mathematics achievement by girls. If we were attempting to design a world that would turn girls off to math, it seems unlikely we could be more successful in funneling females away from math and science than is the case now.

● "What Do I Do on Monday Morning?"

Instructional Responses to Diverse Learners in the Classroom

Many of the following suggestions are effective instructional techniques that were developed throughout this text. Although these techniques are applicable for all students, they are particularly crucial for those students at risk for failure in school. The long-term goal of these recommendations is to build self-efficacy in students and to promote self-regulation.

- *Help students set proximal goals.* Students' goals should be individualized and obtainable, but teachers should make sure the goals the students set present a challenge. As part of this process, the teacher needs to communicate high expectations for all students (see also Chapter 2).
- *Teach students effective learning strategies.* Many students do not access effective learning strategies on their own but can make good use of strategies in which they receive instruction (see also Chapter 4).
- *Provide metacognitive instruction to help students monitor and regulate their use of strategies.* Students need to develop good metacognition in order to use strategies on their own. This includes understandings of where, when, and why strategies are useful (see also Chapter 4).
- *Encourage students to make appropriate attributions for success and failure.* Students who attribute success to their efforts and strategy use are more likely to exert effort and use strategies on future tasks. Similarly, students who attribute failures to low effort or poor strategy selection are more likely to exert effort in the future than students who attribute failure to low ability (see also Chapter 2).
- *Help students become aware of their successes.* Make sure students compare their new performance with their own past performances rather than to that of other students.
- *Teach students to use self-instruction.* Self-instruction can help students regulate their strategy use (as described earlier in this chapter), focus their attention, and reduce impulsivity. The teacher first describes and

models the self-instruction. Then the teacher monitors the students as they attempt to self-instruct. The teacher guides students toward whispering rather than verbalizing the self-instruction out loud. Finally, the students are able to "think" the self-instruction. As part of this process, students learn to monitor their performance and to reward themselves for successful behavior (see also Chapter 7).

- *Provide access to appropriate models.* These models include peers who struggle and then eventually succeed with the benefits of strategy instruction. It may also include members of the community who have special talents.

- *Assist students' ability to access knowledge.* Highlight useful background knowledge the students may possess. Diminish the effects of limitations of working memory by reducing the capacity demands of tasks. Communicate important concepts and relationships in multiple formats such as lecture, discussion, written materials, videotapes, graphs, maps, and role-playing (see also Chapters 3 and 4).

Differences in Thinking Abilities Across the Life Span

Now more than ever, education occurs across the life span. It is not unusual at all for university-level and graduate students to be in their thirties, forties, and fifties. Many of these people are returning to school, perhaps fulfilling an educational dream that was suspended some years before in favor of marriage or children or because of economic hardships. In addition to college-level returnees, there are many who seek to complete high school equivalency work. Others are remediating deficiencies in basic skills, with national efforts now underway to reduce adult illiteracy. There are parts of the United States in which 10 percent to 20 percent of the population are illiterate in the sense that they cannot read with comprehension at a fourth-grade level. With so many adults being educated, there is a real need for educators to understand adult thinking and learning abilities.

Strategies and Metacognition

In a large number of studies, older adults were presented some basic memory task, such as paired-associate or list learning. Adults in one condition were taught a strategy well matched to the task, such as making interactive images for paired associates or organizing list materials by categories; adults in the control group were left to their own devices to process the material. The older adults who were given the strategy instruction consistently outperformed the control subjects (B. J. F. Meyer, Young, & Bartlett, 1989; A. Roberts, 1983). Typically, if left to their own devices, older adults are not as strategic as they could be. Nonetheless, they are quite capable of carrying out a number of strategies if provided brief instruction about how to do so.

One of the most important ways that metacognition has been studied in adults has been with metacognitive questionnaires. Because of a decline in memory with increasing age, metamemory has been assessed more than other types of metacognition. For example, here are some items that appear on one questionnaire (adapted from Gilewski & Zelinski, 1986, Table 11.7, and Kausler, 1991, Table 9.3):

How would you rate your memory in terms of the kinds of problems you have?

How is your memory compared to the way it was one year ago?

How often does remembering names present a problem to you?

As you are reading a novel, how often do you have trouble remembering what you have read?

How well do you remember things that occurred . . . last month, last year?

The most striking finding from the metacognitive questionnaires is that older adults are extremely pessimistic about their memory capabilities and attribute the difficulties they are experiencing to mental decline. They often do not monitor their memories as well as younger adults do, as measured by the discrepencies between how people believe they will perform a task and how well they actually perform the task. Some studies report declines in accuracy among the elderly, but others report equally accurate monitoring in younger and older adults (Devolder, Brigham, & Pressley, 1990).

Motivation

A variety of motivational hypotheses have been advanced to explain, at least in part, the lower performances of older compared with younger adults:

- Older adults have slightly less need for cognitive stimulation than do younger adults, resulting in less engagement in cognitive activities by the elderly (Salthouse, Kausler, & Saults, 1988).
- Older adults have difficulties inhibiting task-irrelevant behaviors and thoughts compared to younger adults. That is, older adults have difficulty staying on task (Hasher, Stoltzfus, Zacks, & Rypma, 1991).
- Older adults are more likely than younger adults to believe their performances are out of their control. That is, older adults are more likely to attribute their cognitive difficulties to impaired ability, whereas younger adults attribute performance differences to controllable factors such as effort and use of inappropriate strategies (Devolder & Pressley, 1992).

Thus, there are multiple influences on the motivation of older adults that may help to explain their lower cognitive performances.

Processing Efficiency: Interactions Among Working Memory, Speed of Processing, and Knowledge

A person continues to acquire knowledge throughout the adult life span (see the discussion of crystallized intelligence in Chapter 13). Thus, there are differences in the quantity of knowledge possessed by younger and older people. Are there also qualitative differences in the knowledge possessed by younger and older people? In general, the commonalities in the knowledge possessed by younger and older adults are greater than the differences. Older adults, however, are less likely than younger adults to use their knowledge to assist them in meeting intellectual demands, such as remembering information. For example, older adults make less use of their semantic memory to organize, study, and recall than younger adults do. Older adults who are asked to learn lists of words that can be grouped into categories are less likely than younger adults to group the words into categories as they study (Kausler, 1991).

With advancing age, the processing of information slows (Salthouse, 1982). In addition, the capacity of working memory declines with advancing age in adulthood (Kausler, 1991). Older adults also are less likely to use their prior knowledge to chunk information into fewer, more meaningful pieces (Taub, 1974). In short, there are a variety of factors that combine to undermine the efficiency of thinking by older adults compared with younger adults.

Chapter Summary

- Legislation specifying that the education of students with special needs should take place in the least restrictive environment has led to the practice of mainstreaming students with disabilities in regular education classrooms. For each of these students, an individualized education program (IEP) must be developed.
- In comparison to normally achieving classmates, students with mental retardation or learning disabilities are likely to use fewer strategies, be less metacognitively aware, possess more dysfunctional motivational beliefs, and know less in general.
- Gifted people have more and better strategies, metacognition, knowledge, and motivation than typical learners. In addition, their information processing is faster and more efficient.
- In general, evidence of strategy use increases going from retarded to learning disabled to normally achieving to gifted students, as does evidence of metacognition, extensive world knowledge, and motivation supporting academic behaviors. Although it is not possible to know whether the amount of neurological capacity allocated for short-term processing differs between these classifications, functional short-term capacity certainly does. Performance on short-term memory tasks improves steadily going from retarded to learning disabled to normally achieving to gifted classifications.
- Children who live in poverty, do not speak the majority language, experience serious illness, or have been exposed to chemical assaults are at risk for difficulties in school. There are ways in which the school environment can be adapted to reduce this risk.
- There are few cognitive differences between males and females, and the ones that exist are small. Females tend to have greater verbal abilities. Males tend to be superior in measures of spatial ability, field independence, and quantitative skills.
- The differences in the thinking of the young, healthy adult and the older, healthy adult are not very great. There are some subtle differences, nonetheless. Older adults are not as quick in their thinking. They are less likely to adopt newly offered strategies. They do not apply prior knowledge to tasks as certainly, and their motivation for many tasks is less than that of younger adults.

Return to the Classroom Predicament

Has reading this chapter helped you formulate responses to the questions raised in the beginning of this chapter? As we have seen, it is not unusual to find diverse learners in one classroom. What are the special educational needs of each of these students?

Jason has difficulty sustaining his attention, exhibits hyperactive behavior, and is impulsive in his schoolwork. He is likely to be identified as ADHD and placed on medication. He would also benefit from training in self-instruction to focus his attention and control his hyperactivity and impulsivity.

Keesha exhibits superior metacognition, strategy use, and processing efficiency. She is also a very motivated learner who needs help in structuring individual goals and academic challenges. Perhaps pairing Keesha with a member of the community with similar interests can provide her with additional challenges.

Mateo most likely has a learning disability in reading. He needs help in strategy instruction, in the development of metacognition, and in making appropriate attributions for his successes and failures.

Amalia is likely to be identified as having mental retardation. As with Mateo, she also needs help in strategy instruction, in developing metacognition, and in making appropriate attributions for her successes and failures.

Joseph is at risk for failure in school because of his lack of English fluency and a cultural mismatch with the school's environment. He would benefit from a bilingual education program or, at the very least, from more of an emphasis on collaborative learning in the classroom.

Glossary

accommodation   In Piaget's theory of cognitive development, the modification of existing cognitive structures in response to environmental stimuli.

adding on   A strategy for subtraction in which children start with the smaller number and count up to reach to the larger number.

advance organizers   Materials that activate prior knowledge to help students learn new information.

alternate-forms reliability   A measure of a test's reliability established by administering two forms of the test to test takers. The correlation between performance on one form of the test and performance on the other form measures the test's reliability.

analogy   A similarity that is found between a new concept and a familiar one to help make the new concept more understandable.

analytic grading   A method of grading essays in which the teacher prepares a model response in advance and assigns points to key components of the model answer. Students' essays are then compared to the model.

animism   The belief that inanimate objects are alive.

anoxia   The reduction of an infant's air supply during birth, which can cause brain injury.

assimilation   In Piaget's theory of cognitive development, the incorporation of environmental stimuli into an existing scheme.

attention deficit–hyperactivity disorder (ADHD)   A syndrome of learning and behavioral problems that makes it difficult for students to sustain attention and inhibit responses.

attention span   The length of time and the quantity of material someone can attend to at any one time.

attributions   Explanations for behaviors, often for successes or failures.

auditory processing   A process of intelligence measured by the ability to perceive sound patterns.

authentic assessments   Assessments that are directly linked to the goals of instruction.

authoritarian parents   Parents who are demanding and unresponsive and who make demands that they expect to be met without question.

authoritative parents   Parents who are demanding and responsive and who have firm rules but will consider others' points of view.

automaticity theory   The theory that explains the tremendous comprehension advantage readers obtain when they can read words by sight and orthographic chunks.

automatizing   Executing procedures quickly and with ease.

axon   A part of a cell that conducts impulses away from the cell body.

behavioral contracting   An agreement between teacher and student that specifies what the student's goal will be, what reinforcement might be earned, and how much progress toward the goal is required for reinforcement.

behavioral models   People who display behaviors that are imitated.

behavior modification   The use of procedures to manage behavior based on the principles of reinforcement and punishment.

bridging inferences   Inferences that are derived from world knowledge and that produce coherence between propositions obtained from reading textual material.

cardinal number   The last number uttered in a count of objects.

cell assemblies   Closed paths that include a number of neurons synaptically connected to one another.

cipher   A code that maps all the letter-sound relationships necessary for word decoding.

classical conditioning   The conditioning of a stimulus to elicit a particular response. Classical conditioning occurs when a neutral stimulus is paired with an unconditioned stimulus that elicits an unconditioned response. The neutral stimulus becomes a conditioned stimulus when the conditioned stimulus presented alone elicits what is now the conditioned response.

class inclusion problems   Problems that require the ability to answer questions about subset relationships between groups of items.

classroom procedures   Procedures that are directed at a particular classroom activity. A classroom procedure might be not to leave the classroom until dismissed by the teacher.

classroom rules   General standards of classroom behavior. A classroom rule might be to show respect to others.

coefficient alpha   The average of all possible split-half reliabilities for a given test.

cognitive behavior modification   An instructional approach that emphasizes using self-verbalizations to modify behavior.

cognitive conflict   According to Piaget's theory of cognitive development, the situation that occurs when a learner does not have cognitive structures that permit understanding of environmental stimuli.

cognitive modules   Distinct capacities that are inherited.

compensation   In conservation tasks, the recognition that change on one dimension can be compensated for by changes on another dimension.

concept   A mental representation of a category of related items.

concept maps   Diagrams that depict concepts and the relationships among them.

conceptual change strategy   A method by which students, when confronted with incongruency between their prior knowledge and new information, work at understanding the discrepancy in order to refine their thinking.

concrete operational stage   The third stage of Piaget's theory of cognitive development, in which concrete operators can apply cognitive operations to problems involving concrete objects.

conditional knowledge   Knowledge of when and where strategies are useful.

conditioned reinforcers   Reinforcers, such as money, that acquire their reinforcement properties by being paired with unconditioned reinforcers.

conditioned response   The response elicited by a conditioned stimulus.

conditioned stimulus   A neutral stimulus that has been paired with an unconditioned stimulus to evoke a conditioned response.

confirmability   In a qualitative study, the point at which multiple indicators all support the same conclusion.

confounding variables   Variables unrelated to the experimental treatment that may be influencing the outcome.

connectionist model   A model in which the basic building blocks of understanding are the connections between units of information.

conservation tasks   Tasks that typically require children to watch the transformation of a substance that does not alter its basic characteristics but changes its appearance.

construct validity   The standard of a test that establishes how well the test measures the construct it is intended to measure.

content validity   The standard of a test that establishes whether the test includes the content it is purported to cover.

conventional morality   According to Kohlberg's theory of moral development, the stages at which individuals focus on maintaining social order.

cooperative learning   An instructional technique in which students work together in small groups. Each student is individually accountable and has equal opportunity for success.

corpus callosum   The bundle of fibers connecting the two hemispheres of the brain.

correct decision speed   A process of intelligence corresponding to the quickness of response for complicated tasks.

correlation   A relationship between two variables.

correlation coefficient   A number, ranging between −1.00 and +1.00, that indicates the size and direction of a relationship between two variables.

counting down from given   A strategy for subtraction in which children count down from the larger number by the number of the smaller number.

counting on from first   A strategy for addition in which children start with the first addend and count up the number specified by the second addend.

counting on from larger   A strategy for addition in which children start with the larger addend and count up the number specified by the smaller addend.

count-to-cardinal transition   The understanding that the cardinal number, the last number uttered in a count, is the number of objects in the set counted.

credibility   The degree to which the grounded theory generated by qualitative research captures the reality of the situation studied.

criterion-referenced tests   Tests in which a student's performance is compared to a predefined performance standard of what should be learned.

criterion validity   The standard of a test that establishes whether or not the test makes the distinctions it is supposed to make, such as whether or not the test predicts scores on some criterion measure.

critical periods   Time periods of great sensitivity to environmental input.

cross-cultural study   A study that helps to evaluate the influence of setting effects.

cross-sectional study   The study of developmental variations carried out by examining age differences among different people at different age levels at one point in time.

crystallized intelligence   The knowledge acquired through the processes of intelligence.

cumulative rehearsal–fast finish   A strategy for remembering information in which the learner repeats all the items in a series, in order, as each new item is presented. After the last item is presented, the learner "dumps out" the last item or two and then recalls the earlier items in their given order.

declarative knowledge   Knowledge about things; knowledge that something is the case.

deferred imitation   The ability to represent learned behaviors so that the behavior can be imitated long after it was witnessed.

defining features   The necessary and sufficient features required for an item to qualify as representative of a concept.

dendrites   Branchlike extensions of the cell body that transmit impulses from other cells toward the cell body.

dependability   In qualitative research, the strength of the argument that most people would come to the same conclusions based on the data.

diffusion   An identity status in which people have not experienced identity crisis or commitment to an identity.

direct explanation and teacher modeling   A teacher-directed method for teaching academic processes that provides explanations and mental modeling, and proceeds with scaffolded instruction.

direct instruction   A teaching method in which instruction is teacher-directed and presented in a sequenced and structured fashion. Direct instruction focuses on teaching academic content.

discovery learning   A teaching method in which teachers facilitate learning by providing rich opportunities for students to discover and construct understandings.

disequilibrium   In Piaget's theory of cognitive development, the realization that two contradictory ways of thinking about the world cannot both be true.

distinctive features   Features critical to differentiating a set of items.

distributed cognition   Thinking that is not the product of one student but of several students in interaction with one another.

distributed practice   Practice that is spaced out over a period of time, leading to better performance than that resulting from massed practice.

domain-specific knowledge   Knowledge about a particular topic.

Down syndrome   A genetic disorder that is the most common cause of severe mental disabilities. Individuals with Down syndrome have distinctive facial and physical features.

dual coding model   A model that describes knowledge as associative networks of verbal and imaginal representations.

dualistic thinking   The belief that one and only one perspective is right and all others are wrong.

dyscalculia   The inability to calculate mathematical problems. Acquired dyscalculia results from some type of brain injury, and developmental dyscalculia refers to calculating difficulties experienced by otherwise normal children.

dyslexia   The inability to decode words well despite substantial reading instruction. Acquired dyslexia results from some type of brain injury, and developmental dyslexia refers to reading difficulties experienced by otherwise normal children.

effect size   A measure of the size of the mean difference between experimental and control conditions, which allows comparisons across studies.

egocentric speech   Speech of young children directed to themselves about what they are doing.

egocentrism   The inability to perceive the perspectives of others.

ego involvement   A determination of success whereby students compare their performances to those of others.

elaboration   A strategy for remembering information by constructing a meaningful context, either visual or verbal.

emergent literacy   The reading and writing behaviors observed in infancy through the preschool years that develop into literacy.

encoding   Creating durable memory traces.

engagement   A high level of investment and commitment on the part of students to mastering what is presented in school.

entity theory   The belief that intelligence is fixed.

episodic memory   The memory of personally experienced events.

equilibration   In Piaget's theory of cognitive development, the process by which a learner constructs new cognitive structures in response to disequilibrium in order to return to equilibrium.

ethnic identity   The feelings, perceptions, and behavior arising from membership in an ethnic group.

executive processing space   The number of pieces of information a student can have active in memory at any one time.

experience-dependent synapses   Synapses that respond to whatever environmental stimulation an individual encounters.

experience-expectant synapses   Synapses that are genetically programmed to respond to certain stimulation.

expository text structures   The schemata for factual texts.

external validity   In a research study, the criterion of resembling closely the real-life issue the researcher is trying to investigate.

extinction   The process by which classically conditioned responses cease (are extinguished) when subsequent experiences of the stimulus are not followed by the conditioned response.

factor analysis   A statistical technique that identifies clusters of items, or "factors," that correlate with one another.

fading   In behavior modification programs, a gradual reduction in the use of reinforcement once the behavioral goals are reached.

feature comparison theory   A theory in which concepts are defined according to the necessary and sufficient features required to qualify as a representative of a concept.

fetal alcohol syndrome (FAS)   Birth defects, such as learning difficulties and mental retardation, caused by damage to the central nervous system as a result of maternal alcoholism.

fluid intelligence   The reasoning ability that allows the acquisition of knowledge.

foreclosure   An identity status in which people have committed to an identity without experiencing an identity crisis.

formal operational stage The last stage of Piaget's theory of cognitive development, in which formal operational thinkers are capable of complex problem solving and of "thinking in possibilities," "thinking ahead," and "thinking in hypotheses."

formative evaluation Often an informal evaluation in which practice tests serve as checks on students' progress, providing feedback to both students and teachers.

frequency distribution A listing of every score and the number of times that score appeared in the distribution of scores on a test.

genotype The genes possessed, which specify a potential range of outcomes.

grounded theory A theory constructed from interpretations of data.

guided discovery A teaching method, more explicit than discovery learning, in which teachers pose questions in order to lead students to solve problems.

guided participation A teaching method in which teachers explicitly direct processing done by students.

habituation The tendency of familiar stimuli to attract less attention after frequent exposure. Susceptibility to habituation is one way to measure intelligence in infants.

heritability The variation in intelligence that is due to genetic variability.

higher-order questions Questions that require the manipulation of information and reflection.

histogram A bar graph that displays the frequencies of scores derived from a frequency distribution.

holistic grading A method of grading essays in which teachers compare an essay response as a whole to some general standard of an "A," "B," or "C" paper.

horizontal décalage In Piaget's cognitive developmental theory, the inability of individuals to master all problems requiring the same logical operations at the same time.

identity In conservation tasks, the basic characteristics of a substance, which remain the same despite perceptual transformations.

identity achieved An identity status in which people have undergone identity crises and have committed to an identity.

images Information stored in mental pictures.

immersion programs Programs whose goal is to stimulate the acquisition of both first and second languages. In immersion programs, much of the instruction is provided in the target language.

impulsivity The tendency to respond quickly without considering alternatives.

inclusion An implementation of the principle of least restrictive environment in which students with disabilities receive all instruction in the regular classroom, often in collaboration with special education teachers or other specialists.

incremental theory The belief that intelligence is modifiable by experience.

individualized education program (IEP) A program that describes a student's disability and outlines an educational plan to address the student's learning difficulties.

indulgent/permissive parents Parents who are undemanding and responsive and who make few demands of their children but are responsive to them.

inner speech An abbreviated and fragmentary internal dialogue that according to Vygotsky plays an important role in thinking.

inquiry teaching A specific example of guided discovery in which teachers present students with a series of questions designed to guide student discovery.

instructional objectives Simple statements of desired student change that indicate the behaviors and skills students should exhibit after instruction.

intermittent reinforcement Reinforcers that are presented only on occasion rather than continuously, thus making behaviors more resistant to extinction.

internal validity In a research study, the criterion of there being no other plausible competing interpretations of the results.

interval reinforcement schedule Intermittent reinforcement that is provided at certain time intervals.

intrinsic motivation   Motivation generated from within the learner.

item analysis   A procedure used in evaluating multiple-choice questions in order to determine item difficulty, item discrimination, and distractor analysis.

item difficulty   A test item characteristic that is determined by computing the percentage of test takers who answered a given item correctly.

item discrimination   A test item characteristic that indicates a test item's ability to distinguish between more and less knowledgeable students.

item distractor analysis   A test item characteristic that indicates whether or not the item distractors are working as planned.

juku   After-school tutoring common in Japan.

knowledge   Information or understanding gained through experience.

knowledge telling   An immature approach to writing in which writers do not plan but instead tell all they know about a writing topic.

labeling   A strategy used by young children on serial recall tasks in which the name of an item is said as it is presented.

learned helplessness   The belief that there is nothing one can do that will lead to success.

least restrictive environment   A term interpreted as meaning that students with disabilities must be educated with their nondisabled peers to the maximum extent appropriate.

logographic reading   A technique for decoding words by focusing on the salient visual characteristics of a word.

longitudinal study   The study of developmental differences carried out by following the same people for a period of time.

long-term memory   A memory store in which information is stored for extended period of time.

lower-order questions   Questions that require only simple recall of information.

magnetic resonance imaging (MRI)   A diagnostic technique that measures changes in the orientation of atomic nuclei.

mainstreaming   The practice of placing students with disabilities as often as possible in regular classrooms with their nondisabled peers.

maintaining   Continuing to use a strategy when it is appropriate.

manipulative investigations   Studies in which researchers control variation by randomly assigning people to one educational treatment or another.

massed practice   Practice that is crammed into one long episode, leading to lower performance than that resulting from distributed practice.

mastery learning   An instructional method in which course content is broken up into manageable units and students progress at their own rates, mastering each unit in a logical sequence.

mastery-oriented   A term describing students who focus on mastering the material presented in class.

mean   An arithmetic average of all scores.

member checking   Qualitative researchers' taking emerging categories back to those being studied and asking them to evaluate the credibility of the categories.

mental modeling   As used in direct explanation and teacher modeling, a strategy by which the teacher shows students how to apply a strategy by simply thinking out loud when using the strategy.

meta-analysis   A method for comparing effect sizes across studies.

metacognition   Knowledge about and awareness of thinking, including the knowledge of when and where to use acquired strategies.

monitoring   Being aware of and keeping track of mental processes.

moratorium   An identity status in which people are in ongoing crisis, actively exploring potential identities.

motivation   Goal-directed behavior.

motor schemes   Patterns of action used in interaction with the environment developed during the sensorimotor stage of cognitive development.

multivoicedness   The ability to use different social languages in different situations.

myelin   A layer of axon sheathing that permits more rapid firing of axons.

narrative text structures   The schemata for fictional stories.

negative reinforcers   The cessation of aversive stimulation following a response, thus increasing the likelihood of the response.

neglecting parents   Parents who are undemanding and unresponsive to their children.

neural networks   Connections linking units of information.

neurogenesis   A period of rapid cell growth.

nonmanipulative investigations   Studies in which researchers systematically analyze naturally occurring differences between people or settings.

norm   A typical level of performance for a clearly defined reference group.

normal distribution   A frequency distribution of scores on a test that resembles a bell-shaped curve, with most of the scores falling near the mean and fewer scores falling further away from the mean.

norm-referenced tests   Tests in which a student's performance is compared to the performance of other students.

note taking   A strategy used to remember information from text or lectures.

objective test questions   Questions in which the evaluation of the response is not open to different interpretations.

objectivity   The use of measures that are publicly observable and clearly measurable.

object permanence   A child's understanding that objects continue to exist regardless of whether or not the child can see or touch them.

operant conditioning   Conditioning that, depending on the consequences (reinforcement or punishment), increases or decreases the likelihood of a response.

operational schemes   The logical patterns of thinking that characterize the concrete and formal operational stages of Piaget's theory of cognitive development.

organization   A strategy for remembering information by grouping items on some characteristic.

orthographic patterns   A meaningful string of letters, such as prefixes, that can be processed as wholes.

outlining   A strategy used to summarize and organize text.

pattern recognition productions   Productions that are used to identify a situation and to determine whether conditions are met for an action sequence.

percentile ranks   An expression of scores in terms of relative position within a norm group.

performance-oriented   A term describing students who focus on performing well and getting good grades.

phenotype   The observed outcome of the genotype, or how the genes are expressed.

phonemic awareness   The awareness that words are composed of separable sounds, a critical competency for reading success during the elementary school years.

phonetic cue reading   A method to decode words that uses cues of salient letter-sound relationships.

phonics rules   Generalizations that may help in sounding out words.

plastic   As used in describing the brain, having fundamental physical properties, including the size and number of synaptic connections, that vary with environmental stimulation.

plus-one approach   An approach to moral education in which students argue about moral dilemmas to induce cognitive conflict and growth in understanding.

portfolios   Collections of objects compiled for an identified purpose.

positive reinforcement   A stimulus that increases the future likelihood of a response when presented following the response.

positron emission tomography (PET)   A method of brain imaging that detects radiation being emitted by an active site in the brain.

possible selves   Envisioning what one might become. Learners are motivated to reduce the difference between their current selves and their possible selves.

postconventional morality   According to Kohlberg's theory of moral development, the stages at which individuals focus on shared principles and standards.

PQ3R (Preview, Question, Read, Reflect, Recite)   A strategy students can use to help remember material.

preconventional morality   According to Kohlberg's theory of moral development, the stages at which individuals focus on self-interest in decision making.

preoperational stage   The second stage of Piaget's theory of cognitive development, in which thinking benefits from the development of symbolic schemes.

primary mental abilities   According to Thurstone's theory of intelligence, the nine primary mental abilities: inductive reasoning, deductive reasoning, practical problem reasoning, verbal comprehension, associative short-term memory, spatial abilities, perceptual speed, numerical competence, and word fluency.

private speech   Thoughts spoken out loud by someone working on a task.

proceduralization   The movement, developed with practice, from a declarative representation of a sequence of actions to a single procedure.

procedural knowledge   Knowledge of how to do things.

processing speed   A process of intelligence corresponding to thinking speed for simple tasks.

prodigies   Those who display extremely high aptitude for a particular activity.

productions   Knowledge representations that specify some action and when the action should occur.

propositional networks   The way in which propositions are connected through associations.

propositions   Descriptions that specify relationships between things and properties of things; the smallest unit of thought that can be judged true or false.

prototype   An abstract representation of a typical member of a concept.

prototype theory   A theory of concept learning suggesting that people classify concepts on the basis of resemblance to a prototype.

punishment   The presentation of aversive stimulation after a response, thus decreasing the future likelihood of the response.

quantitative intelligence   The ability to understand and apply the concepts and skills of mathematics.

random assignment   A method of ensuring that before an experiment begins, each participant has an equal chance of being assigned to any treatment.

ratio reinforcement schedule   Intermittent reinforcement that is provided after a certain number of desired responses.

reaction range   The range of possible phenotypes based on a given genotype.

reciprocal teaching   An instructional reading method consistent with Vygotskian principles in which the teacher initially explains and models comprehension strategies, the students practice the strategies in a group context, and the teacher provides scaffolding to support the group process.

reciprocity principle   A principle of writing stating that in order to construct a text that makes sense, the writer must be aware of what the potential reader knows already.

reconstruction   The use of prior knowledge to recall unclear memories that often result in distortions.

rehearsal   A strategy of repeating information to be remembered.

relativisitic thinking   The belief that the appropriateness of a perspective often depends on the context.

reliability   The likelihood of obtaining the same results consistently.

representational image   A mental picture of material to be learned that does not involve transformation of the content.

resource room   A place where a student with disabilities can receive special services.

response cost   A form of punishment used in some behavior modification programs in which unwanted behavior results in the loss of token reinforcers.

responsive elaboration Providing additional input and elaborations in response to the needs of particular learners as required in direct explanation and teacher modeling.

retrieving Accessing memory traces from long-term memory.

reversibility In conservation tasks, the understanding that an operation can be undone by reversing it.

scaffolding An instructional technique in which teachers provide help to students on an as-needed basis.

schemata Generalized knowledge about objects, situations, and events.

scheme A coordinated pattern of thought or action that organizes an individual's interaction with the environment.

self-concept The organized representation of a learner's theories, attitudes, and beliefs about himself or herself.

self-contained classrooms Classrooms where students with disabilities are taught by special education specialists and where these students have little contact with regular instructional programs.

self-controlled training Instruction that involves teaching a strategy, encouraging students to evaluate the gains, and instructing students to remind themselves to use the strategy using self-verbalizations.

self-efficacy A learner's perception of his or her capability of reaching a desired goal or a certain level of performance.

self-fulfilling prophecy The tendency of students to live up (or down) to expectations.

self-questioning A strategy used to prompt elaboration.

self-reference effect The tendency to access information about oneself when learning new material.

self-regulated Regulated by oneself to keep on task and guide one's own thinking.

self-schemas Knowledge structures about the self that organize interpretations of experience and guide behavior.

semantic memory Organized knowledge of the world that is independent of specific experiences.

semantic networks The way in which concepts are connected to each other in a pattern of associations.

sensorimotor stage The first stage of Piaget's theory of cognitive development, in which thinking is organized by motor schemes and a major accomplishment is object permanence.

serial recall task A task in which students are asked to remember items in the order they were presented.

seriating Ordering objects on some dimension.

shaping Molding behavior by reinforcing closer and closer approximations of the desired response.

short-term memory A memory store of limited capacity and duration; also called working memory.

signals Text conventions, such as "first of all," that flag the structure of the text.

situated cognition or knowledge Knowledge that cannot be separated from the actions that give rise to it or from the culture in which those actions occur.

social languages Languages that are appropriate in specific situations.

social learning theory A theory of learning that emphasizes learning through observation of behavioral models.

split-half reliability A criterion of a test's reliability that is measured by correlating the scores for half the items on the test with scores on the other half of the test items.

spreading activation The way in which concepts connected to each other in a semantic network are activated.

standard deviation An index of how much individual scores on a test differ from the mean.

standardized tests Tests that are given under controlled conditions so that every student taking the test has the same examination experience.

standard scores   An expression of scores on standardized tests that can be compared across contexts.

stanines   Standard scores with only nine possible categories, corresponding to ordered regions of the normal distribution.

storybook reading   The practice of an adult reading to a young child, which is an important emergent literacy experience during the preschool years.

strategies   Plans of action that may result in a solution to a problem or in achieving some goal.

subitizing   The ability of young children to identify the number for small sets of objects.

summative evaluation   A formal evaluation of what students have learned, which is an important component of grade assignment.

symbolic play   Play that incorporates children's capabilities for symbolic representation so that play objects are used to represent other items.

symbolic schemes   Cognitive structures, developed during the preoperational stage of cognitive development, that allow the representation of objects or events by means of symbols such as language, mental images, and gestures.

synaptic connections   Physical connections between neurons formed through an axon's meeting a dendrite, a cell body, or another axon.

table of specifications   In test preparation, a concise way to represent the content of instruction, the types of cognitive performance expected from students, and the number and type of questions expected to elicit such performance.

task involvement   A determination of success whereby students evaluate their own personal improvement.

teratogens   Environment agents such as disease or chemicals that can damage a developing brain.

test-retest reliability   A test's reliability that is established by administering the same test twice to a group of test takers. The correlation between the two scores earned by test takers on each testing occasion indicates whether the test is measuring consistently.

theoretical saturation   The point in qualitative research when all data are explained adequately.

theory of multiple intelligences   A theory that people have a set of specific intelligences—including linguistic intelligence, musical intelligence, logic-mathematical intelligence, spatial intelligence, body-kinesthetic intelligence, interpersonal intelligence, and intrapersonal intelligence—that are biologically determined.

thinking aloud   A research technique in which subjects think aloud as they accomplish a task.

time-out   A form of punishment sometimes used in behavior modification programs in which a student is physically removed from other students or activities (i.e., potential reinforcers) for a short period of time.

token reinforcement   Reinforcements that uses symbolic reinforcers, such as chips or marbles, that can be accumulated and traded for other reinforcers.

tracking   The practice of grouping students by ability.

transactional strategies instruction   A reading strategy instruction in which interpretations of text are codetermined by teacher-student-text interactions.

transferring   Applying strategies to new situations and tasks.

transferability   In qualitative research, an indication of the representativeness of the setting.

transformational image   A mental picture of material to be learned that involves recoding some part of the original message into something concrete that is then embedded in an image with other elements.

triangulation   In qualitative research, multiple indications of a phenomenon.

triarchic theory   A process-oriented theory of intelligence that is composed of three subtheories: contextual (sociocultural context), experiential (role of experiences), and componential (metacomponents, performance components, and knowledge-acquisition components—the mental structures that underlie intelligent behavior).

unconditioned reinforcers   Reinforcers that satisfy biological deprivations such as thirst or hunger.

unconditioned response   The response elicited by an unconditioned stimulus.

unconditioned stimulus   A stimulus that evokes a particular response, the unconditioned response.

utility knowledge   Knowledge of the potential benefits of using a strategy.

validity   Relevance and meaningfulness, as a test that measures what it is purported to measure.

vicarious experiences   In social learning theory, experiences that are observed in others.

visual processing   The process of intelligence measured by tasks involving visualization, such as imaging the way objects appear in space.

volition   The extent to which students persist in performing a task.

wait time   The time teachers allow students to think before responding to a question.

writer's workshop   An instructional method used for writing process instruction in which students share their writing and receive feedback from teachers and peers.

zone of proximal development   A range of achievements that includes tasks that learners cannot accomplish independently but can accomplish with assistance.

z-score   A type of standard score that tells how many standard deviations above or below the mean a raw score is.

References

Achenbach, T., & Zigler, E. (1968). Cue-learning and problem-learning strategies in normal and retarded children. *Child Development, 3,* 827–848.

Adams, A., Carnine, D., & Gersten, R. (1982). Instructional strategies for studying content area texts in the intermediate grades. *Reading Research Quarterly, 18,* 27–53.

Adams, M. J. (1990). *Beginning to read.* Cambridge, MA: Harvard University Press.

Ahn, W. (1987). *Schema acquisition from a single example.* Unpublished master's thesis. University of Illinois, Department of Psychology, Urbana.

Ahn, W., & Brewer, W. F. (1988). Similarity-based and explanation-based learning of explanatory and nonexplanatory information. *Proceedings of the Tenth Annual Conference of the Cognitive Science Society* (pp. 524–530). Hillsdale, NJ: Erlbaum.

Ahn, W., Mooney, R. J., Brewer, W. F., & DeJong, G. F. (1987). Schema acquisition from one example: Psychological evidence for explanation-based learning. *Proceedings of the Ninth Annual Conference of the Cognitive Science Society* (pp. 50–57). Hillsdale, NJ: Erlbaum.

Airasian, P. W. (1994). *Classroom assessment* (2nd ed.). New York: McGraw-Hill.

Ajewole, G. A. (1991). Effects of discovery and expository instructional methods on the attitude of students in biology. *Journal of Research in Science Teaching, 28,* 401–409.

Allen, J. B., Clark, W., Cook, M., Crane, P., Fallon, I., Hoffman, L., Jennings, K. S., & Sours, M. A. (1989). Reading and writing development in whole language kindergartens. In J. Mason (Ed.), *Reading and writing connections* (pp. 121–146). Needham Heights, MA: Allyn & Bacon.

Allen, V. L. (Ed.). (1976). *Children as teachers: Theory and research on tutoring.* New York: Academic Press.

Allington, R. [L] (1977). If they don't read much, how they ever gonna get good? *Journal of Reading, 21,* 57–61.

Allington, R. L. (1983). The reading instruction provided readers of differing ability levels. *Elementary School Journal, 83,* 548–559.

Allington, R. L. (1991a). Effective literacy instruction for at-risk children. In M. S. Knapp & P. M. Shields (Eds.), *Better schooling for the children of poverty: Alternatives to conventional wisdom* (pp. 9–30). Berkeley, CA: McCutchan.

Allington, R. L. (1991b). The legacy of "slow it down and make it more concrete." In J. Zutell & S. McCormick (Eds.), *Learner factors/teacher factors: Issues in literacy research and instruction: Fortieth Yearbook of the National Reading Conference* (pp. 19–29). Chicago: National Reading Conference.

Allington, R. L., & McGill-Franzen, A. (1989). School response to reading failure: Chapter 1 and special education students in grades 2, 4, & 8. *Elementary School Journal, 89,* 529–542.

Allington, R. L., & McGill-Franzen, A. (1991). *Unintended effects of educational reform in New York state.* Unpublished paper. Albany: State University of New York, School of Education.

Almasi, J. F. (1993). *The nature of fourth graders' sociocognitive conflicts in peer-led and teacher-led discussions of literature.* Unpublished dissertation. University of Maryland, Department of Curriculum and Instruction, College Park.

Alvermann, D. E., & Hague, S. A. (1989). Comprehension of counter-intuitive science text: Effects of prior knowledge and text structure. *Journal of Educational Research, 82,* 197–202.

Alvermann, D. E., & Hynd, C. R. (1991). The effects of varying prior knowledge activation modes and text structure on nonscience majors' comprehension of physics text. *Journal of Educational Research, 83,* 97–102.

Alvermann, D. E., & Moore, D. W. (1991). Secondary school reading. In R. Barr, M. L. Kamil, P. B. Mosenthal, & P. D. Pearson (Eds.), *Handbook of reading research* (Vol. II, pp. 951–983). New York: Longman.

Alvermann, D. E., Smith, L. C., & Readence, J. E. (1985). Prior knowledge activation and the comprehension of compatible and incompatible texts. *Reading Research Quarterly, 20,* 420–436.

Ames, C. (1984). Competitive, cooperative, and individualistic goal structures: A motivational analysis. In R. Ames & C. Ames (Eds.), *Research on motivation in education* (Vol. 1, pp. 117–207). New York: Academic Press.

Ames, C. (1990). Motivation: What teachers need to know. *Teachers College Record, 91,* 409–421.

Ames, C., & Ames, R. (1981). Competitive versus individualistic goal structures: The salience of past performance information for causal attributions and affect. *Journal of Educational Psychology, 73,* 411–418.

Ames, C., & Archer, J. (1988). Achievement goals in the classroom: Students' learning strategies and motivation processes. *Journal of Educational Psychology, 80,* 260–270.

Anastasi, A. (1988). *Psychological testing* (6th ed.). New York: Macmillan.

Anastasiow, N. J. (1990). Implications of the neurobiological model for early intervention. In S. J. Meisels & J. P. Shonkoff (Eds.), *Handbook of early childhood interventions* (pp. 196–216). Cambridge, UK: Cambridge University Press.

Anderson, C. W., Sheldon, T. H., & Dubay, J. (1990). The effects of instruction on college nonmajors' conceptions of respiration and photosynthesis. *Journal of Research in Science Teaching, 27,* 761–776.

Anderson, D. R., & Collins, P. A. (1988). *The impact on children's education: Television's influence on cognitive development* (Office of Research Working Paper No. 2). Washington, DC: U.S. Department of Education, Office of Educational Research and Improvement.

Anderson, J. R. (1983). *The architecture of cognition.* Cambridge, MA: Harvard University Press.

Anderson, J. R. (1984). Spreading activation. In J. R. Anderson & S. M. Kosslyn (Eds.), *Tutorials in learning and memory: Essays in honor of Gordon Bower* (pp. 61–90). San Francisco: Freeman.

Anderson, L., Jenkins, L. B., Leming, J., MacDonald, W. B., Mullis, I. V. S., Turner, M. J., & Wooster, J. S. (1990). *The civics report card.* Washington, DC: U.S. Department of Education, Office of Educational Research and Improvement.

Anderson, R. C., Hiebert, E. H., Scott, J. A., & Wilkinson, I. A. G. (1985). *Becoming a nation of readers.* Washington, DC: National Institute of Education.

Anderson, R. C., & Ortony, A. (1975). On putting apples into bottles: A problem of polysemy. *Cognitive Psychology, 7,* 167–180.

Anderson, R. C., & Pearson, P. D. (1984). A schema-theoretic view of basic processes in reading. In P. D. Pearson (Ed.), *Handbook of reading research.* New York: Longman.

Anderson, R. C., & Pichert, J. W. (1978). Recall of previously unrecallable information following a shift in perspective. *Journal of Verbal Learning and Verbal Behavior, 17,* 1–12.

Anderson, R. C., Reynolds, R. E., Schallert, D. L., & Goetz, E. T. (1977). Frameworks for comprehending discourse. *American Educational Research Journal, 14,* 367–382.

Anderson, R. C., Shirey, L. L., Wilson, P. T., & Fielding, L. G. (1987). Interestingness of children's reading material. In R. E. Snow & M. J. Farr (Eds.), *Aptitude, learning, and instruction: Vol. 3, Cognitive and Affective Process Analyses* (pp. 287–299). Hillsdale, NJ: Erlbaum.

Andre, T., & Anderson, T. (1978–1979). The development and evaluation of a self-questioning study technique. *Reading Research Quarterly, 14,* 605–623.

Anglin, J. M. (1977). *Word, object, and concept development.* New York: Norton.

Annett, J. (1989). Training skilled performance. In A. M. Colley & J. R. Beech (Eds.), *Acquisition and performance of cognitive skills* (pp. 61–84). Chichester, UK: Wiley.

Applebee, A. N. (1984). *Contexts for learning to write.* Norwood, NJ: Ablex.

Applebee, A. N., & Langer, J. A. (1983). Instructional scaffolding: Reading and writing as natural language activities. *Language Arts, 60,* 168–175.

Applebee, A. N., Langer, J., & Mullis, I. (1986). *The writing report card: Writing achievement in American schools.* Princeton, NJ: Educational Testing Service.

Applebee, A. N., Langer, J., & Mullis, I. (1988). *Crossroads in American education: A summary of findings.* Princeton, NJ: Educational Testing Service.

Armbruster, B. B., & Anderson, T. H. (1981). Research synthesis on study skills. *Educational Leadership, 39,* 154–156.

Armbruster, B. B., Anderson, T. H., & Ostertag, J. (1987). Does text structure/summarization instruction facilitate learning from expository text? *Reading Research Quarterly, 22,* 331–346.

Arnaudin, M. W., & Mintzes, J. J. (1985). Students' alternative conceptions of the human circulatory system: A cross-age study. *Science Education, 69,* 721–733.

Asarnow, J. R., & Meichenbaum, D. (1979). Verbal rehearsal and serial recall. *Child Development, 50,* 1173–1177.

Aslin, R. N. (1981). Experimental influence and sensitive period in perceptual development: A unified model. In R. N. Aslin & F. Peterson (Eds.), *The development of perception* (Vol. 2, pp. 45–93). Orlando, FL: Academic Press.

Ault, C. S. (1985). Concept mapping as a study strategy with earth science. *Journal of College Science Teaching, 15,* 38–44.

Ausubel, D. P. (1960). The use of advance organizers in the learning and retention of meaningful verbal learning. *Journal of Educational Psychology, 51,* 267–272.

Ausubel, D. P. (1968). *Educational Psychology: A cognitive view.* New York: Holt, Rinehart & Winston.

Azmitia, M., & Hesser, J. (1993). Why siblings are important agents of cognitive development: A comparison of siblings and peers. *Child Development, 64,* 430–444.

Babad, E., Bernieri, F., & Rosenthal, R. (1991). Students as judges of teachers' verbal and nonverbal behavior. *American Educational Research Journal, 28,* 211–234.

Babad, E. Y., & Budoff, M. (1974). Sensitivity and validity of learning potential measurements in three levels of ability. *Journal of Educational Psychology, 66,* 439–447.

Baddeley, A. (1986). *Working memory.* New York: Oxford University Press.

Bailey, S. M. (1993). The current status of gender equity research. *Educational Psychologist, 28* (4), 321–339.

Bakan, P. (1969). Hypnotizability, laterality of eye movement, and functional brain asymmetry. *Perceptual and Motor Skills, 28,* 927–932.

Baker, E. L., Freeman, M., & Clayton, S. (1991). Cognitive assessment of history for large-scale testing. In Wittrock & E. L. Baker, *Testing and cognition* (pp. 131–153). New York: Allyn & Bacon.

Baker, E. L., O'Neil, H. F., & Linn, R. L. (1993). Policy and validity prospects for performance-based assessment. *American Psychologist, 48*(12), 1210–1218.

Baker, L. A., Vernon, P. A., & Ho, H.-Z. (1991). The genetic correlation between intelligence and speed of information processing. *Behavior Genetics, 21,* 351–367.

Baker-Ward, L., Ornstein, P. A., & Holden, D. J. (1984). The expression of memorization in early childhood. *Journal of Experimental Child Psychology, 37,* 555–575.

Bakhtin, M. M. (1981). *The dialogic imagination: Four essays by M. M. Bakhtin* (M. Holquist, Ed.; C. Emerson & M. Holquist, Trans.). Austin: University of Texas Press.

Baltes, P. B. (1968). Longitudinal and cross-sectional sequences in the study of age and generation effects. *Human Development, 11,* 145–171.

Baltes, P. B., Reese, H. W., & Nesselroade, J. R. (1977). *Life-span developmental psychology: Introduction to research methods.* Monterey, CA: Brooks/Cole.

Bandura, A. (1965). Vicarious processes: A case of no-trial learning. In L. Berkowitz (Ed.), *Advances in experimental social psychology* (Vol. 2, pp. 1–55). New York: Academic Press.

Bandura, A. (1969). *Principles of behavior modification.* New York: Holt.

Bandura, A. (1977a). Self-efficacy: Toward a unifying theory of behavioral change. *Psychological Review, 84,* 191–215.

Bandura, A. (1977b). *Social learning theory.* Englewood Cliffs, NJ: Prentice-Hall.

Bandura, A. (1982). Self-efficacy mechanism in human agency. *American Psychologist, 37,* 122–147.

Bandura, A. (1986). *Social foundations of thought and action: A social cognitive theory.* Englewood Cliffs, NJ: Prentice-Hall.

Bandura, A., & Cervone, D. (1983). Self-evaluative and self-efficacy mechanisms governing the motivational effects of goal systems. *Journal of Personality and Social Psychology, 45,* 1017–1028.

Bandura, A., & Cervone, D. (1986). Differential engagement of self-reactive influences in cognitive motivation. *Organizational Behavior and Human Decision Processes, 38,* 92–113.

Bandura, A., Grusec, J. E., & Menlove, F. L. (1966). Observational learning as a function of symbolization and incentive set. *Child Development, 37,* 499–506.

Bandura, A., & Jefferey, R. W. (1973). Role of symbolic coding and rehearsal processes in observational learning. *Journal of Personality and Social Psychology, 26,* 122–130.

Bandura, A., Jeffrey, R. W., & Bachicha, D. L. (1974). Analysis of memory codes and cumulative rehearsal in observational learning. *Journal of Research in Personality, 7,* 295–305.

Bandura, A., & McDonald, F. J. (1963). Influence of social reinforcement and the behavior of models in shaping children's moral judgments. *Journal of Abnormal and Social Psychology, 67,* 274–281.

Bandura, A., & Schunk, D. H. (1981). Cultivating competence, self-efficacy, and intrinsic interest through proximal self-instruction. *Journal of Personality and Social Psychology, 41,* 586–598.

Bandura, A., & Walters, R. H. (1963). *Social learning and personality development.* New York: Holt, Rinehart & Winston.

Banks, J. A. (1993). The canon debate, knowledge construction, and multicultural education. *Educational Researcher, 22* (5), 4–14.

Banks, J. A. (1994). *Multiethnic education: Theory and practice* (3rd ed.). Boston: Allyn & Bacon.

Banks, M. S., & Salapatek, P. (1983). Infant visual perception. In M. M. Haith & J. J. Campos (Volume Ed.) and P. H. Mussen (General Ed.), *Handbook of child psychology: Vol. II, Infancy and developmental psychology* (pp. 435–571). New York: Wiley.

Barclay, C. R. (1979). The executive control of mnemonic activity. *Journal of Experimental Child Psychology, 27,* 262–276.

Barker, T. A., Torgesen, J. L., & Wagner, R. K. (1992). The role of orthographic processing skills on five different reading tasks. *Reading Research Quarterly, 27,* 334–345.

Barnhart, J. E. (1991). Criterion-related validity of interpretations of children's performance on emergent literacy tasks. *Journal of Reading Behavior, 23,* 425–444.

Baron, J. (1977). Mechanisms for pronouncing printed words: Use and acquisition. In D. LaBerge & S. J. Samuels (Eds.), *Basic processes in reading: Perception and comprehension* (pp. 175–216). Hillsdale, NJ: Erlbaum.

Baroody, A. (1987). *Children's mathematical thinking.* New York: Teachers College Press.

Barr, P., & Samuels, M. (1988). Dynamic assessment of cognitive and affective factors contributing to learning difficulties in adults. *Professional Psychology: Research and Practice, 19,* 6–13.

Barr, R. C. (1974–1975). The effect of instruction on pupil reading strategies. *Reading Research Quarterly, 10,* 555–582.

Barrass, R. (1984). Some misconceptions and misunderstandings perpetuated by teachers and textbooks of biology. *Journal of Biological Education, 18,* 201–206.

Bartel, N. R., & Thurman, S. K. (1992). Medical treatment and educational problems in children. *Phi Delta Kappan, 74,* 57–61.

Basili, P. A., & Sanford, J. P. (1991). Conceptual change strategies and cooperative group work in chemistry. *Journal of Research in Science Teaching, 28,* 293–304.

Bassarear, T., & Davidson, N. (1992). The use of small group learning situations in mathematics instruction as a tool to develop thinking. In N. Davidson & T. Worsham (Eds.), *Enhancing thinking through cooperative learning* (pp. 235–250). New York: Teachers College Press.

Bauer, R. H. (1977a). Memory processes in children with learning disabilities. *Journal of Experimental Child Psychology, 24,* 415–430.

Bauer, R. H. (1977b). Short-term memory in learning disabled and nondisabled children. *Bulletin of the Psychonomic Society, 10,* 128–130.

Baumrind, D. (1980). New directions in socialization research. *American Psychologist, 35,* 639–652.

Baumrind, D. (1983). Rejoinder to Lewis's reinterpretation of parental control effects: Are authoritative families really harmonious? *Psychological Bulletin, 94,* 132–142.

Beal, C. R. (1987). Repairing the message: Children's monitoring and revision skills. *Child Development, 58,* 401–408.

Beal, C. R. (1989). Children's communication skills: Implications for the development of writing strategies. In C. B. McCormick, G. Miller, & M. Pressley (Eds.), *Cognitive strategy research: From basic research to educational applications* (pp. 191–214). New York: Springer-Verlag.

Bean, T. W., & Steenwyk, F. L. (1984). The effect of three forms of summarization instruction on sixth graders' summary writing and comprehension. *Journal of Reading Behavior, 16,* 297–306.

Bechtel, W., & Abrahamsen, A. (1991). *Connectionism and the mind.* Cambridge, MA: Basil Blackwell.

Beckwith, L., & Parmelee, A. H., Jr. (1986). EEG patterns of preterm infants: Home environments and later IQ. *Child Development, 57,* 777–789.

Beichner, R. J. (1990). The effect of simultaneous motion presentation and graph generation in a kinematics lab. *Journal of Research in Science Teaching, 27,* 803–815.

Bell, R. Q. (1968). A reinterpretation of the direction of effects in studies of socialization. *Psychological Review, 75,* 81–95.

Belmont, J. M., Butterfield, E. C., & Ferretti, R. P. (1982). To secure transfer of training: Instruct self-management skills. In D. K. Detterman & R. J. Sternberg (Eds.), *How and how much can intelligence be increased* (pp. 147–154). Norwood, NJ: Ablex.

Bennett, F. C. (1987). The effectiveness of early intervention for infants at increased biologic risk. In M. J. Guralnick & F. C. Bennett (Eds.), *The effectiveness of early intervention for at-risk and handicapped children* (pp. 79–112). Orlando, FL: Academic Press.

Bennett, W. L. (1984). *To reclaim a legacy: A report on humanities in higher education.* Washington, DC: National Endowment for the Humanities.

Ben-Zvi, R., Eylon, B., & Silberstein, J. (1987, July). Students' visualization of a chemical reaction. *Education in Chemistry,* 117–120.

Bereiter, C., & Scardamalia, M. (1982). From conversation to composition: The role of instruction in a developmental process. In R. Glaser (Ed.), *Advances in instructional psychology* (Vol. 2, pp. 1–64). Hillsdale, NJ: Erlbaum.

Bereiter, C., & Scardamalia, M. (1987). *The psychology of written communication.* Hillsdale, NJ: Erlbaum.

Berg, J. M. (1985). Physical determinants of environmental origin. In A. M. Clarke, A. D. B. Clarke, & J. M. Berg (Eds.), *Mental deficiency: The changing outlook* (4th ed., pp. 99–134). New York: Free Press.

Berk, L. E. (1986). Relationship of elementary school children's private speech to behavioral accompaniment to task, attention, and task performance. *Developmental Psychology, 22*(5), 671–680.

Berkowitz, S. J. (1986). Effects of instruction in text organization on sixth-grade students' memory for expository reading. *Reading Research Quarterly, 21,* 161–178.

Berliner, D. [C.] (1986). In pursuit of the expert pedagogue. *Educational Researcher, 15* (7), 5–13.

Berliner, D. C. (1988). *The development of expertise in pedagogy.* Washington, DC: American Association of College for Teacher Education.

Berninger, V. W., & Hart, T. M. (1992). A developmental neuropsychological perspective for reading and writing acquisition. *Educational Psychologist, 27* (4), 415–434.

Best, D. L. (1993). Inducing children to generate mnemonic organizational strategies: An examination of long-term retention and materials. *Development Psychology, 29,* 324–336.

Best, D. L., & Ornstein, P. A. (1986). Children's generation and communication of mnemonic organizational strategies. *Developmental Psychology, 22,* 845–853.

Binet, A., & Simon, T. (1905a). Sur la nécessité d'établit un diagnostic scientifique des états inferieurs de l'intelligence. *L'Année Psychologique, 11,* 163–190.

Binet, A., & Simon, T. (1905b). Methodes nouvelles pour le diagnostic du niveau intellectual des anormaux. *L'Année Psychologique, 11,* 191–244.

Binet, A., & Simon, T. (1905c). Application des methodes nouvelles au diagnostic du niveau intellectual chez des enfants normaux et anormaux d'hospice et d'école primaire. *L'Année Psychologique, 11,* 245–336.

Bird, T. (1990). The schoolteacher's portfolio: An essay on possibilities. In J. Millman & L. Darling-Hammond (Eds.), *Handbook of teacher evaluation: Elementary and secondary personnel,* (2nd ed., pp. 241–256). Newbury Park, CA: Sage.

Bissex, G. (1980). *GNYS at work: A child learns to write and read.* Cambridge MA: Harvard University Press.

Bjorklund, D. F. (1985). The role of conceptual knowledge in the development of organization in children's memory. In C. J. Brainerd & M. Pressley (Eds.), *Basic processes in memory development: Progress in cognitive development research* (pp. 103–142). New York: Springer-Verlag.

Bjorklund, D. F. (1987). How age changes in knowledge base contribute to the development of children's memory: An interpretive review. *Developmental Review, 7,* 93–130.

Bjorklund, D. F. (1989). *Cognitive development.* Monterey, CA: Brooks/Cole.

Black, J. E., & Greenough, W. T. (1991). Developmental approaches to the memory process. In J. L. Martinez, Jr., & R. P. Kesner (Eds.), *Learning and memory: A biological view,* (2nd ed., pp. 61–91). San Diego: Academic Press.

Blackman, L. S., & Lin, A. (1984). Generalization training in the educable mentally retarded: Intelligence and its educability revisited. In P. H. Brooks, R. Sperber, & C. McCauley (Eds.), *Learning and cognition in the mentally retarded* (pp. 237–263). Hillsdale, NJ: Erlbaum.

Blackwood, R. (1970). The operant conditioning of verbally mediated self-control in the classroom. *Journal of School Psychology, 8,* 257–258.

Blakenay, R., & Blakenay, C. (1990). Reforming moral misbehaviour. *Journal of Moral Education, 19,* 101–113.

Blatt, M., & Kohlberg, L. (1975). The effects of classroom moral discussion upon children's level of moral judgment. *Journal of Moral Education, 4,* 129–161.

Block, N. J., & Dworkin, G. (Eds.). (1976). *The IQ controversy.* New York: Pantheon Books.

Bloom, B. S. (1968, May). Mastery learning. In *Evaluation comment* (Vol. 1, No. 2). Los Angeles: UCLA, Center for Evaluation of Instructional Programs.

Bloom, B. S. (1985). *Developing talent in young people.* New York: Ballantine Books.

Bloom, B. S. (1986). *Taxonomy of educational objectives.* New York: Longman.

Bloom, B. S. (1987). A response to Slavin's Mastery Learning reconsidered. *Review of Educational Research, 57,* 507–508.

Bloom, L. (1973). *One word at a time.* The Hague, Netherlands: Mouton.

Bogen, J. E. (1975). The other side of the brain. VII: Some educational aspects of hemispheric specialization. *UCLA Educator, 17,* 24–32.

Bomba, P. C., & Siqueland, E. R. (1983). The nature and structure of infant form categories. *Journal of Experimental Child Psychology, 35,* 294–328.

Borko, H., & Livingston, C. (1989). Cognition and improvisation: Differences in mathematics instruction by expert and novice teachers. *American Educational Research Journal, 26,* 473–498.

Borkowski, J. G. (1985). Signs of intelligence: Strategy, generalization, and metacognition. In S. R. Yussen (Ed.), *The growth of reflection in children* (pp. 105–144). Orlando, FL: Academic Press.

Borkowski, J. G., Carr, M., Rellinger, E. A., & Pressley, M. (1990). Self-regulated strategy use: Interdependence of metacognition, attributions, and self-esteem. In B. F. Jones (Ed.), *Dimensions of thinking: Review of research* (pp. 53–92). Hillsdale, NJ: Erlbaum.

Borkowski, J. G., & Kurtz, B. E. (1987). Metacognition and executive control. In J. G. Borkowski & J. D. Day (Eds.), *Cognition in special children: Comparative approaches to retardation, learning disabilities, and giftedness* (pp. 123–152). Norwood, NJ: Ablex.

Borkowski, J. G., & Peck, V. A. (1986). Causes and consequences of metamemory in gifted children. In R. J. Sternberg & J. E. Davidson (Eds.), *Conceptions of giftedness* (pp. 182–200). Cambridge, UK: Cambridge University Press.

Bouchard, T. J., Jr., & McGue, M. (1981). Familial studies of intelligence: A review. *Science, 212,* 1055–1059.

Bowen, C. W. (1990). Representational systems used by graduate students while problem solving in organic synthesis. *Journal of Research in Science Teaching, 27,* 351–370.

Bower, G. H. (1972). Mental imagery and associative learning. In L. Gregg (Ed.), *Cognition in learning and memory* (pp. 51–87). New York: Wiley.

Bower, G. H., & Clapper, J. P. (1989). Experimental methods in cognitive science. In M. I. Posner (Ed.), *Foundations of cognitive science.* Cambridge: MIT Press.

Bower, G. H., & Hilgard, E. R. (1981). *Theories of learning,* (5th ed.). Englewood Cliffs, NJ: Prentice-Hall.

Bowers, C. A., & Flinders, D. J. (1990). *Responsive teaching: An ecological approach to classroom patterns of language, culture, and thought.* New York: Teachers College Press.

Boyes, M. C., & Chandler, M. (1992). Cognitive development, epistemic doubt, and identity formation in adolescence. *Journal of Youth and Adolescence, 21,* 277–304.

Boysen, S. T., & Berntson, G. G. (1990). The development of numerical skills in the chimpanzee (*Pan troglodytes*). In S. T. Parker & K. R. Gibson (Eds.), *"Language" and intelligence in monkeys and apes* (pp. 435–450). Cambridge, UK: Cambridge University Press.

Bracht, G. H., & Glass, G. V. (1968). The external validity of experiments. *American Educational Research Journal, 5,* 437–474.

Bradley, L., & Bryant, P. E. (1983). Categorizing sounds and learning to read—A causal connection. *Nature, 301,* 419–421.

Bradley, R. H., Whiteside, L., Mundfrom, D. J., Casey, P. H., Caldwell, B. M., & Barrett, K. (1994). Impact of the Infant Health and Development Program (IHDP) on the home environments of infants born prematurely and with low birthweight. *Journal of Educational Psychology, 86* (4), 531–541.

Brainerd, C. J. (1978a). Learning research and Piagetian theory. In L. S. Siegel & C. J. Brainerd (Eds.), *Alternatives to Piaget: Critical essays on the theory* (pp. 69–109). New York: Academic Press.

Brainerd, C. J. (1978b). *Piaget's theory of intelligence.* Englewood Cliffs, NJ: Prentice-Hall.

Brainerd, C. J. (1978c). The stage question in cognitive developmental theory. *Behavioral and Brain Sciences, 1,* 173–213.

Bransford, J. D., & Johnson, M. K. (1972). Contextual prerequisites for understanding: Some investigations of comprehension and recall. *Journal of Verbal Learning and Verbal Behavior, 11,* 717–726.

Bransford, J. D., Stein, B. S., Vye, N. J., Franks, J. J., Auble, P. M., Mezynski, K. J., & Perfetto, J. A. (1982). Differences in approaches to learning: An overview. *Journal of Experimental Psychology: General, 111,* 390–398.

Brasell, H. (1987). The effect of real-time laboratory graphing on learning graphic representations of distance and velocity. *Journal of Research in Science Teaching, 24,* 385–395.

Brennan, W. M., Ames, E. W., & Moore, R. W. (1966). Age differences in infants' attention to patterns of different complexity. *Science, 151,* 354–356.

Bretzing, B. H., & Kulhavy, R. W. (1981). Notetaking and passage styles. *Journal of Educational Psychology, 73,* 242–250.

Brewer, N. (1987). Processing speed, efficiency, and intelligence. In J. G. Borkowski & J. D. Day (Eds.), *Cognition in special children: Comparative approaches to retardation, learning disabilities, and giftedness* (pp. 15–48). Norwood, NJ: Ablex.

Brigham, M. C., & Pressley, M. (1988). Cognitive monitoring and strategy choice in younger and older adults. *Psychology and Aging, 3,* 249–257.

Brody, E. B., & Brody, N. (1978). *Intelligence: Nature, determinants, and consequences.* New York: Academic Press.

Brody, N. (1992). *Intelligence.* San Diego: Academic Press.

Brophy, J. (1981). Teacher praise: A functional analysis. *Review of Educational Research, 51,* 5–32.

Brophy, J. (1985). Teacher-student interaction. In J. B. Dusek (Ed.), *Teacher expectancies* (pp. 303–328). Hillsdale, NJ: Erlbaum.

Brophy, J. (1986, October). *On motivating students.* (Occasional Paper No. 101). East Lansing: Michigan State University, Institute for Research on Teaching.

Brophy, J. (1987). Socializing students' motivation to learning. In M. L. Maehr & D. A. Kleiber (Eds.), *Advances in motivation and achievement: Enhancing motivation* (Vol. 5, pp. 181–210). Greenwich, CT: JAI Press.

Brophy, J., & Evertson, C. (1976). *Learning from teaching: A developmental perspective.* Boston: Allyn & Bacon.

Brophy, J., & Good, T. (1970). Teachers' communication of differential expectations for children's classroom performance: Some behavioral data. *Journal of Educational Psychology, 61,* 365–374.

Brophy, J., & Good, T. (1974). *Teacher-student relationships: Causes and consequences.* New York: Holt, Rinehart, & Winston.

Brown, A. L. (1974). The role of strategic behavior in retardate memory. In N. R. Ellis (Ed.), *International review of research in mental retardation* (Vol. 7). New York: Academic Press.

Brown, A. L. (1978). Knowing when, where, and how to remember: A problem of metacognition. In R. Glaser (Ed.), *Advances in instructional psychology* (Vol. 1, pp. 55–111). Hillsdale, NJ: Erlbaum.

Brown, A. L., Bransford, J. D., Ferrara, R. A., & Campione, J. C. (1983). Learning, remembering, and understanding. In J. H. Flavell & E. M. Markman (Eds.), *Handbook of child psychology: Vol. III, Cognitive development* (pp. 77–166). New York: Wiley.

Brown, A. L., & Campione, J. C. (1978). Permissible inferences from cognitive training studies in developmental research. In W. S. Hall & M. Cole (Eds.), *Quarterly Newsletter of the Institute for Comparative Human Behavior, 2* (3), 46–53.

Brown, A. L., & Day, J. D. (1983). Macrorules for summarizing texts: The development of expertise. *Journal of Verbal Learning and Verbal behavior, 22,* 1–14.

Brown, A. L., Day, J. D., & Jones, R. S. (1983). The development of plans for summarizing texts. *Child Development, 54,* 968–979.

Brown, A. L., & French, L. (1979). The zone of proximal development: Implications for intelligence testing in the year 2000. *Intelligence, 3,* 253–271.

Brown, A. L., & Palincsar, A. S. (1989). Guided, cooperative learning and individual knowledge acquisition. In L. B. Resnick (Ed.), *Knowing, learning, and instruction: Essays in honor of Robert Glaser* (pp. 393–451). Hillsdale, NJ: Erlbaum.

Brown, I. (1976). Role of referent concreteness in the acquisition of passive sentence comprehension through abstract modeling. *Journal of Experimental Child Psychology, 22,* 185–189.

Brown, I. (1979). Language acquisition: Linguistic structure and rule-governed behavior. In G. J. Whitehurst & B. J. Zimmerman (Eds.), *The functions of language and cognition* (pp. 141–173). New York: Academic Press.

Brown, J. S., Collins, A., & Duguid, P. (1989). Situated cognition and the culture of learning. *Educational Researcher, 18*(1), 32–42.

Brown, R. (1973). *A first language: The early stages.* Cambridge, MA: Harvard University Press.

Brown, R. G. (1991). *Schools of thought.* San Francisco: Jossey-Bass.

Bruck, M. (1990). Word-recognition skills of adults with childhood diagnoses of dyslexia. *Developmental Psychology, 26,* 439–454.

Bruner, J. S. (1961). The art of discovery. *Harvard Educational Review, 31*(1), 21–32.

Bruner, J. S., Olver, R. R., & Greenfield, P. M. (1966). *Studies in cognitive growth.* New York: Wiley.

Bryk, A. S., & Thum, Y. M. (1989). The effects of high school organization on dropping out: An exploratory investigation. *American Educational Research Journal, 26,* 353–383.

Budoff, M. (1987). The validity of learning potential assessment. In C. S. Lidz (Ed.), *Dynamic assessment: An interactional approach to evaluating learning potential* (pp. 52–81). New York: Guilford Press.

Budoff, M., & Friedman, M. (1964). Learning potential as an assessment approach to the adolescent mentally retarded. *Journal of Consulting Psychology, 28,* 434–439.

Budoff, M., Gimon, A., & Corman, L. (1974). Learning potential measurement with Spanish-speaking youth as an alternative to IQ tests: A first report. *Intraamerican Journal of Psychology, 8,* 233–246.

Burack, J. A. (1990). Differentiating mental retardation: The two-group approach and beyond. In R. M. Hodapp, J. A. Burdack, & E. Zigler (Eds.), *Issues in the developmental approach to mental retardation* (pp. 27–48). Cambridge, UK: Cambridge University Press.

Burgess, D. M., & Streissguth, A. P. (1992). Fetal alcohol syndrome and fetal alcohol effects: Principles for educators. *Phi Delta Kappan, 74,* 24–30.

Burkell, J., Schneider, B., & Pressley, M. (1990). Mathematics. In M. Pressley & Associates, *Cognitive strategy instruction that really improves children's academic performance* (pp. 147–177). Cambridge, MA: Brookline Books.

Butkowski, I. S., & Willows, D. M. (1980). Cognitive-motivational characteristics of children varying in reading ability: Evidence for learned helplessness in poor readers. *Journal of Educational Psychology, 72,* 408–422.

Butler, R., & Neuman, O. (1995). Effects of task and ego achievement goals on help-seeking behaviors and attitudes. *Journal of Educational Psychology, 87*(2), 261–271.

Butterfield, E. C., & Belmont, J. M. (1977). Assessing and improving the executive cognitive functions of mentally retarded people. In I. Bialar & M. Sternlicht (Eds.), *Psychological issues in mental retardation* (pp. 277–318). New York: Psychological Dimensions.

Calderhead, J. (1983, April). *Research into teachers' and student teachers' cognitions: Exploring the nature of classroom practice.* Paper presented at the annual meeting of the American Educational Research Association, Montreal.

Calderhead, J., & Robson, M. (1991). Images of teaching: Student teachers' early conceptions of classroom practice. *Teaching and Teacher Education, 7,* 1–8.

Cameron, J., & Pierce, W. D. (1994). Reinforcement, reward, and intrinsic motivation: A meta-analysis. *Review of Educational Research, 64*(3), 363–423.

Campbell, D. T., & Stanley, J. C. (1966). *Experimental and quasi-experimental designs for research.* Chicago: Rand McNally.

Canfield, J., & Wells, H. C. (1994). *100 ways to enhance self-concept in the classroom: A handbook for teachers, counselors, and group leaders* (2nd ed.). Boston: Allyn & Bacon.

Cannell, J. J. (1987). *Nationally normed elementary achievement testing in America's public schools: How fifty states are above the national average.* Daniels, WV: Friends for Education.

Cannell, J. J. (1989). *How public educators cheat on standardized achievement tests.* Albuquerque, NM: Friends for Education.

Cantor, N., Markus, H., Niedenthal, P., & Nurius, P. (1986). On motivation and self-concept. In R. M. Sorrentino & E. T. Higgins (Eds.), *Motivation and cognition: Foundations of social behavior* (pp. 99–127). New York: Guilford Press.

Caplan, D. (1992). *Language: Structure, processing, and disorders.* Cambridge: MIT Press.

Cardelle-Elawar, M. (1990). Effects of feedback tailored to bilingual students' mathematics needs on verbal problem solving. *Elementary School Journal, 91,* 165–175.

Carey, S. (1985). *Conceptual change in childhood.* Cambridge: MIT Press.

Cariglia-Bull, T., & Pressley, M. (1990). Short-term memory differences between children predict imagery effects when sentences are read. *Journal of Experimental Child Psychology, 49,* 384–398.

Carlsen, W. S. (1991). Questioning in classrooms: A sociolinguistic perspective. *Review of Educational Research, 61*(2), 157–178.

Carpenter, T. P., Hiebert, J., & Moser, J. M. (1981). Problem structure and first-grade children's initial solution processes for simple addition and subtraction problems. *Journal for Research in Mathematics Education, 12,* 27–39.

Carpenter, T. P., Lindquist, M. M., Matthews, W., & Silver, E. A. (1983). Results of the third NAEP mathematics assessment: Secondary school. *Mathematics Teacher, 76*(9), 652–659.

Carpenter, T. P., & Moser, J. M. (1982). The development of addition and subtraction problem-solving skills. In T. P. Carpenter, J. M. Moser, & T. A. Romberg (Eds.), *Addition and subtraction: A cognitive perspective* (pp. 9–24). Hillsdale, NJ: Erlbaum.

Carr, J. (1975). *Young children with Down syndrome.* London: Butterworth.

Carr, J. (1985). The effect on the family of a severely mentally handicapped child. In A. M. Clarke, A. D. B. Clarke, & J. M. Berg (Eds.), *Mental deficiency: The changing outlook* (4th ed., pp. 512–548). New York: Free Press.

Carr, M., & Borkowski, J. G. (1989). Attributional training and the generalization of reading strategies with underachieving children. *Learning and Individual Differences, 1,* 327–341.

Carr, M., Kurtz, B. E., Schneider, W., Turner, L. A., & Borkowski, J. G. (1989). Strategy acquisition and transfer: Environmental influences on metacognitive development. *Developmental Psychology, 25,* 765–771.

Carraher, T. N., Carraher, D. W., & Schliemann, A. D. (1985). Mathematics in the street and in schools. *British Journal of Developmental Psychology, 3,* 21–29.

Carrier, C., & Titus, A. (1981). Effects of note-taking pretraining and test mode expectations on learning from lectures. *American Educational Research Journal, 18,* 385–397.

Carroll, J. (1963). A model of school learning. *Teachers College Record, 64,* 723–733.

Carter, K., Cushing, K., Sabers, D., Stein, P., & Berliner, D. (1988). Expert-novice differences in perceiving and processing visual classroom information. *Journal of Teacher Education, 39,* 25–31.

Carter, K., Sabers, D., Cushing, K., Pinnegar, S., & Berliner, D. C. (1987). Processing and using information about students: A study of expert, novice, and postulant teachers. *Teaching and Teacher Education, 3,* 147–157.

Case, R. (1985). *Intellectual development: Birth to adulthood.* Orlando, FL: Academic Press.

Case, R. (1991). A developmental approach to the design of remedial instruction. In A. McKeough & J. L. Lupart (Eds.), *Toward the practice of theory-based instruction.* (pp. 117–147). Hillsdale, NJ: Erlbaum.

Cattell, R. B. (1987). *Intelligence: Its structure, growth, and action.* Amsterdam: North-Holland.

Cattell, R. B., & Horn, J. L. (1978). A check on the theory of fluid and crystallized intelligence with description of new subtest designs. *Journal of Educational Measurement, 15,* 139–164.

Cazden, C. B. (1988). *Classroom discourse: The language of teaching and learning.* Portsmouth, NH: Heinemann.

Ceci, S. J., & Liker, J. K. (1986). A day at the races: A study of IQ, expertise, and cognitive complexity. *Journal of Experimental Psychology: General, 115,* 255–266.

Center, Y., Wheldall, K., Freeman, L., Outhred, L., & McNaught, M. (1995). An evaluation of Reading Recovery. *Reading Research Quarterly, 30*(2), 240–263.

Chall, J. S. (1967). *Learning to read: The great debate.* New York: McGraw-Hill.

Champagne, A. B., & Bunce, D. M. (1991). Learning-theory-based science teaching. In S. M. Glynn, R. H. Yeany, & B. K. Britton (Eds.), *The psychology of learning science* (pp. 21–41). Hillsdale, NJ: Erlbaum.

Chan, C. K. K., Burtis, P. J., Scardamalia, M., & Bereiter, C. (1992). Constructive activity in learning from text. *American Educational Research Journal, 29,* 97–118.

Charles, R. I., & Silver, E. A. (Eds.). (1989). *The teaching and assessing of mathematical problem solving* (Vol. 3). Hillsdale, NJ: Erlbaum and National Council of Teachers of Mathematics.

Charness, N. (1989). Expertise in chess and bridge. In D. Klahr & K. Kotovsky (Eds.), *Complex information processing: The impact of Herbert A. Simon* (pp. 183–208). Hillsdale, NJ: Erlbaum.

Chase, C. I. (1986). Essay test scoring: Interaction of relevant variables. *Journal of Educational Measurement, 23*(1), 33–41.

Chase, H. (1973). The effects of intrauterine and postnatal undernutrition on normal brain development. *Annals of the New York Academy of Sciences, 205*, 231–244.

Chase, W. G., & Ericsson, K. A. (1981). Skilled memory. In J. R. Anderson (Ed.), *Cognitive skills and their acquisition.* Hillsdale, NJ: Erlbaum.

Chase, W. G., & Ericsson, K. A. (1982). Skill and working memory. In G. H. Bower (Ed.), *The psychology of learning and motivation* (Vol. 16). New York: Academic Press.

Chase, W. G., & Simon, H. A. (1973). Perception in chess. *Cognitive Psychology, 4*, 55–81.

Cheney, L. V. (1987). *American memory: A report of the humanities in the nation's public schools.* Washington, DC: National Endowment for the Humanities.

Cheyne, J. A., & Walters, R. H. (1969). Intensity of punishment, timing of punishment, and cognitive structure as determinants of response inhibition. *Journal of Experimental Child Psychology, 7*, 231–244.

Chi, M. T. H. (1978). Knowledge structure and memory development. In R. S. Siegler (Ed.), *Children's thinking: What develops?* (pp. 73–96). Hillsdale, NJ: Erlbaum.

Chi, M. T. H., Feltovich, P. J., & Glaser, R. (1981). Categorization and representation of physics problems by experts and novices. *Cognitive Science, 5*, 121–152.

Chi, M. T. H., Glaser, R., & Farr, M. J. (1988). *The nature of expertise.* Hillsdale, NJ: Erlbaum.

Chiesi, L., Spilich, G. J., & Voss, J. F. (1979). Acquisition of domain-related information in relation to high and low domain knowledge. *Journal of Verbal Learning and Verbal Behavior, 18*, 257–273.

Childs, C. P., & Greenfield, P. M. (1980). Informal modes of learning and teaching: The case of Zinecanteco weaving. In N. Warren (Ed.), *Studies in cross-cultural psychology* (Vol. 2, pp. 269–316). London: Academic Press.

Chipeur, H. M., Rovine, M. J., & Plomin, R. (1990). LISREL modeling: Genetic and environmental influences on IQ revisited. *Intelligence, 14*, 11–29.

Chomsky, N. (1965). *Aspects of the theory of syntax.* Cambridge: MIT Press.

Chomsky, N. (1980a). Initial states and steady states. In M. Paittelli-Palmarini (Ed.), *Language and learning: The debate between Jean Piaget and Noam Chomsky* (pp. 97–130). Cambridge, MA: Harvard University Press.

Chomsky, N. (1980b). Rules and representations. *Behavioral and Brain Sciences, 3*, 1–61.

Churchland, P. S., & Sejnowski, T. J. (1992). *The computational brain.* Cambridge: MIT Press.

Clandenin, D. J. (1986). *Classroom practice: Teacher images in action.* London: Falmer Press.

Clark, E. V. (1973). What's in a word? On the child's acquisition of semantics in his first language. In T. E. Moore (Ed.), *Cognitive development and the acquisition of language* (pp. 65–110). New York: Academic Press.

Clark, H. H., & Clark, E. V. (1977). *Psychology and language.* New York: Harcourt Brace Jovanovich.

Clark, J. M., & Paivio, A. (1991). Dual coding theory and education. *Educational Psychology Review, 3*, 149–210.

Clay, M. M. (1985). *The early detection of reading difficulties: A diagnostic survey with recovery procedure.* Portsmouth, NH: Heinemann.

Clay, M. M. (1991). *Becoming literate: The construction of inner control.* Portsmouth, NH: Heinemann.

Clay, M. M., & Cazden, C. B. (1990). A Vygotskian interpretation of Reading Recovery. In L. C. Moll (Ed.), *Vygotsky and education: Instructional implications and applications of sociohistorical psychology* (pp. 206–222). Cambridge, UK: Cambridge University Press.

Clement, J., with the assistance of Brown, D., Camp, C., Kudukey, J., Minstrell, J., Palmer, D., Schultz, K., Shimabukuro, J., Steinberg, M., & Veneman, V. (1987). Overcoming students' misconceptions in physics: The role of anchoring intuitions and analogical validity. In J. Novak (Ed.), *Proceedings of the second international seminar: Misconceptions and educational strategies in science and mathematics* (Vol. III, pp. 84–97). Ithaca, NY: Cornell University Press.

Clement, J., Brown, D. E., & Zeitsman, A. (1989). Not all preconceptions are misconceptions: Finding "anchoring conceptions" for grounding instruction on students' intuition. *International Journal of Science Education, 11,* 554–565.

Clifford, M. M. (1975). Validity of expectation: A developmental function. *Alberta Journal of Educational Research, 21,* 11–17.

Clifford, M. M. (1978). The effects of quantitative feedback on children's expectations of success. *Journal of Educational Psychology, 48,* 220–226.

Clifford, M. M. (1984). Thoughts on a theory of constructive failure. *Educational Psychologist, 19,* 108–120.

Clymer, T. (1963). The utility of phonic generalizations in the primary grades. *Reading Teacher, 16,* 252–258.

Cognition and Technology Group at Vanderbilt University (1992). The Jasper series as an example of anchored instruction: Theory, program description, and assessment data. *Educational Psychologist, 27,* 291–315.

Cohen, J. (1988). *Statistical power analysis for the behavioral sciences* (Rev. ed.). Hillsdale, NJ: Erlbaum.

Cohen, P. (1995). Understanding the brain: Educators seek to apply brain research. *Education Update, 37*(7), 1, 4–5.

Coleman, J. S. (1961). *The adolescent society.* New York: Free Press of Glencoe.

Collins, A. (1992). Portfolios for science education: Issues in purpose, structure, and authenticity. *Science Education, 76,* 451–463.

Collins, A., Brown, J. S., & Newman, S. E. (1989). Cognitive apprenticeship: Teaching the crafts of reading, writing, and mathematics. In L. B. Resnick (Ed.), *Knowing, learning, and instruction: Essays in honor of Robert Glaser* (pp. 453–494). Hillsdale, NJ: Erlbaum.

Collins, A., & Stevens, A. L. (1982). Goals and strategies of inquiry teachers. In R. Glaser (Ed.), *Advances in instructional psychology* (Vol. 2, pp. 65–119). Hillsdale, NJ: Erlbaum.

Collins, A. M., & Loftus, E. F. (1975). A spreading-activation theory of semantic processing. *Psychological Review, 82,* 407–428.

Collins, A. M., & Quillian, M. R. (1969). Retrieval time from semantic memory. *Journal of Verbal Learning and Verbal Behavior, 8,* 240–247.

Collins, W. A., Wellman, H., Keniston, A. H., & Westby, S. D. (1978). Age-related aspects of comprehension and inference from a televised dramatic narrative. *Child Development, 49,* 389–399.

Comstock, G., & Paik, H. (1991). *Television and the American child.* San Diego: Academic Press.

Confrey, J. (1990). A review of the research on student conceptions in mathematics, science, and programming. In C. B. Cazden (Ed.), *Review of Research in Education* (Vol. 16, pp. 3–56). Washington, DC: American Educational Research Association.

Connelly, F. M., & Clandenin, D. J. (1985). Personal practical knowledge and the modes of knowing: Relevance for teaching and learning. In E. Eisner (Ed.), *Learning and teaching the ways of knowing (84th yearbook of the National Society for the Study of Education).* (Part II, pp. 174–198). Chicago: University of Chicago Press.

Constantino, G. (1992). Overcoming bias in the educational assessment of Hispanic students. In K. F. Geisinger (Ed.), *Psychological testing of Hispanics* (pp. 89–98). Washington, DC: American Psychological Association.

Cook, L. K., & Mayer, R. E. (1983). Reading strategy training for meaningful learning from prose. In M. Pressley & J. R. Levin (Eds.), *Cognitive strategy research: Educational applications* (pp. 87–131). New York: Springer-Verlag.

Cook, L. K., & Mayer, R. E. (1988). Teaching readers about the structure of scientific text. *Journal of Educational Psychology, 80*(4), 448–456.

Cooney, J. B., & Swanson, H. L. (1990). Individual differences in memory for mathematical story problems: Memory span and problem perception. *Journal of Educational Psychology, 82,* 570–577.

Cooper, E., Blackwood, P., Bolschen, J., Giddings, M., & Carin, A. (1985). *Science,* (Level 4). Orlando, FL: Harcourt Brace Jovanovich.

Cooper, G., & Sweller, J. (1987). Effects of schema acquisition and rule automation on mathematical problem-solving transfer. *Journal of Educational Psychology, 79,* 347–362.

Cooper, H. (1989). *Homework.* New York: Longman.

Cooper, H. M. (1989) Does reducing student-to-instructor ratios affect achievement? *Educational Psychologist, 24,* 79–98.

Corno, L. (1989). Self-regulated learning: A volitional analysis. In B. J. Zimmerman & D. H. Schunk (Eds.), *Self-regulated learning and academic achievement: Theory, research, and practice* (pp. 111–141). New York: Springer-Verlag.

Courage, M. (1989). Children's inquiry strategies in referential communication and in the game of twenty questions. *Child Development, 60,* 877–886.

Covington, M. V. (1987). Achievement motivation, self-attributions, and the exceptional learner. In J. D. Day & J. G. Borkowski (Eds.), *Intelligence and exceptionality* (pp. 355–389). Norwood, NJ: Ablex.

Covington, M. V., & Omelich, C. L. (1979a). It's best to be able and virtuous too: Student and teacher evaluative responses to successful effort. *Journal of Educational Psychology, 71,* 688–700.

Covington, M. V., & Omelich, C. L. (1979b). Effort: The double-edged sword in school achievement. *Journal of Educational Psychology, 71,* 169–182.

Covington, M. V., & Omelich, C. L. (1981). As failures mount: Affective and cognitive consequences of ability demotion in the classroom. *Journal of Educational Psychology, 73,* 796–808.

Covington, M. V., & Omelich, C. L. (1984). Task-oriented versus competitive learning structures: Motivational and performance consequences. *Journal of Educational Psychology, 6,* 1038–1050.

Crandall, V. C. (1969). Sex differences in expectancy of intellectual and academic reinforcement. In C. P. Smith (Ed.), *Achievement-related behaviors in children.* New York: Sage.

Crawford, M., & Chaffin, R. (1986). The reader's construction of meaning: Cognitive research on gender and comprehension. In E. A. Flynn & P. P. Schweickart (Eds.), *Gender and reading: Essays on readers, texts, and contexts* (pp. 3–30). Baltimore: Johns Hopkins University Press.

Cronbach, L. J. (1951). Coefficient alpha and the internal structure of tests. *Psychometrica, 16,* 297–334.

Cronbach, L. J. (1990). *Essentials of psychological testing* (5th ed.). New York: Harper & Row.

Crutcher, K. A. (1991). Anatomical correlates of neuronal plasticity. In J. L. Martinez, Jr., & R. P. Kesner (Eds.), *Learning and memory: A biological view* (2nd ed., pp. 93–146). San Diego: Academic Press.

Cuban, L. (1984). Policy and research dilemmas in the teaching of reasoning: Unplanned designs. *Review of Educational Research, 54,* 655–681.

Dabbs, J. (1980). Left-right differences in cerebral blood flow and cognition. *Psychophysiology, 17,* 548–551.

Dansereau, D. F., Collins, B. A., McDonald, C. D., Holley, J. C., Garland, J. C., Diekhoff, G. M., & Evans, S. H. (1979). Development and evaluation of an effective learning strategy program. *Journal of Educational Psychology, 79,* 64–73.

Dark, V. J., & Benbow, C. P. (1990). Enhanced problem translation and short-term memory: Components of mathematical talent. *Journal of Educational Psychology, 82,* 420–429.

Dark, V. J., & Benbow, C. P. (1991). Differential enhancement of working memory with mathematical versus verbal precocity. *Journal of Educational Psychology, 83,* 48–60.

Darling, N., & Steinberg, L. (1993). Parenting style as context: An integrative model. *Psychological Bulletin, 113*(3), 487–496.

Darling-Hammond, L., & Snyder, J. (1992). Curriculum studies and the traditions of inquiry: The scientific tradition. In P. W. Jackson (Ed.), *Handbook of research on curriculum* (pp. 41–78). New York: Macmillan.

Das, J. P., & Gindis, B. (Eds.). (1995). Lev S. Vygotsky and contemporary educational psychology (Special issue). *Educational Psychologist, 30* (2).

Davey, B., & McBride, S. (1986). Generating self-questioning after reading: A comprehension assist for elementary students. *Journal of Educational Research, 80*(1), 43–46.

Davidson, N. (1985). Small-group learning and teaching in mathematics: A selective review of the research. In R. Slavin, S. Shara, S. Kagan, R. Hertz-Lazarowitz, C. Webb, & R. Schmuck (Eds.), *Learning to cooperate, cooperating to learn* (pp. 211–230). New York: Plenum.

Davidson, N., & Kroll, D. L. (1991). An overview of research on cooperative learning related to mathematics. *Journal for Research in Mathematics Education, 22,* 362–365.

Davidson, N., & Worsham, T. (Eds.). (1992). *Enhancing thinking through cooperative learning.* New York: Teachers College Press.

Day, J. D. (1983). The zone of proximal development. In M. Pressley & J. R. Levin (Eds.), *Cognitive strategy research: Vol. 1, Psychological foundations* (pp. 155–175). New York: Springer-Verlag.

Day, J. D., Borkowski, J. G., Dietmeyer, D. L., Howsepian, B. A., & Saenz, D. S. (1994). Possible selves and academic achievement. In L. Winegar & J. Valsiner (Eds.), *Children's development within social contexts.* Hillsdale, NJ: Erlbaum.

Day, J. D., Cordon, L. B., & Kerwin, M. L. (1989). Informal instruction and development of cognitive skills: A review and critique of research. In C. B. McCormick, G. Miller, & M. Pressley (Eds.), *Cognitive strategy research: From basic research to educational applications* (pp. 83–103). New York: Springer-Verlag.

deCharms, R. (1968). *Personal causation.* New York: Academic Press.

Deci, E. L. (1971). Effects of externally mediated rewards on intrinsic motivation. *Journal of Personality and Social Psychology, 18,* 105–115.

de Groot, A. D. (1965). *Thought and choice in chess.* The Hague, Netherlands: Mouton.

de Groot, A. [D.] (1966). Perception and memory versus thought: Some old ideas and recent findings. In B. Kleinmuntz (Ed.), *Problem solving* (pp. 19–50). New York: Wiley.

Delclos, V. R., Burns, M. S., & Kulewicz, S. J. (1987). Effects of dynamic assessment on teacher's expectations of handicapped children. *American Educational Research Journal, 24,* 325–336.

DeLoache, J. S., Cassidy, D. J., & Brown, A. L. (1985). Precursors of mnemonic strategies in very young children's memory. *Child Development, 56,* 125–137.

DeLoache, J. S., & DeMendoza, O. A. P. (1987). Joint picturebook interactions of mothers and 1-year-old children. *British Journal of Developmental Psychology, 5,* 111–123.

Demana, F., & Leitzel, J. (1988). Establishing fundamental concepts through numerical problem solving. In A. F. Coxford & A. P. Shulte (Eds.), *The ideas of algebra K–12: 1988 yearbook of the National Council of Teachers of Mathematics.* Reston, VA: National Council of Teachers of Mathematics.

Dempster, F. N. (1985). Short-term memory development in childhood and adolescence. In C. J. Brainerd & M. Pressley (Eds.), *Basic processes in memory development: Progress in cognitive development research* (pp. 209–248). New York: Springer-Verlag.

Dempster, F. N. (1988). The spacing effect: A case study in the failure to apply the results of psychological research. *American Psychologist, 43,* 627–634.

Deno, S. L. (1986). Formative evaluation of individual programs: A new role for school psychologists. *School Psychology Review, 15,* 358–374.

Deno, S. L. (1987). Curriculum-based measurement. *Teaching Exceptional Children, 20,* 41.

Deno, S. L., & Fuchs, L. S. (1987). Developing curriculum-based measurement for special education problem solving. *Focus on Exceptional Children, 19*(8), 1–16.

Derry, S. J. (1984). Effects of an organizer on memory for prose. *Journal of Educational Psychology, 76,* 98–107.

Deshler, D. D., & Schumaker, J. B. (1988). An instructional model for teaching students how to learn. In J. L. Graden, J. E. Zins, & M. J. Curtis (Eds.), *Alternative educational delivery systems: Enhancing instructional options for all students* (pp. 391–411). Washington, DC: National Association of School Psychologists.

Desrochers, A., & Begg, I. (1987). A theoretical account of encoding and retrieval processes in the use of imagery-based mnemonic techniques: The special case of the keyword method. In M. A. McDaniel & M. Pressley (Eds.), *Imagery and related mnemonic techniques: Theories, individual differences, and applications* (pp. 56–77). New York: Springer-Verlag.

Devine, T. G. (1987). *Teaching study skills: A guide for teachers.* New York: Allyn & Bacon.

Devolder, P. A., Brigham, M. C., & Pressley, M. (1990). Memory performance awareness in younger and older adults. *Psychology and Aging, 5,* 291–303.

Devolder, P. A., & Pressley, M. (1992). Causal attributions and strategy use in relation to memory performance differences in younger and older adults. *Applied Cognitive Psychology, 6,* 629–642.

Dewey, J. (1933). *How we think: A restatement of the relation of reflective thinking to the education process.* Boston: Heath.

Diamond, A. (1985). Development of the ability to use recall to guide action, as indicated by performance on AB. *Child Development, 56,* 868–883.

Diamond, A. (1990a). Developmental time course in human infants and infant monkeys, and the neural bases, of inhibitory control in reaching. In A. Diamond (Ed.), *The development and neural bases of higher cognitive functions* (pp. 637–676). New York: New York Academy of Sciences.

Diamond, A. (1990b). The development and neural bases of memory functions as indexed by the A[not]B and delayed response tasks in human infants and infant monkeys. In A. Diamond (Ed.), *The development and neural bases of higher cognitive functions* (pp. 267–317). New York: New York Academy of Sciences.

Diamond, A. (1991). Frontal lobe involvement in cognitive changes during the first year of life. In K. R. Gibson & A. C. Petersen (Eds.), *Brain maturation and cognitive development: Comparative and cross-cultural perspectives* (pp. 127–180). New York: Aldine de Gruyter.

Diamond, M. C. (1988). *Enriching heredity: The impact of the environment on the anatomy of the brain.* New York: Free Press.

Diamond, M. C. (1991). Environmental influences on the young brain. In K. R. Gibson & A. C. Petersen (Eds.), *Brain maturation and cognitive development: Comparative and cross-cultural perspectives* (pp. 107–124). New York: Aldine de Gruyter.

Diamond, M. C. (1992, October). Plasticity of the brain: Enrichment versus impoverishment. In C. Clark & K. King (Eds.), *Television and the preparation of the mind for learning.* Washington, DC: U.S. Department of Health and Human Services.

DiClemente, R. J., Pies, C. A., Stoller, E. J., Straits, C., Olivia, G. E., Haskin, J., & Rutherford, G. W. (1989). Evaluation of school-based AIDS education curricula in San Francisco. *The Journal of Sex Research, 26,* 188–198.

DiClemente, R. J., Zorn, J., & Temoshok, L. (1986). Adolescents and AIDS: A survey of knowledge, attitudes, and beliefs about AIDS in San Francisco. *American Journal of Public Health, 76,* 1443–1445.

DiClemente, R. J., Zorn, J., & Temoshok, L. (1987). The association of gender, ethnicity, and length of residence in the Bay Area to adolescents' knowledge and attitudes about acquired immune deficiency syndrome. *Journal of Applied Social Psychology, 17,* 216–230.

Diegmueller, K. (1994, June 22). S.A.T. to realign scores for the first time in half a century. *Education Week,* p. 3.

Dillon, J. T. (1985). Using questions to foil discussion. *Teaching and Teacher Education, 1,* 109–121.

Dillon, J. T. (1991). Questioning the use of questions. *Journal of Educational Psychology, 83,* 163–164.

DiPardo, A., & Freedman, S. W. (1988). Peer response groups in the writing classroom: Theoretic foundations and new directions. *Review of Educational Research, 58,* 119–149.

DiVesta, F. J., & Gray, G. S. (1972). Listening and notetaking. *Journal of Educational Psychology, 63,* 8–14.

Dixon, F. W. (1972). *The Hardy Boys detective handbook.* New York: Grosset & Dunlop.

Dobbing, J. (1974). The later growth of the brain and its vulnerability. *Pediatrics, 53,* 2–6.

Dole, J. A., Duffy, G. G., Roehler, L. R., & Pearson, P. D. (1991). Moving from the old to the new: Research on reading comprehension instruction. *Review of Educational Research, 61,* 239–264.

Dole, J. A., Valencia, S. W., Greer, E. A., & Wadrop, J. L. (1991). *Reading Research Quarterly, 26*(2), 142–159.

Doman, R. J., Spitz, E. B., Zucman, E., Delacato, C. H., & Doman, G. (1960). Children with severe brain injuries. *Journal of the American Medical Association, 174,* 219–223.

Donlon, T. F. (1992). Legal issues in the educational testing of Hispanics. In K. F. Geisinger (Ed.), *Psychological testing of Hispanics* (pp. 55–78). Washington, DC: American Psychological Association.

Dooling, D. J., & Lachman, R. (1971). Effects of comprehension on retention of prose. *Journal of Experimental Psychology, 88,* 216–222.

Dorsey, J. A., Mullis, I. V. S., Lindquist, M. M., & Chambers, D. L. (1988). *The 1986 mathematics report card.* Princeton, NJ: Educational Testing Service, National Assessment of Educational Progress.

Doyle, W. (1986). Classroom organization and management. In M. C. Wittrock (Ed.), *Handbook of research on teaching* (3rd ed., pp. 392–431). New York: Macmillan.

Driscoll, M. P. (1994). *Psychology of learning for instruction.* Boston: Allyn & Bacon.

Duffy, G. G., & Roehler, L. R. (1989). Why strategy instruction is so difficult and what we need to do about it. In C. B. McCormick, G. Miller, & M. Pressley (Eds.), *Cognitive strategy research: From basic research to educational applications* (pp. 133–154). New York: Springer-Verlag.

Duffy, G. G., Roehler, L. R., Sivan, E., Rackliffe, G., Book, C., Meloth, M., Vavrus, L., Wesselman, R., Putnam, J., & Bassiri, D. (1987). Effects of explaining the reasoning associated with using reading strategies. *Reading Research Quarterly, 22,* 347–368.

Duit, R. (1991). Students' conceptual frameworks: Consequences for learning science. In S. M. Glynn, R. H. Yeany, & B. K. Britton (Eds.), *The psychology of learning science* (pp. 65–85). Hillsdale, NJ: Erlbaum.

Dunlap, L. K., & Dunlap, G. (1989). A self-monitoring package for teaching subtraction with regrouping to students with learning disabilities. *Journal of Applied Behavior Analysis, 22,* 309–314.

Dunn, B., Dunn, D., Andrews, D., & Languis, M. L. (1992). Metacontrol: A cognitive model of brain functioning for psychophysiological study of complex learning. *Educational Psychologist, 27*(4), 455–472.

Durkin, D. (1978–1979). What classroom observations reveal about reading comprehension instruction. *Reading Research Quarterly, 14,* 481–533.

Dweck, C. S. (1986). Motivational processes affecting learning. *American Psychologist, 41,* 1040–1048.

Dweck, C. [S.] (1987, April). *Children's theories of intelligence: Implications for motivation and learning.* Paper presented at the annual meeting of the American Educational Research Association, Washington, DC.

Dweck, C. S., & Leggett, E. L. (1988). A social-cognitive approach to motivation and personality. *Psychological Review, 95,* 256–273.

Early, M. M. (1991). Major research programs. In J. Flood, J. M. Jensen, D. Lapp, & J. R. Squire (Eds.), *Handbook of research on teaching the English language arts* (pp. 3–17). New York: Macmillan.

Eccles, J. S. (1985). Sex differences in achievement patterns. In T. Sonderegger (Ed.), *Nebraska Symposium on Motivation* (Vol. 32). Lincoln: University of Nebraska Press.

Eccles, J. S. (1989). Bringing young women to math and science. In M. Crawford & M. Gentry (Eds.), *Gender and thought: Psychological perspectives* (pp. 36–58). New York: Springer-Verlag.

Eccles, J. S., & Blumenfeld, P. (1985). Classroom experience and student gender: Are there differences and do they matter? In L. C. Wilkinson & C. B. Marrett (Eds.), *Gender influences in classroom interaction* (pp. 79–114). New York: Academic Press.

Eccles, J. S., & Jacobs, J. (1986). Social forces shape math participation. *Signs, 11,* 367–380.

Eccles, J. [S.], MacIver, D., & Lange, L. (1986, April). *Classroom practice and motivation to study math.* Paper presented at the annual meeting of the American Educational Research Association, San Francisco.

Edmonds, R. R. (1979). Effective schools for the urban poor. *Educational Leadership, 37*(1), 15–24.

Educational Research Service (1978). *Class size: A summary of research.* Arlington, VA: Educational Research Service.

Educational Testing Service (1985). *The reading report card.* Princeton, NJ: Educational Testing Service.

Edwards, H. (1973). *Sociology of sport.* Homewood, IL: Dorsey Press.

Edwards, R., & Edwards, J. (1987). Corporal punishment. In A. Thomas & J. Grimes (Eds.), *Children's needs: Psychological perspectives* (pp. 127–131). Washington, DC: National Association of School Psychologists.

Ehri, L. C. (1991). Development of the ability to read words. In R. Barr, M. L. Kamil, P. B. Mosenthal, & P. D. Pearson (Eds.), *Handbook of reading research* (Vol. 2, pp. 383–417). New York: Longman.

Ehri, L. C., & Wilce, L. S. (1985). Movement into reading: Is the first stage of printed word learning visual or phonetic? *Reading Research Quarterly, 20,* 163–179.

Eitzen, D. S. (1992). Problem students: The sociocultural roots. *Phi Delta Kappan, 73,* 584–590.

Elkind, D. (1994). *A sympathetic understanding of the child* (3rd ed.). Boston: Allyn & Bacon.

Elliott, R. (1992). Larry P., PASE, and social science in the courtroom: The science and politics of identifying and educating very slow learners. In H. C. Haywood & D. Tzuriel (Eds.), *Interactive assessment* (pp. 470–503). New York: Springer-Verlag.

Ellis, N. R. (Ed.). (1979). *Handbook of mental deficiency: Psychological theory and research.* Hillsdale, NJ: Erlbaum.

Emmer, E. T., Evertson, C. M., Clements, B. S., & Worsham, M. E. (1994). *Classroom Management for Secondary Teachers* (3rd ed.). Needham Heights, MA: Allyn & Bacon.

Englert, C., & Raphael, T. (1988). Constructing well-formed prose: Process, structure, and metacognitive knowledge. *Exceptional Children, 54,* 513–520.

Enright, R. D., Lapsley, D. K., & Levy, V. M. (1983). Moral education strategies. In M. Pressley & J. R. Levin (Eds.), *Cognitive strategy research: Educational applications* (pp. 43–83). New York: Springer-Verlag.

Eraut, M. (1985). Knowledge creation and knowledge use in professional scientists. *Studies in Higher Education, 10,* 117–133.

Ericsson, K. A., & Charness, N. (1994). Expert performance: Its structure and acquisition. *American Psychologist, 49*(8), 725–747.

Ericsson, K. A., & Polson, P. G. (1988). An experimental analysis of the mechanisms of a memory skill. *Journal of Experimental Psychology: Learning, Memory, and Cognition, 14,* 305–316.

Ericsson, K. A., & Staszewski, J. J. (1989). Skilled memory and expertise: Mechanisms of exceptional performance. In D. Klahr & K. Kotovsky (Eds.), *Complex information processing: The impact of Herbert A. Simon* (pp. 235–267). Hillsdale, NJ: Erlbaum.

Erikson, E. H. (1968). *Identity, youth, and crisis.* New York: Norton.

Estrada, M. T. (1990). *Improving academic performance through enhancing possible selves.* Unpublished master's thesis. University of Notre Dame, Notre Dame, IN.

Evans, J. A., & Hamerton, J. L. (1985). Chromosomal anomalies. In A. M. Clarke, A. D. B. Clarke, & J. M. Berg (Eds.), *Mental deficiency: The changing outlook* (pp. 135–213). New York: Free Press.

Evertson, C. M. (1989). Classroom organization and management. In M. C. Reynolds (Ed.), *Knowledge base for the beginning teacher* (pp. 59–70). New York: Pergamon Press.

Evertson, C. M., Emmer, E. T., Clements, B. S., & Worsham, M. E. (1994). *Classroom Management for Elementary Teachers* (3rd ed.). Needham Heights, MA: Allyn & Bacon.

Fagan, J. F. (1991). The paired-comparison paradigm and infant intelligence. In A. Diamond (Ed.), *The development and neural bases of higher cognitive functions.* New York: New York Academy of Sciences.

Fagan, J. F., & McGrath, S. (1981). Infant recognition memory and later intelligence. *Intelligence, 5,* 121–130.

Fantuzzo, J.[W.], King, J., & Heller, L. R. (1992). Effects of reciprocal peer tutoring on mathematics and school adjustment: A component analysis. *Journal of Educational Psychology, 84,* 331–339.

Fantuzzo, J. W., Riggio, R. E., Connelly, S., & Dimeff, L. A. (1989). Effects of reciprocal peer tutoring on academic achievement and psychological adjustment: A component analysis. *Journal of Educational Psychology, 81,* 173–177.

Fantz, R. L., & Nevis, S. (1967). Pattern preferences and perceptual-cognitive development in early infancy. *Merrill-Palmer Quarterly, 13,* 77–108.

Farnham-Diggory, S. (1992). *The learning-disabled child.* Cambridge, MA: Harvard University Press.

Farr, R., & Beck, M. D. (1991). Formal methods of evaluation. In J. Flood, J. M. Jensen, D. Lapp, & J. R. Squire (Eds.), *Handbook of research on teaching the English language arts* (pp. 489–501). New York: Macmillan.

Feldhusen, J. F. (1986). A conception of giftedness. In R. J. Sternberg & J. E. Davidson (Eds.), *Conceptions of giftedness* (pp. 112–127). Cambridge, UK: Cambridge University Press.

Feldhusen, J. F., & Kolloff, M. B. (1981). Me: A self-concept scale for gifted students. *Perceptual and Motor Skills, 53,* 319–323.

Feldman, D. H. (1979). The mysterious case of extreme giftedness. In A. H. Passow (Ed.), *The gifted and the talented: Their education and development.* The Seventy-Eighth Yearbook of the National Society for the Study of Education. Chicago: University of Chicago Press.

Feldman, D. H. (1982). *Developmental approaches to giftedness and creativity.* San Francisco: Jossey-Bass.

Feldman, D. H., with the assistance of Benjamin, A. C. (1986). Giftedness as a developmentalist sees it. In R. J. Sternberg & J. E. Davidson (Eds.), *Conceptions of giftedness* (pp. 285–305). Cambridge, UK: Cambridge University Press.

Feldman, D. H. (1988). *Nature's gambit: Child prodigies and the development of human potential.* New York: Basic Books.

Feltz, D. L., Landers, D. M., & Becker, B. J. (1988). A revised meta-analysis of the mental practice literature on motor skill performance. In D. Druckman & J. A. Swets (Eds.), *Enhancing human performance: Issues, theories and techniques: Background papers* (pp. 1–65). Washington, DC: National Research Council.

Fernandez, R. J., & Samuels, M. A. (1986). Intellectual dysfunction: Mental retardation and dementia. In M. A. Samuels (Ed.), *Manual of neurologic therapeutics* (pp. 30–50). Boston: Little, Brown.

Feuerstein, R. (1979). *The dynamic assessment of retarded performers: The Learning Potential Assessment Device, theory, instrument, and techniques.* Baltimore: University Park Press.

Feuerstein, R. (1980). *Instrumental enrichment: An intervention program for cognitive modifiability.* Baltimore: University Park Press.

Feuerstein, R., & Kozulin, A. (1995). *The Bell Curve:* Getting the facts straight. *Educational Leadership, 52* (7), 71–74.

Finn, C. E., Jr. (1991). *We must take charge: Our schools and our future.* New York: Free Press.

Finn, J. D., & Achilles, C. M. (1990). Answers and questions about class size: A statewide experiment. *American Educational Research Journal, 27,* 557–577.

Firestone, W. A. (1991). Educators, researchers, and the effective schools movement. In J. R. Bliss, W. A. Firestone, & C. E. Richards (Eds.), *Rethinking effective schools research and practice* (pp. 12–27). Englewood Cliffs, NJ: Prentice-Hall.

Fishbein, H. D., Eckart, T., Lauver, E., Van Leeuwen, R., & Langmeyer, D. (1990). Learners' questions and comprehension in a tutoring setting. *Journal of Educational Psychology, 82,* 163–170.

Fitzgerald, J. (1992). Variant views about good thinking during composing: Focus on revision. In M. Pressley, K. R. Harris, J. T. Guthrie (Eds.), *Promoting academic competence and literacy in school* (pp. 337–358). San Diego: Academic Press.

Fitzgerald, J., & Markham, L. (1987). Teaching children about revision in writing. *Cognition and Instruction, 4,* 3–24.

Fixsen, D. L., Phillips, E. L., & Wolf, M. M. (1973). Achievement Place: Experiments in self-government with pre-delinquents. *Journal of Applied Behavior Analysis, 6,* 31–47.

Flavell, J. H. (1971). Stage-related properties of cognitive development. *Cognitive Psychology, 2,* 421–453.

Flavell, J. H. (1972). An analysis of cognitive-developmental sequences. *Genetic Psychology Monographs, 86,* 279–350.

Flavell, J. H. (1985). *Cognitive development.* Englewood Cliffs, NJ: Prentice-Hall.

Flavell, J. H., Beach, D. H., & Chinsky, J. M. (1966). Spontaneous verbal rehearsal in a memory task as a function of age. *Child Development, 37,* 283–299.

Flavell, J. H., Friedrichs, A. G., & Hoyt, J. D. (1970). Developmental changes in memorization processes. *Cognitive Psychology, 1,* 324–340.

Flower, L., & Hayes, J. (1980). The dynamics of composing: Making plans and juggling constraints. In L. Gregg and E. Steinberg (Eds.), *Cognitive processes in writing* (pp. 31–50). Hillsdale, NJ: Erlbaum.

Flower, L., Stein, V., Ackerman, J., Kantz, M. J., McCormick, K., & Peck, W. C. (1990). *Reading to write: Exploring a cognitive and social process.* New York: Oxford University Press.

Flowers, D. L., Wood, F. B., & Naylor, C. E. (1991). Regional cerebral bloodflow correlates of language processes in reading disability. *Archives of Neurology, 48,* 637–643.

Fodor, J. A. (1983). *The modularity of mind.* Cambridge, MA: MIT Press.

Forrest-Pressley, D. L., & Gilles, L. A. (1983). Children's flexible use of strategies during reading. In M. Pressley & J. R. Levin (Eds.), *Cognitive strategy research: Educational applications.* New York: Springer-Verlag.

Forrest-Pressley, D. L., & Waller, T. G. (1984). *Cognition, metacognition, and reading.* New York: Springer-Verlag.

Fox, N. A., & Bell, M. A. (1990). Electrophysiological indices of frontal lobe development: Relations to cognitive and affective behavior in human infants over the first year of life. In A. Diamond (Ed.), *The development and neural bases of higher cognitive functions* (pp. 677–704). New York: New York Academy of Sciences.

Francis, P. L., Self, P. A., & Horowitz, F. D. (1987). The behavioral assessment of the neonate: An overview. In J. D. Osofsky (Ed.), *Handbook of infant development* (pp. 723–779). New York: Wiley.

Franklin, M. E. (1992). Culturally sensitive instructional practices for African-American learners with disabilities. *Exceptional Children, 59,* 115–122.

Frearson, W. M., & Eysenck, H. J. (1986). Intelligence, reaction time (RT), and a new "odd-man-out" RT paradigm. *Personality and Individual Differences, 7,* 807–817.

Friedman, L. (1989). Mathematics and the gender gap: A meta-analysis of recent studies on sex differences in mathematical tasks. *Review of Educational Research, 59,* 185–213.

Fuchs, D., & Fuchs, L. S. (1986). Test procedure bias: A meta-analysis of examiner familiarity effects. *Review of Educational Research, 56,* 243–262.

Fuchs, L. S., & Fuchs, D. (1990). Curriculum-based assessment. In C. R. Reynolds & R. W. Kamphaus (Eds.), *Handbook of psychological and educational assessment of children: Intelligence and achievement* (pp. 435–455). New York: Guilford Press.

Fuchs, L. S., Fuchs, D., & Maxwell, L. (1988). The validity of informal measures of reading comprehension. *Remedial and Special Education, 9*(2), 20–29.

Fuson, K. [C.] (1988). *Children's counting and concept of numbers.* New York: Springer-Verlag.

Fuson, K. C. (1992). Research on learning and teaching addition and subtraction of whole numbers. In G. Leinhardt, R. Putnam, & R. A. Hattrup (Eds.), *Analysis of arithmetic for mathematics teaching* (pp. 53–187). Hillsdale, NJ: Erlbaum.

Fuson, K. C., & Fuson, A. M. (1991). Instruction supporting children's counting on for addition and counting up for subtraction. *Journal for Research in Mathematics Education, 22,* 72–78.

Fuson, K. [C.], & Willis, G. (1988). Subtraction by counting up: More evidence. *Journal for Research in Mathematics Education, 19,* 402–420.

Gaddes, W. H. (1985). *Learning disabilities and brain function* (2nd ed.). New York: Springer-Verlag.

Gagné, R. M. (1965). *The conditions of learning.* New York: Holt.

Gagné, R. M., & Brown, L. T. (1961). Some factors in the programming of conceptual learning. *Journal of Experimental Psychology, 62,* 313–321.

Gagné, R. M., & Dick, W. (1983). Instructional psychology. *Annual Review of Psychology, 34,* 261–295.

Galaburda, A. [M.] (1983). Developmental dyslexia: Current anatomical research. *Annals of Dyslexia, 33,* 41–53.

Galaburda, A. M., Sherman, G. F., Rosen, G. D., Aboitz, F., & Geschwind, N. (1985). Developmental dyslexia: Four consecutive patients with cortical anomalies. *Archives of Neurology, 35,* 812–817.

Galotti, K. M. (1989). Gender differences in self-reported moral reasoning: A review and new evidence. *Journal of Youth and Adolescence, 18,* 475–488.

Galotti, K. M., Kozberg, S. F., & Farmer, M. C. (1991). Gender and developmental differences in adolescents' conceptions of moral reasoning. *Journal of Youth and Adolescence, 20,* 13–30.

Gambrell, L. B., & Bales, R. J. (1986). Mental imagery and the comprehension-monitoring performance of fourth- and fifth-grade poor readers. *Reading Research Quarterly, 21,* 454–464.

Garcia, J. (1981). The logic and limits of mental ability testing. *American Psychologist, 36,* 1172–1180.

Gardner, E. (1975). *Fundamentals of neurology,* (6th ed). Philadelphia: Saunders.

Gardner, H. (1983). *Frame of mind: The theory of multiple intelligences.* New York: Basic Books.

Gardner, H. (1993). *Multiple intelligences: The theory in practice: A reader.* New York: Basic Books.

Gardner, R. C. (1980). On the validity of affective variables in second language acquisition: Conceptual, contextual, and statistical considerations. *Language Learning, 30,* 255–270.

Gardner, R. C. (1983). Learning another language: A true social psychological experiment. *Journal of Language and Social Psychology, 2,* 219–239.

Gardner, R. [C.], & Lambert, W. (1972). *Attitudes and motivation in second language learning.* Rowley, MA: Newbury House.

Gardner, W., & Rogoff, B. (1982). The role of instruction in memory development: Some methodological choices. *Quarterly Newsletter of the Laboratory of Comparative Human Cognition, 4,* 6–12.

Garner, R., Alexander, P. A., Gillingham, M. G., Kulikowich, J. M., & Brown, R. (1991). Interest and learning from text. *American Educational Research Journal, 28,* 643–660.

Garner, R., Gillingham, M. G., & White, C. S. (1989). Effects of "seductive details" on macroprocessing and microprocessing in adults and children. *Cognition and Instruction, 6,* 41–57.

Gaskins, I. W., & Elliot, T. T. (1991). *Implementing cognitive strategy instruction across the school: The Benchmark manual for teachers.* Cambridge, MA: Brookline Books.

Gates, B. (Guest Ed.) (1990). Special Issue: Perspectives on morality and moral education east and west. *Journal of Moral Education, 19* (3).

Gayford, C. (1992). Patterns of group behavior in open-ended problem solving in science classes of 15-year-old students in England. *International Journal of Science Education, 14,* 41–49.

Geary, D. C. (1990). A componential analysis of an early learning deficit in mathematics. *Journal of Experimental Child Psychology, 49,* 363–383.

Geisenger, K. F. (1992). Fairness and selected psychometric issues in the psychological testing of Hispanics. In K. F. Geisinger (Ed.), *Psychological testing of Hispanics* (pp. 17–42). Washington, DC: American Psychological Association.

Gelman, R., & Baillargeon, R. (1983). A review of some Piagetian concepts. In J. H. Flavell & E. M. Markman (Eds.), *Handbook of child psychology; Vol. 3, Cognitive development.* New York: Wiley.

Gelman, R., & Gallistel, C. R. (1978). *The child's understanding of number.* Cambridge, MA: Harvard University Press.

Gelman, R., Massey, C. M., & McManus, M. (1991). Characterizing supporting environments for cognitive development: Lessons from children in a museum. In L. Resnick, J. M. Levine, & S. D. Teasley (Eds.), *Perspectives on socially shared cognition* (pp. 226–256). Washington, DC: American Psychological Association.

Ghatala, E. S. (1986). Strategy-monitoring training enables young learners to select effective strategies. *Educational Psychologist, 21,* 43–54.

Ghatala, E. S., Levin, J. R., Pressley, M., & Goodwin, D. (1986). A componential analysis of the effects of derived and supplied strategy-utility information on children's strategy selections. *Journal of Experimental Child Psychology, 41,* 76–92.

Ghiselin, B. (Ed.) (1952). *The creative process.* New York: Mentor.

Gibbs, J. C., Arnold, K. D., & Burkart, J. E. (1984). Sex differences in the expression of moral judgment. *Child Development, 55,* 1040–1043.

Gibson, E. J. (1969). *Principles of perceptual learning and development.* New York: Appleton-Century-Crofts.

Gibson, K. R. (1991a). Basic neuroanatomy for the nonspecialist. In K. R. Gibson & A. C. Petersen (Eds.), *Brain maturation and cognitive development: Comparative and cross-cultural perspectives* (pp. 13–25). New York: Aldine de Gruyter.

Gibson, K. R. (1991b). Myelination and behavioral development: A comparative perspective on questions of neoteny, altriciality and intelligence. In K. R. Gibson & A. C. Petersen (Eds.), *Brain maturation and cognitive development: Comparative and cross-cultural perspectives* (pp. 29–63). New York: Aldine de Gruyter.

Gibson, K. R., & Petersen, A. C. (1991). Introduction. In K. R. Gibson & A. C. Petersen (Eds.), *Brain maturation and cognitive development: Comparative and cross-cultural perspectives* (pp. 3–12). New York: Aldine de Gruyter.

Gick, M. L., & Holyoak, K. J. (1980). Analogical problem solving. *Cognitive Psychology, 12,* 306–355.

Gick, M. L., & Holyoak, K. J. (1983). Schema induction and analogical transfer. *Cognitive Psychology, 15,* 1–38.

Gickling, E. E., Shane, R. L., & Croskery, K. M. (1989). Developing mathematical skills in low-achieving high school students through curriculum-based assessment. *School Psychology Review, 18,* 344–355.

Gilewski, M. J., & Zelinski, E. M. (1986). Questionnaire assessment of memory complaints. In L. W. Poon (Ed.), *Handbook for clinical memory assessment of older adults* (pp. 93–107). Washington, DC: American Psychological Association.

Gilligan, C. (1982). *In a different voice: Psychological theory and women's development.* Cambridge, MA: Harvard University Press.

Gilligan, C., & Attanucci, J. (1988). Two moral orientations. In C. Gilligan, J. V. Ward, & J. M. Taylor with B. Bardige (Eds.), *Mapping the moral domain: A contribution of women's thinking to psychological theory and education* (pp. 73–86). Cambridge, MA: Harvard University Press.

Gilligan, C., Kohlberg, L., Lerner, E., & Belensky, M. (1971). Moral reasoning about sexual dilemmas: The development of an interview and scoring system. In *Technical Report of the Commission on Obscenity and Pornography* (Vol. 1, No. 5256–0010). Washington, DC: Superintendent of Documents, U.S. Government Printing Office.

Glaser, B., & Strauss, A. (1967). *The discovery of grounded theory.* Chicago: Aldine.

Glaser, R., & Chi, M. T. H. (1988). Introduction: What is it to be an expert? In M. T. H. Chi, R. Glaser, & M. J. Farr (Eds.), *The nature of expertise* (pp. xv–xxiix). Hillsdale, NJ: Erlbaum.

Glass, G. V., McGaw, B., & Smith, M. L. (1981). *Meta-analysis in social research.* Newbury Park, CA: Sage.

Glass, G. V., & Smith, M. L. (1979). Meta-analysis of the research on class size and achievement. *Educational Evaluation and Policy Analysis, 1,* 2–16.

Gleitman, L. R. (1986). Biological preprogramming for language learning. In S. L. Friedman, K. A. Klivington, & R. W. Peterson (Eds.), *The brain, cognition, and education* (pp. 120–151). Orlando, FL: Academic Press.

Glover, J. A. (1989). The "testing" phenomenon: Not gone but nearly forgotten. *Journal of Educational Psychology, 81,* 392–399.

Glynn, S. M. (1991). Explaining science concepts: A teaching-with-analogies model. In S. M. Glynn, R. H. Yeany, & B. K. Britton (Eds.), *The psychology of learning science* (pp. 219–240). Hillsdale, NJ: Erlbaum.

Glynn, S. M., Yeany, R. H., & Britton, B. K. (1991). A constructive view of learning science. In S. M. Glynn, R. H. Yeany, & B. K. Britton (Eds.), *The psychology of learning science* (pp. 3–19). Hillsdale, NJ: Erlbaum.

Goetz, E. T., Schallert, D. L., Reynolds, R. E., & Radin, D. I. (1983). Reading in perspective: What real cops and pretend burglars look for in a story. *Journal of Educational Psychology, 75,* 500–510.

Goldberg, S., & DeVitto, B. A. (1983). *Born too soon: Preterm birth and early development.* San Francisco: Freeman.

Goldberger, A. S. (1977). Twin methods: A skeptical view. In P. Taubman (Ed.), *Kinometrics: Determinants of socioeconomic success between and within families.* Amsterdam: North-Holland.

Golden, C. J., Zillmer, E., & Spiers, M. (1992). *Neuropsychological assessment and intervention.* Springfield, IL: Charles C Thomas.

Goldenberg, C. (1989). Parents' effects on academic grouping for reading: Three case studies. *American Educational Research Journal, 26,* 329–352.

Goldenberg, C. (1992). The limits of expectations: A case for case knowledge about teacher expectancy effects. *American Educational Research Journal, 29,* 517–544.

Goldman-Rakic, P. S. (1987). Development of cortical circuitry and cognitive function. *Child Development, 58,* 601–622.

Goldman-Rakic, P. S., Isseroff, A., Schwartz, M. L., & Bugbee, N. M. (1983). The neurobiology of cognitive development. In M. M. Haith & J. J. Campos (Volume Eds.) and P. H. Mussen (General Ed.), *Handbook of child psychology: Vol. II, Infancy and developmental psychobiology* (pp. 281–344). New York: Wiley.

Good, T. L., & Brophy, J. E. (1986). School effects. In *Handbook of research on teaching* (3rd ed., pp. 570–602). New York: Macmillan.

Gooden, W. E. (1989). Development of black men in early adulthood. In R. L. Jones (Ed.), *Black adult development and aging* (pp. 63–89). Berkeley, CA: Cobb & Henry.

Goodlad, J. I. (1984). *A place called school: Prospects for the future.* New York: McGraw-Hill.

Goodman, J. F. (1990). Infant intelligence: Do we, can we, should we assess it? In C. R. Reynolds & R. W. Kamphaus (Eds.), *Handbook of psychological and educational assessment of children: Intelligence and achievement* (pp. 183–208). New York: Guilford Press.

Goodman, K. S., & Goodman, Y. M. (1979). Learning to read is natural. In L. B. Resnick & P. A. Weaver, *Theory and practice of early reading* (Vol. 1, pp. 137–154). Hillsdale, NJ: Erlbaum.

Goodman, R. (1987). The developmental neurobiology of language. In W. Yule & M. Rutter (Eds.), *Language development and disorders* (pp. 129–145). Oxford, UK: Blackwell.

Goswami, U., & Bryant, P. (1992). Rhyme, analogy, and children's reading. In P. B. Gough, L. C. Ehri, & R. Treiman (Eds.), *Reading acquisition* (pp. 49–63). Hillsdale, NJ: Erlbaum.

Gottesman, I. I. (1963). Genetic aspects of intelligent behavior. In N. Ellis (Ed.), *Handbook of mental deficiency*. New York: McGraw-Hill.

Gough, P. B., Juel, C., & Griffith, P. L. (1992). Reading, spelling, and the orthographic cipher. In P. B. Gough, L. C. Ehri, & R. Treiman (Eds.), *Reading acquisition* (pp. 35–48). Hillsdale, NJ: Erlbaum.

Gould, S. J. (1981). *The mismeasure of man*. New York: Norton.

Graham, S. (1990). The role of production factors in learning disabled students' compositions. *Journal of Educational Psychology, 82*, 781–791.

Graham, S., & Harris, K. R. (1988). Instructional recommendations for teaching writing to exceptional children. *Exceptional Children, 54*, 506–512.

Graham, S., & Harris, K. R. (1989). A components analysis of cognitive strategy instruction: Effects on learning disabled students' composition and self-efficacy. *Journal of Educational Psychology, 81*, 353–361.

Graham, S., & MacArthur, C. (1988). Improving learning disabled students' skill at revising essays produced on a word processor: Self-instructional strategy training. *Journal of Special Education, 22*, 133–152.

Grayson, D. A. (1989). Twins reared together: Minimizing shared environmental effects. *Behavior Genetics, 19*, 593–603.

Graziano, W. G., Varca, P. E., & Levy, J. C. (1982). Race of examiner effects and the validity of intelligence tests. *Review of Educational Research, 52*, 469–498.

Greenfield, P. M. (1984). A theory of the teacher in the learning activities of everyday life. In B. Rogoff & J. Lave (Eds.), *Everyday cognition: Its development in social context* (pp. 117–138). Cambridge, MA: Harvard University Press.

Greenfield, P. M., & Savage-Rumbaugh, E. S. (1990). Grammatical combination in *Pan paniscus:* Processes of learning and invention in the evolution and development of language. In S. T. Parker & K. R. Gibson (Eds.), *"Language" and intelligence in monkeys and apes* (pp. 540–578). Cambridge, UK: Cambridge University Press.

Greeno, J. G. (1991). Number sense as situated knowing in a conceptual domain. *Journal for Research in Mathematics Education, 22*, 170–218.

Greeno, J. G. (1992). Mathematical and scientific thinking in classrooms and other situations. In D. F. Halpern (Ed.), *Enhancing thinking skills in the sciences and mathematics* (pp. 39–62). Hillsdale, NJ: Erlbaum.

Greenough, W. T. (1993). Experience and brain development. *Child Development, 58*, 539–559.

Greenough, W. T., Black, J. E., & Wallace, C. S. (1987). Experience and brain development. *Child Development, 58*, 539–559.

Greenough, W. T., & Juraska, J. M. (1986). *Developmental neuropsycho-biology*. Orlando, FL: Academic Press.

Greenwood, C. R., Delquadri, J. C., & Hall, R. V. (1989). Longitudinal effects of classwide peer tutoring. *Journal of Educational Psychology, 81*, 371–383.

Griffith, D. R. (1992). Prenatal exposure to cocaine and other drugs: Developmental and educational prognoses. *Phi Delta Kappan, 74*, 30–34.

Grinder, R. E. (1985). The gifted in our midst: By their divine deeds, neuroses, and mental test scores we have known them. In F. D. Horowitz & M. O'Brien (Eds.), *The gifted and talented: Developmental perspectives* (pp. 5–35). Washington, DC: American Psychological Association.

Groen, G. J., & Parkman, J. M. (1972). A chronometric analysis of simple addition. *Psychological Review, 79*, 329–343.

Groen, G. [J.], & Resnick, L. (1977). Can preschool children invent addition algorithms? *Journal of Educational Psychology, 69*, 645–652.

Grossman, H., & Grossman, S. H. (1994). *Gender issues in education*. Needham Heights, MA: Allyn & Bacon.

Grossman, H. J. (Ed.). (1983). *Manual on terminology and classification in mental retardation* (3rd rev.). Washington, DC: American Association on Mental Deficiency.

Guba, E. G. (Ed.). (1990). *Paradigm dialog*. Newbury, CA: Sage.

Guba, E. G., & Lincoln, Y. S. (1982). Epistemological and methodological bases of naturalistic inquiry. *Educational Communication and Technology Journal, 30,* 233–252.

Guilford, J. P. (1967). *The nature of human intelligence.* New York: McGraw-Hill.

Guthke, J., & Wingenfeld, S. (1992). The learning test concept: Origins, state of the art, and trends. In H. C. Haywood & D. Tzuriel (Eds.), *Interactive assessment* (pp. 64–93). New York: Springer-Verlag.

Guthrie, J. T., & Dreher, M. J. (1990). Literacy as search: Explorations via computer. In D. Nix & R. Spiro (Eds.), *Cognition education and multimedia: Exploring ideas in high technology.* Hillsdale, NJ: Erlbaum.

Guttentag, R. E. (1984). The mental effort requirement of cumulative rehearsal: A developmental study. *Journal of Experimental Child Psychology, 37,* 92–106.

Guttentag, R. E., Ornstein, P. A., & Siemens, L. (1987). Children's spontaneous rehearsal: Transitions in strategy acquisition. *Cognitive Development, 2,* 307–326.

Guttmann, J., Levin, J. R., & Pressley, M. (1977). Pictures, partial pictures, and young children's oral prose learning. *Journal of Educational Psychology, 69,* 473–480.

Guzzetti, B. J., Snyder, T. E., Glass, G. V., & Gamas, W. S. (1993). Promoting conceptual change in science: A comparative meta-analysis of instructional interventions from reading education and science education. *Reading Research Quarterly, 28,* 117–159.

Haberlandt, K. (1980). Story grammar and reading time of story constituents. *Poetics, 9,* 99–116.

Haertel, E. H. (1991). Should the National Assessment of Educational Progress be used to compare the states? *Educational Researcher, 20*(3), 17.

Haier, R. J., Siegel, B. V., Nuechterlein, K. H., Hazlett, E., Wu, J. C., Paek, J., Browning, H. L., & Buchsbaum, M. S. (1988). Cortical glucose metabolic rate correlates of abstract reasoning and attention studied with positron emission tomography. *Intelligence, 12,* 199–217.

Haladyna, T. [M.] (1994). *Developing and validating multiple-choice test items.* Hillsdale, NJ: Erlbaum.

Haladyna, T. M., Nolen, S. B., & Haas, N. S. (1991). Raising standardized achievement test scores and the origins of test score pollution. *Educational Researcher, 20*(5), 2–7.

Hall, E. R., Esty, E. T., & Fisch, S. M. (1990). Television and children's problem-solving behavior: A synopsis of an evaluation of the effects of *Square One* TV. *Journal of Mathematical Behavior, 9,* 161–174.

Hall, V. C., & Merkel, S. P. (1985). Teacher expectancy effects and educational psychology. In J. B. Dusek (Ed.), *Teacher expectancies* (pp. 67–92). Hillsdale, NJ: Erlbaum.

Halpern, D. F. (1992). *Sex differences in cognitive abilities* (2nd ed.). Hillsdale, NJ: Erlbaum.

Halstead, W. C. (1947). *Brain and intelligence.* Chicago: University of Chicago Press.

Hampson, E. (1990a). Estrogen-related variations in human spatial and articulatory-motor skills. *Psychoendrocrinology, 15*(2), 97–111.

Hampson, E. (1990b). Variations in sex-related cognitive abilities across the menstrual cycle. *Brain and Cognition, 14*(1), 26–43.

Hampson, E., & Kimura, D. (1988). Reciprocal effects of hormonal fluctuations on human motor and perceptual-spatial skills. *Behavioral Neuroscience, 102,* 456–495.

Haney, W. (1991). We must take care: Fitting assessments to functions. In V. Perrone (Ed.). *Expanding student assessment* (pp. 142–163). Alexandria, VA: Association for Supervision and Curriculum Development.

Hansen, J. (1992). Literacy portfolios: Helping students know themselves. *Educational Leadership, 49*(8), 66–68.

Hansen, J., & Pearson, P. D. (1983). An instructional study: Improving the referential comprehension of good and poor fourth grade readers. *Journal of Educational Psychology, 75,* 821–829.

Hardiman, P. T., Pollatsek, A., & Weil, A. D. (1986). Learning to understand the balance beam. *Cognition and Instruction, 3,* 1–30.

Haroutunian-Gordon, S. (1991). *Turning the soul: Teaching through conversation in the high school.* Chicago: University of Chicago Press.

Harrell, R., Capp, R., Davis, D., Peerless, J., & Ravitz, L. (1981). Can nutritional supplements help mentally retarded children? *Proceedings of the National Academy of Science, 78,* 574–578.

Harrell, T. W., & Harrell, M. S. (1945). Army General Classification Test scores for civilian occupations. *Educational and Psychological Measurement, 5,* 229–239.

Harris, K. R. (1988, April). *What's wrong with strategy intervention research: Intervention integrity.* Paper presented at the annual meeting of the American Educational Research Association, New Orleans.

Harris, K. R., & Graham, S. (1992). Self-regulated strategy development: A part of the writing process. In M. Pressley, K. R. Harris, & J. T. Guthrie (Eds.), *Promoting academic competence and literacy in school* (pp. 277–309). San Diego: Academic Press.

Harry, B. (1992). An ethnographic study of cross-cultural communication with Puerto Rican-American families in the special education system. *American Educational Research Journal, 29,* 471–494.

Hart, L. M., & Goldin-Meadow, S. (1984). The child as a nonegocentric art critic. *Child Development, 55,* 2122–2129.

Harter, S. (1981). A new self-report scale of intrinsic versus extrinsic orientation in the classroom: Motivational and informational components. *Developmental Psychology, 17,* 300–312.

Harter, S. (1990). Causes, correlates and the functional role of self-worth: A life span perspective. In R. J. Sternberg & J. Kolligian (Eds.), *From childhood to adolescence: A transition period* (pp. 205–239). Newbury Park, CA: Sage.

Hartup, W. W. (1989). Social relationships and their developmental significance. *American Psychologist, 44*(2), 120–126.

Hasher, L., Stoltzfus, E. R., Zacks, R. T., & Rypma, B. (1991). Age and inhibition. *Journal of Experimental Psychology: Learning, Memory, and Cognition, 17,* 163–169.

Hatano, G., Amaiwa, S., & Shimuzu, K. (1987). Formation of a mental abacus for computation and its use as a memory device for digits: A developmental study. *Developmental Psychology, 23,* 832–838.

Hatano, G., & Inagaki, K. (1991). Sharing cognition through collective comprehension activity. In L. Resnick, J. M. Levine, & S. D. Teasley (Eds.), *Perspectives on socially shared cognition* (pp. 331–348). Washington, DC: American Psychological Association.

Hayes, J. R. (1985). Three problems in teaching general skills. In S. F. Chipman, J. W. Segal, & R. Glaser (Eds.), *Thinking and learning skills: Vol. 2, Research and open questions.* (pp. 391–405). Hillsdale, NJ: Erlbaum.

Hayes, J. R., Waterman, D. A., & Robinson, C. S. (1977). Identifying relevant aspects of a problem text. *Cognitive Science, 1,* 297–313.

Hayes-Roth, B., & Thorndyke, P. W. (1979). Integration of knowledge from text. *Journal of Verbal Learning and Verbal Behavior, 18,* 91–108.

Haywood, H. C., Tzuriel, D., & Vaught, S. (1992). Psychoeducational assessment from a transactional perspective. In H. C. Haywood & D. Tzuriel (Eds.), *Interactive assessment* (pp. 38–63). New York: Springer-Verlag.

Heath, S. B. (1989). Oral and literate traditions among black Americans living in poverty. *American Psychologist, 44*(22), 367–373.

Hebb, D. O. (1949). *The organization of behavior.* New York: Wiley.

Hedges, L. V., & Stock, W. (1983). The effect of class size: An examination of rival hypotheses. *American Educational Research Journal, 20,* 63–85.

Hembree, R. (1992). Experiments and relational studies in problem solving: A meta-analysis. *Journal for Research in Mathematics Education, 23,* 242–273.

Hembree, R., & Dessart, D. (1986). Effects of hand-held calculators in precollege mathematics education: A meta-analysis. *Journal for Research in Mathematics Education, 17,* 83–99.

Henderson, V. L., & Dweck, C. S. (1990). Motivation and achievement. In S. S. Feldman & G. R. Elliott (Eds.), *At the threshold: The developing adolescent* (pp. 308–329). Cambridge, MA: Harvard University Press.

Herman, J. L., & Winters, L. (1994). Portfolio research: A slim collection. *Educational Leadership, 52*(2), 48–55.

Herrnstein, R. J., & Murray, C. A. (1994). *The bell curve: Intelligence and class structure in American life.* New York: Free Press.

Hershenson, M., Munsinger, H., & Kessen, W. (1965). Preferences for shapes of intermediate variability in the newborn human. *Science, 147,* 630–631.

Hertzog, C. (1989). Influences of cognitive slowing on age differences in intelligence. *Developmental Psychology, 25,* 636–651.

Hertzog, C., & Schear, J. M. (1989). Psychometric considerations in testing the older person. In T. Hunt & C. J. Lindley (Eds.), *Testing older adults: A reference guide for geropsychological assessments* (pp. 24–50). Austin, TX: PRO-ED.

Hess, R. D., Chih-Mei, C., & McDevitt, T. M. (1987). Cultural variations in family beliefs about children's performance in mathematics: Comparisons among People's Republic of China, Chinese-American, and Caucasian-American families. *Journal of Educational Psychology, 79,* 179–188.

Hidi, S. (1990). Interest and its contribution as a mental resource for learning. *Review of Educational Research, 60,* 549–571.

Hier, D. B., LeMay, M., Rosenberger, P. B., & Perlo, V. P. (1978). Developmental dyslexia: Evidence for a subgroup with a reversal of cerebral asymmetry. *Archives of Neurology, 35,* 90–92.

Higgins, A. (1987). A feminist perspective on moral education. *Journal of Moral Education, 16,* 240–247.

Higgins, A. T., & Turnure, J. E. (1984). Distractibility and concentration of attention in children's development. *Child Development, 55,* 1799–1810.

Hill, D. (1991). Tasting failure: Thoughts of an at-risk learner. *Phi Delta Kappan, 73,* 308–310.

Hill, K. T., & Wigfield, A. (1984). Test anxiety: A major educational problem and what can be done about it. *The Elementary School Journal, 85*(1), 105–126.

Hinsley, D., Hayes, J. R., & Simon, H. A. (1977). From words to equations. In P. Carpenter & M. Just (Eds.), *Cognitive processes in comprehension.* Hillsdale, NJ: Erlbaum.

Hirsch, E. D., Jr. (1987). *Cultural literacy: What every American needs to know.* Boston: Houghton Mifflin.

Hirsch, E. D., Jr. (1991). *What your second grader needs to know: Fundamentals of a good second-grade education.* New York: Doubleday.

Hirsch, E. D., Kett, J. F., & Trefil, J. (1988). *The dictionary of cultural literacy.* Boston: Houghton Mifflin.

Hitchcock, G., & Hughes, D. (1989). *Research and the teacher: A qualitative introduction to school-based research.* New York: Routledge.

Hobbs, S. A., & Lahey, B. B. (1983). Behavioral treatment. In T. H. Ollendick & M. Hersen (Eds.), *Handbook of child psychopathology* (pp. 427–460). New York: Plenum.

Hoffman, H. S. (1969). Stimulus factors in conditioned suppression. In B. A. Campbell & R. M. Church (Eds.), *Punishment and aversive behavior* (pp. 185–234). New York: Appleton-Century-Crofts.

Hoffman, M. L. (1970). Moral development. In P. H. Mussen (Ed.), *Carmichael's manual of child psychology* (3rd ed., Vol. 2, pp. 261–360). New York: Wiley.

Holland, A., & Andre, T. (1987). Participation in extracurricular activities in secondary school: What is known, what needs to be known? *Review of Educational Research, 57,* 437–466.

Holland, J. G., & Skinner, B. F. (1961). *The analysis of behavior.* New York: McGraw-Hill.

Holloway, S. D. (1988). Concepts of ability and effort in Japan and the United States. *Review of Educational Research, 58,* 327–345.

Hopkins, K. D., & Stanley, J. C. (1981). *Educational and psychological measurement and evaluation* (6th ed.). Englewood Cliffs, NJ: Prentice-Hall.

Hoptman, M. J., & Davidson, R. J. (1994). How and why do the two cerebral hemispheres interact? *Psychological Bulletin, 116*(2), 195–219.

Horn, C. C., & Manis, F. R. (1987). Development of automatic and speeded reading of printed words. *Journal of Experimental Child Psychology, 44,* 92–108.

Horn, J. L. (1985). Remodeling old models of intelligence. In B. Wolman (Ed.), *Handbook of intelligence* (pp. 267–300). New York: Wiley.

Horn, J. L., & Cattell, R. B. (1967). Age differences in fluid and crystallized intelligence. *Acta Psychologica, 26,* 107–129.

Horn, J. L., & Hofer, S. M. (1992). Major abilities and development in the adult period. In R. J. Sternberg & C. A. Berg (Eds.), *Intellectual development* (pp. 44–99). Cambridge, UK: Cambridge University Press.

Horn, J. L., & Stankov, L. (1982). Auditory and visual factors of intelligence. *Intelligence, 6,* 163–185.

Horton, M. S. (1982). *Category familiarity and taxonomic organization in young children.* Unpublished doctoral dissertation. Stanford University, Stanford, CA.

Howe, K. R. (1988). Against the quantitative-qualitative incompatibility thesis. *Educational Researcher, 17*(8), 10–16.

Howe, M. J. A. (1970). Using students' notes to examine the role of the individual learner in acquiring meaningful subject matter. *Journal of Educational Research, 64,* 61–63.

Howell, K. W., & Morehead, M. K. (1987). *Curriculum-based evaluation for special and remedial education: A handbook for deciding what to teach.* Columbus, OH: Merrill.

Howlin, P., & Rutter, M. (1987). The consequences of language delay for other aspects of development. In W. Yule & M. Rutter (Eds.), *Language development and disorders* (pp. 271–294). Philadelphia: Lippincott.

Huba, M. E. (1984). The relationship between linguistic awareness in prereaders and two types of experimental instruction. *Reading World, 23,* 347–363.

Hubel, D. H., & Wiesel, T. N. (1970). The period of susceptibility to the physiological effects of unilateral eye closure in kittens. *Journal of Physiology, 206,* 419–436.

Huberman, M. (1987). How well does educational research really travel? *Educational Researcher, 16*(1), 5–13.

Hudson, J. [A.], & Nelson, K. (1983). Effects of script structure on children's story recall. *Developmental Psychology, 19,* 625–635.

Hudson, J. A., & Shapiro, L. R. (1991). From knowing to telling: The development of children's scripts, stories, and personal narratives. In A. McCabe & C. Peterson (Eds.), *Developing narrative structure* (pp. 89–136). Hillsdale, NJ: Erlbaum.

Hudson, J. A., & Slackman, E. A. (1990). Children's use of scripts in inferential text processing. *Discourse Processes, 13,* 375–385.

Hulme, C., & MacKenzie, S. (1992). *Working memory and severe learning difficulties.* Hillsdale, NJ: Erlbaum.

Humes, A. (1983). Putting writing research into practice. *Elementary School Journal, 81,* 3–17.

Hunt, E., Lunneborg, C., & Lewis, J. (1975). What does it mean to be high verbal? *Cognitive Psychology, 7,* 194–227.

Hunt, N., & Marshall, K. (1994). *Exceptional children and youth: An introduction to special education.* Boston: Houghton Mifflin.

Hunter, J. E., & Hunter, R. F. (1984). Validity and utility of alternative predictors of a job performance. *Psychological Bulletin, 96,* 72–98.

Huston, A. C., & Carpenter, C. J. (1985). Gender differences in preschool classrooms: The effects of sex-typed activity choices. In L. C. Wilkinson & C. B. Marrett (Eds.), *Gender influences on classroom interaction* (pp. 143–165). Orlando, FL: Academic Press.

Hutchins, E. (1991). The social organization of distributed cognition. In L. Resnick, J. M. Levine, & S. D. Teasley (Eds.), *Perspectives on socially shared cognition* (pp. 283–307).

Huttenlocher, P. R. (1979). Synaptic density in human frontal cortex-developmental changes and effects of aging. *Brain Research, 163,* 195–205.

Hyde, J. S., Fennema, E., & Lamon, S. J. (1990). Gender differences in mathematics performance: A meta-analysis. *Psychological Bulletin, 107,* 139–155.

Hyman, I. A. (1990). *Reading, writing, and the hickory stick: The appalling story of physical and psychological abuse in American schools.* San Diego: Lexington Books.

Hyman, I. A., & Wise, J. H. (Eds.). (1977). *Corporal punishment in American education.* Philadelphia: Temple University Press.

Hynd, C. R., & Alvermann, D. E. (1986). The role of refutation text in overcoming difficulty with science concepts. *Journal of Reading, 29,* 440–446.

Hynd, G. W., & Semrud-Clikeman, M. (1989). Dyslexia and brain morphology. *Psychological Bulletin, 106,* 447–482.

Idol, L. (1987). Group story mapping: A comprehension strategy for both skilled and unskilled readers. *Journal of Learning Disabilities, 20,* 196–205.

Idol, L., & Croll, V. J. (1987). Story-mapping training as a means of improving reading comprehension. *Learning Disability Quarterly, 10,* 214–229.

Inagaki, K. (1981). Facilitation of knowledge integration through classroom discussion. *The Quarterly Newsletter of the Laboratory of Comparative Human Cognition, 3,* 26–28.

Inagaki, K., & Hatano, G. (1989). *Learning histories of vocal and silent participants in group discussion.* Paper presented at the annual meeting of the Japanese Psychological Association, Tsukuba, Japan.

Infant Health and Development Program (1990). Enhancing the outcomes of low-birth-weight premature infants. *Journal of the American Medical Association, 263,* 3035–3042.

Itakura, K. (1967). Instruction and learning of concept "force" in static based on Hypothesis-Experiment-Instruction: A new method of science teaching. *Bulletin of the National Institute for Educational Research, 52,* 1–121.

Iversen, S., & Tumner, W. E. (1993). Phonological processing skills and the reading recovery program. *Journal of Educational Psychology, 85,* 112–120.

Iwasa, N. (1992). Postconventional reasoning and moral education in Japan. *Journal of Moral Education, 21,* 3–16.

Jackson, N. E., & Butterfield, E. C. (1986). A conception of giftedness designed to promote research. In R. J. Sternberg & J. E. Davidson (Eds.), *Conceptions of giftedness* (pp. 151–181). Cambridge, UK: Cambridge University Press.

Jackson, N. E., & Myers, M. G. (1982). Letter naming time, digit span, and precocious reading achievement. *Intelligence, 6,* 311–329.

Jacobsen, B., Lowery, B., & DuCette, J. (1986). Attributions of learning disabled children. *Journal of Educational Psychology, 78,* 59–64.

Jamieson, D. W., Lydon, J. E., Stewart, G., & Zanna, M. P. (1987). Pygmalion revisited: New evidence for student expectancy effects in the classroom. *Journal of Educational Psychology, 79,* 461–466.

Jaynes, G. D., & Williams, R. M., Jr. (1989). *A common destiny: Blacks and American society.* Washington, DC: National Academy Press.

Jensen, A. R. (1969). How much can we boost IQ and scholastic achievement? *Harvard Educational Review, 39,* 1–123.

Jensen, A. R. (1972). *Genetics and education.* New York: Harper & Row.

Jensen, A. R. (1973). *Educability and group differences.* New York: Harper & Row.

Jensen, A. R. (1976, December). Test bias and construct validity. *Phi Delta Kappan,* 340–346.

Jensen, A. R. (1980). *Bias in mental testing.* New York: Free Press.

Jensen, A. R. (1981). *Straight talk about mental tests.* New York: Free Press.

Jensen, A. R. (1982). Reaction time and psychometric g. In H. J. Eysenck (Ed.), *A model for intelligence.* Berlin: Springer-Verlag.

Jensen, A. R. (1992). Understanding g in terms of information processing. *Educational Psychology Review, 4,* 271–308.

Jernigan, T. L., Hesselink, J. R., Sowell, E., & Tallal, P. A. (1991). Cerebral structure on magnetic resonance imaging in language- and learning-impaired children. *Archives of Neurology, 48,* 539–545.

Johnson, D. K. (1988). Adolescents' solutions to dilemmas in fables: Two moral orientations—two problem-solving strategies. In C. Gilligan, J. V. Ward, & J. M. Taylor with B. Bardige (Eds.), *Mapping the moral domain: A contribution of women's thinking to psychological theory and education* (pp. 49–72). Cambridge, MA: Harvard University Press.

Johnson, D. W., & Johnson, R. (1985). Classroom conflict: Controversy over debate in learning groups. *American Educational Research Journal, 22,* 237–256.

Johnson, D. [W.], Maruyama, G., Johnson, R., Nelson, D., & Skon, L. (1981). Effects of cooperative, competitive, and individualistic goal structures on achievement: A meta-analysis. *Psychological Bulletin, 89,* 47–62.

Johnson, J. S., & Newport, E. L. (1989). Critical period effects in second language learning: The influence of maturational state on the acquisition of English as a second language. *Cognitive Psychology, 21,* 60–99.

John-Steiner, V. (1985). *Notebooks of the mind: Explorations of thinking.* Albuquerque: University of New Mexico Press.

Jones, L. V. (1984). White-black achievement differences: The narrowing gap. *American Psychologist, 39,* 1207–1213.

Jordan, B. (1989). Cosmopolitical obstetrics: Some insights from the training of traditional midwives. *Social Science and Medicine, 28,* 925–944.

Juel, C. (1990). Effects of reading group assignment on reading development in first and second grade. *Journal of Reading Behavior, 22,* 233–254.

Just, M. A., & Carpenter, P. A. (1987). *The psychology of reading and language comprehension.* Needham Heights, MA: Allyn & Bacon.

Kagan, J., Moss, H., & Sigel, I. (1963). Psychological significance of types of conceptualization. *Monographs of the Society for Research in Child Development, 28* (2, Serial No. 86).

Kagan, S. (1995). Group grades miss the mark. *Educational Leadership, 52*(8), 68–71.

Kahle, J. (1984). *Girl-friendly science.* Paper presented at the annual meeting of the American Association for the Advancement of Science, New York. (Cited in Eccles, 1989.)

Kail, R. (1991). Processing time declines exponentially during childhood and adolescence. *Developmental Psychology, 27,* 259–266.

Kail, R. (1992). Processing speed, speech rate, and memory. *Developmental Psychology, 28,* 899–904.

Kamii, C. K. (1985). *Young children reinvent arithmetic.* New York: Teachers College Press.

Kamphaus, R. W. (1993). *Clinical assessment of children's intelligence.* Boston: Allyn & Bacon.

Kamphaus, R. W., Kaufman, A. S., & Harrison, P. L. (1990). Clinical assessment practice with the Kaufman Assessment Battery for Children (K-ABC). In C. R. Reynolds & R. W. Kamphaus (Eds.), *Handbook of psychological and educational assessment of children: Intelligence & achievement* (pp. 259–276). New York: Guilford Press.

Kandel, E. R. (1991). Brain and behavior. In E. R. Kandel, J. H. Schwartz, & T. M. Jessel (Eds.), *Principles of neural science* (pp. 5–17). New York: Elsevier.

Kanfer, F., & Zich, J. (1974). Self-control training: The effect of external control on children's resistance to temptation. *Developmental Psychology, 10,* 108–115.

Kaniel, S., & Tzuriel, D. (1992). Mediated learning experience approach in the assessment and treatment of borderline psychotic adolescents. In H. C. Haywood & D. Tzuriel (Eds.), *Interactive assessment* (pp. 399–418). New York: Springer-Verlag.

Kasik, M. M., Sabatino, D. A., & Spoentgen, P. (1987). In S. J. Ceci (Ed.), *Handbook of cognitive, social, and neuropsychological aspects of learning disabilities.* (Vol. 2, pp. 251–272). Hillsdale, NJ: Erlbaum.

Kaufman, A. S. (1990). *Assessing adolescent and adult intelligence.* Boston: Allyn & Bacon.

Kaufman, A. S., & Kaufman, N. L. (1983). *The Kaufman Assessment Battery for Children* (K-ABC). Circle Pines, MN: American Guidance Services.

Kaufman, A. S., Reynolds, C. R., & McLean, J. E. (1989). Age and WAIS-R intelligence in a national sample of adults in the 20- to 74-year-old age range: A cross-sectional analysis with education level controlled. *Intelligence, 13,* 235–253.

Kausler, D. H. (1991). *Experimental psychology, cognition, and human aging.* New York: Springer-Verlag.

Kavale, K. A., & Forness, S. R. (1992). History, definition, and diagnosis. In N. N. Singh & I. L. Beale (Eds.), *Learning disabilities: Nature, theory, and treatment* (pp. 3–43). New York: Springer-Verlag.

Keating, D. P., & Bobbitt, B. (1978). Individual and developmental differences in cognitive processing components of mental ability. *Child Development, 49,* 155–169.

Keeney, F. J., Cannizzo, S. R., & Flavell, J. H. (1967). Spontaneous and induced verbal rehearsal in a recall task. *Child Development, 38,* 953–966.

Keller, C. E., & Sutton, J. P. (1991). Specific mathematics disorders. In J. E. Obrzut & G. W. Hynd (Eds.), *Neuropsychological foundations of learning disabilities* (pp. 549–571). San Diego: Academic Press.

Kersh, B. Y. (1958). The adequacy of "meaning" as an explanation of superiority of learning by independent discovery. *Journal of Educational Psychology, 49,* 282–292.

Kerwin, M. L. E., & Day, J. D. (1985). Peer influences on cognitive development. In J. B. Pryor & J. D. Day (Eds.), *The development of social cognition* (pp. 211–228). New York: Springer-Verlag.

Ketcham, R., & Snyder, R. T. (1977). Self-attitudes of the intellectually and socially advantaged student: Normative study of the Piers-Harris' children's self-concept scale. *Psychological Reports, 40,* 111–116.

Kiernan, C. (1985). Behaviour modification. In A. M. Clarke, A. D. B. Clarke, & J. M. Berg (Eds.), *Mental deficiency: The changing outlook* (pp. 465–511). New York: Free Press.

Kiewra, K. A. (1989). A review of note-taking: The encoding-storage paradigm and beyond. *Educational Psychology Review, 1,* 147–172.

Kiewra, K. A., & Benton, S. C. (1988). The relationship between information-processing ability and notetaking. *Contemporary Educational Psychology, 13,* 33–44.

Kiewra, K. A., DuBois, N. F., Christian, D., & McShane, A. (1988). Providing study notes: Comparison of three types of notes for review. *Journal of Educational Psychology, 80,* 595–597.

Kiewra, K. A., DuBois, N. F., Christian, D., McShane, A., Meyerhoffer, M., & Roskelley, D. (1991). Note-taking functions and techniques. *Journal of Educational Psychology, 83,* 240–245.

Kimball, M. M. (1989). A new perspective on women's math achievement. *Psychological Bulletin, 105,* 198–214.

King, A. (1989). Effects of self-questioning training on college students' comprehension of lectures. *Contemporary Educational Psychology, 14,* 366–381.

King, A. (1990). Enhancing peer interaction and learning in the classroom through reciprocal questioning. *American Educational Research Journal, 27,* 664–687.

King, A. (1992). Comparison of self-questioning, summarizing, and notetaking-review as strategies for learning from lectures. *American Educational Research Journal, 29,* 303–323.

King, A. (1994). Guiding knowledge construction in the classroom: Effects of teaching children how to question and how to explain. *American Educational Research Journal, 31*(2), 338–368.

Kintsch, W. (1974). *The representation of meaning in memory.* Hillsdale, NJ: Erlbaum.

Kintsch, W. (1982). Text representations. In W. Otto & S. White (Eds.), *Reading expository material* (pp. 87–102). New York: Academic Press.

Kintsch, W. (1983). Memory for text. In A. Flammer & W. Kintsch (Eds.), *Discourse processing* (pp. 186–204). Amsterdam: North-Holland.

Kintsch, W. (1988). The role of knowledge in discourse comprehension: A construction-integration model. *Psychological Review, 95,* 163–182.

Kintsch, W. (1994). Text comprehension, memory, and learning. *American Psychologist, 49*(4), 294–303.

Kintsch, W., & Greene, E. (1978). The role of culture-specific schemata in the comprehension and recall of stories. *Discourse Processes, 1,* 1–13.

Kintsch, W., & Keenan, J. M. (1973). Reading rate and retention as a function of the number of propositions in the base structure of sentences. *Cognitive Psychology, 5,* 257–279.

Kintsch, W., Mandel, T. S., & Kozminsky, E. (1977). Summarizing scrambled stories. *Memory and Cognition, 5,* 547–552.

Kintsch, W., & van Dijk, T. A. (1978). Toward a model of discourse comprehension and production. *Psychological Review, 85,* 363–394.

Kintsch, W., & Yarbrough, C. J. (1982). Role of rhetorical structure in text comprehension. *Journal of Educational Psychology, 74,* 828–834.

Kirsch, I. S., & Jungeblut, A. (1986). *Literacy: Profile of America's young adults.* Princeton, NJ: Educational Testing Service.

Klausmeier, H. J. (1990). Conceptualizing. In B. F. Jones & L. Idol (Eds.), *Dimensions of thinking and cognitive instruction.* (pp. 93–138). Hillsdale, NJ: Erlbaum.

Kliegl, R., Smith, J., & Baltes, P. B. (1990). On the locus and process of magnification of age differences during mnemonic training. *Developmental Psychology, 26,* 894–904.

Kloster, A. M., & Winne, P. H. (1989). The effects of different types of organizers on students' learning from text. *Journal of Educational Psychology, 81,* 9–15.

Knight, P. (1992). How I use portfolios in mathematics. *Educational Leadership, 49*(8), 71–72.

Kohlberg, L. (1969). Stage and sequence: The cognitive-developmental approach to socialization. In D. Goslin (Ed.), *Handbook of socialization theory and research.* New York: Rand McNally.

Kohlberg, L. (1981). *The philosophy of moral development: Moral stages and the idea of justice: Essays on moral development,* (Vol. 1). San Francisco: Harper & Row.

Kohlberg, L. (1984). *The psychology of moral development: Essays on moral development* (Vol. 2). San Francisco: Harper & Row.

Kohlberg, L., & Candee, D. (1984). The relationship of moral judgment to moral action. In W. Kurtines & J. Gewirtz (Eds.), *Morality, moral behavior, and moral development.* New York: Wiley.

Kohlberg, L., Kauffman, K., Sharf, P., & Hickey, J. (1974). *The just community approach to corrections.* Cambridge, MA: Moral Education Research Foundation.

Kohlberg, L., Yaeger, J., & Hjertholm, E. (1968). Private speech: Four studies and a review of theories. *Child Development, 39,* 691–736.

Komarovsky, M. (1985). *Women in college: Shaping new feminine identities.* New York: Basic Books.

Konner, M. (1991). Universals of behavioral development in relation to brain myelination. In K. R. Gibson & A. C. Petersen (Eds.), *Brain maturation and cognitive development: Comparative and cross-cultural perspectives* (pp. 181–223). New York: Aldine de Gruyter.

Koretz, D. M. (1991). State comparisons using NAEP: Large costs, disappointing benefits. *Educational Researcher, 20*(3), 19–21.

Kounin, J. (1970). *Discipline and group management in classrooms.* New York: Holt, Rinehart & Winston.

Kozol, J. (1991). *Savage inequalities: Children in America's schools.* New York: Crown.

Krajcik, J. S. (1991). Developing students' understanding of chemical concepts. In S. M. Glynn, R. H. Yeany, & B. K. Britton (Eds.), *The psychology of learning science* (pp. 117–147). Hillsdale, NJ: Erlbaum.

Krajcik, J. S., & Peters, H. (1989). *Molecular velocities* [microcomputer program]. Oakdale: Conduit, University of Iowa.

Krasner, S. M. (1985). *Developmental aspects of communication in children with Down's syndrome.* Unpublished Ph.D. thesis. University of St. Andrews, Scotland.

Kuhl, J. (1985). Volitional mediators of cognition-behavior consistency: Self-regulatory processes and action versus state orientation. In J. Kuhl & J. Beckmann (Eds.), *Action control: From cognition to behavior.* West Berlin: Springer-Verlag.

Kulik, C. L. C., Kulik, J. A., & Bangert-Drowns, R. L. (1990). Effectiveness of mastery learning programs: A meta-analysis. *Review of Educational Research, 60,* 265–299.

Kurtz, B. E. (1990). Cultural influences on children's cognitive and metacognitive development. In W. Schneider & F. E. Weinert (Eds.), *Interactions among aptitudes, strategies, and knowledge in cognitive performance* (pp. 177–199). New York: Springer-Verlag.

LaBerge, D., & Samuels, S. J. (1974). Toward a theory of automatic information processing in reading. *Cognitive Psychology, 6,* 293–323.

Lange, G. (1973). The development of conceptual and rote recall skills among school age children. *Journal of Experimental Child Psychology, 15,* 394–406.

Lange, G. (1978). Organization-related processes in children's recall. In P. A. Ornstein (Ed.), *Memory development in children* (pp. 101–128). Hillsdale, NJ: Erlbaum.

Lange, G., MacKinnon, G. E., & Nida, R. E. (1989). Knowledge, strategy, and motivational contributions to preschool children's object recall. *Developmental Psychology, 25,* 772–779.

Larry P. v. Riles 343 F. Supp. 1306 (N. D. Cal. 1979), aff'd 502 F. 2d (9th Cir. 1974); 495 F. Supp. 926 (N. D. Cal. 1979), aff'd. in part and rev'd in part, 793 F. 2d 969 (9th Cir. 1984).

Larsen, J. P., Hoien, T., Lundberg, I., & Ødegaard, S. (1990). MRI evaluation of the size and symmetry of the planum temporale in adolescents with developmental dyslexia. *Brain and Language, 39,* 289–301.

Larson, K. A., & Gerber, M. M. (1992). Metacognition. In N. N. Singh & I. L. Beale (Eds.), *Learning disabilities: Nature, theory, and treatment* (pp. 126–169). New York: Springer-Verlag.

Lasky, R. E. (1974). The ability of six-year-olds, eight-year-olds, and adults to abstract visual patterns. *Child Development, 45,* 626–632.

Laughan, P. (1990). The dynamic assessment of intelligence: A review of three approaches. *School Psychology Review, 19,* 459–470.

Lau v. Nichols (1974). 414 U.S. 563.

Lave, J., & Wenger, E. (1991). *Situated learning: Legitimate peripheral participation.* Cambridge, UK: Cambridge University Press.

LaVoie, J. C. (1973). Punishment and adolescent self-control. *Developmental Psychology, 8,* 16–24.

LaVoie, J. C. (1974). Cognitive determinants of resistance to deviation in seven-, nine-, and eleven-year-old children of low and high maturity of moral judgment. *Developmental Psychology, 10,* 393–403.

Lawton, M. (1993, September 8). Verbal, math scores on S.A.T. up for second straight year. *Education Week,* p. 10.

Lazar, I., Darlington, R., Murray, H., Royce, J., & Sipper, A. (1982). Lasting effects of early childhood education: A report from the consortium for longitudinal studies. *Monographs of the Society for Research in Child Development, 47* (2–3, Whole No. 195).

Lee, V. E., & Bryk, A. S. (1986). Effects of single-sex secondary schools on student achievement and attitudes. *Journal of Educational Psychology, 78,* 381–395.

Lee, V. E., & Bryk, A. S. (1989). Effects of single-sex schools: Response to Marsh. *Journal of Educational Psychology, 81,* 647–650.

Leinhardt, G. (1986). Expertise in mathematics teaching. *Educational Leadership, 43*(7), 34–39.

Leinhardt, G., & Greeno, J. G. (1986). The cognitive skill of teaching. *Journal of Educational Psychology, 78,* 75–95.

Lepper, M. R. (1983). Extrinsic reward and intrinsic motivation: Implications for the classroom. In J. M. Levine & M. C. Wang (Eds.), *Teacher and student perceptions: Implications for learning.* Hillsdale, NJ: Erlbaum.

Lepper, M. R., Aspinwall, L. G., Mumme, D. L., & Chabey, R. W. (1990). Self-perception and social-perception processes in tutoring: Subtle social control strategies of expert tutors. In J. M. Olson & M. P. Zanna (Eds.), *Self-inference processes: The Ontario symposium* (pp. 217–237). Hillsdale, NJ: Erlbaum.

Lepper, M. R., Greene, D., & Nisbett, R. E. (1973). Undermining children's intrinsic interest with extrinsic rewards: A test of the "overjustification" hypothesis. *Journal of Personality and Social Psychology, 28,* 129–137.

Lepper, M. R., & Hodell, M. (1989). Intrinsic motivation in the classroom. In C. Ames & R. Ames (Eds.), *Research on motivation in education: Vol. 3, Goals and cognitions* (pp. 73–105). San Diego: Academic Press.

Lepper, M. R., & Malone, T. W. (1987). Intrinsic motivation and instructional effectiveness in computer-based education. In R. E. Snow & M. J. Farr (Eds.), *Aptitude, learning, and instruction: Vol. 3, Conative and affective process analyses* (pp. 255–286). Hillsdale, NJ: Erlbaum.

Lerner, J. W., Lowenthal, B., & Lerner, S. W. (1995). *Attentional deficit disorders: Assessment and teaching.* Pacific Grove, CA: Brooks/Cole.

Lesgold, A. M. (1984). Acquiring expertise. In J. R. Anderson & S. M. Kosslyn (Eds.), *Tutorials in learning and memory* (pp. 31–60). San Francisco: Freeman.

Lesgold, A. [M.], Glaser, R., Rubinson, H., Klopfer, D., Feltovich, P., & Wang, Y. (1988). Expertise in a complex skill: Diagnosing X-ray pictures. In M. T. H. Chi, R. Glaser, & M. J. Farr (Eds.), *The nature of expertise* (pp. 311–342). Hillsdale, NJ: Erlbaum.

Levin, J. R. (1976). What have we learned about maximizing what children can learn? In J. R. Levin & V. L. Allen (Eds.), *Cognitive learning in children.* New York: Academic Press.

Levin, J. R. (1982). Pictures as prose-learning devices. In A. Flammer & W. Kintsch (Eds.), *Discourse processing* (pp. 412–444). Amsterdam: North-Holland.

Levin, J. R. (1983). Pictorial strategies for school learning: Practical illustrations. In M. Pressley & J. R. Levin (Eds.), *Cognitive strategy research: Educational applications* (pp. 213–237). New York: Springer-Verlag.

Levin, J. R. (1985). Educational applications of mnemonic pictures: Possibilities beyond your wildest imagination. In A. A. Sheikh (Ed.), *Imagery in education: Imagery in the educational process* (pp. 63–87). Farmingdale, NY: Baywood.

Levin, J. R. (1986). Four cognitive principles of learning strategy research. *Educational Psychologist, 21,* 3–17.

Levin, J. R., McCabe, A. E., & Bender, B. G. (1975). A note on imagery-inducing motor activity in young children. *Child Development, 46,* 263–266.

Levin, J. R., & Pressley, M. (1981). Improving children's prose comprehension: Selected strategies that seem to succeed. In C. M. Santa & B. L. Hayes (Eds.), *Children's prose comprehension* (pp. 44–71). Newark, DE: International Reading Association.

Levy, J. (1976). Cerebral lateralization and spatial ability. *Behavior Genetics, 6,* 171–188.

Lewontin, R. C. (1974). *The genetic basis of evolutionary change.* New York: Columbia University Press.

Lewontin, R. C., Rose, S., & Kamin, L. J. (1984). *Not in our genes: Biology, ideology, and human nature.* New York: Pantheon Books.

Lhyle, K. G., & Kulhavy, R. W. (1987). Feedback processing and error correction. *Journal of Educational Psychology, 79,* 320–322.

Licht, B. (1983). Cognitive-motivational factors that contribute to the achievement of learning-disabled children. *Journal of Learning Disabilities, 16,* 483–490.

Licht, B. (1992). Achievement-related beliefs in children with learning disabilities. In L. J. Meltzer (Ed.), *Strategy assessment and instruction for students with learning disabilities: From theory to practice* (pp. 195–220). Austin, TX: PRO-ED.

Licht, B. G., Kistner, J. A., Ozkaragoz, T., Shapiro, S., & Clausen, L. (1985). Causal attributions of learning disabled children: Individual differences and their implications for persistence. *Journal of Educational Psychology, 77,* 208–216.

Lickona, T. (Ed.). (1976). *Moral development and behavior.* New York: Holt, Rinehart & Winston.

Lickona, T. (1991). *Educating for character: How our schools can teach respect and responsibility.* New York: Bantam Books.

Lieberman, P. (1984). *The biology and evolution of language.* Cambridge, MA: Harvard University Press.

Lieberman, P. (1989). Some biological constraints on universal grammar and learnability. In M. L. Rice & R. L. Schiefelbusch (Eds.), *The teachability of language* (pp. 199–225). Baltimore: Brookes.

Lincoln, Y. S., & Guba, E. G. (1985). *Naturalistic inquiry.* Newbury Park, CA: Sage.

Lindow, J., Marrett, C. B., & Wilkinson, L. C. (1985). Overview. In L. C. Wilkinson & C. B. Marrett (Eds.), *Gender influences on classroom interaction* (pp. 1–15). Orlando, FL: Academic Press.

Linn, R. L. (1994). Performance assessment: Policy promises and technical measurement standards. *Educational Researcher, 23*(9), 4–14.

Lockheed, M. E. (1985). Some determinants and consequences of sex segregation in the classroom. In L. C. Wilkinson & C. B. Marrett (Eds.), *Gender influences on classroom interaction* (pp. 167–184). Orlando, FL: Academic Press.

Locurto, C. (1988). On the malleability of IQ. *The Psychologist, 11,* 431–435.

Locurto, C. (1990). The malleability of IQ as judged from adoption studies. *Intelligence, 14,* 275–292.

Locurto, C. (1991a). Beyond IQ in preschool programs? *Intelligence, 15,* 295–312.

Locurto, C. (1991b). Hands on the elephant: IQ, preschool programs, and the rhetoric of innoculation—A reply to commentaries. *Intelligence, 15,* 335–349.

Locurto, C. (1991c). *Sense and nonsense about IQ: The case for uniqueness.* New York: Praeger.

Loehlin, J. C., & Nichols, R. C. (1976). *Heredity, environment, and personality.* Austin: University of Texas Press.

Lou, H. C., Henriksen, L., & Bruhn, P. (1984). Focal cerebral hypoperfusion in children with dysphasia and/or attention deficit disorder. *Archives of Neurology, 41,* 825–829.

Ludeke, R. J., & Hartup, W. W. (1983). Teaching behaviors of 9- and 11-year-old girls in mixed-age and same-age dyads. *Journal of Educational Psychology, 75,* 909–914.

Luhmer, K. (1990). Moral education in Japan. *Journal of Moral Education, 19,* 172–181.

Lundeberg, M. A. (1987). Metacognitive aspects of reading comprehension: Studying understanding in legal case analysis. *Reading Research Quarterly, 22,* 407–432.

Luria, A. R. (1982). *Language and cognition.* New York: Wiley.

Luther, M., & Wyatt, F. (1989). A comparison of Feuerstein's method of LPAD assessment with conventional IQ testing on disadvantaged North York high school students. *International Journal of Dynamic Assessment and Instruction, 1,* 49–64.

Lyman, F., Jr. (1992). Think-pair-share, thinktrix, thinklinks, and weird facts: An interactive system for cooperative learning. In N. Davidson & T. Worsham (Eds.), *Enhancing thinking through cooperative learning* (pp. 169–181). New York: Teachers College Press.

MacArthur, C. Schwartz, S., & Graham, S. (1991). Effects of a reciprocal peer revision strategy in special education classrooms. *Learning Disabilities Research and Practice, 6,* 201–210.

Maccoby, E. E. (1988). Gender as a social category. *Developmental Psychology, 24*(6), 755–765.

Maccoby, E. [E.], & Martin, J. (1983). Socialization in the context of the family: Parent-child interaction. In E. M. Hetherington (Ed.), *Handbook of child psychology: Vol. 4, Socialization, personality and social development* (pp. 1–101). New York: Wiley.

MacKinnon, D. W. (1978). *In search of human effectiveness.* Buffalo, NY: Creative Education Foundation.

MacMillan, D. L., & Knopf, E. D. (1971). Effects of instructional set on perceptions of event outcomes by EMR and nonretarded children. *American Journal of Mental Deficiency, 76,* 185–189.

MacPherson, E. M., Candee, B. L., & Hohman, R. J. (1974). A comparison of three methods for eliminating disruptive classroom behavior. *Journal of Applied Behavior Analysis, 7,* 287–297.

Madison, P. (1969). *Personality development in college.* Reading, MA: Addison-Wesley.

Malcolm, S. (1984). *Equity and excellence: Compatible goals.* Washington, DC: AAAS Publications.

Mallory, M. E. (1989). Q-sort definition of ego identity status. *Journal of Youth and Adolescence, 18,* 399–412.

Malone, T. W., & Lepper, M. R. (1987). Making learning fun: A taxonomy of intrinsic motivation for learning. In R. E. Snow & M. J. Farr (Eds.), *Aptitude, learning, and instruction: Vol. 3, Conative and affective process analyses* (pp. 223–253). Hillsdale, NJ: Erlbaum.

Mandler, J. M. (1978). A code in the node: The use of a story schema in retrieval. *Discourse Processes, 1,* 14–35.

Mandler, J. M. (1984). *Stories, scripts, and scenes: Aspects of schema theory.* Hillsdale, NJ: Erlbaum.

Mandler, J. M. (1987). On the psychological reality of story structure. *Discourse Processes, 10,* 1–29.

Mandler, J. M., & DeForest, M. (1979). Is there more than one way to recall a story? *Child Development, 50,* 886–889.

Mandler, J. M., & Goodman, M. S. (1982). On the psychological validity of story structure. *Journal of Verbal Learning and Verbal Behavior, 21,* 507–523.

Mandler, J. M. & Johnson, N. S. (1977). Remembrance of things parsed: Story structure and recall. *Cognitive Psychology, 9,* 111–151.

Manning, B. H. (1988). Application of cognitive behavior modification: First and third graders self-management of classroom behaviors. *American Educational Research Journal, 25,* 193–212.

Manning, B. H. (1990). Cognitive self-instruction for an off-task fourth grader during independent academic tasks: A case study. *Contemporary Educational Psychology, 15,* 36–46.

Manning, B. H. (1991). *Cognitive self-instruction for classroom processes.* Albany: State University of New York Press.

Maosen, Li (1990). Moral education in the People's Republic of China. *Journal of Moral Education, 19,* 159–171.

Maple, S. A., & Stage, F. K. (1991). Influence on the choice of math/science major by gender and ethnicity. *American Educational Research Journal, 28,* 37–60.

Maratsos, M. P. (1989). Innateness and plasticity in language acquisition. In M. L. Rice & R. L. Schiefelbusch (Eds.), *The teachability of language* (pp. 105–125). Baltimore: Brookes.

Marcia, J. E. (1966). Development and validation of ego-identity status. *Journal of Personality and Social Psychology, 3,* 551–558.

Markman, E. M., & Callanan, M. A. (1983). An analysis of hierarchical classification. In R. Sternberg (Ed.), *Advances in the psychology of human intelligence* (Vol. 2, pp. 325–365). Hillsdale, NJ: Erlbaum.

Markstrom-Adams, C., & Spencer, M. B. (1994). A model for identity intervention with minority adolescents. In S. Archer (Ed.), *Interventions for adolescent identity development* (pp. 84–104). Thousand Oaks, CA: Sage.

Markus, H. (1977). Self-schemata and processing information about the self. *Journal of Personality and Social Psychology, 35*(2), 63–78.

Markus, H., & Nurius, P. (1986). Possible selves. *American Psychologist, 41,* 954–969.

Marmor, G. S. (1975). Development of kinetic images: When does the child first represent movement in mental images? *Cognitive Psychology, 7,* 548–559.

Marsh, H. W. (1989a). Effects of attending single-sex and coeducational high schools on achievement, attitudes, behaviors, and sex differences. *Journal of Educational Psychology, 81,* 70–85.

Marsh, H. W. (1989b). Effects of single-sex and coeducational schools: A response to Lee and Bryk. *Journal of Educational Psychology, 81,* 652–653.

Marsh, H. W. (1992). Extracurricular activities: Beneficial extension of the traditional curriculum or subversion of academic goals? *Journal of Educational Psychology, 84,* 553–562.

Marshall, H. H. (1989). The development of self-concept. *Young Children, 44*(5), 44–51.

Marston, D., & Magnusson, D. (1985). Implementing curriculum-based measurement in special and regular education settings. *Exceptional Children, 52,* 266–276.

Martin, V. L., & Pressley, M. (1991). Elaborative-interrogation effects depend on the nature of the question. *Journal of Educational Psychology, 83,* 113–119.

Martindale, C. (1991). *Cognitive psychology: A neural-network approach.* Pacific Grove, CA: Brooks/Cole.

Mastropieri, M. A., & Scruggs, T. E. (1989). Constructing more meaningful relationships: Mnemonic instruction for special populations. *Educational Psychology Review, 1,* 83–111.

Mathews, M. M. (1966). *Teaching to read: Historically considered.* Chicago: University of Chicago Press.

Mathison, S. (1988). Why triangulate? *Educational Researcher, 17*(2), 13–17.

Matsuzawa, T. (1990). Spontaneous sorting in human and chimpanzee. In S. T. Parker & K. R. Gibson (Eds.), *"Language" and intelligence in monkeys and apes* (pp. 451–468). Cambridge, UK: Cambridge University Press.

Mayer, R. E. (1979). Can advance organizers influence meaningful learning? *Review of Educational Research, 49,* 371–383.

Mayer, R. E. (1981). Frequency norms and structural analysis of algebra story problems into families, categories, and templates. *Instructional Science, 10,* 135–175.

Mayer, R. E. (1982). Memory for algebra story problems. *Journal of Educational Psychology, 74,* 199–216.

Mayer, R. E., Larkin, J. H., & Kadane, J. (1984). A cognitive analysis of mathematical problem solving ability. In R. Sternberg (Ed.), *Advances in the psychology of human intelligence* (pp. 231–273). Hillsdale, NJ: Erlbaum.

McCarthy, K. A., & Nelson, K. (1981). Children's use of scripts in story recall. *Discourse Processes, 4,* 59–70.

McCarthy, R. A., & Warrington, E. K. (1990). *Cognitive neuropsychology: A clinical introduction.* San Diego: Academic Press.

McCauley, C., Kellas, G., Dugas, J., & DeVillis, R. F. (1976). Effects of serial rehearsal training of memory search. *Journal of Educational Psychology, 68,* 474–481.

McClelland, J. L., & Rumelhart, D. E. (1981). An interactive activation model of context effects in letter perception: Part 1. An account of basic findings. *Psychological Review, 88,* 375–407.

McClelland, J. L., & Rumelhart, D. E. (1988). *Explorations in parallel distributed processing: A handbook of models, programs, and exercises.* Cambridge, MA: MIT Press.

McCloskey, M. (1983). Naive theories of motion. In D. Gentner & A. Stevens (Eds.), *Mental models* (pp. 299–324). Hillsdale, NJ: Erlbaum.

McCloskey, M. (1992). Cognitive mechanisms in numerical processing: Evidence from acquired dyscalculia. *Cognition, 44,* 107–157.

McCormick, C. B., Busching, B. A., & Potter, E. F. (1992). Children's knowledge about writing: The development and use of evaluative criteria. In M. Pressley, K. R. Harris, & J. T. Guthrie (Eds.), *Promoting academic competence and literacy in school* (pp. 311–336). San Diego: Academic Press.

McCormick, C. B., & Levin, J. R. (1987). Mnemonic prose-learning strategies. In M. A. McDaniel & M. Pressley (Eds.), *Imagery and related mnemonic processes: Theories, individual differences, and applications* (pp. 407–427). New York: Springer-Verlag.

McCutchen, D., & Perfetti, C. A. (1983). Local coherence: Helping young writers manage a complex task. *Elementary School Journal, 84,* 71–75.

McDaniel, E. (1994). *Understanding educational measurement.* Madison, WI: Brown & Benchmark.

McDonnell, J., & Ferguson, B. (1989). A comparison of time delay and decreasing prompt hierarchy strategies in teaching banking skills to students with moderate handicaps. *Journal of Applied Behavior Analysis, 22,* 85–91.

McGill-Franzen, A. M. (1987). Failure to learn to read: Formulating a policy problem. *Reading Research Quarterly, 22,* 475–490.

McKoon, G., & Ratcliff, R. (1979). Priming in episodic and semantic memory. *Journal of Verbal Learning and Verbal Behavior, 18,* 463–480.

McNamee, G. D. (1979). The social interaction origins of narrative skills. *Quarterly Newsletter of the Laboratory of Comparative Human Cognition, 1,* 63–68.

Mealy, D. L., & Host, T. R. (1988). Coping with test anxiety. *College Teaching, 40*(4), 147–150.

Means, M., & Voss, J. (1985). Star Wars: A developmental study of expert and novice knowledge structures. *Journal of Memory and Language, 24,* 746–757.

Meece, J. L., Blumenfeld, P. C., & Hoyle, R. H. (1988). Students' goal orientations and cognitive engagement in classroom activities. *Journal of Educational Psychology, 80,* 514–523.

Mehan, H. (1979). *Social organization in the classroom.* Cambridge, MA: Harvard University Press.

Mehrens, W. A., & Lehmann, I. J. (1991). *Measurement and evaluation in education and psychology* (4th ed.). Fort Worth, TX: Holt, Rinehart & Winston.

Meichenbaum, D. (1977). *Cognitive behavior modification.* New York: Plenum.

Meichenbaum, D. (1990). Cognitive perspective on teaching self-regulation. *American Journal of Mental Deficiency, 94,* 367–369.

Meichenbaum, D., & Asarnow, J. (1979). Cognitive-behavioral modification and metacognitive development: Implications for the classroom. In P. C. Kendall & S. D. Hollon (Eds.), *Cognitive-behavioral interventions* (pp. 11–35). New York: Academic Press.

Meichenbaum, D., & Goodman, J. (1971). Training impulsive children to talk to themselves: A means of developing self-control. *Journal of Abnormal Child Psychology, 77,* 115–126.

Meisels, S. J., & Plunkett, J. W. (1988). Developmental consequences of preterm birth: Are there long-term effects? In P. B. Baltes, D. L. Featherman, & R. M. Lerner (Eds.), *Life-span development and behavior* (Vol. 9, pp. 87–128). Hillsdale, NJ: Erlbaum.

Meltzoff, A. N. (1985). Immediate and deferred imitation in fourteen- and twenty-four-month-old infants. *Child Development, 56,* 62–72.

Meltzoff, A. N., & Gopnik, A. (1989). On linking nonverbal imitation, representation, and language learning in the first two years of life. In G. E. Speidel & K. E. Nelson (Eds.), *The many faces of imitation in language learning* (pp. 23–51). New York: Springer-Verlag.

Meltzoff, A. N., & Moore, M. K. (1977). Imitation of facial and manual gestures by human neonates. *Sciences, 198,* 75–78.

Meltzoff, A. N., & Moore, M. K. (1983). Newborn infants imitate adult facial gestures. *Child Development, 54,* 702–709.

Mensh, E., & Mensh, H. (1991). *The IQ mythology.* Carbondale: Southern Illinois University Press.

Merighi, J., Edison, M., & Zigler, E. (1990). The role of motivational factors in the functioning of mentally retarded individuals. In R. M. Hodapp, J. A. Burack, & E. Zigler (Eds.), *Issues in the developmental approach to retardation* (pp. 114–134). Cambridge, UK: Cambridge University Press.

Meyer, B. J. F. (1975). *The organization of prose and its effects on memory.* Amsterdam: North-Holland.

Meyer, B. J. F., Brandt, D. H., & Bluth, G. J. (1980). Use of top-level structure in text: Key for reading comprehension of ninth-grade students. *Reading Research Quarterly, 16,* 72–103.

Meyer, B. J. F., Young, C. J., & Bartlett, B. J. (1989). *Memory improved: Reading and memory enhancement across the life span through strategic text structures.* Hillsdale, NJ: Erlbaum.

Meyer, D., Schvaneveldt, R. W., & Ruddy, M. G. (1975). Loci of contextual effects on word recognition. In P. M. A. Rabbitt & S. Dornic (Eds.), *Attention and performance V* (pp. 98–118). London: Academic Press.

Meyers, J., Gelzheiser, L., Yelich, G., & Gallagher, M. (1990). Classroom, remedial, and resource teachers' views of pullout programs. *Elementary School Journal, 90,* 533–545.

Michael, B. (Ed.). (1990). *Volunteers in public schools.* Washington, DC: National Academy Press.

Mikulecky, L. (1987). The status of literacy in our society. In *Research in literacy: Thirty-seventh yearbook of the National Reading Conference* (pp. 24–34). Chicago: National Reading Conference.

Miles, H. L. W. (1990). The cognitive foundations for reference in a signing orangutan. In S. T. Parker & K. R. Gibson (Eds.), *"Language" and intelligence in monkeys and apes* (pp. 511–539). Cambridge, UK: Cambridge University Press.

Miller, A. I. (1984). *Imagery in scientific thought: Creating 20th-century physics.* Boston: Birkhaüser.

Miller, G. A. (1956). The magical number seven, plus-or-minus two: Some limits on our capacity for processing information. *Psychological Review, 63,* 81–97.

Miller, P. H., Woody-Ramsey, J., & Aloise, P. A. (1991). The role of strategy effortfulness in strategy effectiveness. *Developmental Psychology, 27,* 738–745.

Miltenberger, R. G., & Thiesse-Duffy, E. (1988). Evaluation of home-based programs for teaching personal safety skills to children. *Journal of Applied Behavior Analysis, 21,* 81–87.

Mitchell, J. V., Jr. (Ed.). (1985). *The ninth mental measurements yearbook* (Vol. 1–2). Lincoln: The Buros Institute of Mental Measurements of the University of Nebraska-Lincoln.

Mitchell, R. (1992). *Testing for learning: How new approaches to evaluation can improve American schools.* New York: Free Press.

Moely, B. E. (1977). Organizational factors in the development of memory. In R. V. Kail & J. W. Hagen (Eds.), *Perspectives on the development of memory and cognition* (pp. 203–236). Hillsdale, NJ: Erlbaum.

Moely, B. E., Olson, F. A., Halwes, T. G., & Flavell, J. H. (1969). Production deficiency in young children's clustered recall. *Developmental Psychology, 1,* 26–34.

Mokros, J. R., & Tinker, R. F. (1987). The impact of microcomputer-based labs on children's abilities to interpret graphs. *Journal of Research in Science Teaching, 24,* 369–383.

Mooney, R. J. (1990). Learning plan schemata from observation: Explanation-based learning for plan recognition. *Cognitive Science, 14,* 483–509.

Morgan, B., & Gibson, K. R. (1991). Nutritional and environmental interactions in brain development. In K. R. Gibson & A. C. Petersen (Eds.), *Brain maturation and cognitive development: Comparative and cross-cultural perspectives* (pp. 91–106). New York: Aldine de Gruyter.

Morine-Dershimer, G. (1979). *Teacher plan and classroom reality: The S. Bay study, part 4.* Research Monograph, Institute for Research on Teaching, University of Michigan.

Morocco, C., & Neuman, S. (1986). Word processors and the acquisition of writing strategies. *Journal of Learning Disabilities, 19,* 243–247.

Morrow, L. M. (1983). Home and school correlates of early interest in literature. *Journal of Education Research, 76,* 221–230.

Morrow, L. M. (1989). *Literacy development in the early years: Helping children read and write.* Boston: Allyn & Bacon.

Morrow, L. M. (1990). Preparing the classroom environment to promote literacy during play. *Early Childhood Research Quarterly, 5,* 537–554.

Morrow, L. M., & Smith, J. K. (1990). The effects of group size on interactive storybook reading. *Reading Research Quarterly, 25,* 213–231.

Morrow, L. M., & Weinstein, C. S. (1986). Encouraging voluntary reading: The impact of a literacy program on children's use of library corners. *Reading Research Quarterly, 21,* 330–346.

Morse, L. W., & Handley, H. M. (1985). Listening to adolescents: Gender differences in science classroom interactions. In L. C. Wilkinson & C. B. Marrett (Eds.), *Gender influences on classroom interaction* (pp. 37–56). Orlando, FL: Academic Press.

Mortimore, P. (1991). Effective schools from a British perspective: Research and practice. In J. R. Bliss, W. A. Firestone, & C. E. Richards (Eds.), *Rethinking effective schools research and practice* (pp. 76–90). Englewood Cliffs, NJ: Prentice-Hall.

Mullis, J. V. S., Owen, E. H., & Phillips, G. W. (1990). *Accelerating academic achievement.* Princeton, NJ: National Assessment of Educational Progress, Educational Testing Service.

Munsinger, H., & Weir, M. W. (1967). Infants' and young children's preference for complexity. *Journal of Experimental Child Psychology, 5,* 69–73.

Mussen, P. H. (Ed.) (1983). *Handbook of child psychology* (4th ed). New York: Wiley.

Myles-Worsley, M., Johnston, W. A., & Simons, M. A. (1988). The influence of expertise on X-ray image processing. *Journal of Experimental Psychology: Learning, Memory, and Cognition, 14*(3), 553–557.

Naglieri, J. A., & Prewett, P. N. (1990). Nonverbal intelligence measures: A selected review of instruments and their use. In C. R. Reynolds & R. W. Kamphaus (Eds.), *Handbook of psychological and educational assessment of children: Intelligence and achievement* (pp. 348–370). New York: Guilford Press.

National Center for Education Statistics (1992). *Digest of education statistics.* Washington, DC: U.S. Department of Education.

Necka, E. (1992). Cognitive analysis of intelligence: The significance of working memory processes. *Personality and Individual Differences, 13,* 1031–1046.

Needleman, H. L. (1992). Childhood exposure to lead: A common cause of school failure. *Phi Delta Kappan, 74,* 35–37.

Needleman, H. L., & Bellinger, D. (1991). The health effects of low level exposure to lead. *Annual Review of Public Health, 12,* 111–140.

Neely, J. H. (1976). Semantic priming and retrieval from lexical memory: Evidence for facilitatory and inhibitory processes. *Memory and Cognition, 4,* 648–654.

Neely, J. H. (1977). Semantic priming and retrieval from lexical memory: Roles of inhibitionless spreading activation and limited capacity attention. *Journal of Experimental Psychology, 106,* 226–254.

Neisser, U. (1967). *Cognitive psychology.* New York: Appleton-Century-Crofts.

Nelson, J., & Hayes, J. R. (1988). *How the writing context shapes college students' strategies for writing from sources* (Technical Report No. 16.). Berkeley: University of California and Carnegie-Mellon University, Center for Study of Writing at University of California and Carnegie-Mellon.

Nelson, K. (1978). How children represent their world in and out of language. In R. S. Siegler (Ed.), *Children's thinking: What develops?* (pp. 255–273). Hillsdale, NJ: Erlbaum.

Nelson, K., & Gruendel, J. (1981). Generalized event representations: Basic building blocks of cognitive development. In A. Brown & M. Lamb (Eds.), *Advances in developmental psychology* (Vol. 1, pp. 231–247). Hillsdale, NJ: Erlbaum.

Neman, R., Roos, P., McCann, B. M., Menolascino, F., & Heal, L. W. (1974). Experimental evaluation of sensorimotor patterning with mentally retarded children. *American Journal of Mental Deficiency, 79,* 372–384.

Nettelbeck, T., & Brewer, N. (1981). Studies of mild mental retardation and timed performance. In N. R. Ellis (Ed.), *International review of research in mental retardation* (Vol. 10, pp. 61–106). New York: Academic Press.

Neuman, S. B., & Roskos, K. (1992). Literacy objects as cultural tools: Effects on children's literacy behaviors in play. *Reading Research Quarterly, 27,* 202–225.

Neves, D. M., & Anderson, J. R. (1981). Knowledge compilation: Mechanisms for the automatization of cognitive skills. In J. R. Anderson (Ed.), *Cognitive skills and their acquisition* (pp. 251–272). Hillsdale, NJ: Erlbaum.

Newman, L. S. (1990). Intentional and unintentional memory in young children: Remembering versus playing. *Journal of Experimental Child Psychology, 50,* 243–258.

Newman, P., & Newman, B. (1978). Identity formation and the college experience. *Adolescence, 13,* 311–326.

Newman, R. S. (1990). Children's help-seeking in the classroom: The role of motivational factors and attitudes. *Journal of Educational Psychology, 82,* 71–80.

Newman, R. S., & Goldin, L. (1990). Children's reluctance to seek help with schoolwork. *Journal of Educational Psychology, 82,* 92–100.

Newmann, F. [M.] (1988). Can depth replace coverage in the high school curriculum? *Phi Delta Kappan, 68*(5), 345–348.

Newmann, F. [M.] (1990a). Higher-order thinking in social studies: A rationale for the assessment of classroom thoughtfulness. *Journal of Curriculum Studies, 22,* 41–56.

Newmann, F. [M.] (1990b). Qualities of thoughtful social studies classes: An empirical profile. *Journal of Curriculum Studies, 22,* 253–275.

Newmann, F. [M.] (1991a). Higher-order thinking in the teaching of social studies: Connections between theory and practice. In J. F. Voss, D. N. Perkins, & J. W. Segal (Eds.), *Informal reasoning and education* (pp. 381–400). Hillsdale, NJ: Erlbaum.

Newmann, F. M. (1991b). Promoting higher order thinking in social studies: Overview of a study of 16 high school departments. *Theory and Research in Social Education, 19,* 324–340.

Newmann, F. M. (1991c). Student engagement in academic work: Expanding the perspective on secondary school effectiveness. In J. R. Bliss, W. A. Firestone, & C. E. Richards (Eds.), *Rethinking effective schools research and practice* (pp. 58–75). Englewood Cliffs, NJ: Prentice-Hall.

Newmann, F. [M.] (1991d). The prospects for classroom thoughtfulness in high school social studies. In C. Collins (Ed.), *Building the quality of thinking in and out of our schools in the twenty-first century.* Hillsdale, NJ: Erlbaum.

Newmann, F. [M.], Onosko, J., & Stevenson, R. (1990). Staff development for higher-order thinking: A synthesis of practical wisdom. *Journal of Staff Development, 11*(3), 48–55.

Nicholls, J. G. (1989). *The competitive ethos and democratic education.* Cambridge, MA: Harvard University Press.

Nicholls, J. G., & Thorkildsen, T. A. (1987, October). *Achievement goals and beliefs: Individual and classroom differences.* Paper presented at the meeting of the Society for Experimental Social Psychology, Charlottesville, VA.

Noddings, N. (1984). *Caring: A feminine approach to ethics and moral education.* Berkeley: University of California Press.

Nolte, R. Y., & Singer, H. (1985). Active comprehension: Teaching a process of reading comprehension and its effects on reading achievement. *Reading Teacher, 39,* 24–31.

Northcutt, N. (1975). *Adult functional competency: A summary.* Austin, TX: Adult Performance Level Project.

Novak, J. D., & Gowin, D. B. (1984). *Learning how to learn.* New York: Cambridge University Press.

Novak, J. D., & Musonda, D. (1991). A twelve-year longitudinal study of science concept learning. *American Educational Research Journal, 28*(1), 17–153.

Nunnally, J. C. (1978). *Psychometric theory* (2nd ed.). New York: McGraw-Hill.

Nussbaum, J., & Novick, S. (1982). Alternative frameworks, conceptual conflict and accommodation: Toward a principled teaching strategy. *Instructional Science, 11,* 183–200.

Nystrand, M. (1986). *The structure of written communication: Studies in reciprocity between writers and readers.* New York: Academic Press.

Oakes, J. (1985). *Keeping track: How schools structure inequality.* New Haven, CT: Yale University Press.

Oakes, J. (1987). Tracking in secondary schools: A contextual perspective. *Educational Psychologist, 22,* 129–154.

Oden, G. C. (1987). Concept, knowledge, and thought. *Annual Review of Psychology, 38,* 203–227.

Okebukola, P. A. (1990). Attaining meaningful learning of concepts in genetics and ecology: An examination of the potency of the concept-mapping technique. *Journal of Research in Science Teaching, 27,* 493–504.

Olson, L. (1994, June 15). Writing still needs work, report finds. *Education Week,* pp. 1, 10.

O'Neil, J. (1992). Putting performance assessment to the test. *Educational Leadership, 49*(8), 14–19.

Onosko, J. (1989). Comparing teachers' thinking about promoting students' thinking. *Theory and Research in Social Education, 17,* 174–195.

Onosko, J. (1991). Barriers to the promotion of higher-order thinking in social studies. *Theory and Research in Social Education, 19,* 340–365.

Onosko, J. (1992). Exploring the thinking of thoughtful teachers. *Educational Leadership, 49*(7), 40–43.

Onosko, J. J., & Newmann, F. M. (1994). Creating more thoughtful learning environments. In J. Mangieri & C. C. Block (Eds.), *Advanced educational psychology: Enhancing mindfulness.* Fort Worth, TX: Harcourt Brace Jovanovich.

Ornstein, P. A., Naus, M. J., & Liberty, C. (1975). Rehearsal and organizational processes in children's memory. *Child Development, 46,* 818–830.

Ornstein, R. (1977). *The psychology of consciousness.* New York: Harcourt Brace Jovanovich.

Ornstein, R. (1978). The split and whole brain. *Human Nature, 1,* 76–83.

Orr, J. (1990). Sharing knowledge, celebrating identity: Community memory in a service culture. In D. S. Middleton & D. Edwards (Eds.), *Collective remembering: Memory in society* (pp. 169–189). Beverly Hills, CA: Sage.

Ory, J. C., & Ryan, K. E. (1993). *Tips for improving testing and grading.* Newbury Park, CA: Sage.

O'Sullivan, J. T., & Pressley, M. (1984). Completeness of instruction and strategy transfer. *Journal of Experimental Child Psychology, 38,* 275–288.

O'Sullivan, P. J., Ysseldyke, J. E., Christenson, S. L., & Thurlow, M. L. (1990). Mildly handicapped elementary students' opportunity to learn during reading instruction in mainstream and special education settings. *Reading Research Quarterly, 25,* 131–146.

Owen, E., & Sweller, J. (1989). Should problem solving be used as a learning device in mathematics? *Journal for Research in Mathematics Education, 20,* 322–328.

Paivio, A. (1971). *Imagery and verbal processes.* New York: Holt, Rinehart & Winston.

Paivio, A. (1986). *Mental representations: A dual-coding approach.* New York: Oxford University Press.

Palincsar, A. S., & Brown, A. L. (1984). Reciprocal teaching of comprehension-fostering and monitoring activities. *Cognition and Instruction, 1,* 117–175.

Palmer, E. L. (1984). Providing quality television for America's children. In J. P. Murray & G. Salomon (Eds.), *The future of children's television* (pp. 103–124). Boys Town, NE: Boys Town Center.

Panksepp, J. (1986). The neurochemistry of behavior. *Annual Review of Psychology, 7,* 77–108.

Paris, S. G., Lawton, T. A., Turner, J. C., & Roth, J. L. (1991). A developmental perspective on standardized achievement testing. *Educational Researcher, 20*(5), 12–20.

Paris, S. G., Lipson, M. Y., & Wixson, K. K. (1983). Becoming a strategic reader. *Contemporary Educational Psychology, 8,* 293–316.

Park, H. S., & Gaylord-Ross, R. (1989). A problem-solving approach to social skills training in employment settings with mentally retarded youth. *Journal of Applied Behavior Analysis, 22,* 373–380.

Parke, R. D. (1969). Effectiveness of punishment as an interaction of intensity, timing, agent nurturance and cognitive structuring. *Child Development, 40,* 213–236.

Parke, R. D. (1974). Rules, roles, and resistance to deviation in children: Explorations in punishment, discipline and self-control. In A. D. Pick (Ed.), *Minnesota symposium on child psychology* (Vol. 8., pp. 111–144). Minneapolis: University of Minnesota Press.

Parker, S. T., & Gibson, K. R. (Eds.). (1990). *"Language" and intelligence in monkeys and apes.* Cambridge, UK: Cambridge University Press.

Parks, R. W., Loewenstein, D. A., Dodrill, K. L., Barker, W. W., Yoshii, F., Chang, J. Y., Emran, A., Apicella, A., Sheramata, W. A., & Duara, R. (1988). Cerebral metabolic effects of a verbal fluency test: A PET scan study. *Journal of Clinical and Experimental Neuropsychology, 10,* 565–575.

Pascarella, E. T., & Terenzini, P. T. (1991). *How college affects students.* San Francisco: Jossey-Bass.

Patterson, C. J., & Mischel, W. (1976). Effects of temptation-inhibiting and task-facilitating plans on self-control. *Journal of Personality and Social Psychology, 33,* 209–217.

Pea, R. D., & Kurland, D. M. (1984). On the cognitive effects of learning computer programming. *New Ideas in Psychology, 2,* 137–168.

Pearl, R. (1982). LD children's attributions for success and failure: A replication with a labeled LD sample. *Learning Disability Quarterly, 5,* 173–176.

Pearl, R., Bryan, T., & Herzog, A. (1990). Resisting or acquiescing to peer pressure to engage in misconduct: Adolescents' expectations of probable consequences. *Journal of Youth and Adolescence, 19,* 43–55.

Pearson, P. D., Hansen, J., & Gordon, C. (1979). The effect of background knowledge on young children's comprehension of explicit and implicit information. *Journal of Reading Behavior, 11,* 201–209.

Pellegrini, A. D., & Horvat, M. (1995). A developmental contextualist critique of Attention Deficit Hyperactivity Disorder. *Educational Researcher, 24*(1), 13–19.

Pellegrini, A. D., Perlmutter, J. C., Galda, L., & Brody, G. H. (1990). Joint reading between black Head Start children and their mothers. *Child Development, 61,* 443–453.

Pennock-Román, M. (1992). Interpreting test performance in selective admissions for Hispanic students. In K. F. Geisinger (Ed.), *Psychological testing of Hispanics* (pp. 99–136). Washington, DC: American Psychological Association.

Perlmutter, B. F. (1987). Personality variables and peer relations of children and adolescents with learning disabilities. In S. J. Ceci (Ed.), *Handbook of cognitive, social, and neuropsychological aspects of learning disabilities* (Vol. 1, pp. 339–359). Hillsdale, NJ: Erlbaum.

Perlmutter, M., Behrend, S. D., Kuo, F., & Muller, A. (1989). Social influences on children's problem solving. *Developmental Psychology, 25,* 744–754.

Perrone, V. (1991). *Expanding student assessment.* Alexandria, VA: Association for Supervision and Curriculum Development.

Perry, M., VanderStoep, S. W., & Yu, S. L. (1993). Asking questions in first-grade mathematics classes: Potential influences on mathematical thought. *Journal of Educational Psychology, 85,* 31–40.

Perry, W. (1970). *Forms of ethical and intellectual development in the college years.* New York: Holt.

Perry, W. (1981). Cognitive and ethical growth. In A. Chickering (Ed.), *The modern American college: Responding to the new realities of diverse students and a changing society.* San Francisco: Jossey-Bass.

Petersen, S. E., Fox, P. T., Posner, M. I., Mintun, M., & Raichle, M. E. (1988). Positron emission tomographic studies of the cortical anatomy of single-word processing. *Nature, 331,* 585–589.

Petersen, S. E., Fox, P. T., Snyder, A. Z., & Raichle, M. E. (1990). Activation of extrastriate and frontal cortical areas by visual words and word-like stimuli. *Science, 249,* 1041–1044.

Petersen, P. L., & Comeaux, M. A. (1987). Teachers' schemata for classroom events: The mental scaffolding of teachers' thinking during classroom instruction. *Teaching and Teacher Education, 3,* 319–331.

Pfundt, H., & Duit, R. (1991). *Bibliography: Students' alternative frameworks and science education* (3rd ed.). Kiel, Germany: IPN.

Phelps, M. E., Mazziotta, J. C., & Huang, S.-C. (1982). Study of cerebral function with positron computed tomography. *Journal of Cerebral Blood Flow Metabolism, 2,* 113–162.

Phillips, E. L. (1968). Achievement Place: Token reinforcement procedures in a home-style rehabilitation setting for "pre-delinquent" boys. *Journal of Applied Behavior Analysis, 1,* 213–223.

Phillips, E. L., Phillips, E. A., Fixsen, D. L., & Wolf, M. M. (1971). Achievement Place: Modification of the behaviors of pre-delinquent boys within a token economy. *Journal of Applied Behavior Analysis, 4,* 45–59.

Phillips, G. W. (1991). Benefits of state-by-state comparisons. *Educational Researcher, 20*(3), 17–19.

Piaget, J. (1929). *The child's conception of the world.* London: Routledge & Kegan Paul.

Piaget, J. (1965). *The moral judgment of the child.* New York: Free Press.

Piaget, J. (1967). *Biologie et connaissance.* Paris: Gallimard.

Piaget, J. (1972). Intellectual evolution from adolescence to adulthood. *Human Development, 15,* 1–12.

Piaget, J. (1983). Piaget's theory. In W. Kesson (Ed.) & P. H. Mussen (General Ed.), *History, theory, and methods: Vol. 1, Handbook of child psychology* (pp. 103–128). New York: Wiley.

Pichert, J. W., & Anderson, R. C. (1977). Taking different perspectives on a story. *Journal of Educational Psychology, 69,* 309–315.

Pikulski, J. J. (1991). The transition years: Middle school. In J. Flood, J. M. Jensen, D. Lapp, & J. R. Squire (Eds.), *Handbook of research on teaching the English language arts* (pp. 303–319). New York: Macmillan.

Pinnell, G. S. (1989). Reading recovery: Helping at-risk children learn to read. *Elementary School Journal, 90,* 161–183.

Pleiss, M. K., & Feldhusen, J. F. (1995). Mentors, role models, and heroes in the lives of gifted children. *Educational Psychologist, 30*(3), 159–169.

Plomin, R., DeFries, J. C., & Fulker, D. W. (1988). *Nature and nurture during infancy and early childhood.* New York: Cambridge University Press.

Plomin, R., DeFries, J. C., & McClearn, G. E. (1990). *Behavioral genetics: A primer* (2nd ed.). New York: Freeman.

Poche, C., Yoder, P., & Miltenberger, R. (1988). Teaching self-protection to children using television techniques. *Journal of Applied Behavior Analysis, 21,* 253–261.

Polya, G. (1954a). *Mathematics and plausible reasoning: (a) Induction and analogy in mathematics.* Princeton, NJ: Princeton University Press.

Polya, G., (1954b). *Patterns of plausible inference.* Princeton, NJ: Princeton University Press.

Polya, G. (1957). *How to solve it.* New York: Doubleday.

Polya, G. (1981). *Mathematical discovery* (combined paperback edition). New York: Wiley.

Popham, W. J. (1995). *Classroom assessment: What teachers need to know.* Boston: Allyn & Bacon.

Porter, A. C. (1991). Good teaching of worthwhile mathematics to disadvantaged students. In M. S. Knapp & P. M. Shields (Eds.), *Better schooling for the children of poverty: Alternatives to conventional wisdom* (pp. 125–148). Berkeley, CA: McCutchan.

Posner, M. I. (1969). Abstraction and the process of recognition. In G. H. Bower & J. T. Spence (Eds.), *The psychology of learning and motivation* (Vol. 3, pp. 43–100). New York: Academic Press.

Posner, M. I., & Keele, S. W. (1968). On the genesis of abstract ideas. *Journal of Experimental Psychology, 77,* 353–363.

Posner, M. I., & Keele, S. W. (1970). Retention of abstract ideas. *Journal of Experimental Psychology, 83,* 304–308.

Posner, M. I., Petersen, S. E., Fox, P. T., & Raichle, M. E. (1988). Localization of cognitive operations in the human brain. *Science, 240,* 1627–1631.

Powell, A. G., Farrar, E., & Cohen, D. K. (1985). *The shopping mall high school.* Boston: Houghton Mifflin.

Powell, R. E., Locke, D. C., & Sprinthall, N. A. (1991). Female offenders and their guards: A programme to promote moral and ego development of both groups. *Journal of Moral Education, 20,* 191–203.

Power, F. C., Higgins, A., & Kohlberg, L. (1989). *Lawrence Kohlberg's approach to moral education.* New York: Columbia University Press.

Power, F. C., & Power, M. R. (1992). A raft of hope: Democratic education and the challenge of pluralism. *Journal of Moral Education, 21,* 193–205.

Prechtl, H. F. R. (1986). New perspectives in early human development. *European Journal of Obstetrics, Gynecology, and Reproductive Biology, 21,* 347–354.

Premack, D. (1965). Reinforcement theory. In D. Levine (Ed.), *Nebraska Symposium on Motivation* (Vol. 13). Lincoln: University of Nebraska Press.

Pressey, S. L. (1926). A simple apparatus which gives tests and scores—And teaches. *School and Society, 23,* 373–376.

Pressley, G. M. (1976). Mental imagery helps eight-year-olds remember what they read. *Journal of Educational Psychology, 68,* 355–359.

Pressley, M. (1979). Increasing children's self-control through cognitive interventions. *Review of Educational Research, 49,* 319–370.

Pressley, M. (1983). Making meaningful materials easier to learn. In M. Pressley & J. R. Levin (Eds.), *Cognitive strategy research: Educational applications* (pp. 239–266). New York: Springer-Verlag.

Pressley, M., & Afflerbach, P. (1995). *Verbal protocols of reading.* Hillsdale, NJ: Erlbaum.

Pressley, M., Borkowski, J. G., & Johnson, C. J. (1987). The development of good strategy use: Imagery and related mnemonic strategies. In M. A. McDaniel & M. Pressley (Eds.), *Imagery and related mnemonic processes: Theories, individual differences, and applications* (pp. 274–301). New York: Springer-Verlag.

Pressley, M., Borkowski, J. G., & O'Sullivan, J. T. (1984). Memory strategy instruction is made of this: Metamemory and durable strategy use. *Educational Psychologist, 19,* 94–107.

Pressley, M., Borkowski, J. G., & O'Sullivan, J. T. (1985). Children's metamemory and the teaching of memory strategies. In D. L. Forrest-Pressley, G. E. MacKinnon, & T. G. Waller (Eds.), *Metacognition, cognition, and human performance* (pp. 111–153). New York: Academic Press.

Pressley, M., Borkowski, J. G., & Schneider, W. (1987). Cognitive strategies: Good strategy users coordinate metacognition and knowledge. In R. Vasta & G. Whitehurst (Eds.), *Annals of child development* (Vol. 5, pp. 89–129). Greenwich, CT: JAI Press.

Pressley, M., Borkowski, J. G., & Schneider, W. (1989). Good information processing: What it is and what education can do to promote it. *International Journal of Educational Research,* 13, 857–867.

Pressley, M., & Brewster, M. E. (1990). Imaginal elaboration of illustrations to facilitate fact learning: Creating memories of Prince Edward Island. *Applied Cognitive Psychology, 4,* 359–370.

Pressley, M., Cariglia-Bull, T., Deane, S., & Schneider, W. (1987). Short-term memory, verbal competence, and age as predictors of imagery instructional effectiveness. *Journal of Experimental Child Psychology, 43,* 194–211.

Pressley, M., El-Dinary, P. B., & Brown, R. (1992). Skilled and not-so-skilled reading: Good information processing and not-so-good information processing. In M. Pressley, K. R. Harris, & J. T. Guthrie (Eds.), *Promoting academic competence and literacy: Cognitive research and instructional innovation* (pp. 91–127). San Diego: Academic Press.

Pressley, M., El-Dinary, P. B., Gaskins, I., Schuder, T., & Bergman, J. L., Almasi, J., & Brown, R. (1992). Beyond direct explanation: Transactional instruction of reading comprehension strategies. *Elementary School Journal, 92,* 513–556.

Pressley, M., Forrest-Pressley, D. [L.], Elliott-Faust, D. L., & Miller, G. E. (1985). Children's use of cognitive strategies, how to teach strategies, and what to do if they can't be taught. In M. Pressley & C. J. Brainerd (Eds.), *Cognitive learning and memory in children* (pp. 1–47). New York: Springer-Verlag.

Pressley, M., & Ghatala, E. S. (1989). Metacognitive benefits of taking a test for children and young adolescents. *Journal of Experimental Child Psychology, 47,* 430–450.

Pressley, M., & Ghatala, E. S. (1990). Self-regulated learning: Monitoring learning from text. *Educational Psychologist, 25,* 19–34.

Pressley, M., Ghatala, E. S., Woloshyn, V., & Pirie, J. (1990). Sometimes adults miss the main ideas and do not realize it: Confidence in responses to short-answer and multiple-choice comprehension questions. *Reading Research Quarterly, 25*(3), 22–249.

Pressley, M., Harris, K. R., & Marks, M. B. (1992). But good strategy instructors are constructivists! *Educational Psychology Review, 4,* 3–31.

Pressley, M., Heisel, B. E., McCormick, C. G., & Nakamura, G. V. (1982). Memory strategy instruction with children. In C. J. Brainerd & M. Pressley (Eds.), *Progress in cognitive development research: Vol. 2, Verbal processes in children* (pp. 125–159). New York: Springer-Verlag.

Pressley, M., Johnson, C. J., Symons, S., McGoldrick, J. A., & Kurita, J. A. (1989). Strategies that improve children's memory and comprehension of text. *Elementary School Journal, 90,* 3–32.

Pressley, M., & Levin, J. R. (1977a). Developmental differences in subjects' associative learning strategies and performance: Assessing a hypothesis. *Journal of Experimental Child Psychology, 24,* 431–439.

Pressley, M., & Levin, J. R. (1977b). Task parameters affecting the efficacy of a visual imagery learning strategy in younger and older children. *Journal of Experimental Child Psychology, 24,* 53–59.

Pressley, M., Levin, J. R., & Ghatala, E. S. (1984). Memory strategy monitoring in adults and children. *Journal of Verbal Learning and Verbal Behavior, 23,* 270–288.

Pressley, M., Levin, J. R., & McDaniel, M. A. (1987). Remembering versus inferring what a word means: Mnemonic and contextual approaches. In M. G. McKeown & M. E. Curtis (Eds.), *The nature of vocabulary acquisition* (pp. 107–127). Hillsdale, NJ: Erlbaum.

Pressley, M., & MacFadyen, J. (1983). Mnemonic mediator retrieval at testing by preschool and kindergarten children. *Child Development, 54,* 474–479.

Pressley, M., Ross, K. A., Levin, J. R., & Ghatala, E. S. (1984). The role of strategy utility knowledge in children's strategy decision making. *Journal of Experimental Child Psychology, 38,* 491–504.

Pressley, M., Schuder, T., SAIL Faculty and Administration, Bergman, J. L., & El-Dinary, P. B. (1992). A researcher-educator collaborative interview study of transactional comprehension strategies instruction. *Journal of Educational Psychology, 84,* 231–246.

Pressley, M., Snyder, B. L., & Cariglia-Bull, T. (1987). How can good strategy use be taught to children? Evaluation of six approaches. In S. M. Cormier & J. D. Hagman (Eds.), *Transfer of learning: Contemporary research and applications* (pp. 81–120). San Diego: Academic Press.

Pressley, M., Symons, S., McDaniel, M. A., Snyder, B. L., & Turnure, J. E. (1988). Elaborative interrogation facilitates acquisition of confusing facts. *Journal of Educational Psychology, 80,* 268–278.

Pressley, M., Wood, E., Woloshyn, V. E., Martin, V., King, A., & Menke, D. (1992). Encouraging mindful use of prior knowledge: Attempting to construct explanatory answers facilitates learning. *Educational Psychologist, 27,* 91–110.

Price, J. H., Desmond, S., & Kukulka, G. (1985). High school students' perceptions and misperceptions of AIDS. *Journal of School Health, 55,* 107–109.

Prince, G. (1978). Putting the other half of the brain to work. *Training: The Magazine of Human Resources Development, 15,* 57–61.

Pritchard, R. (1990). The effects of cultural schemata on reading processing strategies. *Reading Research Quarterly, 25,* 273–295.

Puckering, C., & Rutter, M. (1987). Environmental influences on language development. In W. Yule & M. Rutter (Eds.), *Language development and disorders* (pp. 103–128). Philadelphia: Lippincott.

Putnam, R., Lampert, M., & Peterson, P. L. (1990). Alternative perspectives on knowing mathematics in elementary schools. In C. B. Cazden (Ed.), *Review of Research in Education* (Vol. 16, pp. 57–150). Washington, DC: American Educational Research Association.

Rabinowitz, M., Freeman, K., & Cohen, S. (1992). Use and maintenance of strategies: The influence of accessibility on knowledge. *Journal of Educational Psychology, 84,* 211–218.

Rabinowitz, M., & Glaser, R. (1985). Cognitive structure and process in high competent performance. In F. D. Horowitz & M. O'Brien (Eds.), *The gifted and talented: Developmental perspectives* (pp. 75–98). Washington, DC: American Psychological Association.

Rabinowitz, M., & McAuley, R. (1990). Conceptual knowledge processing: An oxymoron? In W. Schneider & F. E. Weinert (Eds.), *Interactions among aptitudes, strategies, and knowledge in cognitive performance* (pp. 117–133). New York: Springer-Verlag.

Radford, J. (1990). *Child prodigies and exceptional early achievers.* New York: Free Press.

Ramey, C. T. (1992). High-risk children and IQ: Altering intergenerational patterns. *Intelligence, 16,* 239–256.

Ramey, C. T., & Campbell, F. A. (1987). The Carolina Abecedarian Project: An educational experiment concerning human malleability. In J. J. Gallagher & C. T. Ramey (Eds.), *The malleability of children*. Baltimore: Brookes.

Rand, Y., & Kaniel, S. (1987). Group administration of the LPAD. In C. Lidz (Ed.), *Dynamic assessment* (pp. 196–214). New York: Guilford Press.

Raschke, D. (1981). Designing reinforcement surveys—Let the student choose the reward. *Teaching Exceptional Children, 14,* 92–96.

Ravitch, D., & Finn. C. (1987). *What do our 17-year-olds know?* New York: Harper & Row.

Rawls, J. (1971). *A theory of justice*. Cambridge, MA: Harvard University Press.

Raymond, C. (1992). Sex differences in gifted math students' achievement. *APS Observer, 5*(4), 5.

Rayner, K. (1988). Word recognition cues in children: The relative use of graphemic cues, orthographic cues, and grapheme-phoneme correspondence rules. *Journal of Educational Psychology, 80,* 473–479.

Rayner, K., & Pollatsek, A. (1989). *The psychology of reading*. Englewood Cliffs, NJ: Prentice-Hall.

Redfield, D. L., & Rousseau, E. W. (1981). A meta-analysis of experimental research on teacher questioning behavior. *Review of Educational Research, 51,* 237–246.

Reed, S. K. (1972). Pattern recognition and categorization. *Cognitive Psychology, 3,* 382–407.

Reeder, G. D., McCormick, C. B., & Esselman, E. D. (1987). Self-referent processing and recall of prose. *Journal of Educational Psychology, 79*(3), 243–248.

Reisner, E. R., Petry, C. A., & Armitage, M. (1989). *A review of programs involving college students as tutors or mentors in grades K–12*. Washington, DC: Policy Study Associates.

Renninger, K. A. (1990). Children's play interests, representation, and activity. In R. Fivush & J. Hudson (Eds.), *Knowing and remembering in young children* (pp. 127–165). Cambridge, MA: Cambridge University Press.

Renzulli, J. S. (1986). The three-ring conception of giftedness: A developmental model for creative productivity. In R. J. Sternberg & J. E. Davidson (Eds.), *Conceptions of giftedness* (pp. 53–92). Cambridge, UK: Cambridge University Press.

Resnick, L. B., Levine, J. M., & Teasley, S. D. (Eds.). (1991). *Perspectives on socially shared cognition*. Washington, DC: American Psychological Association.

Rest, J. (1968). *Developmental hierarchy in preference and comprehension of moral judgment*. Unpublished Ph.D. dissertation. University of Chicago.

Rest, J. R., in collaboration with Barnett, R., Bebeau, M., Deemer, D., Getz, I., Moon, Y., Schlaefli, A., Spickelmier, J., Thoma, S., & Volker, J. (1986). *Moral development: Advances in research and theory*. New York: Praeger.

Reynolds, C. R., Chastain, R. L., Kaufman, A. S., & McLean, J. E. (1987). Demographic characteristics and IQ among adults: Analysis of the WISC-R standardization sample as a function of the stratification variables. *Journal of School Psychology, 25,* 323–342.

Reynolds, C. R., & Kaiser, S. M. (1990a). Bias in assessment of aptitude. In C. R. Reynolds & R. W. Kamphaus (Eds.), *Handbook of psychological and educational assessment of children: Intelligence & achievement* (pp. 611–653). New York: Guilford Press.

Reynolds, C. R., & Kaiser, S. M. (1990b). Test bias in psychological assessment. In T. B. Gutkin & C. R. Reynolds (Eds.), *The handbook of school psychology* (pp. 487–525). New York: Wiley.

Rice, M. L., Huston, A. C., Truglio, R., & Wright, J. (1990). Words from "Sesame Street": Learning vocabulary from viewing. *Developmental Psychology, 26,* 421–428.

Richardson, S. A., & Koller, H. (1985). Epidemiology. In A. M. Clarke, A. D. B. Clarke, & J. M. Berg (Eds.), *Mental deficiency: The changing outlook* (4th ed., pp. 356–400). New York: Free Press.

Richert, E. S. (1991). Rampant problems and promising practices in identification. In N. Colangelo & G. A. Davis (Eds.), *Handbook of gifted education* (pp. 81–96). Boston: Allyn & Bacon.

Rickards, J. P., & August, G. J. (1975). Generative underlining strategies in prose recall. *Journal of Educational Psychology, 66*, 860–865.

Rinehart, S. D., Stahl, S. A., & Erickson, L. G. (1986). Some effects of summarization training on reading and studying. *Reading Research Quarterly, 21*, 422–438.

Ringness, T. A. (1961). Self-concept of children of low, average, and high intelligence. *American Journal of Mental Deficiency, 65*, 453–461.

Rips, L. J., Shoben, E. J., & Smith, E. E. (1973). Semantic distance and the verification of semantic relations. *Journal of Verbal Learning and Verbal Behavior, 12*, 1–20.

Risberg, J. (1986). Regional cerebral blood flow in neuropsychology. *Neuropsychologia, 24*, 135–140.

Ritter, K. (1978). The development of knowledge of an external retrieval cue strategy. *Child Development 49*, 1227–1230.

Rivera v. City of Wichita Falls, 665 F. 2d 531 (1982).

Roberts, B. (1992). The evolution of the young child's concept of *word* as a unit of spoken language. *Reading Research Quarterly, 27*, 124–138.

Roberts, P. (1983). Memory strategy instruction with the elderly: What should memory training be the training of? In M. Pressley & J. R. Levin (Eds.), *Cognitive strategy research: Psychological foundations* (pp. 75–100). New York: Springer-Verlag.

Roberts, T., & Kraft, R. (1987). Reading comprehension performance and laterality: Evidence for concurrent validity of dichotic, dichhaptic, and EEG laterality measures. *Neuropsychologia, 25*(5), 817–828.

Robinson, C. S., & Hayes, J. R. (1978). Making inferences about relevance in understanding problems. In R. Revlin & R. E. Mayer (Eds.), *Human reasoning*. Washington, DC: Winston.

Robinson, F. P. (1961). *Effective study* (Rev. ed.). New York: Harper & Row.

Robinson, J. A., & Kingsley, M. E. (1977). Memory and intelligence: Age and ability differences in strategies and organization of recall. *Intelligence, 1*, 318–330.

Rodriguez, O. (1992). Introduction to technical and societal issues in the psychological testing of Hispanics. In K. F. Geisinger (Ed.), *Psychological testing of Hispanics* (pp. 11–16). Washington, DC: American Psychological Association.

Roehler, L. R., & Duffy, G. G. (1984). Direct explanation of comprehension processes. In G. G. Duffy, L. R. Roehler, & J. Mason (Eds.), *Comprehension instruction: Perspectives and suggestions* (pp. 265–280). New York: Longman.

Rogers, H., & Saklofske, D. H. (1985). Self-concept, locus of control and performance expectations of learning disabled children. *Journal of Learning Disabilities, 18*, 273–278.

Rogers, T. B., Kuiper, N. A., & Kirker, W. S. (1977). Self-reference and the encoding of personal information. *Journal of Personality and Social Psychology, 35*, 677–688.

Rogoff, B. (1990). *Apprenticeship in thinking: Cognitive development in social context*. New York: Oxford University Press.

Rohwer, W. D., Jr. (1973). Elaboration and learning in childhood and adolescence. In H. W. Reese (Ed.), *Advances in child development and behavior* (Vol. 8, pp. 1–57). New York: Academic Press.

Rohwer, W. D., Jr. (1980). An elaborative conception of learner differences. In R. E. Snow, P. A. Federico, & W. E. Montague (Eds.), *Aptitude, learning, and instruction: Vol. 2, Cognitive process analysis of learning and problem solving* (pp. 23–46). Hillsdale, NJ: Erlbaum.

Rohwer, W. D., Jr., & Litrownik, J. (1983). Age and individual differences in the learning of a memorization procedure. *Journal of Educational Psychology, 75*, 799–810.

Romberg, T. A., & Carpenter, T. C. (1986). Research on teaching and learning mathematics: Two disciplines of scientific inquiry. In M. C. Wittrock (Ed.), *Handbook of research on teaching* (3rd ed., pp. 850–873). New York: Macmillan.

Rosch, E. (1973). On the internal structure of perceptual and semantic categories. In T. Moore (Ed.), *Cognitive development and the acquisition of language* (pp. 111–144). New York: Academic Press.

Rosch, E. (1975). Cognitive representations of semantic categories. *Journal of Experimental Psychology: General, 104,* 192–233.

Rosch, E. (1978). Principles of categorization. In E. Rosch & B. Lloyd (Eds.), *Cognition and categorization* (pp. 9–31). Hillsdale, NJ: Erlbaum.

Rosch, E., & Mervis, C. (1975). Family resemblance studies in the internal structure of categories. *Cognitive Psychology, 7,* 575–605.

Rosen, M. G. (1985). Factors during labor and delivery that influence brain disorders. In J. Freeman (Ed.), *Prenatal and perinatal factors associated with brain disorders* (NIH Publication No. 85–1149, pp. 237–262). Washington, DC: U.S. Department of Health and Human Services.

Rosenblatt, L. M. (1978). *The reader, the text, the poem: The transactional theory of the literary work.* Carbondale: Southern Illinois University Press.

Rosenblatt, L. M. (1991). Literary theory. In J. Flood, J. M. Jensen, D. Lapp, & J. R. Squire (Eds.), *Handbook of research on teaching the English language arts* (pp. 57–62). New York: Macmillan.

Rosenshine, B. V. (1979). Content, time, and direct instruction. In P. L. Peterson & H. J. Walberg (Eds.), *Research on teaching: Concepts, findings, and implications* (pp. 28–56). Berkeley, CA: McCutchan.

Rosenshine, B. [V.], & Chapman, S. (1992, April). *Instructional elements in studies which taught students to generate questions.* Paper presented at the annual meeting of the American Educational Research Association, San Francisco.

Rosenshine, B. [V.], & Meister, C. (1994). Reciprocal teaching: A review of the research. *Review of Educational Research, 64*(4), 479–530.

Rosenshine, B. [V.], & Trapman, S. (1992, April). *Teaching students to generate questions: A review of research.* Paper presented at the annual meeting of the American Educational Research Association, San Francisco.

Rosenshine, B. V., & Stevens, R. (1984). Classroom instruction in reading. In P. D. Pearson, R. Barr, M. L. Kamil, & P. Mosenthal (Eds.), *Handbook of reading research* (pp. 745–798). New York: Longman.

Rosenshine, B. [V.], & Stevens, R. (1986). Teaching functions. In M. C. Wittrock (Ed.), *Handbook of research on teaching* (3rd. ed., pp. 376–391). New York: Collier Macmillan.

Rosenthal, R. (1985). From unconscious experimenter bias to teacher expectancy effects. In J. B. Dusek (Ed.), *Teacher expectancies* (pp. 37–65). Hillsdale, NJ: Erlbaum.

Rosenthal, R., & Jacobson, L. (1968). *Pygmalion in the classroom: Teacher expectation and pupils' intellectual development.* New York: Holt, Rinehart & Winston.

Rosenthal, T. L., & Zimmerman, B. J. (1978). *Social learning and cognition.* New York: Academic Press.

Ross, H. S., & Balzer, R. H. (1975). Determinants and consequences of children's questions. *Child Development, 46,* 536–539.

Ross, H. S., & Killey, J. C. (1977). The effect of questioning on retention. *Child Development, 48,* 312–314.

Ross, J. A. (1988). Controlling variables: A meta-analysis of training studies. *Review of Educational Research, 58,* 405–437.

Ross, L. E., & Ross, S. M. (1984). Oculomotor functioning and the learning and cognitive processes of the intellectually handicapped. In P. H. Brooks, R. Sperber, & C. McCauley (Eds.), *Learning and cognition in the mentally retarded* (pp. 217–235). Hillsdale, NJ: Erlbaum.

Roth, K. J. (1990). Developing meaningful conceptual understanding in science. In B. F. Jones & L. Idol (Eds.), *Dimensions of thinking and cognitive instruction* (pp. 139–175). Hillsdale, NJ: Erlbaum.

Roth, K. J. (1991). Reading science texts for conceptual change. In C. M. Santa & D. E. Alvermann (Eds.), *Science learning: Processes and applications* (pp. 48–63). Newark, DE: International Reading Association.

Roth, W. M. (1990). Neo-Piagetian predictors of achievement in physical science. *Journal of Research in Science Teaching, 27,* 509–521.

Rotheram-Borus, M. J., & Wyche, K. F. (1994). Ethnic differences in identity development in the United States. In S. Archer (Ed.), *Interventions for adolescent identity development* (pp. 62–83). Thousand Oaks, CA: Sage.

Rothman, R. (1993a, January 20). Achievement in math improves, NAEP data find. *Education Week,* pp. 1, 23.

Rothman, R. (1993b, April 14). 8th graders in 18 of 37 states show math gains, NAEP reports. *Education Week,* pp. 1, 21.

Rotter, J. B. (1954). *Social learning and clinical psychology.* Englewood, Cliffs, NJ: Prentice-Hall.

Rowan, B., & Guthrie, L. F. (1989). The quality of Chapter 1 instruction: Results from a study of twenty-four schools. In R. E. Slavin, N. L. Karweit, & N. A. Madden (Eds.), *Effective programs for students at risk.* Boston: Allyn & Bacon.

Royer, J. M., Marchant, H. G., III, Sinatra, G. M., & Lovejoy, D. A. (1990). The prediction of college course performance from reading comprehension performance: Evidence for general and specific prediction factors. *American Educational Research Journal, 27,* 158–179.

Rulon, D. (1992). The just community: A method for staff development. *Journal of Moral Education, 21,* 217–224.

Russell, T., & Johnston, P. (1988, March). *Teachers learning from experiences of teaching: Analysis based on metaphor and reflection.* Paper presented at the annual meeting of the American Educational Research Association, New Orleans.

Russow, R. A., & Pressley, M. (1993). *Use of graphing calculators increases students' conceptual understanding of graphing: A quasi-experimental and true experimental evaluation.* Technical Report. College Park: University of Maryland, Department of Human Development (Educational Psychology).

Ruth, L. P. (1991). Who determines policy? Power and politics in English language arts education. In J. Flood, J. M. Jensen, D. Lapp, & J. R. Squire (Eds.), *Handbook of research on teaching the English language arts* (pp. 3–17). New York: Macmillan.

Rutter, M. (1983). School effects of pupil progress: Research findings and policy implications. In L. Shulman & G. Sykes (Eds.), *Handbook of teaching and policy* (pp. 3–41). New York: Longman.

Sabers, D. S., Cushing, K. S., & Berliner, D. C. (1991). Differences among teachers in a task characterized by simultaneity, multidimensionality, and immediacy. *American Educational Research Journal, 28,* 63–88.

Sadoski, M. (1983). An exploratory study of the relationship between reported imagery and the comprehension and recall of a story. *Reading Research Quarterly, 19,* 110–123.

Sadoski, M. (1985). The natural use of imagery in story comprehension and recall: Replication and extension. *Reading Research Quarterly, 20,* 658–667.

Sadoski, M., & Quast, Z. (1990). Reader response and long-term recall for journalistic text: The roles of imagery, affect, and importance. *Reading Research Quarterly, 25,* 256–272.

Salthouse, T. A. (1982). *Adult cognition: An experimental psychology of human aging.* New York: Springer-Verlag.

Salthouse, T. A. (1985). Speed of behavior and its implications for cognition. In J. E. Birren & K. W. Schaie (Eds.), *Handbook of the psychology of aging* (2nd ed., pp. 400–426). New York: Van Nostrand Reinhold.

Salthouse, T. A. (1988). The role of processing resources in cognitive aging. In M. I. Howe & C. J. Brainerd (Eds.), *Cognitive development in adulthood* (pp. 139–185). New York: Springer-Verlag.

Salthouse, T. A. (1992). The information-processing perspective on cognitive aging. In R. J. Sternberg & C. A. Berg (Eds.), *Intellectual development* (pp. 261–277). Cambridge, UK: Cambridge University Press.

Salthouse, T. A., Kausler, D. H., & Sault, J. S. (1988). Investigation of student status, background variables, and the feasibility of standard tasks in cognitive aging research. *Psychology and Aging, 3,* 29–37.

Sameroff, A. J. (1975). Early influences on development: Fact or fancy? *Merrill-Palmer Quarterly, 21,* 267–294.

Sameroff, A. J., & Fiese, B. H. (1990). Transactional regulation and early intervention. In S. J. Meisels & J. P. Shonkoff (Eds.), *Handbook of early childhood intervention* (pp. 119–149). Cambridge, UK: Cambridge University Press.

Samuels, M. T., Killip, S. M., MacKenzie, H., & Fagan, J. (1992). Evaluating preschool programs: The role of dynamic assessment. In H. C. Haywood & D. Tzuriel (Eds.), *Interactive assessment* (pp. 251–271). New York: Springer-Verlag.

Samuels, M. T., Lamb, C. H., & Oberholtzer, L. (1992). Dynamic assessment of adults with learning difficulties. In H. C. Haywood & D. Tzuriel (Eds.), *Interactive assessment* (pp. 275–299). New York: Springer-Verlag.

Samuels, M. [T.], Tzuriel, D., & Malloy-Miller, T. (1989). Dynamic assessment of children with learning disabilities. In R. T. Brown & M. Chazan (Eds.), *Learning difficulties and emotional problems* (pp. 145–165). Calgary: Detselig.

Samuels, S. J., Schermer, N., & Reinking, D. (1992). Reading fluency: Techniques for making decoding automatic. In S. J. Samuels & A. E. Farstrup (Eds.), *What research has to say about reading instruction* (pp. 124–144). Newark, DE: International Reading Association.

Sandoval, J. H., & Mille, M. P. W. (1980). Accuracy judments of WISC-R items difficulty for minority groups. *Journal of Consulting and Clinical Psychology, 48,* 249–253.

Santa, C. M., & Havens, L. T. (1991). Learning through writing. In C. M. Santa & D. E. Alvermann (Eds.), *Science learning: Processes and applications* (pp. 122–133). Newark, DE: International Reading Association.

Sattler, J. M. (1992). *Assessment of children* (Revised and updated 3rd ed.). San Diego: Sattler.

Saxe, G. B. (1988). The mathematics of child street vendors. *Child Development, 59,* 1415–1425.

Scarborough, H. S. (1990). Very early language deficits in dyslexic children. *Child Development, 61,* 1728–1743.

Scardamalia, M., & Bereiter, C. (1986). Research on written composition. In M. C. Wittrock (Ed.), *Handbook of research on teaching* (3rd ed., pp. 778–803). New York: Macmillan.

Scarr, S., & Kidd, K. K. (1983). Developmental behavior genetics. In M. M. Haith & J. J. Campos (Eds.) & P. H. Mussen (Gen. Ed.), *Handbook of child psychology: Vol. II, Infancy and developmental psychobiology* (pp. 345–433). New York: Wiley.

Scarr, S., & McCartney, K. (1983). How people make their own environments: A theory of genotype-environment effects. *Child Development, 54,* 424–435.

Scarr, S., & Weinberg, R. A. (1976). IQ test performance of black children adopted by white families. *American Psychologist, 31,* 726–739.

Scarr, S., & Weinberg, R. A. (1983). The Minnesota adoption studies: Genetic differences and malleability. *Child Development, 54,* 260–268.

Schade, J. P., & van Groeningen, W. B. (1961). Structural organization of the human cerebral cortex. I. Maturation of the middle frontal gyrus. *Acta Anatomica, 47,* 74–85.

Schaie, K. W. (1980). Age changes in intelligence. In R. L. Sprott (Ed.), *Age, learning ability, & intelligence* (pp. 41–77). New York: Van Nostrand Reinhold.

Schaie, K. W. (1990). Intellectual development in adulthood. In J. E. Birren & K. W. Schaie (Eds.), *Handbook of the psychology of aging* (3rd ed., pp. 291–309). San Diego: Academic Press.

Schaie, K. W., & Labouvie-Vief, G. V. (1974). Generational versus ontogenetic components of change in adult cognitive behavior: A fourteen-year cross-sequential study. *Developmental Psychology, 10,* 305–320.

Schauble, L. (1990). Belief revision in children: The role of prior knowledge and strategies for generating evidence. *Journal of Experimental Child Psychology, 49,* 31–57.

Shearer, B., Coballes-Vega, C., & Lundeberg, M. (1993, December). *How do teachers who are professionally active select, read, and use professional journals?* Paper presented at the annual meeting of the National Reading Conference, Charleston, SC.

Schiefele, U. (1991). Interest, learning, and motivation. *Educational Psychologist, 26,* 299–324.

Schloss, P. J. (1992). Special issue: Integrating learners with disabilities in regular education programs. *Elementary School Journal, 92*(3).

Schmeiser, C. B. (1992). Reactions to technical and societal issues in testing Hispanics. In K. F. Geisinger (Ed.), *Psychological testing of Hispanics* (pp. 79–88). Washington, DC: American Psychological Association.

Schneider, W., Borkowski, J. G., Kurtz, B. E., & Kerwin, K. (1986). Metamemory and motivation: A comparison of strategy use and performance in German and American children. *Journal of Cross-Cultural Psychology, 17,* 315–336.

Schneider, W., & Körkel, J. (1989). The knowledge base and text recall: Evidence from a short-term longitudinal study. *Contemporary Educational Psychology, 14,* 382–393.

Schneider, W., Körkel, J., & Weinert, F. E. (1989). Domain-specific knowledge and memory performance: A comparison of high- and low-aptitude children. *Journal of Educational Psychology, 81,* 306–312.

Schneider, W., & Pressley, M. (1989). *Memory development between 2 and 20.* New York: Springer-Verlag.

Schoenfeld, A. (1979). Explicit heuristic training as a variable in problem-solving performance. *Journal for Research in Mathematics Education, 10,* 173–187.

Schoenfeld, A. [H.] (1985). *Mathematical problem solving.* New York: Academic Press.

Schoenfeld, A. H. (1988). When good teaching leads to bad results: The disasters of a "well-taught" mathematics classroom. *Educational Psychologist, 23*(2), 145–166.

Schoenfeld, A. [H.] (1992). Learning to think mathematically: Problem solving, metacognition, and sense making in mathematics. In D. A. Grouws (Ed.), *Handbook of research on mathematics teaching and learning* (pp. 334–370). New York: Macmillan.

Schön, D. A. (1983). *The reflective practitioner: How professionals think in action.* London: Temple Smith.

Schön, D. A. (1987). *Educating the reflective practitioner.* San Francisco: Jossey-Bass.

Schön, D. A. (1988). Coaching reflective teaching. In P. P. Grimmett & G. L. Erickson (Eds.), *Reflection in teacher education* (pp. 17–29). New York: Teachers College Press.

Schrage, M. (1990). *Shared minds: The new technologies of collaboration.* New York: Random House.

Schunk, D. H. (1985). Participation in goal setting: Effects on self-efficacy and skills of learning disabled children. *Journal of Special Education, 19,* 307–317.

Schunk, D. H. (1989). Social cognitive theory and self-regulated learning. In B. J. Zimmerman & D. H. Schunk (Eds.), *Self-regulated learning and academic achievement* (pp. 83–110). New York: Springer-Verlag.

Schunk, D. H. (1990). Goal setting and self-efficacy during self-regulated learning. *Educational Psychologist, 15*(1), 71–86.

Schunk, D. H. (1991). Self-efficacy and academic motivation. *Educational Psychologist, 26,* 207–232.

Schunk, D. H., Hanson, A. R., & Cox, P. D. (1987). Peer-model attributes and children's achievement behaviors. *Journal of Educational Psychology, 79,* 54–61.

Scott, D. T. (1987). Premature infants in later childhood: Some recent followup results. *Seminary Perinatology, 11,* 191–199.

Scott, J. A., & Ehri, L. C. (1990). Sight word reading in prereaders: Use of logographic vs. alphabetic access routes. *Journal of Reading Behavior, 22*(2), 149–166.

Scruggs, T. E., & Mastropieri, M. A. (1992). *Teaching test-taking skills: Helping students show what they know.* Cambridge, MA: Brookline Books.

Secada, W. G. (1991). Selected conceptual and methodological issues for studying the mathematics education of the disadvantaged. In M. S. Knapp & P. M. Shields (Eds.), *Better schooling for the children of poverty: Alternatives to conventional wisdom* (pp. 149–168). Berkeley, CA: McCutchan.

Secada, W. G. (1992). Race, ethnicity, social class, language, and achievement in mathematics. In D. A. Grouws (Ed.), *Handbook of research on mathematics teaching and learning* (pp. 623–660). New York: Macmillan.

Seidel, J. F. (1992). Children with HIV-related developmental difficulties. *Phi Delta Kappan, 74,* 38–40, 56.

Selfridge, O. G. (1959). Pandemonium: A paradigm for learning. In D. V. Blake & A. M. Uttley (Eds.), *Proceedings of the symposium on the mechanization of thought processes.* London: H. M. Stationery Office.

Semb, G. B., Ellis, J. A., & Araujo, J. (1993). Long-term memory for knowledge learned in school. *Journal of Educational Psychology, 85,* 305–316.

Service, V., Lock, A., & Chandler, P. (1989). Individual differences in early communicative development: A social constructivist perspective. In S. von Tetzchner, L. S. Siegel, & L. Smith (Eds.), *The social and cognitive aspects of normal and atypical language development* (pp. 23–49). New York: Springer-Verlag.

Seymour, P. H. K., & Elder, L. (1986). Beginning reading without phonology. *Cognitive Neuropsychology, 3,* 1–36.

Shade, B. J. (1982). Afro-American cognitive style: A variable in school success. *Review of Educational Research, 52,* 219–244.

Sharp, A. M. (1987). What is a 'community of inquiry'? *Journal of Moral Education, 16,* 37–45.

Sharp, D., Cole, M., & Lave, C. (1979). Education and cognitive development: The evidence from experimental research. *Monographs of the Society for Research in Child Development, 44* (Serial No. 178).

Shavelson, R. J., Baxter, G. P., & Pine, J. (1992). Performance assessments: Political rhetoric and measurement reality. *Educational Researcher, 21*(4), 22–27.

Shaywitz, S. E., & Shaywitz, B. A. (1992). Learning disabilities and attention deficits in the school setting. In L. J. Meltzer (Ed.), *Strategy assessment and instruction for students with learning disabilities: From theory to practice* (pp. 221–241). Austin, TX: PRO-ED.

Shepard, R. N., & Metzler, J. (1971). Mental rotation of three-dimensional objects. *Science, 171,* 701–703.

Sherman, L. W. (1988). A comparative study of cooperative and competitive achievement in two secondary biology classrooms: The group investigative model versus an individually competitive goal structure. *Journal of Research in Science Teaching, 26,* 55–64.

Shimmerlik, S. M., & Nolan, J. D. (1976). Reorganization and the recall of prose. *Journal of Educational Psychology, 68*(6), 779–786.

Shimron, J. (1975). Imagery and the comprehension of prose by elementary school children (Doctoral dissertation, University of Pittsburgh, 1974). *Dissertation Abstracts International, 36,* 795–A (University Microfilms No. 75–18, 254).

Shinn, M. R., Rosenfeld, S., & Knutson, N. (1989). Curriculum-based assessment: A comparison of models. *School Psychology Review, 18,* 299–316.

Shonkoff, J. P., & Marshall, P. C. (1990). Biological bases of developmental dysfunction. In S. J. Meisels & J. P. Shonkoff (Eds.), *Handbook of early childhood intervention* (pp. 35–52). Cambridge, UK: Cambridge University Press.

Short, E. J., & Ryan, E. B. (1984). Metacognitive differences between skilled and less skilled readers: Remediating deficits through story grammar and attribution training. *Journal of Educational Psychology, 76,* 225–235.

Shurkin, J. N. (1992). *Terman's kids: The groundbreaking study of how the gifted grow up.* Boston: Little, Brown.

Siegler, R. S. (1988). Individual differences in strategy choices: Good students, not-so-good students, and perfectionists. *Child Development, 59,* 833–851.

Siegler, R. S. (1989). Hazards of mental chronometry: An example from children's subtraction. *Journal of Educational Psychology, 81,* 497–506.

Siegler, R. S., & Shrager, J. (1984). Strategy choices in addition and subtraction: How do children know what to do? In C. Sophian (Ed.), *Origins of cognitive skills* (pp. 229–293). Hillsdale, NJ: Erlbaum.

Sigman, M., Neumann, C., Jansen, A. A., J., & Bwibo, N. (1989). Cognitive abilities of Kenyan children in relation to nutrition, family characteristics, and education. *Child Development, 60,* 1463–1474.

Silver, E. A. (1987). Foundations of cognitive theory and research for mathematics problem solving instruction. In A. Schoenfeld (Ed.), *Cognitive science and mathematics education* (pp. 33–60). Hillsdale, NJ: Erlbaum.

Simmons, P. E. (1991). Learning science in software microworlds. In S. M. Glynn, R. H. Yeany, & B. K. Britton (Eds.), *The psychology of learning science* (pp. 241–256). Hillsdale, NJ: Erlbaum.

Simon, H. A., & Chase, W. G. (1973). Skill in chess. *American Scientist, 61,* 394–403.

Sizer, T. R. (1984). *Horace's compromise: The dilemma of the American high school.* Boston: Houghton Mifflin.

Skinner, B. F. (1953). *Science and human behavior.* New York: Free Press.

Skinner, B. F. (1961). Why we need teaching machines. *Harvard Educational Review, 31,* 377–398.

Skinner, B. F. (1977). Corporal punishment. In I. A. Hyman & J. H. Wise (Eds.), *Corporal punishment in American education* (pp. 335–336). Philadelphia: Temple University Press.

Skinner, B. F. (1987). *Upon further reflection.* Englewood Cliffs, NJ: Prentice-Hall.

Slavin, R. E. (1984). Meta-analysis in education: How has it been used? *Educational Researcher, 13,* 6–15.

Slavin, R. [E.] (1985a). An introduction to cooperative learning research. In R. Slavin, S. Sharan, S. Kagan, R. H. Lazarowitz, C. Webb, & R. Schmuck (Eds.), *Learning to cooperate, cooperating to learn* (pp. 5–15). New York: Plenum.

Slavin, R. [E.] (1985b). Team-assisted individualization: Combining cooperative learning and individualized instruction in mathematics. In R. Slavin, S. Sharan, S. Kagan, R. H. Lazarowitz, C. Webb, & R. Schmuck (Eds.), *Learning to cooperate, cooperating to learn* (pp. 177–209). New York: Plenum.

Slavin, R. E. (1987a). Grouping for instruction in the elementary school. *Educational Psychologist, 22,* 109–128.

Slavin, R. E. (1989). Class size and student achievement: Small effects of small classes. *Educational Psychologist, 24,* 99–110.

Slavin, R. E. (1990). Achievement effects of ability grouping in secondary schools: A best-evidence synthesis. *Review of Educational Research, 60,* 471–499.

Slavin, R. E. (1991). Synthesis of research on cooperative learning. *Educational Leadership, 1,* 71–77.

Smith, E. E., & Medin, D. L. (1981). *Categories and concepts.* Cambridge, MA: Harvard University Press.

Smith, G., Spiker, D., Peterson, C., Cicchetti, D., & Justice, P. (1984). Use of megadoses of vitamins with minerals in Down syndrome. *Journal of Pediatrics, 105,* 228–234.

Smith, M. L. (1991a). Meanings of test preparation. *American Educational Research Journal, 28,* 521–542.

Smith, M. L. (1991b). Put to the test: The effects of external testing on teachers. *Educational Researcher, 20*(5), 8–11.

Smith, M. L., & Glass, G. V. (1987). *Research and evaluation in education and the social sciences.* Englewood Cliffs, NJ: Prentice-Hall.

Smith, S. G., & Jones, L. L. (1988). Images, imagination, and chemical reality. *Journal of Chemical Education, 66,* 8–11.

Sodian, B., & Schneider, W. (1990). Children's understanding of cognitive cuing: How to manipulate cues to fool a competitor. *Child Development, 61,* 697–704.

Spearman, C. (1904). "General intelligence" objectively determined and measured. *American Journal of Psychology, 15,* 201–293.

Spencer, M. B., & Markstrom-Adams, C. (1990). Identity processes among racial and ethnic minority children in America. *Child Development, 60,* 290–310.

Spilich, G. J., Vesonder, G. T., Chiesi, H. L., & Voss, J. F. (1979). Text processing of domain-related information for individuals with high and low domain knowledge. *Journal of Verbal Learning and Verbal Behavior, 18,* 275–290.

Spiro, R. J., Feltovich, P. J., Coulson, R. L., & Anderson, D. K. (1989). Multiple analogies for complex concepts: Antidotes for analogy-induced misconception in advanced knowledge acquisition. In S. Vosniadou & A. Ortony (Eds.), *Similarity and analogical reasoning* (pp. 498–531). Cambridge, UK: Cambridge University Press.

Spitz, H. H. (1986a). *The raising of intelligence: A selected history of attempts to raise retarded intelligence.* Hillsdale, NJ: Erlbaum.

Spitz, H. H. (1986b). Preventing and curing mental retardation by behavioral intervention: An evaluation of some claims. *Intelligence, 10,* 197–207.

Spitz, H. H. (1991a). Commentary on Locurto's "Beyond IQ in preschool programs?" *Intelligence, 15,* 327–334.

Spitz, H. H. (1991b). Review of *The Milwaukee Project: Preventing mental retardation in children at risk. American Journal on Mental Retardation, 95,* 482–490.

Spitz, H. H. (1992). Does the Carolina Abecedarian Early Intervention Project prevent sociocultural mental retardation? *Intelligence, 16,* 225–237.

Spreen, O., & Strauss, E. (1991). *A compendium of neuropsychological tests: Administration, norms, and commentary.* New York: Oxford University Press.

Springer, S. P., & Deutsch, G. (1989). *Left brain, right brain* (3rd ed.). New York: Freeman.

Squire, J. R. (1991). The history of the profession. In J. Flood, J. M. Jensen, D. Lapp, & J. R. Squire (Eds.), *Handbook of research on teaching the English language arts* (pp. 3–17). New York: Macmillan.

Stacey, K. (1992). Mathematical problem solving in groups: Are two heads better than one? *Journal of Mathematical Behavior, 11,* 261–275.

Stage, E. K., & Karplus, R. (1981). Mathematical ability: Is sex a factor? *Science, 212,* 114.

Stahl, S. A., & Miller, P. D. (1989). Whole language and language experience approaches for beginning reading: A quantitative research synthesis. *Review of Educational Research, 59,* 87–116.

Stanley, J. C., & Benbow, C. P. (1986). Youth who reason exceptionally well mathematically. In R. J. Sternberg & J. E. Davidson (Eds.), *Conceptions of giftedness* (pp. 361–387). Cambridge, UK: Cambridge University Press.

Stanovich, K. E., & West, R. F. (1989). Exposure to print and orthographic processing. *Reading Research Quarterly, 24,* 402–433.

Staszewski, J. J. (1990). Exceptional memory: The influence of practice and knowledge on the development of elaborative encoding strategies. In W. Schneider & F. E. Weinert (Eds.), *Interactions among aptitudes, strategies, and knowledge in cognitive performance* (pp. 252–285). New York: Springer-Verlag.

Stedman, L. (1988). The effective schools formula still needs changing: A reply to Brookover. *Phi Delta Kappan, 69*(6), 439–442.

Stein, N. L., & Glenn, C. G. (1979). An analysis of story comprehension in elementary school children. In R. O. Freedle (Ed.), *New directions in discourse processing* (Vol. 2). Norwood, NJ: Ablex.

Stein, N. L., & Nezworski, G. (1978). The effects of organization and instructional set on story memory. *Discourse Processes, 1,* 177–193.

Steinberg, L., & Dornbusch, S. M. (1991). Negative correlates of part-time employment during adolescence: Replication and elaboration. *Developmental Psychology, 27,* 304–313.

Steinberg, L., Dornbush, S. M., & Brown, B. B. (1992). Ethnic differences in adolescent achievement: An ecological perspective. *American Psychologist, 47*(6), 723–729.

Steinberg, L., Fegley, S., & Dornbusch, S. M. (1993). Negative impact of part-time work on adolescent adjustment. *Developmental Psychology, 29,* 171–180.

Stern, J. (1985). Biochemical aspects. In A. M. Clarke, A. D. B. Clarke, & J. M. Berg (Eds.), *Mental deficiency: The changing outlook* (pp. 135–212). New York: Free Press.

Sternberg, R. J. (1981). A componential theory of intellectual giftedness. *Gifted Child Quarterly, 25,* 86–93.

Sternberg, R. J. (1985). *Beyond IQ: A triarchic theory of human intelligence.* Cambridge, UK: Cambridge University Press.

Sternberg, R. J., & Davidson, J. E. (1983). Insight in the gifted. *Educational Psychologist, 18,* 51–57.

Sternberg, R. J., & Wagner, R. K. (1985). *Practical intelligence: Origins of competence in the everyday world.* Cambridge, UK: Cambridge University Press.

Sternberg, S. (1966). High-speed scanning in human memory. *Science, 153,* 652–654.

Sternberg, S. (1969). Memory-scanning: Mental processes revealed by reaction-time experiments. *American Scientist, 57,* 421–457.

Stevens, L. J., & Price, M. (1992). Meeting the challenges of educating children at risk. *Phi Delta Kappan, 74,* 18–23.

Stevens, R. J., Madden, N. A., Slavin, R. E., & Farnish, A. M. (1987). Cooperative integrated reading and composition: Two field experiments. *Reading Research Quarterly, 22,* 433–454.

Stevenson, D. L., & Baker, D. P. (1987). The family-school relation and the child's school performance. *Child Development, 58,* 1348–1357.

Stevenson, H. W. (1990). The Asian advantage: The case of mathematics. In J. J. Shields (Ed.), *Japanese schooling: Patterns of socialization, equality, and political control* (pp. 85–95). University Park: Pennsylvania State University Press.

Stevenson, H. W. (1992). Learning from Asian schools. *Scientific American, 267*(6), 70–76.

Stevenson, H. W., Parker, T., Wilkinson, A., Bonnevaux, B., & Gonzalez, M. (1978). Schooling, environment, and cognitive development: A cross-cultural study. *Monographs of the Society for Research in Child Development, 43* (Serial No. 175).

Stiggins, R. [J.] (1987). Design and development of performance assessments. *Educational Measurement: Issues and Practices 6*(3), 33–39.

Stiggins, R. J., & Conklin, N. F. (1992). *In teachers' hands: Investigating the practices of classroom assessment.* Albany: State University of New York Press.

Stigler, J. W. (1984). "Mental abacus": The effect of abacus training on Chinese children's mental calculation. *Cognitive Psychology, 16,* 145–176.

Stillings, N. A., Feinstein, M. H., Garfield, J. L., Rissland, E. L., Rosenbaum, D. A., Weisler, S. E., & Baker-Ward, L. (1987). *Cognitive science: An introduction.* Cambridge: MIT Press.

Stipek, D. J. (1993). *Motivation to learn: From theory to practice* (2nd ed.). Boston: Allyn & Bacon.

Stipek, D. J., & Daniels, D. H. (1988). Declining perceptions of competence: A consequence of changes in the child or in the educational environment? *Journal of Educational Psychology, 80,* 352–356.

Stipek, D. J., & Hoffman, J. M. (1980). Children's achievement-related expectancies as a function of academic performance histories and sex. *Journal of Educational Psychology, 72,* 861–865.

Stipek, D. [J.], & MacIver, D. (1989). Developmental change in children's assessment of intellectual competence. *Child Development, 60,* 521–538.

Storfer, M. D. (1990). *Intelligence and giftedness: The contributions of heredity and early environment.* San Francisco: Jossey-Bass.

Strahan, D. B. (1989). How experienced and novice teachers frame their views of instruction: An analysis of semantic ordered trees. *Teaching and Teacher Education, 5,* 53–67.

Strauss, A., & Corbin, J. (1990). *Basics of qualitative research: Grounded theory procedures and techniques.* Newbury Park, CA: Sage.

Strauss, M. S. (1979). Abstraction of prototypical information by adults and 10-month-olds. *Journal of Experimental Psychology: Human Learning and Memory, 5,* 618–632.

Strauss, S., & Shilony, T. (1994). Teachers' models of children's minds and learning. In L. A. Hirschfeld & S. A. Gelman (Eds.), *Mapping the mind: Domain specificity in cognition and culture* (pp. 455–473). London: Cambridge University Press.

Strong, R., Silver, H. F., & Robinson, A. (1995). What do students really want (and what really motivates them)? *Educational Leadership, 53*(1), 8–12.

Suchman, J. R. (1960). Inquiring training in the elementary school. *Science Teacher, 27,* 42–47.

Sugarman, S. (1983). *Children's early thought.* Cambridge, MA: Cambridge University Press.

Suls, J. (Ed.). (1982). *Psychological perspectives on the self.* Hillsdale, NJ: Erlbaum.

Sulzby, E. (1985). Children's emergent reading of favorite storybooks: A developmental study. *Reading Research Quarterly, 20,* 458–481.

Sulzby, E. (1988). A study of children's early reading development. In A. D. Pelligrini (Ed.), *Psychological bases for early education* (pp. 39–75). Chichester, UK: Wiley.

Sulzby, E., & Teale, W. (1991). Emergent literacy. In R. Barr, M. L. Kamil, P. B. Mosenthal, & P. D. Pearson (Eds.), *Handbook of reading research* (Vol. II, pp. 727–758). New York: Longman.

Svenson, O., & Hedonborg, M. L. (1979). Strategies used by children when solving simple subtractions. *Acta Psychologica, 43,* 477–489.

Symons, S., Woloshyn, V., & Presley, M. (Eds.). (1994). The scientific evaluation of the whole-language approach to literacy development (Special issue). *Educational Psychologist, 29*(4).

Swanson, H. L., & Cooney, J. B. (1991). Learning disabilities and memory. In B. Y. L. Wong (Ed.), *Learning about learning disabilities* (pp. 104–127). San Diego: Academic Press.

Sweller, J., & Cooper, G. A. (1985). The use of worked examples as a substitute for problem solving in learning algebra. *Cognition and Instruction, 2,* 59–89.

Symons, S., & Pressley, M. (1993). Prior knowledge affects text search success and extraction of information. *Reading Research Quarterly, 28,* 250–261.

Szetala, W., & Nicol, C. (1992). Evaluating problem solving in mathematics. *Educational Leadership, 49*(8), 42–45.

Tannen, D. (1990). *You just don't understand: Women and men in conversation.* New York: Morrow.

Tannenbaum, A. J. (1983). *Gifted children: Psychological and educational perspectives.* New York: Macmillan.

Tannenbaum, A. J. (1986). Giftedness: A psychosocial approach. In R. J. Sternberg & J. E. Davidson (Eds.), *Conceptions of giftedness* (pp. 21–52). Cambridge, UK: Cambridge University Press.

Tarver, S. G., Hallahan, D. P., Kauffman, J. M., & Ball, D. W. (1976). Verbal rehearsal and selective attention in children with learning disabilities: A developmental lag. *Journal of Experimental Child Psychology, 22,* 375–385.

Taub, H. A. (1974). Coding for short-term memory as a function of age. *Journal of Genetic Psychology, 125,* 309–314.

Taylor, B. M. (1982). Text structure and children's comprehension and memory for expository material. *Journal of Educational Psychology, 74,* 323–340.

Taylor, B. M., & Beach, R. W. (1984). The effects of text structure instruction on middle-grade students' comprehension and production of expository text. *Reading Research Quarterly, 19,* 134–146.

Tennyson, R. D., & Park, O. (1980). The teaching of concepts: A review of instructional design literature. *Review of Educational Research, 50,* 55–70.

Terman, L. M. (1925). *Genetic studies of genius, mental and physical traits of a thousand gifted children.* Stanford, CA: Stanford University Press.

Terman, L. M., & Childs, H. G. (1912). A tentative revision and extension of the Binet-Simon Measuring Scale of Intelligence. *Journal of Educational Psychology, 3,* 61–74, 133–143, 198–208, 277–289.

Terman, L. M., & Oden, M. H. (1947). *The gifted child grows up: Twenty-five years' followup of a superior group.* Stanford, CA: Stanford University Press.

Terman, L. M., & Oden, M. H. (1959). *The gifted group in midlife: Thirty years followup of the superior child.* Stanford, CA: Stanford University Press.

Thomas, E. (1990). Filial piety, social change and Singapore youth. *Journal of Moral Education, 19,* 192–206.

Thorkildsen, T. A. (1993). Those who can, tutor: High-ability students' conceptions of fair ways to organize learning. *Journal of Educational Psychology, 85,* 182–190.

Thorndike, R. L., Hagen, E. P., & Sattler, J. M. (1986). *Stanford-Binet intelligence scale: Technical manual* (4th ed.). Chicago: Riverside Press.

Thurstone, L. L. (1938). Primary mental abilities. *Psychometric Monographs* (No. 1.). Chicago: University of Chicago Press.

Thurstone, L. L. (1947). *Multiple factor analysis.* Chicago: University of Chicago Press.

Tingle, J. B., & Good, R. (1990). Effects of cooperative grouping on stoichiometric problem solving in high school chemistry. *Journal of Research in Science Teaching, 27,* 671–683.

Tobias, S. (1994). Interest, prior knowledge, and learning. *Review of Educational Research, 64*(1), 37–54.

Tobin, K. (1987). The role of wait time in higher cognitive level learning. *Review of Educational Research, 57,* 69–95.

Tobin, K., & Fraser, B. J. (1990). What does it mean to be an exemplary science teacher? *Journal of Research in Science Teaching, 27,* 3–25.

Tomporowski, P. D., & Simpson, R. G. (1990). Sustained attention and intelligence. *Intelligence, 14,* 31–42.

Torgesen, J. K. (1975). Problems and prospects in the study of learning disabilities. In M. Hetherington & J. Hagen (Eds.), *Review of research in child development* (Vol. 5). Chicago: University of Chicago Press.

Torgesen, J. K. (1977). Memorization processes in reading-disabled children. *Journal of Educational Psychology, 69,* 571–578.

Torgesen, J. K. (1991). Learning disabilities: Historical and conceptual issues. In B. Y. L. Wong (Ed.), *Learning about learning disabilities* (pp. 3–37). San Diego: Academic Press.

Torgesen, J. K., & Goldman, T. (1977). Verbal rehearsal and short-term memory in reading disabled children. *Child Development, 48,* 56–60.

Torgesen, J. K., Kistner, J. A., & Morgan, S. (1987). Component processes in working memory. In J. G. Borkowski & J. D. Day (Eds.), *Cognition in special children: Comparative approaches to retardation, learning disabilities, and giftedness* (pp. 49–85). Norwood, NJ: Ablex.

Tryon, R. M. (1927). Standard and new type tests in the social studies. *The Historical Outlook, 18,* 172–178.

Tulving, E. (1972). Episodic and semantic memory. In E. Tulving & W. Donaldson (Eds.), *Organization of memory* (pp. 381–403). New York: Academic Press.

Tulving, E. (1983). *Elements of episodic memory.* Oxford, UK: Oxford University Press.

Tzuriel, D. (1992). The development of ego identity at adolescence among Israeli Jews and Arabs. *Journal of Youth and Adolescence, 21,* 551–571.

Tzuriel, D., & Feuerstein, R. (1992). Dynamic group assessment for prescriptive teaching: Differential effects of treatment. In H. C. Haywood & D. Tzuriel (Eds.), *Interactive assessment* (pp. 187–206). New York: Springer-Verlag.

Tzuriel, D., & Haywood, H. C. (1992). The development of interactive-dynamic approaches to assessment of learning potential. In H. C. Haywood & D. Tzuriel (Eds.), *Interactive assessment* (pp. 3–37). New York: Springer-Verlag.

Underwood, B. J. (1975). Individual differences as a crucible in theory construction. *American Psychologist, 30,* 128–134.

United States of America v. State of South Carolina, 434 U.S. 1026 (1978).

U.S. Department of Education, National Commission on Excellence in Education (1983). *A nation at risk: The imperative for education reform.* Washington, DC: U.S. Government Printing Office.

Utley, C. A., Haywood, H. C., & Masters, J. C. (1992). Policy implications of psychological assessment of minority children. In H. C. Haywood & D. Tzuriel (Eds.), *Interactive assessment* (pp. 445–469). New York: Springer-Verlag.

Valdez-Menchaca, M. C., & Whitehurst, G. J. (1992). Accelerating language development through picture book reading: A systematic extension to Mexican day care. *Developmental Psychology, 28,* 1106–1114.

van der Meij, H. (1988). Constraints on question asking in classrooms. *Journal of Educational Psychology, 80,* 401–405.

van Dijk, T. A., & Kintsch, W. (1983). *Strategies of discourse comprehension.* New York: Academic Press.

Van Haneghan, J., Barron, L., Young, M., Williams, S., Vye, N., & Bransford, J. (1992). The Jasper series: An experiment with new ways to enhance mathematical thinking. In D. F. Halpern (Ed.), *Enhancing thinking skills in the sciences and mathematics* (pp. 15–38). Hillsdale, NJ: Erlbaum.

Van Houten, R., & Rolider, A. (1989). An analysis of several variables influencing the efficacy of flash card instruction. *Journal of Applied Behavior Analysis, 22,* 111–118.

van Lehn, K. (1990). *Mind bugs: The origins of procedural misconceptions.* Cambridge: MIT Press.

Vasu, E. S., & Howe, A. C. (1989). The effect of visual and verbal modes of presentation on children's retention of images and words. *Journal of Research in Science Teaching, 26,* 401–407.

Vellutino, F. R. (1979). *Dyslexia: Theory and research.* Cambridge: MIT Press.

Vernon, P. A. (1983). Speed of information processing and intelligence. *Intelligence, 7,* 53–70.

Vernon, P. A. (1985). Individual differences in general cognitive ability. In L. C. Hartlage & C. F. Telzrow (Eds.), *The neuropsychology of individual differences.* New York: Plenum.

Vernon, P. A. (1987). New developments in reaction time research. In P. A. Vernon (Ed.), *Speed of information processing and intelligence* (pp. 1–20). Norwood, NJ: Ablex.

Vernon, P. A. (1990). The use of biological measures to estimate behavioral intelligence. *Educational Psychologist, 25,* 293–304.

Vernon, P. A. (1991). Studying intelligence the hard way. *Intelligence, 15,* 389–395.

Veroff, J. (1969). Social comparison and the development of achievement motivation. In C. M. Smith (Ed.), *Achievement-related motives in children* (pp. 47–101). New York: Sage.

Viadero, D. (1993a, August 4). 8th-grade math achievement linked to emphasis on algebra and geometry. *Education Week,* p. 12.

Viadero, D. (1993b, September 22). Students' reading skills fall short, NAEP data find. *Education Week,* pp. 1, 16.

Viadero, D. (1994, March 16). Jittery students are put to test with new S.A.T. *Education Week,* pp. 1, 12.

Voss, J. F. (1991). Informal reasoning and international relations. In J. F. Voss, D. N. Perkins, & J. W. Segal (Eds.), *Informal reasoning and education* (pp. 37–58). Hillsdale, NJ: Erlbaum.

Voss, J. F., Blais, J. Menas, M. L., Greene, T. R., & Ahwesh, E. (1989). Informal reasoning and subject matter knowledge in the solving of economics problems by naive and novice individuals. In L. B. Resnick (Ed.), *Knowing, learning, and instruction: Essays in honor of Robert Glaser* (pp. 217–249). Hillsdale, NJ: Erlbaum.

Voss, J. F., Greene, T. R., Post, T. A., & Penner, B. C. (1983). Problem-solving skill in the social sciences. In G. H. Bower (Ed.), *The psychology of learning and motivation: Advances in research and theory* (Vol. 17, pp. 165–213). New York: Academic Press.

Voss, J. F., Vesonder, G. T., & Spilich, G. J. (1980). Generation and recall by high-knowledge and low-knowledge individuals. *Journal of Verbal Learning and Verbal Behavior, 19,* 651–667.

Voyer, D., Voyer, S., & Bryden, M. P. (1995). Magnitude of sex differences in spatial abilities: A meta-analysis and consideration of critical variables. *Psychological Bulletin, 117*(2), 250–270.

Vurpillot, E. (1968). The development of scanning strategies and their relations to visual differentiation. *Journal of Experimental Child Psychology, 6,* 632–650.

Vygotsky, L. S. (1962). *Thought and language.* Cambridge: MIT Press.

Vygotsky, L. S. (1978). *Mind in society: The development of higher psychological processes.* Cambridge, MA: Harvard University Press.

Vygotsky, L. S. (1981). The genesis of higher mental functions. In J. V. Wertsch (Ed.), *The concept of activity in Soviet psychology* (pp. 144–188). Armonk, NY: M. E. Sharpe.

Vygotsky, L. S. (1987). *Thinking and speech* (N. Minick, Ed. and Trans.). New York: Plenum.

Wagner, D. A. (1974). The development of short-term and incidental memory: A cross-cultural study. *Child Development, 45,* 389–396.

Wagner, D. A. (1978). Memories of Morocco: The influence of age, schooling, and environment on memory. *Cognitive Psychology, 10,* 1–28.

Wagner, D. A., & Spratt, J. E. (1987). Cognitive consequences of contrasting pedagogies: The effects of Quranic preschooling in Morocco. *Child Development, 58,* 1207–1219.

Walberg, H. J., Harnisch, D., & Tsai, S. L. (1986). Elementary school mathematics productivity in twelve countries. *British Educational Research Journal, 12,* 237–248.

Walker, B. J., & Wilson, P. T. (1991). Using guided imagery to teach science concepts. In C. M. Santa & D. E. Alvermann (Eds.), *Science learning: Processes and applications* (pp. 147–155). Newark, DE: International Reading Association.

Walker, C. H. (1987). Relative importance of domain knowledge and overall aptitude on acquisition of domain-related information. *Cognition and Instruction, 4,* 25–42.

Walker, L. (1984). Sex differences in the development of moral reasoning: A critical review. *Child Development, 55,* 677–691.

Walker, L. J., & Moran, T. J. (1991). Moral reasoning in a communist Chinese society. *Journal of Moral Education, 20,* 139–155.

Walters, G. C., & Grusec, J. E. (1977). *Punishment.* San Francisco: Freeman.

Wandersee, J. H. (1988). Ways students read texts. *Journal of Research in Science Teaching, 25,* 69–84.

Wasik, B. A., & Slavin, R. E. (1993). Preventing early reading failure with one-to-one tutoring: A review of five programs. *Reading Research Quarterly, 28,* 178–200.

Waterman, A., & Goldman, J. (1976). A longitudinal study of ego identity development in a liberal arts college. *Journal of Youth and Adolescence, 5,* 361–369.

Watson, D. J. (1989). Defining and describing whole language. *Elementary School Journal, 90,* 129–141.

Weaver, C. (1990). *Understanding whole language: From principles to practice.* Portsmouth, NH: Heinemann.

Webb, N. L. (1992). Assessment of students' knowledge of mathematics: Steps toward a theory. In D. A. Grouws (Ed.), *Handbook of research on mathematics teaching and learning* (pp. 661–683). New York: Macmillan.

Webb, N. M. (1982). Student interaction and learning in small groups. *Review of Educational Research, 52,* 421–445.

Webb, N. M. (1984). Sex differences in interaction and achievement in cooperative small groups. *Journal of Educational Psychology, 76,* 33–34.

Webb, N. M. (1989). Peer interaction and learning in small groups. *International Journal of Educational Research, 13,* 21–39.

Webb, N. M. (1991). Task-related verbal interaction and mathematics learning in small groups. *Journal for Research in Mathematics Education, 22,* 366–389.

Webb, N. M., & Farivar, S. (1994). Promoting helping behavior in cooperative small groups in middle school mathematics. *American Educational Research Journal, 31*(2), 369–395.

Webb, N. M., & Kenderski, C. M. (1985). Gender differences in small-group interaction and achievement in high- and low-achieving classes. In L. C. Wilkinson & C. B. Marrett (Eds.), *Gender influences on classroom interaction* (pp. 209–236). Orlando, FL: Academic Press.

Wechsler, D. (1939). *The measurement of adult intelligence.* Baltimore: Williams & Wilkins.

Wechsler, D. (1949). *Manual for the Wechsler intelligence scale for children.* San Antonio, TX: Psychological Corporation.

Wechsler, D. (1967). *A manual for the preschool and primary scale of intelligence.* San Antonio, TX: Psychological Corporation.

Weed, K., Ryan, E. B., & Day, J. (1990). Metamemory and attributions as mediators of strategy use and recall. *Journal of Educational Psychology, 82,* 849–855.

Weinberg, R. A., Scarr, S., & Waldman, I. D. (1992). The Minnesota transracial adoption study: A followup of IQ test performance at adolescence. *Intelligence, 16,* 117–135.

Weiner, B. (1979). A theory of motivation for some classroom experiences. *Journal of Educational Psychology, 71,* 3–25.

Weinstein, C. F., & Mayer, R. F. (1986). The teaching of learning strategies. In M. C. Wittrock (Ed.), *Handbook of research on teaching* (3rd ed., pp. 315–327). New York: Macmillan.

Weinstein, R. S., Madison, S. M., & Kuklinski, M. R. (1995). Raising expectations in schooling: Obstacles and opportunities for change. *American Educational Research Journal, 32*(1), 121–159.

Wentzel, K. R. (1989). Adolescent classroom goals, standards for performance, and academic achievement: An interactionist perspective. *Journal of Educational Psychology, 81*(2), 131–142.

Werner, E. E. (1990). Protective factors and individual resilience. In S. J. Meisels & J. P. Shonkoff (Eds.), *Handbook of early childhood interventions* (pp. 97–116). Cambridge, UK: Cambridge University Press.

Werner, E. E., & Smith, R. S. (1982). *Vulnerable but invincible: A longitudinal study of resilient children and youth.* New York: McGraw-Hill.

Wertsch, J. V. (1979). From social interaction to higher psychological processes: A clarification and application of Vygotsky's theory. *Human Development, 22,* 1–22.

Wertsch, J. V. (1985). *Vygotsky and the social formation of mind.* Cambridge, MA: Harvard University Press.

Wertsch, J. V. (1991). *Voices of the mind,* Cambridge, MA: Harvard University Press.

Wertsch, J. V., & Minick, N. J. (1990). Negotiating sense in the zone of proximal development. In M. Schwebel, C. A. Maher, & N. S. Fagley (Eds.), *Promoting cognitive growth over the life span* (pp. 71–88). Hillsdale, NJ: Erlbaum.

White, M. (1987). *The Japanese educational challenge: A commitment to children.* New York: Free Press.

Whitehurst, G. J., Falco, F. L., Lonigan, C. J., Fischel, J. E., DeBaryshe, B. D., Valdez-Menchaca, M. C., & Caulfield, M. (1988). Accelerating language development through picture-book reading. *Developmental Psychology, 24,* 552–559.

Whitman, T. L. (1990). Self-regulation and mental retardation. *American Journal on Mental Retardation, 94,* 347–362.

Whittington, D. (1991). What have 17-year-olds known in the past? *American Educational Research Journal, 28,* 759–780.

Widaman, K. F., Little, T. D., Geary, D. C., & Cormier, P. (1992). Individual differences in the development of skill in mental addition: Internal and external validation of chronometric methods. *Learning and Individual Differences, 4,* 167–214.

Wigfield, A., Eccles, J. S., MacIver, D., Reuman, D. A., & Midgley, C. (1991). Transitions during early adolescence: Changes in children's domain-specific self-perceptions and general self-esteem across the transition to junior high school. *Developmental Psychology, 27,* 552–565.

Wigfield, A., & Karpathian, M. (1991). Who am I and what can I do? Children's self-concepts and motivation in achievement situations. *Educational Psychologist 26,* 233–262.

Willerman, L., Schultz, R., Rutledge, J. N., & Bigler, E. D. (1991). *In vivo* brain size and intelligence. *Intelligence, 15,* 223–228.

Willis, S., & Kenway, J. (1986). On overcoming sexism in schooling to marginalize or mainstream. *Australian Journal of Education, 30,* 132–149.

Wilson, S. (1982). Heritability. *Journal of Applied Problems, 19,* 71–85.

Winne, P. H., Woodlands, M. H., & Wong, B. Y. L. (1982). Comparability of self-concept among learning disabled, normal, and gifted students. *Journal of Learning Disabilities, 15,* 470–475.

Wishart, J. G. (1988). Early learning in infants and young children with Down syndrome. In L. Nadel (Ed.), *The psychobiology of Down syndrome* (pp. 7–50). Cambridge: MIT Press.

Wisniewski, K. E., Miezejeski, C. M., & Hill, A. L. (1988). Neurological and psychological status of individuals with Down syndrome. In L. Nadel (Ed.), *The psychobiology of Down Syndrome* (pp. 291–343). Cambridge: MIT Press.

Witkin, H. (1969). *Embedded figures test.* Palo Alto, CA: Consulting Psychologists Press.

Witkin, H., Moore, C., Goodenough, D., & Cox, P. (1977). Field-dependence and field-independence: Cognitive styles and their educational implications. *Review of Educational Research, 47,* 1–64.

Wittrock, M. C. (1966). The learning by discovery hypothesis. In L. S. Shulman & E. R. Keislar (Eds.), *Learning by discovery: A critical appraisal* (pp. 33–75). Chicago: Rand McNally.

Woloshyn, V. E., Pressley, M., & Schneider, W. (1992). Elaborative interrogation and prior knowledge effects on learning of facts. *Journal of Educational Psychology, 84,* 115–124.

Woloshyn, V. E., Willoughby, T., Wood, E., & Pressley, M. (1990). Elaborative interrogation facilitates adult learning of factual paragraphs. *Journal of Educational Psychology, 82,* 513–524.

Wong, E. D. (1991). Beyond the question/nonquestion alternative in classroom discussion. *Journal of Educational Psychology, 83,* 159–162.

Wood, R., & Bandura, A. (1989). Impact of conceptions of ability on self-regulatory mechanisms and complex decision-making. *Journal of Personality and Social Psychology, 56,* 407–415.

Wood, S. S., Bruner, J. S., & Ross, G. (1976). The role of tutoring in problem solving. *Journal of Child Psychology and Psychiatry, 17,* 89–100.

Woods, S. S., Resnick, L. B., & Groen, G. J. (1975). Experimental test of five process models for subtraction. *Journal of Educational Psychology, 67,* 17–21.

Wozniak, R. (1972). Verbal regulation of motor behavior: Soviet research and non-Soviet replications. *Human Development, 15,* 13–57.

Wyatt, D., Pressley, M., El-Dinary, P. B., Stein, S., Evans, P., & Brown, R. (1993). Comprehension strategies, worth and credibility monitoring, and evaluations: Cold and hot cognition when experts read professional articles that are important to them. *Learning and Individual Differences, 5,* 49–72.

Wyatt, M. (1992). The past, present, and future need for college reading courses in the U.S. *Journal of Reading, 36,* 10–20.

Yakovlev, P. I., & Lecours, A. R. (1967). The myelogenetic cycles of regional maturation of the brain. In A. Minkowski (Ed.), *Regional development of the brain in early life* (pp. 3–70). Oxford, UK: Blackwell.

Yarroch, W. L. (1985). Student understanding of chemical equation balancing. *Journal of Research in Science Teaching, 22,* 449–459.

Yates, F. A. (1966). *The art of memory.* London: Routledge & Kegan Paul.

Yeates, K. O., & Selman, R. L. (1989). Social competence in the schools: Toward an integrative developmental model for intervention. *Developmental Review, 9,* 64–100.

Yoakum, C. S., & Yerkes, R. M. (1920). *Army mental tests.* New York: Holt.

Zeamon, D., & House, B. J. (1979). A review of attention theory. In N. R. Ellis (Ed.), *Handbook of mental deficiency: Psychological theory and research* (pp. 63–120). Hillsdale, NJ: Erlbaum.

Zentall, S. S. (1989). Self-control training with hyperactive and impulsive children. In J. N. Hughes & R. J. Hall (Eds.), *Cognitive-behavioral psychology in the schools* (pp. 305–346). New York: Guilford Press.

Zetlin, A., & Murtaugh, M. (1990). Whatever happened to those with borderline IQs? *American Journal of Mental Deficiency, 94,* 463–469.

Zhu, X., & Simon, H. A. (1987). Learning mathematics from examples and by doing. *Cognition and Instruction, 4,* 137–166.

Zigler, E., & Balla, D. (Eds.). (1982). *Mental retardation: The developmental-difference controversy.* Hillsdale, NJ: Erlbaum.

Zigler, E., & Hodapp, R. M. (1986). *Understanding mental retardation.* Cambridge, UK: Cambridge University Press.

Photo Credits

Unless otherwise acknowledged, all photographs are the property of Scott, Foresman and Company. Page abbreviations are as follows: (t)top, (b)bottom, (l)left, (r)right.

Chapter-opening photos: Chapter 2: Kolvoord/Image Works / Chapter 3: John Eastcott/Yva Momatuik/Image Works / Chapter 6: Jeffrey Myers/Stock, Boston / Chapter 7: L. Kolvoord/Image Works / Chapter 8: Lawrence Migdale/Stock, Boston / Chapters 9, 10, 11: SuperStock / Chapter 12: McLaughlin/Image Works / Chapter 13: Ellen Senisi/Image Works / Chapter 15: Bob Daemmrich / Chapter 16: Daemmrich/Image Works

Text photos: 7 Jonathan Nourok/PhotoEdit / 15(t) Charles Gupton/Stock Boston / 15(b) David Woo/Stock Boston / 22 Gail Meese / 31 Tony Freeman/PhotoEdit / 35 Robert B. Tolchin / 42 Robert Brenner/PhotoEdit / 45 Tony Freeman/PhotoEdit / 49 B. Bachmann/Image Works / 56(l) Ray Ellis/Photo Researchers / 56(r) William Johnson/Stock Boston / 58 M. Richards/PhotoEdit / 62 John Coletti/Stock Boston / 66 Jim Pickerell/Stock Boston / 70 Bob Daemmrich/Image Works / 84 Lawrence Migdale/Stock Boston / 88(l) AP/Wide World / 88(r) Keystone/Image Works / 101 Bob Daemmrich/Stock Boston / 115 Mary Kate Denny/PhotoEdit / 121 B. Mahoney/Image Works / 125 Gail Meese / 126 Elizabeth Crews/Image Works / 136 Richard Wood/Picture Cube, Inc. / 137 Peter Southwick/Stock Boston / 141 Mark Newman/Photo Researchers / 149 Mary Kate Denny/PhotoEdit / 169 Bob Daemmrich/Image Works / 172 Jonathan Nourok/PhotoEdit / 174 Mark Richards/PhotoEdit / 184 Stacy Pick/Stock Boston / 189(tr) Tony Freeman/PhotoEdit / 189(br) Seth Resnick/Stock Boston / 190 Ron Sherman/Stock Boston / 203(b) Myrleen Ferguson Cate/PhotoEdit / 204 Tim Barnwell/Stock Boston / 215 Gail Meese / 218(all) Michael Newman/PhotoEdit / 227 Reuters/Corbis-Bettmann / 242 Mary Kate Denny/PhotoEdit / 245 Bob Daemmrich/Stock Boston / 246 Fuji Fotos/Image Works / 247(l) Lawrence Migdale/Stock Boston / 247(r) Skjold/Image Works / 259 Spencer Grant/Stock Boston / 267 Myrleen Ferguson Cate/PhotoEdit / 270 Tony Freeman/PhotoEdit / 271 ©1994 Children's Television Workshop / 280 Bachman/Stock Boston / 287 Russell D. Curtis/Photo Researchers / 289 David Weintraub/Photo Researchers / 299 Tony Freeman/PhotoEdit / 304 Courtesy Texas Instruments / 307 Fuji Fotos/Image Works / 309 Susan McCarthy/Photo Researchers / 311 Myrleen Ferguson/PhotoEdit / 314 Stephen Frisch/Stock Boston / 333(tl) Crandall/Image Works / 333(tr) Robert Brenner/PhotoEdit / 333(bl) Isaac Greenberg/Photo Researchers / 333(br) Jeff Gilbert/Southern Living/Photo Researchers /341 Christopher Brown/Stock Boston / 343 Library of Congress / 362 Gail Meese / 366 Ulrike Welsch/PhotoEdit / 394 Jim Whitmer / 413 Tim Carlson/Stock Boston / 416 Bob Daemmrich/Image Works / 418 George Steinmetz / 419 Guynup/Image Works